History of the City of New York

It's Origin, Rise, and Progress
Volume 1

Mrs. Martha J. Lamb
&
Mrs. Burton harrison

COSIMO CLASSICS
NEW YORK

History of the City of New York: It's Origin, Rise, and Progress -Vol.1

© 2005 Cosimo, Inc.

Cosimo, P.O. Box 416
Old Chelsea Station
New York, NY 10113-0416

or visit our website at:
www.cosimobooks.com

History of the City of New York: It's Origin, Rise, and Progress - Vol.1 originally published by A.S. Barnes & CO. in 1877-1896.

Library of Congress Cataloging-in-Publication Data
A catalog record for this book is available from the Library of Congress

Cover design by www.wiselephant.com

ISBN: 1-59605-283-X

Thus was Manhattan Island again left in primeval solitude, waiting till Commerce should come and claim its own.   Page 85.

PREFACE.

THIS work is the outgrowth of more than a dozen years of careful study and persistent research. The subject is one of unusual interest; and notwithstanding the immense labor involved, it has attracted and diverted rather than wearied the author, and kept the soul stirred with constantly increasing enthusiasm. The outlook will speak for itself to every intelligent reader. A wooded island upon the border of a vast, unexplored, picturesque wild, three thousand miles from civilization, becomes within three centuries the seat of the arrogant metropolis of the Western world. The narrative embraces the condition of Europe which contributed to this remarkable result, the origin and birth of the city in which we take so much pride, its early vicissitudes, the various steps of progress through which it became powerful, the connection of causes and effects, the rise of churches, schools, colleges, charities, and other institutions, the machinery, commercial and political, with all its crudities, breakages, friction, and modern improvements, ever producing unlooked-for events, its wars and rumors of wars, its public characters and foreign relations, and its social thread, knotting and tangling, but yet running through all the years, spinning its own way and coiling itself into every feature of the structure, — the cable, indeed, to hold the multiplicity of parts together. In the language of a prominent leader of public opinion, "hardly did old Rome herself emerge from a more mysterious and fascinating crucible of legend and tradition."

MARTHA J. LAMB.

It would give me pleasure to mention all the sources from which I have obtained assistance in the preparation of these volumes, but they are legion, and the statement would read like a dictionary. I shall, however, make due acknowledgments, as far as space will permit, in the Preface to Volume II. The most eminent scholars of the land are among those who have given me counsel and encouragement. I have never lost sight of the magnitude and importance of the task before me, New York being the central point in all American history, nor have I in any instance indulged fancy at the expense of historical exactness and symmetry. My first aim has been to reach the truth, in which pursuit I have spared no pains. My original purpose to produce a standard authority has been my latest purpose. Facts before finding a place in my pages have been subjected to a searching ordeal. Occasional errors may have escaped even the closest vigilance, but such when discovered will be corrected. On all matters where difference of opinion exists I have examined both sides without prejudice or partiality. I have also listened with deference to and profited by the judgments of the well-informed. But while I have left no stone unturned in the way of securing the broadest light and the most unexceptional aid, I am alone responsible for what I have written.

If, in the treatment of a subject which combines so many sources of thrilling interest, and which is dear to the heart of every American citizen, I have given warmth and color as well as life and expression to realities, and found favor with the great sympathetic reading public, then my labor has not been in vain.

MARTHA J. LAMB.

CONTENTS.

CHAPTER I.

CHAPTER II.

CHAPTER III.

CHAPTER IV.

CHAPTER V.

CHAPTER VI.

CHAPTER XVIII.

CHAPTER XIX.

CHAPTER XX.

CHAPTER XXI.

CHAPTER XXII.

CHAPTER XXIII.

CHAPTER XXIV.

CHAPTER XXV.

LIST OF ILLUSTRATIONS.

FULL–PAGE ENGRAVINGS.

ILLUSTRATIONS IN TEXT.

MAPS.

ARTISTS.

J. D. WOODWARD, ALFRED FREDERICKS, SOL EYTINGE, GEORGE E. WHITE, C. S. REINHART, THOMAS BEACH, ABRAM HOSIER, SAMUEL WALLIN.

ENGRAVERS.

JOHN KARST, J. M. RICHARDSON, JOS. HARLEY, HORACE BAKER, E. CLEMENT, JOHN P. DAVIS, A. BOBBITT, BOOKHOUT, SPEAR, WINHAM, ARNOLD.

HISTORY OF THE CITY OF NEW YORK.

INTRODUCTORY CHAPTER.

EARLY DISCOVERIES.

Manhattan Island. — Earliest Records of America. — The Icelanders. — The Fifteenth Century. — Venetian Commerce. — Christopher Columbus. — England. — The Cabots. — The Portuguese. — Vasco da Gama. — The Fishermen of Brittany and Normandy. — Newfoundland. — The Spaniards. — Verrazano. — Estevan Gomez. — The English again. — The Dutch. — Belgium. — Usselincx and John of Barneveld. — The East and West India Companies.

TWO hundred and sixty-five years ago the site of the city of New York was a rocky, wooded, canoe-shaped, thirteen-mile-long island, bounded by two salt rivers and a bay, and peopled by dusky skin-clad savages. A half-dozen portable wigwam villages, some patches of tobacco and corn, and a few bark canoes drawn up on the shore, gave little promise of our present four hundred and fifty miles of streets, vast property interests, and the encircling forest of shipping. What have been the successive steps of the extraordinary transformation ?

If the lineage, education, experiences, and character of a distinguished personage are replete with interest and instruction, of how much greater moment is the history of a city, which is biography in its most absolute sense ? New York needs no introduction to the reader. It occupies an individual position among the great cities of the world. It is unlike any of its contemporaries. Its population is a singular intermixture of elements from all nations. Its institutions are the outgrowth of older civilizations ; its wisdom and public opinion largely the reflection of a previous intelligence. All the ideas, principles, feelings, and traditions which ever made their appearance have here found a common field in which to struggle for existence, and the result, in so far as it is developed, has naturally been " the survival of the fittest." It would not be fair, however, to demand full fruits from so young a tree. New York

is a city in the vigor of its youth, its final growth yet to be attained;
thus its history the more especially deserves careful and elaborate treatment. If we would correctly estimate the men who laid its foundation-
stones, we must enter into the spirit of the age in which they lived,
and become to a certain degree familiar with the world's progress at
that period. If we would appreciate their proceedings, we must learn
somewhat of national characteristics and the practical operation of government and laws, in the various countries which they represented. The
reader, therefore, is invited first to a brief ancestral disquisition, care
being taken to make plain the causes which led to the discovery and
settlement of Manhattan Island.

The earliest record of the existence of the American Continent is found
among the literary legacies of the Icelanders of the tenth century, who
were superior to the continental people of that age both in mental vigor
and physical endurance. But their discoveries were the result of hap-
hazard adventure rather than scientific probabilities, and their efforts at
colonization were signal failures. From their geographical works we find
that they supposed these western lands to be a part of Europe; and,
while the accounts of their expeditions were carefully preserved, not a
line was committed to parchment until many centuries had passed, so
that there is very little reason for presuming that succeeding generations
were materially benefited by reason of them.

1435.   Christopher Columbus appeared upon the stage of action just
as the world was waking from the long sleep of the Middle Ages.
Marco Polo had made his famous journey across the whole longitude of
Asia, and the manuscript account of his travels, dictated to a fellow-pris-
oner in a Genoese prison, was beginning to attract attention to the vast
and fertile countries he described, — the cities running over with diamonds,
emeralds, rubies, and sapphires, the palaces with floors and roofs of solid
gold, and the rivers hot enough to boil eggs.

The new epoch in the art of printing was also scattering information of
various kinds. The books of the ancients were reproduced, and those who
could afford to read — for it was a luxury confined entirely to the upper
and wealthy classes — discovered that geometrical principles had been applied to the construction of maps by Ptolemy in the second century, and
that the places of the earth had been planned out and described according
to their several latitudes and longitudes. Some geographical knowledge was interwoven with a vast amount of absurd fiction and very little
ascertained fact, but the desire for more light became so great that those
same curious old maps were exhumed and copied and circulated. They
must have been appalling to the pioneers of maritime discovery, for they

bristled from one end to the other with horrid forms and figures, and represented the Occident as the home of demons. A mighty impulse had already been given to navigation by means of the magnetic needle, and the newly printed ancient stories about Carthaginian sailors who had " voyaged through the Pillars of Hercules, and found a strange country supposed to be Asia," and of adventurous Greeks and Persians, who had coasted Africa, filled the very air with speculative romance.

India beyond the Ganges was the mythical land of promise. Its treasures came from hand to hand through caravans and middle men and agents to Constantinople, with which city the Italian States were in constant commercial communication. But some of the shrewdest of the Venetian and Genoese merchants thought to remedy the evils of the painfully long and perilous overland route, and projected enterprises by way of the Persian Gulf and the Mediterranean and Red Seas. They succeeded, but were obliged to pay a heavy tribute in Egypt, and no Christian was at any time allowed to pass through the Egyptian or Mohammedan countries. Thus the producer and the consumer were effectually kept asunder.

| 1651. | 1620. | 1560. | 1605. | 1572. | 1515. |

Group of ladies, showing fashions of the day.

Constantinople fell in 1453, and from that time the business monopoly of the Indies centred with the Venetians. Venice became the great Western emporium, and attained such marvellous riches and rose to such a height of power and grandeur as never were equalled either before or since. The costliness of her magnificent buildings, the elegance of furniture and decorations, and the style of life among her citizens, was quite beyond description. The learned Christians of Constantinople, who had fled before the Turks into Italy, became her schoolmasters, and mathematics, astronomy, and the art of navigation developed with singular rapidity. People began to talk about a new channel of communication with the Oriental countries, where they could change even the bark of trees into money.

Columbus had for his birthright the intellectual restlessness of the age. As a boy, his brain was filled with unformed projects and scientific uncertainties. The new theories as well as the new learning took root within his mind and grew with his growth. He read what Aristotle had written about the small space of sea between Spain and the eastern coast of India. He speculated over what Seneca had said about the ease with which that sea might be passed in a few days by the aid of favorable winds. He pondered again and again the hypothetical doctrine that the earth was a sphere. He became a sailor, and applied his energies to the study of nautical science.

Meanwhile years rolled on. Islands in the Atlantic were discovered, and the coast of Europe, from Iceland to the Cape Verde Islands, was becoming known. Columbus had made several important voyages himself. On one occasion he visited Iceland, which was now a dependent and neglected province of Denmark, and stayed some time in the country and conversed with the inhabitants. Whether he obtained any knowledge of the early adventures of the Northmen it is impossible to determine. But after his return his fancies seem to have taken more definite shape. The question finally settled itself to his satisfaction that the glittering gold regions could be reached by sailing due west; and then he conceived one of the boldest designs in human history, and pursued it to its accomplishment with the firm resolve of a lofty genius. It was from want of a correct estimate of longitude that, like every one else from Ptolemy down, he was so vastly deceived as to the size of the globe. He was a clever politician, and danced attendance before incredulous kings and supercilious courtiers until time whitened his locks, so pronounced were his convictions, and so enthusiastic was he in the success of his enterprise, could he but get funds to put it in execution. But alas ! he could not convince one man that it was possible to sail west and reach east. It remained for him to find in a woman's mind the capacity to appreciate and the liberality to patronize him; and at last he launched forth over unknown seas, trusting to his own stout heart and a mariner's compass, and, reaching an unknown land, planted the chief milestone in the advance of civilization. He aimed for Zipango, and to his dying day believed he had found it, or its outlying isles, very nearly where his calculations had placed it. Never was man's mistake more prolific in great results.

Europe was stunned with admiration, and the Pope of Rome, who up to that time regarded himself as the legal proprietor of all the real estate in Christendom, issued a bull,[1] the material parts of which are still extant, granting the new territory to Spain.

It is interesting to note how all the great plans and projects of the period tended and verged to one point. There was a Venetian merchant living in Bristol, England, who had paid particular attention to science, and who had long housed in his heart a scheme of going to Cathay by the north. It was John Cabot. He was incited to active effort by the prospect of obtaining spices and other valuable articles of trade independent of haughty Venice. His son Sebastian, then a promising youth about nineteen years of age,[2] was, like his sire, stimulated by the fame of Columbus, and anxious to attempt some notable thing. He was a scholar, had been thoroughly drilled in mathematics, astronomy, and the art of navigation, and accompanied the elder Cabot to the Court of Henry VII., in order to obtain the royal consent to their proposed researches. Henry is well known to have been one of the most penurious monarchs who ever sat upon a throne. He listened graciously, and, upon condition that the whole enterprise should be conducted at their own private expense, issued a patent guaranteeing protection and privileges. But he cunningly reserved to himself one fifth of the profits.[3]

The Cabots first steered directly for Iceland, where they stopped for a few days. For some years a steady and profitable commerce **1497.** had been carried on between Bristol and that country. Iceland, although the heroic age of the Northmen had long since passed, was pretty well peopled, and its inhabitants had many wants which their northern land was unable to supply. The English sold them cloth, corn, wheat, wines, etc., and took fish, chiefly cod, in exchange. Some of the Norwegian authors say that in April, 1419, a heavy snow-storm destroyed more than

[1] *Vattel's Law of Nations*, Book I. Chap. 18.

[2] Humboldt, *Kritsche Untersuchungen*, Vol. II. p. 445.

[3] It is a mooted question whether John Cabot, the father, was the leader of the expedition in 1497. Sebastian Cabot lived for more than sixty years afterwards, and became a celebrated personage ; his fame so far eclipsed that of his father as to cause much to be accredited to him that his father actually performed. But his extreme youth and inexperience at that time would hardly induce the belief that the shrewd Henry VII. would intrust him with such an important command. The Venetian ambassador's letters of 1497, preserved in the Sforza archives of Milan, furnish direct evidence in favor of the father. (*Pasqualigo's Letter*, August 23, 1497.) M. d'Avezac, an able French writer, has found what he esteems sufficient proof to establish the fact that the Cabots' first voyage was made in 1494, when they only saw land ; the second in 1497, when they navigated three hundred leagues along the coast ; the third in 1498, by Sebastian alone ; and the fourth in 1517. *M. d'Avezac to Leonard Woods*, dated Paris, December 15, 1868, in *Doc. Hist. Maine ;* by Willis. But the evidence of any voyage in 1494 is so slight that all allusion to it is omitted in the body of this work.

twenty-five English vessels on the coast of Iceland, which gives us an idea of how brisk their commerce must have been. From this point the Cabots proceeded westward, toiling through mountains of ice, but confi-

June 24. dent of final success. On the 24th of June they saw land which they supposed to be an island, but, finding it ran a long distance towards the north, and getting short of provision and into trouble with their crew, they turned back to England. Cabot says in his journal that it was a great disappointment to them. They were absent from England only about three months, and had discovered a continent, but its bleak, uninviting coasts loomed up only as a hateful barrier in the way of the diamond fields beyond.

1498. The Portuguese were at this time the most enlightened nation of Europe. They had very materially enlarged the scope of geo-graphical knowledge by daring voyages along the coast of Africa, under the direction of Prince Henry, third son of John the Great. Their vessels were small but well-built, and their seamen dashed safely along tempestu-ous shores and explored inlets and rivers. Don Emanuel the Fortunate made prodigious efforts to extend the commerce and dominion of Portugal, and his pet problem was a passage to India around Africa. The exploit was actually performed in 1498 by Vasco da Gama. He returned to Portugal with his four ships laden with spices, silks, and other attractive merchandise. All Europe was in the wildest excitement, and the unsuc-cessful venture of the Cabots was hardly noticed. A papal bull granted to Portugal the sole right to trade in the Indies, which were treated as new discoveries. Alas for Venice! It was her mortal stab, and from that day her prosperity rapidly waned. The Portuguese established them-selves at the East, made Cochin their capital, appointed Vasco da Gama governor of the colony, and for nearly a century they supplied the markets of Europe with the Indian produce. Thus the actual results of immedi-ate communication with the Oriental world completely overshadowed the possible advantages to be reaped from lands lying to the west, which were still regarded as merely the unsurmounted obstacle in the path to the Orient. The public could not be satisfied by tales of snow-bound or rocky shores without so much as a city or a castle over which to float a banner.

1503. But little by little the natural wealth of these western re-gions began to be recognized. At what period the fisheries of Newfoundland were first known to the hardy seamen of Brittany and Normandy it is impossible to determine with accuracy; it must have been as early as the commencement of the sixteenth century. Cod, mackerel, and herring were found in abundance, and the demand for them, particularly in France, was greatly increased by the fasts of the church. During the next few years the Spaniards were busy following up the discoveries of Columbus by expeditions to Central and South America, and occupation of portions of those countries. This led to a neglect of their native soil, and seriously and mischievously retarded the rise of Spain to a front rank among powers; but **1522.** it enlarged the boundaries of knowledge, and hastened the good time when the earth should assume its proper form in the minds of men. Prior to the year 1522 the Straits of Magellan had been discovered, the broad Pacific crossed, and the globe circumnavigated. America stood boldly out as an independent hemisphere.

And yet the avaricious merchantmen and navigators gave little heed to its possible resources. They scoured the oceans in every **1524.** latitude, from the Arctic regions to Cape Horn, searching for a gateway through it to the jeweled cities of the East. The chivalric Francis I. of France had in his employ, to accomplish certain deeds of daring, the Italian navigator Verrazano, who in 1524 was sent on a voyage, with the above object in view. He cruised along our coast from the Carolinas to Nova Scotia, landing many times, and learning all that was possible, under the circumstances, of the strange country and its inhabitants. He estimated that America was greater in territorial extent than Europe and Africa combined, but expressed his belief that he could penetrate by some passage to the Indian Ocean. The chart[1] which his brother drew, contributed towards creating the supposition in Europe that at about the 40th degree of latitude such a passage might be found. Verrazano's letter to Francis I. has recently been shadowed with historic doubt, in a volume of nearly two hundred pages, from the facile pen of Hon. Henry C. Murphy; but its uncertain light is by no means extinguished. Neither is it less interesting because of the poverty of actual proof in regard to its authenticity. One paragraph relating to the " *bellissimo lago* at the mouth of the great river" points significantly towards our own sylvan solitudes, as follows : —

" After proceeding one hundred leagues we found a very pleasant situation among some steep hills, through which a large river, deep at the mouth, forced its way into the sea; from the sea to the estuary of the river any ship heavily laden might pass with the help of the tide, which rises eight feet. But as we were riding at anchor in a good berth we would not venture up in our vessel without a knowledge of the mouth, therefore we took the boat, and entering the river we found the country on the

---

[1] A copy of this chart is now in the possession of the American Geographical Society, having been recently obtained from the College of the Propaganda Fide in Rome at the instance of Chief Justice Daly, and is a geographical curiosity.

2

banks well peopled, the inhabitants not differing much from the others, being dressed out with the feathers of birds of various colors. They came towards us with evident delight, raising loud shouts of admiration, and showing us where we could most securely land with our boat. We passed up this river about half a league, when we found it formed a most beautiful lake upon which they were rowing thirty or more of their small boats from one shore to the other, filled with multitudes who came to see us. All of a sudden, as is wont to happen to navigators, a violent contrary wind blew in from the sea, and forced us to return to our ship, greatly regretting to leave this region, which seemed so commodious and delightful, and which we supposed must also contain great riches, as the hills showed many indications of minerals." [1]

The letter was dated, " Ship Dolphin, in the Port of Dieppe, Normandy," was a lengthy document, and, besides furnishing curious evidence of the state of nautical science at that time, gives us a fair picture of the North American Indian as first seen by white men. We are induced to believe that the proprietors of Manhattan Island were an amiable people, and had made some progress in the arts which tend to ameliorate the savage. They were not hostile to visitors, and knew something of agriculture. War was evidently unknown to them, as we can learn of no defenses against hostile attacks. They were, doubtless, of that tribe afterwards called Delawares, or, as they styled themselves, Lenni Lenape, which means original or unmixed men.

It was an entirely different race that Champlain encountered in his wanderings into the State of New York, from the north, in 1609. They were fierce and cruel warriors, somewhat advanced in policy, arts, and agriculture, and had already instituted a confederacy of five independent nations, with a sort of congress of their own, seeming to know somewhat of civilized life and much of warlike achievement, long before they became students of the white man's craft. They called themselves Aquanu Schioni, or the United People. Iroquois is not an Indian, but a French name, and is a generic term, having been bestowed upon that type of language, the dialects of which were spoken by the Five Nations. We have strong reasons for suspecting that during the interim between Verrazano's visit and the subsequent Dutch settlement, the martial Iroquois extended their conquests from the inland lakes to the Atlantic shores, leaving the deteriorating effects of barbarous warfare upon the inhabitants, as, at the latter period, the river Indians and many upon the

[1] *Beschryv van America*, by Jan Huyghen Van Linschotten. (Amsterdam). *N. Y. H. S. Coll.*, Vol. I. (Second Series) pp. 45, 46. *Hakluyt*, III. 360, 361. *Harris's Voyages*, II. 348. *North American Review* for October, 1837. *Belknap's Am. Biog.*, I. 33.

sea-coast were found subject to the Iroquois, acknowledging the same by the payment of an annual tribute.

Of the subsequent career of Verrazano very little is known. We catch fugitive glimpses of him only, enough to excite but not sufficient to satisfy curiosity. There is evidence existing that he commanded an expedition to the Indies for spices, in 1526, and it is supposed that he was engaged also in piratical ventures. He disappeared from public view, after having greatly advanced the knowledge of the new country and given France some claim to an extensive and picturesque territory.[1]

1526.

Group of gentlemen, showing fashions of the day.

1572.   1593.   1620.   1628.   1650   1670.

In 1525 Estevan Gomez, a decoyed Portuguese, who had been the chief pilot of Magellan on his southern voyage, presuming that, since a strait to Cathay had been discovered in the south, there must necessarily be one at the north, sailed in the interests of Spain to find it. He is supposed to have cruised along our coasts as far as the Hudson River, since Rio de Gamas was the first name of European origin which it bore, and there is evidence of his having sailed to the shores of Maine, that land being described upon the Spanish maps as the Tierra de Gomez.[2] He, like Verrazano, drew a chart and it was the more valuable of the two, as the former was entirely unknown down to the year 1582, when it appeared in

---

[1] *Charlevoix, Nouv. Fr.*, I. 78 ; *Bancroft*, I. 13. *Annibale Caro, Lettere Familiari*, Tomo I. let. 12. *Article by Hon. J. Carson Brevoort, in Journals Am. Geog. Soc. N. Y.*, Vol. IV.

[2] *Herrera*, Dec. III. lib. 8. cap. 8. *Navarrete*, I. e. p. 179. *Oviedo (Sommario)*, cap. 10, fol. 14. *Peter Martyr*, Dec. VIII. cap. 9.

the Hakluyt Collection of Voyages. Gomez's draft was embodied in the planisphere made by Ribero, now preserved in the British Museum. At a congress held at Badajos after Gomez's return, at which were present Sebastian Cabot, then pilot-major of Spain, and all the most distinguished geographers of both Spain and Portugal, the outlines of America were fixed for the first time, the chart of Gomez was adopted by the official chart-makers, and from their works, with occasional amendments, passed into all the charts and maps of the sixteenth century, and some of the seventeenth. Beyond the information thus obtained, Gomez's voyage was very meager in results. He caught a few Indians to carry as trophies to the Spanish king, Charles I.; but when he arrived at Coruna, the courier who was despatched by post with the news, mistook slaves (*esclavos*) for cloves, which was what Gomez had promised to bring home with him should he reach Cathay, and there was great excitement among the courtiers and nobles until the ludicrous blunder was corrected. " Then," says the quaint chronicler of the event, " there was much laughter."[1] From that time Spain had no confidence in any northern enterprise. " To the South ! to the South !" was the cry, and all the strength and resources she could spare from her home wars was directed towards the prosecution of her discoveries and conquests in South America. " They that seek riches," said Peter Martyr, " must not go to the frozen North !"

For the next three fourths of a century the wilds and wastes of North America received comparatively little notice from the European powers. It was visited at different points and dates by fishermen and private adventurers, and a few flags were raised and colonies planted, but its geography, farther than its coast-outline, remained almost wholly unknown. During the interval France was too much occupied by her fruitless expeditions into Italy, and her unequal contest with the power and policy of Charles I. of Spain, and also by the civil wars with which she was desolated for nearly half a century, to speculate amidst her miseries upon possibilities, or lay plans for the future extension of her territories except upon parchment. England, too, through most of that period, was agitated and weakened by intestine broils or unwise interference in foreign affairs. Her immense navy, which has since enabled her to give law to the ocean, was then scarcely in embryo ;[2] and her commerce about the year 1550 had become so nearly extinct that bankruptcy appeared for a time

---

[1] *Gomara*, chap. 40 (1st edition, 1552). *History of the West Indies*, by Peter Martyr (1530). *Historia de las Indias Occidentales*, by Antonio de Harrera (edition 1601), Tomo III. Dec. III. cap. 8.

[2] *Robertson's Historical Disquisition on Ancient India*, sect. 4, p. 154.

inevitable. Native produce was in no demand, foreign importations had ceased, and a singular monopoly, consisting chiefly of the factors of extensive mercantile houses in Antwerp and Hamburg, had obtained control of her markets, and, vampire-like, was sucking her remnant of strength. The statesmen and the merchants of the realm met **1555.** in consultation, and took counsel of the aged and justly celebrated Sebastian Cabot, who, although he had thrice made the attempt to reach Asia by the north without success, had never given up his hobby, that " some great good lay in store for the world by the way of the Polar Seas." He advised that the northern coasts of Europe be explored for new markets, and an effort made to reach Cathay by a Siberian route.

A company was accordingly formed, which was called " The Society for the Discovery of Unknown Lands," and an expedition was fitted out in 1553, the expenses of which were mostly borne by private subscription. It was placed under the command of Sir Hugh Willoughby, and the bold Richard Chancellor was made pilot-major of the fleet. The vessels became separated during a storm, and Willoughby with two of them, after the most terrific hardships, reached an obscure harbor on the desolate coast of Lapland, where he and his men finally perished. Chancellor, with heroic persistence, pushed his way through frozen waters where sunlight was perpetual, and landed in safety at Archangel. Russia was then scarcely known to Western Europe. Chancellor made good use of his opportunities. He journeyed by sledge to Moscow, and was invited to a personal interview with Emperor Ivan the Terrible. A lucrative and permanent trade was established between the two countries, which was the foundation of the commercial and political relations that have continued with slight interruptions to the present time. By it a fresh impulse was given to productive industry in England, and her credit was improved, while intercourse with the English secured to the Russians civilization, intelligence, and comfort. When Chancellor returned in 1554 to England, he was the bearer of a letter from Ivan the Terrible to Edward IV. The Muscovy Company, as it was afterwards styled, obtained a formal charter from the Crown, dated February 6, 1555, in which Sebastian Cabot was named as its first governor. It was granted a charter of privileges also by the Russian Emperor, and commenced energetic operations. The same company, after a brilliant career of more than three hundred years, is still in existence. For full fifty years after its organization it absorbed the energy and the surplus capital of the English nation; and nothing was attempted in America save a few unimportant settlements, which came to nothing.

Meanwhile the Dutch were preparing for a marvelous leap into public notice. When, in 1580, Philip II. united Portugal to Spain, and presently began his war upon England, his ports were closed against English vessels. Therefore England was forced to buy her spices, silks, and other Indian produce of the Dutch. But the revolt of the Netherlands followed in quick succession, and Dutch vessels were excluded from Lisbon, which had been so long the European depot for Indian wares. Although the Dutch were not a creative people, there was no nation under the sun which, being strongly pushed in one direction, was more sure to succeed than they. They had begun already to reap large profits from their English trade. Prices had gone up on all India goods; that of pepper by two hundred per cent. They were compelled, as it were, to seek a direct passage to the Orient. Thus originated the great commercial corporation known as the Dutch East India Company. Their vessels followed in the track of the Portuguese around Africa. The directors were mostly city nobles of the old school, and so prosperous became the company that in twenty years they divided more than four times their original capital among the shareholders, besides having acquired a vast amount of property in colonies, fortifications, and vessels.

East India Company's House.

While struggling for freedom, amid the smallest beginnings, and at war with the nation the shadow of whose haughty flag waved over half a conquered world, and whose fashions and language controlled the courts of Europe, the Dutch received the impetus which raised them to the rank of a great power. More than one hundred Protestant families, the very pith of the nation, were driven from Belgium by the Spaniards, and found their homes in Holland and Zealand. The ruin of the ancient trade and opulence of Belgium and the sudden expansion of the Dutch Republic were two sides of the same event. But the exiled Belgians had no intention of remaining permanently in Northern Netherlands. They breathed a new element of commercial strength into the atmosphere, and at the same time were putting their shrewd heads together to devise some method by which Belgium might be delivered from the Spanish yoke. They well knew that the wide possessions of Spain were open to the resolute attacks of a vigorous foe. Finally, they originated the gigantic scheme of a warlike company of private adventurers, who should conquer or ruin the Spanish settlements, seize the Spanish transports, and cut off all communication with her Transatlantic dependencies. And they proposed to name it, very appropriately, the West India Company.

The obstacles in the way of putting so vast a project into execution were very great. John of Barneveld was at the head of affairs in the Dutch Republic, and advocated peace. He was too practical a philosopher not to appreciate the enormous advantages his country had just gained. The victorious return of the Belgians to their native province would only remove commerce and political lead to the south, and was in no case to be desired. He was fully determined to prevent the existence of any such warlike corporation as the one under consideration. But the Belgians found energetic allies. The lower classes in the Holland towns favored them because that Barneveld was hated for his aristocratic proclivities. Influential men from the other Dutch provinces lent their aid because the Advocate aimed at an overweening influence for Holland. The House of Orange gave them the hand of fellowship because this great family aspired to wider dominion and to a less limited authority than they had hitherto possessed.

The leader of the Belgian party was William Usselincx, an exiled Antwerp merchant of noble descent, whose force of will was simply marvelous, and whose magnetic influence over his countrymen was so great that they seemed to think with his brain and act with his hand. His ready pen kept the political life of Holland in one continual ferment. He was opposed to peace with Spain under any circumstances. He said the quarrel was in its nature irreconcilable and eternal, because it was despotism sacerdotal and regal arrayed against the spirit of rational human liberty. His arguments were convincing, and his wit was as flashing and as quickly unsheathed as a sword.

The Dutch revolt was in itself the practical overthrow of religious tyranny. It was a healthy and, for the age, an enlightened movement. But theological disputes arose upon the ruins of popular delusions, even among the Protestants themselves. Arminius, from the ancient University of Leyden, undertook the difficult task of justifying before the tribunal of human reason the doctrine of the condemnation of sinners predestined to evil. He publicly taught, also, that the ministers of the church ought to be dependent upon the civil authority. The municipalities caught at the cleverly thrown bait, and attempted to free themselves from the pretensions of the established clergy. Gomar, a celebrated scholar and a religious fanatic, defended the doctrines of the established Protestant church and its principles of ecclesiastical polity. He was an intimate associate of Usselincx ; and both, being courageous, crafty, far-seeing men, were anxious to prolong a war which would render **1606.** the absolute government of the magistrates impossible, and submission to the Prince of Orange a political necessity.

Thus two parties were formed which lasted down to the French Revolution, and even at the present day there remains of them nearly as much as of whiggism and toryism in England. They were divided in almost every question of public interest. The Belgian party were strict Calvinists and democrats, and their policy was to carry on the war with Spain until Belgium should be freed. The Barneveld party were Arminians, aristocrats, republicans, and quite content to give Belgium over to the Spaniards.

The question of the West India Company was agitated for nearly thirty years. Its actual existence dates from the year 1606. That is, commissioners were named from the Assembly at that period, and discussions were frequent in regard to it. But Barneveld, who was at the head of the Assembly, never seriously thought of confirming the corporation. He only wished to use it as a threat for the intimidation of Spain, and it was chiefly by this menace that the twelve years' truce was accomplished, which played so important a part in the history of the Netherlands.

The wrangling between the two political parties grew more fierce as the details of the peace negotiations became known. The river Scheldt was to be closed, Antwerp thus ruined, Belgium given up, and all attacks upon the Spanish forbidden. The peace party maintained the principle of excluding strangers from every employment, and of concentrating all public offices in a few patrician houses of the old stock. The impoverished, but proud and fiery Belgian exiles looked with dismay at their gloomy prospects in the event of the truce being agreed upon, and put forth all their energies towards the accomplishment of the West India Company. Usselincx wrote a series of pamphlets, in style simple and effective, and which belong to the most remarkable productions of that class of literature. They created such a sensation, and attracted to such a degree the attention of contemporary historians, that the most distinguished of them all, Emanuel van Meteren, reprinted one of them entire.

But the pamphlets, like the plan for the West India Company, only served to accelerate the conclusion of the truce. The Advocate made a singular use of his adversary's weapons. A cessation of hostilities for twelve years was signed by the representatives of the two nations in 1609. It was a signal victory for the aristocratic party. **1609.**

But ten years later the great statesman paid for it with his life. No sooner had the Calvinistic faction gained the ascendency than the West India Company became a fixed fact. And it was due almost entirely to the herculean exertions of Usselincx. It is singular that a man who has earned so honorable a place in history should be so little known to the world. It is true that he never held an official position, yet he founded two great commercial companies, which were so prolific in results that, had justice been properly meted out, his name would have been immortalized. He contributed more than any power to annihilate Spain. He brought to New York the nation in which the principle of free communities — the vital principle of American liberty — was carried out to its full extent. He made Sweden a maritime power. And by the success of his enterprises, he was, in 1629, instrumental in saving Holland from the Spanish yoke, — an act so vast in its consequences that for it alone he deserves the eternal gratitude of all Germanic Europe.

In the mean time, and just about the date of the conclusion of the twelve years' truce with Spain, the East India Company had unwittingly discovered Manhattan Island, with which account the next chapter opens.

Portrait of John of Barneveld.

CHAPTER II.

1609 – 1614.

HENRY HUDSON.

HENRY HUDSON. — HIS VOYAGES. — HE DISCOVERS MANHATTAN ISLAND. — HIS VOY-
AGE UP THE HUDSON RIVER. — HIS VISIT TO AN INDIAN CHIEF. — HIS TRAGICAL
FATE. — AMERICAN FURS. — SETTLEMENT OF VIRGINIA. — VOYAGES TO MANHATTAN.
— THE FUR TRADE. — BURNING OF THE TIGER. — BUILDING OF A SHIP AT MAN-
HATTAN. — DESCRIPTION OF MANHATTAN ISLAND. — THE MANHATTAN INDIANS. —
CUSTOMS AND DRESS. — MONEY AND POLITICS. — TRADING PRIVILEGES.

OF the personal history of the illustrious navigator Henry Hudson
very little is known. The first view we have of him is in the
church of St. Ethelburge, Bishopsgate Street, London, in the summer of
1607, whither he had gone with his crew to partake of the sacrament
before sailing under the auspices of the Muscovy Company in search of a
passage to "Asia across the North Pole." His whole life as known to
the world extends only over a period of about four years; and there is
no portrait of him, not even a contemporaneous print of doubtful authenticity. This is the more remarkable as he lived in an age when it was
quite the fashion to preserve the pictures of celebrities.[1] He appears before us a manly man in middle life, well educated, courageous, cool, an
expert in seamanship, and of wide experience in his country's service.
Who he was, has been a matter of much speculation. His father was
probably Christopher Hudson, one of the factors of the Muscovy Company, and their agent in Russia as early as 1560, a personage who a
little later was made governor of the company, — an office he retained
with honor until 1601. The grandfather of the discoverer of New York
is supposed to have been the Henry Hudson who, in 1554, figured among
the founders, and was the first assistant, of the Muscovy Company.

---

[1] *Purchas His Pilgrimes and Pilgrimage. Hakluyt Collection of Voyages.* Vol. I. *N. Y.
H. S. Coll.* (First Series). *Henry Hudson in Holland,* by Hon. Henry C. Murphy. *Henry
Hudson the Navigator,* by Dr. Asher, member of the Hakluyt Society of London. *Histori-
cal Inquiry concerning Henry Hudson,* by General John M. Read, Jr. *Sailing Directions of
Henry Hudson,* by Rev. B. F. de Costa.

Hudson's voyage in 1607 resulted only in his attaining a much higher degree of northern latitude than any of his predecessors. **1607.**

The next year he sailed north again, but returned without having achieved any further measure of success. **1608.**

The news that such voyages were in progress traveled in due course of time to Holland, and rendered the Dutch East India Company uneasy lest the discovery of a short route to India by their industrious rivals should suddenly deprive them of a lucrative trade. The learned historian, Van Meteren, was the Dutch minister at the Court of St. James, and through him messages were transmitted inviting Hudson to visit Holland.

It was not long ere the famous sea-captain arrived at the Hague, and was received with much ceremony. The officers of the company met, and all that had been discovered concerning the northern seas was carefully discussed. **1609.** The Dutch had not been behind their neighbors in daring exploits. Even while raising enormous sums of money towards carrying on the war with Spain, they had bent every energy towards extending their commerce. Merchant companies and private adventures had been encouraged and assisted by the government. A number of expeditions had endeavored to reach " China behind Norway," and trading monopolies had been established in Guinea and at Archangel ; in short, the sails of the nation whitened the waters of almost every clime. The noblemen who directed the affairs of the East India Company were as cautious as they were enterprising. Some of them had been so influenced by the representations of the sorely disappointed De Moucheron, Barentsen, Cornelissen, Heemskerck, and others, that they declared it would be a waste of time and money to attempt again the navigation of the vast oceans of ice. But Hudson stood before them full of enthusiasm, and expressed his ardent conviction that Asia might be reached by the northeast. Peter Plantius, a clergyman of the Reformed Dutch Church in Amsterdam, who had been engaged with Usselincx in trying to found the West India Company, opened a correspondence with Hudson, and sent him some of his own published works. Plantius had a profound knowledge of maritime affairs, the result of unwearied investigations, and he warmly seconded the effort to search for a northeastern passage. He said that the failure of Heemskerck in 1596 was due to his trying to go through the Straits of Weygate, instead of keeping to the north of the island of Nova Zembla.

After much delay, an expedition was finally planned and Hudson placed in command. The Amsterdam Chamber defrayed the expenses. They furnished a yacht, or Dutch galliot, — an awkward, clumsy kind of a brig, with square sails upon two masts. It was a tolerably safe craft, but a slow sailer, of forty lasts' or eighty tons' burden, and was called the

2

Half Moon. It was manned with a crew of twenty men, partly English and partly Dutch sailors. Hudson was instructed to pass by the north and northeast of Nova Zembla, towards the Straits of Anian, and to search for no other routes or passages but the one in question. He obeyed his employers to the letter, until the cold grew so intense that the seamen of the East India Company, who had been accustomed to warmer climates, became chilled and unfit for duty. Once or twice the vessel escaped as by a miracle from unknown currents, then mountains of ice encompassed it, and the crew were so terrified that they arrayed themselves in open rebellion. Hudson's only alternative was to turn back. He at once gave his attention to searching for a passage to Asia through the American Continent. He was familiar with Verrazano's charts and

Hudson's Ship.

reports, and he was a personal friend of Captain John Smith, whose adventures in America were watched in England with critical interest. He had good reasons for supposing that there was some communication with the South Sea at about the fortieth degree of latitude. He accordingly sailed southward as far as Virginia, then cruised along the shore in a northerly direction until the 2d of September, when he anchored in sight of the beautiful hills of Neversink, which hold the post of honor near the portals to our island. The next day he ventured a little farther into the lower bay, and found what he supposed to be three great rivers, one of which he tried to enter, but was prevented by "the very shoal bar before it."

Sept. 2.

Sept. 3.

On the morning of September 4th he sent out a small boat to explore and sound the water, and a good harbor was found where

Sept. 4.

the sea "was four and five fathoms, two cables' length from shore." A great many fine fish were also discovered. Indians were seen along the shores, and towards evening they came prospecting around the *Half Moon* in small canoes. They were dressed in skins, wore feathers in their hair, and were adorned with clumsy copper ornaments. They brought with them green tobacco, and offered it as a peace-offering. They were so civil that a party of the sailors landed among them the next day, and were very well and deferentially treated. In addition to **Sept. 5.** tobacco, they seemed to have a great abundance of maize, or Indian corn, dried currants, and hemp.

On the 6th, John Coleman, an Englishman, who had been with Hudson on his previous polar voyages, was sent with four seamen **Sept. 6.** to sound the Narrows. They passed through Kill von Kull to Newark Bay. The sweetness of the inner land, and the crisp saltness of the distant sea, were mixed in one delicious breeze, and they reported the country " as pleasant with grass and flowers as any they had ever seen." While returning to the *Half Moon* late in the afternoon, they were attacked by some Indians in canoes, and John Coleman was killed by one of their arrows. The Indians doubtless fired at random, as there is no evidence that hostilities were continued, or any attempt made to capture the boat, which in the confusion might have been done with the greatest ease. Night came on, and the frightened sailors lost their light and their way, and were tossed about on the troubled sea until ten o'clock the next morning, when, with the remains of their murdered officer, **Sept. 7.** they were at last received upon the *Half Moon.* Coleman was buried upon a point of land near by, which was called Coleman's Point.

For some days afterward Hudson spent his time in examining the shores, sounding the waters, and bartering with the Indians. The latter were closely watched, but manifested no knowledge of the fatal affray by which John Coleman had lost his life. On the 11th the *Half Moon* was cautiously guided through the Narrows, and anchored **Sept. 11.** in full view of Manhattan Island. How little Hudson dreamed that it would one day become the home of Europe's overflowing population! His mind was occupied with visions of a different character. He was encouraged to believe that he had at last found the passage to Cathay; for the river stretching off to the north was of such gigantic proportions as to dwarf almost to insignificance the comparative streamlets of the eastern continent! He determined to proceed at all hazards; but the wind was ahead, and he could move only with the flood tide, hence it was not until the 14th that he commenced the ascent of the **Sept. 14.** river in earnest.

If Hudson had been a trained detective he could not have been sharper-
eyed in his observations of the country along his route than his circumstantial journal indicates.   The Indians hovered about his vessel, anxious
to trade their produce for the buttons, ornaments, and trinkets of
the sailors.   On the 17th he anchored at a point just above the
present city of Hudson, and the next day accompanied an old Indian
chief to his home on the shore.   It was a circular wigwam, and upon the
Englishman's entrance, mats were spread upon the ground to sit upon,
and eatables were passed round in a well-made red wooden bowl.   Two
Indians were sent in quest of game, and returned with pigeons.   A fat
dog was also killed, and skinned with sharp shells.   Hudson was served
to a sumptuous repast, but he declined an invitation to spend the night
with his royal host, and the Indians, supposing it was because he was
afraid of their bows and arrows, broke them in pieces and threw them in
the fire.

Sept. 17.

They proceeded on their way up the river for a few days, but
at last navigation became obstructed, and a boat was sent eight
or nine leagues in advance to measure the water.   "Seven foot and
unconstant soundings" deterred the bold mariner from proceeding farther.   He had gone as far as he could, and Asia was not yet.   There
are conflicting opinions as to the precise point reached by the *Half Moon*,
but it is generally supposed that it attained about the latitude of Castle
Island, just below Albany.

Sept. 23.

The glowing description which Hudson gave of the country and its resources was incorporated in an elaborate work by the Dutch historian
De Laet, one of the directors of the West India Company some years
later.   Hudson wrote "that the land was of the finest kind for tillage,
and as beautiful as the foot of man ever trod upon."   He made himself,
it seems, very agreeable to the natives.   On one occasion he persuaded
two old Indians and their squaws, and two maidens of sixteen and seventeen years, to dine with him in the cabin of his vessel, and said that
"they deported themselves with great circumspection."   At another time
he treated some of the sachems to wine until they were merry, and one
of them was so very drunk that he could not leave the *Half Moon* until
the next day.[1]

Hudson commenced his return on the 23d, and, eleven days afterwards,
"went out of the mouth of the great river," and sailed for Europe.   On
the 7th of November he arrived safely at Dartmouth, England, where he
was detained by the English authorities, who denied his right to enter

---

[1] At this very moment the eminent French navigator, Champlain, was upon the waters of
the lake which bears his name, and within one hundred miles of Hudson.

into the service of a foreign power. He forwarded a report of his adventures to the Dutch East India Company, with a proposal to change six or seven of his crew and allow him to try the frozen seas again. His communication did not reach Holland for several months, and his employers were ignorant of his arrival in England. When they were at last apprised of the fact, they sent a peremptory order for him to return with the *Half Moon.* He would have obeyed, but the arm of the English law withheld him. The vessel, however, was sent with its cargo to Holland.

The Muscovy Company made immediate arrangements to avail themselves of Hudson's valuable services, and fitted out another expedition to the north seas. The expenses were defrayed by private English gentlemen, one of whom was Sir Dudley Diggs. Hudson sailed towards the northeast again until the ice obstructed his progress, then proceeded westward, and after many trials and hardships discovered the bay and strait which have immortalized his name ; but his superstitious crew greatly magnified the dangers by which they were surrounded, and at last arose in open mutiny. They placed their heroic commander in a small boat, to drift helplessly over the dreary waste of frozen waters, which are, alas ! his tomb and his monument. To fully appreciate the character of such a man as Henry Hudson, we must never lose sight of the fact that the real hazards of those early voyages were exceedingly great, and the imaginary perils infinite. Even now, after the lapse of nearly three centuries, we cannot dwell upon his tragic fate without mourning that such a life could not have been spared to the world a little longer, and that he who accomplished so much for posterity should have had so slight a comprehension of the magnitude of his labors and discoveries.

The aristocratic Dutch East India Company regarded all Hudson's reports with indifference. They had a great aversion to America, and ignored it altogether. They had been coining wealth too long and too easily from the immense profits on their India goods to be interested in anything short of the Orient. They actually sent again two vessels to the North in 1611, to explore among the icebergs for a direct route to Asia, hoping to soften the edge of former disappointments.

But there were traders in the Netherlands whose eyes were opened to a hidden mine of wealth through the skins with which the returned *Half Moon* had been laden. Furs were much worn in the cold countries of Europe, and the Dutch reveled in the costly extravagance. These furs were obtained mostly through the Russian trade. From sixty to eighty Holland vessels visited Archangel every year, agents were stationed at Novogorod and other inland towns, and a brisk traffic was kept **1610.**

up with ancient Muscovy. The wise Russian Emperor had courted this prosperous commerce, but had laid a duty of five per cent on all imported goods, and allowed an equivalent amount to be exported duty free. Whoever exported more than he imported paid a duty of five per cent on the difference.[1]

If the same and similar goods could be obtained in the New World in exchange for the veriest bawbles, and command a remunerative market at home, it was a golden opportunity. At all events, it was worth an investigation. A partnership was organized, and a vessel fitted out and laden with small wares. A portion of the crew of the *Half Moon*[2] were secured, and the ship was placed under the command of an experienced officer of the East India Company. Hudson River was again visited, and a cargo of skins brought back to Holland. The account of the voyage was published, and the friendly disposition of the Indians much descanted upon.

It was at a period when the press everywhere was teeming with pamphlets of travel and descriptions of the earth as far as known. Geography was becoming with some few a life-study, and every added grain of knowledge was seized with avidity.

England had already begun to think seriously of planting colonies in the New World. The timid James I., perplexed to know how to provide for the great numbers of gallant men of rank and spirit who had served under Queen Elizabeth both by sea and by land, and who were out of employment, had permitted a company to be formed in London for the purpose of settling Virginia, and in 1606 granted it a patent which embraced the entire Atlantic coast from Cape Fear to Nova Scotia, excepting Acadia, then in actual possession of the French. Many of the impoverished noblemen immediately embarked for their new home, and had been tilling the fertile soil of Virginia for three years prior to the discovery of Manhattan Island. These general facts were well known in Holland, and the States-General in 1611, through Caron, their ambassa-
1611. dor at London, made overtures to the British government to join them in their Virginian Colony, and also to unite the East India trade of the two countries. But the statesmen of England were unfavorably inclined towards either project. Their reply was, " If we join upon equal terms, the art and industry of your people will wear out ours." [3]

---

[1] *Richesse de la Hollande,* I. 51. *Muilkerk.* *McCullagh's Industrial History.*

[2] *Heckewelder, New York Hist. Soc. Coll. Yates and Moulton.*

[3] *Winwood's Memorial,* III. 239. *Extract of a letter* from Mr. John Moore to Sir Francis Winwood, the English ambassador at the Hague, dated London, December 15, 1610. *Corps Dip.,* V. 99 - 102. *Grotius,* XVIII. 812. *Van Meteren.*

During the summer of 1611, Captain Hendrick Christiaensen, while returning from a voyage to the West Indies, where many Dutch vessels obtained salt every year, necessary for curing herrings, found himself in the vicinity of the "great river," the Hudson (which the Belgian Dutch called " Mauritius," in honor of the Prince of Orange), and but that his ship was heavily laden would have ventured in. As soon as he arrived in Holland he entered into a partnership with Adriaen Block; they chartered a small vessel, took goods on commission, and sailed for Manhattan. The Indians were glad to see them, and they had no difficulty in freighting their craft with skins. They also persuaded two young Indian chiefs, Orson and Valentine, to accompany them to Holland.

Block wrote a long and graphic account of his voyage, which was published and circulated in all the Dutch cities. Its object was to awaken public interest in the American fur-traffic. The two Indians were taken from place to place to create a sensation, and with pretty good success. Erelong three wealthy merchants, Hans Hongers, Paulus Pelgrom, and Lambrecht Van Tweenhuysen, formed a partnership and equipped two vessels for Manhattan. They were the *Fortune* and the *Tiger*, and were intrusted to the command of Christiaensen and Block. Presently some gentlemen in North Holland sent two vessels to trade at Manhattan. One of them, the *Little Fox*, was commanded by Captain John de Witt, an uncle of the celebrated Dutch statesman who was grand pensionary of the Netherlands in 1652. The other was the *Nightingale*, and was in charge of Captain Thys Volckertsen. Within three months the owners of the *Fortune* and the *Tiger* sent out a third vessel, commanded by Captain Cornelis Jacobsen May, who ten years later was made Director-General of New Netherland. Their success was flattering, for the Indians were captivated by the trinkets which were offered in exchange for skins.

It is worth noting that from the very first the admirable commercial position of Manhattan Island indicated it, as if by common consent, as the proper place where furs collected in the interior **1613.** could be most readily shipped for Europe. Christiaensen, having won the confidence of his employers, became a legally appointed agent, and by means of trading-boats visited every creek, bay, river, and inlet in the neighborhood where an Indian settlement was to be found. He often took, also, long journeys into the country on foot, and was everywhere treated by the savages with kindness and consideration.

One clear cold night in November the *Tiger* took fire at its anchorage, just off the southern point of Manhattan Island, and Block and his crew escaped with much difficulty to the shore. The vessel burned to the water's edge, and as the other ships had all sailed for Holland there was

3

no possible hope of any assistance from white men before spring. Block accepted the situation like a true philosopher, and erected four small habitations on the island at about the present site of 39 Broadway. Of their architecture we have no means of information, but they were doubtless of the wigwam family. The Indians were hospitably inclined, bringing food out of their abundance, and the sailors were enabled to exist with comparative comfort until spring. Block was a plain man, of no inconsiderable tact and capacity. He had been bred to the law, but had deserted his profession to study the science of navigation. He must have had a versatile genius, for he set himself at work with great energy to construct a new vessel upon the charred remains of the *Tiger.*[1]

Burning of the Tiger.

It was an arduous undertaking with the slender materials at command. Indeed, it requires considerable stretch of the imagination, in this age of mechanical luxury, to understand how such a feat could have been accomplished at all. But it is one of the facts of history, and early **1614.** in the spring of 1614 the justly famous yacht of 16 tons' burden was found seaworthy, and launched in the waters of the Upper Bay.

It was significantly called the *Restless.* Block set forth in it to explore

---

[1] *Plantagenet's New Albion. Brodhead,* 48, note. *Breeden Raedt aen de Vereeinghde Nederlandsche Provintien* contains a statement made by the Indians, that "when the Dutch lost a ship we provided the white men with food until the new ship was finished." *De Laet* says : "To carry on trade with the Indians our people remained all winter." *De Vries* repeats the same. A record of the burning of the Tiger exists in the Royal Archives at the Hague under date of August 18, 1614.

the tidal channels to the east, where no large ships had yet ventured. He passed the numerous islands, and the dangerous strait called Hell Gate, and to his amazement found himself in a "beautiful inland sea," which extended eastward to the Atlantic. He was the first European navigator, as far as we have any precise knowledge, who ever furrowed the waters of Long Island Sound.

About the same date, Captain May again reached the American shores and, hovering along the eastern and southern boundaries of Long Island, proved that it was indeed an island. Finding his business soon transacted at Manhattan, he visited Delaware Bay, and bestowed his name upon its northern cape. Block, meanwhile, interested himself in the peculiarities of the southern coast of Connecticut, and sailed up the great Fresh River as far as where the city of Hartford now stands.[1] He then proceeded to Cape Cod, where he unexpectedly met Christiaensen. After some discussion they finally exchanged vessels, and Block sailed for Holland in the larger and safer craft of his comrade, while Christiaensen continued to make explorations along the coast in the *Restless.*

Thus was Manhattan Island again left in primeval solitude, waiting till commerce should come and claim its own. To the right, the majestic North River, a mile wide, unbroken by an island ; to the left, the deep East River, a third of a mile wide, with a chain of slender islands abreast ; ahead, a beautiful bay fifteen miles in circumference, at the foot of which the waters were cramped into a narrow strait with bold steeps on either side ; and astern, a small channel dividing the island from the mainland to the north, and connecting the two salt rivers. Nature wore a hardy countenance, as wild and untamed as the savage landholders. Manhattan's twenty-two thousand acres of rock, lake, and rolling table-land, rising in places to an altitude of one hundred and thirty-eight feet, were covered with somber forests, grassy knolls, and dismal swamps. The trees were lofty ; and old, decayed, and withered limbs contrasted with the younger growth of branches, and wild-flowers wasted their sweetness among the dead leaves and uncut herbage at their roots. The wanton grape-vine swung carelessly from the topmost boughs of the oak and the sycamore, and blackberry and raspberry bushes, like a picket-guard, presented a bold front in all the possible avenues of approach. Strawberries struggled for a feeble existence in various places, sometimes under foliage through which no sunshine could penetrate, and wild rose-bushes and wild currant-bushes hobnobbed, and were often found clinging to frail footholds among the ledges and cliffs, while apple-trees pitifully beckoned with their dwarfed fruit, as if to be relieved from too intimate an association with the giant

[1] *De Laet. Mass. Hist. Coll.,* XV. 170. *Brodhead,* I. 57.

progeny of the crowded groves. The entire surface of the island was bold and granitic, and in profile resembled the cartilaginous back of a sturgeon. Where the Tombs prison now casts its grim shadow in Center Street, was a fresh-water lake, supplied by springs from the high grounds about it, so deep that the largest ships might have floated upon its surface, and pure as the Croton which now flows through the reservoirs of the city. It had two outlets, — small streams, one emptying into the North, the other into the East River.

It was not an interesting people whom the Dutch found in possession of Manhattan Island   They have ever been surrounded with darkness and dullness, and we can promise very little entertainment while we call them up before us, with all their peculiarities of life, language, and garb, and with a few touches sketch them as a whole. They were tall, well made, broad of shoulder and slender in the waist, with large round faces, mild black eyes, and a cinnamon complexion. The distinguished scholar, Dr. O'Callaghan, says : " It was first supposed that this color was the effect of climate, but it has since been discovered to have been produced by the habitual use of unctuous substances, in which the juice of some root was incorporated, and by which this peculiar tinge was communicated to the skin of the North American Indian." They lived in huts which were built by placing two rows of upright saplings opposite each other, with their tops brought together and covered with boughs. These dwellings were skillfully lined with bark to keep out the cold. They were often large enough to accommodate several families ; but it must be remembered that each Indian only required space enough to lie down straight at night, and a place to keep a kettle and one or two other housekeeping articles. Windows and floors were unknown ; fires were built on the ground in the center, and the smoke escaped through a small aperture in the roof.

The Indians never located permanently, but moved about from one place to another, selecting such points as were naturally clear of wood. The men understood the use of the bow and arrow, and spent much of their time in hunting and fishing. They made fish-lines of grass or sinews, with bones or thorns for hooks. *Wigwas* was a process of fishing after dark, similar to that termed *bobbing* at the present day. They gathered shell-fish and oysters in great abundance, so that, wherever the land has been found covered with the *débris* of shells, it has been regarded as a certain indication that an Indian village once existed there. The Dutch found one such locality on the west side of Fresh-Water Pond, which they named Kalch-Hook, or Shell-Point. In course of time this name was abbreviated into Kalch or Collech, and was applied to the pond itself.

The women, as usual among uncivilized nations, performed most of the field-work. The savages raised large quantities of corn and patches of tobacco, and even pumpkins were cultivated in a rude, primitive way. They used sharpened shells for knives, and with them cut down trees and constructed canoes. Although they had no tables nor ceremonies of eating, they were by no means indifferent to the quality of their food. It is even reported by some of the Dutch pioneers in the wilderness that much of their cookery was very palatable. *Yockey* was a mush made of pounded corn and the juice of wild apples. *Suppaen* was corn beaten and boiled in water. *Succotash* was corn and beans boiled together. Corn was often roasted upon the ear. Fish and meat were boiled in water, undressed, entrails and all; dog's flesh was one of their greatest delicacies. Hickory-nuts and walnuts they pounded to a fine pulp, and, mixing it with water, made a popular drink. Supplies for winter they lodged under ground in holes lined with bark. But, like the South American Indians, they had no letters, and had never broken in a single animal to labor. They conveyed their ideas by hieroglyphics, like the ancient Egyptians, and were extremely superstitious.

Of dress both sexes were extravagantly fond. The mantle of skins worn by the men was often elaborately trimmed. The hair was tied on the crown of the head, and adorned with gay-colored feathers. The hair of the women was dressed very much like Guido's picture of "Venus adorned by the Graces." It was sometimes braided, and sometimes flowing loose down the back with the appearance of having been crimped. The same style may now be seen in some recent paintings made by artists who have visited the Southwestern Indians, and it is not unusual in the pictures of the old masters and in the busts of the Grecian sculptures. A highly ornamented petticoat, made of whale-fins and suspended from a belt or waist girdle, was very costly. Its value is said to have been equal to eighty dollars of our currency. Chains of curious workmanship, sometimes only a collection of stones, were much worn upon the necks of both men and women, and wrought copper was suspended from their ears in a very Oriental manner.

Gold was regarded by them with contempt on account of its color. Red and azure were their favorite hues. *Wampum* was their money, while at the same time it was used as an ornament for their persons. It consisted of small cylindrical beads manufactured from the white lining of the conch and the purple lining of the mussel shells. The purple beads were worth just twice as much as white beads. From a circulating medium among the Indians, it became the recognized currency of the early white settlers, and the Dutch called it *sewan*. In like manner, a species of shells are used at the present day as money in the interior of Africa.

Public affairs were managed by a council of the wisest, most experienced, and bravest of their number, called sachems. They had no salary nor fees, to make office an object of ambition. Authority was secured by personal courage and address, and lost by failure in either of those qualities. Law and justice, in our acceptation of the terms, were unknown to them. When a murder was committed, the next of kin was the avenger. For minor offences there was rarely ever any punishment. Prisoners of war were considered to have forfeited all their rights of manhood, and towards them no pity or mercy was shown. With excessive thirst for excitement and display, war became their common lot and condition. The whole tendency of their lives and habits was to that point, and to be a great warrior was the highest possible distinction. They had crude and confused opinions respecting the creation of the world and a future existence, and held vague ideas of a discrimination between the body and soul, but to all systems of religion they were entire strangers. Such was the race which gave way to modern civilization.

Sept. 1. On Block's return to Holland,[1] with the *Fortune* (Christiaensen's vessel, which he had exchanged for the *Restless*), his patrons received him with enthusiasm, and made immediate preparations to avail themselves of a new feature of governmental favor towards enterprising trade.

March 27. The States-General, anxious to encourage the foreign commerce of Holland, in January, 1614, had granted a charter to an association of merchants for prosecuting the whale fishery in the neighborhood of Nova Zembla, and for exploring a new passage to China. One of the directors of this new company was Lambrecht Van Tweenhuysen, one of the owners of Block's vessel, the *Tiger*. The importance of a similar grant of privileges to those at whose expense new avenues of trade were being opened in the vicinity of Manhattan was almost immediately discussed. A petition to that effect was sent to the States.[2] The States recommended it to the general government. On the 27th of March the following was entered upon their records : " Whosoever shall from this

---

[1] A story has been many times repeated, how Captain Samuel Argall of Virginia, while returning from an inglorious expedition against the French colony at Acadia, in November of 1613, stopped at Manhattan and compelled the Dutch who were there to submit to the king of England. Such may have been in accordance with the facts, for it would have been in keeping with Argall's coarse, self-willed, and avaricious character ; but it is not supported by authentic state papers.

[2] "The States " of Holland must not be confounded with the States-General. The difference was as great as between the representation of the State of New York and the Federal Congress at Washington.

time forward discover any new passages, havens, lands, or places shall have the exclusive right of navigating to the same for four voyages." It was required that reports of discoveries should be made to the States-General within fourteen days after the return of the exploring vessels, in order that the parties entitled to them should receive the specific trading privileges. When simultaneous discoveries should be made by different parties, the promised monopoly was to be enjoyed by them in common.

View of the Vyverberg at the Hague.

CHAPTER III.

1614 – 1625.

THE HAGUE.

The Hague. — John of Barneveld. — New Netherland. — New England. — The First Fort at Manhattan. — Political Commotion in Holland. — John of Barneveld's Execution. — Imprisonment of Grotius. — The West India Company. — The Amsterdam Chamber. — The First Settlers of New Netherland. — Death of the Prince of Orange. — Death of James I. — The Marriage of Charles I. — The First Governor of New Netherland.

THE Hague was the seat of government in the United Provinces. It was a fine old city, with broad, straight streets, lined with trees and traversed by canals. It owed its origin to a hunting-seat built by the counts of Holland, and its name to the enclosing *haeg* or hedge **1614.** which surrounded their magnificent park. It derived its importance from the constant presence of gifted and illustrious men. The princes of Orange, the officers of State, and the foreign ministers accredited to the Republic, resided within its limits. It was the home of the ancient nobility, and the favorite resort of persons of culture and distinction from all portions of modern Europe. It was a city of palaces. Among its public buildings was the *Binnehof,* or inner court, the ancient palace of the counts of Holland. It contained a magnificent Gothic hall, the rival of Westminster. Opposite was a smaller apartment, superbly decorated, in which were held the " dignified and extraordinary " meetings of the States-General.

The management of the Seven United Provinces was vested in five chief powers, — the States-General, the Council of State, the Chamber of Accounts, the Stadtholder, and the College of the Admiralty. The States-General had the most influence and authority, but it was hardly a representative body. It was, more properly speaking, a deputation from the Seven Provinces, who were bound to obey their constituents to the letter. It was composed chiefly of noblemen. Twelve usually assembled at its ordinary meetings. Prominent among them was the founder of the Dutch Republic, — he who had organized a political system out of chaos; a man who had no superior in statesmanship, in law, in the science of government, in intellectual power, in force of character. It was John of Barneveld. He bore an ancient and knightly name. He was of tall and commanding presence. While he cared more for the substance than the graces of speech, he was noted for his convincing rhetoric and magnetic eloquence. He had now reached his sixty-eighth year. He was austere and unbending in manner, with thin white hair pushed from a broad forehead which rose dome-like above a square and massive face. He had a chill blue eye, not winning but commanding, high cheek-bones, a solid, somewhat scornful nose, a firm mouth and chin, the latter of which was enveloped in a copious white beard, and the whole head not unfitly framed in the stiff, formal ruff of the period. His magisterial robes were of velvet and sable, and thus we have him in our mind's eye as he sat at the head of the oval council table on October 11, 1614.

In the midst of the transaction of weighty affairs of state, a committee of Amsterdam merchants was announced. They were admitted without delay. The chief speaker among them was Captain Block. He told his story of adventure and discovery, and displayed a " Figurative map " of the country at the mouth of the Hudson River and thereabouts, which had been executed artistically under his own supervision, and which was spread upon the council table and examined with interest. Barneveld asked many questions, all of which Block answered promptly and intelligently. Barneveld remarked that, " in course of time those extensive regions might become of great political importance to the Dutch Republic." Several of the Statesmen expressed the same opinion.

The merchants were before them to petition for a special trading license to the Hudson country, and the " high and mighty lords " were so favorably inclined, that their secretary was at once ordered to draw up a minute of a trading charter, the original of which is in existence, and records in almost illegible characters the first use of the term NEW NETHERLAND. This instrument was sealed and attested before the applicants left; and by it they were granted the full and exclusive right to trade in New Netherland for four successive voyages to be made within three years from the 1st of January, 1615. It expressly forbade any other party from sailing out of the United Provinces to that territory, or frequenting the same, within the time specified, under pain of confiscation of vessels and cargoes, and a fine of fifty thousand Netherland ducats to the benefit of the grantees of the charter.[1] It was a distinct act of

---

[1] The original charter was brought to light by Mr. Brodhead during his researches in the archives of the Hague.

sovereignty over the country between New France and Virginia, which was called "New Netherland," a name which it continued to bear for half a century. It was entirely without boundary lines, and extended westward as far as the Dutch might be supposed ever to explore. Yet the charter, after all, was only an assurance to the associated merchants of a monopoly of trade against the competition of other Dutch subjects, without, for the present, asserting the right to exclude the outside world. No political powers were granted for the government of the new province, and nothing was at the time contemplated but discovery and traffic.

1615.

It is a singular coincidence, that, during the same summer in which Block was exploring Long Island Sound, Captain John Smith was visiting the bays and coasts of Maine and Massachusetts. And about the very time that the States-General were granting the above charter, the Crown Prince of England was confirming the name "NEW ENGLAND," which Smith had given to the territories north of Cape Cod.

Block never revisited this country, where he holds an honorable place in the annals of its discovery, and where his name will ever be remembered as the first ship-builder. The enterprising Van Tweenhuysen sent him north on a whaling voyage, as his services were esteemed more valuable in that direction.

The merchant company were not slow to draw from their new possessions the largest returns. They fitted out several vessels for the Hudson or Mauritius River, and sent with them some of the shrewdest traders in Holland. They ordered Christiaensen to erect a trading-house, which he did on an island a little below the present city of Albany. It was thirty-six feet long by twenty-six wide, and around it was raised a stockade fifty feet square, which was encircled by a moat eighteen feet wide, the whole being defended by two pieces of cannon, and eleven stone guns mounted on swivels. The post was called Fort Nassau, was garrisoned with twelve men, and placed under the command of Jacob Eelkens, who had a rare talent for making friends with the Indians. Christiaensen had scarcely completed his work, when he was murdered by one of the young chiefs whom he had taken to Holland three years before, thus finding a grave in the country to which he had made more successful voyages than any one man up to that time.

In the early part of the spring, a building was erected on the lower point of Manhattan Island, to answer the double purpose of storehouse and fort. It was a small structure of logs, without any very practicable defences of any kind. A few huts sprung up around it after this wise. A square pit was dug in the ground, cellar fashion, six or seven feet deep and from twelve to thirty feet long, floored with plank, and roofed with spars, bark and sods being added when necessary to exclude the cold. The traders lived usually in their ships, but it was found convenient to have a few men on shore to guard the warehouse, and to keep the furs gathered, ready for shipment to Holland.

Thus two years passed. No event of any note happened until the spring of 1617, when Fort Nassau was nearly washed away by a freshet on the breaking up of the ice on the Hudson River. The traders desired to remain in the vicinity of this great eastern terminus of **1617.** the Indian thoroughfare, and built a new fort on an eminence, which the Mohawks called *Twass-gunshe*, near the mouth of the *Twasentha* River. Soon after taking possession of these new quarters, a formal treaty was concluded with the chiefs of the Five Nations. The ceremonies were imposing, each dusky tribe having an ambassador present. The pipe of peace was smoked and the hatchet buried, the Dutch agreeing to build a church over the instrument of death, so that to exhume it would be to overturn the sacred edifice. It was a politic movement on the part of the Dutch, for they thus secured the quiet possession of the Indian trade to the filling of their coffers, while the Indians were well satisfied, for they had learned the use of fire-arms from the French, and were now eager to get them and maintain their supremacy over the neighboring tribes.

On the 1st of January, 1618, the trading charter expired by its own limitation, and, when the associated merchants tried to renew it, the States-General only consented to give a special license to trade at New Netherland from year to year. The Dutch Republic was **1618.** once more in commotion from centre to circumference, and the West India Company was the chief point at issue. Since the ministers of state were unable to prophesy probable results, they were careful not to involve themselves in American affairs. Usselincx had been quietly at work since 1609, and, although he was well aware that the establishment of the desired company must necessarily be postponed until the expiration of the truce, yet there were many obstacles to be removed, and, in his judgment, it was none too early to be taking the preliminary steps. In all his movements he was effectually aided by Maurice, Prince of Orange.

The outward shape of the strife was religious. A theological battle was in progress between Arminianism and strict Calvinism. A conspiracy against Barneveld was rapidly approaching its crisis. He was a liberal Christian, and had all his life advocated religious toleration. The Belgians called him "Pope John." They charged him with being a traitor bought with Spanish gold. Poisonous pamphlets appeared day

3

after day, until there was hardly a crime in the calendar that was not laid at his door.   It was a horrible personal assault upon the venerable statesman who had successfully guided the counsels of the infant commonwealth at a period when most of his accusers were in their cradles, and when mistake would have been ruin to the Republic.   He stood in the way of the formation of the West India Company, and the Belgians were determined to get rid of him.   Prince Maurice was an ambitious general, and although Barneveld had been the first to elevate him to his father's position as Stadtholder, and inspire the whole country with respect for his military skill and leadership, yet the truce with Spain deprived him of a large share of his authority and influence, and he felt himself so thwarted by the power of the patriotic advocate, that he helped to organize the campaign against him, making no secret of his hatred, and determination to crush him from off the face of the earth.

At last the Advocate was arrested by the order of Maurice, and closely confined in one of the apartments of the Prince.   The shower of pamphlets and lampoons and libels began afresh, filled with dark allusions to horrible discoveries and promised revelations.   Even the relatives of the fallen statesman could not appear in the streets without being exposed to insult, and without hearing all manner of obscene verses and scurrilous taunts howled in their ears.   The clergy upheld Maurice, because, having been excluded from political office, they were in active opposition to the civil authorities.   They helped to spread the story that Spain had bribed Barneveld to bring about the truce and kill the West India Company ; and also that the Advocate had plotted to sell the whole country and drive Maurice into exile.   The nobles, the states, the municipal governments, and every man who dared defend Barneveld, were libeled and accused of being stipendiaries of Spain. The war waxed so serious that soldiers were kept constantly on duty to prevent bloodshed in the streets.   And at this critical moment, the weak king of England inflamed the mischief by personal intermeddling.

Aug. 29.

The National Synod of Dordrecht was finally appointed, and foreign churches invited to send delegates.   It came together on the 13th of November, 1618, and sat for more than seven months, at a cost to the Republic of a million of guilders.   It resulted in a Calvinist victory, the Arminians being pronounced "innovators, rebellious, leaders of faction, teachers of false doctrine, and disturbers of church and nation."

Nov. 13.

The president said, in his address to the foreign members at the close of the session, that "the marvelous labors of the Synod had made hell tremble."

1619.

May 9.

Meanwhile, Barneveld had been for several months confined in a dreary garret room, and kept in complete ignorance of even the most insignificant every-day events. On the 18th of March he was brought to trial, but not permitted the help of lawyer, clerk, or man of business. His papers and books were denied him, also pen, ink, *Mch. 18.* and writing materials. He made his own defence with indignant elo- quence, but it availed him nothing. Four days after the termination of the Synod, on the morning of the 13th of May, the majestic old man was led into the vast hall, which had so often in other days *May 13.* rung with the sounds of mirth and revelry, and received the sentence of death. Then he was taken to a scaffold in the hollow square in front of the ancient palace, and beheaded. He was within five months of the completion of his seventy-second year. His property was confiscated to the state, and his proud and prosperous family reduced to beggary.

His principal adherents were imprisoned for life. Hugh Grotius, who was a powerful opponent to the prospective West India Company, was sent to the Castle of Loevenstein, which stood on an island formed by the Waal and the Meuse. He was an illustrious Dutch jurist and author, and influenced a large class of people who were not directly involved in the theological controversy. He was so closely guarded in his prison for a time, that not even his father or his wife were allowed an interview with him. His wife at last obtained permission to share his fate. In her society and in close study he passed two years, during which time he wrote some very important works. His wife had been in the habit of receiving books in a large chest, and, finding that the guards had grown somewhat careless in its examination, she ingeniously managed one morn- ing to have Grotius carried out in it. He disguised himself as a mason, and with trowel and rule made his escape to Antwerp. He afterward took up his abode in Paris, and was protected by the French government.

Immediately after the removal of the chief antagonist, Usselincx started a subscription list for the West India Company, but it was *1619.* filled out slowly. The States-General were unwilling that a foreign element should create to itself so mighty an arm. They had no sym- pathy with its grand purpose, which was to combat and worry Spain, and gather its recompense from the spoils. The East India Company openly and persistently opposed the whole project. For a year scarcely any progress was made. Finally the English unwittingly added the straw which was to turn the scale. They had taken cognizance *1620.* of the Dutch traffic on the Hudson River, and instructed their minister at the Hague to remind the States-General of the patent which James I. granted to the Plymouth and London companies, and of its broad juris- diction. He was also directed to warn the Dutch statesmen of the impropriety of their permitting Dutch vessels to visit English coasts for purposes of traffic. There was an animated diplomatic correspondence on the subject, each government trying to define its own position, and justify its own acts, and establish its own rights. But no definite results were attained, save that the States-General were sharp-sighted enough to discover that the only power by which they could possibly hold New Netherland was absolute possession. In the newly drafted constitution of the West India Company was a clause by which the corporation would be obligated to people the so-called Dutch territory of North America. The prospective company, therefore, was suddenly regarded with less disfavor. In a few weeks it received decided and direct encouragement from the Dutch government; and, after many birth-throes, it became an accomplished fact.

1621. Probably no private corporation was ever invested with such enormous powers. But the right to the vast and valuable lands in America, with which it was endowed by the States-General, was not legally established, and was the seed for a bountiful harvest of discontent. The company was organized into almost a distinct and separate government. It might make contracts and alliances with the princes and the natives comprehended within the limits of its charter. It might build forts. It might appoint and discharge governors, soldiers, and public officers. It might administer justice. It might take any step which seemed desirable for the promotion of trade. And its admirals on distant seas were empowered to act independently of administration. It was required, it is true, to communicate with the States-General from time to time of its treaties and alliances, and to furnish detailed statements of its forts and settlements, and to submit to their high mightinesses for approval, all instructions for prominent officials, and apply to them for high commissions. It took upon itself, however, — and without properly appreciating the magnitude of the undertaking, — one of the greatest of public burdens, the naval war against a powerful enemy, and assumed at once a thoroughly dangerous position. Warfare is always so manifestly unprofitable, that to undertake it without the aid of government, in any event, is sheer folly. " Needful assistance " was promised, but the company soon found that they had no means of enforcing the fulfilment of such a promise. And to increase their future difficulties, the Barneveld party recovered strength, and, in course of years, found in the De Witts even more powerful leaders than Barneveld himself had been.

The West India Company was modelled after the East India Company. It was guaranteed the trade of the American and African shores of the Atlantic, precisely as the East India Company had been granted the right to send ships to Asia, to the exclusion of the other inhabitants of the Dutch provinces. It was divided, like the East India Company, into five chambers, or boards, which were located in the five cities of Amsterdam, the Meuse, North Holland, Zealand, and Friesland. Each of these chambers was a separate society, with members, directors, and vessels of its own. The capital of the company was six million florins, — about $ 2,500,000. This sum, however, was not divided equally between the five chambers, but Amsterdam had four ninths; Zealand, two ninths; and each of the other three chambers, one ninth. In nearly the same proportion was the representation in the general committee of nineteen directors who conducted the common affairs of the company, and were called the " College of the XIX." [1] They adopted the democratic prin-

West India Company's House.

ciples of the Belgians, and accorded to the shareholders a voice in all important proceedings, which was a constant reproach to the East India Company, and created no inconsiderable amount of slanderous misrepresentation and cavil.

As soon as the provisional existence of the company had become a permanent one, there was a change in the tone of public sentiment. Those who had used their pens with the utmost virulence to prevent its accomplishment, turned about and declared it to be the first move on the direct road to national prosperity. Its final organization was delayed two

---

[1] Charter at length, in *Groot, Placaat Book*, I. 566 ; *Hazard; Brodhead; Lambrechtsen; De Laet; Doc. History of N. Y.; O'Callaghan; Biographical and Historical Essay on the Dutch Books and Pamphlets*, by G. M. Asher, LL. D.

years longer; during which time two questions occupied the minds of all interested parties. " Shall the Guinea trade and the salt trade be integral parts of the patent of the company ? " The affirmative gained the day. Then arose pecuniary complications. The opposition of the East India Company had created a panic in regard to the credit and character of the new company, and the directors were not able to collect a sufficient amount of capital to commence operations until they had twice declared the list of subscribers closed. The original charter was also twice amplified in certain points of detail, and articles of internal improvement adopted. It was formally approved by the States-General on the 21st of June, 1623.

1623.   The extraordinary company struck out boldly. Its fleets often numbered as many as seventy armed vessels each. It seemed destined to humble Spain, whether it suppressed or promoted piracy. It met with many brilliant successes. Prizes were captured of such value, that, during the first few years, the shareholders received from twenty-five to seventy-five per cent upon their investments. Although the six millions of capital had been brought together with difficulty, twelve millions were easily added. The first ten years of its existence were marked by three events of historic importance, — the taking of Bahia in 1624; the capture in 1628 of the Silver fleet, which consisted of large armed transports conveying silver and gold from the South American mines to Spain; and the conquest of Pernambuco in 1630: all of which are fondly remembered in Holland. But its history might have been foretold. There were defects in its organization which rendered it unable to establish a thriving commerce or flourishing settlements. And the possessions which it obtained were never governed properly.

Within a month after its incorporation, three ships were sent to the West Indies, and an armed expedition dispatched for an attack upon

Brazil. New Netherland received only such attention as was necessary to satisfy the States-General that it would ultimately be colonized, according to contract, by the company. New Netherland affairs were intrusted to the Amsterdam Chamber. The treasure was sufficient to have enriched them if they had known how to develop its valuable trade and fertile lands. They blundered, as bodies of men with more light and wider experience have been continually blundering ever since their time. They desired to make money in some more swift and easy manner, and failed to put their efforts in the right place. They however erected the indefinite territory into a province, with a grant from the States-General of the armorial distinctions of a count. The seal was a shield bearing a beaver proper, surmounted by a count's coronet, encircled by the words "SIGILLUM NOVI BELGI."

The directors of the Amsterdam Chamber were John De Laet, the historian, Kiliaen Van Rensselaer, Michael Pauw, Peter Evertsen Hulft, Jonas Witsen, Hendrick Hamel, Samuel Godyn, and Samuel Blommaert. They were all men of wealth and education. But they were none of them very deeply interested in the wild Indian country. However, they took measures to secure a party of Protestant Walloons, to send over to their new possessions. These people were that portion of the Belgians who were of Celtic origin, and were ingenious as well as brave and industrious. They had applied the year before to the English for permission to emigrate to Virginia, but the conditions offered by the Virginia Company had been such that they had seen fit to decline them. A ship called the *New Netherland*, commanded by Captain May, conveyed thirty of these families to our shores. They brought with them a knowledge of the arts in which they were proficient, and were distinguished for their extraordinary persistence in overcoming difficulties. A young man by the name of Dobbs was one of the passengers in this vessel. He was the ancestor of a large and influential family, among whom was Dr. Benjamin P. Aydelott, a well-known physician in the time of Dr. Hosack and Dr. Francis. Upon their arrival, two families and six men were sent to the great Fresh River, and the remainder proceeded to the fort on the Hudson River, excepting eight of the men, who remained at Manhattan. A new fort was immediately projected on the alluvial soil now occupied by the business portion of Albany, and called Fort Orange, in honor of Maurice, who was greatly beloved by the Belgians.

About the same time preparations were made for occupying the genial valley of the South or Delaware River. A few traders selected a spot on its east bank, near the present town of Gloucester, in New Jersey, and built a fort which they called Fort Nassau. Later in the season other vessels came from Holland, bringing settlers, and about eighteen persons were added to the colony at Albany. Adrian Joris, the second to Captain May in command, sent his vessel to Holland in charge of his son, and stayed with them all winter. Eelkens was arrested in January for imprisoning a Sequin chief on board his yacht, and Peter Barentsen was made commander of the post in his place.

The income from the fur-trade of New Netherland during that first year amounted to twenty-eight thousand guilders. The West India Company, who were already elated with their victories in Brazil,

1624.

1625.

were gratified, and began to discuss the project of building a town upon Manhattan Island, which was represented as a point of great natural beauty, and favorably located for commerce. To test the disposition of adventurers, they publicly offered inducements to such as might wish to emigrate to America. Volunteers were not wanting in populous Holland, and three large ships were soon freighted, also one fast sailing yacht. Six entire families and several single men, forty-five persons in all, with household furniture, farming utensils, and one hundred and three head of cattle, were conveyed to Manhattan. One of the party, William Verhulst, succeeded Captain May in the government, as the latter was suddenly called to Holland on important private business.

The year 1625 was marked by two important European events which had a direct bearing upon the future prospects of New Netherland. The first was the death of the accomplished Maurice, at the Hague. In him the West India Company lost one of their most zealous and influential champions, and the national army their commander-in-chief. The office of Stadtholder was conferred upon Frederick Henry, who excelled the military Maurice in political capacity, and succeeded him as Prince of Orange.

The other event was the death of James I. of England, and the consequent accession of Charles I. to the throne. England was already at war with Spain. James had been exasperated at the failure of his projects in relation to the marriage of Charles with the Infanta, Donna Maria, who subsequently became the wife of the Emperor of Germany. He had been plunged into hostilities, which the resources of England were illy able to sustain, and Charles had no sooner taken the scepter in his hand than he commenced negotiating an alliance with the Dutch Republic against the common enemy. Meanwhile he married Henrietta Maria, daughter of Henry IV. of France. She came to England with a train of Roman Catholic priests and attendants, which quickly stirred the English people into a commotion, and intensified the hatred which they bore towards Roman Catholic queens. Charles was a monarch of elegant, gentleman-like tastes, of dignified manners, and of great obstinacy of purpose. He could not apparently conceive of any obligation on the part of a king to his subjects. He set himself deliberately at work, in defiance of all law, to introduce into his own country the system of government which prevailed in France. He had not by any means the wretched excuse of a wife's influence. Henrietta had indeed refused to be crowned, lest she should join in the rites of the Church of England. But she was a mere child in years, totally uncultivated, and ignorant of the language and history of her husband's country, and knew nothing whatever about the Anglican religion. She had been not only betrothed, but married to Charles by proxy. The Duke de Chevreuse, a near kinsman of the king, acted in that capacity. At the ceremony, which took place in the porch of Nôtre Dame, he was attired in black velvet, and wore a scarf flowered with diamond roses. The bride wore a magnificent white satin robe, threaded with gold and silver, and flowered with French lilies in gems and diamonds. The Queen mother, Marie de Medicis, shone like a pillar of precious stones, and her long train was borne by two princes of the blood, Condé and Conti. But out of respect to the religious feelings of Charles, the English ambassadors, and even the proxy himself, withdrew from the Nôtre Dame during the concluding mass. The cortège of the bride landed at Dover, June 23d, just after sunset. At ten the next morning the king arrived while Henrietta was breakfasting. She rose from the table, hastily, and ran down a pair of stairs to greet him, and offered to kneel and kiss his hand; but he was too full of gallantry to permit her to do so, and caught her in his arms and folded her to his heart with many loving caresses. She had been taught to say, " Sir, I have come to your Majesty's country to be commanded by you," but the set speech failed her, and she burst into tears. Charles became very fond of her and took great pride in her beauty and musical powers, but he never discussed matters of state with her. Pope Urban VIII. was exceedingly averse to the marriage. He said, " If the Stuart king relaxes the bloody penal laws against the Roman Catholics, the English will not suffer him to live long ! If those laws are continued, what happiness can the French princess have in her wedlock ? " These words were prophetic, as we shall see in future chapters.

Finally, through much astute diplomacy, the treaty of alliance, offensive and defensive, was concluded between England and the United Netherlands ; each nation agreeing to furnish fleets for the purpose of destroying the Spanish commerce in the East Indies.[1] It was also stipulated that the war and merchant vessels of the two countries should be free to enter the ports of each other. One of the first-fruits of this new relationship[2] was a meeting of the West India Company for the transaction of special business. The moment had arrived when the colonization of New Netherland might be attempted without probable English inter-

---

[1] *Corps Dip.*, Vol. II. 458, 478. *Clarendon State Papers*, I. 41, 53. *Aitzema*, I. 671, 1226. *Lon. Doc.*, I. 36.

[2] About the middle of October, King Charles sent the Duke of Buckingham and the Earl of Holland as ambassadors extraordinary to the States-General to negotiate a still closer alliance. *Wassenaar*, XII. 39 ; XVI. 13. *De Laet. Doc. Hist. N. Y.*, III. 46, 47.

ference. A system of government for the new province was considered, and various plans discussed for inducing settlers to emigrate across the Atlantic. A governor was named, and three weeks later received his appointment. It was Peter Minuet, of Wesel, in the kingdom of Westphalia. He sailed from Amsterdam in December, in the ship *Sea Mew*, Captain Adrian Joris, and arrived at Manhattan on the 4th of the following May (1626).[1]

[1] Leonard Kool came to New Netherland in the *Sea Mew*, as private secretary for Peter Minuet. His name may now be found attached to grants of land in connection with that of the governor. He was the ancestor of the Cole family in this State; the orthography of the name having passed through a variety of phases. *Rev. David Cole's genealogical tree.*

Landing of the Walloons at Albany.

CHAPTER IV.

1626 – 1633.

PURCHASE OF THE SITE OF NEW YORK.

PETER MINUET. — THE FIRST BUILDINGS. — THE HORSE-MILL. — THE FIRST GIRL BORN
IN NEW NETHERLAND. — DIPLOMATIC CORRESPONDENCE. — THE EMBASSY TO PLYM-
OUTH. — NEW NETHERLAND NOT A PECUNIARY SUCCESS. — THE CHARTER OF FREE-
DOM AND EXEMPTIONS. — THE MANORIAL LORDS. — KILIAEN VAN RENSSELAER. — THE
VAN RENSSELAER MANOR-HOUSE. — THE GREAT SHIP. — GOVERNOR MINUET AND
RECALL. — WRANGLING AMONG THE DIRECTORS OF THE COMPANY.

THE rocky point of Manhattan Island, near what is now known as
the Battery, was, on the 6th of May, 1626, the scene of one of the
most interesting business transactions which has ever occurred **1626.**
in the world's history. It was the purchase of the site of the **May 6.**
city of New York. The West India Company had instructed Peter
Minuet to treat with the Indians for their hunting-grounds, before he
took any steps towards the erection of buildings. He accordingly made
a somewhat superficial survey of the island, which had been designated
as the field for pioneer operations, and estimated its area at about twenty-
two thousand acres.[1] He then called together some of the principal
Indian chiefs, and offered beads, buttons, and other trinkets in exchange
for their real estate. They accepted the terms with unfeigned delight,
and the bargain was closed at once. The value of the baubles which
secured the title to the whole of Manhattan Island was about sixty
guilders, equal in our currency to twenty-four dollars. On the part of
the Dutch, it was merely a politic measure to establish future amicable
relations with the natives of the country, although it was subsequently
made the basis of the company's claim to the territory. It was, in
itself, a commonplace event; but, in its relation to what has since taken
place, it assumes peculiar significance, and stands out in immortal char-

---

[1] In Dutch phraseology "it was eleven thousand morgens in size." The Rhineland rod
was the Dutch measure for land. It contained twelve English feet four and three fourths
inches. There are five rods to a Dutch chain, and six hundred square Dutch rods constitute
a morgen. *Peter Fauconnier's Survey Book*, 1715 – 1734.

acters as the chief starting-point of the great commercial capital of the west.

Governor Minuet was a man of rare energy and fully equal to the situation. He had had some East Indian experience, and, during the last two years, had spent several months in South America. He was of middle age, hair slightly flecked with gray, a somewhat dull black eye, and a full-sized robust frame. He was permeated with the spirit of adventure, without being hampered with habits of luxury and indolence, like his Virginia contemporaries. He was brusque, and coarse, and self-willed, but kind-hearted, and was admirably successful in winning the confidence of the Indians. His duties were multifarious, but not remarkably difficult, since the people to rule over were few in numbers and obediently disposed.

He organized the government of the province as soon as he had obtained the title deed to Manhattan Island. The supreme authority, executive, legislative, and judicial, had been vested in him by the company, with an advisory council of five of the best men in the colony. These were Peter Byvelt, Jacob Ellertsen Wissinck, Jan Jansen Brouwer, Simon Dircksen Pos, and Reynert Harmenssen. He was empowered with the administration of justice, except in capital cases, when the offender, after being convicted, must be sent with his sentence to Holland. The secretary of the council board, and also of the province, was Isaac De Rasiers, a well-educated young Hollander who arrived in the same vessel with Minuet. After him, in order of position, was the *Schout-Fiscal,* a sort of civil factotum, half sheriff and half attorney-general, and the special custom-house officer. Jan Lampo, of Cantleburg, received the appointment; but he knew very little of law, and was very inefficient in every particular. He was allowed to sit in the council during its deliberations, but had no voice in official proceedings. His compensation was in the civil fines and penalties, and such portion of criminal fines and confiscated wages as the governor and council after prosecution might see fit to bestow upon him. He had no part in captured prizes, and was forbidden to receive presents under any circumstances.

Minuet brought over with him a competent engineer, Kryn Fredrick, who was to superintend the construction of a fort, that being wisely deemed the first business to be dispatched. It did not take long to discover a triangular spot of earth hemmed in by ledges of rock, as if modelled by Nature herself for a fortress. It had a commanding view of the Bay and Narrows, and was but a short distance from the water's edge. This was chosen; but when the work was accomplished it reflected no remarkable credit upon its projectors, except so far as it responded to their immediate necessities, for it was simply a block-house with red-cedar palisades.

About the same time was erected a warehouse of Manhattan stone, having a roof thatched with reeds. It was primitive even to ugliness, without one redeeming touch of architectural finish, but we honor it as the pioneer of all the present long miles of costly business edifices. One corner of it was set apart as the village store, and was the depot of sup-

The First Warehouse.

plies for the colony. It grew erelong to be much haunted by the Indians, who came to sell their furs and drink the " white man's fire-water."

In the course of a few weeks several vessels arrived from Holland, each laden with passengers. The population of the island was thus increased to nearly two hundred; thirty or more cheap dwellings were built around the fort, and the prospect was animated and encouraging. Governor Minuet, Secretary De Rasiers, and Sheriff Lampo occupied a habitation together for nearly three years. Negro servants performed the labor of the household.

The most notable building, as well as one of the most useful, which was speedily erected, was a horse-mill. It was located on June. what is now South William Street, near Pearl. The loft was furnished with a few rough seats and appropriated to the purposes of religious worship. Thus we may observe that, while the settlement of the province had been undertaken with no higher aim than commercial speculation, the moral and spiritual necessities of its people were not entirely overlooked. Two " comforters of the sick " had been sent over with the governor, and it was among their specified duties to read the Bible and lead in devotional exercises every Sabbath morning. Two years later, the learned and energetic Jonas Michaelius was employed to officiate at religious meetings and instruct the children. He was a warm personal friend of Governor Minuet, and exerted a very wholesome influence in the community. An event occurred late in the autumn which, from its sad consequences, deserves special mention. A Weekquaesgeek Indian came from West Chester, accompanied by his young nephew,' to sell beaver-skins to the Dutch. When near the Fresh Water Pond, he was met by three of the governor's negro servants, who seized and robbed, and then murdered him. The boy witnessed the scene and ran away, vowing vengeance. He grew up to manhood, cherishing the terrible oath in his heart, and many long years afterward carried into execution his Indian ideas of justice. The murder was concealed from the authorities, and the murderers escaped punishment.

The fur-trade was so prosperous that the company were quite elated with their operations upon Manhattan Island. Perhaps the reader will be grateful for a glimpse of this remarkable commerce, as pictured in a letter from Peter Schagen of Amsterdam, dated November 5, 1626, in which he announces to the company the arrival of the ship *Arms of Amsterdam*, direct from New Netherland. He writes : —

Nov. 5.

"They had all their grain sowed by the middle of May, and reaped by the middle of August. Our people are in good heart and live in peace there. They send thence samples of summer grain : such as wheat, rye, barley, oats, buckwheat, canary-seed, beans, and flax. The cargo of the aforesaid ship is : —

7,246 ·beaver-skins.	36 wild-cat skins.
178½ otter-skins.	33 minck-skins.
675 otter-skins.	34 rat-skins.
48 minck-skins.	Much oak and hickory timbers."

The same letter contains a record of the birth of the first girl in New Netherland, — Sarah Rapaelje, daughter of Jan Joris Rapaelje, born June 9, 1625.[1]

---

[1] There have been various statements in regard to the residence of Rapaelje at the time of the birth of Sarah. But the depositions of his wife, Catelina Trico, made in New York before Governor Dongan, the year prior to her death, establish the time of her arrival in this country and her first residence. *Doc. Hist. N. Y.*, III. 49 – 51. They went first to live at Fort Orange, Albany, where they remained three years, and where Sarah, the *"first-born Christian daughter in New Netherland,"* was born. They afterwards removed to Manhattan, and from thence to the Walebogbt on Long Island. The age of Catelina Trico, at the time her depositions were taken, was eighty-three years. She stated that she came to this country in 1623 or 1624, in a ship called the *Unity* or *Eendragt*, commanded by Adraen Joris, and that there were four women came along with her who were married on shipboard. Wassenaer, whose

The Dutch were by no means ignorant of their near proximity to the English settlement at Plymouth, and after a while began to discuss the propriety of establishing friendly intercourse with their neigh-bors.   Minuet wrote two letters to the governor of Plymouth, one in Dutch and the other in English, which contained the most polite expressions of good-will, and an offer of various kinds of goods in exchange for beaver and otter skins and other wares. *1627.* *March 9.*

A courteous response came promptly from Governor Bradford. He assured Governor Minuet that for the current year they were fully supplied with necessaries, but would trade at some future time should the rates be reasonable.   He took care, however, to throw out some very marked hints on the questionable propriety of the Dutch traffic with the Indians within the limits of the king's patent.   After writing it in English, he translated his letter into the Dutch language, and sent both copies. *March 29.*

Governor Minuet wrote again in August.   His language was expressed in the same general friendly terms, but he firmly maintained the right to trade in the disputed localities, quoting the States-General and Prince of Orange as authority.   As an evidence, however, of continued good feeling, he sent to Governor Bradford " *a rundlet of sugar and two Holland cheeses.*" *Aug. 7.*

Governor Bradford replied with great apparent deference of manner, only deprecating the "over-high titles" which Dutch politeness required, but which Puritan usage rejected, and repeated his warning respecting the boundary question, requesting that a commissioner be sent to confer personally in the case.[1] *Aug. 24.*

The secretary, Isaac De Rasiers, was accordingly dispatched as ambassador extraordinary to Plymouth.   He was a man of fine address and pleasing manners, and in other respects well fitted for this mission, which was of as much importance in those primitive days as *Sept. 5.*

account was contemporaneous, calls the ship the *New Netherland.*   Sarah Rapaelje, who gave birth to fourteen children, was the maternal ancestor of several of the most notable families of King's County.   At the age of twenty-nine she was the widow of Hans Hansen Bergen, the ancestor of the Bergen family, with seven children.   She afterwards married Theunis Gysbert Bogaert, the ancestor of the Bogaert family in this country.   Some travelers in 1679 visited Catelina Trico, who lived "in a little house by herself, with a garden and other conveniences," and evidently regarded her as a distinguished historical personage.   *Long Island H. S. Coll.*, Vol. I. 342.   It will be observed, that the statement calling her daughter Sarah "the first-born *Christian daughter* in New Netherland," does not conflict with the statement of Jean Vigne, that he was the first *male* born of European parents in this province.

[1] Bradford's correspondence in *N. Y. H. S. Coll.*, I. (Second Series), 355, 360.   *Baillie's Mem. of Plymouth*, I. 146, 147.   *Prince, N. E. Chron.*, 249.   *Mass. Hist. Coll.*, III. 51.   *Morton's Memorial*, 133.   *Moulton*, 378.

the more stately embassies are at the present time. The bark *Nassau* was brushed up and freighted with a few articles of trade, and manned by a retinue of soldiers and trumpeters. Early in October he arrived at Manomet, the advanced post of the English colony, near an Indian village at the head of Buzzard's Bay, the site of the present village of Monument, in the town of Sandwich, and from there he dispatched a courier to Plymouth to announce his presence in the neighborhood. Governor Bradford immediately sent a boat for him and his cargo, and he was escorted with many and imposing ceremonies to the town.[1] He was pleasantly entertained for several days, and sold a large quantity of Indian corn, which enabled the English to better carry on their lucrative trade with the natives. He established a commercial relation, which, but for the subsequent petty quarrels, might have been mutually advantageous to the two lone European colonies. It is interesting to know that the whole tonnage of New England then consisted of "*a bass-boat, shallop, and pinnace.*"[2]

October.

When he returned to Manhattan, De Rasiers brought another letter from Bradford to Minuet, in which, saving always their allegiance to the king of England, he pledged the performance by his colony of all good offices toward the Dutch in New Netherland.

Just about that time, the commander at Fort Orange committed a terrible blunder, whereby he not only lost his own life, but imperiled the lives of all the settlers in that region. He joined a party of Mohicans on the war-path against the Mohawks, which was in disobedience of orders, for the Dutch were pledged to principles of neutrality in reference to all differences among the Indian tribes. In the battle which followed he was killed, also three of his men.

His folly was particularly felt in the sense of insecurity which it threw over the colony; and Minuet, although he succeeded in restoring good feeling with the Mohawks, deemed concentration a necessary policy, and recalled the families from the exposed points, Fort Orange, Fort Nassau, and Verhulsten Island, to Manhattan, where they could be better protected in their interests as well as their homes. Sixteen soldiers only were left at Fort Orange, and the traffic to the South River was limited to the voyages of one small yacht for the present.

1628.

The crop of furs in 1628, amounting to four ship-loads, yielded fifty-six thousand guilders; and two cargoes of ship-timber from Manhattan

---

[1] Winslow's account in *Young's Chronicles*, 306. *Prince*, 208. *Book of Court Orders*, Vol. III. 82. *Pilgrim Memorials*, 122 – 124.

[2] *De Rasiers' Letter*, 350. *Bradford's Letter Book*, 364.

Island sold at Amsterdam for sixty-one thousand guilders. But, after all, the New Netherland colony was not self-supporting. None of the soil was reclaimed, save what supplied the wants of a few farmers and their families; and the only exports were the spontaneous productions of the forest. The mode of life pursued by the people was irregular, and the current expenses of the plantation more than the receipts. It was an unpalatable fact. The company had won brilliant victories by sea, and infatuating wealth had poured into its treasury. Between 1626 and 1628, it had captured one hundred and four Spanish prizes. The nation shared in the glory, but the company alone received the spoils of this marvelous war. Its dividends were advanced suddenly to fifty per cent. Insignificant indeed, in comparison, were the returns from New Netherland. The very subject of North American trade became painfully uninteresting, and the directors avoided allusions to it whenever possible. Finally, at one of their meetings a plan was introduced for a systematic and extended colonization of the whole province of New Netherland. It was discussed at several subsequent meetings, and resulted in a selfish commercial scheme, with a view to drawing private capitalists into the company's ventures.

The scheme was a charter of Freedoms and Exemptions, ma- **1629.** tured and adopted by the company, and confirmed by the States- **June 7.** General, on the 7th of June, 1627. It comprised thirty-one important articles, and was remarkable for being tinctured with the peculiar social ideas of that era, and of promising to transfer to America the most objectionable features of the modern feudalism of Continental Europe.

It offered to any member of the West India Company who should found a colony of fifty adults in any portion of New Netherland, — except Manhattan Island, which was reserved to the company, — and satisfy the Indians for a tract of land not exceeding sixteen miles on one side or eight miles on both sides of a navigable river, and extending inland indefinitely, the title of Patroon, or

Dutch Wind-Mills.

feudal chief of such colony or territory; and the colonists under such patroonships were to be for ten years entirely free from taxation, but would

4

be bound to the patroon in almost absolute servitude. The chief himself would be invested with full property rights, and granted freedom in trade, — except furs, which the company reserved to themselves, — with sundry and various limitations, restrictions, and duties, and the privilege of hunting and fishing within his own domain. The company prohibited manufactures under penalty of the law, but promised protection to the colonists and defence against all enemies; the completion of a suitable citadel on Manhattan Island; and a supply of negro servants. Each patroon was required to provide, immediately, for the support of a minister and schoolmaster, and to make an annual return of the condition of his colony to the local authorities at Manhattan, for transmission to the company. In all its provisions, the charter carefully recognized the commercial monopoly and political supremacy of the West India Company, and was in harmony with the aristocratic sentiment which grew with the acquisition of wealth in Holland. Almost all the real estate there, outside the walls of the towns, was in possession of old families of the nobility, who were unwilling to part with any portion of it. In the wonderful new country it was very apparent that a man might become an extensive landholder and a person of importance with comparative ease. While the company thus made great show of caring for the rights of the aboriginal owners, and held out inducements of labor, capital, religion, and education, it selfishly scattered the seeds of slavery and aristocracy.

As might have been expected, there were men among the directors of the company who stood ready to seize upon the choicest localities, to the discouragement of independent emigrants for whom the charter was intended. Samuel Godyn and Samuel Blommaert, who had had agents prospecting for months, purchased through them a beautiful tract of land extending from Cape Henlopen thirty-two miles up the west shore of Delaware Bay, and opposite sixteen miles square, including **1630.** Cape May. They called it Swaanendael. The title was attested **June.** by Governor Minuet and his council at Manhattan, July 15, 1630, and is the only instrument in existence which bears the original signature of that august body.[1] The purchase was actually effected on the 1st day of June, 1629, seven days before the bill became a law, and was registered at Manhattan on the 19th of the same month.

Kilien Van Rensselaer was one of the oldest and wealthiest of the directors. He had been for many years a pearl and diamond merchant,

---

[1] This original patent was found by Mr. Brodhead in the West India House, at Amsterdam, in 1841, and is now deposited in the secretary's office at Albany. It has the only signatures known to exist of Minuet and his council. *Brodhead,* I. 200. *O'Callaghan,* I. 122.

and had taken a very active part in the formation of the West India Company. Several of his own vessels had been placed at the disposal of the corporation, and he had twice advanced money to save its credit, and hasten its final organization. He was descended from a long line of honorable ancestors, and was himself an educated and refined gentleman of the old school. Early in life he had married Hellegonda Van Bylet, by whom he had one son, Johannes. In 1627, he was married the second time, to Anna Van Wely, and by her he had four sons and four daughters.[1] In the mean time he had sent an agent to New Netherland, and traded with the Indians for land upon the west side of the Hudson River, from about twelve miles south of Albany to Smack's Island, "stretching two days into the interior." Soon after, he concluded the purchase of all the land on the east side of the same river, both north and south of Fort Orange, and " far into the wilderness." This great feudal estate included the entire territory comprised in the present counties of Albany, Columbia, and Rensselaer, and was named Rensselaerswick. Van Rensselaer himself remained in Holland, but managed his affairs through a well-chosen director. His sons took up their abode here after his death, and were successive lords of the colony. Jeremias[2] married Maria, daughter of Oloff S. Van Cortlandt; and Nicolaus married Alida Schuyler. The Van Rensselaer name has been handed down to us through every generation of men who have since had their day in New York, and is interwoven with all that is historical in city and State. The family brought with them the social distinctions of the Fatherland. They brought massive and elaborately carved furniture, and large quantities of silver-plate which bore the family arms. They brought portraits of their ancestors, executed in a

[1] The names of the children of Kiliaen Van Rensselaer were : 1st, Johannes, who married his cousin, Elizabeth Van Twiller ; 2d, Maria ; 3d, Jeremias, who married Maria Van Cortlandt ; 4th, Hellegonda ; 5th, Jan Baptist, who married his cousin, Susan Van Wely ; 6th, Elenora ; 7th, Susan, who married Jan De Lacourt ; 8th, Nicolaus, who married Alida Schuyler ; 9th, Rickert, who married Anna Van Beaumont.

[2] Jeremias Van Rensselaer and Maria Van Cortlandt had a daughter Anna, who married her cousin, Kiliaen, the son of Johannes Van Rensselaer. He died shortly after, and she was married the second time to William Nicolls of New York. Her daughter Mary, in 1713, became the wife of Robert Watts, the ancestor of the Watts family in this country. Jeremias Van Rensselaer and Maria Van Cortlandt had also a son Kiliaen, who married his cousin, Maria Van Cortlandt, and who died in 1701, leaving sons, Jeremias and Stephen, successive lords of the manor. Stephen died 1747, and left a son Stephen, who married Catharine Livingston, and died in 1769. The son of this last was General Stephen Van Rensselaer, who was born in 1764, and who was lieutenant-governor of New York in 1795 and 1798. His first wife was Margaret Schuyler, and their son Stephen was the late patroon. His second wife was Cornelia Patterson, and they had nine children. The other branches of the Van Rensselaer family we shall refer to hereafter.

superior manner for the period, and many original paintings. A manor-house was erected, which in its internal arrangement and finish was very similar to the Holland residence of the Van Rensselaers. There the lord resided among his tenantry, and maintained the same dignity and authority as the landed lords in Europe.

Van Rensselaer had peculiar facilities for peopling his new dominion, and sent out his own ships with laborers and emigrants and implements of husbandry. There was system in his management, and there was order and method in the entire regulation of the colony itself. Hence it was prosperous, while the rest of the province was disturbed by faction, inefficient rulers, and Indian wars.

Van Rensselaer Manor-House in 1874.

About the same time that Rensselaerswick was founded, Michael Pauw purchased Staten Island, Hoboken, Paulus Hook, and the Jersey shore opposite Manhattan, extending inland a great distance. He gave it the pleasant-sounding name of Pavonia. He planted a little colony, which was called The Commune, and the point where they first settled is commemorated by the present romantic little village of Communipauw.

Thus three of the most important localities in the province were artfully secured before the rest of the company were fairly awake. The storm of discontent which arose has scarcely been equalled in the history of private corporations. The new patroons were accused of fraud and double-dealing, and the quarrel assumed alarming proportions. There was an indignant denial of any endeavor to take an unfair advantage of the spirit of the charter, and, as a process of conciliation, other members of the company were taken into partnership in the speculation. Van Rensselaer divided his purchase into five shares, retaining two for himself. He sold one to John De Laet, the historian, and two to Samuel Blommaert. Godyn and Blommaert divided their Delaware property with Van Rensselaer, De Laet, and Captain David Pietersen De Vries. The latter had just returned from a three-years' voyage to the East Indies, where he had been engaged in several notable maritime enterprises. By request of the new firm, he took charge of an expedition to the Delaware, conveying thither thirty settlers, with all the necessaries for the cultivation of tobacco and grain. He landed them, directed in the work of preparing their fields, and not until their first seed was sown did he turn his face again to Holland. It was the purpose of these patroons to prosecute the whale-fishery on the Delaware coast, copying after the French, who had made the business so lucrative in a more northern latitude.

1631.

This matter of feudal estates took up the whole attention of the company for a time. Manhattan Island was scarcely noticed, and improvements were entirely ignored. The houses which were standing were only sufficient for the actual accommodation of the people; and, as we have seen, they were exceedingly simple in construction. The best of them were of hewn plank, roofed with reeds. Many were built entirely of bark. But few trees as yet were cut away, except for shipment to Holland. Not a ridge was smoothed down, and only a few little patches of earth had been brought under cultivation. The fur-trade absorbed what there was of energy and industry.

It was soon found that the patroons were trading with the Indians independently of the corporation. Another quarrel ensued, this time more immediately among the directors of the Amsterdam Chamber. It was finally referred to the College of the XIX. The patroons were self-willed and self-opinionated. They had enormous interests at stake, and they persisted in their right to the fur traffic, under a too liberal construction of the charter. Able lawyers were employed on both sides, and the dispute became so violent that for a long time bloodshed was apprehended.

Meanwhile, two Belgian ship-builders visited Manhattan and tried their skill in converting some of the fine timber into an immense ship. Minuet encouraged them, and supplied them from the company's funds. They accomplished the undertaking; and a vessel of eight hundred tons' burden, which carried thirty guns, was launched in New York Bay. It proved before it was finished more costly than had been expected; and when the bills came before the directors of the company in Holland, the whole proceeding was severely criticised. The States-General regarded it as a sample of the bad management of the corporation. The shareholders grumbled because they were obliged to help pay for such an exhibition of folly. The press censured the Amsterdam Chamber in unsparing terms; and the people talked about the ship in their workshops and stores, and speculated upon the wonderful trees in America. It was full two hundred years, however, before another vessel of such mammoth proportions was built in this country. The fame of this extraordinary naval architecture was, as a matter of course, carried to the ends of the earth, and excited the envy of all the European powers. And it paved the way for the States-General to enter into a rigid examination of the affairs of the West India Company. They decided against the patroons, who were accused of being vastly more interested in filling their coffers with the proceeds of private trade with the Indians, to which they were not entitled, than in the proper colonization of the country. Minuet was suspected of working in their interests, as he had officially ratified their purchases; and the company was advised to recall him. It was accordingly done. Conrad Notleman was appointed sheriff of New Netherland, and sent over to supersede Lampo; he was intrusted with letters, instructing Minuet to report himself immediately in Holland.

1632. Minuet left his government in the hands of his council, of **March 19.** which Jan Van Remund was secretary, De Rasiers having fallen into disgrace with the governor some time before. He sailed in the *Eendragt*, March 19, 1632. Lampo and a number of discontented families were also passengers. They were driven into Plymouth, England, by a terrible storm, and were detained there on a charge of illegally trading in King Charles's dominions.

April 8. Minuet promptly communicated the intelligence to the company, and also to the Dutch minister at Whitehall. The latter hastened to Newmarket, where the king and his court were at that moment, obtained audience of his Majesty, and remonstrated earnestly against the injustice of the whole proceeding, asking for an order for the *Eendragt's* immediate release. Charles declined giving it, on the ground that he " was not quite sure what his rights were."

The main features of the minister's interview with the king were soon laid before the States-General. It provoked another spirited correspondence between the two nations. The Dutch statesmen claimed that they had discovered the Hudson River in 1609; that some of their people had returned there in 1610; that a specific trading charter had been granted in 1614; that a fort and garrison had been maintained there until the formation, in 1623, of the West India Company, which had since occupied the country; and great stress was laid upon the purchase of the land from its aboriginal owners.

May 5. The English based their claims upon the discovery of America by Cabot, and upon the patents granted by James I. They declared that the Indians were not *bona fide* possessors of the soil, and that even if they were, they could not give a legal title, unless all of them jointly contracted with the purchaser. They kindly offered to allow the Dutch to remain in New Netherland if they would submit themselves to the

English government, otherwise they would not be permitted "to encroach upon a colony of such importance as New England."

Sir John Coke was the author of most of the English state papers relating to this subject; but in June of the same year, Sir Francis Windebanke was appointed Secretary of State. It was hardly considered advisable to embarrass the foreign relations of a country, when its own private affairs were already sufficiently complicated : hence Charles contented himself with the assumption of superiority, and did not press the question for a settlement. In the course of a few weeks the Lord Treasurer quietly released the *Eendragt*.

May 27.

The interference of the States-General did not settle the unfortunate disputes among the directors of the company. Upon Minuet's arrival in Holland, commissaries were dispatched to New Netherland to post in every settlement the company's proclamation, forbidding any person, whether patroon or vassal, to deal in sewan, peltries, or maize. The large appropriations of territory were bad enough, but not half so exasperating as individual interference in a trade which was the company's only source of profit, and through which alone it could hope to recompense itself for the expenditure already occasioned by the unprofitable province of New Netherland. "But," said Van Rensselaer, "we patroons are privileged, not private persons." Again and again were the various clauses in the charter analyzed and interpreted. It was a knotty tangle ; and amidst the wrangling over the water, the population of Manhattan Island diminished rather than increased.

Purchase of Manhattan Island.

CHAPTER V.

1633–1638.

GOVERNOR VAN TWILLER.

Wouter Van Twiller. — Captain De Vries. — Van Twiller and the English Vessel. — Captain De Vries and the Governor. — The First Minister. — The First Church and Parsonage. — The First Schoolmaster. — Buildings and Improvements. — New Amsterdam. — Beginnings of Hartford — Troubles with the English. — Quarrels with the Patroons. — Quarrels with the English. — Fort Amsterdam. — Excess and Irregularities. — Purchase of Lands. — Governor Van Twiller's Recall.

THE Amsterdam Chamber, having at last, as was believed, obtained mastery over the patroons, decided to establish forts and mills in New Netherland, in order to give wider scope to their mercantile operations. Despite his private interests, Van Rensselaer had great **1633.** influence among the directors, and succeeded in procuring the appointment of Wouter Van Twiller, one of his relations by marriage, to the command of the colony. It was a politic measure as far as he was concerned; and it was a stupid concession on the part of the company.

Van Twiller had been a clerk in the company's warehouse at Amsterdam for nearly five years, and in the mean time had made two voyages to the Hudson River in the employ of Van Rensselaer, who had select-

Autograph of Van Twiller.

ed him as a fit person to attend to the shipment of cattle to Rensselaerswick. Van Twiller claimed to know all about affairs in New Netherland. He was in point of fact a shrewd trader; but he had no practical knowledge of government, and was ill-qualified to manage the general concerns of a remote province, shaken with internal jealousies and threatened with outside aggressions. He was a short stout man, with close-cropped sandy hair, small pale-blue eyes set deep in a full round face, and an uncertain mouth. He was good-natured and kind-hearted, but irresolute, easily swayed by stronger wills, narrow-minded, slow of thought, word, and deed, and grievously deficient in his understanding of men and their motives.

He arrived at Manhattan early in the spring. His vessel, the *Zoutberg*, captured a Spanish caravela during the voyage, and anchored it safely in front of Manhattan Island. The new governor was attended by one hundred and four soldiers, the first military force which landed upon our shores. His advent was hailed with cheers and enthusiasm; and with much wine and ceremony he was ushered into authority. His council consisted of Jacob Hansen Hesse, Martin Gerritsen, Andries Hudde, and Jacques Bentyn. They were men of comprehensive minds, who had been reared to habits of industry in Holland, and were able to render material assistance to the heavy, indolent Van Twiller. The secretary of the colony, Van Remund, was intelligent, and also helped towards smoothing the pathway of that dull-witted ruler and inexperienced traveler on the road to fame. Cornelis Van Tienhoven, a bright young man of good education, was appointed book-keeper of monthly wages, and Michael Paulusen was made commissary of Pauw's colony at Pavonia. Paulus Hook, now Jersey City, derived its name from him.

A few days after the arrival of Van Twiller at Manhattan, a yacht was seen coming into the bay; and ere the sun set Captain April 16. De Vries announced himself at the fort. He had left Holland some time before the sailing of the *Zoutberg*, as early as November, and when he had reached Swaanendael, found the little post destroyed, and the ground bestrewed with the heads and bones of his murdered people. After various stratagems, he succeeded in persuading some of the Indians into coming on board his vessel, and through attractive presents drew from them the story of a terrible tragedy. The Dutch, in keeping with their time-honored customs, had erected a pillar, and fastened to it a piece of tin, upon which was inscribed the arms of Holland. An Indian chief, thinking it no harm, had stolen the shining metal to make himself a tobacco-pouch. Hossett, the commander of the post, was indiscreet enough to express great indignation, and thereupon some Indians who were particularly attached to him killed the chief who had confiscated the tin. Hossett rebuked them for committing such a crime, and they went away. But a few days afterwards the friends of the murdered chieftain resolved to be revenged, and, coming suddenly upon the men as they were at work in the tobacco-fields, massacred them all. De Vries wisely treated with the same Indians for peace; and when they were at last induced to bring with them their chief, he formed a circle after their own fashion, and gave them blankets, bullets, axes, and trinkets, with which they were greatly pleased, and they went away promising that he should not be harmed.

March 11.　He then tried to establish a whale-fishery, but after spending some time in fruitless efforts, decided that it would not prove paying business there, and sailed to the James River, where he was cour-

Portrait of De Vries.

teously received by Sir John Harvey, the governor of Virginia. He remained several days, greatly admiring the country, which was already under a high state of cultivation, with well-stocked gardens, and Provence roses, apple, cherry, pear, and peach trees about the houses.

Harvey, with genial frankness, produced a map, and tried to convince De Vries that the whole country in the region of Swaanendael was the property of the king of England; but he was very amiably disposed towards the Dutch on the North River, notwithstanding, and a pleasant intercourse was opened between the two colonies.

Captain De Vries was a bronzed, weather-beaten sailor of the old school, without family ties, who had seen the world from many points of observation, and had been on terms of intimacy with the most cultivated men and the rudest barbarians. He was tall, muscular, and hard-visaged, but soft-voiced as a woman, except when aroused by passion. He was quick of perception, with great power of will, and rarely ever erred in judgment. He was the guest of Van Twiller while stopping at Manhattan, and a more striking contrast than the two men presented could hardly be imagined.

The second day after his arrival, the English ship *William* anchored in the bay; and it was soon discovered that Eelkins, who had been dismissed from Fort Orange for misconduct some years before, was on board as supercargo. The governor and several of his officers were invited to dine on the vessel, and were accompanied by Captain De Vries. The immoderate use of wine and consequent disorder astonished the English sailors, who were under strict discipline, and measured the authority of the feeble Dutch governor accordingly. They stayed some days in front of the little town, and then announced their intention of sailing to Fort Orange, and trading with the Indians, with whom Eelkins was well acquainted. Van Twiller was startled as from a dream, and issued orders to the contrary; but the *William* quietly weighed anchor, and went on her way in the most defiant manner. We clip the following from the deposition of one of her crew, as it best explains the scene : —

April 18.

" The Dutch there inhabitinge send and command all our companye (excepte one boye) to come to their forte where they staide about twoe houres, and the governor commande his gunner to make ready three peeces of ordnance, and shott them off for the Prince of Orange and sprede the Prince's coloures, whereupon Jacob Eelekins the merchant's factor of the shippe the William commande William fforde of Lymehouse (the gunner) to goe abord the shippe and sprede her coloures and shoote off theire peeces of ordnance for the king of England."[1]

Van Twiller regarded the audacious movement with incredulous wonder. Then he ordered a barrel of wine to be brought and opened, and, after drinking, waved his hat and shouted, " All those who love the Prince of Orange and me, emulate me in this, and assist me in repelling the violence of that Englishman !"

[1] *N. Y. Coll.* MSS., Vol. I. 74.

But the Englishman was already out of harm's way, sailing up the river, and the crowd only laughed and filled their glasses, saying, they "guessed they would not trouble the English who were their friends. As for the wine, they knew how to get to the bottom of a barrel; if there were six they could master them."

Captain De Vries walked up and down in silent indignation while this was going on. But at the governor's dinner-table, later in the day, he expressed his opinion of the whole transaction in terms more earnest than polite. He told Van Twiller that he had acted very indiscreetly; that the Englishman had no commission, only a custom-house clearance to sail to New England, not to New Netherland; that if it had been his case he should have helped him to some eight-pounders from the fort, and put a stop to his going up the river at all. As it was, he advised, most energetically, that the ship *Zoutberg* be sent to force him out of the river, and teach him better manners. ·

April 28. The governor was convinced of the wisdom of the counsel, and, after mature deliberation, made a move in the proper direction by sending an armed force to Fort Orange, where Eelkins had pitched a tent and commenced a brisk trade with the Indians. The tent was speedily folded, and the intruder conducted to his vessel and to Manhattan. The English said: "The Dutch came along with us in their shallope, and they sticked greene bowes all about her and drank strong waters, and sounded their trumpet in a triumphing manner over us."

Eelkins was obliged to disgorge his peltries and leave the harbor, with a friendly warning in his ears never more to attempt any interference with Dutch trade. Van Twiller then issued an order to the effect that no one should sign any paper in reference to the treatment which Eelkins had received.

May 20. Very soon afterward the governor, who was sure to act promptly on inopportune occasions, attempted to vindicate his statesmanship at the expense of De Vries. The latter had two vessels, one of which was a small yacht; and before returning to Europe he wished to send it toward the north on a trading cruise along the coast. The governor forbade his doing so, and, seeing De Vries making preparations in defiance of his authority, valiantly ordered the guns of the fort turned upon him. De Vries, who tells the story, says : —

"I ran to the point of land where Van Twiller stood with the secretary and one or two of the council, and told them it seemed to me the country was full of fools ! If they must fire at something, they ought to have fired at the Englishman who violated the rights of their river against their will. This caused them to desist from troubling me further."

"'I ran to the point of land where Van Twiller stood with the Secretary and one or two of the Council, and told them it seemed to me the country was full of fools'" Page 70

The yacht sailed, and was soon winding her way through the channel of Hellegat (or Hell-Gate, as it is still called), which in certain times of the tide indulged in all sorts of wild paroxysms. Some go so far as to say that the Dutch named it out of sheer spleen, because it hectored their tub-built barks until the sailors were so giddy that they solemnly gave the yawning gulf over to the Devil.

In the same vessel which brought Wouter Van Twiller to Manhattan, Dominie Bogardus, the first clergyman of New Netherland, was a passenger. He was a man of a certain order of talent in large measure, and was honored for his piety. He was large, graceful, sinewy, strong, with a fine, broad, open, frank face, high cheek-bones, a dark piercing eye, and mouth expressive of the very electricity of good-humor, which was partly hidden, however, by a beard cut in the peculiar fashion prescribed for ecclesiastics during the reign of Henry IV. of France. He was not without prominent faults. He had a hot and hasty temper, was brusque in his manner, and addicted to high living; but he was greatly superior in both mind and character to Van Twiller, and his sterling qualities stood forth in such bold relief, that now, at the very mention of his name, a figure seems to leap forth from the mist of centuries, instinct with hearty, vigorous life. Fearless in the performance of his own duties, he never allowed any failure on the part of others to pass by unreproved. In several instances the governors in authority were severely castigated from the sacred desk.

He desired a more convenient place for public worship than the loft in the horse-mill; and the West India Company displayed their zeal for the preservation of the blessings of education and religion to their infant colony by building him a church. It was a plain wooden edifice, of a pattern similar to the New England barn of the present day, and was located on a high point of land fronting the East River, near what is now Pearl Street, between Whitehall and Broad. It was a conspicuous object to vessels coming up through the bay; and English travelers, who were accustomed to a different style of architecture, criticised it in anything but flattering terms. But it was satisfactory to the conscientious and devout worshipers who assembled there every week, and thought only of the eloquent words of their beloved dominie; and it is to be respected as the first church edifice on Manhattan Island.

Near it, and a little to the right, they built a parsonage. It was a small Dutch cottage, with the gable-end turned towards the street. The front door was ornamented with an elegant brass knocker brought from Holland. Dominie Bogardus had been accustomed not only to the comforts, but also to the luxuries of life, and knew how to surround himself with much that was pleasing to the eye and gratifying to the taste, even in the new, wild country. With his own hands he laid out and planted a garden. And in the fresh summer days pinks and tulips winked and blinked across the graveled pathways, coquetting with young vegetables. Pretty vines clambered to the very house-top, and lilacs and roses, jessamines and syringas, vied with each other in gorgeous display, and helped to render the place for many years the pride of Manhattan, and one of the chief objects of attraction for strangers.

Another noted but far less worthy personage came over in the *Zoutberg*, and enjoyed for several years the distinction of being the first and only schoolmaster in New Netherland. His name was Adam Roelandsen. From some cause, perhaps because " people did not speak well of him," he could not make a living at his vocation, and so took in washing. There is a curious lawsuit recorded in the old Dutch manuscripts, which shows that on the 20th of September, 1638, Adam Roelandsen demanded payment of one Gillis De Voocht for washing his linen. The defendant made no objection to the price charged, but refused to pay until the end of the year. The court decided that Roelandsen should wash for De Voocht during the time agreed upon, and then collect his money. He lived at first quite out of town; but there is on record an agreement for building a house on Stone Street, near the brewery of Oloff S. Van Cortlandt, which was to be thirty feet long, eighteen feet wide, and eight feet high, to be tight-clapboarded, and roofed with reeden thatch, have an entry three feet wide, two doors, a pantry, a bedstead, a staircase, and a mantel-piece, to be ready on the 1st of May, 1642, for which $140 was to be paid by Adam Roelandsen, one half when the timber was on the ground, and the other half when the building was finished.

That the *bedstead* should be named in the contract for building a house requires some explanation. It was called " slaap-banck," and was a sleeping-bench, constructed like a cupboard in a partition, with doors closing upon it when unoccupied. Two ample feather-beds upon it, one to sleep on and the other for a covering, made up in comfort what it lacked in display, and the whole arrangement was a great economy in the matter of room. A sleeping-apartment in the small Dutch tavern of early New Netherland often accommodated several travelers at night, while during the day it was only a public room, quite unencumbered in appearance. Schoolmaster Roelandsen could not have enjoyed his house for a very long period; for on the 17th of December, 1646, he was tried for a very grave offence, found guilty, and sentenced to be " publicly flogged, and banished from the country."

Van Twiller was not slow to carry out the ideas of his employers in the matter of public improvements. The fort was scarcely anything more than banks of earth, eight or ten feet high, with decayed palisades, and without ditches. The Dutch, as we have seen, had already introduced negro slavery into their colony; and a number of recently imported Africans were employed, under the superintendence of Jacob Stoffelsen, to repair this dilapidated and never particularly strong structure. A guard-house and barracks were also built within the fort for the newly arrived soldiers; and three expensive wind-mills were erected, but injudiciously located so near the other buildings that the south-wind was frequently intercepted. However, they gave the little community something more homelike to look at, and were particularly acceptable.

For himself, Van Twiller built a very substantial brick house within the fort, by far the most elaborate private dwelling which had as yet been attempted in this country; and it served for the residence of successive chiefs of the colony during the remainder of the Dutch dynasty. Several smaller brick and frame dwellings were erected for the officers, all being done at the expense of the company. A farm had been laid out some time prior to this date, called the Company's Farm. It extended north from Wall to Hudson Street (we can designate localities only by thus using the present names), and upon this property Van Twiller built a house, barn, brewery, boat-house, etc., for his own private accommodation. Another farm belonging to the company he set apart as a tobacco plantation. He built several small buildings for the tradespeople, and laid out a graveyard on the west of Broadway, above Morris Street. He also built two houses at Pavonia, another at Fort Nassau on the Delaware River, and at Fort Orange one "elegant large house with balustrades, and eight small houses." He did not seem to know where to stop, having once commenced the work of spending his employers' money.

But during all this time no independent farmers attempted the cultivation of the soil. The agricultural improvements lay entirely in the hands of the patroons, and the sound of the hammer was heard only where it was likely to be advantageous to the special business of the West India Company. The little town on Manhattan Island received the name of New Amsterdam, as the governor's new broom swept over it, and was invested with the prerogative of "staple right," by virtue of which all the merchandise passing up and down the river was subject to certain duties. This right gave the post the commercial monopoly of the whole province.

Van Twiller displayed less and less adaptation to his field of labor as the months wore on, and his mismanagement was the topic of conversation among the intelligent men of the colony. Dominie Bogardus wrote him several letters on the subject, and is said to have once **1634.** called him a "child of the Devil," and threatened him with "a shake from the pulpit." The attention of the States-General was again attracted to the affairs of New Netherland through the complaints that were entered by the owners of the ship *William,* who estimated the damages they had sustained by reason of the Dutch on the North River at £ 4,000, and demanded payment. There was a tedious litigation, but it never came to a definite settlement.

One of the most onerous duties imposed upon the unlucky governor by the West India Company was to obtain a title to the lands on the banks of the Fresh or Connecticut River, which had occasionally been visited by the Dutch for trading purposes ever since its original discovery by **June 8.** Adriaen Block, in 1614. They had recently learned that it had been included in a grant to the Earl of Warwick by the king of England, and deemed it politic to get a formal Indian deed before Warwick's grantees should take any steps towards its occupation. Accordingly, Jacob Van Curler and six other agents were sent to accomplish the feat, as also to finish the trading-house, or redoubt, which had been projected in 1623, on the west bank of the river, on the site of the present city of Hartford. They had no difficulty in treating with the Pequods, who had just conquered the Sequeens, and who stipulated only that the ceded territory should always be neutral ground, where all the tribes might come to trade, and no wars ever be waged; and then the little post was completed and fortified with two cannons, and named Good Hope.[1]

Governor Winthrop thought it well to assert promptly the superior title of the English to the whole of the Connecticut valley, in a letter to the Dutch authorities, and received in reply a very courteous and respectful document from Governor Van Twiller, asking the governor of Plymouth to defer all his claims until their respective governments should agree about the limits of their territories, not presuming "two great powers would fall into contention about a little portion of such heathenish countries."

But although the Massachusetts authorities were not disposed to interfere, the Plymouth people were determined to establish a counter-claim to the land where the Hollanders were now in quiet possession, under their

---

[1] The ruins of the old fort have been traced, by persons now living, on the bank of the Connecticut near the seat of the Wylls family. Several yellow Dutch bricks used in its construction are preserved by residents of Hartford. *Public Records of Connecticut,* by J. H. Trumbull. *Holmes, Am. Ann.,* I. 219, note.

threefold supposed right, by original discovery, constant visitation, and legal purchase. So they managed to buy a tract of land, just north of Fort Good Hope, of a party of Indians who had been driven out of that country by the Pequods; and Lieutenant William Holmes, a land surveyor, with a company of English farmers, accompanied by the banished Indians, proceeded there as rapidly as they could make their way through the forests. While passing the Dutch post they were hailed by Van Corlear, who threatened to shoot them if they did not stop instantly. Their reply was, "Fire! we shall go on if we die"; and they went on, and the Dutch did not fire. Arriving at the point where Windsor now stands, they clapped up the frame of a house which they had brought with them, and landed their provisions. Afterwards they "palisadoed" their house about, and fortified themselves better, for they were afraid of the Pequods, who were much offended that they should bring home and restore the Sachem Natuwannute to his rights.

When the news of these proceedings reached Van Twiller, he sent a formal order to Holmes to depart forthwith from the lands on the Fresh River; but Holmes, who had already defied the guns of Fort Good Hope, was not to be moved by the power of speech. He replied that he was there in the name of the king of England, and there he should stay.[1] Van Twiller submitted his perplexities to the Amsterdam Chamber, but, before any reply could reach him, serious difficulties occurred between the Connecticut River Dutch colonists and the Pequods, and the latter entered into an alliance with the English. When the order came from Holland to send an armed force to dislodge the intruders, Van Twiller dispatched seventy men for the purpose; but the Windsor colony put themselves on the defensive, and, fearful of Indian hostilities, the Dutch thought it wise to withdraw.

The most important event of the year 1634 was an advantageous treaty of peace concluded with the Raritan Indians, which, considering the weak state of the colony, was a master stroke of policy.

Meanwhile, Captain De Vries, upon his return to Holland, had found the directors of the company still at variance in regard to the meddling with the fur-trade by the patroons. Even the few beaver-skins which he had brought over in his vessel provoked high words, and, seeing the turn events were taking, he retired from his partnership on the Delaware, and entered into a speculation with some merchants who were trading on the coast of Guiana. But he did not hesitate to speak his mind freely concerning the incapacity of the New Netherland officials, and through

---

[1] Winthrop; Bradford, in *Hutch. Mass.*; Prince; Trumbull; Broadhead; O'Callaghan.   5

his efforts and influence the drunken and dishonest sheriff Notelman was superseded by Lubbertus Van Dincklagen, an educated lawyer, and a man of great excellence of character.

1635. Both the directors of the company and the patroons appealed to the States-General for redress of grievances ; but the latter, finding the question very knotty, prudently postponed a decision. In the mean time, Godyn had died, and the remaining patroons of Swaanendael commenced legal proceedings against the company for damages, which they had sustained through neglect of the company to defend them from inland and foreign wars, as was promised in their charter. The Assembly of the XIX., tiring of these continual discords, determined **Feb. 7.** to purchase the rights and property of the South River patroons ; which they accordingly did, for the sum of fifteen thousand six hundred guilders.

Early in the following summer the vacant Fort Nassau was seized by some Englishmen from Point Comfort, under command of George Holmes. Thomas Hall, one of Holmes's men, deserted, and brought prompt intelligence **June 1.** to Van Twiller, who sent an armed force, dislodged the party, and brought all captives to New Amsterdam. But he did not know what to do with them, and took counsel of De Vries, who was again with his vessel in New York Bay, and about to sail for the **Sept. 10.** Chesapeake. The result was that they were reshipped "pack and sack" for Point Comfort, and thus ended the first English aggression on the South River.

Success was awaiting the English in the Connecticut Valley, notwithstanding the Dutch fort at Hartford. In the autumn, the Pequods **Nov. 24.** visited Boston and sold all their right and title to Governor Winthrop. To whom then did it belong ? Soon afterward, John Winthrop, the younger, arrived from England, commissioned by Lord Warwick's grantees as " agent for the River of the Connecticut with the places adjoining thereto," and brought with him men and ammunition and two thousand pounds in money to begin a fortification at the mouth of the river. A few weeks later he proceeded to take possession and erect some buildings upon the very land which the Dutch had purchased of the Indians three years before, and contemptuously tore down the arms of the States-General which was affixed to a tree, painting a ridiculous face in its place. Van Twiller, who had lost all faith in wordy protests, sent a sloop to dislodge them ; but Winthrop had two pieces on shore, and would not suffer the Dutch to land. The English named the point Saybrook, in compliment to Lord Say and Lord Brook.

Fort Amsterdam was completed this summer ; but although considerable expense had been lavished upon the repairs, if there had been a hostile attack from any source whatever, the question of holding it would have been decided very briefly. The northwest bastion only was faced with stone, and not a fence surrounded it to keep off the goats and other animals which ran at large through the town. Its only redeeming feature was its elegant regularity.

The houses were small and simple in their construction, and nearly all of them were located within a few yards of the quaint little citadel. Some were built of rough stone.

First View of New Amsterdam.

The above sketch of the fort and the buildings around it was originally made by a Dutch officer in 1635, and the picture was engraved in Holland. As a work of art it is certainly curious. It was undoubtedly the production of a strong memory, and, even allowing for the omission of Governor's Island, which is ingrafted upon Long Island, and the distance of Paulus Hook, which appears not more than the length of three of the canoes, there is no view extant which can give us a better idea of the tender infancy of our proud city.

The wind-mill was near a creek which is now Broad Street. The gibbet, or whipping-post, was close by the water's edge. Upon this transgressors were hoisted by the waist, and suspended such length of time as their offense warranted.

And yet, such was the peaceful disposition of the inhabitants, that

police regulations were almost entirely unknown. Not even a sentinel
1636. was kept on duty at night. A very ludicrous incident occurred
May 8. on the morning of the 8th of May, 1636. It was just at daybreak that the boom of a strange gun shook the island from center to
circumference. The people were alarmed, the soldiers in the fort rushed
to their posts, and the corpulent Van Twiller, in a state of mind not to
be envied, ran, holding a pistol in one hand while he tried to dress himself with the other, towards the shore. It was all explained presently.
Captain De Vries had returned, and after having piloted his vessel
through the Narrows in the dead of night, humorously determined to
speak in his own behalf and watch the result. He was heartily welcomed and invited home with the governor to breakfast.

June 25. It is through the writings of this celebrated sea-captain that
we learn of much of the irregularity existing at that time in New
Netherland. Nearly every one drank wine and stronger liquors to excess
when they could be obtained. For instance, a new agent arrived for
Pauw's colony at Pavonia, one Cornelis Van Vorst, and brought with
him some good claret. De Vries called there one day, and found the governor and the minister making merry ; and finally they quarreled with
Van Vorst about a manslaughter which had been committed in his
colony a few days before, but made it up in the end, and started for home.
Van Vorst ran to give a salute to the governor from a stone gun which
stood on a pillar near his house, and a spark fell upon the thatched roof,
setting it on fire. There being no means of putting it out, in less than
half an hour the whole building was consumed.

Aug. 8. On another occasion the gunner gave a frolic, and all the dignitaries were present. The tent was erected in one of the angles of the
fort, and tables and benches were placed for the guests. When the glee was
at its height, the trumpet began to blow, which occasioned a quarrel, and
the koopman of the stores and the koopman of the cargasoons found fault
and called the trumpeter hard names. He turned round and gave them
each a thrashing, and they ran for their swords, uttering terrible threats.
The trumpeter hid from them that night, but the next morning, when the
wine had evaporated, " they feared him more than they sought him."

Aug. 13. The natural beauties of Staten Island attracted the attention
Aug. 15. of De Vries, and before he left for Holland, on the 15th of August,
he arranged with Van Twiller to enter it for him on the records of the
company, as he wished to found a colony there.

On the 16th of June, prior to this date, Jacob Van Corlear had purchased a tract of land from the Indians on Long Island, and employed
Thomas Hall, the English deserter, to superintend the plantation. About

the same time Andries Hudde, one of the governor's council, in partnership with Wolfert Gerritsen, purchased the flats next Corlear's property. On the 16th of July, Van Twiller himself secured the tempting lands farther to the east. These purchases, including nearly 15,000 acres, seem to have been made without the knowledge or approbation of the Amsterdam Chamber. Upon them was founded the town of New Amersfoordt, now Flatlands.

There was another grant of which it is interesting to take notice, and

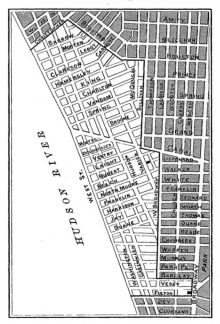

Map of what was Anetje Jans's Farm.

which occurred not far from the same date, — sixty - two acres to Roelof Jans, beginning south of Warren Street, and extending along Broadway as far as Duane Street, thence northwesterly a mile and a half to Christopher Street, thus forming a sort of unequal triangle with its base upon the North River. This was the original conveyance of the very valuable estate since known as the Trinity Church property.[1]

Rensselaerswick was at this time improving more 1637. rapidly than any other part of the province. The farmers wrote home glowing descriptions of the soil and productions, which, published in Holland, brought out colonists in large numbers, and some of them were men of substantial means. Early in the spring of 1637 Van Rensselaer purchased of the Indians a large addition to his already extensive property, and tradition says that he paid a brief visit to his manor about that time.

Van Twiller also inspected and bought for himself Nutten Island,

[1] Roelof Jans died soon after the grant, leaving a wife and four children. His widow Anetje married Dominie Bogardus in the year 1638, and her farm was known as the "Dominie's bouwery." After Bogardus's death in 1647, this grant was confirmed by the English government to the heirs, who sold it in 1671 to Colonel Lovelace, at which sale one of the heirs failed to be present. It was afterward incorporated into the king's farm, and in 1703 was presented by Queen Anne to Trinity Church. Anetje Bogardus died in 1668 in Beverwyck. *Benson's Memoir*, 119. *Rensselaerswick MSS. Paige's Chancery Reports.*

since which it has been called Governor's Island.[1] The water was so shallow between it and Long Island at that time as to be easily forded at low tide. The next month he bought Great Barn and Blackwell's Island. By these acquisitions he became one of the richest land-owners in the province. He stocked his nice farms with valuable cattle, and the colonists wondered how it all came about! The high-toned officer Van Dincklagen could not rest in silence, and remonstrated with the governor in the plainest manner, finally threatening to expose him if he did not desist from his dishonorable proceedings. All the fierce obstinacy of Van Twiller's nature was thus aroused, and in a fit of rage he caused the bold sheriff to be arrested on a charge of contumacy, and sent him as a prisoner to Holland, retaining his salary, which was three years in arrears.

June 16. (margin note)

July 16. (margin note)

Van Dincklagen had no sooner arrived there than with his facile pen he reviewed Van Twiller's government in a memorial to the States-General, which was immediately sent to the Amsterdam Chamber with the suggestion that they had better make prompt reparation to their injured officer. They at first refused, but the resolute Van Dincklagen was well known and respected, and his second memorial was supported by some very stinging remarks from Captain De Vries, about "promoting a fool from a clerkship to a governorship simply to act farces," so that finally it was decided to recall Van Twiller, and appoint Wilhelm Kieft in his place. The new governor, in presence of the States-General, took his oath of office on September 2, 1637.

Sept. 2. (margin note)

Van Dincklagen's complaints were not confined to the civil authorities of New Netherland. Dominie Bogardus was censured, and to such an extent that when the news reached his church in New Amsterdam the consistory felt it their duty to take ecclesiastical proceedings against the complainant, which a long time after they were obliged to defend before the Classis of Amsterdam.

It was years before Van Dincklagen collected his salary, although the States-General signified it as their pleasure that he should at once be

---

[1] Coincident with the governor's purchase, John (George) Jansen De Rapaelje bought of the Indians 335 acres on Long Island near Waal-Bogt, or the Bay of the Foreigners. Prior to this William Adriaense Bennet and Jacques Bentyn had bought 930 acres at Gowanus, and at these two isolated points were formed the nuclei of the present city of Brooklyn. One Jonas Bronck also bought a valuable tract in West Chester "over against Haarlem," and from him the Bronx River derived its name. The West India Company bought the island of Quotenius in Narragansett Bay, also an island near the Thames River, which was for many years known as Dutchman's Island. And not far from the same time they purchased from Michael Pauw, Pavonia and his other lands, which abated a great nuisance in the shape of an independent colony on those shores.

paid. He afterwards returned to New Amsterdam, and filled with honor one of the most important offices under the government.

Notwithstanding the loss of business on the Connecticut, the fur-trade during the last year of Van Twiller's administration had increased. The Dutch had opened a profitable commerce with New England ; and the scarcity of commodities there, owing to the bloody war which was raging with the Pequods, affected prices to a considerable degree in New Nether-land. A schepel — three pecks — of rye sold readily for eighty cents. A laboring man commanded eighty cents per day during harvest. Corn rose to the extraordinarily high price of twelve shillings a bushel. A good cow brought thirty pounds, a pair of oxen forty pounds, and a horse forty pounds, while the price of a negro was on an average sixteen dollars.

Trading with the Indians.

CHAPTER VI.

1638 – 1641.

GOVERNOR WILHELM KIEFT.

Governor Wilhelm Kieft. — The Extraordinary Council. — Abuses. — Proclamations. — The Dominie's Wedding. — A Curious Slander Case. — The First Ferry to Long Island. — Encroachments of the Swedes. — A new Policy. — Captain De Vries's Arrival. — The Pioneer Settlers. — Oloff Stevensen Van Cortlandt. — English Ambition. — Captain De Vries's Travels and what he saw. — Purchase of Indian Lands. — Trouble with the Indians. — The new Charter of Freedoms and Exemptions. — The Store-Keeper. — The Six Murderers. — Municipal Regulations. — The first Marine Telegraph in the Harbor.

GOVERNOR WILHELM KIEFT was somewhat coolly received when, after a long and tedious voyage in the *Herring*, he landed on Manhattan Island, March 28, 1638. Rumors to his disadvantage had preceded him. It was said that he had once failed in the mercan-
1638. tile business in Holland, and, according to custom, his portrait had been affixed to the gallows in consequence. That, in Dutch estimation, was a lasting disgrace. Since then, he had been sent by the government as Minister to Turkey, and had been intrusted with money to procure the ransom of some Christians in bondage. The captives were left in their chains, and the money was never refunded. Such unfortunate antecedents were not calculated to inspire confidence, and the man himself had no personal attractions. He was small in size, fussy, bustling, fiery, and avaricious. He had a wiry look, as if he was constantly standing on guard; prominent, sharp features; and deep-set, restless gray eyes. He was industrious and strictly temperate, not wanting in natural abilities, and far from heedless of the laws of morality; but his education was limited and his self-conceit unrestrained, and in his ignorance of the true principles of government he imagined himself able to legislate, individually, for all mankind.

He seized the reins of authority with the air of a master, the will of a tyrant, and a determination of spirit which would not brook interference. He consulted no one. He showed no deference to the opinions of the intelligent few who were already experienced in the matter of treating with the Indians. He placed himself on a pedestal, and looked loftily over the heads of his subjects. The West India Company had accorded him the privilege of fixing the number of his council. He warily chose one man. The favored individual was Dr. Johannes La Montagne, a learned and highly bred French Huguenot, who had escaped from the rage of religious persecution the year before, and found his Canaan in the Dutch settlement on Manhattan Island. His parents belonged to the *ancienne noblesse* of France, — a fact which he took pains neither to promulgate nor conceal, but which might have revealed itself in a thousand ways, even if his unusual accomplishments and elegant manners had not won universal admiration. He was a widower with four interesting children, upon whom he bestowed great care and affection. He gave them lessons daily, and perfected their education in such a masterly manner that his three daughters grew up to be the most attractive women of their day in the province, and his son became a man of fortune and position. Two of Dr. La Montagne's daughters married physicians, — Dr. Hans Kiersted and Dr. Van Imbroeck. His youngest daughter, Marie, became the wife of Jacob Kip. Dr. La Montagne practiced medicine for many years, and was the only doctor on Manhattan in whom the settlers had any confidence.

Kieft was quick to recognize the prospective value of such a man's advice in state affairs ; but, as a governor, he was resolved to hold the supreme command himself in every particular. He therefore curiously arranged that his *one* councilor should be entitled to one vote, while he reserved to himself two votes. Such a high-handed act of despotism would not have been tolerated a day in any part of the Dutch Republic ; and it only serves to illustrate the inattention of the West India Company to the best interests of their colony. Indeed, the company were discussing the question at that very time, " whether it would not be expedient to place the district of New Netherland at the disposal of the States-General."

Kieft patronizingly declared his willingness to admit an invited guest, perhaps two, into his extraordinary council board, on occasions when special cases were to be tried in which either himself or Dr. La Montagne were supposed to be interested ; but as long as it was judged a high crime to appeal to any other tribunal, the condescension was sneeringly commented upon by the democratic colonists. Cornelis Van Tienhoven won his way into the new governor's favor through a little adroit flattery, and was made secretary of the province at a salary of two hundred and fifty dollars per year. A few days later, Ulrich

Lupold was appointed sheriff, although his qualifications for that office · were bitterly questioned.

Kieft sent, with his first letter to Holland, a formal statement of the ruinous condition in which he had found the colony. He said : —

" The fort is open at every side except the stone point ; the guns are dismounted ; the houses and public buildings are all out of repair ; the magazine for merchandise has disappeared ; every vessel in the harbor is falling to pieces ; only one wind-mill is in operation ; the farms of the company are without tenants, and thrown into commons ; the cattle are all sold, or on the plantations of Van Twiller."

Not very cheerful news for the disheartened company. Van Twiller had retired to private life, and taken up his abode in the house which he had built upon the company's farm. Immediately upon Kieft's arrival, the ex-governor commenced negotiations for hiring both house and farm, and in a few days succeeded in concluding an arrangement at a yearly rent of two hundred and fifty guilders, together with a sixth part of the produce. The inventory of his private property was in startling contrast to the general state of decay and dilapidation throughout the colony, and his manner of living was so ostentatious that he was regarded with scorn by the honest portion of the little community.

Abuses existed in every department of the public service. Private individuals were constantly smuggling furs and tobacco, and selling firearms to the Indians, in open disregard of orders. Law seemed fast becoming obsolete. Kieft commenced the reformatory work by proclamations. They were written in a plain hand and pasted on posts, trees, barns, and fences. All selling of guns or powder to the Indians was prohibited, under pain of death. Illegal traffic in furs was forbidden. Tobacco was made subject to excise. The retailing of liquors was limited to wine, " in moderate quantities." Hours were fixed for laborers to stop work ; sailors were ordered not to leave their ships after night-fall. All the vices were forbidden. No person might leave the island without a passport. Thursday of each week was appointed for the regular sitting of the council.

Presently, the self-sufficient lawgiver ordered that no attestations or other public writings should be valid before a court in New Netherland unless they were written by the colonial secretary. This arbitrary regulation provoked opposition, and was declared on all sides to be oppressive, and intended to restrain popular rights. The policy of the measure was defended by the sycophantic Van Tienhoven, who declared that most of the parties who went to law for the redress of their grievances were illiterate countrymen or sailors, who could read or write but indifferently or not at all.

Dominie Bogardus, when he heard of the charges which Van Dincklagen had preferred against him before the Classis of Amsterdam, petitioned the governor for leave to return to Holland and defend himself.

Autograph of Everardus Bogardus.

Kieft entered warmly into the feelings of the church and people, and finally resolved "to retain Dominie Everardus Bogardus, that the interests of God's Word may in no wise be prevented"; and he also prayed the Classis of Amsterdam "for the protection of their esteemed preacher." [1]

Not long after, the principal families and personages at Manhattan were invited to attend the marriage of the Dominie to the famous Anetje Jans, who, although she may not have seemed rich in the days when great landed estates were to be bought for a few strings of beads, yet is reverenced by her numerous descendants as among the very goddesses of wealth. She was a small, well-formed woman, with delicate features, transparent complexion, and bright, beautiful dark eyes. She had a well-balanced mind, a sunny disposition, winning manners, and a kind heart; and soon became very dear to the people of the church over which her husband was pastor, besides being a distinguished and valuable counselor to her own numerous family of children.

A curious regulation was instituted about that time in relation to the ringing of the town bell. Its chief office was to call the devout to church on the Sabbath; but Kieft ordered it rung every evening at nine o'clock, to announce the hour for retiring; also every morning and evening at a given hour, to call persons to and from their labor; and, on Thursdays, to summon prisoners into court. We take the following from the unpublished Dutch manuscripts at the New York City Hall : [2] —

" October 14th, 1638. For scandalizing the governor, Hendrick Jansen is

---

[1] Cor. Cl. Amsterdam, 19th Nov., 1641 ; 1st April, 1642, *ante*, p. 273.

[2] The official records of New Netherland have fortunately been preserved in an almost unbroken series from the time of Kieft's inauguration, and afford authentic and copious materials for the historian.

sentenced to stand at the fort entrance, *at the ringing of the bell,* and ask the governor's pardon."

Under the same date, —

" For drawing his knife upon a person, Guysbert Van Regerslard is sentenced to throw himself three times from the sailyard of the yacht *Hope,* and to receive from each sailor three lashes, *at the ringing of the bell.*"

And, —

" Grietje Reiniers, for slandering the Dominie Everardus Bogardus, is condemned to appear at Fort Amsterdam, *at the sounding of the bell,* and declare before the governor and council that she knew the minister to be an honest and pious man, and that she had lied falsely."

The records give us an insight into the cause as well as the merits of this slander case. Mrs. Bogardus went to pay a friendly visit to a neighbor; but, on getting into the " entry," discovered that Grietje Reiniers, a woman of questionable reputation, was in the house, and thereupon turned about and went home. Grietje was greatly offended at this " snubbing " from the Dominie's lady, and followed her, making disagreeable remarks. While passing a blacksmith's shop, where the road was muddy, Mrs. Bogardus raised her dress a little, and Grietje was very invidious in her criticisms. The Dominie thought fit to make an example of her; hence the suit. Grietje's husband being in arrears for church dues, Bogardus sent for him and ordered payment, and, not getting it, finally sued for the amount.

In some respects Kieft brought order out of chaos, and improved the appearance of the town. Most of the houses were in clusters without regard to streets, and grouped near the walls of the fort. Pearl Street was then a simple road on the bank of the river. It is at no very distant date that Water, Front, and South Streets were reclaimed from the water. Pearl was undoubtedly the first street occupied for building purposes, and Kieft selected it for the best class of dwellings, on account of its fine river-prospect. The lone wind-mill stood on State Street, and was, as seen from the bay, the most prominent object on the island. Not far from it were the bakery, brewery, and warehouse of the company.

A ferry to Long Island had been established before Kieft's arrival, from the vicinity of Peck's Slip to a point a little below the present Fulton Ferry. Cornelis Dircksen, who had a farm in that vicinity, came at the sound of a horn, which hung against a tree, and ferried the waiting passengers across the river in a skiff, for the moderate charge of three stivers in wampum. Many thousands now cross the Brooklyn ferries daily at about the same place.

There was a road which had been formed by travel from the fort towards the northern part of Manhattan Island, crooking about to avoid hills and ravines, and which might have been more truly called a path. Upon either side of it, although at considerable distances apart, farms were laid out, and some English colonists, who removed to this hitherto uncul-

First Ferry to Long Island.

tivated district from Virginia, brought with them cherry and peach trees, and soon rendered it somewhat interesting to agriculturists. Kieft was extravagantly fond of flowers, and encouraged gardening after the most approved European standard. He also stocked the farms with fine cattle.

Sweden all at once appeared as a competitor with France, England, and Holland for a foothold in North America. Peter Minuet had offered to that power the benefit of his colonial experience; and an expedition was placed under his direction, with fifty emigrants, a Lutheran minister, goods for the Indian trade, and the necessaries for making a little colony comfortable in a strange land. They came to the Delaware Bay country, where Minuet bought of the sachem Mattehoorn, for "a kettle and other trifles," as much land as would serve to build a house upon and make a plantation. For this land a deed was given, written in Low Dutch, as no Swede could interpret the Indian language. Upon the strength of this conveyance, the Swedes claimed to have bought all the territory on the west side of the Delaware River, from Cape Henlopen to the Falls of Trenton, and as far inland as they might want.[1]

April 15.

[1] *Acrelius* in 11 *N. Y. H. S. Col.*, Vol. I. 409. *New York Col.* MSS. *Hudde's Report.* *Hazard, Am. Penn,* 42, 43. *Brodhead*, Vol. I. p. 282. *Letter of Jerome Hawley, Treasurer of Virginia, to Secretary Windebanke*, May 8, 1638, in London Documents. *O'Callaghan,* I. 190. *Ferris,* 42, 45. *Holm,* 85.

As soon as Kieft heard the news, he wrote Minuet a letter of remonstrance, of which the latter took no heed, but went on building his fort, which he called Fort Christiana, in honor of the young queen of Sweden. Before midsummer, he went to Europe with the first cargo of furs. Kieft was uncertain what course to pursue, and wrote to the company for instructions. Sweden was, however, just then, too powerful a kingdom and too dangerous a neighbor to pick a quarrel with, for the company was already on the decline; therefore the Swedes became the first European occupants of the State of Delaware.

By this time the company, in sheer despair, had matured a more liberal policy, by which they hoped to improve their mismanaged province of New Netherland. Every emigrant should be accommodated, according to his means, with as much land as he could properly cultivate. He should be conveyed to New Netherland, with his cattle and merchandise, in the company's ships,. at a duty of ten per cent *ad valorem,* paid to the company. A quit-rent of one tenth of the produce was exacted, but legal estates of inheritance were assured to the grantees of all the land. Ministers, schoolmasters, and negro slaves were promised; and also protection and assistance in case of war. Forts and public buildings were to be kept in repair, and law and order maintained by the company; and each new settler was required to declare under his signature that he would voluntarily submit to existing authorities. It was a step in advance, although far short of the emergency, and arrangements for removal to America were immediately made by many persons of capital and influence in Holland.

Captain De Vries sailed in September, with a party of emigrants, to take possession of Staten Island. When they arrived off Sandy Hook, winter had set in, and all were homesick and disheartened. The captain of the vessel proposed going to the West Indies, to stay until spring; but De Vries objected, and offered to pilot the ship into port, which he accordingly did. He was always a welcome visitor at New Amsterdam, but perhaps never more so than now, as no ship was expected at such a season of the year, and its coming was an agreeable break in the monotony of colonial life. De Vries was invited to the governor's house and treated with distinguished attention. His people remained on the vessel for a few days, when they proceeded to Staten Island, and constructed some log-cabins, to live in until spring.

Sept. 25.

Dec. 27.

Kieft, in looking about him, thought it was well to secure more land to the company; and he purchased from the Indian chiefs, during that and the following year, nearly all the territory now comprising the county of Queen's.[1] A few months afterward, he secured a large tract of land in West Chester, which is supposed to include the present town of Yonkers.[2] Portions of these lands were soon deeded away to **1639.** enterprising settlers; for, by reason of the more liberal system of the company, a rapid impulse had been given to the settlement of the province. In August of this year, Antony Jansen Van Vaas, **Aug. 1.** a French Huguenot, from Salée, bought two hundred acres on the west end of Long Island, and a part of the present towns of New Utrecht and Gravesend, of which he was the pioneer settler. On the 28th of November following, Thomas Bescher received a patent for a **Nov. 28.** tobacco plantation " on the beach of Long Island," supposed to be a portion of the site of Brooklyn. About the same time, George Holms, the leader of the expedition against Fort Nassau, who **Nov. 15.** had returned to cast his fortunes among the Dutch at Fort Amsterdam, entered into partnership with his countryman, Thomas Hall, and bought a large farm on Deutal Bay, a small cove on the East River, now known as Turtle Bay,[3] where they built a very comfortable house. Attracted by the greater religious freedom among the Dutch, numbers came from New England and settled at various points on Long Island, at West Chester, and at New Amsterdam. Among them was Captain John Underhill, who had distinguished himself in the Pequod war, and had since been governor of Dover. That is, he made arrangements for removal, and sent several of·his people; but he was himself detained to undergo ecclesiastical proceedings from the " proud Pharisees," as he called them, and only arrived in New Amsterdam in 1643. But there was an influx of the poorer class from Virginia which was not beneficial, except so far as their experience in tobacco and fruit culture was concerned; for they were English convicts, sent out as laborers, and glad to escape as soon as their term of service had expired. They were very much given to drinking and lawlessness.

In the early part of the summer, New Amsterdam had been visited by two somewhat remarkable men, who were so much pleased with what they saw that they returned to Europe and soon after came back to establish themselves here with their families. These were Jochem Pietersen Kuyter, of Darmstadt, who had held a high position in the

---

[1] *Thomson's Long Island. Dr. Stiles's History of Brooklyn.*
[2] *Bolton's West Chester,* 11, 401. *Alb. Rec. G. G.*, 59, 62.
[3] The Dutch name Deutal, which the English corrupted to Turtle, signified a peg with which casks were secured. These pegs were short, but broad at the base; and as the bay was narrow at the entrance, but wide within, the resemblance suggested the name. *Judge Benson's Memoir,* 96,

East Indies under the government of Denmark; and Cornelis Melyn, of Antwerp. They were both men of property and ability, of some culture, and of wide experience in the ways of the world, and they soon rose to prominence in the colony. Thirty or more farms were now under successful cultivation, and the country began to wear an air of healthy activity. The only obligation required from foreigners was an oath of allegiance similar to that which was imposed upon the Dutch colonists.

In July, Ulrich Lupold was removed from the post of sheriff to that of commissary of wares, and Cornelis Van der Huygens was appointed in his place. Jacob Van Corlear and David Provoost were made inspectors of tobacco, and Oloff Stevensen Van Cortlandt was appointed commissary of the shop. This latter personage came out in the same vessel

Van Cortlandt Manor-House.

with Kieft from Holland, as a soldier in the service of the company, and this was his first promotion. He was a lineal descendant of the Dukes of Courland in Russia. His ancestors, when deprived of the duchy of Courland, emigrated to Holland. The family name was

Stevens, or Stevensen, van (from) Courland, and they adopted the latter as a surname, the true orthography in Dutch being Kortelandt, signifying *short-land*.[1]

Michel Evertsen was clerk of the customs, — the first record in New Netherland of an honorable Dutch name, which has been handed down to many highly respected families in the State of New York and elsewhere. Gerrit Schult and Hans Kiersted were regularly bred surgeons, sent out from Holland by the West India Company. The latter married Sarah, the eldest daughter of Dr. La Montagne. Gysbert Op Dyck was sent as commissary to Fort Good Hope.

---

[1] The above statements are founded upon Burke's *History of the English Commoners, The Heraldic Bearings and Family Tradition.* "Let those who would disparage the origin of this noble family go to work and disprove what has long ago been asserted of them." — Rev. Robert Bolton to the Author, November 11, 1872.

The state of morals in New Amsterdam was by no means healthy, owing to the great variety of persons who were coming into the town; and prosecutions and punishments for dishonesty and public executions for murder and mutiny were not infrequent. The governor was continually on the alert, but, from his irritable nature, commanded no respect, and was obliged to enforce obedience. Assuming sovereignty and refusing counsel, he soon committed an act of the greatest indiscretion. He levied a tribute of "maize furs or sewan" upon the Indians, under the plea that on their account the company was ^{Sept. 15.} burdened with the heavy expenses of fortifications and garrisons. In case they refused to pay it, he threatened to compel them to do so.[1] The disastrous consequences, we shall soon have occasion to relate.

In the mean time, the indomitable New-Englanders had been pushing westward, and had established themselves at a place which the Dutch called Roodeberg, or Red Hill, but to which the English gave the name of New Haven; and so rapidly had the settlement filled up, that they had already a handsome church built, and more than three hundred houses. They had bought large tracts around them and planted numerous smaller towns. Captain De Vries went on a voyage of observation up the Connecticut River, during the summer of 1639, and was agreeably entertained by the English governor at Hartford, which was quite a thriving place, with a church and a hundred or more houses. Captain De Vries was very frank with his English host, and told him that it was not right to take lands which the West India Company had bought and paid for. The reply was, that those lands were uncultivated, and no effort made to improve them, and it seemed a sin to let such valuable property go to waste, when fine crops could be raised with a little care. De Vries noticed that the English lived there, to quote his exact words, "very soberly." "They only drank three times at a meal, and those who got tipsy were whipped on a pole, as thieves were in Holland"; and their whole government was rigorous in the extreme.

The Dutch held their one small foothold near by; but it was of very little use to them, for the English openly denied even their right to the ground about the redoubt. From words it came to blows, and Evert Duyckingck, one of the garrison of fourteen men, was cudgeled while sowing grain in the spring of 1640. Disgusted with the command of a post without adequate force to protect it from insult, Op Dyck resigned his office, and Jan Hendricksen Roesen succeeded him.

With a boldness fostered by the consciousness of superior numbers, smart little towns were started all along the Connecticut River to its

---

[1] The Amsterdam Chamber denied any knowledge of this measure.

mouth, where a strong fort was in existence, and where Saybrook, under the command of Colonel Fenwick, who had just arrived from England, accompanied by his beautiful wife, the Lady Alice, had become quite a flourishing settlement. On the borders of the Sound, De Vries saw also other evidences of English enterprise. At the mouth of the Housatonic the village of Stratford already contained more than fifty houses. Men, like stray bees, were beginning to build at Norwalk and Stamford, and even at Greenwich two houses were erected. One of these was occupied by Captain Daniel Patrick, who had been an officer in the Pequod war, and had had ample opportunity for inspecting the country, and who had married a Dutch lady at the Hague. The other was occupied by Robert Feake, whose wife was the daughter-in-law of Governor Winthrop,[1] and who afterward purchased a title to the whole region, and held it for two years in defiance of Dutch authority.

Returning to his plantation on Staten Island, De Vries found it languishing for want of proper colonists, because his partner in Holland had not fulfilled his agreement to send them. He spent a few days there and then visited New Amsterdam, where two vessels had just arrived, one of which belonged to the company ; the other was a private ship, laden with cattle, and belonged to Captain Jochem Pietersen Kuyter.

1640.
Feb. 10.
Later in the season, De Vries found a better situation, about six miles above the fort on the Hudson River, where there were some sixty acres of "corn land," and no trees to cut down. There was, besides, hay enough upon it for two hundred head of cattle. He accomplished its purchase of the Indians, and determined to live half of the time there. On the 15th of April, he sailed on a voyage up the

April 15.
Hudson, and his circumstantial journal gives a very interesting picture of the country along its banks. From this trip he did not return until December, and then immediately commenced improving his new estate, which he called Vriesendael.

As yet there were few Dutch colonists east of the Harlem River; and Kieft, rendered anxious by English progress, sent Secretary Van

April 19.
Tienhoven to purchase the group of islands at the mouth of the Norwalk River, together with the adjoining territory on the mainland, and to erect thereon the standard of the States-General, "so as to effectually prevent any other nation's encroachment." These directions were executed, and the West India Company thereby obtained the Indian title

May 10.
to all the country between the Norwalk and North Rivers. On the 10th of May of the same year, Kieft also bought of the great chief Penhawitz the territory forming the present county of Kings, on

---

[1] Robert Feake married the widow of Henry Winthrop.

Long Island. All the lands east of Oyster Bay, which form the county of Suffolk, remained, however, in the hands of its aboriginal lords.

What was the surprise of the governor of New Netherland when, one morning, a Scotchman, named Farrett, presented himself at Fort Amsterdam and claimed the whole of Long Island, under a commission from the Earl of Stirling! He had already confirmed Lion Gardiner's purchase of Gardiner's Island [1] from the Indians, and empowered him to make and put in practice all necessary laws of Church and State. He had made an agreement with several persons from Lynn, Massachusetts, by which they might settle upon and cultivate any lands on Long Island which they should buy of the Indians. Farrett was contemptuously dismissed by Kieft; but the Lynn emigrants soon after arrived at the head of Cow Bay, pulled down the Dutch arms, and put up a house very quickly. The sachem Penhawitz hurried to New Amsterdam with the news, and Van Tienhoven was dispatched with an armed force to arrest the whole party and bring them before the governor. Satisfied, however, upon examination, that they were not in fault, Kieft dismissed them after they had signed an agreement to intrude no more upon Dutch territory. This led to the immediate settlement of Southampton; for Farrett discovered that the Dutch, although they derided Lord Stirling's claim, were chiefly anxious to maintain possession of the western extremity of Long Island, and he, with his associates, removed and settled unmolested farther east.

Up to this time the relations between the Dutch and the Indians had been upon the whole friendly. But many of the colonists had neglected their farms for the quicker profits of traffic. To prosper in this they had allured the savages to their homes, fed them bountifully, and treated them to "fire-water." In many instances the jealousies of the latter had been excited against each other. They had also been frequently employed as house and farm servants by the settlers; which was unwise, because they would sometimes steal, and then run away and tell their tribes about the habits, mode of life, and numerical strength of the Dutch.

The unhappiest thing of all was supplying the red-men with fire-arms. The Iroquois warriors at first considered a gun "the devil," and would not touch it. Champlain taught them its power, and then they were eager to possess it. For a musket they would willingly give twenty beaver-skins. For a pound of powder they were glad to barter the value of several dollars. It mattered not that the West India Company forbade the traffic under penalty of death, and that their executive officer at Manhattan was not in the least averse to capital punishment. Such im-

---

[1] The price paid for Gardiner's Island was one large black dog, one gun, some powder and shot, some rum, and a few Dutch blankets : in value about £5.

mense profits were too tempting, and the Mohawks were already well armed. It was less easy to deal with the river tribes without discovery, and the latter began to hate the Dutch in consequence. Kieft's taxes were the final blow to their friendship.

In July, rumors of some intended hostile demonstration reached the governor, and he ordered all the residents of New Amsterdam to arm themselves, and, at the firing of three guns, to repair, under their respective officers, equipped for warfare, to a place of rendezvous. Without waiting to be attacked, he soon found an excuse to become the aggressor. It happened that some persons in the company's service, on their way to Delaware River in July, had landed at Staten Island for wood and water, and stolen some swine which had been left in charge of a negro by De Vries. The innocent Raritan Indians, who lived twenty miles or more inland, were accused of this theft, and also of having stolen the canoe of a trading party.

Kieft thought to punish them, and sent Secretary Van Tienhoven, with fifty soldiers and twenty sailors, to attack them, and unless they made prompt reparation, to destroy their corn. The men accompanying Tienhoven, knowing the governor's temper, were anxious to kill and plunder at once. This Tienhoven refused to permit; but finally, vexed with their importunity, he left them, and they attacked the Indians, several of whom were killed and their crops destroyed. Thus was the seed sown for a long and bloody war.[1]

Meanwhile the directors of the West India Company had not ceased wrangling with each other and with the patroons; but they agreed upon a new Charter of Freedoms and Exemptions, which amended materially the obnoxious instrument of 1629. All good inhabitants of New Netherland were to select lands and form colonies, to be limited to one mile along the shore of a bay or navigable river, and two miles into the country. The right of way by land or water was to be free to all, and disputes were to be settled by the governor, under all circumstances. The feudal privileges of jurisdiction, and the exclusive right of hunting, fishing, fowling, grinding corn, etc., were continued to the patroons as an estate of inheritance, with descent to females as well as males. Manufacturers were permitted. Another class of proprietors was soon established. Masters or Colonists they were called, and were such as should convey fine-grown persons to New Netherland, and might occupy one hundred acres of land. Commercial privileges were very greatly extended, al-

---

[1] *Breeden Raedt. Chalmers's Political Annals. De Vries,* in 11 *N. Y. H. S. Col. Albany Records.* Kieft is accused of having given to the soldiers themselves, at the moment of embarkation, even harsher orders than he gave to Van Tienhoven. *O'Callaghan,* I. 227, note.

though the company adhered to the system of onerous imposts for its own benefit. The company renewed their pledge to furnish negroes, and appoint and support competent officers, "for the protection of the good and the punishment of the wicked." The governor and his council were still to act as an orphans' and surrogate's court, to judge in criminal and religious affairs, and administer law and justice. The Dutch Reformed religion was to be publicly taught and sanctioned, and ministers and schoolmasters were to be sustained.

The people in and around New Amsterdam were generally supplied with necessary goods of all descriptions from the company's store. But it was well known that they were sold at an advance of fifty per cent on their cost, and many were the complaints. The store-keeper, Ulrich Lupold, who had never been regarded as trustworthy, was finally detected in extortion, and removed from his position. The first liquor ever made in this country was produced from a private still on Staten Island, erected by Kieft in 1640, and run by Willem Hendricksen, for twenty-five guilders per month.

In the early part of the year 1641, great excitement was occasioned by the intelligence that a murder had been committed **1641.** near the fort. Six of the company's slaves had killed one of their fellow-negroes. There was no evidence against them; and so torture, the common expedient of the Dutch law in such cases, was resorted to for the purpose of extorting self-accusation. To avoid this terrible engine the negroes confessed they had all jointly committed the deed. The court was in a dilemma. Laborers were scarce, and six were too many to lose. Lots were drawn, in order to determine which should be executed; for justice could not be defrauded. The lot fell on a stalwart fellow, who was called "the giant," and he was sentenced to be hanged. January 24th was the great day appointed for his execution, and the whole community turned out to witness the terrible scene. He was placed on a ladder in the fort, with two strong halters about his neck. The fatal signal was given, the ladder pulled from under him, when both ropes broke, and the negro fell to the ground. The bystanders cried so loudly for pardon that the governor granted the culprit his life, under a pledge of future good conduct.

Kieft was constantly issuing new municipal regulations, and there was great need. We find, under date of April 11th, one **April 11.** by which "the tapping of beer during divine service, and after one o'clock at night," was forbidden; whereat the Dutch were as much exercised as their German cousins have been in later times. He also took measures to prevent the deterioration of the currency, which was in a mixed state.

The coins of Europe were rarely seen here. Wampum was in use, but
April 18. had no standard value, until he fixed it by a law. To promote
Sept. 5. agriculture, the governor established two fairs to be held annually; one of cattle on the 15th of October, and one of hogs on the 1st
of November.

In March of that year, Myndert Myndertsen Van der Horst secured a
plantation, about an hour's walk from Vriesendael, where De Vries was
busy putting up buildings, planning orchards and gardens, and making
his property singularly attractive. It extended north from Newark Bay
towards Tappaen, including the valley of the Hackinsack River; the
headquarters of the settlement being only five or six hundred paces from
the village of the Hackinsack Indians.[1]   Van der Horst's people immediately erected a small fort, to be garrisoned by a few soldiers. In August, Cornelis Melyn returned to New Amsterdam with a full-fledged
grant from the West India Company to settle on Staten Island. This
astonished De Vries, who knew that the company was aware of his own
purchase of the whole of that property. Kieft, who had his distillery
and a buckskin manufactory already there, persuaded the liberal-minded
patroon to permit Melyn to establish a plantation near the Narrows, and
then conferred upon the spirited Belgian a formal patent as patroon over
all the island not reserved by De Vries. A small redoubt was immediately erected upon the eastern headland, where a flag was raised whenever a vessel arrived in the lower bay. This is the first record of a marine
telegraph in New York Harbor.[2]

[1] The name of the Indian tribe was Achkinkeshacky, which was corrupted by the early
settlers into Hackinsack.
  De Vries, 11 *N. Y. H. S. Col.,* I. 264.   *O'Callaghan* I. 228, 229.   *Brodhead,* I. 314.
Albany Records.

First Marine Telegraph.

CHAPTER VII.

1641–1643.

INDIAN VENGEANCE.

INDIAN VENGEANCE. — THE FIRST POPULAR ASSEMBLY. — KIEFT'S DISAPPOINTMENT. — DEATH OF PETER MINUET. — EFFORT OF THE "TWELVE MEN" TO INSTITUTE REFORMS. — THE GOVERNOR'S PROCLAMATION. — THE DUTCH AND ENGLISH. — DISCUSSION OF THE BOUNDARY QUESTION. — A FLAW IN THE TITLE TO NEW NETHERLAND. — RELIGIOUS PERSECUTION. — THE FIRST TAVERN. — THE NEW CHURCH. — RAISING MONEY AT A WEDDING. — THE FIRST ENGLISH SECRETARY. — "THE YEAR OF BLOOD." — THE BLOOD ATONEMENT. — THE SHROVETIDE DINNER-PARTY. — THE INHUMAN MASSACRE. — GENERAL UPRISING OF THE INDIANS. — OVERTURES FOR PEACE. — THE HOLLOW TRUCE. — THE SECOND REPRESENTATIVE BODY. — A PAGE OF HORRORS.

BY this time the effects of Kieft's imprudences with the Indians were fast becoming apparent. The Raritans cajoled him with peaceful messages, but suddenly attacked De Vries's unprotected plantation on Staten Island, killed four of his planters and burned all **1641.** his buildings. Folly begets folly. The governor no sooner heard **June.** how the Raritans had avenged their wrongs, than he determined upon their extermination. In an ostentatious proclamation, he offered a bounty of ten fathoms of wampum for the head of any or **July 4.** every one of the tribe, and twenty fathoms for each head of the actual murderers. Some of the River Indians were incited by these bounties, and attacked the Raritans. In the autumn, a chief of the Haverstraw tribe came one day in triumph to the fort, and exhibited a dead man's hand hanging on a stick, which he presented to Kieft, as the hand of the chief who had killed the Dutch.

Meanwhile blood had been shed on the island of Manhattan. **Aug.** An old man, Claes Smits, lived in a little house near Deutal Bay, and worked at the trade of a wheelwright. The nephew of the Indian who was murdered near the Fresh Water Pond during Minuet's administration, and who, as a boy, had sworn vengeance, went to the old man's house under pretense of bartering some beaver-skins for duffels, and,

7

while the unsuspecting Smits was stooping over the great chest in which he kept his goods, the savage seized an ax and killed him with one blow, then plundered the house and escaped. Kieft sent at once to the chief of the Weekquaesgeek tribe, to demand satisfaction. The latter refused to give up the criminal, on the ground that he was but an avenger, after the manner of his race. Some soldiers were then sent out from the fort to arrest the assassin, but they could not find him. Kieft was exasperated and would have openly declared war, careless of probable consequences, had not some of his friends told him of the

Aug 20.

state of public feeling, and how the people accused him of aiming to provoke hostilities on purpose to make "a wrong reckoning with the company"; even charging him with personal coward-ice, for they said, "He knew full well that he could

Dutch Architecture in New Amsterdam.

secure his own life in a good fort." He, therefore, paused in his mad course, and summoned together all the patroons, masters, and heads of families in the vicinity to the fort, "to resolve upon something of the first necessity." This was the pioneer of popular meet-ings upon Manhattan Island.

Aug. 23.

When the people assembled on the day appointed, the governor submitted three propositions.

Aug. 28

1st. "Was it not just that the recent murder of Claes Smits should be avenged by destroying the Indian village where the murderer belonged, if he was not given up?"

2d. "In what manner ought this to be accomplished?"

3d. "By whom should it be effected?"

The assembly, after some preamble and a grave discussion of the ques-tions, chose twelve men out of their number to co-operate with the gov-ernor and council. The names of this first representative body were: Captain De Vries, Jacques Bentyn, Jan Dam, Hendrick Jansen, Jacob

Stoffelsen, Maryn Adriaensen, Abram Molenaer, Frederick Lubbertsen, Jochem Pietersen, Gerrit Dircksen, George Rapaelje, and Abram Planck. De Vries was chosen president. Their counsel was for preserving peace with the Indians as long as possible. They believed the murder should be avenged, but thought "God and the opportunity" ought to be consid-. ered. The Dutch were scattered all about the country, and the cattle were in the woods. It was impolitic to get involved in war with the Indians, while there was no adequate means of defense. They, therefore, recommended that the governor send again, yea, for the second or third time, until he obtained the surrender of the prisoner, that he might punish him as he should see fit.

Kieft was greatly dissatisfied with their verdict. He had not willingly made this concession to popular rights, but rather by force of circumstances, and to serve as "a cloak of protection from responsibility or censure"; for he fully intended to attack the Indians, and chafed under the hindrance which was thus put in his way. Before winter set in he called the "Twelve Men" together again, to confer upon the ^{Nov. 1.} same subject, and again they counseled patience. De Vries was opposed to war with the Indians under any circumstances. He reminded the governor of the sentiments of the Amsterdam Chamber, whose order had been distinctly expressed, "Keep peace with the savages"; and the uneasy and indiscreet chief magistrate was silenced, but not convinced.

During the spring prior to these events, the English at New Haven had made an effort to appropriate a portion of the Dutch ^{April 1.} territory on the South River. Some fifty families in all had become dissatisfied with their Connecticut River homes, on account of the sickliness of the climate, and with their effects sailed, about the first of April, in a ship belonging to George Lambertsen a New Haven merchant, and put into New Amsterdam on their way South to communicate their designs to the Dutch authorities. Kieft warned them not to build or plant within the limits of New Netherland, and they promised to select some spot over which the States-General had no authority. They were allowed to go on their way, and shortly after fortified a post on the Schuylkill.

In December, news came of the death of Peter Minuet, who had guarded his little Swedish colony well for three years, although ^{Dec.} they had once or twice suffered great privations. They had been reinforced by a party of Dutch from Holland, and also by a deputation of Swedes, who purchased additional lands from the Indians, and, in token of the sovereignty of their queen, set up "the arms and crown of Sweedland." Peter Hollaendare, a Swede, succeeded to the chief government after the death of Minuet.

1642. As soon as the rivers were frozen over, Kieft summoned the
Jan. 21. "Twelve Men" into council the third time, and insisted upon their acceding to his wishes in relation to the Indians. As the murderer had not been given up, they yielded, though reluctantly. Their assistance in the matter was promised only on condition that the governor should lead the expedition in person, and that the expenses of it, and the necessary care of the wounded men and their families afterward, should be defrayed by the company.

During the same session, the " Twelve Men " took occasion to demand certain reforms in the government. In the Fatherland, domineering arrogance was restrained by the system of rotation in office. The self-reliant men who had won their country from the sea, and their liberties from the relaxing grasp of feudal prerogative, knew that they could govern themselves, and they did govern themselves. The "Twelve," who now sat in judgment, were of the same stock, distinguished not only by talent, but by local experience ; and although they had voluntarily pledged themselves to submit to the government of the West India Company, they believed it to have been more by neglect than ill-will that such a conceited little potentate had been placed over them, and they knew him to be unworthy of so much trust. He had often been heard to compare himself to the Prince of Orange, as above the law ; but the grievance which caused the most feeling was the mock council, which in reality was no council at all. He appointed all public officers, except such as came with commissions from Holland, made laws, imposed taxes, levied fines, inflicted penalties, incorporated towns, and could affect the price of any man's property at pleasure by changing the value of wampum. He also decided all civil and criminal questions without the aid of jury, and settled controversies and appeals from inferior courts. The memorial, which had been previously prepared, was presented, with all due deference, to the governor. It called for an addition of four men to the council, two of whom should be chosen each year from the "Twelve Men" elected by the people, and demanded that judicial proceedings should be had only before a full board ; that the militia should be mustered annually ; that the people should have the same privilege as in Holland of visiting vessels from abroad, and the right to trade in neighboring places subject to the duties of the company ; that the English should be prohibited from selling cattle within the province, and that the value of the currency should be considerably increased.

Kieft was confounded. He regretted exceedingly having made any show of parliamentary government. But he was also politic, and he replied to the assembly that he expected a complete council in one of the first ships from Holland, and graciously acceded to all the other requirements, without, however, fulfilling a single promise. Then he wound up the meeting adroitly by telling the gentlemen that they had never been invested with greater powers than to give advice respecting the murder of Claes Smits.

A short time afterward, the following poster appeared in various places : — Feb. 18.

" Whereas, The people have at our request commissioned ' Twelve Men ' to communicate their good council and advice concerning the murder of Claes Smits, which now being done, we thank them for the trouble they have taken, and shall make use of their written advice, with God's help and fitting time ; and we propose no more meetings, as such tend to dangerous consequences, and to the great injury, both of the country and of our authority ; — we, therefore, do hereby forbid the calling of any assemblies or meetings, of whatever sort, without our express order, on pain of punishment for disobedience.

" Done in Fort Amsterdam, February 18th, 1642, in New Netherland.

" WILHELM KIEFT."

Having disposed of the " Twelve Men," Kieft made preparations and dispatched a party of eighty soldiers, under Ensign Van March 5. Dyck, against the Weekquaesgeeks, with orders to exterminate them by fire and sword. The guide professed to know the way to the Indian village, but he lost the track just at nightfall; and, as they had crossed the Harlem River with no little difficulty, the commanding officer finally lost his temper, and the twin losses resulted in an overwhelming gain, for the party returned to New Amsterdam innocent of the death of a single Indian. The mortifying failure enraged the governor ; but the Indians were quick to discover the trail of the soldiers, and were so much alarmed as to come at once to New Amsterdam and sue for peace. A treaty was concluded with them, one of the stipulations of March 28. which was the surrender of the murderer, — a promise which, either from unwillingness or inability, was never fulfilled.

This treaty was scarcely concluded before rumors were afloat that the Connecticut savages were planning to destroy the colonists throughout New England. Hartford and New Haven concerted measures of defence, and anxiety and alarm were everywhere felt. Under these circumstances the settlers at Greenwich thought it wise, as a measure of self-protection, to submit themselves to the government of New Neth- April 9. erland ; and Captain Patrick and his friends, after swearing allegiance, were invested with all the rights of patroons. But the difficulties between the Dutch garrison and the English at Hartford continued; and

April 3. Kieft, finding that his protests were of no effect, prohibited all trade and commercial intercourse with the Hartford people. He soon

May 15. after heard that the New Haven party, who went to the South River, were living upon the company's lands without his permission. He immediately dispatched two sloops with a strong force to require

May 22. them to withdraw, and, in case of refusal, to arrest them and destroy their trading-posts. These orders were executed so promptly that the English had not two hours to prepare for their departure, and they were brought with their goods to New Netherland, and afterwards landed at New Haven. The excitement on the subject there was intense; particularly after Lambertsen, who was considered by the Dutch as the principal instigator of the injury to their trade, had been compelled,

Aug. 28. while passing New Amsterdam, to give an account of what peltries he had obtained on the Delaware, and to pay duties on them all.

The Hartford authorities found the prohibition against intercourse with

May 11. the New Amsterdam settlers very inconvenient, to say the least, and finally sent a committee to confer with Kieft on the subject. He received them pompously, conceded nothing, talked about the antiquity of the Dutch title to the country on the Connecticut River, and graciously offered to lease to them a portion of the lands there, on certain terms. The ambassadors went home to report, having accomplished no part of their mission. Both the Hartford and the New Haven people were more incensed than ever, and vented their annoyance upon every Dutch man or woman who came in their way. The agents from New England who went to London about that time brought the subject into general notice there, and it was discussed with no little acrimony by the courtiers of Charles I. Lord Say told the Dutch Minister that the conduct of the New-Netherlanders was haughty and unbearable in the extreme, and dropped a few meaning hints in regard to their being forcibly ejected from the Connecticut Valley, if the difficulties were not shortly arranged. The Dutch Minister wrote to his government; the States-General took the matter up, and much bitterness appears in the subsequent correspondence, although, as in previous instances, the question was left unsettled.

It is a singular fact that, while the Dutch in New Netherland were at this time so few in proportion to their wide and fine territory, the English had spread themselves over a great part of New England, and were, to all outward appearances, far the more prosperous. In natural advantages New Netherland immeasurably outrivaled New England,

and the difference in the progress of the two colonies may be traced directly to the want of wisdom by which the statesmen at the Hague endowed a commercial corporation with the maintenance of a dependency for their own material gain. New England was founded in religious persecution. As it could contribute little resource to the mother-country, under any circumstances, it was allowed to work out its own combinations of policy in Church and State. The mere facts of a colonial condition tend to entail the same species of subjection which ordinarily appertains to infancy in a family; but the New England colony stands out exceptional in history, as having elicited no particular interest in any quarter of the Old World as to its possible future value, and religious controversies and religious education occupied a reading population who were content with a bare living, and stood quite aloof from mercantile speculations. On the other hand, New Netherland was treated solely as an investment for the eventual accumulation of wealth at home, while at the same time the enormous monopoly of the West India Company comprehended interests in comparison with which the immediate affairs of a little State were esteemed insignificant.

When the New-Englanders crossed the supposed boundary lines, the Dutch in power wondered why their impotent protests were unheeded. Those protests were based upon the supposed right of the West India Company to the territory which they claimed, and the quarrels thus engendered produced some interesting state papers. Later, John De Witt made the most strenuous efforts to establish a good understanding with Oliver Cromwell, and sent some of his ablest diplomatists to the Protector's court. The subject of the boundary line of New Netherland attracted much attention. In the several documents which were drawn up by the West India Company to substantiate their rights, the principal historical statements were audacious fictions, and the writer of them was evidently aware that there was a flaw in the Dutch title, and that, in a court of law, not a foot of the vast territory could be held as a *bona fide* possession. The Dutch ministers to England must have entertained similar views, judging from the gingerly care with which they handled the delicate and perplexing question.

As the New England settlements grew more rapidly, and their institutions received more attention from the people than those of New Netherland, so also did the spirit of intolerance take root among them, until they became the most relentless persecutors of the age. " The arm of the civil government," says Judge Story, " was constantly employed in support of the denunciations of the Church, and, without its forms, the Inquisition existed in substance, with a full share of its terrors and its violence." Many important families were driven by this means into finding homes elsewhere; and not a few, perceiving the larger liberty of opinion which would be vouchsafed in the Dutch dominion, made application to Kieft, and were welcomed right heartily, being required only to take the same oath of allegiance as the Dutch subjects. Roger Williams, a promising young minister, whose ideas of religious liberty shocked the General Court of Massachusetts to such an extent that they sentenced him to perpetual exile, went into the wilderness of Rhode Island and commenced the settlement of that State. That was as early as 1635. Others were banished through the workings of the same peculiar ecclesiastical system. Annie Hutchinson, who was a lady of rare cultivation, and styled by her contemporaries "a masterpiece of wit and wisdom," was accused of "weakening the hands and hearts of the people towards the ministers," because she maintained the "paramount authority of private judgment." She was worried by her clerical examiners for several hours, although the verdict had evidently been agreed upon before the session commenced, and at last she was declared "unfit for society," and ordered to depart from the province. She went, at first, to Rhode Island, accompanied by quite a number of families of personal friends, and persons of the same phase of religious belief. But fearing the implacable vengeance of Massachusetts would reach her even there, she removed to New Netherland in 1642, selecting for her residence the point now known as Pelham Neck, near New Rochelle, which received the name of "Annie's Hoeck."[1] Near by her settled John Throgmorton and thirty-five English families. Kieft granted them all the franchises which the charter of 1640 allowed, with freedom to worship God in the manner which suited them best.

The terms were so agreeable that a large emigration in the same direction would have speedily set in, had not the General Court of Massachusetts taken alarm, and sought to dissuade their own citizens from seeking thus to strengthen "their doubtful Dutch neighbors." But they went on with their political and moral and religious instruction, acting most self-complacently on the conviction that their system of teaching was the very best in the world, and their interpretation of the Scriptures the one and only true way to Heaven.

When, at rare intervals, some bold progressionist tried to open the eyes of the people to the pretenses of pompous ignorance masked in the guise of scholarship and sanctity, or to promulgate some new tenet or article of faith, they were stricken so quickly that the places that had known them knew them not much longer. Rev. Francis Doughty was dragged

---

[1] Hoeck is a Dutch word signifying *point*. It is sometimes spelt Hoek.

from an assembly at Cohasset for venturing to say in his sermon that "Abraham's children should have been baptized." A large number of his friends determined to join him on a pilgrimage to New Netherland. They bought more than thirteen thousand acres at Newtown, Long Island, near where a number of persons from Lynn and Ipswich had settled a short time before. For this large landed property Kieft granted them an absolute ground-brief, and afforded every facility in his power for the erection of substantial houses and the proper cultivation of the soil.

These accessions to the population of New Netherland were of marked value to the prosperity of the province. But there were other arrivals about the same time which were less to be desired. ^{April 13.} A great number of fugitive servants, both from New England and Virginia, flocked into New Amsterdam, trying to get employment. They were full of mischief, idle, indolent, and dishonest, and occasioned great trouble and complaint among the people. Kieft found it necessary to issue new police regulations, one of which was to forbid any family giving to strangers more than one meal, or more than one night's lodging, without first sending notice of the same to the governor.

It would seem that visitors had hitherto been entertained by the citizens. Noteworthy persons had enjoyed the hospitality of the governor himself. The growth of the town, and the increasing number of travelers, rendered this a great inconvenience. The subject of building a public house had been for some time agitated, and Kieft finally concluded to erect it at the company's expense. It was completed this year, a great clumsy stone tavern, and it was located on the northeast corner of Pearl Street and Coenties Slip, fronting the East River.

A short time after this famous old building had been put in use, Captain De Vries was one day dining with the governor, as was his custom when he happened to be at the fort, and, in the course of conversation, the host congratulated himself upon the architecture and workmanship of the new edifice. De Vries said it was, indeed, an excellent thing for travelers, but that the next thing they wanted was a decent church for the people. In New England, the first thing they did, after building some dwellings, was to erect a fine church; and now, when the English passed New Amsterdam, they only saw a "mean barn," in which the Dutch worshiped their Creator. The West India Company had the credit of being very zealous in protecting the Reformed Church [1] against Spanish tyranny, and there was no reason why their settlements should not be supplied with church edifices. There were

---

[1] Calvinist.

Stadthuys.

materials enough at hand, — fine oak timber and good building stone, and lime made from oyster-shells, far better than the lime in Holland.

Kieft was interested, and asked who would like to superintend such a building ?

De Vries told him that no doubt some of the friends of the Reformed religion could be found who would be only too glad to do so.

Kieft, smiling, told De Vries that he supposed he was one of them, and asked if he would contribute one hundred guilders to the enterprise.

De Vries very quickly responded in the affirmative; and then they decided that Jochem Pietersen Kuyter, who was a good Calvinist, and had plenty of workmen, would be the most suitable person to procure timber, and Jan Jansen Dam, who lived near the fort, should be the fourth one of the consistory to superintend the building. The governor promised to furnish a few thousand guilders of the company's money, and the rest was to be raised by private subscription.

A few days afterward, the daughter of Dominie Bogardus was married, and, at the wedding party, the governor and Captain De
May. Vries, thinking it a rare opportunity to raise the requisite amount of funds, took advantage of the good-humor of the guests, and passed round the paper, with their own names heading the list. As each one present desired to appear well in the eyes of his neighbor, a handsome

sum was contributed. In the morning, some few appealed to the governor for permission to reconsider the matter ; but his Excellency would permit no names to be erased from the paper.

An arrangement was at once effected with John and Richard Ogden,[1] of Stamford, for the mason-work of a stone church, seventy-two feet long, fifty wide, and sixteen high, at one thousand dollars for the job, and a gratuity of forty dollars more should the work be

May 20.

Inside of Fort, with Governor's House, and Church.

satisfactory. The agreement was signed and sealed on the 20th of May. The church was to be located in the fort, that it might not be exposed to Indian depredations ; although many objected, on the ground that the fort was overcrowded already. The walls were soon up, and the roof covered with oak shingles, which, from exposure to the weather, became blue like slate. Kieft caused to be erected in the front wall a marble slab with this inscription : —

"ANNO DOMINI, 1642,
WILHELM KIEFT DIRECTEUR GENERAL.
HEEFT DE GEMEENTE DESEN TEMPEL DOEN BOUWEN."

When the fort was demolished, in 1787, to make room for the Government House, this slab was discovered buried in the earth, and was removed to the belfry of the old Dutch Church in Garden Street, where it remained until the burning of that church, in 1835, when it totally disappeared.

It was now becoming necessary to observe regularity in drawing boundary and division lines ; hence Andries Hudde was appointed surveyor, with a salary of eighty dollars per annum and a few additional fees. The first record of the sale of city lots, we find this year. There is one extant, showing that Abraham Van Steenwyck sells to Anthony Van Fees a lot on Bridge Street, thirty feet front by one hundred and ten deep, for the sum of nine dollars and sixty cents ![2]

The influx into the Dutch settlements of persons who spoke only the English language occasioned no little embarrassment. Kieft himself

---

[1] These Ogdens were the ancestors of the present families of that name in New York and New Jersey. *Alb. Rec.*, III. 31. *O'Callaghan*, I. 261, 262. *N. Y. H. S. Col.*, II. 293.
[2] The street was not then named.

7

could speak it fluently, but many of his officers did not understand a word, and it was finally thought best to have an official interpreter. George Baxter received the appointment, at an annual salary of two hundred and fifty guilders.

Meanwhile, Adrian Van der Donck, a lineal descendant of Adrian Van Bergen, a graduate of Leyden University, and a man of acknowledged scholarship, had, in 1641, leased the westerly half of Castle Island. He was appointed sheriff of the colony at Rensselaerswick, and specially instructed to repress the spirit of lawlessness which seemed to pervade that district. He went to work energetically. He made it his first business to induce the patroon to send over the learned clergyman, Dr Johannes Megapolensis, "for the edifying improvement of the inhabitants and Indians thereabouts." The Amsterdam Chamber approved the call; the reverend gentleman was promised a new church and parsonage, and a small theological library, together with an annual salary of one thousand guilders. A number of families accompanied him to his new field of labor. They arrived at New Amsterdam in August, 1642.
August 1. From that point Van Rensselaer had requested that the further transportation of the party should be left entirely to the advice and discretion of Kieft, to whom he sent, as a present for his trouble, a handsome saddle and bridle. To obviate as much as possible the dangers of life among the Indians, the patroon required that all his colonists, except the farmers and tobacco-planters, should live near each other, so as to form a church neighborhood. Ships sometimes remained at Manhattan a fortnight before news of their arrival reached Rensselaerswick; but in this instance prompt measures were resorted to, and by the 11th of the month the names of the new settlers had been registered at their destination by Arendt Van Corlear, the commissary.

It was about the same time that intelligence of the capture of some
Aug. 11. French missionaries by the Iroquois reached Fort Orange. With characteristic Dutch benevolence, Van Corlear and two stout-hearted friends went on horseback to the Mohawk country to attempt their rescue. They carried presents, which were thankfully received by the great warriors, who saluted them with musket-shots from each of their castles as they approached, fed them with turkeys during their stay, and seemed greatly pleased with their visit. Van Corlear invited the chiefs into council, and urged the release of their prisoners, one of whom was a celebrated Jesuit scholar. Their reply was, "We shall show you every friendship in our power, but on this subject we shall be silent." Several days were spent to no purpose. Six hundred guilders' worth of goods were offered for the Frenchmen's ransom, and coldly refused. Van

Corlear's eloquence only elicited from the Indians a promise not to kill their prisoners; and then the baffled diplomats set out for Fort Orange, conducted by an embassy of ten armed savages. They had hardly departed from the encampment, when the restrained braves clamored for blood, and one of the Frenchmen was struck dead with a tomahawk; but the life of Father Jacques was spared, although his subsequent sufferings, throughout a dreary winter, among a class of vindictive savages, who hated the cross and reviled his holy zeal, were most intense.

The year that followed was emphatically "a year of blood." It was ushered in with the wildest stories of a general war by the **1643.** New England and New Netherland Indians against the English and the Dutch. If a benighted traveler halloed in the woods, a panic was immediately caused, lest savages were torturing some captive. The fireside gossips contributed greatly to the general anxiety and terror by accusing the Indians of trying to poison and bewitch those in authority. Thoughtful men censured Kieft severely for having allowed the colonists to settle wherever they liked, all over the country, so that now they were almost entirely defenseless. He had done nothing to prepare them for war; he had not even a sufficient stock of powder to allow each colonist a half-pound, if it should be required.

And war, with all its horrors, was on the wing. It came soon, surely and swiftly. Captain De Vries, while rambling through **January.** the woods near his plantation at Vriesendael, met a drunken Indian. The savage stroked the patroon over his arms, in token of friendship, and called him "a good chief," and then said he had come from Van der Horst's place at Hackinsack, where they had sold him brandy, and stolen his beaver coat. The enraged savage vowed a bloody revenge, and the peace-loving De Vries tried in vain to soothe him. Before night, he had shot Garret Jansen Van Vorst, who was thatching the roof of one of Van der Horst's houses. The chiefs of the Hackinsacks and Reckawancks hurried to Vriesendael to tell the news, and counsel with De Vries, whom they held in the highest esteem : they would have gone to the governor, but were afraid he might detain them as prisoners. De Vries, however, assured them that the latter would be best, and accompanied them in person to the fort, where they made their confession, and offered two hundred fathoms of wampum, a blood atonement of money, as a purchase for peace. This universal custom among the Indians of North America was in singular accordance with the usages of Greece : —

> " If a brother bleed,
> On just atonement we remit the deed ;
> A sire the slaughter of the son forgives,
> The price of blood discharged, the murderer lives."

The chiefs deplored the murder, but pleaded for the murderer. They told Kieft that he was the son of a chief; that brandy should not have been sold him, for he was not used to it, and it crazed him. " Even your own men," they said, " get drunk and fight with knives; if you will sell no more strong drink to the Indians, you will have no more murders," — an early warning which the whites would have done well to observe, even to this day. Kieft refused to accept any expiation less than the head of the fugitive, and the Indians would not bind themselves to surrender him; for they said he had gone two days' journey away among the Tankitekes, and it would be impossible to overtake him. The governor immediately sent a peremptory message to Pacham, the chief of the Tankitekes, for the surrender of the criminal.

Feb. 19.   Before the demand could possibly have been acceded to, under any circumstances, a band of Mohawks made a descent upon the Weekquaesgeek and Tappaen tribes, for the purpose of levying tribute. These Indians were terror-stricken, and came flying, half naked, to the Dutch for protection, leaving seventy of their number dead and many of their women and children captives. They were kindly received in New Amsterdam. They seemed to have almost supreme faith in the superior power of the white man, — a confidence which, by a wise policy, might have been strengthened. But public sentiment was divided. De Vries, at the head of one party, breathed kindness and caution in every syllable he uttered. Others sympathized with Kieft in his insane wish to exterminate the savages. Some inkling of the state of feeling must have reached the Indians, for they suddenly scattered in various directions; some flying to Pavonia, some to Vriesendael, and some to Corlear's bouwery.

Feb. 24.   A few days after, there was a Shrovetide dinner-party at the house of Jan Jansen Dam, the governor being present; and nearly every person in the company became merry with wine. The chief topic of conversation was the Indians. Secretary Van Tienhoven, at the suggestion of Dam, Adriaensen, and Planck, drew up a petition to the governor, urging in the name of the "Twelve Men" an immediate attack upon the defenseless savages, " whom God had thus delivered into their hands." The paper was no sooner read, than Kieft, in a significant toast, announced approaching hostilities. His next move was to dispatch Van Tienhoven and Corporal Hans Steen to Pavonia, to reconnoiter the situation.

Consternation quickly took the place of hilarity. Dominie Bogardus hastened to the governor, sharply reproved him for his " hot-headed rashness," and foretold certain consequences. The usually unmoved and dignified Dr. La Montagne pleaded with Kieft excitedly, for a postponement of his terrible purpose. " Wait, for God's sake," he exclaimed, "until the arrival of the next ship from Holland!" Captain De Vries raised his voice in anxious entreaty, and also in persuasive argument. He told Kieft that the petition was not from the "Twelve Men"; only three had signed it; all the rest were opposed to such a dangerous proceeding. Words, however, were thrown away upon the obstinate governor. He had made up his mind. De Vries walked home with him, and talked incessantly; but Kieft only smiled, and under pretense of showing the Captain his new parlor, which he had just completed, asked him into the hall upon the side of the house, where the soldiers could be seen preparing to start for Pavonia. "My order has gone forth," he said, "and cannot be recalled."

The story of that night is a blot upon the pages of New Netherland's history. It was the most shocking massacre that ever disgraced a civilized nation. Sergeant Rodolf crossed with his troops to Pavonia, and butchered eighty Indians in their sleep, sparing not a woman or a child. It makes humanity blush to record such an atrocious deed. Another band of troops marched to Corlear's Hook, and murdered forty Indians who were encamped there. Not one was spared, and every cry for mercy was unheeded.

De Vries sat all night by the kitchen fire in the governor's house, with an aching heart. The shrieks of the hapless victims reached his ears from Pavonia, while a solemn stillness settled over New Amsterdam. All at once an Indian and his squaw appeared in the doorway, and, overcome with terror, asked him to hide them in the fort. They lived near Vriesendael, and had escaped in a small skiff. As De Vries rose to meet them, they exclaimed, "The Mohawks have fallen upon us!" "No," said De Vries, pityingly, "no Indians have done this; it is the work of the Dutch. It is no time to hide yourselves in the fort"; and leading them to the gate, he directed them towards the north, and watched them until they disappeared in the woods. Feb. 26.

The extraordinary conquerors returned at sunrise with thirty prisoners and the heads of several of their victims. Kieft praised them for their valor, and there was much shaking of hands and many congratulations. Feb. 27.

The following day, a party of Dutch and English went over to Pavonia to pillage ·the stricken encampment. In vain the soldiers on guard warned them of the consequences. Dirk Straatmaker and his wife were both killed by some concealed Indians, whose wigwam they were robbing, and several others very narrowly escaped with their lives.

Stimulated by the success of this discreditable exploit, some of the Long Island settlers sought permission of the governor to attack the

Indians in that neighborhood. De Vries and Dominie Bogardus and Dr. La Montagne remonstrated with so much earnestness, that Kieft finally refused to consent, on the ground that the Long Island Indians were "hard to conquer," but added the unfortunate proviso that "if they proved hostile, each man might resort to such means of defense as he should see fit." Before long some covetous persons, in punishment for an injury which they claimed to have sustained, robbed the Indians of their corn. Three of the latter, while defending their property, were killed. It needed only this crowning act of injustice to fill the measure of Indian endurance. Eleven tribes immediately united and declared war against the Dutch. The result, as may well be imagined, was terrible beyond description. The swamps and thickets were full of vindictive savages, watching opportunities to slay and plunder. From the shore of the Housatonic to the valley of the Raritan, death, fire, and captivity threatened unspeakable horrors. In one week the smiling country was transformed into a frightful and desolate wilderness. The rich and the poor, the strong and the helpless, the old and the young, shared the same fate. Blood flowed in rivers ; and, what was often worse, children were carried into hopeless captivity. Those who escaped fled to the fort, where the valiant governor remained safe from all possible bodily harm, but where he was obliged to listen to the fiery wrath of ruined farmers, childless men, and widowed women, who were soon united in a common purpose of returning to Holland. Not knowing what else to do, he proclaimed a day of general fasting and prayer. But while the people humbled themselves before their Maker, they held their chief magistrate strictly accountable for their calamities. In alarm, he tried to moderate the popular feeling by taking all the unemployed men into the pay of the company, to serve as soldiers for two months.

March 1.

March 4.

One incident deserves special notice. The Indians, in their work of destruction, attacked Vriesendael, burned the barns, killed the cattle, and were preparing to destroy the beautiful manor-house of De Vries. His people had all gathered there for safety, as it was constructed with loop-holes for musketry. Suddenly the same Indian whose life De Vries had saved, on the night of the Pavonia massacre, came running to the scene, and so eloquently declaimed to the savages of the goodness of the "great chief," that they paused in their work, expressed great sorrow that they had destroyed so much already, and quietly went away.

De Vries was full of indignation with the governor, and said to him, with fire flashing from his eyes, "It was our own nation you murdered when you sent men to Pavonia to break the Indians' heads ! Who shall now make good our damages ? "

Kieft saw his error, but it was too late. Willing to make what amends remained in his power, he sent a messenger with an overture of peace to the Long Island Indians, which they rejected with scorn. Standing afar off, they derided the Dutch, calling out, " Are you our friends ? You are corn thieves."

When this report was brought to New Amsterdam, the people were so maddened that they talked of deposing Kieft and sending him in chains to Holland. He tried to exculpate himself by fastening the blame of the Pavonia massacre upon Adriaensen and others, whose advice he pretended to have followed. This was one drop too much for the unprincipled Adriaensen, who had lost all his valuable property since the war commenced, and was not disposed to shoulder any of Kieft's sins. He therefore armed himself, and rushed into the governor's room, intending to kill him on the spot. But strong men were present, and the would-be assassin was seized, disarmed, and imprisoned, and on ^{March 21.} the sailing of the first vessel was sent to Holland, notwithstanding the open resistance of his friends.

Early on the morning of March 24, three Indian messengers from the great chief Penhawitz approached Fort Amsterdam, ^{March 24.} bearing a white flag. None had the courage to go forth and meet them, but De Vries and Jacob Olfersten. The Indians said they had come to ask why some of their people had been murdered, when they had never harmed the Dutch. De Vries assured them that the Dutch did not know that any of their tribe were among the number. They then asked De Vries to come with them and speak to their chief, and he fearlessly consented. They conveyed him and his companion in their boat to a point near Rockaway, where they arrived towards evening, and found the chief with two or three hundred warriors near a village of some thirty wigwams. De Vries was hospitably entertained in the royal cabin, and feasted with oysters and fish. About daybreak he was conducted into the woods, where sixteen chiefs were assembled in a circle, and being placed in the center, the chief speaker among them began to enumerate their wrongs. He charged the Dutch with having repaid their former kindness with cruelty ; told how the Indians had given them their daughters for wives, by whom they had had children ; and accused them of murdering their own blood in a villainous manner. De Vries interrupted him, and begged the chiefs to go with him to the governor and make peace. They were not at all disposed to do so, but De Vries urged them, and his well-known character for justice and honor inspired them at last with confidence, and they repaired to their canoes. Kieft received them gladly, and concluded an informal treaty ; but they were not satis-

8

fied with their presents, and grumbled among themselves afterward. Through their aid and influence, a truce was also effected with some other faithless tribes; but harmony was by no means restored, for both the Dutch and the Indians were smarting from their injuries. The farmers planted their June corn in constant fear of death. Indeed, peace seemed about as full of terror as war.

March 25.

July came. The summer was hot and dry. Men crept about like guilty creatures, and went from place to place, when possible, in bands. An old Indian chief met De Vries one day, and, in response to the cheerful greeting of the popular patroon, said that he was melancholy. Upon being asked the cause, he said that his young men wanted war with the Dutch; that the presents given them were not sufficient recompense for their losses. He had added presents of his own in vain. One had lost a father, another had lost a mother, and so on, and they clamored for revenge. He begged De Vries not to walk alone in the woods, for fear some Indians who did not know him might kill him. De Vries escorted the chief to Fort Amsterdam, where he told the governor the same things; but it was without results. The chief was sorry, but said he feared he should not long be able to quiet his tribe.

July 20.

Soon afterward, there came a rumor that Pacham, the crafty sachem of the Tankitekes, was visiting all the Indian villages, to arrange for a general massacre of the Dutch; and, as if to corroborate its truth, several trading-boats on the North River were attacked and plundered, nine men killed, and one woman and two children carried into captivity. The alarm was so general, that Kieft summoned the people together for advice. "Eight men" were chosen this time by the popular voice, to counsel with the governor. They were Jochem Pietersen Kuyter, Jan Jansen Dam, Barent Dircksen, Abraham Pietersen, Thomas Hall, Gerrit Wolfertsen, and Cornelis Melyn. Their first official act was to eject Jan Jansen Dam from their board, and appoint Jan Evertsen Bout in his place. The result of their first deliberation was a renewal of hostilities with the river Indians, and a resolution to maintain peace with the Long Island tribes.

August 7.

Sept. 13.

Sept. 16.

But the war-whoop sounded almost immediately in another direction. The Weekquaesgeeks stole upon the estate of Annie Hutchinson, at Annie's Hoeck, and murdered her with all her family and people, save a sweet little granddaughter of eight years, whom they carried into captivity. They then proceeded to Vreedeland and attacked Throgmorton's settlement, laying it waste and killing every person whom they found at home.

Sept. 20.

Lady Deborah Moody, who had been "dealt with" by the church at

Salem " for the error of denying baptism to infants," had settled, in the month of June, at Gravesend. Thither the savages hurried in their insane thirst for blood. But the settlement was defended by over forty brave men, and the Indians were obliged to retreat. They went from there to Doughty's settlement at Newtown, where were eighty or more inhabitants, who fled to New Amsterdam, leaving everything belonging to them but the bare land to be destroyed. A few days later, the Hackinsacks made a night attack upon Van der Horst's colony, on Newark Bay, and destroyed the plantation, driving the little garrison, who for a time made a determined resistance, into a canoe, by which they ^{Oct. 1.} escaped to New Amsterdam. The Neversincks caught the infection, and killed some traders near Sandy Hook. The yacht had just reached New Amsterdam with the tidings, when a nearer calamity appalled every heart. Jacob Stoffelsen had married the widow of Van Vorst, Pauw's former superintendent, and lived at Pavonia. He was a favorite with the Indians, and felt secure in his home. They came to his house, however, one afternoon, and having sent him on some false errand to Fort Amsterdam, they killed his wife and children (except the little son of Van Vorst, whom they took off with them), destroyed all his property, and murdered every white inhabitant of Pavonia. The next day Kieft went with Stoffelsen to see De Vries, and earnestly entreated him to follow the Indians and ransom the boy. Being the only man who dared venture into the haunts of the savages, he finally consented, ^{Oct. 2.} and secured the child's freedom.

Thus New Jersey was left in the possession of its aboriginal lords. Melyn, on Staten Island, hourly expected an assault, and was fortified to the extent of his resources. The only tolerable place of safety was Fort Amsterdam, and into it women and children and cattle were huddled promiscuously, while husbands and fathers mounted guard on the crumbling walls. The whole available fighting force of ^{Oct. 5.} the Dutch was not over two hundred men, besides fifty or sixty Englishmen who had been enrolled into service to prevent their leaving New Netherland. This army was under the command of Captain John Underhill; and it was necessary that they should keep guard at all hours, for seven allied tribes, numbering about 1,500 warriors, were likely to descend upon them at any moment.

Just at this juncture, the province lost one of its leading men, and the Indians their best friend. De Vries had had no sympathy with war; he now found himself ruined in consequence of it, and, bidding adieu to the governor with the portentous assurance, " Vengeance for innocent blood will sooner or later fall upon your head," he embarked on a fishing-vessel and sailed for Europe.

CHAPTER VIII.

1643-1647.

APPEALS FOR ASSISTANCE.

CONFISCATION OF SHOES. — THE DOOMED VILLAGE. — TRIALS FOR WANT OF MONEY. — ACTION OF THE WEST INDIA COMPANY. — KIEFT'S QUARRELS. — THE WAR ENDED. — THE GREAT INDIAN TREATY OF PEACE. — MINERALS. — THE NEW SCHOOL. — ADRIAEN VAN DER DONCK. — VAN RENSSELAER'S DEATH. — THE NEW GOVERNOR. — STUYVESANT'S RECEPTION. — GOVERNOR STUYVESANT. — MRS. PETER STUYVESANT. — MRS. BAYARD.

THE front line of progress is never uniform. We can indeed assert with truth that New Netherland generally advanced; but an intimate acquaintance with its early history shows that at many points it was stationary; and now we have come to one where it actually receded, until the only wonder is that the province under that style and power did not become entirely extinct.

Indian wars are never invested with any of the fleeting splendors which embellish other armed conflicts. They add no luster to the pages of history. They furnish little philosophy or instruction. We have in this instance no military skill to chronicle, no marshaling of hosts, no clash of serried columns. A sense of helplessness, an atmosphere of terror, an indefinable dread, take the place of heroism and romance as usually pictured with the shock of battles. The "Eight Men" whom the people of New Netherland had chosen to think and act for them appealed to their English neighbors at New Haven for assistance in their great distress. The reply was cool and courteous, but decidedly negative. It was embodied in these words, "We are not satisfied that your war with the Indians is just."

Just or unjust, they must all perish now without relief. So Oct. 24. they told the whole agonizing story in a most eloquent letter to the Amsterdam Chamber, praying for immediate and decisive help.[1] This document is supposed to have been penned by Cornelis Melyn, who

---

[1] The Eight Men to the Amsterdam Chamber, *Col. Doc.*, Vol. I. 138, 139.

was a man of no mean ability, and who seems to have fully appreciated the mistaken policy of the governor. The winter was setting in with unusual severity. The small, worthless straw huts around the fort were the only shelter which could be given to the homeless suffer- **Nov. 3.** ers who had fled from the tomahawk and scalping-knife. The fort itself was in no condition to meet the emergency of the hour; and provisions and clothing were wholly inadequate to the demand. As help from Holland must come slowly, if, indeed, it came at all before spring, expeditions were planned against some of the Indian villages, the chief object of which was plunder. Meanwhile the "Eight Men" sent to the States-General a bold complaint of the neglect of the West India Company. They said, "We have had no means of defense provided against a savage foe, and we have had a miserable despot sent to rule over us."

About the middle of November, a colony of English emigrants, headed by Robert Fordham, arrived at Hempstede, Long Island, **Nov. 16.** and settled on land which was granted them by Kieft. Their houses were hardly ready for occupation when suspicions of treachery fell upon

Group, showing **Holland** Fashions.

Penhawitz, the sachem of the Canarsee Indians, who since the truce in the spring had, to all outward appeárance, been friendly. Fordham sent a message of this import to the governor, who, without waiting to ascertain the truth of the charge, dispatched one hundred and **1644.** twenty men, under the command of Dr. La Montagne, Cook, **Jan. 2.** and Underhill, to "exterminate" the Canarsees. They sailed in three yachts to Cow Bay, and proceeded to the two Indian villages. The savages, taken by surprise, made little resistance, and one hundred and twenty were killed, while the assailants lost but one man. Two prisoners were taken to New Amsterdam and put to death in the most revolting manner. One, frightfully wounded by the long knives with which Kieft had armed the soldiers instead of swords, at last dropped dead while dancing the death-dance of his race. The other, shockingly mutilated beforehand, was beheaded on a millstone in Beaver Lane, near the Battery.

March 8. The winter was one of the darkest and most disheartening ever known to the colonists. Food was doled out with a sparing hand, and famine seemed ever near. Many had not sufficient clothing for their necessities. One of Van Rensselaer's vessels, laden with goods for his store in Rensselaerswick, chanced to arrive, and Kieft, applying to Peter Wynkoop, the supercargo, tried to buy fifty pairs of shoes for his soldiers. The man declined to trade, and Kieft, in great anger, ordered a forced levy, searched the vessel, and, finding a large supply of ammunition and guns, not included in the manifest, confiscated its whole cargo.

The shoes obtained were immediately put to use. Underhill had just returned from Stamford, where he had been reconnoitering the strength and position of the Connecticut Indians in that vicinity, and Kieft sent him back with one hundred and fifty men to "exterminate" them.

March 11. The word "exterminate" was incorporated into all his orders in such cases. The party went in yachts to Greenwich, and then marched over the country through the snow, arriving about midnight **March 12.** at the doomed Indian village. It was a clear, cold night, and the moon shining on the snow rendered it nearly as light as day. The village contained three rows of wigwams, and was sheltered in a nook of the hills from the northwest winds. The savages were not asleep, but merrily celebrating one of their annual festivals. The Dutch soldiers surrounded the place, and charged upon them, sword in hand. They made desperate resistance; but every attempt to break the line of the troops failed, and in one hour the snow was dyed with the blood of nearly two hundred of the Indians. Having forced the remainder into their wigwams, Underhill, remembering Mason's experiment on the *Mystic,* resolved to burn the village. Straw and wood were heaped about the houses, and in a few moments red flames were shooting into the sky in every direction. The wretched victims who tried to escape were shot, or driven back into the fiery abyss, and not one man, woman, or child was heard to utter a cry. Six hundred fell that night. Of those who, blithe and happy, crowded the little village at nightfall, but eight were left to tell the fearful story to their countrymen. None of the troops were killed, and but fifteen wounded. They bivouacked on the snow until daylight, and then returned, like Roman conquerors, to Fort Amsterdam. For their "brilliant victory," Kieft proclaimed a day of public thanksgiving.[1]

Wishing to turn loose the few cattle they had all winter been stabling in the fort, the governor, as soon as the snow went off, issued an order for the building of a fence across the island from the North to the East River, on the line of the present Wall Street. While a number of men were engaged in its construction, a few tribes of Indians, worn out, it is presumed, with being hunted like wild beasts, came to the fort and entered into a treaty of peace. But the tribes nearest the town, and consequently those most dreaded, kept aloof.

By this time, the "Eight Men" had received from the Amsterdam Chamber a response to their letter, but not the sorely needed funds which had been expected. The financial condition of the company had been for some time on the decline, for the subsidies and other sums due from the provinces had never been promptly paid in; and, not being supported by an extensive trade, their military and naval triumphs had, on the whole, cost more money than they had produced. In 1641, the shaking off of the Spanish yoke by the Portuguese, in which Holland had assisted, made it apparent that the company would in the end lose Brazil; a long series of quarrels with the Directors had just induced Count John Maurice, one of the ablest rulers of the seventeenth century, to leave that South American province in disgust; and through many causes bankruptcy was already threatening the proud corporation. A bill of exchange which Kieft drew upon the Amsterdam Chamber, the previous autumn, came back protested. Pressing need drove him to the dangerous alternative of taxing wine, beer, brandy, and beaver-skins. The "Eight Men" opposed the measure with all their strength, but without avail. The brewers, upon whom the tax fell most heavily, refused to pay it, on the ground of its injustice; they were arrested, and their beer given to the soldiers.

In July, a vessel containing one hundred and thirty Dutch soldiers, who had been driven by the Portuguese out of Brazil, came into port, having been sent to the relief of the New-Netherlanders; and Kieft immediately dismissed his English auxiliaries, and billeted

March 31.

April 15.

June 21.

July 15.

---

[1] This affair is supposed to have taken place on Strickland's Plain. *Doc. Hist. N. Y.*, IV. 16, 17.

the new-comers on the citizens. As they were half naked, he enforced his excise laws, to get the means to clothe them. His conduct engendered private as well as public quarrels ; and there were prosecutions daily and without number, which of course engrossed his attention ; for the governor, it must be remembered, was judge as well as jury. Indians prowled about the town, committing thefts every night, often killing persons less than a thousand paces from the fort. The "Eight Men" tried to improve matters, but they had little power, and Kieft was

Aug. 6.

deaf to their counsels and suggestions. A committee from them went in person to him at one time, and remonstrated so loudly in regard to his negligence respecting the war, that he sent a party of soldiers to the north ; but they soon returned, having accomplished nothing but the murder of eight of the savages.

Oct. 22.

Thus that terrible summer passed in civil anarchy, and every day affairs grew worse. The "Eight Men" bore it until they could bear it no longer ; and finally, in a cutting memorial addressed to

Oct. 28.

the West India Company, they charged the whole blame of the war and their consequent sufferings upon Kieft, and demanded his recall. They particularly warned the company against a "book ornamented with water-color drawings" which Kieft had sent to them, which they said "had as many lies as lines in it," and declared that his Excellency could know nothing about the geography of the country, since, during his whole residence in New Amsterdam, he had never been farther from his bedroom and kitchen than the middle of Manhattan Island.

Dec. 10.

This communication reached Holland at an opportune moment. The College of the XIX was in session, and all who heard the letter felt that the colonists were in earnest, and would return with their wives and children to the Fatherland, as they threatened, if Kieft was not recalled. Melyn's[1] spirited letter to the States-General, which had been sent to the Amsterdam Chamber with appropriate remarks from that august body, came in at the same time for its share of attention. It was finally resolved "to collect and condense all the reports

Dec. 15.

about New Netherland." This was subsequently done by the recently organized "Rekenkamer," or Bureau of Accounts ; and the document is one of the most important state papers in existence, as having determined the future policy of the company.

It was decided to recall Kieft ; but as no one at hand appeared exactly adapted to fill his place, Van Dincklagen was named as a provisional governor for New Netherland. At a meeting of the Direc-

[1] Melyn was the president of the "Eight Men."

tors, on the 3d of March, 1645, it was resolved to vest the provincial government in a Supreme Council, consisting of a Director-Gen- 1645. eral, Vice-Director, and Fiscal, by whom all public concerns March 3. should be managed. Fort Amsterdam should be repaired, and a garrison of fifty-three soldiers constantly maintained. The wishes of the people should be respected, and the Indians appeased. The population of the country should be strengthened, and Amsterdam weights and measures used throughout New Netherland. All the negroes should be imported that the patroons and colonists would buy, and every man should be required to provide himself with a musket and side-arms.

Thus, notwithstanding the discovery that their North American province had fallen into ruin and confusion by reason of Kieft's unnecessary war, without the knowledge and surely not by the order of the company, and against the will and wishes of the people; and that, according to the books of the Amsterdam Chamber, this same province had, in place of being a source of profit, actually cost, since 1626, over five hundred and fifty thousand guilders above the returns, — they evidently felt that it was not entirely beyond hope, and that they need not and ought not to abandon it.

The news of Kieft's recall reached New Amsterdam long previous to the official summons to appear before his employers. He thenceforth labored under a great pressure of untoward circumstances. All classes of the people treated him with marked disrespect. His life was an unbroken chapter of arrests, for he attempted to punish every one who was guilty of disloyalty to himself as their chief magistrate. He fined and imprisoned and banished to his heart's content, allowing no appeal to the Fatherland; a stretch of high-handed tyranny which, but for the expected relief, would probably have cost him his life.

His best friends — if, indeed, he had any friends — could not restrain him from the most injudicious acts. Dominie Bogardus, while remonstrating with him one day, was accused by him of drunkenness and alliance with the malcontents. The next Sabbath morning, the good divine, standing in his cheaply canopied pulpit, said: "What are the great men of our country but vessels of wrath and fountains of woe and trouble? They think of nothing but to plunder the property of others, to dismiss, to banish, and to transport to Holland." Whereupon Kieft, who had been up to that time a noted church-goer, absented himself from the sanctuary, and caused a band of soldiers to practice all sorts of noisy amusements, such as the beating of drums and the firing of cannons, under the church windows.

The dominie did not, however, relax his censures of the governor, and just after the following New Year's Day he was arrested, and **1646.** required to answer to a long list of charges. His answers, being **Jan. 2.** in accordance with his clear sense of justice, were inadmissible before such a tribunal; and at last, to silence the scandal and **Jan. 15.** disorder, mutual friends interfered, the prosecution was terminated, and the governor went to church again, being placated by **July 23.** the compliance of Dominie Bogardus with his request to allow Dominie Mesapolensis, who was in New Amsterdam, to preach the next Sunday.

1645. Meanwhile the Indians, wishing to plant their corn, and after-**April 22.** wards to engage in their usual pastimes of hunting and fishing, sued for peace. A few chiefs appeared at the fort and entered into a treaty, apparently pleased when a salute of three guns was fired in honor of the occasion.[1] They were engaged to secure the good-will of the yet hostile tribes, — a work which was at last accomplished by the diplomacy of Whiteneywen, chief of the Mockgoncocks. He soon returned with friendly messages from the chiefs along the Sound and near Rockaway, and both parties went through the ceremony of a formal treaty.

Aug. 8. Kieft then, accompanied by Dr. La Montagne, made his first visit to Fort Orange, hoping to secure the friendship of the Mohawks and other tribes in that vicinity, who had just made peace with the **Aug. 30** French. This effort was crowned with success, and on the 30th of August the chiefs of all the tribes assembled in New Amsterdam, where they were met by the officers of the government and the people, and with the most imposing ceremonies all pledged themselves to eternal friendship with each other. No armed Indian was henceforth to visit the houses of the Europeans; and no armed European was to **Aug. 30.** visit the Indian villages, without a native escort. So slender, at this time, were the resources of Kieft, that he was obliged to borrow money of Van der Donck, in order to make the customary presents to the savages.

With characteristic thoughtfulness, the Dutch stipulated for the restoration of the little captive granddaughter of Annie Hutchinson; and the Indians, with apparent reluctance, acceded to the proposal. The next July they appeared with her at Fort Amsterdam, and Kieft had the rare pleasure of sending her to her friends in Boston. During her brief captivity, she had forgotten her own language and the faces of her relatives, and was loath to leave the Indians, who had evidently treated her tenderly.

---

[1] The salute was fired by Jacob Jacobsen Roy, who, in the discharge of this duty, unfortunately received a severe injury from an explosion, which long kept him under the care of Surgeon Kiersted, and ultimately deprived him of his arm.

There was joy in New Amsterdam at the bright prospect of a durable peace; but the desolation caused by the needless war was not soon to pass out of sight. It had been easy to commence hostilities, but how were broken hearts and fortunes to be repaired? The day following _{Aug. 31.} the final settlement of the treaty, Kieft issued a proclamation, directing the observance of the 6th of September as a day of general thanksgiving, " to proclaim the good tidings in all the Dutch and English churches."

People began once more to scatter over the country, and to clear and improve the land. The party who had been driven from Newtown, Long Island, returned; but they were bankrupt, their houses and farming utensils were gone, and it was difficult to get another foothold. Doughty exacted purchase-money and quit-rents before he would allow his people to build; but they appealed to the governor, who, thinking it unwise to hinder population, managed so that the minister's land was confiscated. Doughty gave notice that he should appeal from this decision; and he was thereupon imprisoned for twenty-four hours, fined, and compelled to promise in writing that he would never mention what had occurred. He afterwards removed to Flushing, which had just been settled by a party of New England emigrants. These people had bought ^{Sept.} more than sixteen thousand acres of land of Kieft; and Doughty became their minister, with a salary of six hundred guilders per annum.

Two months later, that portion of Long Island adjoining Coney Island, now known as Gravesend, was formally patented to Lady ^{Dec. 19.} Moody, her son Sir Henry Moody, Ensign George Baxter, and Sergeant James Hubbard, who had held it so bravely during all these harassing years.

In pursuance of orders from the West India Company, Kieft investigated the mineral resources of the province. During the ^{Oct. 12.} progress of the treaty in August, some of the Indians had exhibited specimens of minerals they claimed to have found in the Neversinck Hills and elsewhere, which upon analysis yielded what was supposed to be gold and quicksilver and iron pyrites. An officer and thirty men were sent to search for and procure as many specimens as possible for transmission to Holland. They found the article in question, and as a ship was going to leave New Haven in December, they sent their little cargo by it, in charge of Arendt Corssen; but the vessel was lost at sea, and never heard from after it passed out of Long Island Sound.

One of the signs of progress in New Amsterdam was a new school started by Arien Jansen Van Olfendam, who arrived from Holland on March 3d of this year. He had no competitor after Roelandsen's banish-

8

ment, and prospered as well as could have been expected, considering the condition of the country. His terms of tuition were " two beavers " per annum, — beavers meaning dried beaver-skins. He taught in New Amsterdam until the year 1660, and among those he educated were some of the leading personages of the province.

1647. Meanwhile Adriaen Van der Donck, whose name is familiar to **Jan. 17.** the historians of New Netherland, had married the daughter of Rev. Francis Doughty, and wished to remove to Manhattan. He had filled the office of sheriff in Rensselaerswick for nearly five years, and had been of infinite service to the colony. Through his influence the first church had been built there, which, although small, had a canopied pulpit, pews for the magistracy and the deacons, and nine benches for the people, after the fashion of the Fatherland. As previously recorded, it was chiefly through his recommendations that the services of Dominie Megapolensis had been secured; a clergyman who not only preached to his own countrymen, but was the first of the Dutch Church to attempt the instruction of the Indians in religion. For a long time, he knew very little of the Indian language ; and he related in a letter to a friend how, when he preached a sermon, ten or twelve savages would attend, each with a long pipe in his mouth, and would stare at him, and afterward ask why he stood there alone and made so many words, when none of the rest might speak. He taught them slowly and by degrees, as he could make himself understood, that he was admonishing them as he did the Christians, not to drink and murder and steal. Through his voluntary and earnest and unceasing labors, many of the red-men about Fort Orange heard the gospel preached long before New England sent missionaries among the Indians.

Before Van der Donck had completed his arrangements for removal, the pretty cottage in which he lived was burned ; and, as it was in the depth of a remarkably inclement winter, Van Corlear invited his houseless neighbors to share his hospitality. A quarrel soon arose, because Van Curler insisted that Van der Donck was bound by his lease to make good to the patroon the value of the lost house. Van der Donck retorted sharply ; whereupon Van Corlear ordered him from under his roof within two days. Seeking refuge in Fort Orange, Van der Donck was allowed by the new commissary, Van der Bogaerdt, to occupy a miserable hut, " into which," he said, " no one would hardly be willing to enter," until the opening of river navigation, when he proceeded to New Amsterdam.

April 28. Kieft was well disposed towards the man to whom he was indebted for a large amount of borrowed money, and readily granted him the privileges of patroon over some fine lands which he selected, to the north of Manhattan Island, on the Hudson River, which took the name of "Colon Donck," or "Donck's Colony." Many of the Dutch were in the habit of calling this estate "de Jonkheer's Landt," Jonkheer being a title which in Holland was applied to the sons of noblemen. The English corrupted it and called it Yonkers; thus the name Yonkers perpetuates the memory of the first proprietor of the property in that locality. *Early spring.*

During the same summer, Kieft issued a patent to Cornelis Antonissen Van Slyck for the land which is now the town of Catskill, with the privileges of patroon; giving as a reason "the great services which Van Slyck had done this country in helping to make peace and ransom prisoners during the war"; but in so doing the governor openly set at naught the pretensions of the patroon of Rensselaerswick, which, indeed, had already been formally denied in the proceedings against Koorn in 1644.

News of the death of Kiliaen Van Rensselaer soon after reached the colony. By this event the title of the estate descended to his eldest son, Johannes, who, being under age, was, by his father's will, placed under the guardianship of Johannes Van Wely and Wouter Van Twiller, his executors. In November, these guardians of the young patroon, having rendered homage to the States-General, in the name of their ward, sent Brandt Van Slechtenhorst as director to the colony, in place of Van Corlear, who had resigned.

Late in autumn, the company granted the town of Breuckelen, Long Island, municipal privileges; that is, the people were allowed to elect two schepens, with full judicial powers, and a schout, who should be subordinate to the sheriff at New Amsterdam. The village at this time was a mile inland, the hamlet at the water's edge was known as the Ferry. *Nov. 26.*

Kieft was very much harassed, during the entire year of 1646, by difficulties with the Swedes on the Delaware River, and by what he styled the "impudent encroachments" of the New-Englanders. He sent Andries Hudde to succeed Jan Jansen at Fort Nassau, and imprisoned Jansen for fraud and neglect of duty. In the autumn of 1645, he sent him to Holland, for trial. Hudde was equal to the governor in the use of profane language, but, though energetic, he was no match for Printz, the imperious Swedish commander, who nearly annihilated the commerce of the Dutch; and the two neighbors were engaged in a perpetual squabble, which had no dignity, and is hardly worth a place in history, since it was followed by no results. In the same manner ended a long and curiously bitter correspondence between the governor and the New England authorities. While justice, in this instance, seemed to be on the side of the Dutch, the English certainly showed themselves the better diplomatists, and Kieft only injured a good cause by intermeddling.

But events in another part of the world had already prepared the way for a change which was to influence all the future of the province of New Netherland. Peter Stuyvesant, the governor of Curaçoa, which had been wrested from the Spanish during the most brilliant period of the West India Company's history, made an unsuccessful attack upon the Portuguese island of St. Martin in 1644, through which he lost a leg, and was obliged to return to Europe for surgical aid. The company, who held him in great respect, concluded to send him as governor to New Netherland, and revoked Van Dincklagen's provisional appointment. During the summer of 1645, a sharp controversy was going on among the Directors of the company in regard to the proposed reforms in colonial affairs; and

Autograph of Stuyvesant.

their ablest pens were in constant requisition to ward off the attacks of the national Dutch party, who were publishing pamphlets to influence the public mind against their movements, and to show them up as a clique of tyrants, who had squandered the treasures of the country and contracted immense debts. It is curious to read the company's various and numberless resolutions about this time, especially those treating of money matters. They lead us into a better understanding of the difficulties attending such a corporation, which, taking upon itself a part of the duties of the government, would necessarily expect from the latter assistance; and this, coming at all times slowly, at last failed them **1645.** altogether. It was decided in the College of the XIX, that the **July 6.** expenses of New Netherland should no longer be confined to the Amsterdam Chamber, but shared by all the chambers of the company in common. As news of the peace with the Indians had reached them, they were in less haste to send out a new governor: finally, to settle the knotty questions which were engendering a great deal of ill-feeling, and to render instructions clear and comprehensive, Stuyvesant's departure was delayed for more than a year; and even at the last, all the preparations for his voyage were tediously slow.

1646. He received his commission, and took the oath of office before **July 28.** the States-General, July 28, 1646. He sailed on Christmas morning, and after a long *détour*, stopping at Curaçoa and the West India Islands, reached New Amsterdam, May 11, 1647. He was ac- **1647.** companied by Van Dincklagen as Vice-Director, Van Dyck as **May 11.** Fiscal, Captain Bryan Newton, Commissary Adriaen Keyser, and Cap-

Portrait of Peter Stuyvesant.

tain Jelmer Thomas, with several soldiers, a number of free colonists, and a few private traders. The first-named gentlemen, including the governor, had their families with them.

Stuyvesant's reception was very flattering. The guns of the fort were fired, and the entire population of New Amsterdam cheered and waved hats and handkerchiefs as he landed. There was a little informal speech-making, and with great *hauteur* the new chief magistrate assured the crowd that he "should govern them as a father does his children."

The wily little Kieft was foremost in making his successor welcome, and escorted him to the Executive Mansion, which he had already vacated, and in which a sumptuous repast was awaiting His Excellency.

Peter Stuyvesant was the son of a clergyman in Friesland. He had early evinced a taste for military life, and had now been for some years in the employ of the West India Company. He was a proud, scholarly looking man, a little above the medium height, with a remarkably fine physique; and he bore himself with the air of a prince. The highly intellectual features of his face gave evidence of great decision and force of character. His complexion was dark, and a close black cap which he often wore imparted to it a still deeper shade. His chin was bare, and his mouth, indicative of sternness and grave authority, was fringed with a very slight mustache. The inflections of his voice, and his whole appearance when speaking, were rather unattractive; but, in spite of a certain apparent coldness, no one could escape the influence of his magnetic presence. He was a man of strong prejudices and passions, of severe morality, and at times unapproachable aspect; but his heart was large, his sympathies tender, and his affections warm, though his creed was rigid. He was never otherwise than faultlessly dressed, and always after the most approved European standard. A wide, drooping shirt-collar fell over a velvet jacket with slashed sleeves, displaying a full white puffed shirt-sleeve. His hose were also slashed, very full, and fastened at the knee by a handsome scarf tied in a knot, and his shoes were ornamented with a large rosette. His lost leg had been replaced by a wooden one with silver bands, which accounts for the tradition that he wore a silver leg. He was often abrupt in manner, and made no pretensions to conventional smoothness at any time. He had sterling excellences of character, but more knowledge than culture.

The career of Governor Stuyvesant is deeply interesting from its symmetry and its manliness. He came to Manhattan in the employ of a mercantile corporation; but his whole heart and soul became enlisted in the welfare of the country of his adoption. Thenceforward to his latest breath he was intensely American, and the varied fruits of his labors are among the most valuable legacies of the seventeenth century.

A few years prior to this date, he had married Judith Bayard, the daughter of a celebrated Paris divine, who had taken refuge in Holland from religious persecution. Shortly after his own marriage, his sister Anna was espoused to Samuel Bayard, Judith's elder brother. The husband died within a short period, leaving his young widow and three infant sons to the care of her only brother, who deemed it wise to bring them with him to his new home. The two ladies, Mrs.

Stuyvesant and Mrs. Bayard, had hitherto known only luxury and comfort. They were well informed as to the uncertain prospects of colonial life, and possible savage warfare; for the published accounts of the New Netherland horrors had circulated widely in Europe. But they were as brave as they were sensible and self-sacrificing. Mrs. Stuyvesant was a blonde, and very beautiful, spoke both the French and the Dutch language with ease, and in the course of a few years acquired a good knowledge of English. She had a sweet voice and a rare taste for music, which had been cultivated under the best of masters. She was fond of dress, and followed the French fashions, displaying considerable artistic skill in the perfection and style of her attire. She was gentle and retiring in her manners, but was possessed of great firmness of character.

Mrs. Bayard was less attractive in person; she was tall, commanding, and imperious. Her education was of a high order, considering the age in which she lived, and she had great tact and capacity for business. She brought a tutor across the ocean for her three little sons; but after he had been dismissed as unworthy of his position, she taught the children herself in almost every branch of practical education. Of her abilities in that direction we may judge from the fact that her son Nicholas, a mere youth, was appointed, in 1664, to the clerkship of the Common Council, — an office of which the records were required to be kept in both Dutch and English. It will not be amiss perhaps, in this connection, to quote from the historian Brodhead a few words in regard to the women of Holland. He says: "The purity of morals and decorum of manners, for which the Dutch have ever been conspicuous, may be most justly ascribed to the happy influence of their women, who mingled in all the active affairs of life, and were consulted with deferential respect. They loved their homes and their firesides, but they loved their country more. Through all their toils and struggles, the calm fortitude of the men of Holland was nobly encouraged and sustained by the earnest and undaunted spirit of their mothers and wives. And the empire which the female sex obtained was no greater than that which their beauty, good sense, virtue, and devotion entitled them to hold."

It was well for Stuyvesant that he had such a wife and sister near him, for he was entering upon a series of trials which would test his temper and discretion to the utmost. Of their influence and coun-
May 27. sels we catch only occasional glimpses here and there. But his administration was longer and more perplexing than that of any other Dutch governor. It was, at that time, no easy matter to conduct the affairs of a remote settlement, where the machinery of government was

insufficient of itself to control a mixed community, whose interests were in constant conflict with those of the trading company which held the reins of power. The very conditions of his office compelled him to assume individual responsibility, and to depend upon his own private judgment in a thousand instances, the importance of which we can now imperfectly estimate. His faults sometimes glare upon us in a most blinding manner; but with all his apparent fondness for ostentation of command, he does not seem to have been open to the charge of intentional injustice, and his purity of purpose stands out in indelible contrast with the capricious rule of his predecessor.

He was formally inaugurated, May 27. The whole community were present, and listened with eagerness to his well-prepared speech on the occasion. The democratic Belgian, Cornelis Melyn, afterwards wrote, "He kept the people standing with their heads uncovered for more than an hour, while he wore his *chapeau,* as if he were the Czar of Muscovy." Others who had suffered from the petty despotism of Kieft, and who were full of the liberal ideas which

Stuyvesant's Seal.

were the birthright of every Hollander, criticised the haughty bearing of the new governor, and prophesied the character of his future government. When he earnestly promised that "every man should have justice done him," he was loudly applauded. Kieft stood by his side during the ceremony, and seemed to think it fitting that he should say a few words of farewell to the people. He thanked them for their fidelity to him, expressed many kind wishes, and bade them adieu. Only a murmur of dissatisfaction arose in response, and a few voices above the rest were heard to say, "We are glad your reign is over."

CHAPTER IX.

1647 – 1650.

POLITICAL EVENTS IN EUROPE.

POLITICAL EVENTS IN EUROPE. — HOLLAND AND THE HOLLANDERS. — THE SABBATH IN NEW YORK. — THE FIRST SURVEYORS. — KUYTER AND MELYN, AND THEIR TRIAL FOR REBELLION. — THE WRECK OF THE PRINCESS. — KIP. — GOVERT LOOCKERMANS. — FIRST FIRE-WARDENS. — SCHOOLS AND EDUCATION. — RENSSELAERSWICK A POWER. — THE GOVERNOR'S FAILURE. — CIVIL WAR IN ENGLAND. — VAN CORTLANDT. — VAN DER DONCK. — MELYN. — THE QUARREL. — VAN DER DONCK IN HOLLAND. — ISAAC ALLERTON.

FREDERICK HENRY, Prince of Orange, died on the morning of March 14, 1647. He had been stadtholder of the provinces for twenty-two years, and had reached his sixty-third birthday. His death tended directly towards drawing to a close the eighty years' war, which had cost Spain over fifteen hundred millions of ducats. **1647.** His office descended to his son, William II., by an act of reversion which the States passed in 1631. The young prince was the husband of Mary, daughter of Charles I. of England. He was full of military ambition and ready to buckle on his armor, but the nation distrusted his inexperience and entered immediately into negotiations for peace. France was a snag in the way, for a time, through a variety of conflicting interests. The French ministers were bent on preventing the consummation of the treaty, even resorting to countless intrigues when other means failed. It was finally signed by the representatives of the two nations, in January, 1648, at Munster. It was at once ratified by Philip IV. and by the several States of the Netherlands. The recognition of the sovereignty of the Dutch Republic was so absolute that an ambassador was actually sent to the Hague from Spain, before Philip himself received one from the Dutch.[1]

Of the seven Dutch States, Holland was the most important, by reason of its dense population and great wealth; hence its name was often

---

[1] *Corps Dip.*, VI. 429, 450. *Barnage Annales des Prov.*, Un. I. 102. *Grattam*, 262. *Davis*, II. 645, 649.

applied to the confederacy by way of eminence. It embraced but a small portion of territory, chiefly of made ground, which was so loose and spongy that high winds sometimes tore up large trees by the roots. Every inch of the country was rendered available for some good purpose. The soil, steeped in water, produced excellent crops, and the fields and gardens teemed with vegetation. Canals were cut in all directions, and were alive with fleets of barges and with innumerable ships of war and commerce. The trim villas, and the quick succession of great towns, made a profound impression upon travelers and strangers. Throughout the length and breadth of the land there was a uniform appearance of comfort, affluence, and contentment. Houses and grounds were kept in a condition of perfect order, the streets and canals were lined with elegant trees, and the ever-whirling windmills looked as if they came out in fresh robes every morning. In no country were the domestic and social ties of life discharged with greater precision. It matters not that chroniclers have made the Dutch subjects of unmerited depreciation. It has been stated that they were characterized only by slowness; and that the land was barren of invention, progress, or ideas. The seeds of error and prejudice thus sown bear little fruit after the reading of a few chapters of genuine contemporary personal description. As a rule, the Hollanders were not inclined to take the initiative in trade or politics, and were distinguished for solidity rather than brilliancy; but it is absurd to say "they were unequal to the origination of any new thing." We find among them many of the most illustrious men of modern Europe, — politicians, warriors, scholars, artists, and divines. Wealth was widely diffused; learning was held in highest respect; and eloquence, courage, and public spirit were characteristic of the race. For nearly a century after the Dutch Republic first took its place among independent nations, it swayed the balance of European politics; and the acumen and culture of the leading statesmen elicited universal deference and admiration. For an index to the private life of the upper classes, we need but to take a peep into the richly furnished apartments of their stately mansions, or walk through their summer-houses and choice conservatories and famous picture-galleries. As for the peasantry, they were neat to a fault, and industrious as well as frugal.

The liberal commercial policy of the Dutch, and their great latitude of religious faith, attracted people to their shores from all parts of the world. Every language spoken by civilized man was to be heard in their exchange. The floor of the hall in the Stadt Huys at Amsterdam was inlaid with marble, to represent maps of the different nations of the earth.

Such was the country whose people settled New York. All classes emigrated; but those who took the most active part in the direction of our infant institutions were, in intelligence and worldly wisdom, and in all those sterling characteristics which we are wont to respect, above the average of their generation. Their number was small, but its proportion to that of the illiterate laborers and traders who crossed the water was greater than that between the higher and lower classes in any portion of Europe. This fact has generally been overlooked by the writers of American history who have imputed wholesale heaviness and incapacity, except in money-making, to the Dutch founders of the metropolis. As the blood of Holland, France, and England (and, we may add, much of the best blood of those three nations) became mixed in the veins of the people, it is easy to trace the increase of men-

Interior of the Stadt Huys, of Amsterdam.

tal vigor, the softening of national prejudices, and the general amalgamation of opinions, habits, tastes, fashions, and modes of life, until we have a new and distinct species of the human kind in the New York American.

Stuyvesant possessed in an eminent degree that distinguishing element of greatness, perception. He took the colony in at a glance, and saw why there was so much dilapidation and discomfort. The Indian war had destroyed property, until only about fifty farms could be counted in the province. Some of the colonists had been killed, and others had returned to Holland; so that there were not to be found over three hundred capable of bearing arms. The church in the fort was unfinished, and the timbers rotting. Money which had been contributed towards building a school-house had been expended to pay off the troops; and the debt was still in arrears. The public revenue had not been collected, and there were conflicting claims in waiting to be settled with the patroons. In short, the whole situation was chaotic in the extreme.

Whatever Stuyvesant did, he did thoroughly.   As soon as he was inaugurated, he organized his council.   It consisted of Vice- Director Van Dincklagen, a clever politician and a thorough scholar ; Fiscal Van Dyck, of whom little can be said in praise ; the learned and gentlemanly Dr. La Montagne ; Adriaen Keyser ; and Captain Bryan Newton. Van Tienhoven was retained in the office of secretary ; Paulus Van der Grist was made equipage-master ; and George Baxter, an English gentleman of good education, was reappointed English secretary and interpreter.

A court of justice was established, over which Van Dincklagen was appointed presiding judge.   Stuyvesant, however, reserved the right to preside in person whenever he should think proper, and required that his own opinions should be consulted in important matters.

Proclamations were issued with marvelous rapidity.   The first on record relates to the Sabbath.   Experience had long before yielded, upon every hand, its testimonies to the wisdom of the Divine institution. Then, as now, it was esteemed the duty of government to protect it,. and to confirm to the people the material and vital benefits which it is so well calculated to secure.   As a means of social, moral, and physical health, and as a measure of industrial economy, if we had no Sabbath, the ordination of one would come directly within the scope of legislation.   Stuyvesant was possessed with a profound sense of its importance as a direct means for the establishment and perpetuation of a pure Christianity in this country ; and for his sentiments and his efforts in that direction he deserves to be honored to the remotest posterity.   Another proclamation forbade drunkenness and profanity ; and still another prohibited the sale of liquor and fire-arms to the Indians, on pain of death.   Strict laws were instituted for the protection of the revenues, which had been defrauded by the introduction of foreign merchandise in vessels running past Manhattan in the night.   The following is a copy of one of the proclamations on that subject : —

" Any one is interdicted from having the hardihood to go into the interior with any cargoes or any merchandise ; but they shall leave them at the usual places of deposit and there wait for traffic."

The usual place for vessels to anchor was under the guns of the fort, near a queer little hand-board, which stood on the water's edge.   To replenish the treasury, taxes were levied on liquors, and the export duties on peltries were increased.   All outstanding tenths due from the impoverished farmers were called in, but a year's grace for the payment was allowed in consideration of losses by the war.   The people grumbled.   Who will pay taxes with a cheerful countenance, particularly when it is at the supreme command of an individual, and through the withholding of his birthright, the franchise ? But Stuyvesant's military training made him imperious ; and, in point of fact, his instructions from the West India Company gave him less discretionary power than has been generally supposed. He must govern absolutely ; and he was by no means backward in obeying such instructions.

Workmen were employed to put the fort in repair; and others were engaged to complete the church, of which Stuyvesant at once became a member and set an example of devout Sabbath worship. The little village, with its crooked roads winding round hillocks and ^{June 23.} ledges, its untidy houses with hog-pens and chicken-coops in front and tumble-down chimneys in the rear, had some surveyors appointed over it in July, — Van Dincklagen, Van der Grist, and Van Tienhoven. They understood what improvements were needed to make the new *dorp* the miniature of a thrifty Holland town, and were very energetic in their measures. The streets were straightened, even to the removing of some huge obstacles ; nuisances were done away with ; great piles of accumulated rubbish were dumped into the water ; a better class of houses was erected under their supervision ; and all owners of vacant lots were compelled to improve them within nine months after purchase.

In the mean time Kuyter and Melyn were instituting proceedings against Kieft. They had lost heavily by the Indian war, and were determined to compel an investigation of its causes. They proposed that all the leading men of the colony should be summoned into court and examined on oath in regard to it. They prepared a list of questions to be put to them, tending to elicit a train of evidence that would place the matter correctly before the company in Holland.

Stuyvesant appointed a commission to decide upon the propriety of granting such an inquiry ; and, as soon as the members came together, he expressed his opinion emphatically, that *" the two malignant fellows were disturbers of the peace, and that it was treason to complain of one's magistrates, whether there was cause or not."* He had evidently taken alarm at the dangerous precedent of allowing subjects to judge rulers, since his own acts might have to pass the ordeal. Kieft was delighted at this mark of favor from the new governor, and emboldened by it to accuse his accusers. He had a double incentive ; personal and ^{July 11.} revengeful hatred, and the rescue of his own character from ignominy. The following day, Kuyter and Melyn were arrested on a charge of " rebellion and sedition." They were brought to trial almost immediately. This trial occupied several days, and created the wildest excitement. Stuyvesant occupied the bench, and Judge Van Dincklagen sat by his side. Lawyers were rare on this side of the water, hence the prisoners defended themselves, and they did it in an able manner. They produced ample proof to sustain their charges against Kieft, towards whom they said they had no vindictive feelings whatever. They admitted that in the heat of war, and smarting under the loss of property, they had complained to the authorities in Holland, but not to strangers, nor had any deception at any time been used. It was a singular tribunal; their case had been prejudged. They were pronounced GUILTY; and capital punishment was, for a time, seriously contemplated. They were even denied the right of appeal to the Fatherland. "If I were persuaded that you would bring this matter before their High Mightinesses, I would have you hanged on the highest tree in New Netherland," said Stuyvesant, as he pronounced their sentence. Melyn was banished for seven years and fined three hundred guilders. Kuyter was banished for three years and fined one hundred and fifty guilders. The fines were to be given, one third to the attorney-general, one third to the church, and one third to the poor. The prisoners were required to sign a written promise that, in any place to which they might go, they would never complain, or speak in any way, of what they had suffered from Kieft and Stuyvesant. The *Princess* was about to sail for Holland, and they took passage, as did also Dominie Bogardus, who had been so disturbed by Kieft in his ministerial labors that he resigned his charge and obtained permission to defend himself before the Classis of Amsterdam. The church was not left without a pastor, for Dominie Johannes Backerus, formerly clergyman at Curacoa, who had accompanied Stuyvesant to New Amsterdam, was installed as his successor, at a salary of fourteen hundred guilders per annum.

July 25.

Aug. 16.

Kieft had managed, during his few years in office, to acquire a large property, which he turned into money before taking his departure from the province. He had always entertained the idea that minerals abounded in the vicinity of Manhattan. A lump of mineral paint which an Indian displayed during the trial of Kuyter and Melyn had been tried in a crucible, and yielded three guilders' worth of gold. This induced him to obtain, through the aid of the willing Indians, a variety of specimens, which were nicely packed and taken with him to Europe. It was the last of gold-finding in this part of the country; and it is more than probable that all that was discovered was brought from some remote locality. Kieft sailed in the *Princess*, with the minister and the exiles. But the ill-fated vessel never reached its destination. It was wrecked on the rocky coast of Wales, and only about twenty persons were saved. They floated on pieces of the wreck to the shore. Among them were Kuyter and Melyn. Kieft, Dominie Bogardus, a son of Melyn, and eighty-one others perished. In the moment of agony, when all hope was abandoned, Kieft confessed his injustice towards the two men whom he had wronged, and begged their forgiveness. Kuyter and Melyn proceeded to Holland, where the company afterwards reversed their sentence, and they returned with honor to this country.

The sorrowful tidings of the death of Dominie Bogardus fell over the community like a pall. There was universal sorrow. His wife and children, who had remained behind, were the recipients of the most heartfelt sympathy and consideration. But Kieft's fate excited very little feeling; a fact which could not have escaped the notice of Stuyvesant.

Before the middle of September, the pressure of public sentiment had been so great, and the opposition to the payment of the revenues so spirited and determined, that Stuyvesant concluded to recognize to a limited extent the principle of "taxation only by consent," which the Fatherland had maintained since 1477. He called a public meeting, and "Nine Men" were chosen to advise and assist in the affairs of the government. This representative body consisted of Augustine Heermans, Arnoldus Van Hardenburg, Govert Loockermans, Jan Jansen Dam, Jacob Van Couwenhoven, Hendrick Kip, Michael Jansen, Evertsen Bout, and Thomas Hall.

Kip's Arms.

Names are the keys of family history, unlocking for us the secrets of ancestral lineage. It is well known that, in very many cases, members of distinguished families sought here a field of enterprise and action which was denied them at home.

Kip[1] was one of those persons, and his coat-of-arms,[2] engraved upon

---

[1] The De Kype family formerly lived near Alençon, Bretagne, France. Ruloff De Kype was a Roman Catholic. He fell in battle in 1562, and the Protestants under Condé burned his elegant château. His son, Jean Baptiste, who was a priest, secured his burial in a neighboring church, where an altar-tomb was erected to his memory, surmounted by his arms with two crests. The youngest son, Ruloff, settled in Amsterdam, Holland, and became a Protestant. He died in 1596, and left one son, Hendrick (born 1576), who removed to this country in 1635, with his wife and children. He had three sons, Hendrick, Jacob, and Isaac. Both himself and sons secured large tracts of land, and held prominent positions in the New Netherland government. Hendrick married Anna De Sille in 1660, the daughter of Hon. Nacasius De Sille. Jacob married Marie La Montagne in 1654, the daughter of Dr. La Montagne. Rachel, the daughter of the latter, married Lucas Kiersted, in 1683, the grandson of Anetje Jans.

[2] The coat-of-arms was painted also upon the window of the Dutch church in New Amsterdam.

stone, was used ten years later by his son Jacob, who built it firmly into the wall over the front door of the house at Kip's Bay, where it remained until the building was demolished, in 1851. Govert Loockermans, also, was a man of good birth as well as of strong character. He was married twice : first in Amsterdam, February, 1641, to Ariaentie Jans; and second in New Amsterdam, July, 1649, to Maritje (Maria), the widow of Tymen Jansen. His daughter Maria, who married Balthazar Bayard in 1664, was born while on the voyage to America late in the autumn of 1641. His daughter Jannetie (born 1643) became the second wife of Dr. Hans Kiersted. His step-daughter, Elsie Tymens, was twice married, her second husband, whom she wedded in 1663, being the celebrated Jacob Leisler. Two sisters, handsome and accomplished women, accompanied Govert Loockermans to this country, one of whom married Jacob Van Couwenhoven ; the other, Anetje (or Ann, as the name was Anglicised), was married to Oloff S. Van Cortlandt, in the Dutch Church of New Amsterdam, February 26, 1642. Loockermans bought a large tract of land and rented it out to laborers; he owned two or three sailing vessels, erected a store, and became a thriving man of business.

The winter which followed was memorable in the history of Stuyvesant. He had shed his blood on battle-fields before he took up his abode in New Netherland ; but he had never encountered such a snarl of disputes as arose about the boundary lines of the province. It was the same subject continued which had pestered Kieft, and which seemed to grow more unwieldy and less likely to be settled every year. He was harassed also by the encroachments of the Swedes on the Delaware. And in the midst of his efforts to harmonize the contending parties, the Indians exhibited signs of uneasiness because their promised presents were in arrears. They demanded fire-arms, too, of the Dutch ; and, despite the new code of stringent laws, a contraband trade in this commodity was carried on. On one occasion, this crime was charged upon three hitherto respectable men, and they were tried and found guilty. Stuyvesant condemned them to death ; but friends interceded, and their lives were spared, though their property was confiscated. Stuyvesant was engaged in frequent wrangles with the " Nine Men," who acted in the capacity of legislators, and held decided opinions of their own ; and he had still more serious controversies with the patroons, who interfered with the trade of the company, and denied the governor's authority over them. The subordinate officers of the government were captious and sometimes insolent, and all at once the people united with the New-Englanders in

---

[1] A Dutch Bible which once belonged to Govert Loockermans, and which is now in the library of the American Bible Society, contains memoranda of the family, written in Dutch.

one grievous complaint against the high custom-house duties. Verily, the governor's lines had not fallen in pleasant places.

He found time, in the midst of his many and disagreeable duties, to think a little about the feeble settlement, which was certainly in great need of friendly care.

1648.

In June of that year, the first " fire-wardens " were appointed, at his suggestion. They were to inspect the chimneys between the fort and the Fresh Water Pond. Their names were Adriaen Keyser, Thomas Hall, Martin Cregier, and George Woolsey. For a foul chimney, the owner was fined three guilders. If a house was burned through carelessness in that respect, the occupant was fined twenty-five guilders. The fines were to be used to buy hooks, ladders, and buckets; but it was several years before the fund became large enough to invest to any advantage.

June 23.

There were many little taverns springing up all over the lower part of the island, and Stuyvesant took it upon himself to inspect them; for he feared, with reason, that they seriously endangered the morals of the people, since they were but fountains of bad liquor, and the habitual resort of Indians and negroes. He made it therefore an indictable offense to keep one open without a license, and he required all those who received licenses to procure or build better buildings " for the adornment of the town." He also issued a proclamation that no hogs and goats should for the future be pastured between the fort and Fresh Water Pond, except within suitable inclosures. As the autumn rolled round, he established a weekly market, which was held on Mondays. Soon after, in imitation of one of the customs of Holland, he instituted an annual cattle-fair, to commence every first Monday after the feast of St. Bartholomew and continue ten days.

July 8.

Sept. 18.

About that time, Jan Stevensen opened a small private school which was tolerably well patronized. The best families had generally their own private tutors direct from Europe; but there were enough to support a school besides, and the new teacher found himself fully occupied. Stuyvesant was very earnest in the matter of providing means for " the education of every child in the colony." He wrote to the West India Company several times on the subject of establishing a public school, which he said ought to be furnished with at least two good teachers. He related how, for a long time, they had passed round the plate among themselves, but " had only built the school with words, for the money thus collected was always needed for some other purpose." He expatiated upon the great necessity of instructing the youth, not only in reading and writing, but in the knowledge and fear of God. His sugges-

9

tions were treated with marked respect by his employers, and in course of time met with a favorable response.

The colony of Rensselaerswick had become, in the natural course of events, an independent power; and all efforts on the part of the company to induce the patron to cede to them any of his rights had failed. Such a power was looked upon as very injurious to the interests of the province; and, since it could not be bought off, Governor Stuyvesant was instructed to circumscribe its jurisdiction as far as possible. The patroon, understanding what immunities were claimed for manors and municipalities in Europe, would hold no fellowship with a man who arrogated to himself supreme rulership in New Netherland, without proper regard for the feudal privileges granted by the charter of the company. Brant Van Slechtenhorst was the champion of the views of the late Van Rensselaer, as well as of the rights of the infant lord, and, being of a resolute temper, paid no attention to the governor's orders in any respect.

Van Rensselaer Arms on Window.

Stuyvesant finally resolved to visit the colony in person, and with a military escort proceeded up the river. The fort itself and the land immediately about it were the property of the company. Van Slechtenhorst was summoned to answer for his contempt of authority. He did answer, and it was by protest to protest. He charged the governor with having interfered with him, contrary to ancient order and usage; as if he, Stuyvesant, and not Van Rensselaer, were lord of the patroon's colony. Stuyvesant ordered that no buildings should be erected within a prescribed distance from Fort Orange, and Van Slechtenhorst declared such an order an aggression which could not be justified. He said the soil belonged to the patroon. Stuyvesant replied, that "the objectionable buildings endangered the fort." Slechtenhorst hotly pronounced the governor's argument a mere pretext. No definite results were obtained; and, after Stuyvesant's departure, Slechtenhorst continued his improvements precisely as before. We can hardly realize, at this late day, that our republican State of New York once harbored within its borders something so nearly akin to a principality; but such is the fact. Stuyvesant wrote to Van Slechtenhorst that force would be used if he did not desist from erecting buildings; but it only provoked a characteristically

July 21.

impudent retort, and a criticism upon the technical formality of the governor's legal proceedings. Van Slechtenhorst followed up his reply to
Stuyvesant by forbidding the company's commissary at Fort Orange to
quarry stone or cut timber within the boundaries of the colony, while he
himself was actively putting up houses for the patroon within pistol-shot
of the fort.

Stuyvesant, having been informed of this fact, dispatched a military
force to arrest Van Slechtenhorst and demolish the buildings.
Their mission was not performed to the letter, however. Van Sept 21.
Slechtenhorst, who was himself a shrewd lawyer, refused to appear at Fort
Amsterdam with his papers and commissions until a summons should be
legally served ; and he demanded a copy in writing of the governor's claims
and complaints. The Rensselaerswick colonists were angered at Stuyvesant's hostile movements, and the Mohawk savages were with difficulty restrained from attacking the soldiers. After much confusion, the military
company was withdrawn, the houses were left standing, and matters continued unsettled.

Dominie Megapolensis asked his dismission from the church at Rensselaerswick during the summer, as did also Dominie Backerus from
the church at New Amsterdam, both gentlemen wishing to return Aug. 15.
to Europe. The Classis of Amsterdam was then petitioned for "old,
experienced, and godly ministers"; but although every effort was
made, and there were many consultations held in Holland with Sept. 2.
the Directors of the company and the heirs of Van Rensselaer, it was
difficult to find "experienced" ministers willing to undertake such "a
far distant voyage."[1]

The Dutch could not fail to see that the colonies of their English neighbors, where neither patroons nor lords nor princes were known, were much
more flourishing than their own; and they complained bitterly to the governor. He had made the same observations, but could not remedy the
evils that were retarding the progress of New Netherland ; and he was
unreasonably jealous of any attempt on the part of others to institute
reforms. Again a long correspondence about boundaries ensued with the
New England authorities, and the tone of it was exceedingly bitter.

Retaliation was threatened. Then Stuyvesant was accused of trying to
instigate the Indians to rise up against the English. He promptly
vindicated himself and demanded an investigation. In the mean **1649.**
time he had written to the West India Company, praying that the
boundary between the Dutch and English provinces might be settled in
Europe. But, at this time, the distracted condition of affairs there in-

---

[1] Cor. Classis Amst.

duced the company to instruct their governor "to live with his neighbors on the best terms possible."

Every great European event affected the prospects of the American colonies. Civil war was now raging in England. Charles I. was a prisoner in the hands of his subjects. He might perhaps have reigned to the end of a peaceful life, if he had been content to rule as a constitutional sovereign. At the same time, the Parliament party went beyond the limits of the constitution in their desire to preserve the constitution. The unfortunate king was tried, condemned, and executed in front of his own banqueting-hall. As he stood upon the scaffold, Gregory Brandon, his executioner, fell on his knees before him and asked his forgiveness. "No!" said the king; "I forgive no subject of mine who comes deliberately to shed my blood." The king spoke as became the chief magistrate and the source of the laws which were violated in his murder. He took off the medallion of the order of the Garter, and gave it to Juxon, saying with emphasis, "Remember!" Beneath the medallion of St. George was a secret spring which removed a plate ornamented with lilies, under which was a beautiful miniature of his beloved Henrietta. The warning word which has caused so many historical surmises evidently referred to the fact that he had parted with the portrait of his wife only at the last moment of his existence. Queen Henrietta had escaped to the Louvre; and her second son, James, was with her at the time she received the terrible news. Her eldest daughter, Mary, was the wife of William II., Prince of Orange; and thither Charles, Prince of Wales, and his brother James repaired for safety, while the broken-hearted queen retired, with one or two of her ladies, to St. Jacques, the Convent of the Carmelites.

But though England was declared a republic, the monarchical principle survived. There could be no republic; and there was no republic. Political knowledge was not sufficiently advanced. It is as impossible to jump from monarchy to democratic equality, as to lay out new streets in a day through a city that is already crowded with massive structures. Cromwell saw the impossibility of a representative government, and wished to become king; but the army, which was composed of republicans who acted conscientiously, would not allow it. He would have ruled constitutionally if he could; but by him the English would not be so ruled. He, however, managed England's affairs far more wisely than they had ever been managed by a Stuart, though with an iron hand which he did not condescend to cover with a velvet glove.

It was not, therefore, a favorable moment for the Dutch to quarrel with England or her colonies about mere boundary lines. But the "pride and obstinacy " of Stuyvesant (for so his fierce energy was called) was increasing the number of his opponents at an alarming rate. At the second yearly election of the " Nine Men," Adriaen Van der Donck and the able and respected Oloff S. Van Cortlandt were chosen members of the board. Van Cortlandt was a thriving merchant and one of the

Van Cortlandt Arms.

richest men in New Amsterdam. His estate, or a portion of it, lay on the west side of Broadway, near the street which perpetuates his name. The " Nine Men," at one of their subsequent meetings, determined upon sending a delegation to Holland to demand certain reforms and regulations which had been promised by the company, and waited for patiently in vain. They asked permission to convene the people, to confer on the subject " how expenses should be defrayed," etc. Stuyesant declined granting their request, and told them in writing " that communications must be made with the company through the governor, and his instructions followed."

The " Nine Men " thought differently. They promised Stuyvesant to send no document to Holland without giving him a copy, but pronounced his last demand " unreasonable and antagonistical to the welfare of the country." As he would not allow the people to be convened, a committee from the " Nine Men " went from house to house to learn their opinions. This excited the governor's extreme displeasure, and various intrigues were resorted to, on his part, to counteract the influence of the popular tribunes. Among other things, he and his council summoned a meeting of delegates from the militia and towns-people, to consider the question of sending agents to the Fatherland on some important matters, not named.

The " Nine Men " were, nevertheless, determined to carry out their plans. Van der Donck was appointed secretary, and was expected to keep a careful journal of the proceedings. He lodged in the house of Jan Jansen Dam. One day, in his absence, Stuyvesant sent to his chamber and seized all his papers, and the next morning ordered him to be arrested and thrown into prison.

This high-handed measure was followed by a public meeting at the fort, consisting of the governor, council, officers of the militia, and deputations from the citizens. Van Dincklagen, the Vice-Director, had **March 4.** a keen sense of justice ; and, as his superior had acted without his knowl-

edge or approval in the matter of Van der Donck, he demanded that the prisoner be admitted on bail, and heard in his own defense. Stuyvesant refused. Angry words followed, on both sides. It soon became evident that the majority of the council were inclined to treat Van der Donck harshly. Van der Donck himself, seeing the turn events were taking, asked for his journal, that he might correct some errors in it; but the request was refused. He was examined a few days later, and his
March 15. conduct condemned "as tending to bring sovereign authority into contempt"; and he was thereupon excluded from the executive council, and also from all legislative authority in connection with the "Nine Men." Van Dincklagen publicly disclaimed, and with great vehemence, his co-operation in this war against the free exercise of the right of petition.

In the midst of the excitement, Cornelis Melyn, so recently banished in disgrace, suddenly appeared in Manhattan, restored to the full rights of a colonist,[1] and armed with a summons for Stuyvesant to answer for his conduct before the States-General and Prince of Orange without delay, either in person or by attorney. Determined to make his
March 8. triumph as public as his former dishonor had been, he took advantage of a meeting in the church in the fort, and demanded that the paper he held, containing the acts of their High Mightinesses, should be read then and there by one of the "Nine Men." After a noisy debate, he carried his point, and the mandamus and summons were read to the assemblage by Arnoldus Van Hardenburg.

Stuyvesant was stung and humiliated beyond expression, but replied: "I shall honor the States-General by obeying their commands; yet, until I am discharged by the company, an attorney must answer for me in Holland." He refused any conversation or communication with Melyn, and required an apology from each of his subordinates for their share in the transactions at the church. He appointed Van Tienhoven and Jan Jansen Dam, whose daughter Van Tienhoven had married, as his representatives to the Hague. Van Tienhoven was admirably fitted for this mission. He was crafty, cautious, and sharp-witted. When he attempted to defend any plot or scheme, his eloquence had all the charm of sincerity. He is known to have been dishonest in a multitude of ways, and for that reason, as well as others, he had become generally disliked in the colony. He had been so long a servant of the company that he was intelligent as to its concerns; and he knew the people and the condition of affairs as well as any one else, and perhaps better. Having

---

[1] *Mass. Hist. Col.*, IX. 277. John Winthrop, Jr., received a letter from Roger Williams, saying, "Skipper Isaac and Melyn are come with a Dutch ship, bringing letters from the States-General calling home this Dutch governor to answer to many complaints."

quarreled personally with several of the "Nine Men," he was, from mo-tives of policy, a warm advocate for the governor. It is said that his curious tact and strength of will enabled him to maintain extraordinary influence over Stuyvesant for a series of years. He lived on an estate of his own, west of Pearl Street and above Maiden Lane, his land ex-tending towards Broadway.

The favor shown by the States-General to Melyn encouraged the "Nine Men" to persist in their efforts for a hearing. Van der Donck was regarded as a political martyr, and Melyn was just in time to throw fire-brands adroitly in every direction. He was engaged, during his stay, as has since been supposed, in preparing *Breeden Raedt*, a quarto tract of forty-five pages, bearing date 1649, which was afterwards published in Antwerp, his native place. Some writers deny that he was the author of the work, alleging that it must have been written by a lawyer. So far as the dramatic character of various portions of it is concerned, it is one of the best executed and most effective of dialogues. It certainly could have been produced only by a genius.[1] But although very little is known of Melyn, we are not prepared to discredit his claim to its authorship, particularly as the information contained in it must have been founded upon his experience.

It happened, about that time, that Stuyvesant received a case of fire-arms which he had ordered from Holland, agreeably to a suggestion from the company that the best policy was "to furnish them to the Indians with a sparing hand, lest their discontent lead them into ^{April 21.} open war." They were landed at the fort, much to the astonishment and disapprobation of the people, who began to accuse the governor of doing the business of the whole country on his own responsibility. Finding how strongly public opinion was setting against him, he was obliged to produce the communication of his superiors and explain the whole matter.

Meanwhile, the "Nine Men" had prepared a memorial, in which all the desired reforms were distinctly stated, and a *Vertoogh*, or remon-strance, annexed, giving the reasons and detailing the grievances of the people. Both documents were drafted by Van der Donck, and signed by each of the "Nine Men." The "*Vertoogh Van Nieuw Nederlandt*" was printed at the Hague in 1650, in the form of a quarto tract of forty-nine pages. Three of the signers, Van der Donck, Couwen- ^{July 26} hoven, and Bout, were sent as delegates to the Hague, and Van Dinck-lagen wrote a letter of credence by them to the States-General. They

---

[1] Historical Essay. By G. M. Asher.

sailed August 15. Dominie Backerus, who had been waited upon by the governor and forbidden to read from the pulpit any papers not previously sanctioned by the administration, and Melyn, were passengers in the same vessel. Through the earnest entreaties of Stuyvesant, Dominie Megapolensis remained at Manhattan, although his wife had sailed a short time before.

Aug. 15.

Van Tienhoven had already been gone fourteen days when the delegates left New Netherland; but he missed the straight course, and was the last to arrive in Holland. He had with him a mass of exculpatory documents, and letters from Stuyvesant to the States-General, telling them that many of the papers necessary for his justification in the case of Kuyter and Melyn had been lost with the *Princess*, etc. Also that Melyn " had abused their safe-conduct and behaved mutinously," and that he " would rather never have received the commission of their High Mightinesses than have his authority lowered in the eyes of both neighbors and subjects."

Oct. 2.

Both parties appeared before the States-General, and a tedious examination, occupying the whole winter, followed. It had a beneficial effect upon New Netherland, in so far as it brought the distant and almost unknown province squarely before the public. It put the idea of migrating hither into the heads of hundreds of persons. The West India Company were wedded to the existing order of things, and sustained their governor. They said those who took umbrage at his haughtiness " were such as sought to live without either magistrates or law." They were not in favor of investing the " Nine Men " with the administration of justice, in any degree. Melyn, having placed his cause in the hands of an attorney, exerted himself to promote the settlement of Staten Island. He interested one of the influential noblemen of the States-General, Baron Van der Capellen,[1] who, in company with some wealthy merchants, bought and equipped a vessel, *New Netherland's Fortune*, and sent her freighted with farmers and their families to the picturesque island. The States-General embodied a list of reforms as to the management of New Netherland affairs, in a " Report " which was submitted to the Amsterdam Chamber, accompanied by the draft of a *Provisional Order*, providing for a better system of government. It provoked determined opposition from the members of that body, and a renewal of accusations against those who had risen up to injure the company and their servants. A copy of it, however, was forwarded to Stuyvesant by Couwenhoven and Bout on their return, who brought also letters from the

[1] Yonkheer Hendrick Van der Capellen, of Ryssel, was Baron of Essels and Hasselt, and represented the principality of Gebre and the earldom of Zutphen in the States-General.

States-General, forbidding the governor to molest them. Van der Donck remained in Holland, to watch the interests of the New Netherland people, and did not return to America for several years. During that period, he contributed greatly towards bringing this country into notice and improving its institutions. In 1652, he was made Doctor of Laws at Leyden. He died in New Amsterdam in 1655, leaving the colony of Colon Donck, or Yonkers (his baronial estate), to his wife, who subsequently married Hugh O'Neal. The property, after changing owners two or three times, became a part of the celebrated Philipse manor.

In the same vessel with the delegates came Dirck Van Schelluyne, a Hague lawyer, who was licensed to practice his profession in New Amsterdam. He opened an office in one corner of a grocery-store, **1650.** and hung out a sign of "Notary Public." His commissioned duty **April.** was "to serve process and levy executions." He eventually removed to Rensselaerswick, and ten years later was secretary of that colony. In the upper part of the same grocery, a small school was opened during the month of April by Jan Cornelissen.

Early in the spring, men were employed to repair Fort Amsterdam; but the work progressed slowly. The governor issued another proclamation forbidding the running at large of cows, hogs, and goats, without a herdsman, between the fort and the company's farm, and the pasture-ground occupied by Thomas Hall and the house of Mr. Isaac Allerton. Mr. Allerton was an Englishman who came over in the *Mayflower* to Plymouth, and had now taken up his residence at Manhattan.[1] He lived in a stone house on the hill, near Beekman Street; and he also owned a large warehouse or store. He was in partnership with Govert Loockermans. The merchants of those days dealt in every class of merchandise, and raised their own poultry and pork, as well as made their own butter. A general law was passed that year, to the effect that "inasmuch as the hogs spoil the roads and make them difficult of passage for wagons and carts, every man must stick rings through the noses of such animals as belong to him."

---

[1] Isaac Allerton is said to have had the best head for business, and to have been one of the most stirring persons, among the first settlers of Massachusetts. He made five voyages to England in the interests of the colony before 1631. He finally quarreled with Plymouth and removed to Marblehead, where he built a large fishing-house and several vessels. It was he who sent to Ipswich for Parson Avery; and it was his ill-fated shallop which was dashed against the rock, since known as "Avery's Rock," — a disaster, the story of which has been retold in one of Whittier's rarest poems. Allerton soon quarreled with Winthrop's General Court, which gave him "leave to depart from Marblehead." The impulse which he gave to trade was never wholly lost; and, at this moment, the finest building in that ancient town, for business purposes, is "Allerton Block," a name the history of which is almost unknown.

Brewing seems to have been a favorite occupation, and was a source of much profit. Pieter and Jacob Couwenhoven, brothers, who came to New Amsterdam in 1633, made quite a fortune in that way, and carried on at the same time a brisk trade in flour, which was bolted in windmills. A law, in the early part of 1650, required bakers to make their bread of the standard weight, and to use nothing but pure wheat and rye flour, as it came from the mill. This precaution was to silence the complaints about the "poverty and leanness" of the common bread. The crops were not good this year, in consideration of which a law was made, in the autumn, forbidding any one to malt or brew wheat, and also decreeing that no wheat, rye, or baked bread should be sold out of the province.

Apr. 14.

The winter of 1650 was one of great severity. It was so cold that "ink froze in the pen." There was much distress, as food was scarce and prices necessarily high. When the governor, in the face of it, victualed the company's vessels on their way to Curacoa, the "Nine Men" were surprised and indignant, and not only remonstrated but accused him openly of "wanton imprudence" in thus diminishing supplies which were already too scanty. It was about the time that the delegates arrived from Holland. They brought with them arms and a stand of colors for the burgher guard; an act which infuriated Stuyvesant, who refused to have them delivered. A great commotion ensued in consequence. The "Nine Men" pronounced it a tyrannical outrage, and for their persistent interference with his prerogative Stuyvesant publicly deprived them of their pew in church. Both parties wrote letters of accusation to the authorities in Holland; and, what is remarkable, the English residents in the province defended the governor, and endorsed his sentiments, charging all the "schisms" upon the returned delegates.

In September, the long-contemplated and repeatedly postponed meeting of the Dutch and New England worthies took place at Hartford. It was hoped to settle beyond any further question the boundary line between the two territories. Stuyvesant traveled in state, with quite a train of attendants. The voyage occupied four days. He was received with much ceremony, and courteously entertained by the governor of Hartford. When the commission assembled, Stuyvesant proposed to carry on the negotiations in writing. He gave two reasons for this which had sufficient weight to prevent any objections from his opponents : that it would give greater accuracy to the proceedings, and that it would save time, as he could not speak the English language with fluency. But his first paper provoked sharp argument on account of its date, "New Netherland," and the New England gentlemen declined to go on with

Sept. 17.

the business until " Connecticut " was substituted instead. Stuyvesant apologized. He said the draft of the paper had been substantially agreed upon by himself and council before he left New Amsterdam, and translated and copied by his English secretary, George Baxter, on the voyage ; as for the date, he supposed it was proper, but was entirely willing to comply with their wishes. After that, the discussion of national and territorial and individual rights proceeded slowly, but with considerable tact and discretion as well as earnestness. Over a week had been consumed, when they finally agreed to submit the issue to arbitrators. Simon Bradstreet and Thomas Prince were chosen for New England, and Thomas Willett and George Baxter for New Netherland. Their decision was accepted. It was, however, never ratified in England ; and the fact that Stuyvesant had confided the interests of the Dutch to two Englishmen raised a storm of discontent in his own province. ^{Sept. 29.} Vice-Director Van Dincklagen had had no voice in the matter, and was greatly offended. The " Nine Men " declared that " the governor had ceded away territory enough to found fifty colonies each four miles square." There was a grand union of sentiment that it was an insult to the Dutch for Englishmen to be appointed to fix the English boundaries. Stuyvesant remained in Hartford some days after his business was accomplished, hoping to make arrangements whereby the Indians should be placed upon a permanent footing of good behavior. He was treated by his well-bred neighbors with a distinguished attention, at which he was much pleased. His return voyage was exceedingly rough, and his welcome home by an angry community anything but cordial. The freedom of speech of the " Nine Men " was so exasperating, that he threatened the body with dissolution. At the next election, he absolutely refused to select from the nominations to fill vacancies in their board. Again they appealed to the States-General for the reformation of this " grievous and unsuitable government " ; and Melyn, at the Hague, used his influence to the utmost against the New Netherland governor.

Seal of New Netherlands, 1623.

CHAPTER X.

1650 – 1654.

THE SPIRIT OF POPULAR FREEDOM.

THE CONFISCATED VESSEL. — GOVERNOR STUYVESANT'S BODY-GUARD. — RENSSELAERSWICK. — THE SCHUYLER FAMILY. — THE NAVIGATION ACT. — REV. SAMUEL DRISIUS. — AFRICAN SLAVERY. — THE BIRTH OF THE CITY. — THE FIRST CITY FATHERS. — ALLARD ANTHONY. — WILLIAM BEEKMAN. — THE PRAYER OF THE CITY FATHERS. — MILITARY PREPARATIONS. — VAN DER DONCK. — HON. NICASIUS DE SILLE. — THE DIET OF NEW AMSTERDAM. — OLIVER CROMWELL. — PEACE BETWEEN ENGLAND AND HOLLAND.

"OUR great Muscovy duke keeps on as of old; something like the wolf, the longer he lives the worse he bites." Thus wrote Van Dincklagen to Van der Donck. The West India Company, unwilling to relinquish any of its power, was arrayed like a bulwark of iron against the spirit of popular freedom which the colonists were urging
1650. and which was countenanced by the States-General. It was a struggle for the elective franchise, and its long subsequent effects were of such a character that, while few portions of our history are more obscure, none are more important or instructive.

In this extraordinary controversy, the governor, the West India Company, and the English residents of New Netherland were on one side, and the States-General and the Dutch colonists on the other. "The power to elect a governor among ourselves would be our ruin," was the expression of the English residents, in a *Memorial* sent to the company. "I shall do as I please," was Stuyvesant's reply more than once, when his attention was called to some order. or suggestion from the States-General which had not been indorsed by the Amsterdam Chamber. His mind was vigorous and acute, and he never lacked the courage to carry out to the very letter the peculiar policy of his immediate employers.

Van Dincklagen was a constant thorn in the governor's side. He was a quick-witted, sagacious politician, — a man who was considered eligible to the highest office, and who had accepted a subordinate position with a bad grace. He stood ready to seize upon every mistake of executive judgment, and, with caustic satire, to hold it up to the popular view in its most unfavorable light. He was an advocate of no mean pretensions; and when Melyn arrived in the *New Netherland's Fortune*, it was he who investigated the cause of the unusually long voyage. He discovered that boisterous seas had delayed the vessel, that "water had fallen short," and the "last biscuit been divided among the passengers," and that the captain had been obliged to put into Rhode Island to refit and replenish his stores. Stuyvesant took his seat upon the bench beside Van Dincklagen, and pronounced a remarkable decision. It was one of the regulations of the West India Company that vessels should not "break bulk" between Holland and New Amsterdam; and he took the ground that the delay in this case was "needless and unjustifiable," and proceeded to seize the ship and cargo, supposing them to belong to Melyn. The ship was sold to Thomas Willett, who sent it on a voyage to Virginia and Holland. At the latter place it was replevied by Baron Van der Capellen, and after a protracted litigation the company was obliged to pay heavy damages.

Melyn again took possession of his lands on Staten Island, which, in order to promote his greater security, Van Dincklagen had formerly purchased of the Raritans in the name of Baron Van der Capellen; but he was presently summoned to New Amsterdam by the governor to answer to various charges. Dreading the encounter, he failed **1651.** to obey; and, in consequence of this, his house and lot in the city were confiscated and sold by the government. Expecting that an effort would be made to arrest him at his country-house, he established and fortified a manorial court on one of the petty eminences overlooking what is now the village of Clifton. He was not disturbed, but he was soon after accused of trying to influence the Indians against Stuyvesant, and the council were induced to pass a resolution that the governor should henceforth be constantly attended by a body-guard of four halberdiers.

Van Dincklagen ridiculed this action on the part of his colleagues. He denied the absurd stories in regard to Melyn. He even volunteered to bring the chiefs of the Raritan and other tribes to the fort, to prove the falsity of the charge that "one hundred and seventeen savages had been supplied with arms and ammunition!"

About the same time, Van Dincklagen, with the assistance of Van Dyck, prepared and sent an elaborate *protest* to the States-General, in which he claimed to picture the popular griefs and the general dissatisfaction of the colonists with the administration. When it **Feb. 28.** came to the knowledge of Stuyvesant, he was thoroughly enraged.

Without a moment's hesitation, he ordered Van Dincklagen to be expelled from the council board. The Vice-Director·flatly refused to leave, on the ground that his commission was from the same supreme authority as that of the governor himself. However that might be as a question of law, Stuyvesant waited only until a file of soldiers could be summoned, before ordering Van Dincklagen to be dragged from the room and thrown into prison. The affair created an intense sensation. Van Dincklagen's wife and daughter went to the prison to see him, and were denied admittance. Stuyvesant was denounced by many as jealous and exacting, and by others warmly applauded for his prompt action. He was sustained by the majority of the council. In the course of a few days, Van Dincklagen was released from confinement, but was allowed no further participation in the government. He retired to Melyn's manor-house on Staten Island, where he met with cordial sympathy. Van Dyck, because of the part he had taken in the complaint, was removed from office; and the lawyer, Schelluyne, who attested the *protest*, was forbidden to practice his profession. Loockermans and Heermans, who lent some assistance, were prosecuted and heavily fined.

While these and similar events were agitating Manhattan, Van Tienhoven, at Amsterdam, was amusing himself by playing the gallant lover to the pretty young daughter of a respectable fur-merchant. Pretending to be a single man, he won her affections under promise of marriage, and finally persuaded her to elope with him to America. Having submitted an able defense of Stuyvesant and his officers to the States-General, he was about to embark, when a message sent in hot haste to the Amsterdam Chamber ordered him to report immediately at the Hague for examination by their High Mightinesses. The summons required also the presence of his father-in-law, Jan Jansen Dam. The *protest* of Van Dincklagen had been received, and Van der Donck had replied to Van Tienhoven's defense in a spirited and effective manner. Greatly annoyed at the delay, Van Tienhoven proceeded to the Hague. He was arrested, the very evening of his arrival, on the charge of adultery. In the course of two or three days he made his escape, and reached the vessel bound for New Amsterdam in time to secure his passage. The capture of the cargo of a Portuguese merchant-vessel on the voyage is supposed to have subsequently secured his acquittal ; but he was hopelessly disgraced. His return to New Amsterdam was a misfortune to the community. He was likened to "an evil spirit scattering torpedoes."

Rensselaerswick was so far from the capital that it was not affected by these disturbances. It continued to grow, while the progress of New Amsterdam was seriously retarded. Van Slechtenhorst had stood out boldly against the governor, and extended the limits of the patroon's colony, until he had at last been arrested and imprisoned for four months in the fort at New Amsterdam. He made his escape by secreting himself on a sloop bound for Albany, the skipper of which he had fully indemnified against possible harm. Stuyvesant arrested the skipper on his return, and fined him two hundred and fifty guilders and costs. Van Slechtenhorst estimated the whole expense of his luckless trip down the Hudson at about one thousand guilders. He soon after issued an order that all the householders and freemen of his colony should take the oath of allegiance to the patroon and his representatives. The occasion of this was the fear that Stuyvesant would execute his threatened purpose of extending the jurisdiction of Fort Orange, and so severing from the colony the populous little village of Beverwyck, Nov. 28. which lay close to and around the citadel, and which was every day becoming more valuable. Among those who bound themselves " to maintain and support offensively and defensively " the interests of Rensselaerswick, was John Baptist Van Rensselaer, a younger half-brother of the patroon, who had just been appointed to the magistracy of the colony.[1] Philip Pietersen Schuyler, the ancestor of the American family of Schuylers, had been in Rensselaerswick a little more

Schuyler Arms on Window.

than a year, and had also taken the oath of allegiance to the patroon. He had recently married Margritta, one of the daughters of the cool and fearless Van Slechtenhorst. He was a young man of ability, and was already actively assisting in the management of public affairs. To prepare the reader for an acquaintance with the different members of his family as they shall be introduced from time to time in future chapters, we digress a moment to speak of his ten children.[2] Guysbert was the eldest son, — a man of whom very little is known. Gertrude was the eldest daughter, beautiful, educated, and high-bred, — indeed, the belle of Rensselaerswick, prior to her marriage and removal to New Amsterdam as Mrs. Stephanus Van Cortlandt. Alida, the second daughter, was scarcely less attractive than her sister. She married, when only seven-

[1] *Holgate's American Geanology.*
[2] *O'Callaghan*, II. 174, 177. *La Potherie's History of North America.*

teen, the Rev. Nicolaus Van Rensselaer; and, after his death, the famous
Robert Livingston.   Peter, the next son in the order of age, was the first
mayor of Albany.   He was the great colonel whose wise counsels and

personal exertions at one
period preserved the province from an Indian war;
and who, at another, es-
corted five Indian chiefs
to England to persuade
the government to drive
the French out of Canada.
In 1719, as the oldest
member of the executive
council, he assumed, for a

Schuyler Mansion at the Flats in 1875.

ment of New Netherland.[1]
nius for trade than for
quite young, to New Amsterdam,

season, the entire govern-
Brandt, who had more ge-
command, went, when
where he married, in 1682,
Cornelia Van Cortlandt, the daughter of Oloff S. Van Cortlandt, and
sister of Stephanus.   Arent likewise took up his abode in the metropolis.[2]
Sibylla died in infancy.   Philip settled in Albany.   John, the youngest
son, held a captain's commission in 1690, when only twenty-three years of
age, and led into Canada an expedition which achieved a brilliant victory
over the French and Indians.   He was the grandfather of General Philip
Schuyler, of Revolutionary memory.   The youngest daughter was Margritta.   The elder Schuyler died at Albany, March 9, 1684.   His will
bears date May 1, 1683, O. S.

On New Year's evening, the soldiers at Fort Orange became hilarious,
and a few of them started out on a frolic.   Coming in front of the house

1652. of Van Slechtenhorst, they ignited some cotton and threw it upon

Jan. 1. the roof.   The inmates almost immediately discovered the fire,
and by active exertions saved the building from destruction.   The next
day, a son of Van Slechtenhorst met some of the soldiers in the street, and

Jan. 2. accosting them in relation to the mischief they had occasioned,
threatened them sharply; whereupon they charged upon him,
threw him down, and having severely beaten him, dragged him through
the mud.   Schuyler hastened to the assistance of his brother-in-law;
but Dyckman, the commander of the fort, who stood by, swore he
would run him through with his drawn sword if he did not keep out of
the way.   Others who rushed into the fray received severe blows.

[1] He married, Oct. 25, 1672, Maria, daughter of Kilian Van Rensselaer.
[2] The ancestor of the New Jersey branch of the family.

The friends of Van Slechtenhorst vowed revenge; and, this coming to Dyckman's ears, he ordered the guns of the fort to be loaded with grape and turned upon the patroon's house, declaring he would batter it down. While things were in this chaotic state, there arrived from Stuyvesant some placards, which declared the jurisdiction of Fort Orange to extend over a circumference of six hundred paces (about one hundred and fifty rods) around the fortress. These Dyckman was ordered to publish. With nine armed men, the military commander proceeded to the court-room where the magistrates of the colony were in session, and demanded that the placards should be published through the colony with the sound of a bell. As it was contrary to law for any man to enter another's jurisdiction with an armed *posse* without the previous consent of the local authorities, Van Slechtenhorst ordered the intruder to leave the room, exclaiming, " It shall not be done as long as we have a drop of blood in our veins, nor until we receive orders from their High Mightinesses and our honored masters."

Feb. 8.

Dyckman retired, but returned presently with an increased force. He ordered the porter to ring the bell, and that being vigorously opposed, he proceeded to the fort and caused the bell there to be rung three times. He then returned to the steps of the court-house and directed his deputy to read the placards. As the latter was about to obey, Van Slechtenhorst rushed forward and tore the paper from his hands, " so that the seals fell on the ground." Some violent words followed; but young Van Rensselaer, standing by, said to the crowd, " Go home, my good friends ! 't is only the wind of a cannon-ball fired six hundred paces off."

A messenger was sent down the river to Stuyvesant, who at once forwarded another placard to Dyckman, with orders to publish it, and also to affix copies of it to posts erected on the new line, north, south, and west of the fort. Within these bounds, for the future, no house was to be built, except by the consent of the governor and council, or of those authorized to act for them. This act, severing forever the village of Beverwyck from Van Rensselaer's colony, was pronounced illegal, and in direct violation of the sixth article of the charter of 1629. Van Slechtenhorst sent a constable to tear the posters down contemptuously, and drew up a long remonstrance against the unbecoming pretensions of the governor, who he declared had no authority over the colony whatever. The patroon's lands, he said, had been erected into a perpetual fief, which no order emanating from the West India Company was sufficient to destroy. This paper was denounced by the governor and council as a " libellous calumny." Dyckman set afloat a rumor that Stuy-

April 1.

10

vesant was about to visit Fort Orange, and that he was preparing a gallows for Van Slechtenhorst, his son, and young Van Rensselaer.

Stuyvesant, after dealing with a number of refractory persons in New Amsterdam, some of whom he put in confinement and bastinadoed others with a rattan, repaired to the troubled regions at the north. He sent a party of soldiers to Van Slechtenhorst's house with an order to the patroon to strike his flag, which the latter peremptorily refused to do. They then entered the inclosure, fired a volley from their loaded muskets, and hauled down the flag themselves. Stuyvesant immediately erected a court of justice in Beverwyck, apart from and independent of that of Rensselaerswick ; but the notice of this, having been affixed to the courthouse of the latter colony, was torn down, and a proclamation asserting the rights of the patroon posted in its place. The next day, nine armed men broke into Slechtenhorst's house and forcibly conveyed him to Fort Orange, where neither his wife, children, nor friends were allowed to speak with him. His furs, his clothes, and his meat were left hanging to the door-posts. It was not long ere he was conveyed to New Amsterdam ; but he was not confined in the hold of the fort there, as has been asserted. He was under " civil arrest," and spent a portion of his time on Staten Island.

John Baptist Van Rensselaer took Van Slechtenhorst's place provisionally, and was afterwards formally appointed commander of the colony by the patroon. Gerrit Swart succeeded to the office of sheriff; Rev. Gideon Schaets was installed as clergyman, and retained that position for over thirty years. His salary was $ 380 per annum. Before returning to New Amsterdam, Stuyvesant confirmed the authority of the West India Company by issuing patents to some of the principal colonists for tracts of land within the confines of Beverwyck. It was thus that the germ of the present city of Albany was rescued from feudal jurisdiction.

April 18.

Sept 2.

On the 28th of March, Van Tienhoven was appointed to the office of sheriff, which had been made vacant by the removal of Van Dyck. " Were an honorable person to take my place, I should not so much mind it," bewailed the latter ; " but here is a public. notorious, and convicted whoremonger and oath-breaker, who has frequently come out of the tavern so full of strong drink that he was forced to lie down in the gutter, while the fault of drunkenness could not easily be imputed to me."

Mar. 28.

Carel Van Brugge succeeded Van Tienhoven as secretary of the province, and Adriaen Van Tienhoven became receiver-general, in place of his brother.

The death of William II., Prince of Orange, in 1650, left vacant the office of stadtholder, and that dignity remained in abeyance during the minority of William III. This event led to the recognition of the English Commonwealth by the Dutch Republic in January, 1651. Delegates were sent from England to the Hague to negotiate a league of amity and confederation between the two nations. Some of the visionary enthusiasts in Parliament even entertained the idea of making the two republics one, to be governed by a council sitting at London, composed of Dutchmen and Englishmen. To effect this, the embassy was instructed to use the most adroit diplomacy ; but their first act was to demand that all the English fugitives should be expelled from Holland. This decided the matter. The Dutch government at once assumed a haughty air. The people of the Netherlands were attached to the house of Orange, and did not relish the presence of the executioners of the unhappy grandfather of William III.[1] They openly, and on every possible occasion, insulted the ambassadors, who finally returned to England, determined to destroy the commercial ascendency of the Dutch.[2] The celebrated Act of Navigation was accordingly carried through Parliament. Henceforward the commerce between England and her colonies, as well as that between England and the rest of the world, was to be conducted in ships solely owned and principally manned by Englishmen. Foreigners might carry to England nothing but those products of their respective countries which were the established staples of those countries. The act was leveled at the commerce of the Dutch, and destroyed one great source of their prosperity, while some letters of reprisal issued by English merchants brought eighty Dutch ships as prizes into English ports. The act was, after all, but a protection of British shipping. It contained not one clause which related to a colonial monopoly, or was specially injurious to an American colony. In vain did the Dutch expostulate against the breach of commercial amity. England loved herself better than she loved her neighbors. But, as might have been expected, a naval war was the consequence. The first battle between the forces of the Netherlands and the English Commonwealth was fought in the Straits May 29. of Dover, on the 29th of May, 1652. Other battles followed in which the Dutch were victorious, and the triumphant Van Tromp sailed along Dec. 9. the English coast with a broom at his masthead, to indicate that he had swept the Channel of English ships.

The States-General had remonstrated so often and so earnestly with the

---

[1] *Aitzema*, III. 638 – 663. *Thurloe's State Papers*, I. 174, 179, 182, 183, 187 – 195. *Verbael Van Beverning*, 61, 62.

[2] *Common's Journal*, VII. 27. *Anderson*, II. 415, 416. *Lingard*, XI. 128. *Davis*, II. 707 – 710. *Bancroft*, I. 215, 216.

West India Company in regard to the mismanagement of New Netherland, that the Amsterdam Chamber finally deemed it wise to pour a little
oil upon the bleeding wounds of the colonists. They took off the export
duty from tobacco; reduced the price of passage to New Amsterdam;
allowed the colonists to procure negroes from Africa; sent supplies of
ammunition to be distributed at a " decent price "; assented to

April 4. the establishment of a public school; and granted a burgher government to New Amsterdam, similar to that of the cities of the Fatherland. In the vessel which brought these dispatches were several distinguished passengers, among whom was Dominie Samuel Drisius, a
learned divine, who could preach in English, Dutch, and French, and who
came to New Amsterdam as colleague to Dominie Megapolensis, at a
salary of $ 580 per annum.

The public school was opened in one of the small rooms of the great
stone tavern, and Dr. La Montagne offered to teach until a suitable master
could be obtained from Holland. Meanwhile the States-General had resolved to recall Governor Stuyvesant. They prepared their mandate and
intrusted it to Van der Donck, who was about to sail for New Amsterdam.
This extraordinary measure aroused the Amsterdam Chamber; they interfered, and at last persuaded the States-General that, in view of the
rupture with England, they needed a man of Stuyvesant's military character and experience to guard their American possessions. A messenger
was therefore sent to Texel, where Van der Donck was upon the eve of
sailing, and the letter of recall was obtained and destroyed. Thus

April 27. Stuyvesant received nothing of his threatened humiliation. An
order reached him, however, that Schelluyne should be unmolested in his
practice of notary-public.

The towns of Middleburg and Flatbush were commenced this year.
There were also large tracts of land ceded to different parties on Long
Island, in New Jersey, and on the banks of the North River. But prosperity was not ready to bless the slow-growing community, and its off-
shoots and branches developed with strange tardiness. One of the greatest wants of the colony was skilled labor, and, indeed, labor of every kind.
Efforts had been made to procure it from Holland, but with very little
success. Negroes had occasionally been brought to Manhattan and sold,
but the demand for servants was far beyond the supply. The new law of
the company, which permitted the colonists to equip vessels and sail to the
coasts of Angola, in Africa, to procure negroes for themselves, was the
signal for the fitting out of several vessels exclusively for the slave-trade
and the bringing to New Netherland of a large invoice of the colored
population of the torrid zone. Every family who could afford it invested

in this branch of industry. But it was wretchedly unsatisfactory. The slaves were ignorant and intensely stupid. Twenty-five of such as were imported at that time could hardly perform as much work as three, a hundred years later.

While these voyages were occupying the attention of the enterprising merchants of Manhattan, an interesting moment arrived. A new **1653.** city appeared in the annals of the world. Its birth was an- **Feb. 2.** nounced on the evening of February 2, 1653, at the feast of Candlemas. A proclamation of the governor defined its exceedingly limited powers and named its first officers. It was called New Amsterdam. There was nothing in the significant scene which inspired enthusiasm. It came like a favor grudgingly granted. Its privileges were few, and even those were subsequently hampered by the most illiberal interpretations which could be devised. Stuyvesant made a speech on the occasion, in which he took care to reveal his intention of making all future municipal appointments, instead of submitting the matter to the votes of the citizens, as was the custom in the Fatherland ; and he gave the officers distinctly to understand from the first, that their existence did not in any way

Kip's Mansion.

diminish his authority, but that he should often preside at their meetings, and at all times counsel them in matters of importance. They were not to have a sheriff of their own ; but Van Tienhoven, the provincial sheriff, might officiate for the corporation. Neither was it deemed requisite that they should have a scribe ; but Jacob Kip, the newly appointed secretary of the province, was notified to attend their meetings and do such writing as seemed necessary.

He was a young man of spirit and intelligence, tall, handsome, and extremely popular. The following year, he married Marie La Montagne, the daughter of Dr. La Montagne, a beautiful girl of sixteen. He owned a farm of one hundred and fifty acres on the East River, and soon after his marriage erected a house upon it, and went there to reside. The locality was, and is still, known as Kip's Bay.

This Kip mansion subsequently became famous. It was once or twice rebuilt, and five generations of the Kip family were born in it. It was, for a short time, during the American Revolution, the head-quarters of General Washington. It was one of the landmarks of the olden time that was ruthlessly pushed aside by the corporation, at the opening of Thirty-fifth Street, on the direct line of which it stood. The sketch is a fair illustration of the style of the better class of farm-houses on Manhattan Island, during the early period. The new city contained a number of good stone dwellings, which had a substantial and aristocratic air, as if inhabited by people of wealth and cultivated tastes. There were many English and French, as well as Dutch, residents who were well connected in Europe ; and, from whatever cause they had been induced to emigrate, they were not likely to turn barbarians because they were in a new country. Good breeding cannot be taken on and put off so readily. Many struggled along for years with wants unsupplied ; but when, with increase of means, they were able to provide the comforts and luxuries to which they had been born, they were not slow to embrace the opportunity. The refinement and culture of these gave tone, even at that early date, to the social life of the little community.

The cheaper and more common dwellings we find to have been generally built of wood, with checker-work fronts, or rather gable ends, of small black and yellow Dutch bricks, with the date of their erection inserted in iron figures facing the street. The roofs were tiled or shingled, and surmounted with a weathercock. The front door was usually ornamented with a huge brass knocker, with the device of a dog's or lion's head, which was required to be burnished daily. As the facilities for obtaining building materials increased, the huts of the very poor classes gradually assumed a more and more respectable appearance. The old stone tavern was remodeled, cleaned up, and called a Stadthuys, or City Hall ; and there the city magistrates held their meetings on Mondays, from nine o'clock in the morning until noon, and if business was urgent they sometimes had an after-dinner session. Absent members were fined six stuyvers for the first half-hour, twelve for the second, and forty if absent during the meeting.

A pew was set apart in the church for the City Fathers ; and on Sunday mornings these worthies left their homes and families early to meet in the City Hall, from which, preceded by the bell-ringer, carrying their cushions of state, they marched in solemn procession to the sanctuary in the fort. On all occasions of ceremony, secular or religious, they were treated with distinguished attention. Their position was eminently respectable, but it had as yet no emoluments. We shall have occasion hereafter to show how they watched over the tender babyhood of the city, — a city whose infancy was dwarfed by the constant neglect of the parent country; which was exposed to savage hostility and over-looked by the world in general; which was captured while yet in swad-dling-clothes by people of different language, views, and policy; whose youth was a combat with all kinds of untoward circumstances, but whose maturity has so far exceeded the promise of its earlier years, and whose future certainties are so much greater than those of any other city on the face of the earth, that we cannot pass on without extending our cordial fellowship to those who rocked its cradle. Their names we shall rewrite each time with newly awakened emotions.

There were two burgomasters, Arent Van Hattam and Martin Cre-gier. The first was an intelligent Holland speculator, who traveled through the country and amassed a large fortune, but never married, or had any permanent residence in New Amsterdam that we can learn. He was once sent as ambassador to Virginia. Martin Cregier was the captain of the citizens' military company, and went often in command of important expeditions into the interior. He was the pro-prietor of a small tavern opposite the Bowling Green, the site of which he purchased in 1643. He was a conspicuous man in his day; and his descendants are among the most highly respected families in the State of New York.

There were five schepens, — Paulus Van der Grist, Maximilian Van Gheel, Allard Anthony, Peter Van Couwenhoven, and William Beck-man. Paulus Van der Grist was a hale, hearty old sea-captain, who commanded one of the four ships of the fleet which conveyed Governor Stuyvesant to America. Either personally or through an agent, he bought considerable property on Manhattan Island as early as 1644, and took up his permanent residence in New Amsterdam, as naval agent, in 1648. He owned a sloop with which he navigated the waters near by; built himself a nice house on Broadway below Trinity Church; and opened a dry-goods store, keeping groceries and knick-knacks also, according to village custom.

Allard Anthony was a middle-aged man, rich, influential, conceited, and unpopular. He was the consignee of a large firm in Holland; and his store was in the *old church* building erected by Van Twil-ler. Besides his general wholesale business, he engaged in the retail trade; for we learn by the records that he sold a " hanger " to Jan Van Cleef " for as much buckwheat as Anthony's fowls will eat in six months." At another time we learn that his wife complained of some negroes " for killing a few of her pigs." He had a large farm on the island; but his city residence, a first-class stone mansion, was on the corner of Whitehall and Marketfield Streets. He had one son, Nicholas, who was afterwards sheriff of Ulster County; and two daughters, who, it has been said, dressed the most showily and fashionably of all the ladies of New Amsterdam. Peter Couwenhoven has been noticed on a previous page.

William Beekman was the ancestor of the well-known Beekman family, and his name is perpetuated by two streets, William and Beekman. He came from Holland in the same vessel with Stuyvesant, at the age of twenty-one. Full of strong, healthy life, and ambition, he employed every moment that he could spare from his clerkship duties in searching for a spot to plant his money, for he had not come empty-handed from abroad. An opportunity soon offered; he purchased Corlear's Hook of Jacob Corlear, and shortly after fell in love with and married the pretty blue-eyed Catharine Van Boogh. Everybody thought it a good match, and the youthful pair were held in high esteem. In the course of years, he rose to distinction; he was at one time vice-director of the colony on the Delaware, and at another sheriff at Esopus. He was nine years a burgomaster of New Amsterdam. In 1670, he bought the farm formerly owned by Thomas Hall, stretching along the East River for a great distance. His orchard lay upon a side-hill running down to the swamp which was called Cripple Bush, and through which Beekman Street now passes. He had five sons and one only daughter, Marie. This daughter married Nicholas William Stuyvesant, a son of the governor.

The bell-ringer was a notable and useful individual. He was the court messenger, the grave-digger, the chorister, the reader, and sometimes the schoolmaster. He seems also to have been a general waiter upon the city magistrates. He kept the great room in which they assembled in order, placed the chairs in their proper and precise positions, and rang the bell at the hour for coming together. It was the business of the sheriff to convoke and preside over this board, to prosecute offenders, and to execute judgments. City officials in the Fatherland were invested with judicial and municipal powers; but, as no specific charter had been granted to our City Fathers, their authority was not well defined. They heard and settled disputes between parties; tried cases for the recovery of debt, for defamation of character, for breaches of marriage promise, for assault and theft; and even summoned parents and guardians into their presence for withholding their consent to the marriage of their children or wards without sufficient cause. They sentenced and committed to prison, like any other court of sessions.

Feb. 6.

All their meetings were opened with a solemn and impressive form of prayer. As we find it recorded in their minutes, we presume they designed it should go down to posterity; hence we give it in full: —

"Oh God of Gods, and Lord of Lords! Heavenly and most merciful Father! We thank thee that thou hast not only created us in thine image, but that thou hast received us as thy children and guests when we were lost, and in addition to all this, it has pleased thee to place us in the government of thy people in this place.

"O Lord, our God, we, thy wretched creatures, acknowledge that we are not worthy of this honor, and that we have neither strength nor sufficiency to discharge the trust committed to us without thine assistance.

"We beseech thee, oh fountain of all good gifts, qualify us by thy grace, that we may, with fidelity and righteousness, serve in our respective offices. To this end enlighten our darkened understandings, that we may be able to distinguish the right from the wrong, the truth from the falsehood; and that we may give pure and uncorrupted decisions; having an eye upon thy word, a sure guide, giving to the simple, wisdom and knowledge. Let thy law be a light unto our feet, and a lamp to our path, so that we may never turn away from the path of righteousness. Deeply impress on all our minds that we are not accountable unto man, but unto God, who seeth and heareth all things. Let all respect of persons be far removed from us, that we may award justice unto the rich and the poor, unto friends and enemies alike; to residents and to strangers according to the law of truth: and that not one of us may swerve therefrom. And since gifts do blind the eyes of the wise, and destroy the heart, therefore keep our hearts aright. Grant unto us, also, that we may not rashly prejudge any one, without a fair hearing, but that we patiently hear the parties, and give them time and opportunity for defending themselves; in all things looking up to thee and to thy word for counsel and direction.

"Graciously incline our hearts, that we may exercise the power which thou hast given us, to the general good of the community, and to the maintainance of the church, that we may be praised by them that do well, and a terror to evil-doers.

"Incline, also, the hearts of the subjects unto due obedience, so that through their respect and obedience our burdens may be made the lighter.

"Thou knowest, Oh Lord, that the wicked and ungodly do generally contemn and transgress thine ordinances, therefore clothe us with strength, courage, fortitude, and promptitude, that we may, with proper earnestness and zeal, be steadfast unto death against all sinners and evil-doers.

"Oh good. and gracious God, command thy blessing upon all our adopted resolutions, that they may be rendered effectual, and redound to the honor of thy great and holy name, to the greatest good of the trusts committed to us and to our salvation.

" Hear and answer us, Oh gracious God, in these our petitions and in all that thou seest we need, through the merits of Jesus Christ thy beloved Son, in whose name we conclude our prayer."

In view of the disturbances across the water, Stuyvesant, as a precautionary measure, wrote to the authorities in New England and Virginia,

Feb. 26.
expressing friendship and good-will, and proposed that the commercial intercourse of the colonies should continue uninterrupted. He learned before the end of March, however, that military preparations

March 13.
were going on in New England ; but whether these were offensive or defensive, he could not discover.   He called a joint meeting of the Council and the City Fathers, and they resolved that a body of citizens should mount guard every night at the City Hall ; also, that Fort Amsterdam should be put in a proper state of defense, and that the city should defray the cost.   About forty of the principal men of New Amsterdam subscribed a loan of two thousand dollars for the purpose.   The fence which Kieft had built across the island still remained, and it was decided to inclose the city by a ditch and palisades with a breastwork, on about the same line, and every man was required to leave his business and lend a helping hand.   Posts twelve feet high and about seven inches in diameter were erected, and covered on the outside with boards ; a ditch, two feet wide and three deep, was dug upon the inside, and the

May 1.
dirt was thrown up against the fence, thus making a platform of sufficient height to permit the assailed to overlook the stockade. It was completed about the 1st of May.   In the mean time, the people had become seriously alarmed, and had spent the 9th day of April in fasting and prayer throughout the province.

War upon the Dutch colonists was actually in contemplation in New England.   A large party were eager to take the opportunity offered by the hostilities in Europe to grasp New Netherland ; but the General Court of Massachusetts refused to sanction such an enterprise.   In the mean time, Captain John Underhill had grown restless, and agitated a revolt on Long Island.   In a seditious paper addressed to the people, he speaks of " this great autocracy and tyranny too grievous for any good

June 2.
Englishman or brave Christian to tolerate."   But his plot was discovered in time to be prevented, and he was arrested, tried, and

---

[1] *New Ams. Rec.*, I. pp. 105, 106, 107, 108, 109.   The records of the first City Fathers are well preserved.   They have been translated into the English language, and are both curious and entertaining.   The minutes of the proceedings of the burgomasters and schepens in the earliest years of the city furnish an abundant harvest for the antiquary.   The writer of this volume only regrets that its necessary limitations exclude so large a proportion of the interesting matter found in their pages.

banished from the province. The city was full of startling rumors ; and, during the summer that followed, the governor was constantly involved in a variety of unexpected difficulties. A man of less firmness and decision of character would have signally failed in maintaining authority. Allard Anthony was sent to Holland as a special agent to rep- June 5. resent the situation of affairs to the Amsterdam Chamber. Stuyvesant, having called upon the city government for further funds July 29. to invest in fortification, was waited upon by the burgomasters, who peremptorily refused to contribute anything more, unless the Aug. 2. governor gave up the excise on wines and beers.

In the summer, Van der Donck arrived from Holland. He had enlarged his *Vertoogh* by writing out a more accurate description of New Netherland. He had submitted it to the West India Company, who had not only approved of it, but recommended it to the States-General ; and the author had received a copyright. He desired to give it a still broader historical character ; and he applied to the company for permission to examine the records at New Amsterdam. He was cordially referred to Stuyvesant. But the latter gentleman suspected his motives and treated him with cool severity, denying him access to any papers whatever. Van der Donck wished also to practice law in this country. His ability as a lawyer was well known. The directors of the company were disposed to grant him a license, only they said, " What will one great advocate do alone among the savages ? You will have nobody of your stamp to plead against you ! " Van der Donck, Dec. 1. when he found his journey barren of results, sailed again for Europe, where he published the book under the title of *Beschryvinge van Nieuw Nederlandt*. The second edition contained a map reduced from the large one of Visscher, and embellished with a view of New Amsterdam, sketched by Augustine Heermans in 1656.

Heermans was a native of Bohemia, and came to New Amsterdam, with Van Twiller, in 1633, as an officer of the company. He had picked up a great fund of information, as well as an immense quantity of real estate ; and he had a natural taste for sketching, which, however, was never cultivated in any considerable degree. His house stood on the west side of Pearl Street, covering the line of Pine. It was built of stone, and surrounded by an orchard and an extensive garden. He removed afterwards to Maryland, where he became a large landholder.

The governor was cheered in July by the arrival of a personage of importance. The company had selected Hon. Nicasius De Sille, a gentleman of the best culture the time afforded, a thorough July 24. statesman and an experienced lawyer, and commissioned him as first councilor in their provincial government. He was a widower, with two attractive daughters and one son; and he built quite an extensive house on the corner of Broad Street and Exchange Place, where he was in the habit of entertaining a small but very select circle of friends in the same elegant and court-ly manner to which he had been accustomed at the Hague.

Autograph of De Sille.

His eldest daughter, Anna, a brilliant little girl of fourteen, who afterward married Hendrick Kip, presided over his table, with its blue and white china and porcelain, curiously ornamented with Chinese pictures. The teacups were very diminutive in size, according to the prevailing fashion, and the tea was sipped in small quantities alternately with a bite from the lump of loaf-sugar which was laid beside each guest's plate. De Sille brought to this country more silver-plate than any one had done before him, and took special pride in its exhibition. Governor Stuyvesant's family, Mrs. Bayard, the La Montagnes, and the Kips were his most frequent visitors. He selected Tryntie Croegers for his second wife; but the marriage proved unhappy. The parties separated in 1669; and a commission, in which figured such names as Van Cortlandt, De Peyster, and Van Brugh, was appointed to try to bring about a reconciliation. They reported that all affection and love were estranged on both sides, but that the husband was more inclined to a reunion than the wife, and they recommended an equal division of the property. De Sille built the first stone house in New Utrecht, and resided there for many years. He left a brief history of the settlement of that town. Laurence De Sille, his son, married the daughter of Martin Cregier, and was the ancestor of all of the name of De Sille in this country. Mrs. De Sille at her death left the whole of her estate, real and personal, to her cousin, Jacobus Croegers.

Cornelis Van Ruyven was about this time appointed secretary of the province, and Van Brugge was employed in the custom-house. All at once there arose again a great spirit of disaffection among the English on Long Island. How much of it was due to the consummate tact of Captain Underhill we are not prepared to say, but from many of the towns came the bitterest denunciation of the Dutch authorities of New Netherlands. It finally resulted in one of the most important popular meetings ever held in New Amsterdam. The capital itself was represented by delegates, as also Breuckelen, Flatbush, Flatlands, Gravesend, Newtown, Flushing, and Hempstead; and the men who assembled were earnest, thoughtful, liberty-loving citizens. The

Nov. 26.

Dec. 10.

convention, after mutual consultation and discussion, adopted a remonstrance, which, in courteous phraseology, compares well with documents of a similar character at a later day, and which shows upon the

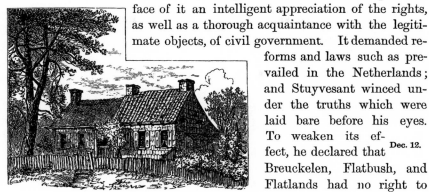

De Sille's House.

face of it an intelligent appreciation of the rights, as well as a thorough acquaintance with the legitimate objects, of civil government. It demanded reforms and laws such as prevailed in the Netherlands; and Stuyvesant winced under the truths which were laid bare before his eyes. To weaken its effect, he declared that Dec. 12. Breuckelen, Flatbush, and Flatlands had no right to jurisdiction, and could not send delegates to a popular assembly. He talked eloquently, and was exhaustive in argument. The delegates prepared a rejoinder, and threatened to send their *protest* to the States-General and the Dec. 13. West India Company, if he did not lend a considerate ear. Then nothing seemed to remain but the exercise of his prerogative. He commanded the delegation to disperse " on pain of our highest displeasure," and closed his message by arrogantly declaring that " we derive our authority from God and the company, not from a few ignorant subjects; and we alone can call the inhabitants together." But the popular voice was not stifled, for the burgomasters and schepens wrote to the West India Company, complaining that their municipal powers were " too narrow," Dec. 24. and asking for such privileges as were granted to their " beloved Amsterdam." The Gravesend magistrates wrote to the States-General, presenting their grievances; and another letter of a similar char- Dec. 27. acter, signed by Martin Cregier, George Baxter, and others, was addressed to the burgomasters and schepens of the city of Amsterdam. Meanwhile the exigencies of the times gave the disaffected community Dec. 30. an excellent opportunity of demonstrating their actual loyalty to the Fatherland. The rapid increase of piracy on the Sound, and the dreaded invasion of the English, made it necessary that a force of men should be raised in each of the towns for the common defense; and the call was responded to with alacrity.

On the 16th of December was established in England the new institute of government, by which Oliver Cromwell was made Lord Dec 16. Protector, and the supreme legislative authority was vested in him and

Parliament. For weeks, during the year past, that country had been as near to anarchy as any civilized nation has ever been; but Parliament was now to be imperial in its character, and the Protector was to be assisted by a council of state.

The spring was just opening, when news reached New Amsterdam that an armed fleet of four ships, direct from England, were in Boston **1654.** raising men for the purpose of attacking the Dutch possessions **June.** in this country. The consternation may readily be imagined. There was nothing talked or thought of but preparations for war. Women and other non-combatants, goods and valuables, were removed with rapidity beyond range of the missiles of destruction. Many of the inhabitants counseled the surrender of the city without bloodshed; but the stern military chieftain visited upon such advisers the full measure of his contempt.

Just as the British force, numbering nine hundred foot and a troop of horse, were victualed and about setting out for New Amsterdam, peace **July 12.** was proclaimed between England and Holland.[1] Cromwell had stipulated his own terms with the United Provinces; but his foreign policy was bold and manly, and, if he had robbed England of her liberty, he at least gave her glory in exchange. The nation which for half a century had been of scarcely more weight than Venice in European **July 18.** politics, suddenly became the most formidable power in the world, and her ruler an object of mingled aversion, admiration, and dread. Nowhere was the news received with such abandonment of delight as in New Amsterdam. Bells rung and cannon boomed, and a day was set apart by the governor for general thanksgiving.

[1] Three hundred of these troops were from Massachusetts, two hundred from Connecticut, one hundred and thirty-three from New Haven, and two hundred from the fleet.

CHAPTER XI.

1654 – 1660.

SALARIES.

CITY TAXATION. — THE SWEDES. — THE LONG ISLAND FERRY. — THOMAS PELL. — LADY MOODY'S LIBRARY. — THE GAY REPAST. — FIRST CITY SEAL. — CHRISTMAS. — NEW YEAR'S. — THE CITY HALL. — THE FIRST CHURCH ON LONG ISLAND. — DOMINIE POLHEMUS. — THE EXPEDITION AGAINST THE SWEDES. — THE INDIAN HORROR. — VAN TIENHOVEN'S DOWNFALL. — THE LUTHERAN PERSECUTION. — CITY PROGRESS. — DOMINIE DRISIUS. — BURGHER RIGHTS. — UNIQUE LAWS. — THE QUAKER PERSECUTION. — HODGSON AT THE WHEELBARROW. — STUYVESANT'S INTERVIEW WITH THE INDIAN CHIEFS. — "WHITEHALL." — STUYVESANT'S COUNTRY-SEAT. — INDIAN HOSTILITIES. — OLIVER CROMWELL'S DEATH.

THE burgomasters and schepens, even before their first year of service had expired, found their duties so arduous, and involving so much time and trouble, that they petitioned for salaries. Stuyvesant, after mature deliberation, granted to each burgomaster one hundred 1654. and forty dollars, and to each schepen one hundred dollars, per annum. They sent in, at the same time, a double set of names from which he might choose officers for the coming year. He, however, retained the same men in office, except that he filled two vacancies in the board of schepens by the appointment of Oloff Stevensen Van Cortlandt and Jochem Pietersen Kuyter. The latter had been successful in the vindication of his character, and was now in possession of his estate in Harlem, and restored to all the rights and privileges of a feudal lord. He lived in a house on the north side of Pearl Street, between Broad Street and Hanover Square. He was commissioned by the Amsterdam Chamber as city sheriff, it having been found necessary, through the rapid increase of business, to separate the office from that of the province; but, unfortunately, before the commission reached New Amsterdam, he had been murdered by the Indians, while on a tour of exploration through the wilderness to the North. The appointment was transferred to Jacques Cortelyou, an educated Frenchman, who was acting as tutor to the sons of Hon. Cornelis Van Werckhoven. He declined to accept it, because of the peculiar nature of the instructions, and it was four years before the city was favored with a sheriff of its own.

There was, from the first, a want of harmony between the governor and the city magistrates. The latter wished to assimilate their municipal government to that of Amsterdam. They never ceased their exertions until they deprived the executive of the absolute power of appointment. They clamored, too, for the management and control of the excise. It seemed eminently proper that this should go into the city treasury, and Stuyvesant finally consented to the arrangement. But he immediately ordered that the city should provide for the support of the troops which had recently arrived from Holland, and for the maintenance of civil and ecclesiastical ministers. The magistrates replied, expressing their willingness to furnish their quota to the amount of one fifth of the whole sum necessary to pay the debt incurred for the repairs of the public works, on condition that they should be empowered to levy taxes on all the real estate within their jurisdiction, sell and convey lands, etc.; they would also pay the salary of one clergyman, one chorister (to act as beadle and schoolmaster), one sheriff, two burgomasters, five schepens, one secretary, and one court messenger; but as to the military, they considered the citizens already overtaxed for the fortifications, and unable to carry a burden which was not for the protection of the city alone, but for the country in general.

When the magistrates rendered their first report of excise income and expenditures, Stuyvesant was greatly displeased to find that the minister's salary had not been paid. As he went on with the examination of the papers, he discovered that they had credited themselves with **Sept. 16.** many items which could not be allowed; as, for instance, the passage-money of François de Bleue, their agent, to Amsterdam. They had not fulfilled their promise to complete the fort; money borrowed for the purpose had been otherwise used; and the men who had advanced the loan were clamoring for repayment. They had not furnished the subsidies which they had promised, and they had failed to contribute their quota towards the public works. He took them severely to task, and by the advice of his council he reassumed the control of the excise which he had **Nov. 23.** already surrendered. The subject was submitted to the Amsterdam Chamber, which instructed the governor to enforce his authority, "so that those men may no longer indulge in the visionary dream that contributions cannot be levied without their consent."

Meanwhile, difficulties had been brewing on the South River. The news of the capture of Fort Casimir by the Swedes reached Stuyvesant while he was in the midst of his hurried preparations to defend New

"As he went on with the examination of the papers, he discovered that the minister's salary had not been paid, and that they had credited themselves with many things that could not be allowed, and he took them severely to task."   Page 179

Netherland from the English. To attempt the recovery of that distant post in a moment of such danger was out of the question, and therefore an account of the affair was sent to Holland, and orders thence were awaited. In September, a Swedish vessel entered the lower bay by ^{Sept. 22.} mistake, and sent to New Amsterdam for a pilot to guide her back into the ocean. Stuyvesant at once ordered the arrest of the boat's crew, and sent soldiers to capture the vessel and bring its captain to the fort. The cargo was removed to the company's warehouse, and a message sent to the Swedish commander of Fort Casimir that the vessel would be detained until such time as "a reciprocal restitution should be made."

The city magistrates, about the same time, demanded and obtained the power to lease the ferry between Manhattan and Long Island, which somewhat mollified their antagonism to their stern superior. Up to this period great inconvenience had been experienced by the community in crossing the East River. Persons had often been compelled to wait a whole day before they could be ferried over ; and the trip was dangerous at its best. An ordinance was accordingly passed, as follows : —

"No one shall be permitted to ferry without a license from the magistrates : the ferryman must keep proper servants and boats, and a house on both sides of the river for the accommodation of passengers, and must pass all officials free. The said ferryman shall not be compelled to ferry any persons, cattle, or goods, without prepayment, and must not cross the river in a tempest." [1]

The toll established by law was, for a wagon and two horses, twenty stuyvers, or one dollar ; for a wagon and one horse, eighty cents ; for an Indian, thirty cents ; for any other person, fifteen cents.

Early in November, news reached the harassed governor that Thomas Pell, an English gentleman and a rank royalist (formerly Gentleman of the Bedchamber to Charles I.), who had been obliged to ^{Nov. 5.} leave New Haven because he refused to swear allegiance to the local government, on the ground that he had already taken an oath in England, had bought of the Indian sachem, Annhook, a tract of land in Westchester, including the estate formerly owned and occupied by Mrs. Annie Hutchinson.[2] Stuyvesant immediately dispatched a marshal to warn the intruder that the same land had long ago been bought of the Indians, and paid for, by other parties, and to forbid the transaction altogether. Pell took no notice of the message, but went on improving his newly

---

[1] *New Amsterdam Records.*

[2] It is supposed that the red chieftain, Annhook, was the one most concerned in the murder of Mrs. Hutchinson, as it was an Indian custom for a warrior to assume the name of some distinguished victim of his prowess.

11

acquired possessions. Thirty-five years later, the acting governor of New York himself purchased the township of New Rochelle of Mr. Pell. From the latter the town of Pelham derived its name; the word being of Saxon origin, compounded of the two words, *Pell* and *ham*. (*Ham* signifies *home*, or *house*.)

During the same month, the governor himself was severely reprimanded by the Amsterdam Chamber. The following paragraph is a key to the document which he received:—

Nov. 23.

"You ought to act with more vigor, and dare to punish refractory subjects as they deserve."

Opportunities for the display of courage were certainly not wanting. At that very moment, some of the English settlers on Long Island were struggling to free themselves from the dominion of the Dutch. The conduct of George Baxter, the former English secretary, and of Mr. Hubbard, of Gravesend, was such that Stuyvesant removed them from the magistracy. Immediately after, he visited the settlement in person, hoping to allay in some measure the acute discontent which prevailed, and to regulate the future choice of magistrates. He was, for several days, the guest of Lady Moody; and Mrs. Stuyvesant, who accompanied her husband, was greatly charmed with the noble English lady. The house of the latter in Gravesend, though primitive in outward construction, was furnished with comparative elegance and good taste, and contained the largest collection of books which had yet been brought into the colony. It was fortified against the Indians, and, in the course of its curious history, sustained several serious attacks.

As the winter advanced, Stuyvesant determined to make a voyage to the West Indies, for the purpose of establishing a commerce between the Spanish plantations and New Netherland. He was to sail, on Christmas eve, in the *Abraham's Sacrifice*, and the city magistrates were impelled to call a special meeting of the Common Council and pass the following significant resolution:—

Dec. 8.

"Whereas, The Right Honorable Peter Stuyvesant, intending to depart, the burgomasters and schepens shall compliment him before he takes his gallant voyage, and shall for this purpose provide a gay repast, on Wednesday next, in the Council Chamber of the City Hall."[1]

Dec. 12.

The list of edibles which was furnished to the committee of arrangements was a long one, and the dinner was a feast indeed. This courtesy to the chief magistrate was productive of sincere good-feeling. Wit and humor for once took the place of dignified austerity. The governor was

---

[1] *New Amsterdam Records.*

genial, even to familiarity.

First Seal of New Amsterdam.

Before the party separated, he presented to the city a long-desired SEAL, which consisted of the arms of Old Amsterdam, — three crosses *saltier*, — with a beaver for a crest. On the mantle above were the initial letters C. W. C. for "Chartered West India Company," for to that corporation the island of Manhattan especially belonged. Underneath was the legend "SIGILLUM AMSTELLODAMENSIS IN NOVO BELGIO," and around the border was a wreath of laurel. [1]

The administration of affairs during Stuyvesant's absence was committed to Vice-Governor De Sille and the council.

The Dutch held national festivals in high esteem. At a meeting of the Common Council, on Monday, December 14, the following was placed on record : — {Dec. 14.}

"As the winter and the holidays are at hand, there shall be no more ordinary meetings of this board between this date and three weeks after Christmas. The court messenger is ordered not to summon any person in the mean time." [2]

Christmas was, at that period, observed as a religious, domestic, and merry-making festival throughout England and Holland, as well as in some other European countries. The Dutch often called it the " children's festival." The evening was devoted to the giving of presents, and " Christmas trees " were everywhere in vogue. The custom originated in the Protestant districts of Germany and Northern Europe. Saint Nicholas, whose image presided as the figure-head of the first emigrant ship which touched Manhattan Island, and for whom the first church had been named, was esteemed the patron saint of New Amsterdam. The hero of the childish legend of Santa Claus — the fat, rosy-cheeked, little old man with a pipe in his mouth, driving a reindeer sleigh over the roofs of houses — is no modern creation of fancy. His expected coming created the same feverish excitement, the same pleasurable expectancy, the same timorous speculations, among sleepy little watchers centuries ago as among the children of New York to-day.

" New Year's " was observed by the interchange of visits. Cake, wine, and punch were offered to guests. It was one of the most important social observances of the year, and was conducted with much ceremony. Gifts, on that day, particularly in families and among intimate {1655.}

---

[1] *Brodhead*, I. 597. *Val Man*, 1848, 384.
[2] *New Amsterdam Records*, II. 76, 77 – 81, 92.

friends, were by no means unusual. The custom of New-Year's visits, which had been handed down from remote ages, prevails at the present time in nearly all the large cities of the world.

The winter wore away quietly. The vice-governor was seriously embarrassed, through the constant uneasiness and the threats of the English colonists, and longed for Stuyvesant's return ; but nothing of any importance occurred. In February, the city took its first step in the direction of police regulations. Dirck Van Schelluyne, the lawyer, **Feb. 6.** was appointed high constable, and furnished with detailed instructions as to his duties. As the spring opened, the city magistrates obtained control of the City Hall for the first time, and ordered it "to be emptied **March 1.** of the vast quantity of salt and other trumpery with which it was encumbered ; its lodgers were also cleared out." They then proceeded to put it in better repair; and it became a very respectable-looking edifice.[1] It faced the East River, but was so closely hemmed in by other buildings that a good view of it was difficult to obtain. The Council Chamber was in the southeast corner of the second story. The prison was a small room on the first floor in the rear. Upon the roof was a handsome cupola, in which hung a bell. In the year 1699, the building gave place to a new City Hall in Wall Street, at the head of Broad, and was sold for one hundred and ten pounds sterling. Its stones, which were very finely cut, may even now be traced in the foundations of some of the stores in that vicinity.

It was found necessary to protect the shore in front of the City Hall against high tides. Prior to this date, a stone-wall had been constructed and the street filled in ; but the water washed between the crevices, and it was resolved to drive planks into the shore and make a uniform "sheet pile" extending the whole distance between Broad Street and the City Hall, for the expenses of which all the lot-owners were taxed. The public school was removed, in May, from the little room in the City Hall to a small building on Pearl Street which had been rented for the purpose, and William Verstius was employed as teacher.

For many years, the people of Long Island used to cross to Manhattan on the Sabbath, to attend public worship, except when some clerical traveler preached in a private house. They had sent several petitions to the government for the establishment of a church, which was accomplished at Midwout (Flatbush) in 1654. Stuyvesant appointed Dominie Megapolensis, John Snedicor, and John Stryker to superintend the erection of a church edifice, which was to be built in the form of a cross, twenty-eight feet wide and sixty feet long, and twelve to fourteen be-

[1] See sketch of City Hall on page 106.

tween the beams. The rear of it was to be used as a minister's dwelling. The construction of this first house of worship in Kings County occupied several years, although it was sufficiently advanced in the summer of 1655 to allow of its being opened for church services.

Dominie Johannes Theodorus Polhemus was installed pastor over this church. He had just arrived in New Netherland from Brazil, where he had been laboring as a missionary. He had sprung from an ancient and highly respectable Holland stock, and was a gentleman of fair education and moderate ability. In 1656, he was joined by his wife and family. He had two sons, Theodore and Daniel, from whom have descended all of the name in this country. In order to accommodate the people scattered here and there over the wild region between Breuckelen and Gravesend, it was arranged that there should be preaching in Flatbush on Sunday mornings, and alternately in Breuckelen and Flatlands on Sunday afternoons. It was not long before Breuckelen began to grow mutinous. The minister's tax was a serious bugbear.[1] The Sunday service was pronounced "poor and meager." The people said "they were getting only a prayer in lieu of a sermon, so short that when they supposed it just beginning it came to an end," — in other words, they were not getting the worth of their money,— and they asked to be relieved from supporting such an unsatisfactory gospel. The governor replied by sending a sheriff to collect their dues. He reproved them sharply for attempting thus to shirk the fulfillment of their promises; and he reminded them that the good minister was in absolute suffering for the want of his salary, — his house being unfinished, and himself, wife, and children obliged to sleep on the floor.

In the month of July, Stuyvesant returned from the West Indies. He had been wholly defeated in the object of his voyage, through Cromwell's peculiar policy,[2] and he was weary, sick, and disappointed. He found orders awaiting him from Holland to proceed against the audacious Swedes at Fort Casimir, and to drive them from every point on the South River. A squadron of armed vessels for his use had already arrived. The city fathers had fitted up another large vessel, to swell the force. Volunteers were enlisted from both town and country. During the month of August, the little city was alive with warlike preparations. Three North River vessels were chartered, pilots were engaged, July.

---

[1] *New York Col.* MSS., VIII. 406. *Stiles's History of Brooklyn*, I. 130 – 134.

[2] Cromwell had issued orders, during 1654, for the management and government of the West Indies ; and the commissioners, on their arrival, laid an embargo on all the Dutch ships in these islands, eight of which were seized at Barbadoes alone. Three of the same were under the command of Governor Stuyvesant. *O'Callaghan*, II. 285.

and provisions and ammunition laid in store.   The 25th of August was observed as a day of fasting and prayer for the success of the undertaking.   On the first Sunday in September, after the close of the morning sermon in the fort, the seven vessels, manned by seven hundred men, sailed out of the harbor.   They were commanded by Governor Stuyvesant in person, who was accompanied by Vice-Governor De Sille, and Dominie Megapolensis, as chaplain of the expedition.

Aug. 25.

In a few days, they entered the Delaware River, passed Fort Casimir, and landed about a mile above.   A flag of truce was sent to the fort, demanding its surrender, which, after some parleying, was acceded to without resistance.   The Swedish commander went on board Stuyvesant's vessel and signed a capitulation.   The Swedes were allowed to remove their artillery; twelve men were to march out with full arms and accouterments; all the rest retained their side-arms, and the officers held their personal property.   At noon, on the 25th of September, the Dutch, with sounding bugles and flying banners, took possession of the fort.   Such of the Swedes as chose were allowed to take the oath of allegiance to the New Netherland government and remain in the country. The next day was Sunday, and Dominie Megapolensis preached to the troops.   Towards evening, a report was brought to the governor that the Swedish commander, Rising, had re-assembled his forces at Fort Christina, two miles farther up the river, and was actively strengthening his position there.

Sept. 25.

The Swedes had an undisputed right to the land about Fort Christina,[1] having made the purchase many years before with the tacit consent of the company.   They had been cultivating gardens and tobacco, and were making fair progress in the erection of dwellings.   There were about two hundred independent settlers.   Stuyvesant moved his fleet to the mouth of the Brandywine River, where he anchored, invested Fort Christina on all sides, and demanded a surrender.   Resistance was hopeless.   Articles of capitulation were quickly signed, and thus came to an end the Swedish dominions on the Delaware.

Meanwhile, a terrible calamity befell New Netherland.   A few days after the governor and military had departed from the peaceful little city on Manhattan Island, Ex-Sheriff Van Dyck shot an Indian woman who was stealing peaches from his orchard, on the west side of Broadway, below Trinity Church.   For ten years the savages had been friendly, and the minds of the people were lulled into a state of security in regard to them.   But the woman's tribe were inflamed by the

Sept. 15.

---

[1] Fort Christina was about thirty-five miles below the present site of Philadelphia, on a small stream called Christina Creek.

murder, and they determined upon revenge. They knew of the absence of the greater part of the male population of New Amsterdam, and availed themselves of the opportunity. About two thousand armed warriors, in sixty-four canoes, suddenly appeared before the city. It was in the early morning, just as daylight was breaking in the east. They landed stealthily, and scattered themselves through the streets, breaking into several houses, under pretense of searching for Indians from the North. The people were stricken with mortal terror. The city officers sprang from their beds, as did also the members of the governor's council, and after a hurried conference, went bravely among the Indians and asked to see their sachems. The latter came to the fort, where they were received and treated in the kindest manner. They finally promised to take their warriors out of the city, and proceeded, after much delay, to their canoes. They crossed over to Nutten Island, but soon after dark they returned, and ran up Broadway to the house of Van Dyck, whom they killed. Paulus Van der Grist, who lived next door, stepped out, hoping to quiet the savages, but was struck down with an ax. The city was in arms at once, and the citizens, with the aid of the burgher-guard, drove the vindictive enemy to their canoes.

But this effected only a change in the scene of carnage. The Indians hurried to Pavonia and Hoboken, and massacred every man, woman, and child they could find. From there they went to Staten Island, where were eleven flourishing plantations, with about ninety settlers, and laid waste the entire land. Thence they carried their devastations into other parts of New Jersey. In three days, one hundred had been murdered and as many more carried into captivity; twenty-eight plantations had been wholly destroyed, and property had been lost to the amount of eighty thousand dollars !

The whole country was struck with horror and fear. The farmers fled with their families to the fort for protection. The English villages on Long Island were threatened, and Lady Moody's house at Gravesend was twice attacked. Prowling bands of savages flitted in and out of the woods on the northern part of Manhattan Island. Mrs. Stuyvesant and her children were at their country-place, in the neighborhood of 13th Street ; and as the citizens were so few in number that it was difficult to spare a guard for her protection, ten resolute Frenchmen were hired for that duty.

As soon as possible, a message was sent to the absent governor, who hastened home, bringing joy and confidence to the distressed community. His policy with regard to the Indians was to give no new _{Oct. 12.} provocation, and to exchange fire-arms for prisoners. He succeeded, after a short time, in inducing the red-men to sue for peace, and then he promptly concluded a treaty with them.

About this time, one great source of misfortune to the province was removed. Van Tienhoven, who had gradually been falling into almost every known vice, was believed to have given serious cause — through imprudence when intoxicated — for the late terrible tragedies. Every honest heart and every honest face was turned against him. Having been suddenly detected in the perpetration of gross frauds upon the revenue, he was arrested. Stuyvesant clung to him to the last. He tried to palliate his misconduct, evidently blinded to the extraordinary profligacy and corruption which had ruined the miserable sheriff, body and soul. Before the time arrived for submitting his defense, Van Tien-hoven absconded, leaving his hat and cane floating on the river, to convey the idea of suicide. His wife begged that his property and papers might not be seized, and the execution was stayed. His brother Adriaen, the receiver-general, disappeared at the same time, and was subsequently recognized in the English service at Barbadoes, in the capacity of cook.

In the midst of these excitements, a few Lutherans attempted to hold religious meetings. Stuyvesant, with all his Christian virtues, was religiously intolerant. He issued a proclamation, forbidding the people to assemble for any religious service not in harmony with the Reformed **1656.** Church. This penal law, the first against freedom of conscience which disgraced the statute-book of New York, was rigorously enforced. Stuyvesant claimed that its purpose was "to promote the glory of God, and the peace and harmony of the country." Any minister who should violate it was to be fined one hundred pounds. Any person who should attend such a meeting was to be fined twenty-five pounds. Complaints were sent to Holland, and the company rebuked the governor for his bigotry. The directors wrote: —

" We would fain not have seen your worship's hand set to the placard against the Lutherans, nor have heard that you oppressed them with the imprisonments of which they have complained to us. It has always been our intention to let them enjoy all calmness and tranquillity. Wherefore you will not hereafter publish any similar placards without our previous consent, but allow all the free exercise of their religion in their own houses."

The Lutherans in Holland soon after sent a clergyman, the Rev. Ernestus Goetwater, to New Amsterdam, to organize a church. It was with the consent of the company, and the movement was thought very noble and tolerant in those dark days of the seventeenth century. There was, however, in the instructions sent to the governor a qualification which he interpreted according to his own arbitrary views. There should be no *conventicles.* The clergy of the Reformed Church in New Amsterdam remonstrated against permitting the Lutheran minister " to do any clerical service whatever." They said it would encourage " heresy and schism," and that the established religion " was the only lawful, being commanded by the Word of God." Stuyvesant finally ordered Goetwater to leave the colony and return to Holland.[1] He even went so far as to compel parents of Lutheran principles to assist at the baptism of their children in the Reformed Church. If they refused, they were imprisoned and fined. The law applied equally to all denominations. There were a few Baptists in Flushing. They met in the house of one of the magistrates of the town, and a man without license preached, administered the sacrament, and baptized several persons in the river. He was arrested, fined one thousand pounds, and banished from the province. The magistrate was removed from office, as a penalty for allowing the meeting to be held in his house.

The city fathers were unceasingly industrious. They enacted laws and ordinances with as much grace as their ruler assumed sovereignty. They condemned all " flag roofs, wooden chimneys, hay-stacks, hen-houses, and hog-pens," which were located on the principal streets. They ordered owners of gardens to either sell or improve them. The penalty for refusal was taxation. They compelled buyers of city lots by the terms of purchase to build upon them without delay. The average price of the best city lots had reached fifty dollars. Houses rented at from fourteen to one hundred dollars per annum. They surveyed and established the streets, seventeen in number. This occurred in July.[2] The next year, they began to pave. The first street honored with paving-stones was De Hoogh, — what is now Stone Street, between Broad and Whitehall. In 1658, De Brugh or Bridge Street, so called from a bridge which had been built across the ditch at Broad Street, was improved in like manner. Within the next two years, all the streets most used were paved. These pavements were of cobble-stones, with the gutters in the middle of the street. Sidewalks were not as yet contemplated.

The census of the city was taken in 1656. The inhabitants were found to number one thousand, of which a large proportion were negro slaves. The adjoining cut is a copy of Augustine Heerman's sketch of New York in 1656, which was widely copied and circulated in Europe.

---

[1] This harsh decree was suspended, out of regard to the feeble health of Rev. Mr. Goetwater.

[2] The names of the streets were : Te Marckvelt, De Heere Straat, De Waal, Te Water, De Perel Straat, Aghter De Perel Straat, De Browner Straat, De Winckel Straat, De Bever Graft, Te Marckvelt Steegie, De Smee Straat, De Smits Valley, De Hoogh Straat, De Brugh Straat, De Heere Graft, De Prince Graft, De Prince Straat.

There was, on the line of Moore Street, one small wharf running out from Pearl, but extending a little farther into the stream than low-water mark. Ships usually moored in the East River, and sent their cargoes ashore in scows, which were compelled to come up to the head of the pier. The increase of the shipping rendered it desirable that this wharf should be elongated about fifty feet, and it was accordingly done. A market-stand for country wagons was established, the same year, on an uninclosed space near the Bowling Green. Allard Anthony opposed the measure in the board of schepens, because the selected site was in front of his own house, and his wife and daughters would object. But he was overruled

View of New York, 1656.

by the majority. Three years later a yearly fair for the sale of cattle was instituted, and the exchange for buyers and sellers was located beside this market-stand. The cattle were fastened to posts, driven for the purpose, on the west side of Broadway, in front of the graveyard.[1] The fair commenced October 20, and closed late in November. It brought strangers to the city from all parts of the country, even from New England, and threw business constantly in the way of the merchants. This fair existed for more than sixty years.

Dominie Drisius lived in a pretty cottage on the north side of Pearl Street, below Broad, — the lot was twenty feet front, extending through to Bridge Street. He exerted a healthful influence over the church, and also took an active interest in political affairs. In 1653, he was sent as ambassador to Virginia, and concluded an important commercial treaty with Governor Bennet, including the concession to New Netherland

---

[1] The first burial-ground in New York was on the west side of Broadway, near Morris Street. Just north of it was the large stone house of Paulus Van der Grist, before mentioned (pp 161, 177). The orchards and gardens of the latter were highly cultivated, and extended to the very edge of the North River. Some years later this fine property was owned and occupied by Hon. Francis Rombouts.

merchants of the power to collect debts due them in Virginia.[1] When the dominie first arrived in New York, he was a middle-aged widower. He subsequently married Lysbeth (Elizabeth), the widow of Isaac Greveraet. She held a large property in her own right, and is often mentioned upon the tax-lists as " Mother Drisius." Dominie Megapolensis owned a small, comfortable house in the vicinity of Beaver Street. The most pretentious house in the city had recently been built by Pieter Cornelisen Vanderveen, a rich merchant, who was described as " old and suitable " for a great burgher. He was for a time one of the schepens, and he had held many offices of trust in the church and community. He married, in 1652, Elsie Loockermans, who, after his death, became the wife of Jacob Leisler. Pearl Street was the favorite locality for building, and was well lined with dwellings.[2] On Bridge Street lived Hendrick Kip. His house was small, but his lot was ninety feet front and seventy deep. His nearest neighbor, Abraham Verplanck,[3] the ancestor of the Verplanck family of New York, was one of the oldest citizens; he also owned a farm near Fulton Street. Thomas Hall lived on a hill in the vicinity of Peck Slip.

On the site of Trinity Church and churchyard there was a fine garden belonging to the company, between which and the Van der Grist estate on the south, Governor Stuyvesant granted to each of his two sons, Nicholas William and Balthazar, a lot containing ninety-three feet front and two hundred and forty-eight feet deep, to the North River shore.

The effort to sustain a good public school appears on nearly every page of the records. As the children increased in numbers, a larger building than the one on Pearl Street was procured. William Verstius was succeeded as teacher by Harmen Van Hoboken, who was also a famous singer and acted as church chorister. Five years afterward, he was superseded by Evert Pietersen, because of alleged inattention to his pupils. The salary was then fourteen and one half dollars per month, with a margin of fifty dollars per annum for board.

About this time, the system of great and small " burgher rights " was introduced into the city. Metropolitan immunities were constantly infringed by peddlers, who sold goods and departed with the proceeds. Stuyvesant's new law required every man to open a store within the city limits and pay a fee of eight dollars before commencing trade. In this way he obtained the small burgher right. All natives of the city, residents of a year and a half, salaried officers of the company, and husbands

---

[1] *Albany Records*, IX. 59.

[2] There were on Pearl Street forty-three houses and a few shops.

[3] Abraham Verplanck had two sons, Gulian and Isaac.

of the daughters of burghers, were entitled to the same privilege. The great burghers comprised burgomasters, schepens, governors, councilors, clergymen, military officers, and all their male descendants. The city officers were, from that time forth, to be chosen from this class. They were to be exempt for one and a half years from watches, expeditions, and arrests by inferior courts. The great burgher right could be secured by the payment of twenty dollars; but not many were disposed to buy a right which all disregarded. The system proved a failure in New Amsterdam as it had done in old Amsterdam, where it originated.

Some of the laws of that period were strikingly unique. It was expressly enjoined upon women that they should not scold. The penalty for this fault was arrest, imprisonment, and fine. In aggravated cases, the grave law-givers resorted even to public whipping.

One Wolfert Weber, the proprietor of a small tavern near the Fresh Water Pond, entered this curious complaint against Judith Verbeth:—

"The defendant has for a long time pestered him; she came with her sister Sara over to his house last week, and beat him [the plaintiff] and afterwards threw stones at him. He pleads that said Judith be ordered to let him live quietly in his own house."

On the 8th of May, 1657, we find Nicholas Verbeth complaining of Wolfert Weber about a pile of stone. Verbeth stated his **1657.** case thus:—

"If anybody removes what belongs to another without his knowledge, it is thieving; my father deposited some stone by the Fresh Water Pond, before his own door, and Weber removed it; whereupon we had words, and Weber promised to deliver other stone instead; we want Weber ordered to bring back to the place the *same stone.*" The court decided for the plaintiff, and ordered the stone returned within eight days.

Hon. Nicasius De Sille prosecuted a man for stealing "three half-beavers, two nose-cloths, and a pair of linen stockings." The court sentenced the offender to be whipped within the Council Chamber and banished from the city. Slander was esteemed a rank offense. A certain Jan Adamzen, for slandering certain respectable persons, was condemned to be "stuck through the tongue with a red-hot iron, and banished from the province."

The severity of sentences, the peculiar modes of punishment, etc., were but a feature of the times. They originated on the other side of the ocean. The city magistrates seem to have had a conscientious regard for equity and justice, and set themselves like flint against Sabbath-breaking, drunkenness, and all the popular vices. It was a mixed population they were trying to control, and the task could have been neither easy nor agreeable. The governor treated his subordinates with profound respect, so long as they were directly in the line of their duties. In his communications to the city magistrates he was exceptionally courteous, always preceding his signature with "Your High Mightinesses' affectionate Friend and Director." But he curtailed their power in all directions. One day, some common people appeared before him, much aggrieved because he had forbidden the servants of the farmers "to ride the goose" at the feast of Shrovetide. He told them "it was unprofitable and unnecessary and criminal to celebrate such pagan and popish feasts, and though it was tolerated in some places in Holland, and connived at by magistrates here, he should enact such ordinances as would tend to the glory of God without the consent of *a little court of justice*"; adding, "I understand my quality and authority, and the nature of my commission, better than others, and hope you will not vex and trouble me continually." [1]

In 1658, a law was enacted forbidding the whipping of negro slaves without first obtaining permission of the city magistrates. Another remarkable law forbade men and women to live together until legally married; for it had been an ancient custom — of much longer standing than the young city — to "bundle" after the publication of the banns.

1658.

The same year, the first fire company was organized. It was called the "Rattle Watch," and consisted of eight men, who were to do duty from nine o'clock in the evening until morning drum-beat. Two hundred and fifty fire-buckets, with hooks and ladders, were imported from Holland, reaching New Amsterdam on the 12th of August.

Long Island was one continual source of anxiety to the men in power at New Amsterdam. George Baxter returned from New England the next year after he was dismissed from the magistracy at Gravesend (he crossed Long Island Sound on the ice), and was arrested in the course of a few days for hoisting the flag of England and "reading seditious papers to the people." For more than a year, he lay in the dungeon of the fort. He was almost forgotten, when Sir Henry Moody and others petitioned so earnestly to have him removed to a more comfortable apartment, that he was released on bail. He immediately drew up a petition to Cromwell to be emancipated from Dutch rule and taken under his protection; and, after obtaining a large number of signers, he left the country. He soon after appeared in England, and was active in trying to vindicate the right of that nation to the entire territory of New Netherland. He was the mortal enemy of Stuyvesant, both at home and abroad. Cromwell's secretary wrote to the English residents of Long Island a long

[1] *New Amsterdam Records.*

letter, which Baxter sent to Gravesend by one of his emissaries, with instructions to have it publicly read. Stuyvesant seized the man and the document. The former he imprisoned; the latter he forwarded to Holland, unopened. It seemed particularly necessary to crush every symptom of rebellion on Long Island, as it was a noted resort for robbers and pirates. "The scum of New England is all drifting into New Netherland," said the venerable Dominie Megapolensis. "Why do you harbor persons who are driven from the other colonies as worse than a pestilence?" asked Dominie Drisius of the governor.

Just at this critical moment, a ship arrived, bringing some Quakers who had been expelled from New England. Of these, two women, with more zeal than discretion, went preaching through the streets. They were arrested, and taken to the prison in the fort, where they were confined in separate apartments. After being examined, they were placed on board a ship bound for Rhode Island. Robert Hodgson, one of the Quakers, went over to Hempstead, intending to preach there. He was arrested while walking in an orchard, and examined by the Hempstead magistrates. A message was sent to the governor, who dispatched an armed party for the poor man, the same evening. His Bible and papers were taken from him, and he was pinioned in a painful position for twenty-four hours. Two women who had entertained him, one of whom had a nursing infant of four months, were also arrested. The latter were tied into a cart, to the rear end of which Hodgson, still pinioned, was fastened with his head downwards ; and thus were they conveyed over the bad roads to the city, where they were placed in separate dungeons. Upon trial, Hodgson was sentenced to two years' hard labor with a negro at the wheelbarrow, or to pay a fine of two hundred and forty dollars. Being destitute both of money and friends, he was, a few days afterwards, brought forth and chained to the wheelbarrow. In vain he argued that he was unused to labor, he was ordered to proceed ; but he refused to move. A tarred rope some four inches thick was then put into the hands of a strong negro, who beat the Quaker until he fell exhausted He was lifted up and again beaten until it was estimated that he had received one hundred blows. All day, standing in the heat of a broiling sun, his body bruised and swollen, he was kept chained to the wheelbarrow. At last he fainted. He was thrown into the cell for the night, and the next day again chained to the wheelbarrow. A sentinel was placed over him, to prevent any conversation with his companion. As before, he refused to work. The third day, he was led forth chained, and was still indomitable in his resistance. Finally, he was taken before the governor.

Stuyvesant told him that he must work ; that he should be whipped every day until he did. The prisoner looked up boldly and demanded to be told what law he had broken. He was not answered, but sent away in contempt, and chained again to the wheelbarrow. He was now confined to his dungeon for two or three days, without even bread and water; but, as this brought no symptoms of surrender, a new torture was tried. He was taken to a private room, stripped to the waist, and suspended from the ceiling by his hands, with a heavy log of wood fastened to his feet. He was then lashed by a negro until his flesh was cut to pieces; and, after two days' respite in his dungeon, this barbarity was repeated. He begged to see some person of his own nation; and at last a poor Englishwoman came and bathed his wounds. She thought he could not live until morning, and informed her husband of his terrible condition. The man hurried to the sheriff, and offered a fat ox to be allowed to remove Hodgson to his house until he recovered; but he was informed that the whole fine must be paid before any mercy could be shown to the prisoner. By this time, the pitiful story, having got well noised about, reached the ears of Mrs. Bayard, the governor's sister, who resolutely interfered in behalf of the sufferer, and obtained his release.

Hodgson was by no means the last of the Quakers of that epoch. Persecution seemed to multiply their numbers and increase their self-confidence. Rumors that they were creeping about among the Long Island towns led to the strictest watchfulness on the part of the magistrates, and any one who ventured to lodge or feed a Quaker, man or woman, was promptly arrested and imprisoned. Mrs. Scott and Mrs. Weeks, having been accused of "absenting themselves from public worship on the Lord's day, to attend a *conventicle* in the woods where there were two Quakers," were imprisoned. At their examination, they justified themselves, declaring that they had broken no law and done no wrong. Nevertheless, they were compelled to pay a heavy fine. There were a great number of similar instances. Three men, suspected of being Quakers, were brought before the governor and council, and at once confessed themselves such. But the tide of feeling had, by this time, become so strong against the tarred rope and wheelbarrow, that the prisoners were only sent back to Communipaw, whence they had come, with an admonition to remain there. The good dominies wrote to the West India Company of the alarming spread of *sectarianism* in New Netherland; but the only answer was a quiet recommendation to allow the people to indulge their various religious beliefs.

All at once, the Indians were again upon the war-path. This time, Esopus was threatened. A messenger came in haste to the city for assistance. The governor responded in person, accompanied by fifty soldiers under

Govert Loockermans. On Ascension Thursday, the settlers, to the number of sixty or more, assembled at the house of Jacob Jansen Stol for religious services. Stuyvesant was present, and took the opportunity to urge the farmers to unite in a village, instead of living so far apart from each other. It seemed almost impossible to accomplish this, as their crops were already in the ground and in need of constant care and protection. They were but just recovering from their previous losses, and could ill afford the time necessary for removal and for the construction of defenses. They begged that the soldiers might remain until after harvest. " No," said Stuyvesant, with emphasis; " but they shall remain with you until the extra work is done, if you will agree at once upon the site of your village."

May 28.

Meanwhile, messengers had been sent to all the great Indian sachems within easy distance, to invite them to an interview with the " big white sachem from Manhattan." They came, sixty or more, including women and children. The interview took place under an immense tree, just outside Mr. Stol's garden-fence. Stuyvesant went out to greet them, without any guard, and attended only by Govert Loockermans, who acted as interpreter. One of the chiefs arose and made a speech. He detailed in full the wrongs practiced upon the Indians for the last twenty years. When the sachem sat down, Stuyvesant was on his feet. His reply was a masterpiece of concentrated eloquence. He said he had nothing to do with events which had occurred before his time; that such remembrances were buried when peace was agreed upon. With his bold dark eye emitting flashes which seemed to penetrate the red skins of the stalwart warriors around him, he demanded, " Has any injury been done you in person or property since the conclusion of peace, or since *I* came into the country ? " They were silent. He paused a moment, and then rapidly enumerated the murders and affronts, the burning of houses and the killing of cattle, which he and his subjects had received at their hands. " You are overbearing and insolent," he said. " I have come to make war upon you, unless you surrender the murderer,[1] and make good all damages. We have not had a foot of your land without paying you for it. You came and asked us to buy this land and make a settlement here; and now you vex and threaten us."

An old chief responded. He said the late murder had been committed by a Minnisinck Indian, who was skulking now at a great distance away. He complained of the selling of fire-water to his tribe, which had made great mischief. He said they had no malice against the white men, but the young men wanted to fight.

---

[1] An Esopus farmer had been killed, and two houses burned.

Stuyvesant sprang to his feet, and hurled defiance at the young braves. "Let them step forth," he shouted, " I will place man against man; yes, I will place twenty against forty of your hot-heads. Now is your time. But it is unmanly and mean and contemptible to threaten farmers and women and children, who are not warriors."

The Indians were humiliated. They dared not accept the challenge. They laid down a few fathoms of wampum, and expressed their sorrow for what had been done to injure the Esopus settlers. In the course of the negotiations, the proposed village was decided upon. A spot about two hundred and ten yards in circumference was chosen at the bend of the creek, where three sides could be surrounded with water. It belonged to the Indians, who at first agreed to sell it, and then formally offered it as a gift to the governor, — " to grease his feet," they said, " because he had taken so long a journey to visit them." They suddenly seemed to hold the " great white sachem " in profound respect. Stuyvesant remained at Esopus until the buildings were removed to the new village, a guard-house was erected, a bridge was thrown across the creek, and temporary quarters were prepared for twenty-four soldiers that he proposed to leave behind, to keep the Indians on their good behavior.

As soon as the governor returned, repairs upon Fort Amsterdam, which had been dragging along for months, were prosecuted with vigor. The negroes, under an overseer, built a stone-wall some three feet thick and ten feet high around the fortress. The governor's house was **1659.** getting old and rusty. He accordingly built for himself a gubernatorial mansion of hewn stone, and called it " Whitehall." It was located upon the street which was subsequently named for it. It was surrounded by gardens on three sides, and a rich velvet lawn in front extended to the water's edge, where lay the governor's barge at the foot of fine cut stone steps. Upon the north side of the grounds there was an imposing gateway.

The governor's country-seat, where he and his family usually spent the summer months, embraced the greater portion of the present Eleventh, Sixteenth, and Seventeenth Wards. It cost him originally sixty-four hundred guilders. His house was a great, commodious, comfortable, home-like specimen of Holland architecture. His gardens were remarkably fine, and his land was in a high state of cultivation. He kept from thirty to fifty negro slaves, besides a number of white servants, constantly employed in the improvement of his grounds. The road to the city had been put in good condition, and shade trees were planted on each side where it crossed the governor's property.

The settlement of Harlem was commenced through an offer by the
12

government to give any twenty-five families who would remove to that remote part of Manhattan Island a court and clergyman of their own and a ferry to Long Island.   Upon the bank of the Harlem River a little tavern was built, which became quite a resort for pleasure-parties from the city.   It was called the "Wedding Place."   The road beyond Stuyvesant's country-seat was little more than a bridle-path through the

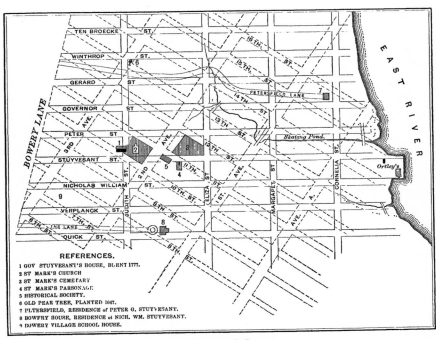

Map of Stuyvesant's Bouwery

woods, crooking about to avoid ledges and ravines.   The land travel at that period was almost exclusively on foot or on horseback ; few wagons had as yet reached the country.

In the mean time, a general fear of the Indians took possession of the public mind.   Stuyvesant had visited Esopus in the autumn, after the dwellings had been collected into a village, and tried to settle certain claims with the sachems.   Only a few came to the interview.   One of their number plead poverty in a studied and cunningly constructed piece of oratory, entirely avoiding the governor's question as to their intentions in regard to the surrender of a certain tract of land in compensation for the injuries they had committed.   When brought back to that point, they went away, pretending that they must consult the absent chiefs.

As they did not return, the governor left a guard of fifty soldiers at the post. A few months later, a sad circumstance enraged the savages far and near. Thomas Chambers had acquired an immense tract of land in the vicinity of Esopus, which had been erected into the manor of Fox-HALL.[1] Some seven or eight Indians in his employ had been husking and shelling corn until late one evening, when they obtained some brandy and had a drunken orgie. Their hideous and unearthly yells, breaking in upon the midnight stillness, startled the settlers, who reconnoitered to find out the cause. The officer in command of the fort forbade his soldiers to molest the poor wretches; but some of the imprudent residents proceeded to the spot where they were lying in a heap together in the bushes, and fired a volley of musketry among them. Several were wounded, and a few ran away. Presently houses, barns, and corn-stacks were set on fire all through the country, and the Esopus fort was besieged for three weeks. News came to Manhattan that several prisoners had been taken by the Indians, and afterwards tortured in the most cruel manner and burned at the stake. The crisis was imminent. Despair seemed to paralyze the fighting men of the colony. Stuyvesant had been suffering from a severe illness; but he met the situation grandly, visiting all the neighboring villages in person and using every effort to stimulate the farmers to fortify and protect themselves. His energy was marvelous, and the resources of his mind abundant. He was delayed several days before he could raise a force sufficient to go to the aid of suffering Esopus; but he succeeded at last, and took command in person. **Oct. 10.** Upon his appearance the Indians fled, and heavy rains prevented his pursuing them. He obtained the co-operation of the Mohawks, and having concluded an armistice with the Esopus tribe, shortly succeeded in obtaining a few of the prisoners in exchange for powder. It was a hollow truce, as everybody understood. During the entire winter after, the air was full of alarms. In the spring there was fighting again, and the Indians were driven back into the country. They were awed and **1660.** made cautious, but not conquered. In July, however, through **July.** the influence of the Mohawks and other friendly tribes, they sued for peace, and an important treaty was concluded.

Staten Island was a dreary waste for long after the massacre of 1650. Baron Van der Capellen sent out fresh colonists, and offered many induce-

---

[1] This grant was confirmed, in 1686, by Governor Dongan, who invested the manor with power to hold Court Leet and Court Baron, besides many other temporal honors. Chambers was a man of much dignity and influence. He was justice of the peace at Esopus, and did notable service in the war with the Indians. He left no descendants in the direct line ; and his name has disappeared, save from the Book of Patents.

ments to encourage the settlers to return; but they were timid. Melyn removed to New Haven. Baron Van der Capellen died, and his heirs sold their entire interest to the West India Company. In 1661, some French Huguenots started a village a little to the south of the Narrows, which was fostered by the government with fatherly care. Dominie Drisius visited them every two months, to preach in French and to administer the sacrament.

A tract of land near the Fresh Water Pond, which had hitherto been used as a common for the pasturing of cattle, was fenced in about this time and more especially devoted to the city cows. A herdsman was employed, who went through the streets every morning blowing a horn, collected his drove, conducted it to the grassy fields, and brought it again through the city gates at nightfall.

As time wore on, the subject of education was discussed with increased earnestness. The schools were imperfect, and it was difficult to remedy the evil. The better class of citizens pressed for the establishment of a higher grade of schools. Now and then, some enterprising schoolmaster opened a private establishment without the consent of the government, and was immediately ordered to close it. Finally, the burgomasters and schepens wrote to the company, petitioning for a suitable master for a first-class Latin School. They said their sons had to be sent to New England for classical instruction. They agreed that the city should build a school-house, if the company would pay the teacher's salary. The company consented, and sent over Dr. Curtius, a physician of some note, who could practice medicine when not engaged with his pupils. At the end of two years, he resigned his position, on account of ill-health; and Dominie Ægidius Luyck, who was a private tutor in the governor's family, was employed in his stead. He soon had twenty pupils, including two from Virginia and two from Albany. The public school was continued, and two private schools for small children were permitted. One of these was taught by Jan Lubbertsen.

Dominie Henricus Selyns [1] arrived in the summer of 1660, to take the pastoral charge of the first church in Breuckelen. He was formally in-

---

[1] Prior to 1660, the only ministers of the Reformed Church in New Netherland were the Reverends Megapolensis and Drisius at New Amsterdam, Schaats at Beverwyck (Albany), Polhemus at Midwout (Flatbush), and Melins at New Amstel. The two first-named had written earnest letters to the Classis of Amsterdam, describing the state of religion in the colony, and entreating that good Dutch clergymen be speedily sent over. These letters were forwarded to the College of the XIX. It was difficult to persuade clergymen to brave the hardships of a newly settled country, but Dominie Selyns received and accepted a call to the Brooklyn church. Dominie Blom came over with him under appointment to preach at Esopus (now Kingston).

stalled on the 7th of September. The ceremony was specially interesting. Vice-Governor De Sille and Martin Cregier were deputed from the governor's council to introduce the minister to the congregation; after which, the call of the Classis and their certificate of examination, also a testimonial from the clergymen of Amsterdam, were read by the dominie himself to the assembly. He then preached his inaugural sermon. The church had twenty members, inclusive of one elder and two deacons. But they had as yet no church edifice, and the installation services took place in a barn.

The next season, Dominie Selyns married a young woman in New Amsterdam. She was very gifted and beautiful. Her portrait he has handed down to us in a charming little birthday ode. The governor, finding that the Breuckelen church could not raise the minister's salary without great embarrassment, offered to advance one hundred dollars per annum towards it, provided Dominie Selyns would preach at his farm on Sunday afternoons. He built a small chapel at his own expense on the site of the present church of St. Mark; and services were held in it on the Sabbath during the remainder of his life.

An event momentous in its consequences upon the future of the little city whose fortunes we are following occurred in the autumn of 1658. It was the death of Oliver Cromwell. The reins of power fell quietly into the hands of his eldest son, Richard. But not for long. The young man was as weak as his father was strong. Within a year, England had disposed of him, and was in imminent danger of sinking under the tyranny of a succession of small men raised up and pulled down by military caprice. General was opposed to general, and army to army. Finally, there was one grand union of sects and parties for the old laws of the nation against military despotism, and thus the way was paved for the return of Charles II. to the throne of his ancestors.

Medal of Oliver Cromwell.

CHAPTER XII.

1660 – 1664.

THE RESTORATION.

THE RESTORATION. — CHARLES II. — THE CONNECTICUT CHARTER. — SIR GEORGE DOWNING.
— GEORGE BAXTER AND JOHN SCOTT. — PROGRESS OF THE CITY. — THE ANTIQUARIAN
MAP. — THE QUAKERS. — DESTRUCTION OF ESOPUS. — THE INDIAN WAR OF 1663. —
GOVERNOR STUYVESANT IN BOSTON. — THOMAS BENEDICT. — THE EMBASSY TO CON-
NECTICUT. — STARTLING CONDITION OF AFFAIRS. — JOHN SCOTT. — HON. JEREMIAS VAN
RENSSELAER. — THE CONVENTION OF 1664. — MRS. DR. KIERSTEDE. — PLANNING OF
CHARLES II. AND HIS MINISTERS. — AN UNFRIENDLY EXPEDITION. — NEW AMSTERDAM
IN DANGER. — PREPARATIONS FOR A SIEGE. — WINTHROP'S INTERVIEW WITH STUYVE-
SANT. --- THE LETTER. — THE APPROACHING STORM. — THE CRISIS. — THE SURRENDER.
— NEW YORK. — CONSEQUENCES OF THE CONQUEST. — STUYVESANT AT THE HAGUE. —
THE STUYVESANT PEAR-TREE. — THE STUYVESANT FAMILY.

ON the 8th of May, 1660, Charles II. set out on his triumphal journey from Breda to London. He was magnificently entertained at the Hague, and parted with the States-General and other officers of the Dutch government with the most profuse pledges of friendship. On **1660.** the 29th of May, he entered England, welcomed and escorted by **May 29.** triumphal processions. A spirit of extravagant joy seemed to pervade the whole nation. London was in raptures. He remarked dryly, "that he could not see for the life of him why he had stayed away so long, when everybody was so charmed with him now that he was at length come back."

For a time, he was more loved by the English people than any of his predecessors had been. The calamities of his house and his own romantic adventures rendered him an object of tender interest to all classes. His return had delivered them from what had become an intolerable bondage. Entertainments were the order of the day. Presently drunkenness overran the kingdom and corrupted the morals of the people; and, through pretenses of religion and profane mockeries of true piety, grave disorders prevailed.

The king was a young man (then about thirty years of age), of pleasing address and elegant manners. He was cheerful in disposition, fond of wit and humor, and a great talker. He understood affairs, and was familiar with matters of government and religion. He was a good mathematician; his apprehension was quick, and his memory excellent. But he was insincere, had an ill opinion of mankind, detested business, and seemed to think the main object of life was to get all the pleasure possible out of every hour of the twenty-four. Like his father, he married a Catholic queen. His marriage festivities with Catharine of Braganza, of Portugal, were brilliantly celebrated at Hampton Court on the anniversary of his birth and restoration, May 29, 1662. But not like his father did he love his Catholic queen; on the contrary, he neglected and wounded her, and rendered her life one of abject misery.

The Convention Parliament which called him home revised the Navigation Act of 1651, and made it more obnoxious to the Dutch than ever. Presently, Lord Baltimore, through an agent at the Hague, ordered the West India Company to surrender the lands on the south side ^{July 24.} of Delaware Bay. The directors were confounded. They promptly declined to yield territory which they held under grant from the States-General, and appealed to the latter for protection. A demand that Lord Baltimore should be ordered to desist from his pretensions until the boundaries were properly established, and that the territory to the east of the Hudson River which the English had usurped should be restored and the inhabitants thereof required to conduct themselves as Dutch subjects, was at once forwarded to the Dutch minister at Whitehall, with directions to seize the first opportunity to lay it before the king.

American affairs were confided to the new " Council of Foreign Plantations," of which Clarendon was the head. Charles declined to trouble his mind with them. He laughed at Lord Baltimore and the Earl of Stirling when they argued their claims, and said " the subject was too heavy for a crowned head." He hoped he should be " spared the stupid task of looking after a batch of restless Western adventurers." But he was reminded of the prospective treaty of commerce and alliance with the Dutch nation, and of the necessity of settling the Delaware Bay controversy, and requiring the Dutch on Long Island to submit to English authority. He promised to give his attention at some more convenient season in the future. Meanwhile, John De Witt, the grand pensionary and real chief magistrate of the Netherlands, grew weary of the procrastination which prefaced the execution of the treaty, and instructed his minister to bring the matter to a close or to leave London. The document was accordingly signed, at Whitehall, September 14, 1662. At that very moment the " Council for Foreign Plantations " was maturing an order for the Virginia governor to cause the Navigation Act to be carefully observed, notwithstanding the well-known intercolonial treaty which **1662.** Stuyvesant had negotiated with Berkeley, and which had given great satisfaction to both provinces. A royal charter was issued, investing Connecticut with jurisdiction over the territory "bounded east by Narraganset Bay, north by the Massachusetts line, south by the sea, and west by the Pacific Ocean, including all the islands thereunto adjoining."

This remarkable charter, under which Connecticut thrived until 1818, **April.** and which was as liberal in its character as any since granted by our republican government, guaranteeing every privilege which freemen could desire, passed the great seal in April. It was obtained by John Winthrop the younger. This gentleman was an elegant and accomplished courtier, and an intimate personal friend of Lord Say, Lord Seal, the Earl of Manchester, and others of the royal household. He was the founder of New London, and the owner of Fisher's Island, where his family resided for some years in a mansion erected by himself. He was actively interested in all the concerns of the Connecticut Colony, and drafted the charter with his own pen, making the voyage to Europe in order to secure for it the sanction of the king. He wore into the royal presence an extraordinary ring which had been given to his grandmother by Charles I. This he took from his finger and presented to Charles II., who was greatly pleased, and tenderly regarded the treasure which had once belonged to a father most dear to him. The opportune moment was seized for presenting the petition from Connecticut, "which was received with uncommon grace and favor"; and Winthrop returned in triumph to America.

When Stuyvesant heard of this transaction, he declared, that, "it was an absolute breach and nullification of the boundary treaty of 1650, and that it would justify the States-General and West India Company in forcibly recovering all their ancient rights, which he had surrendered for the sake of peace." He wrote sharply to Winthrop, who retorted in the same spirit. The latter proceeded to notify the people of Westchester and Long Island to send delegates to the General Court of Connecticut. Stuyvesant appealed to his government for instructions.

Sir George Downing, Winthrop's cousin, was the English minister at the Hague. He was one of the earliest, ablest, and most unprincipled graduates (in 1642) of Harvard College in Massachusetts. Subsequently, he was Cromwell's minister to the Dutch Republic, where he openly insulted his exiled king; but, through consummate tact and management, he obtained forgiveness, and was taken into favor, at the Restoration. His American life rendered him familiar with the whole series of colonial quarrels. He knew every weak point in the Dutch title to New Netherland. He had no scruples of honor, was an ardent hater of the Dutch, and longed for a war which might aggrandize the new king and his satellites. He played a double part on all occasions. Once, after dining with De Witt, and promising with emphasis to use his best endeavor for the righting of the wrong of the "Connecticut encroachments," he went to his own apartments and sent the following private advice to Clarendon : "Wait three or four months, and then answer that the king will write into those parts to be informed of the truth of the matter of fact and right on both sides." He adroitly gathered such information about Dutch affairs as he could turn to English advantage, and all his letters to the lords in power were seasoned with subtle arguments in favor of the undoubted right of England to the whole of New Netherland, which he affirmed to be "the most admirably situated region in North America." [1]

New England never took kindly to the Restoration. Charles was acknowledged with reluctance and grim austerity. The fear that he would install bishops in the colonies induced the Puritans to crowd petition after petition upon the notice of the indolent monarch, and the Church party were quite as voluminous in their complaints of the arrogant and domineering Puritans. Samuel Maverick appeared before the king, to claim redress for many grievances which he had suffered in Massachusetts. He was a zealous Episcopalian. He was accompanied by George Baxter and John Scott, from Long Island, who were smarting from the lash of Governor Stuyvesant. The latter were both extensive landholders ; indeed, Scott claimed to have purchased nearly one third of the island. He had formerly been an officer in the army of Charles I., but for some political misdemeanor had been banished to New England. He was a brilliant logician, and the object of his appeal was to obtain a royal grant for the government of Long Island. The claim of Lord Stirling, however, was in the way. As for New Netherland, a statement was drawn up by Scott and Baxter, assisted by Maverick, to prove the king's title to it ; and it was emphatically asserted, that, "the Navigation Act could never be enforced in America while that rich territory existed as a Dutch plantation."

While Charles and his ministers listened with newly awakened interest, and revolved various plans by which New Netherland might be seized without an open rupture (for Charles disliked as much as some of

---

[1] *Col. Doc.*, II. 224 – 229, 302 – 507 ; III. 47, 48. *Aitzema*, V. 64, 65. *Lister's Clarendon*, III. 276 – 279. *Ogilby's America*, 169. *Brodhead*, II. 12 – 20. *Burnet's History of the Reign of Charles II.*, 136, 137. Sir George Downing was the son of Emanuel Downing, the brother-in-law of Governor John Winthrop. He was born in London, and accompanied his parents to America at the age of thirteen.

his lords desired hostilities), the West India Company and the States-General were mildly protesting against the "unpardonable usurpations," and asking the king to issue orders "for the immediate restoration of the towns and places in their American province which had been invaded by his subjects." At the same time, Stuyvesant, upon this side of the water, was working manfully to sustain his authority and promote the interests of his employers.

During the year 1661, the governor, as a sort of peace-offering, granted village charters to five Long Island towns. Among them was New Utrecht, founded by Jacques Cortelyou, who managed the estate of the deceased Mr. Werckhoven, for the heirs. This property, which embraced the land along the bay, from Gowanus to Coney Island, and which cost originally six coats, six kettles, six axes, six chisels, six small looking-glasses, twelve knives, and twelve combs, had been improved by Werckhoven until it offered special attractions, and the settlement had increased more rapidly than many others.

Between the years 1660 – 1664, the city of New Amsterdam grew in a ratio greatly exceeding that of any previous period. Business of all kinds was brisk. New settlers came and the old ones remained. New houses were built and manufactories established. Several breweries and brick kilns were in successful operation. The potteries of Long Island began to be esteemed equal to those of Delft. Lawyers were finding this lucrative field, and among the most prominent of these was Solomon La Chair. There has recently been exhumed, in the county clerk's office of the City Hall, a written volume of some three hundred pages, which is a careful minute of La Chair's legal proceedings, and a curious relic of that early period. He was a good English, as well as French and Dutch, scholar, and often acted as interpreter before the courts. He had at command a large law library, as evidenced by the numerous quotations in his written arguments. The magistrates of Gravesend employed him, in opposition to Mr. Opdyck, to prosecute their claim to Coney Island.

The accompanying map is the only plan of the city during the Dutch era which is known to exist. It is presumed that the English officers found it after the capture, and gave to it its present shape, adding the date, 1664. It fell into the British Museum, where it remained in obscurity until a few years since, when it was rescued by George H. Moore, the librarian of the New York Historical Society. The outlines of the streets, though apparently drawn without measurement, seem to follow the proper directions, and the general character of the buildings is given without any special attempt at accuracy. But the map itself is a curious memorial, worthy of tender preservation.

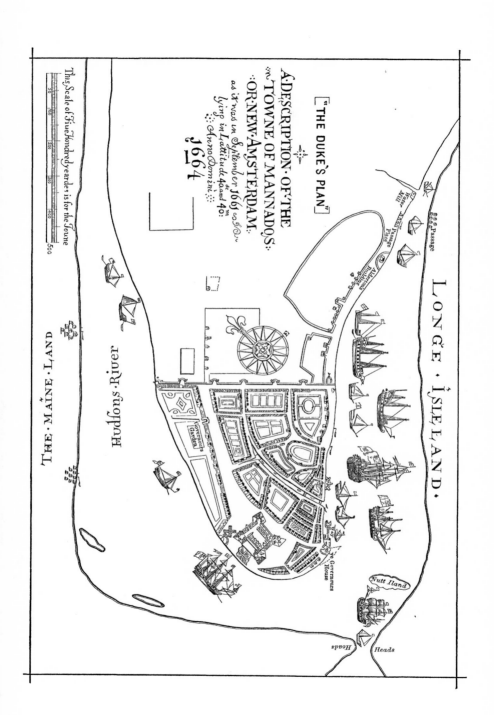

About the time it was issued (1661), a fresh effort was made to assure discontented Puritans and other Englishmen that they would be welcomed and cherished by the Dutch in New Netherland. The States-General caused a proclamation of "conditions and privileges" to be scattered through the British kingdom,[1] appended to which was a glowing description of the country "only six weeks' sail from Holland, . . . land fertile, . . . climate the best in the world; . . . seed may be committed to the soil without preparation, . . . timber and wild fruit of all descriptions, furs, game, fisheries," etc., etc. The picture was attractive. It enlisted attention in various quarters. Among the first who came to look at the country, with a view to investment and permanent settlement, was Hon. Robert Treat and Hon. Benjamin Fenn, as delegates from New Haven. That little republic was in high dudgeon at the prospect of annexation to Connecticut, and seriously contemplated flying from her impending fate. Stuyvesant courteously entertained the gentlemen at his own house, and took them in his barge to the shores of Newark Bay, where they spent some time in exploration, and finally negotiated terms by which the colony might remove bodily to that desirable locality. Events followed rapidly, however, which induced New Haven to throw herself into the arms of Connecticut for protection.

The invitation to "persons of tender conscience" to come freely into New Netherland, by no means referred to the Quakers. These were still heartlessly persecuted. A Quaker divine having stopped on Long Island, at the residence of Henry Townsend, the fact was soon known among the neighbors. The report reached Stuyvesant that a "conventicle" had actually been held in Mr. Townsend's parlor. Presently, soldiers appeared and arrested Mr. Townsend and all who attended the meeting, and a strong guard was placed over the infected district. Quaker meetings were held secretly in Flushing, the headquarters of the sect being at the house of John Bowne, who was accused and arrested, and, for refusal to pay his fine, shipped to Holland, as a terror to evil-doers. John Tilton and his wife Goodie Tilton, of Gravesend, persisted in their heresies, and were peremptorily ordered to quit the province. These rigorous measures were followed by a proclamation from the governor, forbidding the exercise of any but the Reformed religion "in houses, barns, ships, yachts, woods, or fields," under heavy penalties. The Amsterdam Chamber wrote to Stuyvesant shortly after, that, although it was their preference that "sectarians" should not be found in the province, yet it was not well to check population. "You had better let every one remain free," they said, "as long as he is modest, moderate, his political conduct

[1] *O'Callaghan*, II. 443 – 452.

irreproachable, and he does not offend others or oppose the government."

Indian disturbances at the North kept Stuyvesant almost constantly on the wing, passing to and from Albany. In 1662, he met delegates from New England at Fort Orange, and an " accommodation " was effected with the Mohawks and Oneidas by which they liberated a few French and English captives. But Canada was threatened, and the danger was only stayed, not averted.

In 1663, a severe shock of earthquake was felt in New Amsterdam, all along the Hudson River, in Connecticut, Massachusetts, Acadia, **1663.** and Canada. It was followed by a terrible freshet, which destoyed the harvests in the neighborhood of Fort Orange, and inundated many other portions of the country. Upon the heels of this calamity, the small-pox made its appearance and spread with fearful rapidity.[1] The good Puritans of New England declared, that, " the hand of God had gone out against the people of New Netherland by pestilential infections."

In the midst of the panic in New Amsterdam, news came which caused the cheek to blanch and the blood to stand still. A horri- **June 7.** ble massacre had occurred at Esopus. On the morning of June 7, just after the men had gone to their work in the fields, a large number of Indians sauntered carelessly into the village and tried to sell some beans. Fifteen minutes later, a horseman rode at full speed down the road, shouting that the Indians were setting fire to the houses. Instantly the war-whoop was raised, shots were heard in every direction, and battle-axes and tomahawks flashed in the sunlight. Women and children were butchered in the most shocking manner. Many were left wounded and dying, and forty-five were carried into captivity. The men rallied with desperate energy, and, though poorly armed, succeeded eventually in driving the savages into the woods. But what a sight was there ! Twelve houses in the old, and every house in the new, village were mere heaps of smouldering rubbish; husbands were standing over murdered wives ; and fathers were trying to identify the bodies of children who had been burned alive.

Stuyvesant, having hastily called for volunteers, sent to the relief of the sufferers an armed force, commanded by Martin Cregier and Pieter Van Couwenhoven. They pursued the savages for a long distance through the wilderness, finding a guide in the person of Mrs. Dr. Van Imbroeck, the daughter of Dr. La Montagne, who had been one of the captives on the day of the massacre, but who had escaped from her

---

[1] About one thousand Indians died of small-pox, among the Mohawks alone.

captors and succeeded in finding her way back to the settlement. She conducted the party to the Indian castle where she last saw the warriors; but it was vacant. After using it as a shelter from a heavy rain-storm, the pursuers went on, through dense forests, over high hills, and across deep rivers, until they overtook the flying foe, and engaged them in a severe battle which resulted in the recovery of twenty-three prisoners. But the war did not end here. Other expeditions were planned and executed, and ancient treaties were renewed with the neighboring tribes. Still there was no peace. Out-settlers hurried to the forts and held regular watch, day and night; and parties of soldiers scoured the woods all along the Hudson from Rensselaerswick to Manhattan. "Nothing is talked of," said Jeremias Van Rensselaer, in one of his letters, "but the Indians and the war." Late in the autumn, an "armistice" was agreed upon by the Esopus tribes, and all except three of the ^{Oct. 9.} prisoners were restored to their friends.

Lord Baltimore, in the mean time, had resorted to various methods to obtain control of the South River territory. His son, Charles Calvert, came over and visited the region, with a suite of twenty-seven persons, and was entertained, during his stay on the South River, by William Beekman, who was governor of the Dutch colony. The latter tried to discuss the matter of boundaries, but the young nobleman maintained an attitude of non-committal, and to all arguments replied that he would communicate with Lord Baltimore. At last, a transfer was made by the West India Company of all their interests on the South ^{Dec. 3.} River to the city of Amsterdam. De Hinoyossa was appointed governor by the burgomasters and schepens; and he soon arrived, accompanied by one hundred colonists. Beekman was made sheriff at Esopus, in which office he continued until the close of Lovelace's administration, when he returned to New York.

The West India Company was at this time laboring under great pecuniary depression. Its outlay for the province of New Netherland, over and above its receipts, exceeded ten tons of gold; and the province itself was threatened, from the North and the South, by a foreign power. Seeing no hope of obtaining in Europe a settlement of the limits between New Netherland and New England, the directors wrote to Stuyvesant, to see what arrangement he could effect in America. He accordingly made a journey to Boston, to meet the commissioners who had agreed to ^{Sept. 6.} the treaty of 1650. He asked them if they considered the agreement still in force. They were evasive. They talked about the king's rights and the Connecticut charter. They suggested that the whole controversy should undergo a hearing the next year, after advices had been received from

England.   The Connecticut delegates were triumphant, having obtained delay.   Winthrop was able to predict with tolerable accuracy the final action of the English government, while Stuyvesant was perplexed by the extraordinary events which were taking place about him.   He proposed a continuation of trade, and an alliance offensive and defensive against the savages, which was submitted to the General Courts Sept. 23. of Massachusetts and Connecticut.   He returned to New Amsterdam, much chagrined at the meager result of his mission.   On his arrival, he found Long Island in a great ferment.   The messenger who had attempted to read to the people of Gravesend an announcement that " they were no longer under the Dutch government, but under that of Connecticut," had been arrested and conveyed to the city.   The next night, the sheriff's house had been ransacked by a mob of about one hundred and fifty men ; he had escaped in the darkness to the house of his Sept. 26. son-in-law and from there to New Amsterdam, where he had been commended for his prompt action by the administration.

Sept. 29.   Three days later, Sergeant Hubbard was busy getting signatures to a petition to the General Court at Hartford, in which, after a setting forth of the inconveniences " that doe much trouble us," is the following passage :

" As we ar alruddy according to our best information under the scurts of your patten, so you would be pleased to cast over us the scurts of your government and protecktion."

This was signed by Robert Coe, John Strickland, Zachariah Walker, Thomas Benedict, Thomas Benedict, Jr., and twenty-one others.[1]   Thomas Benedict[2] was one of the bearers of the document to Hartford.   He was well known and highly esteemed by Winthrop and his council ; indeed, he was considered the main support of the cause of Connecticut on Long

---

[1] *Towns and Lands*, I. 18, in the Secretary of State's office, Hartford.   *O'Callaghan*, II. 486.   *Benedict Genealogy*, 9 – 12.

[2] Thomas Benedict was from Nottinghamshire, England.   He came to New England in 1638, when only twenty-one years of age.   He married a young Englishwoman who came over in the same vessel with him.   He soon sought the smiling regions of Long Island, and took up his abode at Jamaica.   He became a man of distinction among the men of the period.   He was a magistrate, the officer of a little train band in the neighborhood, a pillar in the church, the arbitrator of differences between the settlers and the Indians, one of the legislative body to create and codify the system of law on Long Island after its conquest from the Dutch, and, subsequently, a member of the Colonial Assembly.   He removed to Norwalk, Connecticut, in 1665, and took an active and prominent part in the affairs of that ancient town.   He died at the latter place in 1689.   He was the ancestor of a large and influential family, about whom, in every generation since, all sorts of offices in church and state have clustered, and have been honorably and usefully filled.   Among the eminent representatives of the family in New York, at the present day, is the Hon. Erastus C. Benedict.

Island. He urged the adoption of measures for the reduction of the Dutch towns.

Stuyvesant sent commissioners at once to Connecticut, to enter, if possible, into some boundary accommodation. The gentlemen chosen for this mission were Secretary Van Ruyven, Burgomaster Oloff S. Van Cortlandt, and John Lawrence. Money was wanted. Indeed, the pressing necessities of the government induced the governor to draw upon the company for four thousand guilders; but no one could be found willing to cash the draft until he pledged four of the brass guns of the fort as security. The commissioners went in a small vessel to Milford, and thence on horseback to Hartford. They called upon Winthrop, who was polite, but not communicative. They made known their errand to the General Court, which appointed a committee to confer with them. They stated their case. The committee sheltered themselves behind the royal patent, and said they *knew of no New Netherland province!* The gentlemen from New Netherland offered to show the charter of the West India Company. The committee said that this was only a charter of commerce, and that its limits were conditional. The retort was, that the right to the territory lay with the States-General, on the ground of discovery, purchase from the Indians, possession, etc. The committee denied that right, and said that it was their duty to make the king's grant known. " How then are we to regard the treaty of 1650 ? " was asked. " As of no force whatever," was the reply.

The commissioners were nonplussed. They began to suspect a " wheel within a wheel "; that the powers beyond the seas were working mischief in some mysterious way; that bloodshed was lurking at their very doors. To prevent the latter, they resolved to propose that, if Connecticut would refrain from assuming any jurisdiction over the English settlements on Long Island until the king and the States-General should agree on a boundary line, New Netherland would abandon all control over Westchester. The Hartford committee declined to agree to this; but, after a long and excited debate, they offered to refrain for twelve months from exercising authority over the specified Long Island towns, provided the Dutch did not attempt any coercive power over them; but Westchester and Stamford must remain under Connecticut.

The commissioners, upon their return, found Stuyvesant seriously alarmed. " What shall I do ? " he asked in despair. " Our treasury is exhausted, Long Island in revolt, and the Esopus war not ended ! " Seventy or eighty men had actually been in arms, marching from village to village on Long Island, in some instances changing the names of the places, and threatening the Dutch with extermination. He did not hesitate, but sent

13

Vice-Governor De Sille, with a posse of soldiers, to check the rebellion, and wrote to Winthrop, accepting the proposition in regard to a mutual forbearance of jurisdiction for twelve months. Shortly after, he heard that twenty New-Englanders had gone to the Raritan River, to buy land of the Indians. He sent Martin Cregier, Govert Loockermans, and Jacques Cortelyou, with a few soldiers, in hot haste, to warn the sachems and prevent the sale.

"You are a band of traitors, and you act against the government of the state," said Loockermans, with dignity.

"Your government!" was the contemptuous response, "the king's patent is of quite another cast."

On the 2d of November, a convention was summoned which adopted a stern remonstrance, to be forwarded to Holland. It charged the responsibility of the disastrous condition of the province upon the West India Company, who seemed to be losing sight altogether of their own best interests. "Why do you not settle the boundary question?" asked Stuyvesant, in a private letter to the directors. "Why is not your original charter solemnly confirmed by a public act of the States-General under their great seal? Why are we left to fight your battles without any legal papers or patents by which we can respond to English impertinence?"

In December, Scott returned to America, bearing royal letters, recommending him to the New England governments. Connecticut gave him the powers of a magistrate over Long Island, and Winthrop administered the oath of office. He proceeded to his field, and immediately commenced the missionary work of "freeing those who had been enslaved by the cruel and rapacious Dutch." He announced that Long Island was about to be given by the king to his brother the Duke of York, henceforth to be an independent government, and that, until then, he was to act as President. He raised a force of one hundred and seventy men, to assist in the reduction of the Dutch villages. He proceeded from place to place, haranguing the people, and making unsuccessful efforts to establish his authority. In Breuckelen, he was jeered and insulted. In a fit of anger, he struck Martin Cregier's son, a bright boy of thirteen years, over the head with his whip, for refusing to take off his hat to the royal flag.

Stuyvesant sent Van Ruyven, Van Cortlandt, and Cregier to Jamaica to treat with Scott, and they were coolly informed that "the Duke of York was soon to possess himself of the whole of New Netherland"! Upon their return, measures for defense were at once discussed. The city offered to appropriate its revenues towards the expense, and to

Nov. 2.

1664.

Jan. 11.

Jan. 14.

raise a loan besides. The State government would do what it could, but it was drifting into bankruptcy.

The confusion on Long Island continued, and, at last, Stuyvesant went

Portrait of Hon. Jeremias Van Rensselaer.

over to hold a personal interview with Scott. The latter, though a man of much boldness, possessed little principle. He had been an officer in the army of Charles I., but was arrested for cut-ting the girths of some of the Parliamentary horses, and was not only fined £500, but also banished to New England. Stuyvesant was at-tended by Van Cortlandt, John Lawrence, Jacob Backer, and a military escort. Scott was surrounded by delegates from some of the English

March 3.

towns, among whom were Daniel Denton, John Underhill, and Adam Mott. The result was only a conditional arrangement, by which the principal English towns on Long Island were to remain under the king without molestation for twelve months, to afford opportunity for settlement in Europe.

By request of the burgomasters and schepens of New Amsterdam, a *Landtdag*, or *Diet*, was called, which assembled in the City Hall April 10. on the 10th of April, for the purpose of taking into consideration the precarious condition of the province. The delegates from New Amsterdam were Burgomaster Cornelis Steenwyck and Schepen Jacob Backer; from Rensselaerswick, Director Jeremias Van Rensselaer and Attorney Van Schelluyne; from Fort Orange, Jan Verbeck and Gerrit Van Slechtenhorst; from Breuckelen, William Bredenbent and Albert Cornelis Wantenaar; from Flatbush, Jan Strycker and William Guilliams; from Esopus, Thomas Chambers and Dr. Van Imbroeck; from Flatlands, Elbert Elbertsen and Coert Stevensen; from New Utrecht, David Jochemsen and Cornelis Beekman; from Boswyck, Jan Van Cleef and Guisbert Teunissen; from New Haerlem, Daniel Terneur and Johannes Verveeler; from Bergen, Englebert Steenhuysen and Herman Smeeman; from Staten Island, David De Marest and Pierre Billou.

The first question which agitated this august assemblage was that of the presidency. New Amsterdam claimed the honor, as the capital; Rensselaerswick, as the oldest colony. The right of the latter was finally admitted, and Hon. Jeremias Van Rensselaer took the chair. The convention next demanded protection of the government against both barbarian and civilized foes; and, if such protection could not be April 11. afforded, it desired to be informed "to whom the people should address themselves." Stuyvesant answered, with dignity and subtle sarcasm, that he had done all and more than his means permitted, and that the object of the convention was to consult, and not to dispute, as to the best

Autograph of Jeremias Van Rensselaer.

method of raising men and money to meet the emergency. The delegates apologized, saying, they wished only to know whether their application should be addressed to the West India Company or the States-General. Stuyvesant accepted the explanation, and proceeded to define the business before the gentlemen assembled. He said New Netherland had never contributed to her own support or defense. He proposed a tax on mills and cattle, and the enrollment of every sixth man in the province on the militia. To this the convention would not assent, but prepared an appeal to the company for the necessary aid.

Before it was sent, a vessel arrived, bringing letters from Europe. Stuyvesant was informed that soldiers were on the way from Holland; and he was instructed to exterminate the Esopus Indians, and to check the arrogance of the English on Long Island. The States-General had actually issued under their great seal a patent confirming the charter of the West India Company, — an important movement, had it come a little earlier. The convention, which had adjourned for a week, came together once more. But it was not in favor of an attempt to re- April 22. duce the English towns. " Let me assure you," said Cornelis Beekman, " that the English rebels are as six to one, and that it would be impossible to subdue them. Connecticut would come to their help and massacre us all."

As for the Indians, they were apparently humbled. Three sachems were, at that moment, in New Amsterdam suing for peace. It was wise to treat with them. The result was a general treaty, concluded in the Council Chamber on the 15th of May. There were present a May 15. large number of chiefs; Governor Stuyvesant, in full robes of state, with Vice-Governor De Sille at his right hand; Abraham Wilmerdoncx, Jr., of the West India Company; Thomas Chambers, of Esopus; and, of the city magistrates, Cornelis Steenwyck, Paulus Van der Grist, Martin Cregier, Govert Loockermans, Jacob Backer, and Pieter Van Couwenhoven. Sarah, the wife of Dr. Hans Kiersted, acted as interpreter. She was the daughter of the celebrated Anetje Jans Bogardus, and was a woman of unusual nerve and strength of character. On many previous occasions, she had filled the office of interpreter with great satisfaction to the sachems, one of whom made her a present of a large tract of land, near the Hackinsack River.[1]

While the people of New Amsterdam were thus engaged, Connecticut had reached across the Sound and spoiled the ambitious projects of President Scott, who was carried to Hartford and imprisoned. Shortly after, when Stuyvesant's messengers went through the Long Island towns

---

[1] After the death of Mrs. Sarah Kiersted, Dr. Kiersted married Jannetje Loockermans, who died about 1710. Dr. Kiersted left five children, whose descendants are numerous and influential at the present day.

with mandatory letters from the States-General, they were forbidden to read them, and the documents were seized and sent to Hartford. Winthrop questioned their authenticity. At all events, he was fortified by the king's patent. About the same time, he authorized Thomas Pell to trade with the Indians for all the land between Westchester and the North River, including Spuyten Duyvel Creek, which the Dutch had bought and paid for, fifteen years before.

Early in June, news came to the city that Winthrop was at Gravesend, and Stuyvesant, accompanied by Secretary Van Ruyven and several other prominent gentlemen, went over to meet him. Winthrop was very courtly and cold, and insisted that the English title was indisputable ; so that the interview was without any favorable results.

Meanwhile, in spite of treaties and at the risk of war, Charles and his ministers had resolved to seize New Netherland. The first important step was to purchase Lord Stirling's interest in Long Island, for which Clarendon agreed to pay three thousand five hundred pounds, in behalf of his son-in-law, James, Duke of York. He then hastened to affix the great seal to a patent, by which the king granted to the Duke of York "the territory comprehending Long Island and the islands in the neighborhood, and all the lands and rivers from the west side of the Connecticut River to the east side of Delaware Bay." This included the whole of New Netherland, and was in utter disregard of the Connecticut Charter.

An expedition against the Dutch in America was at once ordered, but kept a profound secret, lest the States-General should send a squadron to aid their unprotected subjects. The Duke of York, who had been appointed Lord High Admiral of the British dominions, was to manage the enterprise. He borrowed of the king four war-vessels, on which he embarked four hundred and fifty well-trained soldiers, under the command of Colonel Richard Nicolls, the groom of his bedchamber, who was also commissioned as governor of the yet unpossessed territory. Among the commissioned officers serving under Nicolls, were Matthias Nicolls, Daniel Brodhead, Robert Needham, Harry Norwood, and Sylvester Salisbury, some of whom were accompanied by their families.[1] A commission, consisting of Colonel Nicolls, Sir Robert Carr, Sir George Cartwright, and Samuel Maverick, were empowered to attend to the general welfare of the colonies, settle boundaries, etc. The fleet sailed from Portsmouth about the middle of May.[2]

---

[1] Matthias Nicolls settled on Long Island ; Daniel Brodhead and Sylvester Salisbury, in Ulster County, New York. Their descendants are very numerous, and rank among the best families in this country.

[2] *Col. Doc.*, II. 243 – 501 ; III. 66. *Mass. H. S. Coll.*, XXXVI. 527. *Pepys*, IV. 353. *Clarke's James II.*, I. 400. *Valentine's Manual* 1860, 592. *Smith*, I. 16. *Wood*, 144. *Brodhead*, II. 21.

The first intimation New Amsterdam received of these hostile designs was through Richard Lord, of Lyme, a merchant, who was sending vessels to both Boston and New Amsterdam. He heard of it in the former place and communicated the fact to Thomas Willett, with whom he was doing business. Willett hastened to Stuyvesant, and, within an hour, the burgomasters and schepens were in close council with the brave old soldier, devising plans for fortifying the city. Some vessels on the point of sailing for Curaçoa were countermanded, and agents were sent hurriedly to New Haven to buy provisions. Men were stationed at Westchester and Milford, to act the part of spies, and announce the approach of the enemy, who were expected by way of the Sound. A loan of money was obtained from Jeremias Van Rensselaer, and a quantity of powder was secured from New Amstel. At this critical moment, when every hour was more precious than gold, a dispatch from the Amsterdam Chamber to Stuyvesant declared that no danger from England need be apprehended, — that the king had only sent some frigates to introduce Episcopacy into New England.

Confidence was thus restored, and the Curaçoa vessels were permitted to depart. Mischievous quarrels among the Indians to the North induced Stuyvesant to take a trip to Fort Orange. He had ^{Aug. 6.} reached his destination and entered upon the work of reconciling the savages, when an express followed him to say that the English squadron was actually on the way from Boston to New Amsterdam. He hurried home, arriving only three days before the English banners floated over the bay, just below the Narrows. One of his first acts was to set all his own negro slaves and hired workmen at his farm thrashing grain night and day, and carting it to the fort. Three weeks had ^{Aug. 29.} been lost in false security ; the city, alas ! was ill prepared to stand a siege. The fort, and the wall at Wall Street, however strong a defense against the Indians, would avail positively nothing against a civilized foe ; and there was the exposure on two rivers ! Four hundred men were all that could be mustered, to bear arms. Six hundred pounds was the maximum of powder in the fort. Then, the English inhabitants were numerous and would aid the king's forces ; and the latter, before casting anchor, had cut off all communication between the city and Long Island, and had scattered proclamations through the country, promising safe and undisturbed possession of property to all who would quietly submit to the government of England.

Stuyvesant regarded the situation with dismay. The English were in full possession of the harbor. He hastily called in the few soldiers from Esopus and other outposts, and, wishing to ascertain the condition of

14

affairs on Long Island, sent to the English commander four commissioners, representing the council and the city, with a letter inquiring the object
of his coming, and why he remained so long in the harbor without giving
due notice. Nicolls replied, that he had come to reduce the country to
the obedience of the king of England, whose commission he displayed;
and that he would send a letter to the governor on the following day.

Aug. 30. Saturday morning, Sir George Cartwright and three other gentlemen came to the city, and were received with a formal salute from
the guns of the Battery. The interview was ceremonious in the extreme.
They bore from Nicolls to Stuyvesant a formal summons to surrender the
province of New Netherland, with all its towns, forts, etc., at the same
time promising to confirm his estate, life, and liberty to every man who
should submit without opposition to the king's authority.

Nicolls having omitted to sign this summons, it was returned to the
delegates, and time thereby gained. Stuyvesant and his council consulted with the city magistrates. Stuyvesant was determined upon defending his post to the last, and withheld the paper which contained the
terms of surrender, lest it should influence the people to insist upon
capitulation. The city magistrates were strongly in favor of non-resist-
ance, but thought it well to bring the city into as fair a state of defense
as possible, in order to obtain "good terms and conditions." Men worked
all day Sunday on the fortifications, and the officers of the government
were in close council for several hours. On Monday morning, a
Sept. 1. meeting of the citizens was called at the City Hall, and the burgomasters stated publicly that they had been denied a copy of the summons which Nicolls had sent to Stuyvesant, but explained the terms of
surrender. A loud clamor at once arose for the paper itself. Stuyvesant
came to the City Hall and attempted to explain the impossibility of
surrender under any circumstances, the extreme displeasure it would
occasion in Holland, the painful responsibility that was resting upon him,
etc., etc., but, in the end, produced the desired document.

The work of preparation continued through the day; and anxiety and
excitement were everywhere apparent. On Tuesday morning,
Sept. 2. Governor Winthrop, who had joined the fleet, accompanied by his
son Fitz John, Ex-Governor Willys, Thomas Willett, and two Boston gentlemen, visited the city in a row-boat, under a flag of truce. As they
landed at the wharf, a salute was fired, and they were conducted to the
nearest public house. Stuyvesant met them with stately politeness.
Winthrop's mission was to present a carefully written letter from Nicolls
and to use his own utmost endeavor to persuade the Dutch governor into
a peaceful submission. There were many courtly speeches and replies

during the interview, but Stuyvesant was iron-hearted and declined Winthrop's urbane advice. On taking leave, Winthrop handed the following letter, addressed to himself, to Stuyvesant, who read it aloud to the gentlemen of his council and the burgomasters present;

" MR. WINTHROP : As to those particulars you spoke to me, I do assure you that if the Manhadoes be delivered up to his Majesty, I shall not hinder, but any people from the Netherlands may freely come and plant there, or thereabouts ; and such vessels of their owne country may freely come thither, and any of them may as freely returne home, in vessels of their owne country, and this, and much more, is contained in the privilege of his Majesty's English subjects ; and thus much you may, by what means you please, assure the governor from, Sir, Your very affectionate servant,

" RICHARD NICOLLS."

The burgomasters asked permission to read this letter to the citizens. Stuyvesant pronounced such a course injudicious and refused his consent. Van Cortlandt declared that all which concerned the public welfare ought to be made public. High words ensued on both sides, and finally Stuyvesant in a fit of passionate indignation tore the letter in pieces. Steenwyck, in angry tones, condemned the destruction of a paper of so much consequence, and, with the other magistrates, quitted the fort. A crowd had collected about the City Hall, to learn how matters stood. The news was received with lowering brows. Suddenly the work on the palisades stopped, and three of the principal citizens — not belonging to the government — appeared before the governor and council and peremptorily demanded a copy of the letter. They were not disposed to parley. The fragments were shown to them ; but no reasoning would satisfy them. They threatened — covertly at first, and then openly. Stuyvesant hurried to the City Hall and tried in vain to quiet the raving multitude. " It would be as idle to attempt to defend the city against so many as to gape before an oven," was the general cry. Some cursed the governor; others cursed the company ; but all united in a demand for the letter. He argued that it did not concern the commonalty, but only the officers of the government. " The letter ! The letter !" was the only reply. Retiring from this outburst of popular fury, he returned to the fort, and Nicholas Bayard, his private secretary, having gathered the scattered scraps, made a copy of the mutilated document, which was given to the burgomasters.

Meanwhile, Stuyvesant had been preparing an answer to the summons of Nicolls. It was an overwhelming argument, tracing the history of New Netherland through all its vicissitudes, and pointing out the absolute unsoundness of the English claim. He pictured in earnest language the consequences of any violation of the articles of peace so solemnly agreed upon by Charles and the States-General, and warned the English commander against aggression. He sent four of his ablest advisers — two from his council and two from the city — to convey the document to Colonel Nicolls, and to " argue the matter " with him.

Nicolls declined discussion. He said the question of right did not concern him. He must and would take possession of the place. If the reasonable terms he offered were not accepted, he should proceed to attack.

" On Thursday, I shall speak with you at the Manhattans," he said, with dignity.

" Friends will be welcome, if they come in a friendly manner," replied one of the delegates.

" I shall come with my ships and soldiers, and he will be a bold messenger indeed who will dare to come on board and solicit terms," was his rejoinder.

" What, then, is to be done ? " was asked.

" Hoist the white flag of peace at the fort, and I may take something into consideration."

The delegates returned sadly to New Amsterdam. Nicolls, seeing that Stuyvesant was not disposed to surrender, made preliminary arrangements for storming the city. He called the people of Long Island together at Gravesend, and published the king's patent to the Duke of York, and his own commission, in their presence. Winthrop announced, on behalf of Connecticut, that, as the king's pleasure was now fully signified, the jurisdiction which that colony had claimed and exercised over Long Island " ceased and became null." Nicolls promised to confirm all the civil officers who had been appointed by Connecticut, — which gave immense satisfaction. Volunteers, to swell his army, came from all parts of the island. Prospects of plunder seem to have entered largely into their calculations. The citizens of New Amsterdam regarded them as their deadly enemies ; and well they might, at this juncture, for threats and curses filled the air, and rovers talked openly of " where the young women lived who wore chains of gold."

The volunteers were encamped just below Breuckelen, to be ready to storm the city by land. Nicolls sent a few of his troops to join them. It was rumored that six hundred Northern savages and one hundred and fifty Frenchmen had re-enforced the English forces against the Dutch. On the morning of September 5th, Nicolls came up under full sail, and anchored between the fort and Governor's Island.

Sept. 5.

"It is madness," said Domine Megapolensis, laying his hand lovingly upon the Governor's shoulder——"what will our twenty guns do in the face of the sixty-two which are pointed towards us on yonder frigates? Pray, do not be the first to shed blood!" *Page* 218

The crisis had come. New Amsterdam, with its population of fifteen hundred souls, was "encircled round about," without any means of deliverance. "It is a matter of desperation rather than soldiership to attempt to hold the fort," said Vice-Governor De Sille.

Stuyvesant stood in one of the angles of the fort, near where the gunner held a burning match, awaiting the order to fire at the approaching vessels. He had been expostulated with by one and another, who saw only infatuation and ruin in resisting a foe with such extraordinary advantage in point of numbers; but to all he had answered, with emphasis, "I must act in obedience to orders." "It is madness," said Dominie Megapolensis, laying his hand lovingly upon the governor's shoulder. "Do you not see that there is no help for us either to the north or to the south, to the east or to the west? What will our twenty guns do in the face of the sixty-two which are pointed towards us on yonder frigates? Pray, do not be the first to shed blood!"

Just then, a paper was brought to Stuyvesant signed by ninety-three of the principal citizens, including the burgomasters and schepens, and his own son, Balthazar, urging with manly arguments that he would not doom the city to ashes and spill innocent blood, as it was evident the sacrifice could avail nothing in the end. He read the appeal with white lips, and with unspeakable sorrow expressed in every feature. His only remark was, "I had rather be carried to my grave." Five minutes later, the white flag waved above the fort.

Arrangements were immediately made for a meeting, to agree upon articles of capitulation. The time was eight o'clock, on Saturday morning; the place, Stuyvesant's country-house at the farm. Colonel Nicolls appointed his two colleagues, Sir Robert Carr and Sir $^{\text{Sept. 6.}}$ George Carteret, and the New England gentlemen, Governor Winthrop and Ex-Governor Willys of Connecticut, and John Pinchon and Thomas Clarke of Boston, as his commissioners. Stuyvesant selected Hon. John De Decker, Hon. Nicholas Varlett, and Dominie Megapolensis from his council, to represent the province, and Cornelis Steenwyck, Oloff S. Van Cortlandt, and Jacques Cousseau, to represent the city. The proclamation and the reiterated promises of Nicolls formed the basis of the twenty-four articles which were carefully and intelligently discussed on that momentous occasion. The Dutch citizens were guaranteed security in their property, customs, conscience, and religion. Intercourse with Holland was to continue as before the coming of the English. Public buildings and public records were to be respected, and all civil officers were to remain in power until the customary time for a new election. The articles of capitulation were to be ratified by Nicolls and delivered to Stuyvesant by eight o'clock on Monday morning, at the "old mill," on the shore of the East River, near the foot of Roosevelt Street, at the outlet of the brook which ran from the Fresh Water Pond. Within two hours afterward, the fort was to be vacated, the military marching out with all the honors of war.

On Sunday afternoon, after the second sermon, the conciliatory terms by which New Amsterdam was surrendered — terms, perhaps, the most favorable ever granted by a conqueror — were explained to the anxious community. On Monday morning, Stuyvesant and his council affixed their names to the articles of capitulation, and exchanged them with Nicolls. All things being ready, the garrison marched out of the fort, carrying their arms, with drums beating and colors flying, and embarked on a vessel about to set sail for Holland. Colonel Nicolls and Sir Robert Carr formed their companies into six columns, and entered the town as the Dutch garrison departed. The city magistrates were assembled in the council chamber, and with much ceremony proclaimed Nicolls governor of the province. The English flag was raised over the fort, which was now to be called Fort James, and New Amsterdam was henceforth to be known as New York.

Sept. 7.

Sept. 8.

The conquest of Long Island and New Amsterdam has been widely stigmatized as an act of peculiar national baseness. It was matured in secret and accomplished with deliberate deceit towards a friendly government. It provoked a war which disgraced the reign of Charles II.; a war in which Dutch fleets not only swept the Channel, but entered the Thames, burned the warehouses and dock-yards at Chatham, and maddened and terrified the citizens of London with the roar of their cannon. And yet, unjustifiable as it surely was for an undeclared enemy to sneak into a remote harbor and treacherously seize a province, the temptation furnished by the circumstances of the case may perhaps be cited as a sort of palliation of the deed. The West India Company and the States-General had always undervalued New Netherland; it was their neglect of it which had been the most potent stimulus to English ambition; and finally, the event itself could not have been avoided by the Dutch government unless all their previous policy had been reversed and their title planted upon a more tenable basis.

Stuyvesant was mortified and humiliated beyond expression. His solitary heroism, and his loyalty, unshaken to the last, did not protect him from the severe censure of his superiors. He was summoned to Holland to render an account of his administration, and detained there many months. The soulless corporation was dying by inches. The loss of its province had been its death-blow. But it had sufficient vitality left to make a desperate effort to shift the responsibility of its misfortunes upon the head of its faithful servant, notwithstanding abundant proof that, year after year, and by almost every ship which crossed the ocean, he had warned the self-sufficient company of the impossibility of holding the province against any hostile attack without the means to improve its weak and dangerous condition. The peace of Breda put an end to the controversy, and Stuyvesant, whose property interests were all in New York, returned and took up his abode here as a private citizen. While at the Hague, he labored incessantly to secure from the king the ratification of the sixth article in his treaty with Nicolls, which granted free trade with Holland in Dutch vessels. He wrote to Charles, that New York could scarcely be relieved by England during the present season, and that what he asked for would prevent the Indians from diverting their traffic to Canada, as well as enable the Dutch inhabitants to follow their prosperous vocations. His logic was convincing, and Charles authorized the Duke of York to grant " temporary permission for seven years, with three ships only."

Stuyvesant brought with him, on his return voyage to New York, a pear-tree, which he planted in his garden. It survived the storms of two hundred winters. As the city grew, and one old landmark after another disappeared, the solitary pear-tree long continued to put out its blossoms every spring and to bend under the weight of its fruit every summer. It stood for many years, surrounded by an iron fence, on the corner of East 13th Street and 3d Avenue; and when, at last, it fell, many a loyal mourner strove to obtain a fragment of its broken body to preserve in remembrance of by-gone times. The railing which enclosed it may still be seen,

Stuyvesant's Pear-Tree.

and within it a vigorous young offshoot of the parent tree, putting forth its leaves and branches with an appearance of family pride, and a good degree of the family energy.

The life of Governor Stuyvesant was one long romantic history, as well as an instructive lesson. He had marvelous intellectual power, great subtlety of discernment, and yet a peculiar turn of mind which rendered him less successful in politics than were many who had not half his ability. He gave evidence of extensive reading; a fact in itself remarkable, when we take into consideration the age in which he lived, and the difficulty, at that time, of obtaining books in this country. He was a courtly man, from whom the freshness of youth had quite

In this Vault lies buried
PETRUS STUYVESANT,
late Captain-General and Governor in Chief of Amsterdam
in New-Netherland now called New -York
and the Dutch West-India Islands, died in A.D.167½
aged 80 years.

Stuyvesant's Tomb.

departed, when he retired from public life. He was active, however, in all his movements long after a restful repose had settled upon his care-worn features. He interested himself in church affairs and in city improvements, grew social and companionable, frequently dined his English successor at his country-seat, and rendered himself very dear to his family and intimate friends. He gave one the impression of fine rich fruit, not tempting in external show, but sound and sweet to the core. He died in 1672, and was interred in the family vault, in the church upon his farm. One hundred and thirty years afterward, St. Mark's Church was erected upon the same site, and Peter Stuyvesant, the great-grandson of the governor, caused the vault to be repaired and enlarged. Upon the outer wall of St. Mark's Church is the original tablet, of which the sketch is a *fac-simile.*

Governor Stuyvesant had two sons, Balthazar and Nicholas William.

The former was born in 1647, and the latter in 1648. Balthazar removed to the West Indies after the surrender of the province. Nicholas William married Maria, the only daughter of William Beekman, who died without issue. He then married Elizabeth Slechtenhorst, daughter of the famous commander of Rensselaerswick. They had three children, Peter, Anna, and Gerardus. The former died in 1705, having never married. Anna married the Rev. Mr. Pritchard, an Episcopal clergyman. Gerardus married his second cousin, Judith Bayard. They had four sons, only one of whom, Peter, left descendants. He was born in 1727, and married Margaret, daughter of Gilbert Livingston. Their sons, Nicholas William and Peter Gerard, are well remembered by our older citizens; of their daughters, Judith married Benjamin Winthrop, Cornelia married Dirck Ten Broeck, and Elizabeth married Colonel Nicholas Fish and was the mother of Hon. Hamilton Fish, the present Secretary of State for the United States.

PETERSFIELD.   THE BOWERY HOUSE.

["Petersfield" was the residence of Peter Gerard Stuyvesant (many years President of the New York Historical Society), who married, 1, Susan, daughter of Colonel Thomas Barclay; 2, Helen Sarah, daughter of Hon. John Rutherford, of New Jersey. The "Bowery House" was the residence of Nicholas William, the brother of Peter Gerard Stuyvesant. Both mansions were built prior to the Revolution. For location, see map of Stuyvesant estate, page 188. The chief portion of this extensive property is now in possession of the three descendants, Hon. Hamilton Fish (Secretary of State), Benjamin Robert Winthrop, and Louis M. Rutherford, the well-known astronomer.]

CHAPTER XIII.

1664 – 1668.

NEW YORK.

New York. — The Duke of York. — Governor Nicolls. — Mr. and Mrs. Johannes Van Brugh. — The Brodhead Family. — Albany. — The Taking of the Oath of Allegiance to England. — Sir Robert Carr at Delaware Bay. — An Extraordinary Complication. — Connecticut Diplomacy. — The Dividing Line between Connecticut and New York. — New Jersey. — Elizabethtown. — Johannes De Peyster. — Interesting Controversy. — Court of Assizes. — Nicolls a Law-Maker. — The Hempstead Convention. — "The Duke's Laws." — The First Race-Course on Long Island. — The First Vineyard on Long Island. — The First Mayor of New York. — The First Aldermen. — John Lawrence. — Nicholas Bayard. — Symptoms of War. — Secret Orders. — War declared. — Cornelis Steenwyck. — The Plague in London. — The Great Fire in London. — England's Disgrace. — Clarendon's Fall. — New York's Miseries. — Nicolls's Wisdom. — Witchcraft. — The Manors of Gardiner and Shelter Islands. — Nicolls asks for his Recall.

IT has been the destiny of New York to sustain fiercer trials and to gain a wider and more varied experience than any other American State. The first half-century of her existence, though not very fruitful in achievements, greatly surpasses in importance any other equal period, from having projected the impulse and prescribed the law of her subsequent development. When, in 1664, she was geographically united to New England and the Southern British colonies, and exchanged a republican sovereignty for an hereditary king, she possessed the vital element of all her later greatness. The irrepressible forces, political, social, and religious, which were sweeping over the chief nationalities of Europe in that remarkable century, were already here, and pushing to unforeseen ends. Eighteen languages were spoken in our infant capital. The arrivals which followed increased without materially changing the character of the population. The old, stubborn, intensely practical Dutch spirit was firmly planted in this soil; English inflexibility, sagacity, and invigorating life had also taken root; and French industry, refinement, and vivacity flourished, if possible, the most luxuriantly of the three. The

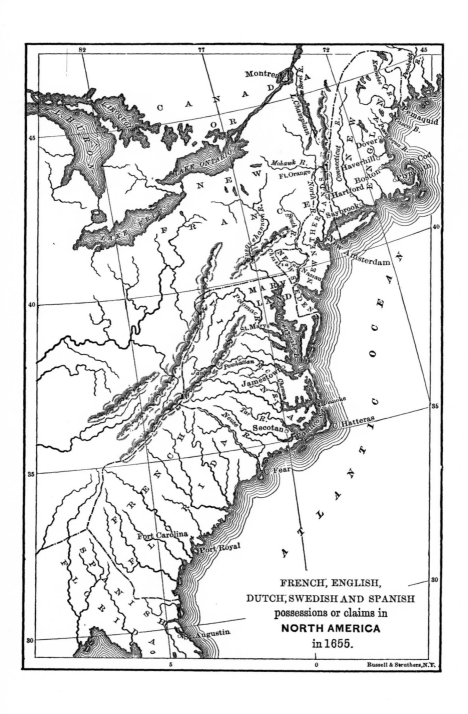

FRENCH, ENGLISH,
DUTCH, SWEDISH AND SPANISH
possessions or claims in
NORTH AMERICA
in 1655.

Russell & Struthers, N.Y.

chief impulse of the Huguenot movement, which had begun in France, both in the capital and in the University, was coeval with the revival of letters. Hence those who fled into voluntary exile were generally of the cultivated and wealthy classes. They transplanted to New York an influence of education and graceful accomplishments, and gave a certain chivalric tone to the new society. We have seen Dr. La Montagne closely associated in the New Netherland government for more than a score of years; and we find that the public documents of the period were written in the French as well as the Dutch language. Swedes, Germans, and some of other nationalities were here, but in smaller numbers. The inhabitants, drawn together from regions so remote, grew to be one people : a fearless, thoughtful, energetic, constructive people, politically alive, religiously free; a people which rejected hereditary leaders and kept those whom it elected under careful limitations. New York, standing midway among the sea-coast colonies, modified with her broader views the narrowness of her neighbors, and, after guarding for a century her long frontier from the attacks of Canada, became the pivot upon which turned the most important events of that gigantic Revolution which gave birth to a nation.

The Duke of York was a practical business man. He had been told that his new territory, if well managed, would yield him thirty thousand pounds per annum. In none of his plans and arrangements did he display more far-sighted common-sense than in his choice of a capable, resolute, and honest governor. Colonel Nicolls was the son of a lawyer of the Middle Temple. His mother was the daughter of Sir George Bruce. He was splendidly educated and accustomed to all the refinements of the higher European circles. Warmly attached to the royal cause, he had shared its fortunes, and spent much time, as an exile, in Holland. He was familiar with the Dutch literature, and spoke the Dutch and French languages as well as he spoke his own. He was about forty years of age ; a little above the medium height ; of fine, stately presence, with a fair, open face, a pleasant, magnetic gray eye, somewhat deeply set, and hair slightly curled at the ends.

He laughed a little at the fort, with its feint of strength, and its quaint double-roofed church within, but found the governor's house very comfortably furnished and quite attractive for a new country. The city pleased him. Its promise was vague and undefined, but he wrote to King James that it was undoubtedly the best of all his towns, and, with a little care, the staple of America might be drawn thither in spite of Boston.

His affability and genial nature won the citizens from the start; at

14

least such as were so fortunate as to come in personal contact with him, either officially or otherwise. On the day after the surrender, the burgomasters and schepens met and transacted their ordinary business, as if nothing unusual had occurred. They afterwards indicated their good-will to the administration through a letter — drawn up by Cornelis Steenwyck, and signed by each member of the board — in which appeared the following passage : " Nicolls is a wise and intelligent governor, under whose wings we hope to bloom and grow like the cedar on Lebanon."

The official counselors of Governor Nicolls were Robert Needham, Thomas Delavall, Thomas Topping, and William Wells. Matthias Nicolls, a thoroughbred English lawyer, was appointed Secretary of the province. All these were from among the new-comers, except William Wells, who had settled previously at Southold, Long Island. Cornelis Van Ruyven, Stuyvesant's provincial Secretary, was appointed collector of the customs. He was called into counsel on many occasions, and rendered material aid to Nicolls. One of the schepens, Johannes Van Brugh, was also invited to the meetings of the council, and his opinions were treated with profound deference. He was a shipping merchant, doing a prosperous business. His wife was a daughter of Anetje Jans. They lived in a stone house near Hanover Square, in front of which several immense forest-trees cast their broad shadows over a handsome green, where the Indians used to camp, during their visits to the city, and where market-wagons were often left standing, while the horses rested and grazed in the cool shade. Mr. and Mrs. Van Brugh were the first of the Dutch residents who gave a dinner-party in honor of the new English governor.

On the Sunday following the surrender, the English Episcopal service was celebrated for the first time in New York, by the chaplain of the English forces. It having been agreed in the capitulation that the Dutch should enjoy all their religious liberties and retain their own church edifice, it was very cordially arranged that the services of the Church of England should take place in the same sanctuary after the close of the usual morning worship. Meanwhile the city magistrates provided for the support of Dominies Megapolensis and Drisius, until the governor should make further arrangements.

Fort Orange, and Esopus, although included in the capitulation, remained to be brought under the Duke's authority. As soon as the safety of the capital was fairly assured, Nicolls dispatched to the former point Colonel Cartwright and his company, armed with various orders and instructions. Colonel Cartwright was a typical Englishman, heavy, grave, often morose, overbearing, of a suspicious temperament, and an excellent hater of the Dutch. The two officers next in command were

.

Captain John Manning and Captain Daniel Brodhead. Captain Manning had formerly commanded a trading vessel between New Haven and New York, but was now in the military service. Captain Brodhead, from an ancient family in Yorkshire, England, was a zealous royalist, in high favor with the king. He was the common ancestor of the Brodhead family in this country, among whom in every generation have been men of culture and distinction, — the most widely known of them all, perhaps, being the late John Romeyn Brodhead, the eminent scholar and historian of New York.

Van Rensselaer was directed to obey Cartwright, and also to bring his title papers respecting Rensselaerswick to Nicolls for inspection. This was subsequently done, and a new patent was issued to the patroon by the Duke. Thomas Willett, and Thomas Breedon, ex-governor of Nova Scotia, accompanied the expedition by request, because they were accustomed to dealing with the savages, and it was esteemed of the first importance to secure the friendship which the Iroquois had cherished towards the Dutch.

The military officers were received with courtesy by Dr. La Montagne and the magistrates of the little town, which was at once named Albany, after the Scotch title of the Duke of York. It was found that John De Decker, one of Stuyvesant's counselors and a signer of the articles of capitulation, had been actively engaged in trying to infuse the spirit of resistance into the people at the north, and he was banished from the province. Few changes were made in the civil government. The Mohawk and Seneca sachems appeared and signed with Cartwright the first treaty between the Iroquois and the English; and Captain Manning was left in command of the fort. Sept. 25.

On his return from Albany, Cartwright landed at Esopus, where he was warmly welcomed by William Beekman, who was confirmed in his authority as sheriff. Thomas Chambers was also retained as commissary. The charge of the garrison was committed to Captain Brodhead. Sept. 30.

Nicolls was quick to see the advantage of influencing as many of the Dutch families as possible to remain in their present homes. By the articles of capitulation he had given them liberty to sell their lands and effects and to remove to Holland. But he resolved to ask the principal Dutch citizens to take the customary oath and become British subjects. He accordingly sent for Ex-Governor Stuyvesant, De Sille, Van Ruyven, Dominies Megapolensis and Drisius, and a few others, to meet him in the chamber of the common council, where the burgomasters and schepens were assembled, and there he addressed them on the subject, explaining that this new obligation did not involve any permanent renunciation of allegiance to the Dutch government. They demurred. Van Ruyven argued that the people had been pronounced "free denizens" by the terms of the surrender, and no provision made for assuming a new allegiance. Van Cortlandt feared such a proceeding would render the articles of capitulation null and void. After much debate, the meeting declined taking the oath, unless Nicolls should add to it, "conformable to the articles concluded on the surrender of this place."

Oct. 14.

The subject was in agitation for several days. Finally, Nicolls said in writing, that "the articles of surrender" were "not in the least broken, or intended to be broken, by any words or expressions in the said oath." This statement proved satisfactory, and, within the subsequent five days, over two hundred and fifty residents of the city and adjacent country took the oath of allegiance to Charles II. and the Duke of York. Among these was Stuyvesant himself; also Van Ruyven, Van Brugh, Van Cortlandt, Van Rensselaer, Beekman, and the two Dutch Dominies.

Oct. 18.

Tonneman, the sheriff, returned to Holland, and the city was called upon to elect his successor. The choice fell upon Allard Anthony, who was at once confirmed in office by the governor. About the same time a provost-marshal was appointed, to keep unruly soldiers from interfering with the citizens.

Dec. 12.

Meanwhile, Sir Robert Carr had gone, with two vessels and a large armed force, to reduce the settlements on the Delaware. He found the Swedes manageable and the Dutch obstinate. Superiority in numbers, however, secured a bloodless victory. It was then that the royal knight began to reveal his true character. He assumed authority independent of Nicolls, and claimed to be the sole disposer of affairs in that region. He shipped the Dutch soldiers to Virginia, to be sold as slaves. He imprisoned the commander Hinnoyssa, and appropriated his comfortable house and flourishing farm to his own use. He gave the stone dwelling, and a large tract of land belonging to Sheriff Van Sweringen, to his son Captain John Carr. He distributed the property of the other settlers as he saw fit. When an account of his high-handed proceedings reached the other commissioners, they were astonished beyond measure. They considered such conduct "presumptuous and disgraceful." They peremptorily required his lordship's return to New York to attend to the further business of the commission, and when he did not make his appearance, Cartwright and Maverick deputed Nicolls to proceed to Delaware Bay and appoint such civil and military

Oct. 10.

officers there as his best judgment dictated. He was accompanied by Counselor Needham. He administered a severe rebuke to Carr and compelled him to disgorge much of his ill-gotten spoil. He regulated affairs as well as he was able, and appointed Captain John Carr as deputy-governor.

Connecticut was all this while in deep distress. The patent of the king had extended her territory to the Pacific Ocean. But here was another patent of the king to his brother, comprising every inch of land west of the Connecticut River. It was a most extraordinary complication.

As for Long Island, the Duke's patent expressly included it by name; moreover, Winthrop, at Gravesend, just before the surrender of New York, had declared that the jurisdiction formerly exercised by Connecticut "ceased and became null." There seemed therefore to be little room for discussion in regard to that region, and it received the name of Yorkshire.

But Hartford herself was included in the Duke's patent, to say nothing of republican New Haven, who had held her head so high, and stoutly refused to bend to Connecticut, because the charter of the latter had been (as was affirmed) surreptitiously obtained, "contrary to righteousness, amity, and peace." Alas, when the choice was finally made between two great evils, Puritan dictation was judged to be far better than foreign annexation. The General Court of Connecticut held a mournful meeting in October. "We must try to conciliate those royal commissioners," said Winthrop. It was voted to present them with five hundred bushels of corn and some fine horses. A committee, consisting of Governor Winthrop, his son Fitz John, Matthew Allyn, Nathan Gold, and James Richards, was appointed to pay a visit of congratulation and to make the presentation. They were empowered to seize any opportunity which might offer, to settle a boundary line between the two patents. Oct. 13.

They reached New York late in November, and were graciously received by Nicolls, Cartwright, and Maverick. After much preamble, the delicate and perplexing question was fairly brought under discussion. The two patents were spread upon the table. Winthrop was reminded that, in obtaining the former, he had promised to submit to any alteration of boundaries which might be made by the king's commissioners. The authority of the later patent could not be shaken. The Connecticut gentlemen pleaded that it should not be enforced to its full extent, thus depriving Connecticut of her "very bowels and principal parts." To this Nicolls readily assented, for his own judg- Nov. 30.

ment condemned a course which would only result in the ruin of a thriving colony, and in lasting dishonor to the king. It was therefore agreed that the dividing line between Connecticut and New York should run about twenty miles from any part of the Hudson River. To define the starting-point and the compass direction, the Connecticut gentlemen inserted a clause in the document by which the line was to be drawn from where the Mamaroneck Creek flows into the Sound, and north-northwest onward to the Massachusetts line.

For the moment, this settlement seemed to be satisfactory to both parties. New Haven submitted to Connecticut and all went well. But Nicolls and his colleagues, being unfortunately ignorant of the geography of the country, were misled into the supposition that the line had been drawn twenty miles, when in reality it was only about ten miles, distant from the Hudson. It was an absurd error, which was never ratified by the Duke or the king, and proved the source of a long-continued and distracting controversy.

While the forces of the expedition against New Netherland were still on the Atlantic, in June, James dismembered his American province and laid the foundation of another State. The treasurer of his house-hold was Lord Berkeley, who was also one of the Admiralty Board. He was a coarse, bold man, arbitrary and unscrupulous, and somewhat inclined to Catholicism. The treasurer of the Admiralty was Sir George Carteret, who had formerly been governor of the Channel Island of Jersey, where he received and entertained Charles, while Prince of Wales, and at which point he gallantly defeated the troops of Cromwell. He rode by the side of the king, when he entered London, at the Restoration, and was made chamberlain of the royal house-hold. Berkeley and Carteret were both members of the Council for Foreign Plantations, and had studied America with careful attention. They expressed a desire to purchase of the Duke a portion of his new territory ; and he, wishing to please two such devoted friends, accepted the small sum they offered, and conveyed to them by deed the section now known as New Jersey, — a name bestowed in com-pliment to Carteret. James had very little idea of the magnitude or importance of this sale, and made no reservation of the right to govern. Thence the purchasers assumed absolute control, engendering controver-sies which were prolonged for many years. They published a constitu-tion for New Jersey, and appointed Philip Carteret, a cousin of Sir George's, governor of the province.

Nicolls knew nothing of all this until the arrival of Governor Carteret off the coast of Virginia, when he immediately wrote to James, protesting against a movement so unexpected and so unwise. Of course, the protest came too late. Carteret reached New York in July, 1665, and received from Nicolls, according to the orders of the Duke which he brought with him, complete and undisputed possession of New Jersey. He landed on Jersey soil, at the head of a party of men, carrying a hoe on his shoulder, to indicate his intention of becoming a planter with them. He chose for the seat of government a charming spot near Newark Bay, where four families had already settled, and named it Elizabethtown, in honor of Lady Elizabeth, the wife of Sir George Carteret.

Nicolls found serious work on all sides of him. In order to win the Dutch, he copied or rather continued, with as little alteration as possible, the form of administration to which they had been accustomed. The burgomasters and schepens of the city, when their terms **1665.** **Feb. 2.** of service expired, named their successors, as formerly. It was just twelve years to a day since Stuyvesant had conferred the powers which they exercised. The new officers were promptly confirmed by Nicolls, and announced to the public after the usual ringing of the bell. They were Cornelis Steenwyck and Oloff S. Van Cortlandt, burgomasters;

Autograph of Johannes De Peyster.

Timotheus Gabry, Johannes Van Brugh, Johannes De Peyster, Jacob Kip, and Jacques Cousseau, schepens; and Allard Anthony, sheriff.

It is noticeable that among these names are three of Huguenot origin. Johannes De Peyster descended from one of the families of the nobility who were driven from France in 1572 by the religious persecutions of Charles IX. He himself was born in Holland. He had been in

Silverware of the De Peysters.

New York for sixteen or more years. He was heir to considerable wealth, some of which was invested in ships which sailed to and from Europe and the West Indies. He brought to this country many valuable articles of furniture, and a large quantity of massive silver. Several

15

specimens of the latter are still in possession of the family, and are esteemed by the curious as masterpieces of art. He filled important positions in the city government and in the church, and was held in great respect. Nicolls said of him that he could make a better plat-form speech than any other man outside of Parliament, only that his knowledge of the English tongue was defective. He was the ancestor of the De Peyster family, which, from its intimate connection with the fortunes of New York, will occupy our attention in future chapters.

Almost immediately, a controversy arose between the city magistrates and the governor and council. It having been stipulated that the city should provide quarters for such soldiers as could not be lodged in the fort, an attempt was made to distribute them among the inhabitants, who were to be paid for their board. In many instances, they were turned out of respectable houses on account of disorderly conduct, and complaints arose on every side. The citizens generally preferred to pay an assessment rather than have any contact with them ; and the matter was finally arranged in this way, to the satisfaction of all concerned.[1]

In fact, Nicolls was a provincial autocrat. Under the Duke's despotic patent, he was the real maker of the laws, and the interpreter of them after they were made. With such tact and moderation, however, did he exercise his delegated powers, that his subordinates actually believed themselves to be sharers in the responsibilities of legislation. He erected a Court of Assizes, consisting of the governor and his council, which was the supreme tribunal of the province. After a time, Long Island, or Yorkshire, was divided into three districts, or ridings. The justices of the peace appointed by the governor were to hold, three times a year in each district, a Court of Sessions over which the governor or any coun-selor might preside ; and these justices, and the high-sheriff of each district, were to sit in the Court of Assizes once a year, — the last Thurs-day in September. But they had no representative character whatever.

The anomalous condition of New York required special laws. Here was a conquered province, which had no charter, like the New England colonies ; which was not a royal domain, like Virginia ; which differed materially from the proprietary of Maryland ; and whose Dutch inhabi-tants, having received special privileges for the sake of peaceable posses-

---

[1] Among those assessed were Peter Stuyvesant, Frederick Philipse, Cornelis Van Ruyven, Oloff S. Van Cortlandt, Paulus Van der Grist, Johannes Van Brugh, Johannes De Peyster, Jacob Kip, Allard Anthony, Evert Duyckinck, Jan Evertsen Bout, Johannes De Witt, Hans Kiersted, Jacob Leisler, Paulus Richards, Simon Jansen Romeyn, Isaac Bedlow, Augustine Heermans, Ægidius Luyck, and many others. Some were taxed four guilders per week, some three, some two, and some one.

sion, were in many respects upon a better footing than the king's English subjects upon Long Island, which had been British territory before the capitulation. Nicolls had promised the Long-Islanders at Gravesend, before the surrender, that they should have a convention of delegates from their towns, to enact laws and establish civil offices. He accordingly proceeded, with the help of his council, to frame a code which should ultimately become the law of the whole province. He carefully studied the laws in actual operation in the several New England colonies; and, for that purpose, obtained copies of those of Massachusetts and New Haven, the latter of which had been printed in London in 1656. He wrote to Winthrop for a copy of the statutes of Connecticut; but they existed only in manuscript, and he did not obtain a transcript in time to make use of it. But, however much Nicolls may have borrowed from the experience and wisdom of his neighbors, he excelled them all in liberality in matters of conscience and religion.

He called a convention at Hempstead on the 28th of February. It consisted of thirty-four delegates, two from each of the Long Island towns, and two from Westchester. These delegates were all notified to bring with them whatever documents related to the boundaries of their respective towns, and to invite the Indian sachems, whose presence might be necessary, to attend the meeting, as there was important business to be transacted, aside from the discussion and adoption of the new code of laws.[1]

Feb. 28.

Nicolls presided in person. At the opening of the exercises, he read the Duke's patent and his own commission. He then proceeded to the settlement of local boundaries, and other minor matters. The laws were delivered to the delegates for inspection. Scarcely a man among them was satisfied. They had expected immunities at least equal to those

---

[1] The delegates to this convention were as follows : Jacques Cortelyou and Mr. Fosse, from New Utrecht ; Elbert Elbertsen and Roeloffe Martense, from Flatlands ; John Stryker and Hendrick Jorassen, from Flatbush ; James Hubbard and John Bowne, from Gravesend ; John Stealman and Guisbert Tennis, from Bushwick ; Frederick Lubbersten and John Evertsen, from Brooklyn ; Richard Betts and John Coe, from Newtown ; Elias Doughty and Richard Cornhill, from Flushing ; Thomas Benedict and . Daniel Denton, from Jamaica ; John Hicks and Robert Jackson, from Hempstead ; John Underhill and Matthias Harvey, from Oyster Bay ; Jonas Wood and John Ketchum, from Huntington ; Daniel Lane and Roger Barton, from Brookhaven ; Counselor William Wells and John Young, from Southold ; Counselor Thomas Topping and John Howell, from Southampton ; Thomas Baker and John Stratton, from Easthampton ; and Edward Jessop and John Quimby, from Westchester. *Brodhead*, II. 68. *Journals New York Legislative Council ; Gen. Ent.*, I. 93 – 95. *Wood*, 87, 88. *Thompson*, I. 131, 132. *Bolton*, II. 180. *Dunlap*, II. App. XXXVII. *Smith*, I. 388. *Hist. Mag.*, VIII. 211. *Trumbull MSS.*, XX. 74. *Col. Doc.*, II. 251 ; III. 86, 88, 114 ; IV. 1154. *Deeds*, II. 1 – 15, 43, 48, 49. *Chalmers*, I. 577, 578, 598.

enjoyed under the charter of Connecticut, with which they were perfectly familiar. The code prepared did not recognize the right of the people to choose their own magistrates or to have a voice in the levying of taxes. Consequently, they objected to some of its clauses, and proposed others. The discussion occupied ten days. Several amendments were accepted by Nicolls. But when the debate waxed warm, it was very promptly checked by his emphatic announcement that all civil appointments were solely in the hands of the governor, and that whoever wished any larger share in the government must go to the king for it. The delegates were thus assured that, instead of being popular representatives to make laws, they were merely agents to accept those already made for them. It was not a pleasant medicine, but it was gracefully swallowed. The code was adopted, and was generally known as " THE DUKE'S LAWS." The subjects were arranged in alphabetical order, and, about a century after, having become obsolete, the document was first printed as an historical curiosity.

Among the provisions of this code were trials by jurymen ; arbitration in small matters ; a local court in each town, from which there was an appeal to the Court of Sessions ; overseers, and constables, and justices of the peace ; assessments, and enforcements of rates imposed. The tenure of real estate was to be from the Duke of York, involving new patents and a harvest of fees ; all conveyances were to be recorded in the Secretary's office, in New York ; no purchase of the Indians was to be valid unless the original owner acknowledged the same before the governor ; no trading with the Indians was to be allowed without a license ; no Indian might pow-wow, or perform outward worship to the Devil, in any town in the province ; negro slavery was recognized, but no Christians were to be enslaved except those sentenced thereto by authority ; death was the punishment for denying the true God, for murder, for treason, for kidnapping, for the striking of parents, and for some other offenses, — but witchcraft was not included in the list ; churches were to be built in every parish and supported, but no one particular Protestant denomination was to be favored above another ; no minister was to officiate but such as had been regularly ordained ; each minister was to preach every Sunday, on the 5th of November (the anniversary of the gunpowder treason), on the 30th of January (the anniversary of the violent death of Charles I.), on the 29th of May (the anniversary of the birth of Charles II. and of the Restoration), to pray for the king, queen, Duke of York, and the royal family, to baptize children, and to marry persons after legal publication ; no person who professed Christianity was to be molested, fined, or imprisoned for differing in opinion on matters of religion. There were numerous regulations respecting the administration of estates,

"As an immediate result of Nicolls' attendance upon the Convention, a race-course was established at Hempsted. The ground selected was sixteen miles long and four wide. It was covered with fine grass, unmarred by stick or stone. Nicolls directed that a plate should be run for, every year, to improve the provincial Dutch, or Flemish, breed of horses." Page 289 boundaries of towns, births and burials, surgeons and midwives, children and servants, weights and measures, and wrecks, and whales, and sailors, and orphans, and laborers, and brewers, and pipe-staves, and casks, and wolves ; and every town was to provide a pillory, a pair of stocks, and a pound.

Nicolls, with great caution, delayed the enforcement of those laws in New York, Esopus, Albany, and the valley of the Hudson. And, in order to mollify the resentment of some of the Long Island delegates, he made several civil appointments upon the adjournment of the convention. Counselor William Wells was commissioned the first high-sheriff of Long Island. John Underhill, of Oyster Bay, who had been so prominent hitherto in New Netherland affairs, was made high-constable and under-sheriff of the North district, or riding, and surveyor-general of the island. Daniel Denton, John Hicks, Jonas Wood, and James Hubbard were appointed justices.

As an immediate result of Nicolls's attendance upon the convention, a race-course was established at Hempstead. The ground selected was sixteen miles long and four wide. It was covered with fine grass, unmarred by stick or stone, and was for many years called "Salisbury Plains." Nicolls directed that a plate should be run for, every year, in order to improve the provincial Dutch, or Flemish, breed of horses, which was better adapted to slow labor than to fleetness or display. The race-course itself was named " Newmarket," after the famous English sporting-ground, and was subsequently a favorite annual resort for the governors of New York and the farmers of Long Island.

Nicolls was ready to favor every important colonial enterprise. There had been much talk about the culture of grapes. Paulus Richards established a vineyard on Long Island for the manufacture of wine. As he was the first planter of vines, it was cordially agreed by the administration that whoever during thirty years should plant vines in any part of the province should pay five shillings for each acre so planted to Richards, in acknowledgment of his pioneer operations. The produce of his vines, if sold at retail by any one house in the city, was to be free from impost for the above period of thirty years, and, if sold in gross, to be free forever.

While Nicolls was busily at work, attending to his own government, his colleagues, Cartwright, Maverick, and Carr, were laboring with " refractory " Massachusetts. It had been the object of the king to work such alteration in the Puritan charters as would give him the appointment of their governors, and of the commanders of their militia. Nothing, however, could be accomplished without the presence of Nicolls. He accordingly made the journey to Boston. It was of no use : Massachusetts was on her dignity. Boston treated the overtures of the royal commissioners with scorn. " Our time and labor is all lost upon men misled by the spirit of independency," said Nicolls. He hurried back to New York; and Cartwright, Maverick, and Carr went eastward to Maine.

May 26.

The first care of Nicolls, after his return, was to alter the city government, so as to make it conform to the customs of England. Wishing to do this in the most conciliatory manner, he selected Thomas Willett for the first mayor of New York. This gentleman had distinguished himself on the Albany expedition, and had so impressed Cartwright that the latter wrote to Nicolls from Boston, " I believe him a very honest and able gentleman, and that he will serve you both for a mayor and counselor." Willett was a Plymouth settler, but had been much in New Netherland, had property interests there, and for a series of years had had constant business relations with the Dutch merchants. He was better acquainted with the country, and with the language, manners, and customs of the Dutch, than any other Englishman, and was popular among all classes.

On the 12th of June appeared the governor's proclamation, which declared that the future government of the city should be administered by persons to be known by the name and style of Mayor, Aldermen, and Sheriff. A separate instrument, under the same date, ordained that all the inhabitants of Manhattan Island "are and shall be forever accounted, nominated, and established as one body politic and corporate." The appointments were as follows : Thomas Willett, mayor ; Thomas Delavall, Oloff S. Van Cortlandt, Johannes Van Brugh, Cornelis Van Ruyven, and John Lawrence, aldermen ; and Allard Anthony, sheriff, — three Englishmen and four Hollanders.

June 12.

They were to be duly installed in office on the 14th of June. When Nicolls entered the Council Chamber, he instantly perceived that there was much dissatisfaction. As soon as the meeting was called to order, Van Cortlandt rose, and, with his silvery locks thrown back and his eyes flashing fire, stated distinctly his objections to the new regulation, which violated the sixteenth article of the capitulation. Nicolls replied elaborately, showing how the old officers had been continued, and, in February, new ones elected who had been retained until now. Van Brugh sprang to his feet and argued at length the superior wisdom of the old Dutch system. Van Ruyven followed him, and, in great heat, opposed the principle of appointments by the governor. Nicolls was bland and deferential, but said he was under orders from the

June 14.

Duke of York to model the government of New York according to that of the cities of England. At the same time, he paid the gentlemen some happy compliments in respect to their recent administration of affairs. The ceremony of swearing in the new magistrates proceeded without interruption; they were duly proclaimed, and shook hands with the polite governor before separating.

John Lawrence was one of three brothers who settled on Long Island in the time of Charles I. He was a lineal descendant of Sir Robert Lawrence (anciently spelled Laurens), who owned in England, during the reign of Henry VII., thirty-four manors, the revenue of which amounted to six thousand pounds sterling per annum. These brothers, John, William, and Thomas, brought considerable property into the province, and all became extensive landholders. John accumulated a fortune in mercantile pursuits. When he was first made an alderman, he had a city as well as a country residence, and owned more slaves than any one on Manhattan Island.

The democratic theory which has since been thoroughly instilled into the American mind, that all men (and perhaps women) are born free and equal, was then among the marvels of the future. An aristocratic sentiment pervaded the little community, and was predominant for more than a century after, which was much the same as in the contemporaneous cities of Europe. The line between master and servant was rigidly drawn. There was no transition state, through which the latter might aspire, by the favor of fortune, to rise to the condition of the former. And the Dutch, with their great republican notions but half developed, were, if possible, more tenacious in the matter of social classification than the English.

Nicholas Bayard, Stuyvesant's nephew, was appointed secretary of the common council, and was required to keep the records both in Dutch and English. He was a mere boy in years and personal appearance; but, thanks to his accomplished mother, he had all the flexibility and self-possession of a veteran. He was industrious, and intelligent in the details of finance and city government. He wrote rapidly, and his penmanship was the pride of the board. He had none of the forwardness common to youth, was courteously deferent to his elders, and remarkably grave and reticent. " He is never in the way, nor ever out of the way," said Willett, — a trait of character which may possibly account for his extraordinary career in after life. He was, however, excessively frivolous in some of his personal tastes, and, when off duty, devoted himself to dancing, horse-racing, and other diversions which greatly distressed his worthy friends.

The schools, so far as they were established, were allowed to continue;

but Nicolls took no steps to increase their number, or, indeed, to promote education in any form. It was sufficient for him, he argued, to see that the Christian ministers were supported. The Lutherans he permitted to build a church of their own and to send to Europe for a clergyman.

But a storm was gathering across the water, which was to involve New York in fresh difficulties. When Charles II. and his ministers settled with convenient logic the question of seizing and appropriating a Dutch province, it was at the risk of war. The States-General had no suspicion of the treachery in progress until the whole facts were revealed. De Witt sought an explanation from Downing, who replied, with stinging sarcasm, that he knew of no such country as New Netherland except in the maps ; the territory had always belonged to the English ! Charles himself laughed heartily when the news reached him of the complete success of Nicolls, and remarked to Sir George Carteret, " I shall have a pleasant time with the Dutch ambassador, when he comes."

The West India Company raved. They applied to the city of Amsterdam and also to the States-General for ships of war and soldiers, to send at once for the reconquest of the province whose concerns they had so fatally neglected. But the commercial monopoly had lost caste, and the popular cry was against lending it any assistance.

A considerable time elapsed before Van Gogh succeeded in obtaining audience of the king. Charles put him off with one excuse after another, but finally admitted him into his presence. Van Gogh denounced the whole proceeding as a vile deception, equally opposed to honor and to justice, and as a palpable infraction of the treaty between the English and Dutch nations. Charles haughtily replied that New Netherland belonged to the English, who had merely allowed the Dutch to settle there, without conferring any authority upon the West India Company. The next day, Clarendon wrote to Downing to tell De Witt that " the king was no more accountable to the Dutch government for what he had done in America than he would be in case he should think fit to proceed against the Dutch who live in the fens of England or in any other part of his dominions."

De Witt did not pause to demonstrate the transparent absurdity of the comparison, but peremptorily replied, " New Netherland must be restored." It was soon apparent to the Dutch statesmen, through the insolent manner of Downing, as well as the tone of Clarendon's correspondence, that no redress from England need be anticipated. Secret orders were therefore given to De Ruyter, who was with a squadron on the coast of Africa, " to reduce the English possessions in that region, and inflict by way of reprisal as much damage and injury as possible, either at Barbadoes,

New Netherland, Newfoundland, or other islands or places under English obedience." Downing secured information in regard to these secret orders, through the aid of skillful spies, who took keys from De Witt's pocket while he was asleep in bed, and extracted papers from his desk which were returned within an hour.[1] He immediately communicated the fact to his own government. Letters of reprisal were at once issued against the "ships, goods, and servants" of the United Provinces, and, without any previous notice, one hundred and thirty Dutch merchant vessels were seized in the English ports.

The Dutch, who lived by commerce, were no longer backward about fighting. Every city offered men and money to the government. The East India Company suspended their herring and whale fisheries, and equipped twenty war-vessels. The West India Company were authorized to attack, conquer, and destroy the English everywhere, both in and out of Europe, on land and on water. Fourteen millions of guilders were voted for the expenses of the war. As De Ruyter was yet in the West Indies, Wassenaar of Opdam was made admiral of the fleet, with the younger Tromp, and other renowned commanders, under him.

On the 4th of March, Charles issued a formal declaration of war against the United Provinces. The House of Commons at once voted two and one half millions of pounds sterling; "a sum," says Macaulay, "exceeding that which had supported the fleets and armies of Cromwell, at the time when his power was the terror of all the world." The public mind of England had been for some time growing discontented with the maladministration of affairs, and the immorality and extravagance of the court; but all prior murmurs were mild compared with the cry of indignation which now burst forth. March 4.

The Duke of York took command of the English fleet, and sent orders to Nicolls to put his province of New York in a posture of defense against the Dutch. Charles wrote to Nicolls himself, telling him of De Ruyter's expedition, and admonishing him to take all possible care to avoid a surprise. Clarendon added his word of warning, telling Nicolls that he must expect the Dutch to do him every possible mischief. Nicolls and Philip Carteret were appointed commissioners in Admiralty, to dispose of all Dutch prizes in the American harbors.

In May, De Ruyter was actually on his way from the West Indies to Newfoundland. He intended to visit New York, and, had he done so, its conquest would have been easy. But, being short of provisions, he was obliged to turn homeward. May.

---

[1] *Pepys*, II. 186, 192. *Davies*, III. 27, 28. *Barnage*, I 714. *De Witt*, IV. 413. *Aitzema*, V. 93, 94. *Col. Doc.*, II. 285–288. III. 85. *Parl. Hist.*, IV. 296–303. *Clarke's James II.*

As for the inhabitants of New York, they feared De Ruyter much less than they did the privateers who were prowling about in pursuit of plunder. Nicolls was painfully embarrassed. He had received no supplies whatever from England since the surrender. The fort was weak; he had no war-vessels; and the soldiers were in want of the commonest necessaries. But he was as loyal as he was brave. He at once issued a proclamation for the confiscation of the West India Company's estate, which had already been attached, and sent orders to New England in relation to Dutch prizes in their ports. He then called a meeting of the citizens, to consult about fortifying the city on the river side. As on many other important occasions, he presided in person. His opening address was a marvel of oratory. He assured the people

June 28.

that he should constrain no one to fight against his own nation. In asking aid in the matter of defense, he agreed to furnish palisades and wampum. Cornelis Steenwyck responded. He was a stanch republican, of the old Belgian stock, intelligent and liberal-minded; and he probably exercised a more healthful influence over the public mind than any other man of his time. He said that he should always be a faithful subject, and would contribute according to his means. But he did not see how the Dutch residents could enlist on the public works until their arms

Portrait of Steenwyck.

were restored to them. One and another arose with the same objection. Some said the town was strong enough as it was. There were many

other excuses. No direct result was obtained. It was evident to Nicolls that he should be able to

Autograph of Steenwyck.

command very little assistance from a community which would welcome the restoration of Dutch authority.

He sent an elaborate statement of New York affairs to the king by Cartwright, who, quite discouraged with his unprofitable labors in Boston, and in great physical torture with the gout, sailed in June for London. He was captured at sea by a Dutch privateer, who, having taken away all his papers, landed him in Spain. " It is for your health, sir," said the humorous sea-captain, as they parted company; "the mild southern climate always cures the gout."

Before the breaking out of hostilities, France had endeavored to reconcile the differences between England and the United Provinces. As the war progressed, Louis secretly sympathized with Charles, while at the same time he wrote to his minister at the Hague, that, from all he could learn, the rights of the Dutch were the best founded. " It is a species of mockery," he went on to say, "to make believe that those who have built and peopled a city, without any one saying a word to hinder them, would have been tolerated as strangers in France or in England ; and habitation, joined to long possession, are, in my judgment, two sufficiently good titles." At the same time he advised that, since New Netherland was already lost to the Dutch, it be abandoned, for the sake of peace. De Witt declining any further overtures in that direction, Louis made propositions once more to Charles without avail, and then reluctantly fulfilled a promise of long standing to assist Holland. He came to this decision on the 20th of January, 1666. The next month, England declared war against France.

In the mean time, a fierce conflict had raged. On the 13th of June, 1665, a battle was fought off the coast of Suffolk, in which the ship of Admiral Opdam was blown up, and the Duke of York returned in triumph to London. An English medal was struck, bearing the words " QUATUOR MARIA VINDICO " — I claim four seas. When the news reached New York, the English residents held a grand jubilee over the personal safety of the Duke. But the bonfire which celebrated the victory in London glared over a doomed city. A pestilence broke out, surpassing in horror any that had visited the British Isles for three centuries. The appalled court fled from Whitehall. The great city was desolated. Within five months, more than one hundred thousand lives were suddenly ended. The awful silence of the streets was only broken by the nightly round of the dead-cart.

Naval defeat almost produced a revolution in Holland. The return of De Ruyter, however, again inspired confidence. Other expeditions were fitted out. De Witt himself went with the troops, and soon came to a perfect understanding of sea affairs. In the effort to get the great clumsy vessels of the Dutch through the Zuyder Zee, he went out in a boat

15

himself, sounding carefully, and by degrees so mastering the elements, that he may be said to have avenged in some sense his former indignities by keeping his ships at sea long after the English fleet was obliged to put in. Several naval engagements occurred, and some frigates were disabled on both sides ; the English were sullen and disappointed, and the Dutch encouraged and hopeful.

Thus departed the year 1665. Parliament still voted supplies ; but the English nation was but a step removed from anarchy. Rents had fallen until the income of every landed proprietor was so **1666.** diminished that a wail of agricultural distress arose from all the shires in the kingdom. The gentry paid their accumulated taxes, breathing curses upon the king's favorites and upon the ignominious war. Algernon Sidney went to the Hague and urged De Witt to invade England, promising him aid ; a strong party in that country having conceived the idea of re-establishing the Commonwealth. This proposition was declined by the great statesman. But, as the spring advanced, another naval contest, occupying four days, took place at the mouth of the **June 11** Thames. Instead of the Duke of York, Prince Rupert and the Duke of Albermarle commanded the English fleet. De Witt went with his generals, and the chain shot which he is said to have invented was at this time first introduced, and so cut to pieces the rigging of the English that the Dutch came off victorious. Before the end of the summer, the fleets engaged again to the advantage of the English, **Aug. 4.** and De Witt swore that he would never sheathe his sword until he had had his revenge.

A terrible conflagration completed England's miseries for 1666. Five sixths of the proud city of London were laid in ashes. The summer had been the driest known for years. The citizens who had been driven away by the plague were returning ; the merchants counted upon peace before winter, and were preparing to go to the Continental markets. On **Sept. 2.** the 2d of September, a fire broke out which lasted four days and nights, and consumed every house, church, and hall in ninety parishes between the Tower and Temple Bar.

The year 1667 opened gloomily. Calamity followed calamity. The incapacity of the English statesmen who were in favor with the **1667.** king became more and more apparent. All schemes of an offensive war were abandoned. Presently it appeared that even a defensive war was too much for the administration. The ships became leaky and the dock-yards were unguarded. De Witt was promptly informed, and sent De Ruyter up the Thames to Chatham, where he burned all the finest vessels in the English navy, sending terror into every heart in the realm.

Charles was compared to Nero, who sang while Rome was burning. At that very moment, he was surrounded by the ladies of his court, and amused himself by hunting a moth about the supper-room.

The English regarded De Witt's success in the light of a national disgrace. The States-General haughtily dictated the terms of a treaty which was soon after signed at Breda. Singularly enough, they surrendered New Netherland, the very occasion and prize of this long ^{July 31.} contention, for Poleron, Surinam, and Nova Scotia. The West India Company shareholders and the regents of Amsterdam took exceptions; but otherwise there was general satisfaction in the United Provinces. The same day another treaty was signed between France and England, by which Acadia was restored to Louis. Bells rang in London, but there was little music in them. No bonfires expressed the national joy, since bonfires were costly, and there was no joy to express. Public sentiment both in and out of Parliament set stronger than ever against the king. What was New York, that it should have been accepted in exchange for such profitable places as Poleron, Surinam, and Nova Scotia? Massachusetts shared largely in the same bitter feeling. Popular indignation was aimed chiefly at Clarendon, and Charles adroitly shielded himself behind his austere and faithful minister. England must have a victim; and Charles, who had really grown weary of Clarendon's imposing ways, deprived him of the Great Seal at the very moment when he was affixing it to the proclamation of the Peace of Breda. "I must assuage the anger of Parliament," was his kingly excuse.

Innocent New York, the cause of all these disturbances, was becoming more interesting abroad than within her own borders. Improvements were at a dead stand. Her merchants were hampered in all their business operations by sea and by land. Her ships were seized by Dutch and French privateers almost within sight of her harbor. Her trade was suspended. Nicolls was compelled to use his own private means for the public good. There was little direct intercourse with England. Necessaries of all kinds grew very scarce. When, after a long captivity, Cartwright reached London, and explained the condition of affairs in the colonies, the Duke sent to New York two ships, laden with supplies. He wrote to Nicolls a letter full of commendation. The king did the same, inclosing a present of two hundred pounds. At the same time, he ordered a strict guard kept against the French in Canada.

This caution had been anticipated. And the meager help came at a moment when Nicolls was well-nigh disheartened in his herculean efforts to harmonize the various elements of discord. In the summer of 1665, a terrible war had broken out between two tribes of Indians at the North.

Two Dutch farmers who lived out in the clearings were killed. Mayor Willett, of New York, went to confer with the Albany magistrates on the subject. Two Indians were arrested for the murder, and, by order of the governor, one of them was hanged and the other sent in chains to Fort James. A great effort was then made to secure peace between the two contending tribes. Nicolls went to Albany, where he was met by Governor Winthrop, of Connecticut, and the arduous work was accomplished. Captain John Baker was left in command of Fort Albany, with nine cannon, and a garrison of sixty men.

On his return, Nicolls visited Esopus, where the towns-people and the soldiers were in a quarrel. His presence, and his discreet counsels, allayed the feverish temper of all parties. Brodhead, as the chief officer of militia, was instructed " to keep constant guard, cause the village authorities to be respected, prevent his soldiers from abusing the Indians, avoid harshness of words on all occasions, seek rather to reconcile differences than to be the head of a party, and abstain from prejudice against the Dutch, who," continued Nicolls, " if well treated, are not as malicious as some will seek to persuade you that they are." He also executed an important treaty with the Esopus Indians, by which he secured for the Duke a large tract of land to the West, to offer as an inducement to planters who might wish to settle in the province.

At the Court of Assizes, held in New York in September of the same year, the sachems of the Long Island Indians appeared, and agreed to submit to the government. Shortly after, David Gardiner, in compliance with the requirement of the code, brought to Nicolls his grant of the Isle of Wight, or Gardiner's Island (which had been originally made to his father, in 1640, by the agent of the Earl of Stirling), and received a new patent of confirmation. An interesting criminal case was also decided at this first Court of Assizes. Ralph Hall and his wife Mary were arraigned by the magistrates of Brookhaven for murder by means of witchcraft. It was claimed that two deaths had been caused by their " detestable and wicked arts." Twelve jurymen, one of whom was the afterwards conspicuous Jacob Leisler, rendered a verdict to the effect that there were suspicious circumstances in regard to the woman, but not of sufficient importance to warrant the forfeit of her life ; the man was acquitted. The court sentenced Hall to give a recognizance for his wife's appearance from sessions to sessions, and guarantee the good behavior of both while they remained under the government.[1]

The owners of Shelter Island, Thomas Middleton, and Constant and

Oct. 5.

---

[1] One of the last acts of Nicolls, just before he left New York, was to release Hall and his wife from their bonds.

Nathaniel Sylvester, soon followed the example of Gardiner, and obtained confirmation of their title. In consideration of seventy-five pounds of beef and seventy-five pounds of pork towards the support of the New York government, they were released forever from taxes and military duty. A patent was issued to the Sylvesters, erecting the island into a manor with all the privileges belonging.[1]

The Long Island inhabitants chafed under what they styled " arbitrary power." They were outspoken and aggressive, and gave Nicolls more trouble than all the Dutch population together. They clamored for a General Court, after the manner of New England. In many instances, they openly defied the Code of Laws. The danger of rebellion was imminent. The governor went among them, but with less success than he had reason to anticipate. Finally, adopting a vigorous course, he made it an indictable offense to reproach or defame any one acting for the government, and arrested, tried, and severely punished several persons.[2] He then declared that every land patent in the province which was not immediately renewed should be regarded as invalid ; the quitrents and fees being actually necessary for the support of the government. In New York, and in the Dutch towns, the payments for new patents were made easy. Van Rensselaer created quite an excitement by claiming Albany as a part of Rensselaerswick. Nicolls wrote to him that the question must be settled by the Duke of York, but added, " Do not grasp at too much authority ; if you imagine there is pleasure in titles of government, I wish that I could serve your appetite, for I have found only trouble."

The natural consequences of the war were apparent on every hand. There were altercations between English and Dutch laborers ; the officers of the garrisons were not always prudent ; and the common soldiers were given to roguery. On one occasion, three of the New York garrison were convicted of having stolen goods from a gentleman's cellar, and it was determined that one of them must die. The fatal lot fell to Thomas

---

[1] The islands of Martha's Vineyard and Nantucket were included by name in the Duke's patent. An independent government had been exercised over them by Thomas Mayhew and his son, who purchased them of Lord Stirling ; but, in January, 1668, Nicolls issued a special commission to Mayhew, thus settling the point of jurisdiction beyond question. Fisher's Island, one of the gems of the Sound, a few miles from Stonington — an island nine miles long and one mile broad — had been granted, in 1640, by Massachusetts to John Winthrop, but as it was included in the Duke's patent, Winthrop was obliged to apply to Nicolls for a confirmation of his title, and it was erected into a manor, and made independent of any jurisdiction whatever. It now forms a part of Suffolk County.

[2] Arthur Smith, of Brookhaven, was convicted of saying " the king was none of his king, and the governor none of his governor," and sentenced to the stocks. William Lawrence, of Flushing, was fined and compelled to make public acknowledgment for a similar remark. *Court of Assizes*, II. 82 - 94.

Weall. On the evening before the day fixed for the execution, some of the women of the city besought the governor to spare the culprit's life. All the privates in the garrison joined in a petition to the same effect; and, yielding to the influence, Nicolls drew up the soldiers on parade and in a characteristic speech pronounced pardon.

A complication of difficulties between the French and the Indians, between the different tribes of Indians, and between the Jesuits, the Indians, and the New York colonists, to the north, kept Nicolls in continual anxiety. He had reason to apprehend mischief from the French; the Mohawks, with all their pledges, were very uncertain; the New England colonies were not in a condition to render efficient aid in an emergency; and the prospect was as dismal as could well be imagined.

Nicolls was so oppressed with financial embarrassments that he wrote to both the Duke and the king, begging to be relieved from " a government which kept him more busy than any of his former positions, and had drawn from his purse every dollar he possessed." His detailed account of the condition of New York affairs was most pitiful. " Such is our strait," he said, " that not one soldier to this day since I brought them out of England has been in a pair of sheets, or upon any sort of bed but canvas and straw."

A response came tardily. The Duke consented to the return of Nicolls ; but it was not until after the Peace of Breda had set his mind **1668.** at rest concerning the immediate possibility of losing his prov-Jan. 1. ince. The news of the treaty came with the same ship which brought the recall of the weary governor. Peace was a charmed word in Dutch as well as English ears; politics, feuds, and bickerings were forgotten, in the universal gladness; vague, wearing, corroding apprehension was succeeded by intense relief; business might again be resumed.

Presently came the official announcement of Nicolls's intended departure, and there was universal sorrow. He had made himself exceedingly popular. The leading Dutch residents were, if possible, more attached to him than his English colleagues ; but all were united in one deep feeling of regret that he must leave the country.

CHAPTER XIV.

1668 – 1673.

COLONEL FRANCIS LOVELACE.

COLONEL FRANCIS LOVELACE. — NICOLLS AND LOVELACE. — CORNELIS STEENWYCK'S HOUSE. — THE CITY LIVERY. — NICHOLAS BAYARD. — FEVER AND AGUE IN NEW YORK. — THE END OF COMMERCIAL INTERCOURSE WITH HOLLAND. — LOUIS XIV. FRANCE. — THE TRIPLE ALLIANCE. — SOCIAL VISITING IN NEW YORK IN 1669. — A PROSPEROUS ERA. — THE DUTCH REFORMED CHURCH. — THE SABBATH IN NEW YORK TWO HUNDRED YEARS AGO. — DRESS OF THE PERIOD. — THE LUTHERAN MINISTER. — WITCHCRAFT. — THE FIRST EXCHANGE. — REBELLION ON LONG ISLAND. — THE PURCHASE OF STATEN ISLAND. — CHARLES II. AND LOUIS XIV. — THE PRINCE OF ORANGE. — ASSASSINATION OF THE DE WITTS. — WAR BETWEEN ENGLAND AND HOLLAND. — FIERCE BATTLES IN EUROPE. — THE DEATH OF COLONEL NICOLLS. — THE FIRST POST BETWEEN NEW YORK AND BOSTON. — LOVELACE IN HARTFORD. — THE DUTCH SQUADRON IN NEW YORK BAY. — CAPTURE OF NEW YORK BY THE DUTCH. — NEW ORANGE.

COLONEL FRANCIS LOVELACE was appointed to succeed Nicolls. He was the son of Baron Richard Lovelace of Hurley. The ancestral home of the family was some thirty miles from London, on the Berkshire side of the Thames ; a great imposing country mansion, which was standing until recently, with spacious grounds and terraced gardens, covering the site of the ancient Benedictine monastery, from which it was named " Lady Place."

1668.

Colonel Lovelace was one of the gentlemen of that focus of political intrigue and fashionable gayety the Court of Charles II. He had been one of the supporters of the royal cause, — zealous, even to the point of incurring imprisonment in the tower by Cromwell, on a charge of high treason. This only increased his favor with the king at the Restoration, and he was made one of the knights of the " Royal Oak," an order instituted as a reward for the faithful. He was a handsome, agreeable, polished man of the world, — upright, generous, and amiable. But he lacked energy, and that discrimination which the successful conduct of government requires at every step. He had a fine perception

16

of probabilities, and a profound conviction of the future destiny of New York. At the same time, he was of the narrow type of mind, inclined to move along a single line of thought, like a railway in its grooves, and he possessed very little of that subtle sagacity which brings conflicting elements into one harmonious whole.

He had visited Long Island in 1650, under a pass from Cromwell's Council of State, and had gone thence to Virginia. But his knowledge of America was limited, and when he reached New York, in the spring of 1668, he was without any valuable preparation for the work before him. The Duke wrote, requesting Nicolls to remain a few months longer, that Lovelace might have an opportunity to study affairs. The first time the latter presided in the Admiralty Court, Nicolls sat by his side. The two governors journeyed together to various parts of the province. They spent one week in Albany, were *fêted* by Van Rensselaer at his manor-house, and smoked the pipe of peace with the Mohawk sachems. On their return, they stopped two days in Esopus, and were the guests of William Beekman. They looked into military and other matters, and visiting Thomas Chambers at his manor, "passed an evening there of great hilarity." They traveled over Long Island on horseback, stopping at all the principal towns. They went to Hartford, and were entertained by Governor Winthrop in his most hospitable and courtly style; and they spent one day with the dignitaries of New Haven.

As the time drew near for Nicolls's departure, the most sincere sorrow was manifested on all sides. He who had come among the people as a conqueror was regarded as a loyal and trustworthy friend. He had ruled with such discretion and moderation, that even they who had disliked his orders had come to love the man that had taken so much pains to avoid the unnecessary wounding of their prejudices. Maverick wrote to Lord Arlington, " he has kept persons of different judgements and of diverse nations in peace and quietness during a time when a great part of the world was in wars; and as to the Indians, they were never brought into such peacable posture and faire correspondence as they now are." Every one delighted in doing him honor. The city corporation gave him a notable dinner, the scene of which was the great square stone house of Cornelis Steenwyck, the mayor, on the corner of Whitehall and Bridge Streets. A slight glimpse of the inside of this antique dwelling may be obtained from the inventory of its furniture, found among the old records, one fragment of which is as follows: " Handsome carpets, marble tables, velvet chairs with fine silver lace, Russia leather chairs, French nutwood book-case, Alabaster images, tall clock, flowered tabby chimney-cloth, tapestry work for cushions, muslin curtains in front parlor and flowered tabby curtains in drawing-room, eleven paintings by old Antwerp masters, etc."

The leading families in the province were represented among the guests on this memorable occasion. Lovelace wrote in a private letter to the king, "I find some of these people have the breeding of courts, and I cannot conceive how such is acquired." On the 28th of August, Nicolls took his final farewell, escorted to the vessel in which he was to embark for Europe by the largest procession of the military and citizens which had as yet been seen on Manhattan Island.

Steenwyck's House.

Cornelis Steenwyck occupied the mayor's chair three years. It was during this period that Thomas Delavall was sent to England by Lovelace on matters of business, and, upon his return, brought from the Duke of York a present of seven gowns for the aldermen, to be worn upon state occasions, and a silver mace to be carried by a mace-bearer, at the head of the procession of city magistrates; also, an English seal for the province of New York. A city livery was from that time worn by beadles and other subordinate officers, the colors being blue tipped with orange. Steenwyck was one of the governor's counselors, and at one time was appointed governor *pro tem.*, during the temporary absence of Lovelace. He was a man of sterling character, and filled his various public positions with dignity and honor.

Lovelace made no attempt to disturb the policy by which Nicolls had administered the government to such general satisfaction. Among his counselors at various dates were, besides Steenwyck, Thomas Willett and Thomas Delavall, former mayors of the city; Ralph Whitfield, Isaac Bedlow, Francis Boone, and Cornelis Van Ruyven, aldermen; Captain John Manning, the city sheriff; Matthias Nicolls, the provincial secretary; and Dudley Lovelace and Thomas Lovelace, the governor's younger brothers. But he found his field of labor hedged in by many thorns. Conflicting claims about lands stirred up quarrels in every part of the province. He had no sooner quelled one than another broke out. The difficulties of the situation were greatly aggravated by the absence of any uniform nationality. Some of the habits and customs were Dutch, some French, some English, some Christian, and some heathen. The lower classes were intemperate, unruly, and sometimes shockingly profane; and the more respectable and religious inhabitants were constantly entering complaints against them. Extremes of evil and good were singularly linked together, and the barbarous punishments which English usage warranted seemed the only safeguard against anarchy.

Nicholas Bayard, who had developed a remarkable talent for mathematics, was appointed surveyor of the province. He was noted, besides, for his varied attainments and for a ready wit, which enabled him to render important service to Lovelace, whom he usually accompanied when the governor was compelled to make personal investigations into the boundaries of farms and manors.

One of the great wants which sorely oppressed Lovelace was that of a printing-press. He sent to Cambridge for a printer, but could not obtain one. There was no restriction in this respect on the part of the Duke of York, as has generally been supposed. It was not until 1686 that James, as king of England, restrained the liberty of printing in New York. The immediate cause of Lovelace's enlightened effort was the desire to publish a catechism, which, together with a few chapters of the Bible, the Rev. Thomas James, the first minister of Easthampton, had translated, under the auspices of Nicolls, for the use of the Indians.[1]

Fever and ague prevailed in the city to such an extent during the autumn of this year, that it was regarded as a serious epidemic, and the governor proclaimed the 21st of November as a day of fasting, humiliation, and prayer on this account.

Nov. 21.

New Jersey, which under the rule of Philip Carteret had now attained the age of three years, was a constant source of annoyance to New York. Nicolls, when he reached London, explained to the Duke that his grant to Berkeley and Carteret had not only deprived him of a vast tract of his very best land, but ceded away some promising Dutch villages within three or four miles of the metropolis. About the same time, Maverick wrote to the Duke in a mournful strain, deprecating the worthlessness of the greater portion of that part of the patent which he still retained. He said, " Long Island is very poor and inconsiderable, and, besides the city of New York, there are but two Dutch towns of any importance, Esopus and Albany. I suppose it was not thought that Lord Berkeley would come so near, nor the inconvenience of his doing so considered." The Duke grew uneasy, and attempted to negotiate an exchange with

---

[1] *Brodhead*, II. 145. *Mass. Hist. Coll.*, XXXVII. 485. *Thomas's History of Printing*, I. 275; II. 90, 286. *Dunlap*, I. 126. *Thompson*, I. 317. *Wood*, 41. *Col. Doc.*, III. 216–219, 331–334, 375.

Berkeley and Carteret for some lands on the Delaware ; but the arrangement fell through, owing undoubtedly to Lord Baltimore's claim to the west side of the Delaware. Staten Island, however, was " adjudged to belong to New York."

Meanwhile the Lords of Trade complained that the English merchants were jealous concerning the business that was lost to them by the continuance of the old commercial intercourse between New York and Holland. They claimed that it was contrary to the spirit of the Navigation Act, and that the sixth and seventh articles of the capitulation had reference only to the first six months after the surrender. The king's promise to Stuyvesant had induced Van Cortlandt, Cousseau, and some others to unite in ordering one large ship from Holland to New York. Another was upon the eve of sailing, when Sir William Temple, who had succeeded Downing as minister to the Hague, was directed to notify interested parties that all passes granted under the order of 23d October, 1667, viz. that " three Dutch ships " might " freely trade with New York for the space of seven years," were henceforth recalled and annulled. When Nicolls heard of this order, he hastened to Whitehall and, in a personal interview with the king, obtained permission for the vessel just prepared to make one voyage. Shortly after, private Dec. 11. letters from New York so plainly revealed the grievous disappointment of some of the merchants, who, relying upon the pledge of Charles, had invested heavily, that this able and justice-loving ex-governor set himself energetically at work and with much difficulty obtained 1669. an order in council for the sailing of one more merchant vessel Feb. 24. from Holland to New York. This was announced as positively the last Dutch ship which should ever " come on that account " to Manhattan.

The English statesmen had long been watching with dismay the steady growth of France. The personal qualities of the French king added greatly to the power and importance of that realm. No sovereign ever sat upon a throne with more dignity and grace. He was his own prime minister, and performed the duties of that office with wisdom and firmness the more remarkable from the fact that from his cradle he had been surrounded with fawning flatterers. He was as unprincipled as Charles II., but by no means as indolent. He was a Roman Catholic, but it was not until a later date that, through austere devotion, he gave his court the aspect of a monastery. His transactions with foreign powers were characterized by some generosity, but no justice. His territory was large, compact, fertile, well placed both for attack and defense, situated in a good climate, and inhabited by a brave, active, and ingenious people, who were implicitly subservient to the control of a single mind. His revenues far exceeded those of any other potentate. His army was excellently disciplined, and commanded by the most noted of living generals. France was, just then, beyond all doubt, the greatest power in Europe and stood like a perpetual menace to the rest of the world. It must be remembered that the Empire of Russia, now so powerful, was then as entirely out of the system of European politics as Abyssinia or Siam ; that the house of Brandenburg was then hardly more important than the house of Saxony ; and that the Republic of the United States had not even begun to exist.

Spain had been, for many years, on the decline ; and France, pressing upon her, was in the full career of conquest. The United Provinces, prosperous and rich as they then were, saw with anxiety that they were no match for the power of so great, ambitious, and unscrupulous a monarch as Louis XIV., should he choose to extend his frontiers. Little help could be expected from England in such an emergency, since her policy had been devoid of wisdom and spirit from the time of the Restoration. It was not easy to devise an expedient to avert the danger.

Two nations were suddenly amazed and delighted. Sir William Temple, one of the most expert diplomatists, as well as one of the most pleasing writers, of the age, had been, for some time, representing to Charles, that it was both advisable and practicable to enter into engagements with the States-General, for the purpose of checking the progress of France. For a time his suggestions had been slighted ; but the increasing ill-humor of Parliament induced the king to try a temporary expedient for quieting discontent which might become serious. Hence Sir William was commissioned to negotiate an alliance with the Dutch Republic. He soon came to an understanding with John De Witt. Sweden, which, small as were her resources, had been raised by the genius of Gustavus Adolphus to a high rank among European powers, was induced to join with England and the States ; and thus was formed the famous coalition known as the " Triple Alliance." Louis was angry ; but he did not think it politic to draw upon himself the hostility of such a confederacy, in addition to that of Spain. He consented, therefore, to relinquish a large portion of the territory which his armies had occupied, and to treat with Spain on reasonable terms. Peace was restored to Europe, and the English government, lately an object of general contempt, was restored to the respect of its neighbors. The English people were specially gratified at this, for the nation was now leagued with a republican government that was Presbyterian in religion, against an arbitrary prince of the Roman Catholic Church. " It was the masterpiece of King Charles's life," said Burnet, " and, if he had stuck to it, it would have been both the strength and glory of his reign."

The news produced intense satisfaction in New York. The English and the Dutch inhabitants became better friends than ever. There was much social visiting during the winter of 1668 – 69. The formal entertainments were not more than five or six in number, but a club was established, comprising the more notable of the Dutch, English, and French families, who met twice a week, at one another's houses in rotation, coming together about six in the evening and separating at nine o'clock. The refreshments were simple, consisting chiefly of wines and brandies, — "not compounded and adulterated as in England," wrote Maverick, — and they were always served in a silver tankard. These gatherings were productive of great good feeling. Lovelace was generally present and rendered himself exceedingly agreeable. To those who would share in any considerable degree the advantages of this coterie, familiarity with three languages — English, Dutch, and French — was almost indispensable. Indeed, education was held in such high esteem, that the difficulties of obtaining it were overcome by the employment of private tutors in all the wealthy families.

Portrait of Steendam.

The earliest poet in New York was Jacob Steendam. A poem which appeared in 1659, " *The Complaint of New Amsterdam to her Mother,*" was from his pen ; also " *The Praise of New Netherland,*" which was published in a small quarto form in 1661. He wrote a variety of verse, some of which was distinguished by great elegance. He indulged in quaint conceits and rhymes, and evinced oftentimes a strong religious feeling. The action of his poems was usually taken from the Scriptures or classical mythology. A few fragments of poetry from the pen of Hon. Nicasius De Sille have been handed down to us from the same remote period ; and a little volume of poems written at a later date by Dominie Selyns is the key to a treasure of genius and culture.

A prosperous era was dawning upon New York. Several Bostonians removed thither and invested largely in real estate. One man bought five houses, which had just been erected on Broadway. Business of all kinds increased. Nine or ten vessels were in port at one time, with cargoes of tobacco from Virginia. Large quantities of wheat were shipped to Boston. A fishing bank was discovered two or three leagues from Sandy Hook, on which, in a few hours, some twelve hundred "excellent good cod" were taken. More than twenty whales were caught during the spring at the east end of Long Island, and several in New York Bay. Lovelace, co-operating with some of the merchants, built a strong and handsome vessel called the "*Good Fame*," which was sent to Virginia and subsequently to England. A smaller and less costly ship was launched about the same time at Gravesend. Some gentlemen, who arrived at this time from Bermuda and Barbadoes, were so much pleased with the prospect, that they bought houses and plantations. Nicolls obtained from the Duke of York the gift of a snug house on Broadway for Maverick, who complained that he had never received the value of a sixpence (one horse excepted) for his services to the government.

Daniel Denton describes New York at that date as "built mostly of brick and stone, and covered with red and black tile; and the land being high, it gives at a distance a pleasing aspect to beholders." The king's cosmographer, John Ogilby, more elaborately pictures it, as "placed upon the neck of the island looking toward the sea"; and as "compact and oval, with fair streets and several good houses; — the rest are built much after the manner of Holland, to the number of about four hundred; upon one side of the town is James'-fort, capable to lodge three hundred soldiers; it hath forty pieces of cannon mounted; it is always furnished with arms and ammunition against accidents, and is well accommodated with a spring of fresh water; the church rises from the fort with a lofty double roof between which a square tower looms up: on one side of the church is the prison and on the other side the governor's house; at the water-side stand the gallows and the whipping-post."

A glowing tribute was paid to Hell Gate, which was represented as sending forth such a hideous roaring as to deter any stranger from attempting to pass it without a pilot, and was therefore an absolute defense against any hostile approach from that direction. Governor's Island had been beautified and rendered attractive through the making of a garden and the planting of fruit trees. Long Island, although so recently pronounced by Maverick "poor and inconsiderable," was described by Denton, whose home was in Jamaica, as almost a paradise. Crops were plentiful; trout and other delicious fish abounded in the crystal streams; fruits grew spontaneously, especially strawberries, of which he says, "they are in such abundance in June that the fields and woods are dyed red." The vast, smooth plains encouraged the breeding of swift horses. Lovelace ordered that trials of speed at the race-course established by Nicolls should take place every May. A subscription-list was filled out by those who were disposed to enter horses for a crown of silver, or its value in good wheat. The swiftest horse was rewarded with a silver cup.

The clergymen of the Reformed Dutch church in New York were Dominie Schaats at Albany, Dominie Polhemus on Long Island, and Dominies Megapolensis and Drisius, colleagues at New York. Early in the spring, Dominie Megapolensis obtained of the governor permission to visit Holland, where he died suddenly, after twenty-seven years of ministerial service in the province. Dominie Drisius was in feeble health, and needed assistance, which could only be furnished by Ægidius Luyck, the Latin teacher, who had studied divinity in Holland, and by the foresinger, Evert Pietersen.

In June, 1670, Lovelace offered one thousand guilders per annum, with a dwelling-house free of rent, and firewood gratis, to any minister from Holland who would come and take charge of the New York church. Dominie Selyns, who was settled in Wavereen, Holland, **1670.** induced his relative, Dominie Wilhemus Van Nieuwenhuysen, to accept the liberal proposition. He duly made the voyage, and, in the summer of 1671, was installed as the colleague of . Dominie Drisius. The new minister was an accomplished scholar, full of fire and eloquence in the pulpit, and highly acceptable to the church and congregation. The governor furnished Dominie Drisius with an allowance from the public revenue, and authorized the consistory to tax the congregation for the support of the pulpit and of the poor. Thus the English rulers virtually established the Dutch Church in New York. The elders and deacons at this time were Ex-Governor Peter Stuyvesant, Oloff S. Van Cortlandt, Paulus Van der Grist, Boele Roelofsen, Jacob Teunissen Kay, and Jacob Leisler.[1]

The English customs in regard to the observance of the Sabbath were as rigid as those of the Dutch, and were sustained by the habits and feelings of the great mass of the population. It was about 1678 that the statute was passed in England which may be regarded as the foundation of our present laws on the subject; although, when the colonies became States, each one legislated more or less for itself, and there was a gradual and universal relaxation of the excessive severity of the earlier years. The statute referred to forbade any person laboring or doing any business or work, except works of charity or necessity, on the " Lord's Day "; and it was enforced to the letter. Any violation of it was vis-

---

[1] *Brodhead*, II. 176. *Corr. Classis of Amst. Records of Collegiate R. D. Church, N. Y. New York City Rec.*, VI. 562 – 750. *Gen. Ent.*, IV. 47. *Council Minutes*, III. 82. *Col. Doc.*, II. 470, 475 ; III. 189. *Murphy's Anthology of N. N.*, 146, 178.

ited with immediate punishment. Ludicrous stories are told of Puritan rigor : how, in Massachusetts, no one was permitted to make beer on Saturday, lest it should " work " on Sunday; and how, in Connecticut, no man was allowed to kiss his wife on the Sabbath. But, with all due allowance for humorous exaggeration, it was practically the same in New York. The Sabbath was consecrated to an entire cessation from worldly labor. With a musical peal of the old Dutch bell the houses poured forth their occupants. Since no power ever decreed adversely to the dressing of one's best on that day, it must have been a bright and impressive scene. Gentlemen wore long-waisted coats, the skirts reaching almost to the ankles, with large silver buttons, sparkling down the entire front; a velvet waistcoat trimmed with silver-lace peeped out, and the shirt-front was elaborately embroidered; breeches were of silver cloth or different colored silks, according to the taste of the wearer ; and the shoe-buckles were of silver. Ladies wore jaunty jackets of silk, velvet, or cloth, over different colored skirts. Sleeves were of the " muttonleg " shape, with large turned-up white cuffs. Not only were chains for the neck much in vogue, but girdle-chains of gold and silver were common, to which were suspended costly bound Bibles and hymn-books for church use. Brooches and finger-rings also were much worn. The hair was dressed high and was frizzed about the face, and the bonnet was very pretty. The mayor and aldermen, in a dress that was peculiarly conspicuous, occupied, in the church, a pew by themselves. Lovelace, in the afternoon, attended the Episcopal service, and occupied the governor's pew, which had been elaborately fitted up by Nicolls. Another pew was set apart for the governor's council.

The Duke of York sympathized with any and every religious creed which dissented from the Church of England. He was by conviction a Roman Catholic ; a fact which was not then without its value, as it served to protect irregular forms of worship, and actually placed him before the world as the friend of religious toleration. He permitted the Lutherans in New York to call a minister, the Rev. Jacobus Fabricus, from Germany. He went first to Albany. But his conduct there was not such as became his calling, and, complaints having been made, Lovelace suspended him from the pulpit at that place, giving him, at the same time, permission to preach in New York. It was soon found that, in addition to a dictatorial and quarrelsome temper, manifested in all his church relations, he was constantly abusing his wife. She spent one whole winter in the garret of their house, suffering all the while from fever and ague. She finally complained to the government, and petitioned, that since the house belonged to herself, that her husband should be ordered to give up the keys and not presume to enter it any more. After a careful investigation, through which they found that the husband was deserving of great blame, the court granted her request. Six months later he defied legal authority by going to his wife's house in an angry and turbulent manner. A woman who tried to prevent his entrance was pushed over her spinning-wheel and severely hurt. Soldiers were summoned to arrest him, and he fought them desperately. He was conquered, tried, fined, and compelled to ask pardon of the court. The clamors against him were so loud, that the governor once more interfered and removed him from the pulpit, giving him permission to proceed to the Delaware.

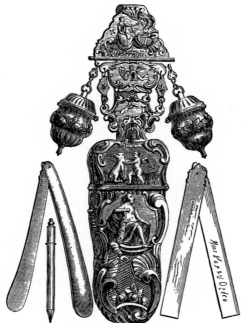

[Gold Chatelaine, worn at this period by Mrs. Jacob Leisler, having been brought to New York by her mother, Mrs. Govert Loockermans. After Mrs. Leisler's death it became the property of her daughter, Hester, and has descended in the direct line to Miss Gertrude S. Ogden, of Newark, N J., in whose possession it is at present, and through whose courtesy the copy has been permitted.]

A meeting for merchants — the first New York Exchange — was established in March of this year. The members were to meet every Friday morning, between eleven and twelve o'clock, at the bridge which crossed the ditch at Broad Street, — the site of what is **March 24.** now Exchange Place. Just above this there was a hill, which was a favorite place with the boys for coasting on their sleds, affording as it did a steep descent from Broadway down to the bridge ; but Lovelace ordered the mayor of the city to see that the meetings were not disturbed.

16

In the autumn, an interesting political event created a considerable sensation. The Court of Assizes levied a tax upon the Long Island towns for the purpose of repairing the fort in New York. They had, for several years, paid a direct tax of a penny in the pound to defray their town charges. They had also submitted graciously to the Duke's custom duties for the support of his government. But this last infliction was the straw too much. If yielded to, it might become a dangerous precedent; they might be required to maintain the garrison, and they knew not what else. They were persuaded that the principle of "taxation only by consent"—which Holland had maintained since 1477, and England had adopted in her Petition of Right in 1628—was their birthright as British subjects. Public meetings were called and protests fearlessly adopted and sent to the governor. At the court, which met at Gravesend, December 21st, Secretary Nicolls presided, and Counselors Van Ruyven, Manning, and Thomas Lovelace were present as justices. It was unanimously agreed that "the said papers were false, scandalous, illegal, and seditious," and they were referred to the governor and his council for such action as should "best tend to the suppression of mischief." Lovelace ordered that, at the next Mayor's Court, they should be publicly burned before the City Hall in New York, and their originators prosecuted.

Oct. 8.

Dec. 21.

But it was easier to burn documents than to control public opinion. The people of Long Island were full of indignation. They accused the governor of despotism, and openly threatened a revolt. Some of the towns had taken out new patents, in conformity with the law of 1666. But Southampton and Southold refused, the latter on the ground that their title from the Indians and New Haven was sufficient : Southampton relied upon theirs from Lord Stirling. The Court of Assizes declared the titles invalid, unless a patent from the Duke's government should be obtained within a certain time. This produced from fifty of the citizens of Southampton a remonstrance, which was so full of reason and spirit, that Lovelace, having promised to appoint commissioners to confer with them, postponed the matter indefinitely.

The most memorable act of Lovelace's administration was the purchase of Staten Island from the Indian sachems, who complained that they had never received full compensation from the Dutch. He quieted all their claims with a quantity of wampum, coats, kettles, guns, powder, lead, axes, hoes, and knives, and obtained a deed in behalf of the Duke of York. Immediate measures were taken to induce persons to settle there. The surveyors called it "the most commodiosest seate and richest land in America."

April 7.

Matthias Nicolls, who had been secretary of the province and one of the governor's council since 1664, was appointed mayor of the city in 1671. Few Englishmen of his time had a keener percep- **1671.** tion of practical necessities, or a character more admirably fitted for the position. The following year, Thomas Delavall — the mayor, in 1666 — was reappointed. He purchased several large estates, among which were Great and Little Barent Islands, now Barn Islands, near Hell Gate, and a cherry orchard of several acres in the neighborhood of Franklin Square. From this orchard, Cherry Street derived its name.

In March, 1671, Lovelace bought the greater portion of the "Dominie's Bouwery." This property consisted of about sixty-two acres of land between the present Warren and Christopher Streets, which **March 9.** formerly belonged to Dominie Bogardus and his wife, Anetje Jans, and had been confirmed to their heirs by Nicolls in 1667. It adjoined the West India Company's farm, which the Duke of York held by virtue of confiscation by Nicolls. Lovelace made the purchase for his own benefit and for some time held it in his own right. It was afterwards vested in the crown, and, by a curious train of events, the farm of the first Dutch minister was merged in the estate now enjoyed by the corporation of Trinity Church.

In the mean time, in England, the king had grown restless under constitutional restraints. The independence, the safety, the dignity of the nation over which he presided were nothing to him. While an **1672.** assembly of subjects could call for his accounts before paying his debts, or could insist upon knowing which of his mistresses or boon companions had intercepted the money destined for the equipping and manning of the national fleet, he could not think himself a king ; and he determined upon emancipating himself. Who, better than the French king, could aid in establishing absolute monarchy in England ? To this end he opened a negotiation ; and his own sister, the beautiful and witty Henrietta, Duchess of Orleans, who was also the sister-in-law of Louis, and a favorite with both monarchs, was made the chief agent at the French court. The offer of Charles was to dissolve the Triple Alliance and join France against the Dutch Republic, if Louis would furnish such military and pecuniary assistance as would render him independent of Parliament. To this arrangement Louis consented, and a secret treaty was signed, by which Charles bound himself to profess the Roman Catholic religion, and employ the whole strength of England by land and by sea to destroy the power of the United Provinces, and to maintain the rights of the house of Bourbon to the throne of Spain. The Duke of York was immensely gratified, and in haste to see the article touching the Roman Catholic religion carried into immediate execution. But Louis was too wise, and decreed that Charles should continue to call himself a Protestant, and, at high festivals, to receive the sacrament according to the ritual of the Church of England.

The Prince of Orange had been, from his birth, an object of serious apprehension to the aristocratic party in Holland, and it was not intended to restore him to the high office of Stadtholder, which had been regarded as hereditary in his family. He was a cold, sullen young man, without health, but full of ambitious ideas and projects. As the nephew of Charles, and a grandson of England, it was thought expedient to bring him if possible into the alliance. Accordingly, he was invited to London, where his birthday was celebrated with great pomp. He was offered the despotic rule of the seven provinces, and the hand of Mary, the daughter of the Duke of York, in marriage, if he would join the allies. He replied, " My country trusts in me ; I will not sacrifice it to my interests, but if need be die with it in the last ditch." When war was actually declared, he chafed under his thraldom and longed to be at the head of armies. As he was of age, there was a strong tide of public sentiment in favor of giving him the supreme command.

De Witt resisted for a long time. It had been his policy to foster the sea, rather than the land forces of the nation ; consequently, while the Dutch fleets under De Ruyter and Tromp fought gloriously and maintained the honor of their flag against England, the French monarch invaded the Netherlands with his armies, numbering two hundred thousand men, to meet twenty thousand Dutch soldiers. The annals of the human race record but few instances of moral power so successfully defying and repelling such superiority of force. The dikes were broken up, and the country was drowned. The son of Grotius, suppressing anger at the ignominious proposals of Louis XIV., who had established his court at Utrecht, protracted the negotiations until the rising waters formed a wide and impassable moat around the cities. At Gronigan, the whole population, without regard to sex, — little children even, — toiled on the fortifications. The suffering and terrified people raged against the government. The Prince of Orange came forward and spoke to the States-General in lofty and inspiring language. He told them that, even if their soil and all the marvels of it were buried under the ocean, all was not lost. They might take refuge in the farthest isles of Asia, and commence a new and glorious existence amid the sugar-canes and nutmeg-trees ! He was presently made Captain-General, and shortly after De Witt resigned his office of Pensionary, and his brother Cornelius was imprisoned. Men in their madness attributed to their ablest statesmen and bravest generals all the disasters which had occurred. One day while De Witt was visiting his brother in the prison, a band of infuriated ruffians burst in the doors, dragged them both out, and brutally assassinated them in front of the Binenhof, at the Hague. Confusion and discouragement seemed at their height. The stern determination of Prince William, however, infused new life into the faltering army, until the French thought it prudent to retire. Holland was saved.

But the landing of English troops upon the soil could only be prevented by naval conflicts. The younger Tromp had been disgraced some time before on the accusation of De Ruyter; hence the two **1673.** commanders were bitter enemies. At the battle of Soulsberg, the Dutch with fifty-two ships of the line engaged an enemy with eighty. De Ruyter was in the full flush of victory, when he discovered that Tromp was nearly overpowered. He magnanimously checked his own career and turned to the relief of the latter. Seeing the movement, the young hero shouted, " There comes grandfather to the rescue ; I will never desert him as long as I breathe."

The issue of that day was uncertain. In the next encounter, the advantage was decidedly with the Dutch, and the English retreated to the Thames. Two months later, one hundred and fifty English **Aug. 11.** and French ships were met by seventy-five Dutch, near the Helder, and a terrible battle ensued. The contesting forces rivalled each other in stubborn valor. The noise of artillery boomed along the low coasts, while the Dutch churches were thronged with people praying for the success of their arms. To the ears of these anxious worshipers, the fluctuating roar of the conflict — now almost dying away into silence, and, again, shaking the earth and filling all the air — was followed at last by the protracted hush which afforded the first intimation of the enemy's retreat. A marvelous victory had been won, and De Ruyter and Tromp shared with William of Orange in the tumultuous gratitude which, like the sea, almost deluged the country.

New York must needs suffer meanwhile. Its progress was checked with the first news of the commotion beyond the seas. Lovelace gave his attention to defenses. An extra company of foot was organized, and that sterling old Dutch officer, Martin Cregier, was placed in command. A volunteer troop of horse was also raised, and Ex-Mayor Cornelis Steenwyck was made its captain. The fort was repaired and other precautions were taken. All ships bound for Europe were compelled to sail in company for mutual protection against privateers. The navigation of the Hudson River was restricted. The merchants were hampered and on the eve of bankruptcy. Commerce was injured with all the colonies along the Atlantic coast. Several New York merchant vessels — among them even the *Good Fame* itself — were captured by the Dutch.

The news that Colonel Nicolls had been killed in the first naval engagement was received in New York with much lamentation,[1] and funeral exercises were held with great solemnity in the Dutch church in the fort.

A compulsory tax for the building of a new battery was not deemed prudent or politic ; hence Lovelace asked for a " benevolence " from each town in the province. A commission, consisting of Francis Rombouts, Thomas Lovelace, Captain Manning, Allard Anthony, Thomas Gibbs, and Captain Richard Morris,[2] was appointed to receive and expend the moneys collected. A legion of knotty questions immediately sprung up in connection with titles and quitrents. While the governor and his council were doing their best to preserve harmony in New York, an arrogant assembly at Elizabethtown deposed Governor Philip Carteret, and appointed his cousin James, the son of Sir George, who had just arrived, in his stead. And Delaware escaped the imminent peril of being absorbed by Maryland.

The times were so disturbed that Lovelace was impressed with the necessity of establishing an overland mail between New York and Boston, for the transmission of intelligence, in case of sudden danger or misfortune, and for the advancement of commerce. He consequently issued a proclamation, on the 10th of December, 1672, that on the first day of January, 1673, and on the first Monday of every following month, a sworn messenger would be dispatched to convey letters and small packets to Boston, taking Hartford and other places on his way. A change of horses would be furnished to the messenger at Hartford on his journey to and from Boston. He was to be paid a small salary, and all the letters were to be free of postage. He was instructed to form a post-road by marking trees, " that shall guide other travelers as well." Lovelace wrote to Winthrop, asking him to give the man advice as to the best route to pursue, and in the same letter informed Winthrop

Jan. 1.

---

[1] In the Ampthill church, Bedfordshire, England, is a monument to Richard Nicolls, on which is represented a cannon-ball with the inscription "*Instrumentum mortis et immortalitatis.*" *Brodhead*, II. 186. *Basnage*, II. 192 – 209. *Sylvius*, I. 191 – 208, 243 – 249. *Evelyn*, I. 335 – 409. *Pepys*, II. 361.

[2] Captain Richard Morris was an English gentleman of fortune, who had been one of the adherents of Cromwell. He came to New York while it was yet a Dutch province, and bought over three thousand acres of land near Harlem. He obtained a grant with baronial privileges and called his property *Morrisania*. His wife died in 1672. He himself died shortly after his appointment recorded above, leaving an infant son, Lewis, a year old. The administration of his estate was granted to Secretary Nicolls. An elder brother of the deceased, Lewis Morris, afterwards removed to Morrisania from Barbadoes, and assumed the guardianship of the boy, who became the famous Governor Morris.

of the latest news from England ; namely, that the Dutch Republic had actually lost three of its provinces, and that there were no tidings of peace. Forty well-equipped men-of-war had just been dispatched from Holland to the West Indies. " It is high time we begin to buckle on our armor," he added.

While the snow was yet upon the ground, Lovelace paid a visit to the manor of Thomas Pell, near " Annie's Hoeck," for the ^{March.} purpose of settling some question about the new postal route. An express followed him from Captain Manning, to announce the appearance of a supposed Dutch squadron off Sandy Hook. He hurried back to the city, and, finding no enemy, was inclined to ridicule the false alarm. However, he summoned the soldiers from Albany, Esopus, and Delaware, and mustered one hundred or more enlisted men. The weeks went quietly by, there was a general training, and, as the Indians were menacing the outposts, the garrisons were sent back to their sta- ^{May.} tions, leaving about eighty soldiers in Fort James.

Lovelace had for months been intending to visit Winthrop on business of importance, and, seeing no special reason to hinder, set ^{July 20.} out for Hartford on the 20th of July, leaving Manning as before in charge of the fort. He had been gone but a few days, when several ships were discovered lying near the present quarantine ground. Man- ^{July 29.} ning immediately dispatched a messenger in hot haste to Lovelace, put the guns of the fort in order, caused drums to be beaten through the streets for volunteers, and seized provisions wherever they could be found. But New York was divided against itself. There were Dutch citizens who visited the hostile fleet and revealed the weakness of the defenses. The Dutch militia even spiked the guns of the new battery, in front of the City Hall. Manning tried to gain time until the governor should return. He sent Captain John Carr, who was accidentally in the city, Counselor Thomas Lovelace, and Attorney John Sharpe to demand " why the fleet had come in such a manner to disturb his Majesty's subjects in this place." A boat passed them on the way, with a messenger from the two admirals, Evertsen and Binckes, bearing an order for the surrender of New York. " We have come to take the place, which is our own, and our own we will have," they said.

Captain Carr informed Captain Manning, on his return, that the enemy were too strong to be withstood, and that the Dutch flag must be hoisted within half an hour or they would fire upon the fort. Meanwhile the fleet had moved nearer, so that the foremost ships were within musket-shot. Sharpe was sent promptly back to ask for a cessa- ^{July 30.} tion of hostilities until the next morning, that advice might be obtained

17

from the mayor and aldermen. But Admiral Evertsen had already written a letter to the city magistrates, guaranteeing to all men their estates and liberties, and this had been read aloud to the citizens from the City Hall. The commanders would grant but one more half-hour, " and the glass was turned up."

At the end of that time, the ships fired a broadside into the fort, killing and wounding several of the garrison, and the fire was returned. At the same moment six hundred men were seen landing just above the "governor's orchard," on the river shore, back of the present Trinity Church. They paraded in the old graveyard adjoining. Manning, at Carr's instigation, ordered a flag of truce to be exhibited ; but Carr, exceeding his orders, struck the king's flag at the same time. Carr, Lovelace, and Gibbs were sent to make the best conditions possible with the invading force. The two latter were detained as hostages, and Carr was sent back to demand the surrender of the garrison in fifteen minutes, as prisoners of war. Carr never delivered the message, but sought his personal safety in another direction. Manning sent Sharpe to meet the column which was rapidly advancing down Broadway, to ask permission to march out of the fort with the honors of war. It was about seven o'clock, on a summer evening. Captain Anthony Colve, who was in command of the Dutch, readily acquiesced. He formed his men in a line in front of the fort, and waited, while Manning marched through the gates, at the head of the garrison, with colors flying and drums beating. They grounded their arms, and were committed to prison in the church, while the Dutch quietly took possession of the citadel. The three-colored ensign of the Dutch Republic rose to its old place on the flag-staff, and New York became once more New Netherland.

This was an absolute conquest by an open enemy in time of war. Every circumstance in connection with it differed from those which had stood out conspicuously when the place was captured by the English, nine years before. A province was annexed to the Dutch Republic ; but the effete West India Company had had nothing whatever to do with the transaction. The old corporation had gone into liquidation soon after the conquest of the place in 1664, and the new company had taken no interest in its recapture. It had greatly increased in value under the English ; the population had more than doubled ; and now the direct authority of the States-General and the Prince of Orange was hailed by all who had a drop of Dutch blood in their veins, and by many others, with unbounded enthusiasm. The city was called New Orange, in honor of the young prince, and the fort received the name of William Hendrick.

CHAPTER XV.

1673–1678.

ADMIRAL EVERTSEN.

ADMIRAL EVERTSEN. — THE NEW MUNICIPAL OFFICERS. — THE CONQUERED TERRITORY. — TAKING THE OATH. — LOVELACE'S PRIVATE LOSSES. — GOVERNOR ANTHONY COLVE. — RUMORS OF WAR WITH NEW ENGLAND. — AUSTRIA AND SPAIN TO THE RESCUE OF HOLLAND. — THE FAMOUS TEST ACT. — MARY OF MODENA. — THE MARRIAGE OF THE DUKE OF YORK. — THE SACRIFICE OF NEW NETHERLAND. — THE TREATY OF WESTMINSTER. SIR EDMUND ANDROS. — LIEUTENANT-GOVERNOR ANTHONY BROCKHOLLS. — NEW JERSEY. — LONG ISLAND. — GOVERNOR COLVE'S FAREWELL. — THE RECEPTION OF GOVERNOR ANDROS. — DOMINIE VAN RENSSELAER. — FREDERICK PHILIPSE. — CAPTAIN MANNING. — STRINGENT MEASURES. — IMPRISONMENT OF LEADING CITIZENS. — INDIAN WAR IN NEW ENGLAND. — ROBERT LIVINGSTON. — ANDROS AND THE CONNECTICUT DELEGATES. — CITY IMPROVEMENTS. — TANNERIES ALONG MAIDEN LANE. — STEPHANUS VAN CORTLANDT. — THE CELEBRATED BOLTING ACT. — INDIAN AND NEGRO SLAVES.

Portrait of Evertsen.

THE two Dutch admirals, Evertsen and Binckes, were obliged to assume the responsibility of governing their conquest until directions should come from the Hague. Never was the Dutch Republic more ably represented than by the cool, honest, and sagacious Admiral Evertsen. He was the eldest son of the renowned Admiral Cornelis Evertsen, who was killed in a battle with the English, in 1666. He had with him in the New York harbor about twenty English prizes, which he had captured in Virginia and elsewhere, and a large number of prisoners. But it was a delicate matter to select from his inferior officers a governor for New Amsterdam.

Captain Anthony Colve was the best fitted among them for such a command. He was accordingly appointed, by the admirals, and a commission was issued for him similar in phraseology to those issued by the crown of England. He was a short, stout, dark-complexioned man, abrupt in his manners, coarse in his language, and of a rough, passionate nature, which had not been improved by military service. He possessed undoubted qualifications for rulership, but he was vain, gluttonous, and excessively given to wine. He put on princely airs, spent money extravagantly, and lived ostentatiously. In the latter respect he outdid any of the governors who had preceded him.

The admirals determined to keep their ships in the harbor until the new government should be firmly established. They evidently distrusted the ability of Colve in many particulars. They sent for Oloff S. Van Cortlandt, Johannes De Peyster, Cornelis Steenwyck, and a few others of the prominent Dutch citizens, and advised with them as to proper persons for official trusts. Nicholas Bayard acted as register of their proceedings, and was finally made secretary of the province. The old form of municipal government was restored, and the commonalty convoked to elect a new board of burgomasters and schepens. The burgomasters were Johannes Van Brugh, Johannes De Peyster, and Ægidius Luyck. The schepens were William Beekman (who had returned from Esopus), Jeronimus Ebbing, Jacob Kip, Lawrence Van der Spiegel, and Gulian Verplanck.

They were from among the wealthiest citizens, and of the Dutch Reformed religion. Jeronimus Ebbing was a man of large property, whose business for seventeen years or more had been along the Hudson River, chiefly at Esopus and Albany, which he visited at stated intervals, to gather and ship to Holland furs and other articles from the Indians. He was by profession a lawyer, and his wife was the daughter of De Laet, the Dutch historian. She was a lady of great personal beauty, and possessed in her own right a large estate, comprising, amongst other property, the tract of land which her father had acquired near Albany, when he was one of the directors of the West India Company. Gulian Verplanck was the son of Abraham Verplanck, who lived on the east side of the town near the river. Gulian was, for many years, the clerk of Allard Anthony, but, about 1656, he went into business for himself and became very prosperous. He married Hendrica Wessells, the belle of New Amsterdam. The venerable Allard Anthony, who, as sheriff, had been so exacting and severe that the common people called him the "hangman," was now removed from that office, and Anthony De Milt was appointed in his place. The latter was a baker, living on the corner of Whitehall and Beaver Streets. He was well known and possessed the good-will of the entire community. His three daughters, Maria, Anna, and Sarah, were at one period the best Latin scholars in the city. He had two sons, Isaac and Pieter, from whom the numerous families of that name are descended.

The new magistrates were duly sworn into office, and the late mayor surrendered the gowns, mace, and seal which the Duke of York had given to the city. These were at once carefully deposited in the fort. The admirals issued a proclamation, confiscating all the property and debts belonging to the kings of France and England, and requiring every person to report such property to Secretary Bayard. The estates of Lovelace, Delavall, Carteret, Manning, Willett, Derval, and others were attached, and those unfortunate officers left penniless.[1] The dwellings of Lovelace and Manning had been plundered by the Dutch troops in the first heat of conquest; and that of John Lawrence, the mayor, would have suffered the same fate, but for the timely interference of some of his Dutch neighbors. Van Ruyven, who was the Receiver-General of the Duke's revenues, was required to render a strict account of all the property in his possession. Aug. 8.

The conquered territory, as described in the commission to Governor Colve, extended from fifteen miles south of Cape Henlopen to the eastern end of Long Island, thence through the middle of the Sound to Greenwich, and so northerly according to the boundary made in 1650, including Delaware Bay and the intermediate territory, as possessed by the Duke of York. As soon as the city was secured, two hundred men were sent up the river in vessels, to reduce Esopus and Albany. They encountered no opposition, the places were surrendered " at mercy," and the soldiers held as prisoners of war. New Jersey submitted peaceably, and the countries on the Delaware followed her example. Some of the Long Island towns came forward with alacrity, to bring their English flags and adopt the colors of Holland; but others were not disposed to yield so easily. Southampton appealed to Hartford for advice and assistance. Connecticut was cautious. Her own affairs were in a critical condition : two delegates from the General Court were just upon the eve of starting for New Orange, with a letter of remonstrance to the Dutch commanders against their arbitrary treatment of British subjects. The admirals gave them a strictly military reception, and replied in writing to their appeal, that it was very strange their enemies should object to the results of war, and that prompt punishment would be visited upon "all who should strive to maintain the said villages in their injustice." While the Connecticut delegates were still at the fort, deputies from Southampton,

---

[1] William Derval to Mr. R. Wolley, September 20, 1673 ; *Col. Doc.*, III. 206.

Easthampton, Southold, Brookhaven, and Huntington arrived. Nathaniel Sylvester came also from Shelter Island, and advised his Long Island neighbors by all means to submit. This they finally decided to do. Sylvester asked and obtained a confirmation of the privileges which Nicolls had granted to Shelter Island in 1666. David Gardiner shortly after took the oath and was confirmed in the possession of Gardiner's Island with all its manor privileges. But there were so many English prisoners that the situation became embarrassing, and three ships were sent to convey them to Europe.

Aug. 9.

While these events were following each other in rapid succession, Governor Lovelace had completed his stay in Hartford and was leisurely returning on horseback through the woods, when he was met near New Haven by an excited messenger, who reported that the Dutch squadron was in the bay. He pushed on as rapidly as possible, but learned at Mamaroneck that the fort had already been taken. Still hoping, however, to retrieve the disaster, he crossed to Long Island for the purpose of arousing the people and raising militia. At the house of Justice Cornwell, near Flushing, he met Secretary Matthias Nicolls, who advised him " to keep out of the enemy's hand." Some of the Dutch ministers gave him counter-advice ; and, having at stake private interests of moment, he finally decided to visit the fort for three days. Admiral Evertsen, having been informed of this, went over in his barge to Long Island, received the superseded governor with courtesy, and conducted him to the city, where he was handsomely entertained by its new masters. Before the expiration of the three days, he was arrested by his creditors for debts which the confiscation of his property. left no means for paying. He wrote to Winthrop : " Are you curious to know the extent of my losses ? it was my all whichever I had been collecting ; too greate to misse in this wilderness." Soon after he sailed for Europe in Admiral Binckes's vessel, accompanied by Thomas Delavall.

By the hand of Van Ruyven, who left for Holland about the same time, the city magistrates wrote to the States-General an eloquent letter, representing the urgent need of reinforcements as soon as the squadron should leave the bay. Finding that Admiral Evertsen proposed sailing sooner than had been anticipated, the citizens laid before him an urgent petition that two ships of war, commanded by superior officers, should be left behind, to prevent the Duke of York from attempting to recover his possessions. This request was granted.

Aug. 31.

The Indians were attracted by the magnificent vessels in the harbor, and some of the sachems visited the fort and congratulated the Dutch upon the recovery of their colony. They said, " We have always been as one flesh ; if the French come down from Canada, we will join the Dutch, and live and die with them." These words of amity were confirmed with a belt of wampum.

When Governor Colve was at last installed in office, he set up a coach, drawn by three horses. Cornelis Steenwyck was his first counselor. Secretary Bayard was efficient in all business matters, and on important occasions the burgomasters and schepens of the city were consulted. When questions arose about the treatment of foreigners or their property, Captain Knyff and Captain Epesteyn, of the Dutch infantry, were added as a council of war.

Everything assumed a military air. A guard was stationed near Sandy Hook, to send the earliest information to the governor of the arrival of ships. Strangers were not allowed to cross the ferries into the city without a pass ; and whoever had not taken the oath of allegiance was expelled from the city. The insecure condition of the fort was improved ; and twenty-one houses that pressed too closely upon the citadel were removed, the owners being compensated with lots in other **Dec.** localities. The Lutheran church which had just been built " without the gate " was demolished, and the Lutherans were allowed to build another at the corner of Broadway and Rector Street, on the site of what was afterwards Grace Church.

Serious difficulties arising about this time with New England, and hostilities having been threatened, it was ordered that no person should enter or depart from New York except through the city gate, *on pain of death.* At sundown the gates were closed, and a watch was set until sunrise. Citizens were forbidden to harbor any stranger, or to hold any correspondence whatever with the people of Massachusetts and Connecticut.

To bring the city more directly under the governor's authority, **1674.** a " Provisional Instruction " was issued, which authorized Captain **Jan. 16.** Knyff to preside over the Court of Burgomasters and Schepens. The honest magistrates rebelled at this ; whereupon Colve pompously threatened to dismiss them and appoint others, and they finally **Feb. 1.** yielded under protest.

To provide for the " excessive expenses," a tax was levied upon every inhabitant of the city worth over one thousand guilders. As it must necessarily take some time to collect this tax, every person who had been assessed more than four thousand guilders was ordered to advance a loan. As it was generally supposed that the Duke would attempt the recapture of the province, precautions were taken on **March 17.** all sides to prevent a surprise.

Meanwhile, a series of remarkable events, affecting the whole future of

New York, were taking place across the water. The movements of the king of France had roused Austria to arms, and the Roman Catholic dynasty of Spain had hastened to support the Protestant Dutch Republic against the common danger. Louis found himself all at once compelled to contend with half of Europe, and was consequently in no condition to furnish funds for England. Parliament was convoked, and both houses reassembled in the spring of 1673. But they doled out money sparingly, considered the war with Protestant Holland unjustifiable, disliked the king's alliance with Roman Catholic France, and suspected the orthodoxy of the Duke of York. The Commons, as the only condition upon which they would vote supplies, extorted the unwilling consent of Charles to a celebrated law known as the Test Act, which continued in force down to the reign of George IV. It required all persons holding office, civil or military, to take the oath of supremacy, and publicly receive the sacrament according to the rites of the Church of England. The Duke of York, who had secretly been a Roman Catholic, was obliged to candidly declare his religious faith, and, in a flood of tears, he resigned all the offices which he held under the Crown, including that of Lord High Admiral. But, as the act did not extend to Scotland and Ireland, or to the American Plantations, his admiralty jurisdiction over the latter remained unchanged.

The king of Spain made it one of the conditions of his signing an alliance with Germany and the United Netherlands, that the latter should consent to a peace with England upon the basis of a mutual restoration of conquests. The House of Commons, having obtained one victory over the king in the matter of the Test Act, declared that no more supplies should be granted for the war, unless it should appear that the enemy had obstinately refused to consent to reasonable terms of peace. Charles then cajoled the nation by pretending to return to the policy of the Triple Alliance. He summoned Sir William Temple from his retirement and sent him again as minister to Holland. The latter, of all the official men of that age, had preserved the fairest character, never having taken any part in the politics which had dictated the war. Through his efforts, a separate treaty of peace was, in course of time, concluded with the United Provinces. The States-General submitted to hard terms, for they were forced to succumb to a political necessity. It was two months before they knew of the conquest of New Netherland, and one month before that important event had actually occurred, that they yielded to the dictation of Spain so far as to promise to sign articles of peace with England.

Never before were two allies by circumstance greater enemies at heart than the uncertain king of England and the statesmen of the Dutch Republic. Charles and the Duke of York both wished, for many reasons, to remain in favor with the French king. Mary of Modena, the beautiful Roman Catholic princess, had been selected as the wife of the Duke, and the future queen of England. Charles approved the match, and Louis gave the bride a splendid dowry. Perhaps the Duke would have been just then more pleased with ships and men and money for the recovery of New York; and the ruined merchants of England would certainly have been better satisfied with some indemnity for their losses, as the privateers of Holland and Zealand had captured twenty-seven hundred British vessels, to say nothing of other property destroyed. But it was a wedding instead.

Mary of Modena was fifteen years of age; tall, and womanly, and beautiful. She read and wrote Latin and French with ease, had some taste in painting, could dance well, and excelled in music. Of history, geography, and the royal sciences, she knew nothing. When her mother announced to her that she had been sought in marriage by the Duke of York, she asked, with great simplicity, who the Duke of York was. When told that he was brother to the king of England and heir-presumptive to that realm, she inquired the whereabouts of England. As for her prospective husband, when she found that he was in his fortieth year, she burst into a fit of weeping, declaring that she would rather be a nun, and implored her aunt to marry the man herself. James, smarting doubly from the consequences of the Test Act and the loss of New York, paid very little attention to his marriage festivities. Instead of choosing a person of his own faith to act as his proxy in France, he sent a member of the Church of England, and the ceremony was performed by an English priest, not only without a dispensation from the Pope, but in defiance of his interdict.

James was in the drawing-room, laughing and chatting with some ladies and gentlemen, when the French ambassador came to him with the news that the marriage service had been concluded. " Then I am a married man," he exclaimed, gayly. He sent a message the same evening to his daughter Mary, that he " had provided a playfellow for her." As for the bride, she cried and screamed two whole days and nights as the time drew near for her to commence her journey to England. She would not be pacified until her mother promised to accompany her. She embarked at Calais on the 21st of November, 1673. The Duke gallantly awaited her on the sands at Dover, and, like his royal father, many years before, received his French bride in his arms. He was charmed with her grace and loveliness, and, though she betrayed a childish aversion to him, he was too well versed in the art of playing the successful wooer to ladies of all ages to notice it, and lavished upon her the most courtly attentions.

From that hour, it became evident that New Netherland was the pivot upon which affairs were likely to turn. The States-General had committed themselves with Spain to a mutual restoration of conquests, while yet ignorant of their recent American acquisition. With the news of their unexpected good fortune came a sense of painful embarrassment. Peace was desirable; and finally they determined upon the sacrifice, and, through the Spanish ambassador at London, offered to restore New Netherland. Charles charged the Dutch with insincerity; but Parliament was alive to the probable consequences of the Duke's marriage, and informed the king that the treaty was inevitable. Perceiving that his lords were bent upon keeping him poor and without an army, Charles suddenly accepted the terms, although he said, " it went more against his heart than the losing of his right hand." When he had committed himself too far to recede, Louis offered him five million and a half dollars and forty ships of war to break off negotiations. James tried to accomplish the same result, for he would have greatly preferred to recover his losses by force of arms. The treaty was signed, however, at Westminster, on the 9th of February, 1674, and peace was soon after proclaimed at London and at the Hague. Thus England escaped a disastrous war, and the Dutch were rendered less apprehensive of Louis, their more dreaded foe.

Feb. 9.

The news reached New Netherland early in June. Governor Colve received instructions from the States-General to restore the province to any person whom the king of England should depute to receive it. The wise heads at the Hague had been denied even one brief moment of exultation in the prospect of rearing the offspring of their offspring, — the child of the selfish corporation which they themselves had fostered. Whatever dreams they may have indulged of building a great empire midway between the Royalist and Puritan colonies of England, to teach the world lessons in civil and religious liberty and patriotic devotion, were now dissipated forever. But the spirits of a few men had already infused into the character of the people elements of greatness destined never to die out, and laid the foundations of a community on principles of freedom and virtue which, through all the mutations of time, will increase the purity and power of the nation.

June 7.

Sir Edmund Andros was the newly appointed English governor. He had been brought up in the king's household, of which his father was the master of ceremonies. He had distinguished himself in the army, and, by the recent death of his father, had succeeded to the office of bailiff of Guernsey, and become hereditary seigneur of the fief of Sausmarez. The proprietor of Carolina had also made him a landgrave, and granted him four baronies in that province. He was about thirty-seven years of age; well informed in the politics of the time, educated in history and language and art, and, as events subsequently developed, possessed of great capacity for statesmanship. His private character, moreover, was without blemish. His wife, Mary, to whom he had been married about three years and who accompanied him to this country, was the daughter of Sir Thomas Craven. His commission authorized him to take possession of New York, in the name of Charles II. He arrived in October.

Portrait of Andros.

An interesting question arose at Whitehall, touching the Duke's title to New York. The most eminent lawyers in England were taken into council, and it was finally decided that all subordinate right and jurisdiction had been extinguished by the Dutch conquest; the king alone was proprietor of New Netherland by virtue of the treaty of Westminster. Charles therefore issued a new patent to his brother, conveying the same territory as before, with absolute powers of government. And the Duke gave elaborate instructions to Andros, which formed the temporary political constitution of New York.

Anthony Brockholls was appointed lieutenant-governor. He was a Roman Catholic; but the Test Act, which would have excluded him from office in England, did not reach these shores. The Duke, still writhing under Protestant intolerance, was thus able to illustrate his own ideas of freedom of conscience.

It is a curious fact, that the king's new patent to the Duke read as if no previous English patent had ever existed. It conveyed, ostensibly for the first time, a territory, which the Netherlands, after conquering and holding it, had by treaty restored. New Jersey was once more the property of James, together with all the territory west of the Connecticut River, Long Island and the adjacent islands, and the region of Pemaquid.

Boundary dissensions, litigations, fines, and heart-burnings were all to begin at the original starting-place and be lived over again. Berkeley and Carteret were slightly moved to anger when they found their former purchases annulled. Berkeley had sold his undivided half of New Jersey for one thousand pounds; and John Fenwick, the buyer, thought he

17

had secured a bargain. Sir George Carteret was vice-chamberlain of the royal household, and a resolute, domineering courtier. These gentlemen suddenly found themselves without any legal right whatever to New Jersey, and were not slow or moderate in their complaints. Carteret wielded the greater influence of the two; and, within three weeks after the commission to Andros was issued, the Duke directed Thomas Wynnington, his attorney-general, and Sir John Churchill, his solicitor-general, to prepare a grant to Carteret, *in severalty*, of a part of the portion which, ten years before, he had conveyed to Berkeley and Carteret *jointly*.[1]

Whatever may be said of the scope of this instrument, its history is remarkable. Before he granted it, James hesitated and demurred. Charles had insisted that something must be done to keep Sir George in a good-humor. And when James at last affixed his signature to the grant, it was after carefully noting that it contained no clause by which the imperious Carteret could claim the absolute power and authority to govern. The commission to Andros comprehended New Jersey, and it was not altered. Yet Carteret, esteeming himself sole proprietor, drew up a paper distinctly recognizing the annihilation of this old right by the Dutch conquest and the recent fresh grant from the Duke, and at the same time commissioned his cousin Philip Carteret as governor over his possessions, and procured his passage in the same vessel with Andros. Lord Berkeley seems to have been ignored altogether.

The Duke, not quite at ease about his title to Long Island, as he had never paid Lord Stirling the sum agreed upon in 1664, negotiated a life pension of three hundred pounds a year for him on condition that he would yield all pretense to right and title. This was satisfactory; and Lord Stirling agreed that, if the Duke would procure for him any employment of the like value, he would release the grant of his annuity.

Oct. 22.   The frigates *Diamond* and *Castle*, with the gubernatorial party, anchored off Staten Island, October 22, 1674. Andros sent Governor Carteret, with Ensign Knafton, to notify Governor Colve of his

---

[1] This grant was described as the tract of land "westward of Long Island and Manhattan Island, bounded on the east partly by the main sea and partly by Hudson's River, and extends southward as far as a certain creek called Barnegat, being about the middle between Sandy Point and Cape May ; and bounded on the west in a strait line from Barnegat to a certain creek in Delaware River next to and below a certain creek called Rankokus Kill ; and from thence up the Delaware River to the northermost branch thereof which is forty-one degrees and forty minutes of latitude ; and on the north crosses over thence in a strait line to Hudson's River in forty-one degrees of latitude ; which said tract is to be called by the name of *New Jersey*." *Brodhead*, II. 267. *Whitehead*, 64. *Leaming and Spicer*, 49. *Chalmers*, I. 617. *Col. Doc.*, III. 229, 240.

arrival, and of his readiness to receive the scepter of command. The latter, by advice of his council, and the burgomasters and schepens, asked for eight days, in which to complete some necessary preliminaries. Cornelis Steenwyck, Johannes Van Brugh, and William Beekman were appointed to pay a visit of welcome to Andros on board the *Diamond*, and to request certain privileges for the Dutch inhabitants of New York. They were courteously received, invited to dine, treated to the choicest of wines, and assured that every Dutch citizen should participate in all the liberties and privileges accorded to English subjects. To the several articles, relating chiefly to the settlement of debts, the validity of judgments during the Dutch administration, the maintenance of owners in the possession of their property, the retention of church forms and ceremonies, etc., Andros replied that he would give such answers as were desired as soon as he had assumed the government. And all his promises were honorably fulfilled.

On the 9th of November, Governor Colve assembled at the old City Hall the burgomasters and schepens, together with all officers, civil or military, who had served under him, and, in a short speech, ^{Nov. 9.} absolved them from their oaths of allegiance to the States-General and the Prince of Orange, and announced that on the morrow he would surrender the fort and province to the new English governor, who represented the king of England. The cushions and the tablecloth in the City Hall were placed in charge of Johannes Van Brugh until they should be claimed by superior authority. Then, with a few words of farewell, he dismissed the assembly.

The next day was Saturday. Andros landed with much ceremony and was graciously greeted by the Dutch commander. The final transfer of the province took place, and the city on Manhattan ^{Nov. 10.} Island became once more and for all the future up to the present time, NEW YORK. One of the most friendly incidents of the occasion occurred just as the setting sun was tinting the western horizon. Ex-Governor Colve sent his coach and three horses with a formal, flattering message, as a gift to Governor Andros.

A quiet Sabbath followed. Dominie Van Nieuwenhuysen was assisted in the morning service, at the old Dutch church in the fort, by Rev. Nicolaus Van Rensselaer, a younger son of the patroon, and ^{Nov. 11.} one of the late arrivals by the *Diamond*.[1] He was an ordained clergyman,

---

[1] Dominie Van Rensselaer had fortunately prophesied to Charles II., when the latter was an exile at Brussels, that he would be restored to the throne. When that event occurred, the dominie accompanied the Dutch ambassador, Van Gogh, to London, as chaplain to the embassy ; and the king, remembering his prediction, gave Van Rensselaer a gold snuff-box

and had been recommended by James to fill one of the Dutch churches in New York or Albany, whenever a vacancy should occur. Andros, who was a member of the Church of England, attended divine service in the afternoon in the same sanctuary, as had been the custom of his predecessors.

Early on Monday morning, Andros wrote a polite note of acknowledgment to Colve for his many courtesies, and thanked him cordially for his unexpected present. He likewise returned the articles which had been submitted to him, nearly all of which had been agreed to, and certified by the newly sworn secretary of the province, Matthias Nicolls. The latter was made one of the governor's chief counselors and also mayor of the city.

Andros appointed the common council by special commission. John Lawrence was made deputy-mayor; and William Derval, Frederick Philipse, Gabriel Minvielle, and John Winder, aldermen. They were to hold their offices until the next October. Thomas Gibbs received the appointment of sheriff; and Captain Dyer, formerly of Rhode Island, that of collector of the revenues.

Frederick Philipse was known, for a full quarter of a century from this time, as the richest man in New York. He was a native of Friesland, and came to this country to seek his fortune, when New York was in her

feeblest infancy. He brought no money across the water, as has been generally supposed. He was a penniless youth, of high birth, with extraordinary tact and talent for business, and a smattering of the carpenter's trade. He worked at the latter until he could measure and master the situation. It is said that he was employed on the old Dutch church in the fort, and actually made the pulpit with his own hands. He finally started in trade and was successful, particularly with the Indians. He was persistently industrious and rose rapidly into notice. He

Philipse's Coat of Arms.

is spoken of as a well-to-do merchant, in 1662. From that time his

with his portrait on the lid, which is still preserved by the family at Albany. After Van Gogh left London, in 1665, because of the Dutch war, Van Rensselaer received Charles's license to preach in the Dutch church at Westminster, was ordained a deacon in the English Church by the Bishop of Salisbury, and was appointed lecturer in Saint Margaret's, Lothbury. Van Nieuwenhuysen's Letter to Cl. Amst., May 30, 1676; *Col. Doc.*, III. 225. *Doc. Hist. N. Y.*, III. 526. *O'Call.*, I. 122, 212 ; II. 552. *Holgate*, 52. *Smith*, I. 49, 388. *Brodhead*, II. 272. *New York Christ. Intell.*, Nov. 2, 1865. *Hist. Mag.*, IX. 352.

advance was rapid. The wealthy Peter Rudolphus De Vries died; and Philipse, marrying the widow, acquired her estate. The lady, however, was strong-minded, quite competent to manage her own affairs, and altogether opposed to taxation without representation. She bought and traded in her own name, and often went to Holland as supercargo in her own ships. She took her children to Europe, and gave them a liberal education. The world pronounced her able, but not amiable. The world sometimes errs in judgment, and may have done so in this instance, for there is no evidence of domestic infelicity in the Philipse family. On the contrary, Mrs. Philipse seems to have been in sympathy with all her husband's plans and projects, and to have greatly advanced his mercantile interests.

He became one of the largest traders with the Five Nations, at Albany; he sent his own vessels to both the East and West Indies; he imported slaves from Africa; and (as we shall see hereafter) there were audible whisperings, when piracy was at its zenith, of his being engaged in unlawful trade with the buccaneers at Madagascar. The latter accusation, however, if true, was never proven. By a fortuitous chain of circumstances, the united avails of several large individual fortunes centered in this one man. After the death of his first wife (about the time of the advent of Governor Sloughter), he married, in 1693, another rich widow. This was Catharine, the daughter of Oloff S. Van Cortlandt, and, besides the large estate bequeathed by her father, she had received from her deceased husband a still more extensive property. She was, moreover, young and attractive, had a sweet disposition, many accomplishments, and charming manners.

Frederick Philipse secured to himself, by purchase of the Indians and grants from the government, all the " hunting-grounds " between Spuyten-Duyvil and the Croton River. In 1693, this vast estate was formally erected by royal charter into a manor, under the style and title of the manor of Philipseborough, with the customary privileges of a lordship, such as holding court-leet, court-baron, exercising advowson, etc. It embraced the romantic site of the present ambitious city of Yonkers, which extends six miles along the Hudson River by three miles inland, and in the very heart of which may now be seen the pioneer manor-house erected in 1682. It was enlarged and improved in 1745, but the practiced eye can readily determine where the products of the two centuries were joined in one harmonious whole. There still swings in the center of the southern front a massive door, which was manufactured in Holland in 1681, and imported by the first Mrs. Philipse in one of her own vessels. It is as dark as ebony, and shows where the upper and lower halves, which formerly opened separately, were fastened together.

This old manor-house has had an eventful history, and finally, in the year 1867, it was purchased by the corporation of Yonkers and converted into a City Hall. Philipse was, for more than twenty years, a member of the governor's council, and on terms of intimacy with all the royal governors, from Andros to Bellamont. His enormous wealth entitled him to constant consideration ; yet he was no favorite with the magnates of his time. He was grave, even to melancholy, and talked so little that he was often pronounced excessively dull. He was not a man of letters, or of any special culture. He was intelligent, apt, a close observer of men and things, and shrewd almost to craftiness. Although an official adviser to the king's commander-in-chief, he never advised. In the political controversies which were more deadly bitter in that remote period than they have ever been since, he never meddled, but laid his hand upon his purse, and waited to see which party was likely to win. He was tall and well proportioned, with a quiet gray eye, which always seemed to hide more than it revealed, a Roman nose, and a mouth expressive of strong will. His movements were slow and measured. He dressed with great care and precision, wearing the full embroidery, lace cuffs, etc., of the time, and his head was crowned with that absurd and detestable monstrosity, — a periwig with flowing ringlets.

The governor and his council were to meet at nine o'clock every Friday morning for the transaction of State business. The first mayor's court was convened on the Wednesday following the surrender. Nov. 13. It was ordered that the records be henceforth kept in English, and that every paper offered to the court be in the same tongue, except in case of poor people who could not afford the cost of translation. This introduced more of the English form into legal proceedings than had heretofore obtained, but it was several years before the custom was well established.

Captain Manning returned to New York with Governor Andros in the *Diamond*. He had sailed for England shortly after the recapture of New York by the Dutch, and, suffering the affliction of losing his wife on the voyage, had arrived in London while the Treaty of Westminster was yet in suspense. The Duke summoned him into his presence, and, after listening to his account of the surrender of New York to the Dutch, censured him severely. The next day, he was closely examined in Lord Arlington's office by the king and the Duke. " Brother," said Charles to James, " the ground could not have been maintained by so few men." Manning was dismissed without reprimand, and the Duke, after a time, paid his expenses from Fayal.

But some of those who had lost heavily by the surrender to the Dutch were disposed to attribute the disaster to the officer in command. Alderman Derval, who was the son-in-law of Thomas Delavall, was very bitter in his denunciations of Manning. Andros was finally compelled to arrest the latter ; and he was tried by a court-martial, composed of the governor and council, Captains Griffith, Burton, and Salisbury, and the mayor and aldermen of the city. Six charges were brought against him, involving neglect of duty, cowardice, and treachery. A number of witnesses testified against him ; and, although he endeavored to explain his conduct, rejected indignantly the idea of treachery or cowardice, and finally threw himself upon the mercy of the court, he was found guilty of all save treachery, and pronounced deserving of death. As he had seen the king and the Duke since the crime was committed, he was allowed the benefit of the proverb, " king's face brings grace," and his life was spared. His sentence was to have his sword broken over his head in front of the " City Hall," and to be rendered incapable of holding any station of trust or authority under the government. He had, before this, purchased a large island in the East River, whither he retired, and where it would seem his disgrace did not disturb his philosophy, for he entertained largely and was one of the most facetious and agreeable of hosts. He settled the island upon Mary, the daughter of his wife by a former husband. This lady married Robert Blackwell, from whom the island received the name it has borne to the present time.

Andros, by the Duke's order, seized the estate of Lovelace, and required all persons possessing any portion of it to render an account. He thus obtained possession of the " Dominie's Bouwery," which was added to the Duke's farm adjoining. He visited in person the towns on the eastern part of Long Island, and soothed the ruffled temper of the people, who prudently avoided any direct opposition to his authority. He afterwards wrote to Winthrop that Connecticut had done well for the king by her interference against the Dutch during the past year, but significantly hinted that henceforth New York would be quite able to stand without neighborly assistance. The town clerk of Newtown was kept an hour upon the whipping-post, in front of the City Hall of the capital, with a paper pinned to his breast, stating that he had signed seditious letters against the government, because he replied to the governor's proclamation reinstating the old town officers, with a frank statement of former grievances under Lovelace.

In March, Andros issued an order requiring every citizen of the province to take the usual oaths of allegiance and fidelity. The mayor and aldermen appointed Monday, March 13, for the purpose, and the mayor's court was in session at an early hour. Some of the

March 13.

18

leading men, including several of the city magistrates, requested that before they proceeded with the business, Andros should confirm the pledge of Governor Nicolls, "that the capitulation of August, 1664, was not in the least broken, or intended to be broken, by any words or expressions in the said oath." As they understood it, this capitulation had been confirmed by the sixth article of the Treaty of Westminster; and such seems to have been the opinion of the Duke himself. The mayor, Matthias Nicolls, claimed to know nothing of any such pledge on the part of the former governor, and evinced much surprise when a copy was produced. The gentlemen declared that they only wished to be assured of future freedom of religion, and exemption from the duty of fighting against their own nation in time of war. But Andros fancied he detected something of covert mutiny, and haughtily required them to take the oath without qualification. Thereupon a petition was drafted, asking the governor to accept the oath in the manner and form approved by Nicolls, or to allow the parties concerned to dispose of their estates and remove elsewhere with their families. It was signed by Cornelis Steenwyck, Johannes Van Brugh, Johannes De Peyster, Nicholas Bayard, Ægidius Luyck, William Beekman, Jacob Kip, and Anthony De Milt. It was promptly rejected by Andros, without discussion, and its eight signers were immediately arrested and imprisoned, on a charge of trying to foment rebellion. Their examination took place in the presence of Andros and his council, Governor Carteret of New Jersey, and Captains Griffith and Burton, of the English frigates. Their case was turned over to the next Court of Assizes, and meanwhile they were released on bail. When their trial came on, De Peyster was acquitted, through the taking of the oath; the other seven were convicted of a violation of the act of Parliament in having traded without taking the oath, and their goods were accordingly forfeited; but eventually the penalties were remitted by the prisoners taking the required oath, and thus the difficulty ended.

About the first of May, Andros wrote to Winthrop, claiming for the Duke of York the country west of the Connecticut River, and sending copies of the Duke's patent and his own commission. The General Court of Connecticut replied that their charter came from the king, and that they should rest upon the boundary arrangement of 1664. Andros demanded possession, which was flatly refused. He then equipped an armed force and sailed up the Sound, anchoring just off Saybrook Point, with the intention of reducing the fort. But he found the people prepared for a determined resistance, and was unwilling to take the responsibility of bloodshed.

May 1.

June 28.

July 8.

He sent one of his sloops to Boston, with supplies for the aid of the New-Englanders, who were fighting the Indians. And, to prevent mischief nearer home, he crossed Long Island on horseback, disarming the Indians everywhere, and reviewing the militia. Upon reaching New York, he sent for the Long Island and New Jersey sachems, and renewed with them the old treaty of peace. The intrigues of the French missionaries among the Iroquois having created disturbance, Andros visited Albany, Schenectady, and the warlike tribes one hundred miles beyond. He was entertained by the savages everywhere, and created a strong sentiment in favor of the English. The sachems, in the happiest temper, renewed their former alliance. Before he left Albany on his homeward journey, he organized a local board of commissioners for Indian affairs, of which he appointed Robert Livingston the secretary.

This gentleman was a scion of an ancient and honorable Scotch family, whose lordly ancestors had drunk wine from king's goblets for centuries. His father was Rev. John Livingston, whose name ranks high in the Scotch Church, and who was one of the commissioners appointed by Parliament to negotiate with Charles the terms of his restoration to the throne, but who was afterward prosecuted with vigorous rancor for non-conformity, and obliged to take refuge in Rotterdam.

Robert Livingston was a bold and adventurous young man, and had been in the country about a year. His ability and promise were so marked, that, within a week after his arrival, he had been made town clerk of Albany. He acquired great influence over the Indians, and retained the office which he received from Andros for a long series of years. He married, in 1683, Alida, the widow of Rev. Nicolaus Van Rensselaer and daughter of Philip Pietersen Schuyler. He was a man

Livingston Coat of Arms.

of strongly marked individuality, of original conceptions, of irrepressible opinions, of obstinate determination, of untiring acquisitiveness, and, for the age in which he lived, of no mean culture. He was, in short, a man to be remembered on his own account, independent of birth or connection. Yet his birth and connection gave him social position in the Old World, and were not without their advantage to him in the New; for, on his frequent visits to England, in after years, the state policy of the colonial government or his own private interests were not infrequently the better served through his standing in the society, and his influence with the ruling classes, of the mother country. He was tall, and well developed in figure, with a somewhat cloudy complexion, brown hair, and dark, inscrutable eyes. He was polished in his manners, but careless of giving pleasure and indifferent to giving pain ; and withal, so icily impertinent at times as never to attain popularity in New York. He was of infinite value to the colony, for his energy and activity set in motion many a wheel which otherwise would have been long in turning.

In October of the same year, the burning of Hadley, Deerfield, North-
Oct. 19. field, and Springfield induced Andros to seriously contemplate engaging the Iroquois to go to the aid of New England against the murderous Indians within her borders. Connecticut declined the offer of such assistance, insinuating certain reflections upon the Dutch, and upon the conduct of Andros. The latter replied satirically and demanded explanations. Samuel Willys and William Pitkin were sent
1676. by Connecticut to hold a personal interview with Andros at the fort. They asked permission to talk with the Iroquois at Albany. They were told that it was strange that a colony so jealous about their own concerns should seek to treat with separate portions of another government. Andros, however, expressed his willingness to do all in his power to procure peace between New England and her Indian enemies. It was a time of great tribulation throughout the whole country. Pemaquid was, shortly after, burned, and Andros dispatched a sloop to Boston
Aug. 12. to bring the sufferers to New York. But Philip, the great Indian chief who had instigated the war, was suddenly slain in a swamp, and these barbarous hostilities came to an end.

The Connecticut boundary was still unsettled. The Duke wrote to Andros that he was willing things should rest as they were for the present. As to assemblies — for which New York had petitioned — he said they were useless and dangerous, apt to assume to themselves too many privileges, and hazardous to the peace of the government ; but he added, " Howsoever, if you continue of the same opinion, I shall be ready to consider any proposals you shall send, to that purpose."

Since the Peace of Westminster, American affairs had been restored to the immediate control of the crown, through the dissolution of the Council for Plantations and the transfer of the records to the Privy Council. It was the intention to strictly enforce the navigation and custom laws in the colonies. This caused, for a time, a cessation of trade between New York and Boston (since no European goods might be imported from one place to the other without the payment of customs in England), and produced misunderstandings and heartburnings between the two colonies.

Andros took an active personal interest in city affairs. He advised and suggested laws for correcting morals, suppressing profanity and intemperance, and punishing Sabbath-breakers. The city gates were closed at nine o'clock and opened at daylight. Every citizen was required to possess a musket, with a small quantity of powder and ball, and to take part in the night watch, when called upon. Masters of vessels coming into port must always furnish the mayor with a full list of their passengers, under penalty of fine. Peddling was prohibited, as freemen and burghers only were allowed to sell goods in the city. A number of good dwellings were erected, and all owners of vacant lots were ordered to improve them, under penalty of having them sold at public auction. Nicholas De Meyer was the mayor in 1676. He was a merchant and an old resident; his wife was the daughter of Hendrick Van Dyck. He was so ambitious for the prosperity of New York, and projected so many improvements, that Andros laughingly called him the " new broom," and charged him with sweeping all the rubbish into the ditch at Broad Street. That famous canal was, during the year, filled and made level with the rest of the land about it. The tan-pits which it had hitherto contained, and which had been complained of as a nuisance by the dwellers in the vicinity, were removed and established along Maiden Lane, where there was a marshy valley and a similar influx of water. One company, consisting of four shoemakers who were also tanners, bought a piece of land bounded by Maiden Lane, Broadway, Ann Street, and a line between William and Gold Streets, and prosecuted a flourishing business. Slaughter-houses were ordered out of the city limits, and were afterwards located over the water at " Smit's Vly," which was so called from a blacksmith who set up a forge on the corner of Maiden Lane and Pearl Street, and intercepted the custom of the Long Island farmers on their way to the city. Six wine and four beer taverns were licensed. No grain was allowed to be distilled unless unfit for flour. Everybody was allowed to cut wood on the island, at a distance of one mile from a house. The fort was repaired. Andros removed the kitchen of the governor's house, over which was the old armory, because the roof was leaky and rotten. Presently arose a new building in its place. He removed the tiles from the roof of the main edifice and substituted shingles. He set stockades around the fort, to protect it from animals, and closed the gate upon the water side. He also placed the arms of the Duke of York over the Broadway entrance.

In 1677, Stephanus Van Cortlandt was appointed mayor. He was the son of Oloff S. Van Cortlandt, and the first native-born citizen who had filled the office. He was some thirty-four years old, of **1677.**

fine presence, with commanding countenance and courtly bearing. He had been trained under a learned tutor in the severe and thorough mental culture which distinguished his parents, and was, in many respects, a brilliant character. His wealth was enormous. His wife — whom he married in 1671 — was the beautiful Gertrude Schuyler of Albany, one of the few chosen friends of Lady Andros. They lived in a handsome and well-furnished house, on the corner of Broad and Pearl Streets, and subsequently built the Cortlandt manor-house on the Hudson.

It was he who carried into execution the digging of the first public wells in the city. They were six in number, each located in the middle of a street. Water was not plentiful in them, and that little was brackish. But they were esteemed a security against fires, if of no greater value. The same year, a new dock was built, at the expense of the property-owners. The old graveyard on the west side of Broadway was sold off in building-lots, each one of which extended to the river's edge. At this date, there were sixty-five dwellings on Broadway. Francis Rombouts's home, upon or near the site of Trinity Church, was the handsomest of them all. It had been lately enlarged and beautified, and its picturesque gardens and grounds extended even to the water below. Rombouts was an educated Frenchman, of high birth and large wealth. In the year following Van Cortlandt's mayoralty he was appointed mayor.

This was the year noted for the passage of the celebrated "Bolting Act," which secured to the citizens of New York the exclusive **1678.** right of bolting flour, and exporting it from the province, — an act which, during the sixteen years of its existence, trebled the wealth of the city. It created great dissatisfaction in the inland towns, and, through their united efforts, it was finally repealed, in 1694. But meanwhile six hundred houses had been erected, land had increased to ten times its former value, and the shipping had multiplied into sixty full-sized vessels, which were in constant use for the transportation of the golden fruits of the monopoly.

The most important measure of the year 1679 had reference to Indian slaves. Many of the natives of the Spanish West Indies were **1679.** held in bondage, and also some of the Indians of New York. It was resolved, that "all Indians here have always been and are free, and not slaves, except those brought from foreign parts. But if any shall be brought hereafter into the province within the space of six months, they are to be disposed of out of the government as soon as possible. After the expiration of six months, all that shall be brought here shall be as other free Indians."

Andros spent the winter of 1678 in England, by special permission.

He told the Duke that the greatest want in New York was that of servants. Few negro slaves had been brought in of late, and their value was greatly increased. They cost from thirty to thirty-five pounds each. He said the value of the estates in the province amounted to about one hundred and fifty thousand pounds. A merchant having five hundred or a thousand pounds was thought substantial; and a planter worth half that in movables was accounted rich. "Ministers were scarce and religions many; but there were no beggars in New York, and all the poor were cared for."

During the absence of Andros, Lieutenant-Governor Brockholls acted as commander-in-chief. Secretary Nicolls was next him in authority, both being instructed to consult, on extraordinary occasions, with the mayor of the city. Lady Andros was invested with a power of attorney to manage the governor's private affairs, and she fulfilled her task with credit.

"At the first interview they stood so appalled as if the ghosts of Luther and Calvin had suffered a transmigration." — Page 284.

CHAPTER XVI.

1678–1683.

EUROPEAN AFFAIRS.

EUROPEAN AFFAIRS. — PRINCE OF ORANGE IN LONDON. — MARRIAGE OF WILLIAM AND MARY. — PEACE BETWEEN HOLLAND AND FRANCE. — JACOB LEISLER. — THE CLIMATE OF NEW YORK. — THE MINISTER'S SUPPER. — CONVERSATION IN LATIN. — ECCLESIASTICAL TROUBLES. — HUNTING BEARS BETWEEN CEDAR STREET AND MAIDEN LANE. — THE TWO LABADISTS. — JEAN VIGNE. — THE TRAVELERS ON LONG ISLAND. — SLEEPING IN A BARN. — THE FIRST CLASSIS IN AMERICA. — MOVEMENT TO BUILD A NEW CHURCH. — THE UNEASY INDIANS. — NEW JERSEY. — ARREST AND TRIAL OF GOVERNOR CARTERET. — EAST AND WEST NEW JERSEY. — FAULTY DEEDS. — IMPERIOUSNESS OF ANDROS. — WILLIAM PENN'S SOPHISTRY. — OPINION OF SIR WILLIAM JONES. — COMPLAINTS AGAINST ANDROS. — FOUNDING OF PENNSYLVANIA. — RECALL OF ANDROS. — CLAMOR FOR AN ASSEMBLY. — LIEUTENANT-GOVERNOR BROCKHOLLS. — ALMOST A COLONIAL REVOLUTION. — LONG ISLAND. — INSUBORDINATION. — AN ASSEMBLY GRANTED. — THOMAS DONGAN. — THE TRIUMPHAL MARCH.

THE constitution of England had recently been violated for the purpose of protecting the Roman Catholics from the penal laws. It created the general fear that a blow was about to be aimed at the Protestant religion ; and the public mind was in such temper, that every movement on the part of the king was regarded with suspicion, as leaning towards Rome.

Louis, still at war with Holland, carefully fomented these jealousies. As a neutral between the two fighting nations, England engrossed the principal commerce of the world. The Dutch, seeing their commerce languish, while that of England flourished, naturally longed for peace with France. The Prince of Orange visited London, to enlist his uncle, the king, in the important undertaking, while negotiations were opened at Nimeguen on the Rhine.

Charles received William cordially and affectionately ; and the young prince remained some weeks at Whitehall, talking with his two uncles about the proposed treaty. He was about to depart for Holland, when the king said to him, " Nephew, it is not good for man to be alone ; I will give you a helpmeet," — and thereupon offered him the hand of his cousin Mary in marriage. James, who had been hitherto bitterly opposed to giving his daughter to a heretic, and who was ambitious withal to marry her to the Dauphin of France, gave his consent with seeming heartiness. William smiled grimly, showing no disposition, as on a former occasion, to decline the splendid alliance. "Nephew," added Charles, "remember that love and war do not agree well together."

The news of the intended marriage spread through the court. All, except the French and the Roman Catholic party, were much pleased with it. Barillon, the French ambassador, was amazed, and predicted that such a son-in-law would be the ruin of James. He sent a courier to the Court of France with the tidings, and Louis was moved more seriously than he would have been by the loss of an army.

The marriage followed quickly. It took place on the 4th of November, William's twenty-seventh birthday. The bride was fifteen **1677.** the preceding April. She had been educated with her sister **Nov. 4.** Anne at the Richmond palace, knew something of science and accomplishments, spoke and wrote French well, sketched a little, read history attentively, and possessed some musical skill. Her chief faults, as a child, were love of eating and gambling. The latter amusement she persistently indulged in on Sunday evenings, to the great distress of her tutor. She had been confirmed in the Church of England by the Bishop of London, in obedience to the orders of the king. When first informed of her future prospects, she wept piteously in her father's arms. The ceremony was performed at nine o'clock in the evening, in her bedchamber, in the presence of the king and queen, the Duke and Duchess of York, and a few official attendants. Bishop Compton officiated, while Charles gave away the sobbing Mary, and, at the same time, little foreseeing the momentous consequences of such Dutch and British nuptials, attempted to overcome her dejection by noisy joviality.

Two days later, Mary was deprived of her position as heiress presumptive to the crown of England by the birth of a son to the Duke of York, and William was complimented with the office of sponsor to the unwelcome relative. But the little life was not destined to be of long duration. The bridegroom might have spared his pretty young bride the unhappiness of seeing him in constant ill-humor during the honeymoon. The whole court was surprised and indignant that she was rarely seen except in tears; and, to add to her griefs, her sister Anne was lying dangerously ill of small-pox. On the 19th of November, Mary sailed with William for Holland, Charles and James accompanying them as far as Erith, where they bade them an affectionate farewell.

The conference at Nimeguen progressed briskly after William's marriage. Parliament voted supplies for a possible war with France, and recalled all English soldiers and sailors who had been on duty under Louis. But the chief source of anxiety was at home. Religious conventicles had just then reached an insufferable pitch, and wild doctrines were being sown in all parts of the kingdom. The Titus Oates perjuries wellnigh produced a convulsion ; and presently the sight of James so inflamed the populace, that the king sent him, with his wife and daughter, to Brussels. Mary met her father with the first sunny face she had worn since her gloomy wedding. He was soon ordered to Scotland, and she accompanied him on the journey as far as the Maesland sluice, parting from him in an agony of sorrow. How, at that moment, she would have recoiled, could the future have been unrolled to her vision !

Peace was at length covenanted between the French and the Dutch. **1678.** Andros watched with interest the progress of events. He reached **Aug. 1.** England in January, and was at once knighted by the king ; after which he took a short holiday, to look after his private affairs at Guernsey. Upon his return to court, he attended the meetings of the Privy Council. Two agents from Massachusetts were present, and in great tribulation because of the seeming ill-favor of their colony at Whitehall. Andros took occasion to add still further to their trials by exposing the behavior of the Puritan colonies towards New York, particularly in connection with the late Indian war, — a subject which was immediately investigated by this supreme tribunal. He also gave a full and specific account of the internal administration of New York. The Duke **May 27.** required him to return immediately to his government, and he sailed May 27, commissioned as Vice-Admiral over all the Duke's territory, and authorized to appoint a Judge, Register, and Marshal in Admiralty, to hold office during his pleasure.

He made it his first business to order that none but New-Yorkers should trade with the Indians at Albany ; also, that no inland **Aug. 8.** towns should "trade over sea," and that all flour must be in- **Aug. 24.** spected in the metropolis.

During this month, news having been received that Jacob Leisler, while on a trading voyage to Europe in one of his own vessels, had been **Aug. 17.** captured by the Turks, the governor issued an order that the church officers should collect money of well-disposed persons in the province for his redemption. Leisler himself paid two thousand

Spanish dollars towards the fund, and was soon after released, together with those who were in captivity with him.[1]

The first Judge in Admiralty appointed by Andros was Mayor Stephanus Van Cortlandt. The aldermen of the city were to be assistants of the Provincial Court of Admiralty. Samuel Leete, the city clerk, was appointed register, and Sheriff Thomas Ashton, marshal, of the court. This organization, substantially, existed for several years.

Some gentlemen crossed the ocean with Andros, on his return voyage, who were destined to become prominent in public affairs ; among them were William Pinhorne, James Graham, and John West. Rev. James Wolley, a recent graduate of Cambridge University, came also as chaplain to the British forces in New York. He was called by his contemporaries "a gentleman of learning and observation ; sociable of habit and charitable in feeling." He published, after his return to England, " A Two Years' Journal in New York," which was highly appreciated. Despite its pedantry, and the fact that it gives a more detailed account of the Indians than of the European settlers, the work abounds in valuable information. One paragraph, in relation to the climate of New York, is too curiously characteristic to be omitted. It is as follows : —

" It is of a sweet and wholesome breath, free from those annoyances which are commonly ascribed by naturalists for the insalubriety of any Country, viz. South or South-east Winds, stagnant Waters, lowness of Shoars, inconstancy of Weather, and the excessive heat of the Summer ; it is gently refreshed, fanned, and allayed by constant breezes from the Sea. It does not welcome Guests and Strangers with the seasoning distempers of Fevers and Fluxes, like Virginia, Maryland, and other Plantations; nature kindly drains and purgeth it by Fontanels and Issues of running waters in its irriguous Valleys, and shelters it with the umbrellas of all sorts of Trees, from pernicious Lakes ; which Trees and Plants do undoubtedly, tho' insensibly, suck in and digest into their own growth and composition those subterraneous Particles and Exhalations, which otherwise wou'd be attracted by the heat of the Sun and so become matter for infectious Clouds and malign Atmospheres. . . . . I myself, a person seemingly of a weakly Stamen and a valetudinary Constitution, was not in the least indisposed in that Climate, during my residence there, the space of three years."

Speaking of the temperature, he says : —

" New York lieth 10 Degrees more to the Southward than Old England ; by which difference according to Philosophy it should be the hotter Climate, but on

---

[1] *Ord. Warr. Passes,* III. 219. *Council Min.,* III. (II.), 178. *Gen. Ent.,* XXXII. 65. *Mass. Rec.,* V. 289. *Col. Doc.,* III. 717. *Doc. Hist.,* II. 2 ; III. 253. *Laws of Maryland,* 1681.

18

the contrary, to speak feelingly, I found it in the Winter Season rather colder for the most part ; . . . . it is adjacent to and almost encompassed with an hilly, woody Country, full of Lakes and great Vallies, which receptacles are the Nurseries, Forges and Bellows of the Air, which they first suck in and contract, then discharge and ventilate with a fiercer dilatation."

The inhabitants of New York he called " a clan of high-flown Religionists "; yet he said they were very hospitable and often invited him to their houses and tables, the last overture usually including a generous bottle of Madeira. He made a personal endeavor to promote good feeling among the clergymen of the different denominations in the city. He says : —

" There were two other Ministers, or Dominies as they were called there, the one a Lutheran, or High-Dutch, the other a Calvinist, or Low-Dutchman, who behaved themselves one towards another so shily and uncharitably as if Luther and Calvin had bequeathed and entailed their virulent and bigoted Spirits upon them and their heirs forever. They had not visited or spoken to each other with any respect for six years together before my being there, with whom I being much acquainted, I invited them both with their Vrows to a Supper one night unknown to each other, with an obligation, that they should not speak one word in Dutch, under the penalty of a bottle of Madeira, alledging I was so imperfect in that Language that we could not manage a sociable discourse. So accordingly they came, and at the first interview they stood so appaled as if the Ghosts of Luther and Calvin had suffered a transmigration, but the amaze soon went off with a *salve tu quoque*, and a Bottle of Wine, of which the Calvinist Dominie was a true Carouzer, and so we continued our *Mensalia* the whole evening in Latine, which they both spoke so fluently and promptly that I blushed at myself with a passionate regret that I could not keep pace with them ; and at the same time could not forbear reflecting upon our English Schools and Universities (who indeed write Latine elegantly) but speak it, as if they were confined to Mood and Figure, Forms and Phrases, whereas it should be their common talk in their Seats and Halls, as well as in their School Disputations and Themes. This with all deference to these repositories of Learning. As to the Dutch Language, in which I was but a smatterer, I think it lofty, majestic and emphatical, especially the High-Dutch, which as far as I understand it is very expressive in the Scriptures, and so underived that it may take place next the Oriental Languages, and the Septuagint." [1]

The Calvinist minister referred to was Dominie Nieuwenhuysen, who died in 1681, and the Lutheran was Dominie Bernhardus Frazius. They were both men of vast scholastic acquirements. The language of Rome

[1] *Wolley's Journal*, 55, 56.

had not then lost its "imperial" character, and to speak it well was much more common than in later times. But the literary accomplishments of the Englishmen of that generation seem to have been less solid and profound than at either an earlier or a later period. Dominie Nieuwenhuysen was an excellent pastor, notwithstanding that, outside of his own flock, he sometimes exhibited more zeal than charity. He took exceptions to the clerical conduct of Dominie Van Rensselaer, whom Andros sent to Albany as colleague to Dominie Schaats, and openly declared that a minister ordained in England by a bishop was not qualified to administer the sacrament in the Reformed Dutch Church. He even went so far as to forbid Dominie Van Rensselaer to baptize children, which occasioned much ill-feeling; but, at the trial of the latter before the governor, Nieuwenhuysen was obliged to admit the validity of English Episcopal ordination. Fresh ecclesiastical troubles broke out the next year (1676), when Jacob Leisler, one of Dominie Van Nieuwenhuysen's deacons, accused Dominie Van Rensselaer of "false preaching" and of uttering "dubious words." Van Rensselaer was arrested and brought to New York for trial; but he was acquitted, and Deacon Leisler and Jacob Milborne were ordered to pay all costs for "giving the first occasion of difference." [1]

Between Cedar Street and Maiden Lane there was an orchard, owned by John Robinson. On one occasion, we are told, Mr. Wolley put off his clerical dignity and went out with a party to hunt bears in that locality. They pursued one until he finally betook himself 1679. to a tree, and crouched upon a high bough. A boy with a club was sent up, who, reaching an opposite branch, knocked away at the paws of Bruin until he came growling down, and fell, with a tremendous thump, to the ground.

Mr. Wolley and his wife were frequent guests of Lord George Russell (then residing in New York), a brother of the celebrated Lord William Russell, who was beheaded in 1683. He speaks also in his Journal of Frederick Philipse, and his great wealth. He says skating was very much in vogue; and he gives some pleasant glimpses into the exchange of presents on New Year's day. On his return to London, he took with him, as American curiosities, "a Gray Squirrel, a Parrot, and a Raccoon." He sailed in a ship commanded by George Heathcote, a Quaker; the same who was imprisoned by the governor of Massachusetts, in 1672, for delivering to his Excellency a letter without taking off his hat.[2]

---

[1] *Council Min.*, III. 54 – 59.   *Doc. Hist. N. Y.*, III. 526, 527.   *Brodhead*, II. 288, 300.

[2] George Heathcote made numerous voyages to New York. At his death, he liberated

In 1679, Jasper Dankers and Peter Sluyter, two travelers, appeared in New York, who had been sent from Europe by a religious sect, called Labadists, to find some suitable spot for a colony. The founder of the sect was Jean De Labadie, a native of Bordeaux, and he had made many converts to his doctrines among persons of learning. His public declaration that he was inspired and specially directed by Christ filled the clergy with dismay, and caused him and his followers to be driven to Westphalia and afterwards to Denmark. De Labadie died in 1674, at Wieward in Friesland, where the community had at last found permanent quarters. Three years later, some of his disciples removed to Surinam, but did not remain there long.

The two envoys to New Amsterdam were passengers on the *Charles*, one of Mrs. Frederick Philipse's vessels. Some of their experiences and observations are interesting enough to be recited. They landed about four o'clock on a September afternoon, and were invited to supper by a fellow-passenger, at the house of his father-in-law, Jacob Swart. Sept. 23. The table was loaded with delicious peaches, pears, and apples. They were invited to spend the night, and graciously accepted the invitation. They went to walk in the fields, and saw trees laden with divers kinds of fruit in such overflowing abundance as they had never seen in Europe in the best seasons. Upon their return to the house in the evening they were regaled with milk and peaches, and retired to rest and sleep, and dream of peaches on the morrow. The next day was Sunday, and, after partaking of an appetizing breakfast of fish and fruit, they went to church, "to avoid scandal," — as they said. They were not pleased, however, with the personal appearance of the minister, or with his manner of explaining the Bible; and as for his congregation, it was "too worldly." In the afternoon they were escorted by Mr. and Mrs. Swart and Mr. Van Duyne to a tavern, where a daughter of the old people lived; but they found the place "uncongenial," and walked in the orchard "to contemplate the innocent objects of nature." They found a mulberry-tree, with leaves as large as a plate. Towards evening they called upon one of Mr. Swart's neighbors. His name was Jean Vigne. He was the first male child born in New York of European parents. The date of his birth, according to these travelers, must have been 1614, the very earliest period of white settlement.[1] His mother owned a farm near Wall and Pearl Streets. He was,

three negro slaves, and gave to Thomas Carlton five hundred acres of land near Shrewsbury, New Jersey, to be called "Carlton Settlement." He also constituted his nephew, Caleb Heathcote, residuary legatee. *Will, dated Nov.,* 1710, *Surrogate's Office, N. Y.*

[1] This statement does not in any manner conflict with the record which confirms Sarah de Rapalje as the first born "Christian *daughter*" in New Netherland. *Long Island Hist. Soc. Coll.,* I. 113. *Benson's Memoir in N. Y. H. S. Coll.,* II. (Second Series) 94.

at this time, in possession of the old homestead, and kept an ancient wind-mill constantly at work upon the hill back of his house. He was a brewer, as well as a farmer; and he was one of the great burghers of the city. He filled the office of schepen in 1663, in 1655, and in 1656. Of his three sisters, Maria married Abraham Verplanck, Cristina was the wife of Dirck Volckertsen, and Rachel the second wife of Cornelis Van Tienhoven. Jean Vigne left no children; but the descendants of his sisters are scattered through the country.

View of the Water Gate (present Wall Street).
(From a pencil-sketch by Dankers and Sluyter.)

On the 29th the explorers made a journey to Long Island. They describe their route from the ferry as "up a hill, along open roads and woody places, and through a village called Breuckelen, which has a small ugly church standing in the middle of the road"! Sept. 29. Peach-trees were everywhere numerous, and laden with fruit; in some instances actually breaking down with their treasures. They visited the oldest resident, a woman who had lived in this country over half a century, and who had seventy children and grandchildren. They spent one night at the house of Simon De Hart, where they supped on raw and roasted oysters, a roasted haunch of venison, a wild turkey, and a goose, and sat before a hickory fire blazing half-way up the chimney, all the chilly autumn evening. The house is still standing, having been in the possession of the descendants of Simon De Hart ever since.

In the morning they went out through the woods to what is now Fort Hamilton, where the *Najack* Indians resided upon land which Jacques Cortelyou had long since bought of the sachems, and at present rented to them for twenty bushels of corn yearly. They rambled along the shore to Coney Island, and from one Indian village to another, eating peaches and wild grapes by the way, and coming every now and then upon "great heaps of watermelons." They visited New Utrecht, and were kindly entertained by Jacques Cortelyou. The town and everything in it had been burned a short time before; but some good stone houses had been rebuilt, and among them this of Cortelyou's. He had two sick sons, and, with his wife, was so occupied in attending to them, that he had little time to devote to his visitors. He invited them to stay as long as it was convenient; but the only place to sleep he could offer them was in the barn. So, after supper, they took up their quarters for the night upon some straw spread with sheep-skins, "in the midst of the continual grunting of hogs, squealing of pigs, bleating and coughing of sheep, barking of dogs, crowing of cocks, and cackling of hens"; much to their discomfort, as would appear from their journal, although they were less disposed to complain when they discovered that they were occupying the usual bed of one of Cortelyou's sons, who had crept into the straw behind them. They said Cortelyou was a mathematician, a sworn land-surveyor, and a doctor of medicine.

View of North Dock.
(From a pencil-sketch by Dankers and Sluyter.)

After an extended tour over Long Island, they returned (October 4) to New York, and remained in the city about a month. On Sunday, October 15th, they attended the Episcopal service in the Dutch church in the fort, conducted by Mr. Wolley. There were not above twenty-five or thirty people present. They said, "after the prayers and ceremonies, a young man went into the pulpit, who thought he was performing wonders: he had a little book in his hand, out of which he read his sermon, which was about a quarter of an hour long. With this the services were concluded, at which we could not be sufficiently astonished."

Oct. 4.

Oct. 15.

They evidently worked with great zeal to make converts to their own faith, and scattered their admonitions loftily among the sinners of the country. The peculiarity of their movements attracted the attention of the better class of the inhabitants, of whom they had seen but little; and when, in January, they returned from Westchester and adjacent towns, they were summoned before the mayor to give an account of themselves, and to explain the object of their travels. This done, they were dismissed with the caution not to attempt to go to Albany without a passport from the governor. After obtaining this document, they sailed, on the 20th of February, up the Hud-

1680.
Jan. 3.

Feb. 20.

son. They also traveled through New Jersey and the Delaware Bay region. And they persuaded many persons (among whom were Ephraim Heermans and Peter Bayard) to leave their wives and join the Labadists. In June they sailed for Europe. Their journal was published, in 1867, by the Long Island Historical Society, under the supervision of Hon. Henry C. Murphy, who procured the original manuscript in Holland. It is deeply to be regretted that the portion relating chiefly to the metropolis has been hopelessly lost.

View of New York from the North.
(From a pencil-sketch by Dankers and Sluyter.)

The first classis ever held in America consisted of Dominies Nieuwenhuysen and Schaats, Dominie Van Zuuren of Long Island, and Dominie Van Gaasbeeck of Esopus. It was formed in 1679, at the suggestion of the Episcopal governor, and for the purpose of examining and ordaining a young licensed Bachelor in Divinity, Peter Tesschenmaeker, who had been called to the church at Newcastle. This novel proceeding was approved by the supreme ecclesiastical judicature at Amsterdam.

June 30.

The church edifice in the fort having become too small to accommodate the congregation, a meeting was called at the suggestion of Andros, in June, 1680, to consider the best measures for building a new one. Several members of the Council and other leading citizens were present, together with the Dutch and English clergymen. It was voted to raise money by " free-will or gift," and not by public tax ; and it was cordially agreed that the new church should be a quarter larger than the old one. The mayor and aldermen appropriated certain fines towards the fund.[1]

---

[1] *Doc. Hist. N. Y.*, III. 244, 265. *Gen. Ent.*, XXXII. 65. *Col. Doc.*, III. 315, 415, 717. *Letter of Dominie Selyns to Classis, October* 28, 1682. *Brodhead*, II. 331. *Records of Collegiate Dutch Church, Liber A,* 161, 162.

Meanwhile, the English claim of sovereignty over the Iroquois, which had been asserted by Andros, roused the French king, Louis. In the unsettled condition of European politics, he could not take a decided stand with respect to his interests in America; hence he resorted to intrigue. The Jesuit missionaries were the instruments of his purpose. They made presents to the Indians and sought to incline them towards the French; while, to prevent this, Andros was compelled to increase his watchfulness. About this time, one of the French ministers argued long and earnestly with his sovereign that a war with New York and New England must redound to the advantage of Canada.

The governor of Maryland wrote to Andros that " strange Indians " were doing mischief along the Susquehanna; the governor of Virginia complained of " unknown Indians " committing thefts and murders within his jurisdiction; and, in the depth of winter, the New York governor sent two Indian interpreters through the snows and storms to summon the Iroquois to a conference in Albany. The difficulty was settled for the time; but, the next season, it broke out afresh in a still more complicated form, and again Governor Andros was compelled to meet the Iroquois warriors, and discuss with them the question of mutual relations and the duties of the future.

New Jersey for a while carried on a direct trade with England. But Andros saw fit to put into rigid execution the Duke's order, that all vessels trading within his original territory should enter at the New York custom-house. Thereupon the Assembly of East Jersey passed an act to indemnify any ship which might be seized by the government of New York for entering and clearing at Elizabethtown. An interesting quarrel was at once inaugurated.

Andros and Carteret were kinsmen, and socially intimate. Carteret was in the habit of attending Sabbath service in the fort, and of dining often at Sir Edmund's table. The wives of the two gentlemen were as devoted to each other as sisters. All at once a chill fell upon this friendly intercourse. Andros seized every Jersey-bound vessel and exacted duties before allowing it to proceed from Sandy Hook to Elizabethtown. Carteret claimed to be the supreme governor of his province, and complained to Sir George. Andros sent Collector Dyer to England, to justify his past course and to ask instruction for the future.

The political storms in his immediate horizon prevented James from giving proper attention to his American possessions. He was, at this moment, absent from England. His secretary admonished Andros to continue the maintenance of the Duke's prerogative throughout his territory. As soon as Dyer returned with the order, Andros notified

Carteret that he should erect a fort at Sandy Hook; and Carteret replied, that he should resist such a proceeding to the last. Andros sent Secretary Nicolls into New Jersey with a proclamation, forbidding Carteret to exercise any further authority within the Duke's province, and demanding the surrender of his person. Carteret appealed to the king. But the people of New Jersey sustained Carteret, to whom they were much attached, and Andros was deterred by their loyalty from resorting to extreme measures.

The latter went over to New Jersey, and the rumor of his coming induced Carteret to collect a large force for defense. But Andros making his appearance unattended by soldiers, he was invited to Carteret's house, where the contending parties dined together and held a long conference over their difficulties. Each produced papers and patents in support of the righteousness of his course, and both were undoubtedly actuated by the honest motive of obedience to superiors. Yet they arrived at no amicable understanding.

Three weeks later, Andros caused the arrest of Carteret. The unguarded country-house of the latter was entered, in the night, by a band of armed men, who dragged him naked from his bed, and ^{April 7.} carried him in this condition to New York, where, after being furnished with clothes, he was thrown into prison. The charge against him was that of "unlawfully assuming jurisdiction over the king's subjects." He was tried before a special Court of Assizes, over which Andros presided in great state. The prisoner was allowed to plead his own cause; and he did so with lawyer-like skill and learning. In the first place, he denied the power of such a court to settle a question which involved the right of a king, and, indeed, refused to acknowledge its jurisdiction. He was quite willing, he said, to have his actions thoroughly investigated; and, expressing his astonishment that Andros should pretend to have never recognized him as governor of New Jersey, he produced several letters addressed by Sir Edmund to himself under that title.

Andros responded quickly, that the letters had been so addressed because Carteret had generally been styled governor, not because he was so in fact. " But," said Carteret, " the king has made me governor, and you, as well as all the world, have acknowledged me as such." The royal commissions to the two men were produced, and it was found that the one to Carteret was older than the one to Andros. " Mine, therefore, should be preferred," said Carteret. " By no means," exclaimed Andros, "mine being the younger, yours is annulled by it." " That remains to be shown," rejoined Carteret; and he produced letters from Charles himself, directed to the governor of New Jersey. The honest verdict of a New York jury set Carteret free; but he was obliged to give security, that, if he was allowed to return home, he would assume no authority, civil or military, until his case was decided in England. Governor and Lady Andros, accompanied by a number of personal friends, escorted Carteret to Elizabethtown, with distinguished ceremony; and Andros proceeded to commission civil and military officers in the principal towns of East Jersey.

West Jersey was under the control of Quakers, who complained most bitterly of Andros and his high-handed proceedings. The root of the trouble was at Whitehall. When Lord Berkeley parted with his undivided interest in New Jersey, he could give only a doubtful title. When William Penn and his associates sent an agent to take possession, Andros, without in any way exceeding his instructions, directed that, as no proper authority had been produced, the parties concerned were not to be treated as proprietors of lands, and all duties were to be collected from them as from other English subjects. Fenwick, the agent, was arrested for disobeying orders, and tried before a special Court of Assizes. The affair created a stir in London; and James persuaded Sir George Carteret to consent to a quinquepartite deed, in partition with Penn and his partners, by which they agreed upon a dividing line from Little Egg Harbor to the most northerly branch of the Delaware River. The two provinces were to be called henceforward East and West New Jersey. This famous instrument was the most remarkable for extraordinary faults of all the extraordinary and faulty parchment deeds in the early American annals.[1] The Duke's secretary wrote to Andros, that his master had no intention of parting with any of his prerogative by this arrangement, but wished to make a show of favor to the imperious Sir George.

The co-proprietors of West New Jersey at once appointed commissioners to look after their government matters, and Fenwick in particular. These commissioners embarked on board the ship *Kent*. As the vessel was lying in the Thames, King Charles came alongside in his pleasure-barge, and, seeing a large number of passengers, and learning where they were bound, asked if they were all Quakers, *and gave them his blessing*. When they arrived at Sandy Hook, the commissioners left the vessel, and went up to the city in a barge to pay a visit to Andros, who received them graciously and inquired if they had brought any orders from the Duke, his master. They replied that they had not, but quoted the transfer of the soil, with which the government of West Jersey was also conveyed. "That will not clear me," replied Andros, with emphasis, "if I

---

[1] *Dixon's Penn.*, 138.   *Whitehead*, 67, 68.   *Gordon*, 38.   *Leaming and Spicer*, 61 – 72. *Proud*, I. 142.   *Brodhead*, II. 304.

should surrender without the Duke's order, it is as much as my head is worth. But if you had but a line or.two from the Duke, I should be as ready to surrender it to you, as you would be to ask it."

The commissioners strenuously asserted their independence, and continued to argue their case, until Andros, losing all patience, sprang to his feet, with head erect and flashing eyes, and, clapping his hand upon his sword, exclaimed, "I shall defend my government against you until such time as I am ordered by the Duke to surrender it."

He softened, however, almost instantly, and assured the commissioners that he would do all in his power to make them easy until they could send to England for instructions; and in the mean time he would commission them to act as magistrates under him, in order that they might proceed to the transaction of business. Fenwick was released from confinement and allowed to proceed with them to the Delaware, on condition that he should report himself in New York in the following October.

The news produced a sensation at Whitehall. James, already threatened with exclusion from the throne on account of his Romish faith, was moody and obstinate. He said that West New Jersey had no right to set up a distinct government. It was amenable to the laws established in New York. The English Secretary of State was consulted, and many of the most astute lawyers in the kingdom. William Penn elaborately argued his own case, and that of his Quaker associates. He insisted that, in Lord Berkeley's conveyance, powers of government were distinctly granted. Then, aware of the impossibility of proving the assertion, he hastened to allude to the Duke's present distressing circumstances and the jealousies of the people, and to suggest that kindness and justice now shown to Englishmen in America would seem to forecast the character of his Royal Highness's administration, in the event of his accession to the throne, and could not fail to enhance his popularity. Penn's peculiar fascination of manner, together with his feint of passive obedience, bound him closely both to the gracious Charles and the arbitrary James. He was much more skillful in reading their characters and practicing upon their weaknesses than they were in penetrating his specious purposes. Besides, he had a special hold on both. His father, Sir William Penn, had been Admiral of England ; and, at his death, the crown was in debt to his estate some sixteen thousand pounds. His subtle sophistry might have turned the scale, had truth been on his side. But, before the question was settled, the furious hate of the populace drove James again into Scotland, and, in his strait, he referred the whole matter to Sir William Jones, "the greatest lawyer in England," but a determined opponent of the "Tories," as the king and his friends were styled.

Jones was a wary Parliamentarian advocate. Believing that an English Parliament had the right, though the sovereign had not, to tax an unrepresented colony, he gave his opinion with great caution. He said, " I am not satisfied by anything I have yet heard that the Duke can legally demand duties from the people of those lands ; and, to make the case stronger against his Royal Highness, these inhabitants claim that, in the original grant to Lord Berkeley and Sir George Carteret, there is no reservation of any profit, or so much as jurisdiction." [1]

It was an ingenious report for a referee wishing to evade a decision or to becloud the truth. Several of the material facts in the case were wholly ignored. For instance, Jones cited only the Duke's **1680.** first grant, in 1664, and left out of the discussion both the Dutch conquest of 1673 (which annihilated that grant) and the king's second patent to his brother, in 1674. But James had neither time nor inclination to contest the matter, and, without waiting for his own counsel to approve, he executed a deed the more firmly to convey West New Jersey **Aug. 6.** to its purchasers, granting them all the powers which were ever intended to be granted to himself by the king.

Scarcely was this accomplished, when Lady Carteret, the widow of Sir George (who had recently died), having received letters from Gov- **Sept. 10.** ernor Philip Carteret, giving a detailed account of the treatment he had suffered from Andros, complained to the worried Duke ; and he, having just released all claim to the government of West New Jersey, and believing that he could do no less by East New Jersey, ordered a deed to that effect to be prepared.

All at once, and from every side, complaints began to pour in upon the Duke concerning Andros. It was insinuated that he favored Dutchmen in trade, made laws hurtful to the English, detained ships unduly for private reasons, and admitted Dutch vessels to a direct trade, or traded himself in the names of others. Moreover, James was receiving constant offers to farm his revenue in New York, which differed " so vastly " from the accounts rendered by Andros, that he commissioned John Lewin as an agent to inspect all accounts and learn the true condition of affairs in his province. At the same time, he ordered Andros to report immediately **1681.** in person. The latter, though surprised, was too good a soldier **Jan. 6.** not to obey the summons to the very letter. He committed the government to Lieutenant-Governor Brockholls, and sailed January 6, 1681, leaving Lady Andros (as he fully expected to return) in New York.

While he was on his voyage to England, a royal parchment founded

---

[1] *Clarke's James* II., I. 588 – 600. *Col. Doc.*, III. 284, 285. *Chalmer's Annals*, I, 240 – 626. *Force's Tracts*, IV. No. IX. *Brodhead*, II. 340 – 342.

the State of Pennsylvania. The subtle William Penn had petitioned the king for a region of wild land in North America, with a vague and undefined boundary, in payment of the debt due to his father's estate; and, with shrewd geographical judgment, he had drafted his own patent. Lord Sunderland, Lord Baltimore, and other gentlemen, to whom the matter was referred, attempted to oppose this monstrous demand; but Penn, having won over to his interests both the king and the Duke, soon accomplished his end. The charter of Pennsylvania, as it passed the Great Seal, granted to William Penn all the powers of a feudal chief, — the making of laws and the execution of the same, the appointment of officers, etc. But all laws were to be subject to the approval of the freemen of his province, and to the pleasure of the king; and no taxes were to be levied nor revenues raised, except by a Provincial Assembly. The supreme power of the Parliament of England was acknowledged in the matter of regulating commercial duties.

After the departure of Governor Andros, New York was in great con-

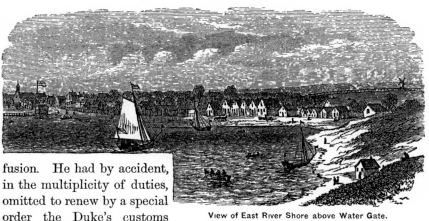

fusion. He had by accident, in the multiplicity of duties, omitted to renew by a special order the Duke's customs duties, which had expired

View of East River Shore above Water Gate.
(From a pencil-sketch by Dankers and Sluyter.)

the November before by their three years' limitation, which was unfortunate indeed. This oversight having been discovered by the traders, they refused to pay duties upon what they imported into the province. Neither did they abate to consumers a farthing from the prices of the goods they were selling. Brockholls and his council decided that there was no power to continue expired taxes without orders from his Royal Highness. The question produced almost a colonial revolution. New Jersey was prospering under free-trade, at the expense of New York. Collector Dyer, at this time mayor of the city, was sued for detaining goods for customs, and forced to deliver them without payment. On the back of this he was accused of high treason for having levied the duties, committed to prison, and arraigned before a court specially summoned for his trial. His indictment was for "traitorously exercising regal power and authority over the king's subjects." A jury was sworn, and twenty witnesses were examined for the prosecution. Dyer pleaded "not guilty," and challenged the authority of the court. He refused to surrender the seal of the city and his commission as mayor, because he had received them from their common superior, Andros. The court finally decided to send him to England, to be dealt with as the king should direct; and his accuser, Samuel Winder, was required to give five thousand pounds security to prosecute him in England. John West, the clerk of the court, excused its irregular action, because of "the novelty of the charge of high treason, and the present discord in the government here."

It was soon noised about, that, in the new province of Pennsylvania, established by the king, no laws could be passed or revenue June. levied without the assent of a majority of colonial freemen represented in a local assembly. The old Dutch principle of "taxation only by consent" was quickly revived in New York. The jury which indicted Dyer declared to the Court of Assizes that the want of a Provincial Assembly was a *grievance*. The clamor became so loud and determined, that John Younge, the high sheriff of Long Island, was appointed to draft a petition to the Duke, and his work was adopted by the court. It represented that the inhabitants of New York had, for many years, groaned under inexpressible burdens by having an arbitrary power used and exercised over them, whereby a revenue had been exacted against their wills, their trade burdened, and their liberty enthralled, contrary to the privileges of a royal subject; so that they had become a "reproach" to their neighbors, who were flourishing "under the fruition and protection of the king's unparalleled form and method of government in his realm of England." The Duke was therefore besought to rule his province henceforth through a governor, council, and assembly, — the latter to be duly elected by the freeholders of the colony, as in the other plantations of the king.

Brockholls wrote to Andros by the same vessel which conveyed Dyer, as a prisoner, and this petition to the Duke, that the customs July 21. were wholly destroyed and the province in the most terrible disorder. Meanwhile, Andros, on reaching London, had sent back an order to Brockholls to act as receiver-general of all the Duke's revenues; but his afterthought came too late. The mischief had been done. Brockholls, from lack of energy or some other cause, conveniently shirked the duty of meddling with the insolent tax-payers. Trade was substantially free. Disorderly gatherings were held in various places, particularly on Long Island, and peace and quiet were seriously disturbed. Brockholls suspended Derval from the council for impertinence; and, in the absence of Secretary Nicolls and Collector Dyer, his only advisers were Frederick Philipse and Stephanus Van Cortlandt. Much of this spirit of insubordination arose from the Duke's own act, in recalling Andros, and sending over Lewin, as a sort of private detective. The latter, stupid and incompetent, was often insulted to his face, and his proceedings were branded as unlawful. When he returned to London, in December, he was examined by Churchill and Jeffreys. ^{Dec.} Secretary Nicolls and Collector Dyer were also questioned. The result was that Andros was exonerated from all blame whatsoever. He was even complimented upon the marvelous success of his administration and made a Gentleman of the king's Privy Chamber. As this honor required him to live near London, he sent to New York for Lady Andros to join him in their ancient home.

However much in after years Sir Edmund may have merited the appellation of "the tyrant of New England," he seems to have governed New York with wisdom and moderation. The position had its peculiar temptations; and besides, he was the executive servant of one of the most obstinate of men, — one who had no proper estimate of character and who was blind to universal principles. If, in trying to rule a mixed community of different nationalities, proclivities, and opinions, a faulty, imperious temper occasionally obtained ascendency over sober judgment, we can grant some measure of indulgence, in view of all the circumstances of the case. Andros was unquestionably diligent and sagacious; and he did much towards bringing New York into a healthy political and financial condition. Certain it is, that, when he laid down the staff of office, anarchy followed almost immediately.

Collector Dyer, after waiting in vain in London for his prosecutor to appear, petitioned the king to be honorably acquitted; and the petition was granted. In recompense for his losses, he was afterwards appointed surveyor-general of the customs in America. ^{1682.}

Long Island seems to have been a constant source of care and trouble to New York. In February, two prominent justices of the peace, Richard Cromwell and Thomas Hicks, were arrested for disaffec- ^{Feb. 17.} tion to the government, and bound over for trial at the next Court of Assizes. The minister of Huntington was "dealt with" for denying baptism to the children of those whom he charged with "loose lives." At Staten Island, and at Albany, there was trouble about their clergymen. In the city of New York, the patriarch Dominie Van Nieuwenhuysen had gone to his rest; and the consistory of the Dutch church called, as his successor, Dominie Henricus Selyns, who returned to America, and entered upon a new and laborious service. There were a multitude of petty disturbances. Connecticut revived the boundary question. Frederick Philipse, having bought a tract of land,

May 11 embracing Sleepy Hollow, and prepared to build a mill upon it, was informed that the Connecticut line ran to the south and west of his property. Thereupon a lively dispute arose between the governors of the two provinces. Brockholls knew that Connecticut was never to approach within twenty miles of the Hudson River, and pronounced the affair an attempt at swindling. Of course, the question was, in the end, referred to the Duke and the king.

Meanwhile, William Penn, with the aid of Algernon Sidney, drew up and published for Pennsylvania a form of government and laws, the large benevolence of which presented a model worthy to be carefully studied by the Duke. Charles dissolved Parliament, being firmly resolved to govern thenceforth without one, and to stand up boldly against those who plotted to exclude James from the throne. The latter ventured to return again from Scotland; and the royal brothers had many conversations about New York. It was clear, that, in order to collect a revenue in that province, an Assembly must be granted. It was simply a question of finance. The property was now a mere drain upon the Duke's purse. He talked seriously of offering it for sale. "No," said William Penn, with his Quaker hand laid lovingly on the shoulder of his Catholic friend, "keep the province, and give it the franchise."

When James had once made up his mind to act upon this closet advice, he was not slow in putting his plans in execution. He fixed

Sept. 30. upon Thomas Dongan as his future governor. This gentleman was a Roman Catholic; but his experience in France (where he had commanded an Irish regiment under Louis, during the French and Dutch war), and his general knowledge of the French character, were powerful recommendations at the present moment, when the delicate relations between New York and Canada required the most consummate diplomacy on the part of the English. He was the younger son of Sir John Dongan, an Irish baronet, and nephew to Richard Talbot, Earl of Tyrconnel. He was trained to the profession of arms, and had distinguished himself on many occasions. He had recently been lieutenant-governor of Tangier, in Africa.

His appointment was confirmed a few days after the first mention of his name in this connection, and a commission was executed similar to

"*The property was now a mere drain upon the Duke's purse He talked seriously of offering it for sale. 'No,' said William Penn, with his Quaker hand laid lovingly on the shoulder of his Catholic friend; 'keep New York, and give it the franchise'*" *Page 298.*

that given to Andros; only, New Jersey was excepted from his juris-diction. The eastern boundary of New York was still declared to be the western bank of the Connecticut River. His special instructions con-tained an order to call a General Assembly.

His departure for New York was delayed for some time. Another New Jersey episode required the attention of James and his min-isters. The grantees under the will of Sir George Carteret had **1683.** conveyed East New Jersey to William Penn, Thomas Rudyard, and ten other Quakers; and these twelve proprietors had each sold half his inter-est to a new associate, thus introducing, among others, the Earl of Perth, the Earl of Melford, and Robert Barclay, the famous author of the "Apology." Barclay was appointed governor, with leave to execute his office by deputy; and he sent, as his representative, Thomas Rudyard, to whom Philip Carteret resigned his authority.[1] The twenty-four proprie-tors, wishing to make their title more secure, asked of the Duke a special grant, which was finally executed, with an order from the king command-ing all persons concerned in the said province of East New Jersey to yield obedience to its lawful owners.

Dongan then sailed, and, arriving at Nantasket in August, completed his journey by land. A number of gentlemen crossed the sea with him, and others hurried from New York to greet him and **Aug. 10.** escort him through the country. Thus, the traveling party was quite an imposing one. They crossed from Connecticut to Long Island and stopped in the most important towns by the way. Everywhere, **Aug. 25.** the people were assured that henceforward their rights as British subjects should be respected, and no taxes should be imposed but by a Legislature of their own choosing. The current of popular feeling set strongly in favor of the new governor. He was easy and affable, and personally mag-netic. His sentiments met with the heartiest applause from all classes. His progress through the country was one triumphal march, and the city itself was in ecstasies at his arrival.

On Monday morning he appeared before the mayor and aldermen at the City Hall, and published his commission and instructions. **Aug. 27.** On Tuesday a dinner was given to him by the corporation. **Aug. 28.**

---

[1] Philip Carteret died shortly after this event, and was buried in New York. His wife was the daughter of Richard Smith, the patentee of Smithtown, and the widow of William Lawrence of New York. She was a lady of more than ordinary endowments and strength of character, and was frequently intrusted with the affairs of the government of New Jer-sey during the absence of her husband. He was at one time in Europe for several months, and the acts of that period are recorded as "passed under the administration of Lady Eliza-beth Carteret." *Whitehead's East New Jersey*, 85. *Hatfield*, 212, 213. *Brodhead*, II. 368. *Thompson's Long Island.*

19

CHAPTER XVII.

1683 – 1686.

GOVERNOR THOMAS DONGAN.

GOVERNOR THOMAS DONGAN. — MAYOR WILLIAM BEEKMAN. — WILLIAM PENN IN NEW
YORK. — THE FIRST NEW YORK ASSEMBLY. — LAWS ENACTED BY THE ASSEMBLY. —
THE NEW YORK COURTS. — THE ACTS OF THE ASSEMBLY. — NEW YORK CONTENTED
AND PROSPEROUS. - - DOMINIE SELYNS'S PARSONAGE. — THE IROQUOIS A WALL OF DE-
FENSE. — A BRUSH WITH CONNECTICUT. — PLOT TO ASSASSINATE CHARLES II. AND THE
DUKE OF YORK. — CONFUSION IN ENGLAND. — ARGUMENTS IN THE PRIVY COUNCIL. —
ARBITRARY MEASURES. — THE CITY CHARTER. — THE SABBATH QUESTION IN 1684. –
HOTELS AND THEIR GUESTS. — FUNERAL CUSTOMS. — POWDER MAGAZINE. — LORD EF-
FINGHAM IN NEW YORK. — THE GREAT INDIAN CONFERENCE. — THE AUSPICIOUS NEW
YEAR. — THE SUDDEN REVULSION. — THE DEATH OF CHARLES II. — SCENES AND INCI-
DENTS. — JAMES II. PROCLAIMED KING OF ENGLAND. — THE NEW KING'S PROMISES. —
THE GRADUAL GRASP OF POWER. — INCONSISTENCIES OF JAMES II. — EFFECT UPON
NEW YORK. — JURIES IN 1685. — MASON AND DIXON'S LINE. — WILLIAM PENN'S IN-
FLUENCE AT COURT. — THE DONGAN CHARTER. — NEW CITY SEAL. — THE ALBANY
CHARTER. — THE LIVINGSTON MANOR. — PHILIP LIVINGSTON.

G OVERNOR THOMAS DONGAN was about fifty years of age, and
a bachelor. He had broad intelligent views on all subjects of
general interest. He was, moreover, an accomplished politician. Perhaps
we do not often enough reflect how effectively the spirit of one
1683. man, or of a few men, may decide the destiny of a state. Cool
tempers and wise heads possess great power to give direction to the common mind. This was a remarkable period. New York was passing
through a crisis. Dongan was essentially a man for the times. He was
a ready talker, bland and deferential to his associates, and fitted to inspire confidence in all around him. He has been justly classed " among
the best of our colonial governors." [1]

One clause in his instructions provided for the appointment of Frederick Philipse and Stephanus Van Cortlandt as members of his council.
It also required him to summon other eminent men, to the number of

---

[1] Some years after, Governor Dongan succeeded to the Earldom of Limerick. At his death,
his estates in America were settled upon three nephews, John, Thomas, and Walter Dongan,
from whom those of the name in New York have descended.

ten, to be sworn into his service as counselors. John Spragg was appointed secretary of the province, in the place of John West, who had filled the office temporarily. West was an energetic and prosperous lawyer: he married Anna, the daughter of Lieutenant-Governor Rudyard of East New Jersey.[1] Lucas Santen was made collector of the revenues. The mayor of the city in 1683, was William Beekman,[2] and he,

Beekman House, Rhinebeck.

with Stephanus Van Cortlandt, Lucas Santen, Gabriel Minvielle, and Captain Mark Talbot, were appointed a committee to report upon the condition of Fort James. Brockholls and Matthias Nicolls were directed to catalogue the provincial records.

As soon as the matters of first necessity were settled in the metropolis, Dongan hurried to Albany. The *Sept. 13.* direct occasion of this sudden trip was a rumor that William Penn was attempting to secure to himself the Upper Susquehanna Valley. He had actually commissioned two agents to treat with the Indians about the purchase. One of these, James Graham, an alderman of New York, was already in Albany on this business when Dongan arrived from England. Nothing less than a personal investigation of the whole matter could enable the new governor to pronounce upon its justice. Penn himself was in Albany, and the two gentlemen held a long conference. The question was a difficult one, since they were both subjects of the same master. Dongan, however, ordered a stop to all Penn's proceedings until the vexatious boundary between New York and Pennsylvania should be arranged; and then courteously invited the wily Quaker to his house in New York, where he entertained him for several days. Penn was engaged in a similar controversy with Lord Baltimore, the proprietor of Maryland, and when he left New York it was to push his claims to territory in that direction.

---

[1] Thomas Rudyard was an eminent London lawyer. He died abroad in 1692. His daughter Anna married, for her third husband, Governor Andrew Hamilton of Pennsylvania. His daughter Margaret married Samuel Winder, the prosecutor of Collector Dyer. *Col. Doc.*, III. 351.

[2] William Beekman purchased all the region of Rhinebeck from the Indians, and built a small stone house, which is still standing. The bricks of the chimney were imported from Holland. The place was named from the river Rhine in Europe, upon the bank of which Beekman was born.

In October, the Mohawks visited Fort James, and agreed to give the
"Susquehanna River" to New York. Dongan informed Penn at
October. once of the fact, "about which," he adds, "you and I shall not
fall out; I desire we may joine heartily together, to advance the interests
of my master and your good friend." But Penn cared less for his "good
friend's" interests than his own; and when, a year later, he asked Dongan's intervention in his difficulty with Lord Baltimore, he also requested
permission to treat with the New York Indians for their Susquehanna
territory. "Mr. Penn has already more land than he can people these
many years," replied Dongan, and coldly dismissed the Quaker agents.
The consequence was soon apparent. Penn became at Whitehall, whither
he returned to keep up his interest at court, Dongan's bitterest enemy.[1]

The most important event of the year 1683 was the institution in New
York of the long-desired colonial Assembly, by which the Duke of York
allowed the inhabitants to participate in legislation. He retained in his
own hands the power to appoint a governor and counselors, and thus
maintained a certain degree of colonial subordination; but he granted to
the new legislative body "free liberty to consult and debate among themselves in all affairs of public concern," and to make laws, which, if approved by the governor, were good and binding until confirmed or rejected
by himself. In one respect, he inaugurated a more democratic government than was enjoyed in the chartered colonies of New England; for he
gave to freeholders the right to elect their own representatives in an
Assembly. He had watched those Puritan oligarchies with interest, and
perceived that they were administered for the chosen few, and not for the
unprivileged many. He abhorred all laws which made distinctions in
religion. But he directed that such as were enacted in his province
should be as similar as possible to those in force in England.

Dongan issued writs for an election; and New York, Long Island,
Staten Island, Esopus, Albany, Rensselaerswick, Pemaquid, and Martha's
Vineyard proceeded to choose representatives. There was some show of
dislike to a Roman Catholic governor among the remote Puritan towns
on Long Island; but the elections, for the most part, went on quietly according to the method prescribed by the governor and council. Eighteen
assemblymen were returned, the majority of whom were Dutch.

It was a memorable day in the history of New York, when the representatives of its freeholders first met together under British rule.
Oct. 17. They took their seats on the 17th of October. Matthias Nicolls
was chosen speaker; and John Spragg, clerk. They sat for three weeks,

---

[1] *Proud*, I. 276. *Penn. Arch.*, I. 76–84. *Council Min.*, V. 10, 11. *Doc. Hist.*, I. 262,
263. *Col. Doc.*, III. 341–422. *Colden*, II. 64.

"'Mr. Penn has already more land than he can people these many years,' replied Dongan, and coldly dismissed the Quaker agents." Page 322.

and passed fourteen several acts, each of which, after three readings, was approved by Dongan and his council. The first and most important of these was "The charter of Liberties and Privileges" granted by the Duke. It was simply and clearly worded in good Saxon English,[1] and embraced the main features of self-government and self-taxation which the people had so earnestly desired. The usual privileges of Parliament were conferred on the members of the Assembly. Entire freedom of conscience and religion was guaranteed to all peaceable persons who professed faith • in God. And, in consideration of "many gracious and royal favors," and for the necessary expenses of the government, to the Duke and his heirs were granted certain specified duties on importations. The latter act was declared to be in force directly after its publication, which took place at the City Hall early on the morning of October 31. ^{Oct. 31.} Dongan by proclamation ordered all persons to report dues to Collector Santen.

The Assembly divided New York into twelve counties. But two of them, Duke's and Cornwall, embracing Nantucket and Martha's Vineyard, Elizabeth Island, No Man's Island, and Pemaquid, with the adjacent islands, were soon after ceded to other governments. Another important act was "to settle Courts of Justice." Four distinct tribunals were established in New York : Town Courts, for the trials of small causes, to be held each month ; County Courts, or Courts of Sessions, to be held quarterly or half-yearly ; a General Court of Oyer and Terminer, with original and appellate jurisdiction, to sit twice every year in each county ; and a Court of Chancery, to be the Supreme Court of the province, composed of the governor and council, with power in the governor to depute a chancellor in his stead, and to appoint clerks and other officers. But any citizen might appeal to the king from any judgment, according to a clause in the patent to the Duke of York. The first judges of the New York Court of Oyer and Terminer appointed by Dongan were Matthias Nicolls and John Palmer, both of whom had been bred to the law in England.

A significant law for naturalizing foreigners was enacted. Louis XIV. was driving out of France all of his subjects who refused to acknowledge the Pope of Rome as the only Vicar of Christ, and numbers of the refugees were already in New York. Strangers from other lands were constantly arriving. The Assembly, as if imbued with the spirit of

---

[1] *Brodhead*, II. 384, Appendix, Note E. *New York Revised Laws*, 1813, II. Appendix, iii., vi. *Munsell's Annals*, IV. 32 – 39. *Chalmers*, I. 584. *Bancroft*, II. 414. *Dunlap*, II. Appendix, xlii. *Smith*, I. 115. *Journals of Legislative Council, Col. Doc.*, III. 341, 357 – 359.

prophecy, ordained, that all actual inhabitants of the province, except slaves, of what foreign nation soever, who professed Christianity, and who had taken or should take the oath of allegiance to the government, were citizens; and that all Christian foreigners who should afterwards come and settle in the province could in like manner become subjects of the king.

The acts of the Assembly were sent to England by Governor Dongan for the Duke's approval. The king objected to the words, "THE PEOPLE," in the expression, "the people met in a General Assembly," as being too democratic, and not in use in any other colonial constitution. · But New York clung to them. Her first State Constitution, in 1777, declared that the style of all her laws should read thus : " *Be it enacted by the People of the State of New York, represented in Senate and Assembly.*" And under her second Constitution, of 1821, she adopted the more direct formula : " *The People of the State of New York, represented in Senate and Assembly, do enact,*" etc. The Duke's secretary wrote to Dongan of several amendments which were proposed in the revenue part of the charter, advising that they be acted upon at the next meeting of the Assembly ; and it was accordingly done. The Duke finally signed and sealed the instrument. Owing, however, to serious events in England, it was not perfected by delivery.

New York had a brief season of apparent content. Addresses of gratitude were sent to the Duke ; the " integrity, justice, equity, and prudence " of Dongan were emphasized ; and loyalty was expressed in the strongest terms. New trading regulations were established, and the merchants of the city subscribed two thousand guineas in a stock company to manage the fisheries and the Indian trade at Pemaquid. Taxes were paid cheerfully, and city improvements began anew. Quite a number of houses and stores were projected, and there was a healthful increase of business of all kinds.

Dominie Selyns wrote to the classis of Amsterdam that his congregation were building him a parsonage " wholly of stone, three stories high, and raised on the foundation of unmerited love." He said Governor Dongan was a gentleman " of knowledge, politeness, and friendliness " ; that he had received a visit from his Excellency, and could call upon him whenever he chose. As for himself, he said, he had too much work for one person, as he could not neglect the surrounding villages, but preached in them on Mondays and Thursdays, administering the communion and attending other services. He spoke of a French colleague, Dominie Petrus Daillé, late professor at Salmurs, and described him as " full of fire, godliness, and learning " ; he conducted

French worship in the old Dutch church in the fort between the hours of the Dutch service in the morning and the Episcopal in the afternoon. Rev. Dr. John Gordon was the English chaplain. Dominie Dellius had just come out from Holland, and been installed as the colleague of Dominie Schaats, at Albany.[1]

The records of the transactions between Dongan and the Indians are among the most valuable and interesting documents of the times. The frontiers of New York had no protection against encroachments from the French, except the valor of the Iroquois. Their fighting men numbered ten times as many then as they did a century later. They were subtle, restless, treacherous allies; and yet their importance, as a wall of separation between an unprotected colony and an always possible foe, was so apparent to the leading minds both in New York and England, that every effort which ingenuity could devise was put forth to win the favor of these renowned warriors. Dongan made the subject a careful study. Schuyler and Livingston, at Albany, were of great assistance to him, being familiar with the language and character of the various tribes. The Five Nations were a sovereign republic in themselves, and all their general business was performed by a congress of sachems, at Onondaga. As subsequent events proved, New York was indebted to them for her present northern boundary; for, had it not been for them, Canada would have embraced the entire basin of the St. Lawrence.

Connecticut had been surly ever since Philipse began to improve his property at Sleepy Hollow. "Castle Philipse," a stone house, was erected, and fortified with great care against the Indians, in 1683 (the same year that the new mill first began to grind the grain from all the country round). This building still survives, and the port-holes and loop-holes for cannon and musketry may yet be seen in its cellar-walls. A few years later (1699) Philipse built at his own expense, op-

Dutch Church: Sleepy Hollow.

posite "Castle Philipse," a substantial church, which is now the oldest church edifice in the State of New York. But it was when Dongan notified the towns of Rye, Greenwich, and Stamford to "make presentment" at the New York Assizes that Connecticut groaned aloud, and

[1] *Corr. Cl. Amst.* *Murphy's Anth.*, 104, 105. *Doc. Hist.*, III. 265, 535, 536.

once more stirred the much-agitated boundary question. She said all
those places "indubitably" belonged to herself. Dongan responded,
Oct. 5. that advantage had been taken in 1664 of Nicolls's want of geographical knowledge by running the line ten miles instead of twenty
miles east of the Hudson River, according to agreement; and that, if the
territory was not yielded, he should proceed to claim the whole of the
Duke's patent to the Connecticut River. It was a perilous time for
English charters, and wisdom clearly seemed the better part of
Nov. 14. valor. Governor Treat, in great tribulation, summoned a special
court at Hartford; and commissioners were appointed to visit and
confer with Dongan. Governor Treat, Nathan Gold, Secretary
Nov. 25. Allyn, and William Pitkin were the appointees, and journeyed
on horseback to the metropolis. Dongan, attended by Counselors Frederick Philipse, Stephanus Van Cortlandt, Anthony Brockholls, and John
Younge, met them, fortified with the testimony of several gentlemen who
knew personally all the details of the boundary settlement of
Nov. 28. 1664. The agents finally appealed to Dongan's magnanimity,
asking to be allowed to retain some of their settlements on the Sound in
exchange for equivalent property inland. After much discussion, it was
amicably arranged, that the boundary line should be removed a few miles
east from Mamaroneck to Byram River, between Rye and Greenwich,
and run thence as it now remains; and that this new line should be
properly surveyed the next October. The Connecticut agents, after their
return, notified the people of Rye that they "could not help" giving up
that town, but that Dongan was a noble gentleman, and would do for
their welfare whatever they should "desire in a regular manner."

At that very moment England was in a political convulsion. A plot
to murder the king and the Duke had been discovered. The details of
the proposed butchery had all been arranged at a small farm near London, from which it was called the "*Rye House Plot.*" There were, in
reality, two plots, one within the other. The greater was a Whig plot,
to raise the nation in arms against the government, and the leaders knew
nothing of the lesser, or "Rye House, Plot," in which only a few desperate
men were concerned, under the delusion that to kill the scions of royalty
was the shortest and surest way to vindicate the Protestant religion and
the liberties of England. There were traitors among them, who divulged
all and more than all, and the two plots were confounded together. The
whole Whig party were implicated, to a certain extent. Men of high
rank were condemned and executed; among them, Lord William Russell
and Algernon Sidney. Politicians, in great numbers, were sent to the
gallows. Convictions were obtained without difficulty from Tory juries,

and rigorous punishments were inflicted by courtly judges. The Court of King's Bench declared the franchise of the city of London forfeited to the crown. Flushed with victory, Charles proceeded to deprive of its charter almost every corporation in his realm. Then he granted new ones, which gave power into the hands of the Tories. These proceedings were accompanied by an act, intended as a sort of pledge to his subjects for the security of their Protestantism; for he was himself nominally the head of the Episcopal Church. Anne, the youngest daughter of James, who, like her sister Mary, had been nurtured a Protestant, he gave in marriage to George, a prince of the orthodox house of Denmark, whose chief recommendations were his dullness and his Lutheranism. This was in opposition to the wishes of James; but Charles said, " Brother, we must mollify England." And England, to a certain degree, was mollified; for James being near the age of the king, even if he should outlive and succeed his brother, his reign would probably be short, and there was the gratifying prospect of a long line of Protestant sovereigns.

Still further emboldened, Charles violated the plain letter of the law, and rewarded James for his acquiescence in the marriage of Anne by dispensing with the Test Act in his favor and restoring him to his old office of Lord High Admiral of England. Soon after, he took him into his Privy Council. It appeared by these successive trials that the nation would endure almost anything which the government had the courage to inflict. The hour of revolution was not quite yet.

The king's acts were not approved by his ministers. Halifax, in particular, objected to the long intermission of Parliaments, regretted the severity with which the vanquished Whigs were treated, and dreaded the reaction of public feeling. He urged the king to send the Duke to Scotland, and the Duke pressed his brother to dismiss Halifax. At one of the last councils which Charles held, the Massachusetts charter was discussed. The king had made void his father's patent to that corporation, on the ground that the rulers there had abused their privileges by excluding from the freedom of their corporation those who did not agree with them in matters of religion. He had no sympathy with Puritanism. But how should Massachusetts be governed? James suggested that the whole power, legislative as well as executive, should abide in the crown. Several of the lords were of the same opinion. Halifax argued with energy in favor of representative government. " Remember," he said, " that a population sprung from English stock and animated by English feelings will not long submit to be deprived of English institutions." James, in great heat, maintained the right of the king to govern his distant countries in the way which should seem to him most convenient.

"Life would not be worth having," exclaimed the unintimidated Halifax, "where liberty and property were at the mercy of one despotic master." Charles hesitated. He was not altogether pleased with his brother's excessive zeal, and he was too indolent to act independently. But, in the end, it was settled that the king's sovereignty was to be resumed. Sir Edmund Andros was suggested as the royal governor for Massachusetts ; but he was at present occupied with private affairs in the Channel Islands, and Colonel Kirke, a dangerous, unprincipled despot, was chosen in his stead. He was commissioned with power to make laws and perform all acts of government, under the king, in New England ; including Massachusetts, New Hampshire, Maine, and New Plymouth : Rhode Island and Connecticut were excepted from his authority. In his instructions, no mention whatever was made of a legislative assembly.

James privately hoped to obtain from his brother (now more than ever indulgent) a special grant of Rhode Island and Connecticut. And all at once came a petition from Dongan and his council, and the mayor and aldermen of the city of New York, that the Duke would, either by purchase or otherwise, if possible, reannex East New Jersey to his province. The reason given was, that, " by reason of the separation, the trade of New York was diverted, to the injury of his Majesty's revenue."

One of Dongan's special instructions from the Duke was, to grant the city of New York " immunities and privileges " beyond what any other parts of his possessions enjoyed. As soon as the Assembly adjourned, the mayor and common council petitioned for a confirmation of the " immunities " granted the corporation by Nicolls, with certain additions, including the division of the city into six wards ; the annual election of aldermen and other officers by the freemen in each ward (the local government of the city to be intrusted to them, and to a mayor and recorder, to be annually appointed by the governor and council), with provisions that a sheriff, coroner, and town clerk be appointed in the same way ; that the corporation appoint their own treasurer ; and, finally, that whatever else was necessary for the welfare of the metropolis should be accorded as fully as to similar corporations in England.

Objections were raised by Dongan to some of the proposed additional articles, but, after explanation and discussion, they were agreed to in almost every particular. The existing officers were reappointed : John West was commissioned city clerk ; and John Tudor, a London lawyer, was made city sheriff. James Graham was commissioned the first recorder of the city of New York, and took his place upon the bench at the right hand of the mayor, Cornelis Steenwyck.

The board proceeded to divide the city into six wards ; assigning

Nicholas Bayard as alderman for the South Ward, John Inians for the Dock Ward, William Pinhorne for the East Ward, Gulian Verplanck for the North Ward, John Robinson for the West Ward, and William Cox for the Out Ward. They adopted various by-laws for the better government of the city. Among them was one, which said, " no youths, maydes, or other persons may meet together on the Lord's day for sporte or play, under penalty of a fine of one shilling." No public houses were allowed to keep open doors, or give entertainment on the Sabbath, except to strangers, under a fine of ten shillings. No manner of work was to be done on the Lord's day, under the same penalty, and double for each repetition. No children were allowed to play in the streets on the Sabbath day ; and not more than four Indian or negro slaves might assemble together in any place, under a penalty of six shillings to their owners.

The Sabbath question was, with the men of that day, one of morals and religion. They believed that the roads which led to Sunday amusements were in a contrary direction from that pointed out by the Christian Church. Their experience, as well as their education, had taught them that the only way to build up and purify a community was to legislate for the proper observance of the Sabbath. Before we welcome that European Sunday of amusements which now seems about to invade our shores, let us well consider the effect of the Dutch and English and American Sabbath upon the character of the people that have been brought under its influence, and what it has contributed to the progress and the glory of three great nations.

It was also enacted, that the proprietors of hotels should report all strangers who arrived, and never entertain any person, man or woman, suspected of a bad character, under penalty of a fine of ten shillings. Flour bolted in the city was to be inspected. Bolting was performed by horse-power, as water and steam had not yet been utilized. Indians were allowed, by a special license, to sell firewood ; also, to vend gutters for houses, — long strips of bark, so curved at the sides as to conduct water. All horses ranging loose were to be branded and enrolled. A reward was offered to all who should destroy wolves.

A committee was appointed to collect ancient records of the city and its laws, for preservation. Surveyors were chosen, to regulate the manner of building, and preserve uniformity in the streets. A constable was appointed, to walk up and down, armed, and see that the laws were obeyed ; a haven-master, also, to look after the shipping and collect the bills. There was a public chimney-sweep, whose duty it was to announce his approach by crying through the streets, and to cleanse the metropolitan chimneys at a compensation of one shilling or eighteen pence apiece, according to the height of the house.

An *Inviter to Funerals* was licensed by the mayor. The first man who served the public in that capacity was Conradus Vanderbeck ; his assistant was Robert Chapman. They were required to serve the poor *gratis*. The customs of the period in respect to funerals were peculiar. No one, of any caste, thought of attending a funeral without invitation. The bearers were presented with mourning rings, silk scarfs, and handkerchiefs. In some cases, all the invited guests were presented with gloves. After the ceremonies of burial, they returned to the house to partake of a banquet, at which, if the means of the family allowed, the best of wines were furnished.

A portion of the slaughter-house at Smits Vly, being at a safe distance from the city, was, this year, converted into a powder magazine, and Garret Johnson was intrusted with its custody.

By advice of the mayor and common council, Dongan issued a proclamation, prohibiting the packing or bolting of flour, or the making of bread for exportation to any place within the government, except the city of New York. This was in addition to the former bolting monopoly, and was approved by the Duke, who was anxious to encourage the metropolis above all other cities. There were twenty-four bakers, who were divided into six classes, one for each working-day in the week. The price established by law for a white loaf of bread, weighing twelve ounces, was six stuyvers in wampum.

In the summer of 1684, Lord Effingham, governor of Virginia, visited New York, accompanied by two of his counselors, for the purpose of inducing Dongan to join him in a war against the Five Nations, **1684.** who had been committing outrages all along the borders of his territory. He was the first British peer upon whom was conferred the distinction of the " freedom of the city." He was the guest of Dongan, and the recipient of all manner of courtesies from the leading families. Sundry dinner-parties were given in his honor, which brought together the Philipses, Van Cortlandts, Bayards, Stuyvesants, De Peysters, Kips, Beekmans, and others.

But serious work was before the government. Dongan and Lord Effingham went to Albany, where they were cordially welcomed by Schuyler and Livingston. Deputies from the Five Nations had been summoned to meet them, and were already on the spot. Counselor Van Cortlandt, who had been appointed agent for Massachusetts, to ratify with gifts and pledges the ancient friendship of New England and the savages, was also present. Lord Effingham opened the stately conference by an address to the sachems, recapitulating the promises broken and the outrages recently committed by them, and proposing to make " a new chain" between them and Virginia and Maryland, "to endure even to the world's end." Dongan followed in a similar strain of oratory. Taking advantage of the good feeling produced, a written sub- July 30. mission to "the Great Sachem, Charles, that lives on the other side of the Great Lake," was obtained from the Iroquois. It was traced in legible characters upon two white dressed deer-skins, which were to be sent to the "Sachem Charles," to put his name and red seal upon. By this instrument, all the Susquehanna River above the "Washuta," and all the rest of the land of the Iroquois, was confirmed to the Duke, as within the limits of New York.[1]

The Indians requested that the Duke's arms should be put upon their castles, supposing that this would protect them from the French. Dongan notified the French commander of Canada that the Duke's territory must not be invaded; but this did not prevent the most persistent and vexatious intermeddling, and a protracted series of annoyances and alarms.

The next day, the sachems promised "to plant a tree of peace, whose tops will reach the sun and its branches spread far abroad, to cover Virginia, Maryland, and Massachusetts." Axes were buried in the southeast end of the Albany court-house yard, and the Indians threw earth upon them.

The inconvenience of having two distinct governments upon one river grew more and more apparent. East New Jersey revived her old claim to Staten Island, which Lady Carteret had tried in vain to establish in 1681; printed circulars, freely distributed, so agitated the landholders that many of them deemed it a matter of prudence to secure their titles by obtaining additional patents from the East New Jersey proprietors. Judge Palmer, and Dongan himself, having purchased valuable estates on Staten Island, are said to have done likewise. The Duke's secretary, who had witnessed the transfer of the Jersey lands, wrote to Dongan that there was no manner of color for such pretensions. The Surveyor-General of New York, Philip Wells, was accordingly ordered to lay out Staten Island in such a way as to regard each owner's patent; and Thomas Lovelace, the sheriff of Staten Island, was directed to summon all persons without proper land titles before the governor and council for examination.

The new year opened auspiciously. New York was in a fair and promising condition. In gorgeous halls across the water, her sovereign, a man of fifty well-rounded years, healthy, robust, and gay   **1685.** almost to frivolity, surrounded by ladies whose charms were the boast and whose vices were the disgrace of the age, and by gambling courtiers

---

[1] *Col. Doc.*, III. 347 – 516. *Colden* (first ed.), 64, 65; ed. 1755, I. 55, 56. *Penn. Arch.*, I. 121 – 125. *Brodhead*, II. 395 – 397. *Doc. Hist. N. Y.*, I. 261 – 266.

winning and losing mountains of gold in a night, was looking forward to a long life of ease and pleasure.

A month rolled round. Scarcely had Charles risen from his bed on the morning of February 2d, than the gentlemen of rank, who had assembled as usual to chat with him while he was being shaved, noticed a strange look upon his face. An instant later, he uttered a loud cry and fell insensible into the arms of Lord Bruce. A physician, who happened to be present, quickly opened a vein, and he was laid upon a bed. The alarm was given, and all the medical men of note in London were summoned to the palace. One prescription was signed by fourteen names. He recovered his senses after a time, yet lay in a condition of extreme danger. The queen hung over him, and the Duke scarcely left his bedside. The news filled London with dismay, for those who most disliked him preferred his unprincipled levity to his brother's stern bigotry. The prelates who were present exhorted him to prepare for death, which was imminent; but he listened to them in silence. The service for the visitation of the sick was read; he said he was sorry for what he had done amiss, and absolution was pronounced, according to the forms of the Church of England ; but when the faithful divines urged that he should declare that he died in the communion of the Episcopal Church, he was apparently unconscious, and made no movement to take the eucharist from the hands of the bishop. A table with bread and wine was brought to his bedside ; but he said there was no hurry, and that he was too weak ; and it was supposed that he was overcome with the stupor which precedes death.

A few persons in his household knew that he had never been a sincere member of the Established Church. In his rarely serious moments, he was at heart a Roman Catholic. The Duke was so much occupied looking after his own interests, the posting of guards through the city, and the preparation for his proclamation as soon as the king should expire, that he was oblivious to the danger of the loss of his brother's soul for the want of the last sacraments. This was the more extraordinary as the Duchess of York had, at the request of the queen, suggested spiritual assistance. The Duchess of Portsmouth finally sent the French ambassador to remind James of his sacred duty. The message was whispered in his ear, and he started, scarcely able to repress tears at the thought of his negligence, and hastily looked about him to see how it might be repaired. The room was filled with Protestant clergymen. Catholicism was the powder magazine of the kingdom. There was not a moment to waste in preliminaries. He commanded every one to stand back, and bending over the dying king said something in a whisper to which Charles answered

Feb. 2.

audibly, "Yes, yes, with all my heart." "Shall I bring a priest?" asked James. "Do, brother, for God's sake do, and lose no time; but no, you will get into trouble"; and his voice grew fainter. "If it costs me my life, I will bring a priest," exclaimed the Duke, with great feeling.

The gentlemen standing about the room were not aware of the purport of the conversation. To find a priest for such a purpose at a moment's notice was no easy thing to do. As the law then stood, it was a capital crime to admit a proselyte into the Roman Catholic Church. A Portuguese nobleman, who was present, undertook to find one of the queen's chaplains; but none of them understood English or French sufficiently. The French ambassador was about to go to the Venetian minister for a clergyman, when they learned that there was a Benedictine monk at Whitehall, named Huddleston, who had, after the battle of Worcester, risked his life to save that of the king, and had ever since been a privileged person. When the nation had been goaded to fury and proclamations issued against popish priests, Huddleston had always been excepted by name. He was willing to put his life in peril again for the king he loved; but he was so illiterate that he had to have instructions as to what was proper to say on such a momentous occasion. He was brought by a confidential servant up the back stairway. The Duke requested all present, except three noblemen whom he dared trust, to withdraw. Then the back door was opened and the monk, whose sacred vestments were concealed under a cloak, entered. When he was announced, Charles faintly answered, "He is welcome." Huddleston went through his part better than was expected, pronounced the absolution, and administered extreme unction. He asked if Charles wished to receive the Lord's Supper. "Surely, if I am not unworthy," was the quick reply. Meanwhile, the courtiers in the outer room were whispering their suspicions, with significant glances. The door was opened, and once more they stood around the king's bed. He retained his faculties during the entire night, conversing at intervals with different persons. Once he apologized for being such an unconscionable time dying, and hoped those who had stood about him so long would excuse it. Soon after daylight his speech failed, and about noon he passed away.

In a quarter of an hour, James came out of the closet, whither he had retired when all was over, and the Privy Counselors, who were assembled in the palace, proclaimed him king. Usage required a speech, and the new monarch expressed a few words of touching sorrow for the loss just sustained, and promised to imitate the singular lenity which had distinguished the late reign. He said he had been accused of an over-fondness for power; but that was one of many falsehoods which had been told of him. He would maintain the established government both in Church and State, and, knowing the Church of England to be eminently loyal, should specially care for, support, and defend it. And he should with his life defend the rights and liberties of his people.

The lords were delighted with his sentiments. When his speech was made public, it produced a pleasing impression. A king, whose very first act was to defend the Church and strictly respect the rights of his people, was certainly fit to wear a crown. His worst enemies did not regard him as one likely to court public favor by professing what he did not feel, or by promising what he had no intention of performing. He would probably have kept his word, had it not involved complicated relations which his mind could not grasp. At a later period, he stated that his unpremeditated expressions touching the Church of England were too strong, and had been made without due consideration.

James knew, when he ascended the throne of England, that it was liable to be overturned in an hour, and his face was fixed on France, in an agony of supplication. His new ministry, of which Halifax was Lord President, in spite of old quarrels, urged the call of a Parliament. There was no other safe course. The customs had been settled for life on Charles only, and could not be legally exacted by the new king. James issued the call, and then apologized deferentially to Louis for taking such a step without coming to him for advice. He asked the French king for a subsidy, and his wants were promptly supplied. When the money was put into his hands, he actually shed tears of gratitude. He became the slave of France. The degrading relation galled him, and he looked about in vain for some way in which to break loose from his thralldom. He grew haughty, punctilious, boastful, and quarrelsome, and evinced tokens of indecision and insincerity. Those who were without the clew were puzzled by his extraordinary conduct. Even Louis could not comprehend the ally, who passed, in a few hours, from homage to defiance and from defiance to homage. It was only within narrow limits that he could conform his actions to a general rule. It was not long before he was assuring the United Provinces, that, as soon as the affairs of England were settled, he would show the world how little he feared France. The patience of the nation caused visions of dominion and glory to rise before his mind.

A little oratory had been fitted up in the palace for Mary, while Duchess of York, and James was in the habit of hearing mass with her there in private. Soon after he became king, he shocked his Protestant subjects by erecting a new pulpit, and throwing open the doors, so that all who came to pay their duty to him might see the Catholic ceremony.

There was a sensation in the antechamber, the Catholics falling on their knees and the Protestants hurrying away. During Lent, a series of sermons was preached there by popish divines, and a little later the rites of the Church of Rome were once more, after an interval of a hundred and twenty-seven years, performed on Easter Sunday at Westminster with regal splendor. The Tories were in the ascendant; hence zealous churchmen brooded over England's wrongs in dignified silence. But, on the day of his coronation, James committed what, in Roman Catholic estimation, was little short of an act of apostasy. He made an oblation on the altar, joined in the litany as chanted by the bishops, received the unction typical of divine influence, and knelt with the semblance of devotion, while that society of heretics (as he believed the Church of England to be) called down upon him the Holy Spirit, of which they were in his opinion the malignant and obstinate foes.

The inconsistencies of James II. furnish a key to the succession of disasters which befell New York. He was quite another person from what he had been as Duke of York. Not less active, if possible more industrious, and equally disposed to manage and control; but his interests were divided, and despotism appeared in the ascendant. The first time after his accession that the affairs of New York were discussed, he presided in person over the Plantation Committee. He re-examined the Charter of Privileges, which he had sealed but never delivered to New York City, and discovered that it was too liberal in its construction. He declined to confirm it, because it tended towards an abridgment of his power; although it was in force until such time as he should see fit to communicate his disapproval to Dongan. He thought it would be well to consolidate New York and New England under one government, and a constitution was discussed, although not acted upon at that time.

A letter bearing his royal signature directed that all men in office in New York should so continue until further orders. It contained no allusion to an Assembly, which accordingly was called in October, and William Pinhorne was chosen speaker. But it was the last representative body permitted to New York, or indeed to any of the American colonies, during the reign of James II. It accomplished very little business of importance. Immediately after its adjournment, a day of thanksgiving was proclaimed by the governor, for the king's victory over the rebels under Argyll and Monmouth. _{March 3.} _{Oct. 20.} _{Nov. 20.}

In 1685, Nicholas Bayard was the mayor of the city and also one of Dongan's council. James Graham was appointed attorney-general of the province, and Isaac Swinton was made clerk in chancery. About this time, Collector Santen proved unfaithful to his trust, and was ordered

20

before the governor and council with his books and accounts, which were rigidly examined. He was a hypochondriac, subject to fits, careless in his business habits, boundlessly arrogant, and extremely violent in temper. He was testy about explanations and was severely reprimanded. He was allowed to execute the duties of his office a short time longer ; but charges accumulated against him, and he was finally suspended, arrested, and sent to England. Stephanus Van Cortlandt and James Graham were appointed to manage the king's revenue until further orders. Dongan wrote to James, asking the privilege of naming a collector from among the old residents of the city, " because," said he, " those who are sent over for the purpose expect to run suddenly into great estate."

It was found necessary to establish a Court of Exchequer, to be held in the city of New York on the first Monday in each month, for the purpose of determining royal revenue cases. There was great hazard in leaving such questions to country juries, who were ignorant, and generally linked together by affinity or swayed by particular humors and interests. Dyer, who was now Surveyor-General of the customs in America, complained that the juries in New Jersey found verdicts in opposition to the most undoubted facts. He also wrote to the Plantation Committee in regard to the mixed condition of affairs in the whole revenue department.

When James found breathing space amid the putting down of the various rebellions which menaced his throne, he gave attention to his American affairs. A temporary government was arranged for Massachusetts, and Joseph Dudley,[1] for whose loyalty Dongan vouched, was appointed president over seventeen counselors. The case of William Penn and Lord Baltimore was next in order. The rival claimants were politically equal, one being a Roman Catholic and the other a Quaker, and their territorial dispute was settled as impartially as possible under the circumstances. It was decided that Delaware did not form a part of Maryland ; and the boundary between Pennsylvania and Maryland was run from Delaware westward by Charles Mason and Jeremiah Dixon, and has ever since been known as " Mason and Dixon's Line."

James regarded the Quakers with a feeling akin to tenderness ; partly because they had never been implicated in any conspiracy against the

---

[1] Joseph Dudley was the son of Governor Thomas Dudley of Massachusetts. He was born in 1647 ; graduated at Harvard in 1665 ; was agent of Massachusetts in England in 1682 ; president in 1685 ; one of Andros's council in 1689 ; one of Governor Sloughter's council, and Chief Justice of New York in 1691. In the latter capacity, he tried and condemned Leisler. He was afterwards member of the British Parliament, lieutenant-governor of the Isle of Wight, and, from 1702 to 1715, governor of Massachusetts. He died in 1720. *Hutchisson's Mass.*, II. 193.

government, but more particularly as the direct result of a potent advocacy at court. William Penn lived in the highest circles and had constant access to the royal ear. His father had held various positions of honor, had sat in Parliament, and had been knighted. The son had a high reputation and many virtues. He was every day summoned from the gallery into the closet, and spent hours with the king, while many a peer was kept waiting in the antechamber. His integrity was not entirely proof against the temptations of that polite but deeply corrupted court, where intrigues of one sort and another were constantly fermenting. His own sect grew suspicious of him, notwithstanding that they received indulgences similar to those granted to the Roman Catholics, while the intermediate or Puritan order of religionists were suffering beyond measure. On one occasion, a list of Quakers against whom proceedings had been instituted for not taking the oaths and for not going to church was made out, and every individual of them discharged. It was generally remarked that William Penn had more power at Whitehall than any of the nobles. It is quite apparent that he knew how to influence James to his own private advantage, for when the plan was matured for consolidating the colonies in America, Pennsylvania alone escaped the forfeiture of her charter. Printing was also permitted in that province at a time when freedom of type was by no means a popular idea in high circles. William Bradford, a young man of twenty-two, a namesake Aug. 6. and favorite of William Penn, who had been apprenticed to a Quaker printer in London and had married his daughter, was allowed to set up a printing-press in Philadelphia. His first work was an almanac for the year 1686, which is at this date (1876) a very unique and interesting curiosity. Hitherto, the only printing-press in the English colonies had been in Massachusetts and under Puritan censorship.

The year 1686 was distinguished by the granting of the "Dongan Charter" to the city of New York. It was drafted by Mayor Nicholas Bayard and Recorder James Graham, and was one of **1686.** the most liberal ever bestowed upon a colonial city. By it sources of immediate income became vested in the corporation. Subsequent charters added nothing to the city property, save in the matter of ferry rights, in immediate reference to which the charters of 1708 and 1730 were obtained.

The Dongan charter confirmed all former "rights and privileges," and conveyed specifically to the corporation the City Hall, the two market-houses, the bridge into the dock, the great dock and wharf connected therewith, the new burial-ground, the ferry, and the waste, vacant, unpatented lands on Manhattan Island reaching to low-water mark, together with the rivers, rivulets, coves, creeks, ponds, waters, and water-courses not before mentioned.[1]

It is an interesting document and is recited at large in the charter of 1730. It is the more remarkable from the fact, that, at the very moment of its creation, James and his ministers were waging war against all chartered rights and privileges throughout the British dominions. The marked partiality thus displayed for New York may be imputed more to the personal character and influence of Dongan, and the spirit and far-sighted intelligence of the leading citizens of the metropolis, than to any private preference on the part of the king. The instrument was the basis of a plan of government for a great city. It was cautiously worded, and shows that the minds in which it originated were possessed of a broad and enlightened sense of the sanctity of corporate and private rights, and by no means disposed to neglect provident guards for their security. It is in itself an ample foundation, and we shall see how it was built upon as exigencies demanded.

Before the end of the year, a new city seal was presented to New York. It was richer and more elaborate than the old Dutch city seal ; but it preserved the beaver, with the addition of a flour-barrel, and the arms of a wind-mill, signifying the prevailing commerce and industry. The whole was supported by two Indian chiefs, and encircled by a wreath of laurel, the motto being, *Sigillum civitatis Novi Eboraci.*

Soon after signing the metropolitan charter, Dongan went up to Albany, and executed a charter agreed upon between himself and the magistrates of that city, giving the corporation large franchises, including the management of the Indian trade. He appointed Peter Schuyler its first mayor ; Isaac Swinton, recorder ; and Robert Livingston, city clerk and sub-collector of the king's revenues at that place. The aldermen and assistants were to be chosen annually by the inhabitants on the Feast of Saint Michael, the 29th of September.

May.

Livingston discovered the peculiar value of the lands south of Van Rensselaer's property, which had never yet been granted by the government to any one, and entered into negotiations with the Indians for their purchase. They conveyed to him, July 12, 1683, just prior to his marriage with Alida, the widow of Rev. Nicolaus Van Rensselaer, two thousand acres on Roelof Jansen's Kill. The deed was executed by two Indians and two squaws. The payment consisted of " three hundred guilders in sewan, eight blankets and two children's blankets, five and

---

[1] *Col. Doc.*, III. 360 – 495 ; IV. 812 ; V. 369. *Council Minutes*, V. 155. *Minutes of Common Council*, I. 272 – 300. *Valentine, Man* 1844, 318 ; 1858, 13 – 24. *Booth's Hist. N. Y.*, Appendix. *Dunlap*, II. Appendix. *Patents*, V. 381 – 406. *Kent's Book of Charters*, 210.

twenty ells of duffels, and four garments of strouds, ten large shirts and ten small shirts, ten pairs of large stockings and ten small pairs, six guns, fifty pounds of powder, fifty staves of lead, four caps, ten kettles, ten axes, ten adzes, two pounds of paint, twenty little scissors, twenty little looking-glasses, one hundred fish-hooks, awls and nails of each one hundred, four rolls of tobacco, one hundred pipes, ten bottles, three kegs of rum, one barrel of strong beer, twenty knives, four stroud coats, two duffel coats and four tin kettles."

During the next two years, Livingston secured the Indian title to, in all, one hundred and sixty thousand acres of the finest land on the Hudson, and in the midst of scenery unsurpassed by any in Europe. He then obtained from Dongan a patent, with manorial privileges, dated July 22, 1685; and this grant was confirmed by royal authority in 1715, with the additional privilege of electing a representative to the General Assembly.

Thus Livingston was one of the largest landholders in New York. His manor was not, however, as rich and valuable as that of Van Rensselaer. It belonged strictly to that class of institutions called close boroughs, which necessarily gave way before the equalizing influences of republicanism. The manor-house which he built on the Hudson, forty miles south of Albany, was for several generations the seat of a princely hospitality. The governors of the province were always entertained there on their trips up and down the river; and every foreigner of distinction who visited this country was cordially welcomed within its walls.

Philip Livingston, the eldest son of Robert, and heir to this great manorial estate, was born at Albany in 1686. He was unlike his father in many respects, — was less bold, less subtle, less persevering, less of financier, and a much handsomer man. In his youthful days, he was dashing and

Clermont. The Lower Manor-House.

gay; he had a winning manner with women, and went about breaking hearts promiscuously. In the course of time, however, he wedded Catharine, the pretty daughter of Peter Van Brugh of Albany. He was by no means destitute of rank and consequence. He was, for several years, deputy agent of Indian affairs under his father, and, from 1722, sole secretary. He was at the taking of Port Royal in 1710 ; a colonel of militia, a member of the Assembly, and, for many years, one of the governor's council. He lived in a style of courtly magnificence.

He was the eldest of five sons and four daughters. Two of the sons and two of the daughters died unmarried ; but he, with his two brothers, Robert and Gilbert, survived to a good old age. Robert, the second son, received from his father thirteen thousand acres of the main estate, as a special reward for having discovered and frustrated an Indian plot. This formed the lower manor of Clermont. A large stone house was built upon it, which, towards the close of his life, he gave to his son Judge Robert R. Livingston, the father of Chancellor Livingston. Gilbert received a large estate near Saratoga, and married Cornelia Beekman. He was the ancestor of a large family, among whom was Rev. John R. Livingston, the celebrated divine.

Livingston Manor-House in 1876.

[Robert, eldest son of Philip, and third lord of the manor, divided the estate (in 1784) equally between his four sons. Walter subsequently conveyed his portion of the manor to his brother Henry, who built the present structure.]

CHAPTER XVIII.

1686–1689.

EFFECTS OF THE MEASURES OF JAMES II.

CATHOLICISM IN NEW YORK. — ABSURD ALARMS. — PERSECUTION IN FRANCE. — THE ASSEMBLY ABOLISHED IN NEW YORK. — SIR EDMUND ANDROS IN BOSTON. — CONNECTICUT AND HER TWO WOOERS. — CONNECTICUT LOSES HER CHARTER. — THE POST-ROUTE. — GOVERNOR DONGAN A STATESMAN. — ALBANY IN DANGER. — THE ENGLISH, FRENCH, AND IROQUOIS. — CONSOLIDATION OF THE COLONIES. — NEW YORK SWALLOWED BY NEW ENGLAND. — SIR EDMUND ANDROS. — THE EXILED HUGUENOTS. — EXTRAORDINARY ACTS OF JAMES II. — THE SEVEN BISHOPS. — BIRTH OF THE PRINCE OF WALES. — MARY, PRINCESS OF ORANGE. — THE CHARACTER OF WILLIAM III. — THE POLITICAL MARRIAGE. -- A DOMESTIC ROMANCE. — WILLIAM'S PURPOSES. — WILLIAM'S EXPEDITION TO ENGLAND. — REVOLUTION IN ENGLAND. — THE KING'S DESPAIR. — ABDICATION OF THE THRONE BY JAMES II. — WILLIAM'S RECEPTION IN LONDON. — WILLIAM AND MARY CROWNED SOVEREIGNS OF ENGLAND.

IT would seem as if the whole world was just at this moment in a religious ferment. The revocation of the Edict of Nantes, in 1685, caused a simultaneous cry of grief and rage through the whole of Protestant Europe. The courts of Spain and Rome, not usually **1686.** backward in applauding a vigorous war upon heresy, were amazed at the injustice of the French king, and took the side of religious liberty. England was filled with dismay. She began immediately to scrutinize the recent acts of her own king. He had ordered the organization of a large military force, and, in defiance of the law, had officered it chiefly with Roman Catholics. Why might it not be employed in England for the same wretched work which the dragoons of Louis had performed in France ? James had publicly promised to respect the privileges of his Protestant subjects ; but had not Louis in like manner pledged himself ? Was there, after all, any reliance to be placed upon kings ?

New York caught the alarm, and suffered, as a feeble child, much more severely than its parent. The rumor was started that James had communicated to Governor Dongan an intention to establish the Roman Catholic religion there. A new Latin teacher who was said to be a Jesuit

21

having been employed in the school, many of the children were hastily removed, and some of them sent to the New England schools. The Catholic officers of the government were watched with jealous eyes, and every movement of the governor was criticised. All confidence in rulers seemed to be fast fading away. A gentleman from London arrived about this time and was hospitably entertained by Governor Dongan. The two appeared together on the streets, and dined with Frederick Philipse and with Nicholas Bayard. It was absurdly reported that the strange guest was a Catholic priest in disguise, sent over on private business by the king ; and the rumor, fostered by that kindly entertainment always furnished in such cases by small communities, speedily assumed the importance of an acknowledged fact. If James himself was constitutionally treacherous, how could any member of his church be trusted ? What sense was there in calling a monarch who rejected the English communion " the Defender of the Faith " of the Episcopalians ! Supposing that he did wear a crown which he owed to the Anglican clergy, and that every tie of gratitude and decency bound him to their support, it was clear that he only waited for some plausible excuse to trample them all under his feet.

Meanwhile James publicly expressed disapproval, and was really at heart distressed by the outrages which Louis was visiting upon the Huguenots. Men and women of all classes were stripped of their possessions, hunted from place to place without sleep and without food, and subjected to the most violent persecution ever recorded upon the pages of history. Men in power even set themselves at work to invent new, methods of cruelty. Nothing could exceed the fury of the inquisitors. Such of the persecuted as attempted to escape were seized, the men committed to the galleys, and the women immured in nunneries, where they were starved, whipped, and otherwise barbarously treated. Those who died were denied burial. And yet thousands upon thousands succeeded in escaping ; the best blood of France was on the wing ; persons of great fame in war, in letters, in the arts, and in the sciences, dressed like the humblest peasants, wandered from place to place, engaging in the most menial occupations, until ingenuity could devise some method of crossing the frontiers. Many reached England, and James assisted them from his own private purse. He did not like to have it appear that Catholics were intolerant. All this came upon him just as he had made up his mind to ask of his Protestant Parliament the fullest toleration for Roman Catholics in England.

June 3. The idea of consolidation for the purpose of bringing New England under the direct authority of the crown was fully matured in the spring of 1686. Sir Edmund Andros was finally commissioned to the supreme command, and the former provisional appointment was revoked. He was empowered to make laws, levy taxes, regulate finances, and control the militia. Humanity and severity were mingled in his instructions. Liberty of conscience was particularly enjoined; but printing-presses were forbidden, except by special license. Whole pages were devoted to the rights of the governed; but assemblies were prohibited, on account of the dangerous power which they invested in the people. The great seal for New England was adorned with the remarkable motto, "*Nunquam libertas gratior extat,*" — Liberty is never more agreeable — than under a pious king!

A similar commission was prepared for Dongan, and by it the Charter of Franchises, which had been so dear to New York, was made void. Dongan was ordered to resume the powers of law-making ^{June 10.} and tax-gathering. He was also directed to swear into his service, as counselors, Frederick Philipse, Stephanus Van Cortlandt, Nicholas Bayard, Anthony Brockholls, Lucas Stanten, John Spragg, Jervis Baxter, and John Younge. These gentlemen were all well and favorably known at Whitehall, and their eligibility had been fully discussed in the Plantation Committee at one of its meetings over which the king in person presided.

In December (1686), Andros reached Boston, "glittering in scarlet and lace," according to the discontented Puritans, who looked gloomily on while his Irish soldiers, under Lieutenant-Governor Nicholson, ^{Dec. 19.} marched through the streets in brilliant uniform, with gay music and banners floating in the breeze. The free-and-easy manner of the newcomers was in the highest degree repulsive to the people. The stiff and formal bigots of Massachusetts, who had persecuted even to banishment and death every man and woman presuming to hold religious opinions different from their own, accused Andros of papacy, and turned upon him the concentrated strength of a long-cherished hatred. Their precious charter had been vacated, and his personal rule had been bestowed upon them in its stead. Had he been an angel from Heaven, under the circumstances, he would hardly have pleased them. His soldierly bearing and administration were, according to their ideas, overbearing and oppressive; and when he was sharp, quick, and decisive in his measures, they called him "the arbitrary and sycophantic tool of a despotic king." It is doubtful whether moderation on his part would not have given even greater offense.

Joseph Dudley, the president of the board which had temporarily administered the government, was appointed Chief Justice of New England.

William Stoughton and Peter Bulkley were made associate judges, and George Farwell, from New York, was the attorney-general. John West resigned his offices under Dongan, and removed to Boston, where he was made Secretary of New England.

One of the first acts of Andros was to rebuke Hinckley, the late governor of Plymouth, for intolerance, in seizing the property of Quakers for the support of other sectarian ministers. Indeed, the statesmanship of Andros was more tolerant and just, and provided more generally for the happiness and prosperity of all classes of inhabitants, than that which it superseded. He was fearless and unconcerned in regard to the public temper, and made and executed laws which indicate a profound regard for the good of the province.

Connecticut, at that period, had two wooers, New York and Boston. Dongan wrote an eloquent letter to the king, recommending the annexation of Connecticut to New York, and suggesting that Pemaquid, which was troublesome and expensive, from being so distant, might be given to New England as an equivalent. Andros, wiser as to the king's intentions, was trying to induce Connecticut to come peaceably under his authority. Some very curious intercolonial intrigues followed. Connecticut coquetted ; giving New York to understand that it would be more agreeable to tend westward than toward the east, and allowing Boston meanwhile to kiss her hand. Andros treated Dongan with extreme official reserve, keeping him in the dark in regard to the true situation of affairs, and, with some show of haughtiness, communicated an order for the surrender of Pemaquid, which was promptly and cheerfully obeyed.

In the course of events, definite instructions reached Andros to demand the charters of Rhode Island and Connecticut. He set out at once to visit the two provinces, accompanied by several of the gentlemen of his council, with an escort of sixty soldiers. He was received in Hartford with distinguished ceremony. The General Court was in session, that same evening. Andros appeared, leaning upon the arm of Governor Treat, and publicly explained the king's policy in bringing his colonies under a single government, that they might the better defend themselves against invasion. Tradition says that Treat remonstrated against the surrender of the charter, and that just as Andros had secured one of the copies of the instrument, the lights were suddenly extinguished, and Joseph Wardsworth escaped from the hall and secretly hid the duplicate copy in a hollow tree, which was ever after known as the "Charter Oak." The authenticity of this story is severely questioned, since neither by contemporary writers, nor in the records of the colony, which were closed in the handwriting of Secretary Allyn, is there any

1687.
Oct. 22.
Oct. 31.

allusion to such an occurrence. The next morning, Andros was conducted in state to the court-house, where his commission was read, and Governor Treat and Secretary Allyn were sworn into ^{Nov. 1.} office as his counselors. Royal courts were established, and the dominion of James rendered supreme over the land of steady habits.[1] Andros then proceeded to New London, and to Newport. The old seal of Rhode Island was broken and the new authority set up. Shortly after, a post-route between Boston and Stamford, on the border of New York, which had been originally suggested by Lovelace and encouraged by Dongan, was established, and John Perry, as the deputy of the provincial postmaster Randolph, was appointed to carry a monthly mail.

Dongan identified himself more and more, as time rolled on, with the state affairs of New York. He learned that the French in Canada were upon the eve of attacking the Iroquois warriors, and made a vigorous effort to prevent mischief in that quarter. He finally decided to spend the winter in Albany, the more readily to influence the Indians in favor of peace with their Canadian neighbors. His able and earnest letters to James, descriptive of the attitude of the belligerents, induced the British ministers to propose the Treaty of Neutrality with France, which was to be observed by the American subjects of both powers. Chancellor Jeffreys, with Barrillon, the French minister, arranged the details, and it was agreed, that notwithstanding any breach which might occur between the two sovereigns, absolute peace and neutrality should be maintained between their subjects in America ; and that neither colonial power should, in any instance, assist the "wild Indians" with whom the other might be at war.

Although no mention of the Iroquois was made in the treaty, Dongan assumed that they were British subjects, and governed himself accordingly. The governor of Canada accused him of duplicity in permitting New York traders to go among these savages, and complained that he had broken the Treaty of Neutrality by advising and protecting them ; and finally, he maintained with boldness, the right of the French to sovereignty over the Iroquois.

Before going to Albany, Dongan empowered Brockholls to sign warrants, papers, and licenses, and to attend to other public business which usually devolved upon the governor. He appointed Stephanus ^{Sept. 20.} Van Cortlandt mayor of the city in place of Nicholas Bayard, and Judge James Graham counselor in place of John Younge, who ^{Oct. 8.}

[1] *Brodhead,* II. 472, 473. *Palfrey,* III. 541, 542. *Col. Rec. Conn.,* III. 248, 249, 386 – 390. *Annals,* I. 298, 306. *Trumbull,* I. 371, 372. *Holmes,* I. 421. *Col. Doc.,* III. 429, 511. *Arnold,* I. 504, 506. *Force's Tracts,* IV. No. 9, pp. 47, 48. *Bancroft,* II. 430.

was not only very old, but lived at the east end of Long Island, one hundred and fifty miles from the city and fort. He reappointed Peter Schuyler mayor of Albany; and confirmed prior legislation by ordering in council that certain Spanish Indians, who had been brought from Campeachy, in Mexico, and sold as slaves, should be set free.

Oct. 11.

Albany was fortified as far as possible; for a party of Mohawks and

Oct. 24.

Mohicans, exasperated against the French in Canada, had besieged Fort Chambly, burned houses, killed several men, and taken a large number of prisoners; and a storm might burst upon the English settlements at any moment. Dongan called upon his council in New York to consider ways and means to defray the expenses which

Governor Dongan's House.

the French movements were causing the province; but they answered in effect that New York was not able to bear so great a burden alone, and that the neighboring colonies should be invited to contribute. The neighboring colonies were invited, but found it "inconvenient" to furnish any special aid. Andros offered a few men from New England, but no money. Pennsylvania withheld and Maryland refused help. Virginia was not disposed to contribute; but her governor, Lord Effingham, sent Dongan five hundred pounds. New Jersey, anxious to stand well with the king, voted a tax for the benefit of New York, which was never levied. Dongan pledged his personal credit, and even mortgaged his farm on Staten Island, to borrow of Robert Livingston two thousand or more pounds for the use of the government.

Judge Palmer went to London during the autumn, bearing dispatches from Dongan, which convinced James that the Treaty of Neutrality was not favorable to English interests. It had given to Louis a positive advantage. The Five Nations sent a touching appeal to the "Great Sachem beyond the Great Lake," for protection against their enemies; and this brought to a crisis the question of European sovereignty over the Iroquois. The king at once ordered Dongan to demand from the governor of Canada all British prisoners, and to build necessary forts, employ militia, and defend those Indians against the Canadians.

Nov. 16.

Louis attempted to argue his claim, and insisted that the Iroquois had acknowledged French sovereignty since 1665. He complained also of Dongan's arrogance, "novel pretensions," and " dishonorable treatment"; but, in the end, an agreement was signed, that, until the ^{Dec. 1.} first day of January, 1689, and afterward, no English or French commander in America should invade or commit any act of hostility against the territories of either king.

New France, with her undefined territory, had the strength of union, while New England, New York, New Jersey, and Pennsylvania were distinct and inharmonious. James, who took a lively personal interest in the details of his administration, resolved to unite his colonies under one vice-regal government. " I will make them a tower of iron," he said. He accordingly decreed that all his American possessions north of the *fortieth degree* of latitude, stretching across the continent from the Atlantic to the Pacific, should be consolidated into one great political whole, to be called New England.[1] Pennsylvania was to be the solitary exception, as he could not afford to offend so useful a favorite as William Penn by the withdrawal of his charter.

As New England was henceforth to be governed by a single viceroy, either Dongan or Andros must be displaced. Both had been twice commissioned by his Majesty. Andros had the larger experience, and excelled in executive talent. He was administering his trust to the entire satisfaction of James and his ministers, and it was thought best to retain him. On the other hand, Dongan was as good a soldier as Andros, with more independence of character. He had not hesitated to foil and embitter Penn, nor to anger Perth and Melfort, in the king's behalf. His policy and firmness had preserved Northern New York to the English, in spite of the French king and his shrewd maneuvers. He had given, indeed, more advice and shown more official zeal than was agreeable to the politicians at Whitehall. He was offered the command of a regiment, with the rank of major-general of artillery in the Brit-^{March 23.} ish army, but saw fit to decline the honor. Andros received his appointment, and hastened to assume almost imperial command over the province which he had left seven years before, and which, in the interval, had gained and lost a popular Assembly. Dongan retired to his farm.

Andros was at this time saddened by the recent death of his wife (whose funeral was attended in Boston, on the 10th of February, " with

[1] *Col. Doc.*, III. 363, 391, 392, 397, 415, 416, 425, 429, 492. *Hutch. Coll.*, 559. *Leaming and Spicer*, 604, 605. *S. Smith*, 204, 206, 211, 568. *Gordon*, 53. *Bancroft*, II. 46, 47. *Brodhead*, II. 500, 501. *Grahame*, II. 299. *Whitehead's E. J.*, 112, 113. *Index to N. J. Col. Doc.*, 13. *Chalmer's Annals*, I. 590, 622. *Proud*, I. 322, 341. *Dalrymple*, II. 89, 90. *Narcissus Luttrell*, I. 461.

great pomp "), and delayed his journey to New York for some weeks.
He arrived finally, with quite an army of attendants, on Satur-
Aug. 11. day, August 11, and was received by Colonel Nicholas Bayard's
regiment of foot and a troop of horse. His commission was read at
Fort James, and afterwards at the City Hall. The Seal of New York
was broken and defaced in his presence, by order of the king, and the
Great Seal of New England was used in its stead.

New York was deeply humiliated with the loss of her provincial individuality. Dutch blood waxed warm, and Dutch wrath could with difficulty be restrained. New York and Massachusetts had been rivals and
antagonists from the start, and differed politically and religiously on almost
all essential points. The former was grand, courteous, hospitable, and
magnanimous ; the latter, sectional, narrow, rigorous, and selfish. Both
erred in persecuting the Quakers ; but the annals of Dutch New York
were not disfigured by the acts of self-righteous despotism which marred
the record of her Eastern neighbor. There had never been so much as a
fugitive spark of love between the two provinces, and New York despair-
ingly pronounced her present " unhappy annexation " an "abhorred and
unmerited degradation."

The counselors of Dongan — Brockholls, Philipse, Bayard, and Van
Cortlandt — were sworn into the new administration, and found their
official importance increased rather than diminished, as they could now
vote on the affairs of Boston as well as New York. As it was necessary
for Andros to make Boston his headquarters, some of the New York records were transferred to Boston for his convenience, and Lieutenant-Governor Nicholson was left in charge of New York affairs.

The Protestants of New York appear to have rejoiced to some extent
in the change of governors. However noble and discreet Dongan's course
might have been, the fact that he worshiped, every Sabbath, with a few
Roman Catholics, in a small chamber in Fort James, had caused uneasiness. Dominie Selyns wrote to the Classis of Amsterdam, " Sir Edmund
Andros has now stepped into this government of New York and New
Jersey, and is of the Church of England ; and, understanding and speaking the Low Dutch and French, he attends mine and Mr. Daillé's preaching." It was hoped that papists would not henceforth come so freely to
settle in the province.

James was, at this moment, actually engaged in trying to change the
religion of his kingdom. The cardinals at Rome were dismayed at his
blunders. "We must excommunicate him, or he will destroy the little
of Catholicity which remains in England," they said. James had, some
time before, apologized to Louis for the discourtesy shown to France in

favoring the exiled Huguenots, and in directing Dongan to encourage
them to settle in New York, with the promise of letters of denization.
He had also admonished the
Huguenot ministers to speak
reverentially of their oppres-
sor in their public discourses.
When his advisers ventured to
remonstrate at these concessions, "One king should always
stand by another king," was
his apology; and then he went
on intrusting civil and military power to Roman Catholics.
He multiplied Catholic chap-
els; he favored the establish-

The First French Church in New York.

ment of convents in different parts of London; he encouraged the appearance of monks and friars, clad in the habits of their orders, in
the streets, and even in the Court itself; he attempted to proselyte
the Protestants about him; he held private interviews, which he called
"closetings," with various members of Parliament, and, when they
did not accede to his wishes, he removed them, unless they resigned of
themselves, and gave their places to Catholics; and he made direct attack
upon the Established Church by granting equal franchises to every religious sect.

A few days after he executed the commission to Andros, he issued his
second declaration of the liberty of conscience, in which he renewed
the abrogation of all test oaths and laws against dissenters. The ^April 27.^
act was unconstitutional, and every Catholic of good judgment, from the
Pope downward, was alarmed for the cause it was intended to advance.
Then he invaded Oxford, that its rich endowments might be shared by
the Catholics. The University plucked up courage and resisted; and, in
consequence, twenty-five of its officers were expelled and rendered incapable of holding any church preferment. As a last plunge, preparatory
to the tumble from his throne the blind king resolved to have his declaration of liberty of conscience read in every church in the realm.
Little did he dream of the spirit he was provoking. Archbishop ^May 4.^
Sancroft, of Canterbury, and six other bishops, in a petition refused to
obey the command. The next day was the Sunday fixed for the
reading, and only about two hundred out of ten thousand clergy- ^May 18.^
men complied with the requisition. Against all advice, the seven bishops
were committed to the Tower. They were taken to that dismal prison

by water; and, as they passed along, the crowds of people, who had assembled in startling numbers, fell upon their knees, and wept and prayed for them. When they entered the iron gates, the officers and soldiers on guard besought their blessing. During their confinement, the soldiers of the army every day drank, with loud shouts, to their release. When they were arraigned before the Court of King's Bench, they were surrounded by a throng of noblemen and gentlemen and a multitude of sympathizing people. The jury brought in a verdict of "NOT GUILTY," and such a shout went up as had never before been heard in Westminster Hall, and was passed on from street to street, away to Temple Bar, and to the Tower, and westward, till it reached the camp at Hounslow, where fifteen thousand soldiers took it up, and echoed it again and again. The king heard the mighty roar, and asked in alarm what it meant ? "It is nothing but the acquittal of the Bishops," answered one of his Lords. "Call you that nothing?" exclaimed his Majesty. "It is so much the worse for them."

Between the petition of the Bishops and the trial, the queen gave birth to a son. The prospect of a Catholic successor, which was a great consolation to James, since both of his daughters were Protestants, produced for him an unlooked-for and extraordinary result. Several of the leading noblemen of the realm, among whom was the Earl of Shrewsbury, the Earl of Danby, the Earl of Devonshire, Lord Lumley, the Bishop of London, Admiral Russel and Colonel Sidney, on the evening after the acquittal of the Bishops, sent a secret invitation to the Prince of Orange to come over to England.

June 10.

June 30.

Admiral Russel had visited the Hague in May, while it was still uncertain whether or not the declaration would be read in the churches, and had held a long interview with Prince William, advising him to appear in England at the head of a strong body of troops and call the people to arms. William was inclined to suspect the courage of those who talked about sacrificing their lives and fortunes in such an enterprise, and finally declined giving the subject consideration until distinct invitations and pledges of support should come to him from responsible sources. He ordered prayers to be said under his own roof for his little brother-in-law, and sent a formal message of congratulation to London. Presently the rumor reached him that not more than one person in ten believed[1] the child to have really been born of the queen. Mary partook of the prevailing suspicion, and the prayers for the Prince of Wales ceased in her private chapel. If she had ever loved her father, this supposed attempt

---

[1] *Clarendon's Diary,* 1688. *Correspondence between Anne and Mary in Dalrymple. Clarke's Life of James II. Burnet. Macaulay's Hist. of Eng. Ronquillo.*

to deprive her of her rights must have alienated her affections. It was many years since she had seen him. He had done nothing since her marriage to call forth tenderness on her part. On the contrary he had tried to disturb her domestic happiness, and had introduced spies, eaves-droppers, and tale-bearers under her roof.

The direct influence exerted by Prince William Henry upon the fortunes of New York seems to demand a brief glance at his person and character. He was less than forty years of age, with a face of fifty, and a wasted, attenuated body, that seemed scarcely able to sustain the burden of existence. His faculties ripened at a time of life, when, in ordinary men, they have scarcely begun to blossom. While but a lad, he astonished the fathers of the Dutch Commonwealth by his gravity and self-control. At twenty-three, he was famous all over Europe as a soldier and a politician. He had been weak and sickly from his birth; and his feeble frame was constantly shaken by

Portrait of William III.

a hoarse asthmatic cough. He never slept unless his head was propped by several pillows, and he could scarcely draw his breath in any but the purest air. He was the victim of severe nervous headaches, and exertion quickly fatigued him. He was neither a happy nor a good-humored man. His pale, thin face was deeply furrowed, and a cloud seemed ever to rest upon his thoughtful brow. His eyes were bright, keen, and restless; his nose curved like the beak of an eagle; and his compressed lips gave to his whole aspect an air of pensive severity.

21

But he was endowed with the qualities of a great ruler. He had a hard and invincible will, which forced him at times into the performance of the most herculean labors. He could praise and reprimand, reward and punish, with the stern tranquillity of an Indian chieftain. When enraged, the outbreak of his passion was something terrible to witness, and it was scarcely safe, at such times, to approach him. His affection was as impetuous as his wrath; although, to the world in general, he appeared to be one of the coldest and most unfeeling of men. When death separated him from the object of his love, the few who witnessed his agonies trembled for his reason and his life.

He was not, in a fashionable or a literary sense, accomplished; and, in social intercourse, he was either ignorant or negligent of the little graces which increase the value of a favor and take away the sting of a refusal. He understood Latin, Italian, and Spanish, and spoke and wrote French, English, and German, fluently, although inelegantly. He cared little for science, but was intensely interested in all questions of international usage, of finance, and of war. He was a born statesman. His theology had been molded by the faith of his ancestors, the discussions in the synod of Dort, and the austere and inflexible logic of the Genevese school. The tenet of predestination was the keystone of his religion, but he openly avowed his fixed aversion to intolerance and persecution.

His marriage had been purely a political consideration. He devoted himself to public business, field sports, and some of the beautiful ladies of Mary's Court, and proved himself one of the most negligent of husbands. For nine years, he and his young wife lived estranged, but Mary's gentleness gradually won upon his esteem. There was one cause by which they were kept asunder, of which Mary had not the slightest suspicion. A time might come when she would be Queen of England, while her husband, with the same royal blood in his veins, ambitious, versed in diplomacy, understanding the state of every court in Europe, and bent on enterprises of magnitude, could only hold power from her bounty and during her pleasure. It was but natural that a man so fond of authority and so conscious of strength should have been stung with jealousy, in view of his humiliating position. Bishop Burnet, Mary's spiritual director and confidential adviser, blurted the truth to her, one morning, and she thus learned, for the first time, that, when she became Queen of England, William would not share her throne. She tearfully sought the remedy. Burnet explained to her, that, when she received the crown, she might, if she desired, easily induce Parliament to give the regal title to her husband, and even transfer to him by legislative act the administration of the government. Mary was delighted with this opportunity of showing her magnanimity and her attachment, and sent Burnet at once in quest of William, and sweetly assured the latter with her own lips that he should always bear rule, only asking him in return to observe the precept which enjoins husbands to love their wives. Her generosity melted the ice of so many years' formation, and the warmest affection took the place of painful indifference. Bishop Burnet thereby rendered to his country a service of the gravest moment, for it was not long before the public safety depended upon the mutual confidence and perfect concord of William and Mary.

The difficulties in the way of their accession to the throne of England were very many, and appeared insurmountable. But they were all comprehended in the grasp of one capacious mind which planned their solution with consummate skill. Mary sympathized in her husband's every movement, and regarded the contemplated undertaking as just and holy. William's objects seemed incompatible with each other, — to lead enthusiastic Protestants on a crusade against Popery with the good wishes of almost every Popish government, and even of the Pope himself. But whether he rightly estimated the meaning and the direction of the great movements of the time, and was conscious that all through Europe there was the stirring of a new intellectual power and an irresistible tendency towards democratic conditions of society, or was prompted purely by a desire to resist the power of France and the progress of tyranny and persecution, and to rescue Protestantism and constitutional liberty in England, he certainly accomplished all, and more than all he contemplated. The history of ancient and modern times records no other such triumph in statesmanship.

His future course once decided upon, William urged his preparations with indefatigable activity. A military and naval expedition was quietly and skillfully organized in the Netherlands. For a time, neither James nor Louis was aware of its object. Rumors, however, reached the ears of the former which caused him great anxiety. At last, a dispatch told the whole story : the blood left the cheeks of the now thoroughly awakened king, and he remained for some time speechless. The first easterly wind would bring a hostile army to the shores of England. All Europe, one power only excepted, was impatiently waiting for his downfall. He was overcome by absolute fear. He tried to conciliate the Tories, forgetting that concessions had always been the ruin of kings. But the Tories stood aloof.

All at once, William's expedition landed at Torbay. It produced less excitement than had been anticipated. A full week elapsed before any man of note joined the invaders. If James had acted **Nov. 5** with ordinary efficiency, even then his cause might not have been lost. William, who had hazarded everything, was excessively mortified at the coolness of his reception. He became so indignant, that he threatened to return to Holland. Several parties of consequence were, however, on their way to join his standard. One example stimulated another. His forces swelled rapidly. John, Lord Lovelace, of Hurley, the brother of the former governor of New York, with his command, and Edward, Lord Cornbury, who was in command of three regiments of cavalry, went quietly to William's quarters, and their troops were pressed into the new service through the offer of a bounty equal to a month's pay. The tidings of Cornbury's defection reached the king just as he was sitting down to dinner. He turned quickly away, swallowed a crust of bread and a glass of wine, and retired to his closet. Meanwhile, several gentlemen in whom he had implicit confidence were rejoicing over the occurrence in the next room, and laughing heartily. When the queen heard the news she broke out in screams of agonizing sorrow.

The quarters of William at Exeter soon presented the appearance of a court. More than sixty noblemen and gentlemen were there assembled, and the display of rich liveries, and of coaches each drawn by six horses, gave to the Cathedral Close something of the splendor of Whitehall. Bishop Burnet drew up a paper, which was approved and eagerly signed by the English adherents, by which they promised to stand by William until the liberties and the religion of the nation should be effectually secured.

James bustled, and prepared to maintain his honor by force of arms. All at once, Churchill went over to the Protestants. Confusion reigned in the royal camp. News came that Kirke had followed Churchill. No one knew whom to trust or whom to obey. James was in despair. At the supper-table, in Andover, he had the company of his son-in-law, Prince George, and the Duke of Ormond. Both were intending to join Churchill at the earliest possible moment, and were silent and taciturn. Prince George was always stupid. It was his habit, when he heard a piece of news, to exclaim in French, " *Est-il possible ?* " So, when he was told that Churchill was missing, his first and only response was, " *Est-il possible ?* " And at every fresh report of ill-tidings, he uttered in the same tone, " *Est-il possible ?* " They finished their supper, and the king retired to rest. Prince George and the Duke of Ormond left the table, mounted their horses, and rode to the Protestant camp. When James was informed of this new defection, on the following morning, " What !" he exclaimed, " is *est-il possible* gone too ? After all, a good trooper would have been a greater loss."

On the morning of the 26th, the apartments of the Princess Anne, at Whitehall, were found empty. She had abandoned her father, to follow her husband and William. This affliction forced a cry ^{Nov. 26.} of agony from the king's lips. "God help me," he said, "my own children have forsaken me!"

He instituted negotiations with William, in order to gain time to send the queen and the Prince of Wales into France. He then made immediate preparations to abdicate the throne. At three o'clock in the morning of the 11th of December, he rose from his bed, ordered the lord of his bedchamber not to open the door until the usual hour, and, passing down the back stairway, set out in the disguise of a servant, accompanied by Sir Edward Hales, on a fishing-boat to France. He threw the Great Seal into the Thames, where it was found by a fisherman some months afterward. He was arrested by some sailors, who were watching for priests and other delinquents, and taken to Feversham. Having told his captors who he was, a great crowd came together to see the proud king in such mean hands. It was a trifling incident, and yet it proved to be the origin of the Jacobites. Until now, the king had scarcely had a party; but from this moment one budded into existence which was long active for his interests.

William regretted most keenly that James failed in his attempt to escape. It was a tender point, how to dispose of his person. With the desertion of the sovereign, the nation was free, and at liberty to secure itself. William would not consent to make the father of his wife a prisoner. It was necessary to send him out of London, and a guard was ordered to attend him, not to hamper his movements, but for his protection and defense. It had the appearance of forcible expulsion and elicited sympathy in his behalf in various quarters, creating much mischief for those who came after him. He left finally on the last day of the year and reached France in safety.

Even before he arrived in London, William ordered that the papists should be secured from all violence. He was warmly welcomed by the different bodies ; such as, first the bishops, then the clergy, the city officials, and others, in the order of their importance. When the lawyers came, William took notice of one who was nearly ninety years of age, and said to him, "You must have outlived all the men of the law of your time." "Yes," he replied, "and I should have outlived the law itself, if your Highness had not come over."

The government once assumed, William published a proclamation, continuing in office all magistrates, and another, ordering the collection of the revenue. He remodeled the army, reappointing many of the officers whom James had removed. The Common Council of London raised in forty-eight hours the sum of two hundred thousand pounds, to extricate him from his financial difficulties. The disturbances which had been occasioned by the suspension of all regular government were soon at an end, and a sense of security was implanted throughout the kingdom.

1689. The Catholics were treated with the utmost kindness, and the Spanish minister reported to the Pope, that no one of that faith need feel any scruple of conscience on account of the late Revolution in England.

William called a Convention Parliament, which declared that the English throne was vacant by the abdication of the king. It then

Jan. 22. cordially offered the crown to William and Mary, by whom it was accepted. The very night before this was to be done, Mary arrived in

Feb. 12. safety from Holland. On the 13th of February the whole affair

Feb. 13. was consummated and William and Mary were proclaimed king and queen of England.

Louis took the part of James. He spoke of the Revolution as a frightful domestic tragedy. The politics of a long and glorious line of kings had been confounded in a day. William's conquest was admired even in France, but he was personally abhorred. The conduct of the unnatural daughters of James was execrated; the queen and her infant son were objects of pity and romantic interest. Louis set an example of royal munificence in providing for the hapless king and his family, and lavished upon them every courtly attention.

Second Seal of the City of New York.
(For description see page 318.)

CHAPTER XIX.

1689.

THE REVOLUTION.

TWO days after the coronation, a new privy council was chosen. It was composed chiefly of Whigs; but the names of a few **1689.** eminent Tories appeared on the list. It was thereby understood **Feb. 16.** that William did not intend to proscribe any class of men who were willing to support his throne. Even the new Committee for Foreign Plantations were noblemen from both political parties. This committee met at once, and prepared drafts of Proclamations, to send to the American colonies. They also wrote letters to the colonial governors, **Feb. 18.** signifying the pleasure of William that all men in office under the late king should be so continued until further notice.

The irregular convention which had conferred the monarchy of England upon the new sovereigns was transformed into a Parliament, and went on making laws, as if it had unimpeachable authority. **Feb. 20.** It did not extend the Test Act to the colonies, but it required every person holding office to take an oath of allegiance to William and Mary; and it simply abjured the Pope's authority, ecclesiastical and spiritual, throughout the realm of England. While not a single new right was

22

given to the people, order was preserved. The nation supported the throne, and thus the revolution — of all revolutions in history the least violent — proved a peace revolution. The executive power and the legislative power no longer impeded each other in the passage of such laws as were found necessary for the public weal.

The agents of Massachusetts in England, Sir William Phipps and Rev. Dr. Increase Mather, watched events with keen interest. Sir William was the son of a Pemaquid farmer and one of a family of twenty-six children. In his boyhood he had tended sheep, and at the age of eighteen had learned the trade of a ship-carpenter. He grew up illiterate and ill-mannered, and having adopted a seafaring life, chanced, through a series of fortuitous circumstances, to come under the notice of King James, who was pleased with his bustling energy and made him commander of one of his frigates. Soon afterward, in consideration of some valiant service, James knighted him, and presently offered him the government of Massachusetts; but, as the offer was made just prior to the abdication, no further action was ever taken in the matter.

Rev. Dr. Increase Mather, the son of Rev. Richard Mather, was born in Massachusetts in 1639. After graduating at Harvard College in 1656, he went to Europe, and in 1658 was made Master of Arts in the Dublin University. He married the daughter of the celebrated Rev. John Cotton, of Boston, and had ten children.[1] He was pastor of the North Church in Boston from 1664 to 1723, a period of fifty-nine years, and was the author of ninety-two publications, besides many short fugitive articles. He was a gentleman, as well as one of the profoundest scholars of his time, — a Puritan, whose whole anxiety was for the future of the New England colonies.

Sir Henry Ashurst was a steadfast friend of Massachusetts and influential in the House of Commons. He was a personal friend of Dr.
March 16. Mather, and together with the latter, and Sir William Phipps, was chiefly instrumental in pushing through the House a bill to restore the corporations both at home and abroad to their original condition in 1660. When this act was shown to William, he was seriously annoyed. Such a law could not but imperil his prerogative. It was consequently delayed in the House of Lords until the Convention Parliament was dissolved.

Meanwhile, Dr. Mather had been for some time in correspondence with Abraham Kick, an eminent Hollander. The latter had contrived to surprise Mary, before she left the Hague, into a promise that she would favor New England. Upon the strength of her unguarded words, Dr.

---

[1] The distinguished Rev. Cotton Mather was the son of Dr. Increase Mather, and was the author of three hundred and eighty-two distinct publications.

Mather and Sir William appeared before the king with a petition that Governor Andros should be removed, and that Massachusetts, Plymouth, Rhode Island, and Connecticut should be restored to their former privileges and the rule of their former governors.

William was confounded. He had no intention of disuniting his royal dominion of New England. But he was too cautious a statesman to speak his whole mind in such a crisis. He listened graciously, and, knowing that Sir William and Sir Edmund were sworn foes, signified in general terms his willingness to remove the latter. To Dr. Mather he intimated the possibility of a new charter and a colonial assembly. Yet, notwithstanding this apparent compliance with their requests, he was so coldly non-committal that neither of the gentlemen was satisfied, and they learned shortly after, to their dismay, that he was being urged by his Whig advisers to carry into vigorous execution some of the most rigid colonial measures of his predecessor, in order to bring those remote dominions into a nearer dependence upon the crown.

There were no deep-sea cables in those days and news crossed the Atlantic tardily and uncertainly. It was in January that the first intimation of the hostile movements of the Prince of Orange reached the American shores. Even then, the report was not well authenticated. A Virginia coasting-vessel brought it to New York. Captain Greveraet called upon Lieutenant-Governor Nicholson, and repeated the story, which had come verbally and at second hand to him, and which sounded altogether incredible. "Nonsense!" exclaimed Nicholson, laughing contemptuously, "if the report is true the very 'prentice boys of London will drive him out again. He will have no better success than Monmouth."

In the latter part of February, Jacob Leisler, while in Maryland on business, heard a rumor to the same effect, and, on his return to New York, put it into general circulation. The first day of March, Nicholson received, through a Quaker traveler, a letter from Governor Blackwell of Pennsylvania, saying that he had examined one Zagharia Whitepaine, a sailor recently arrived, who declared upon oath that the Prince of Orange had invaded England. Seventeen other letters to different persons in New York were brought from Pennsylvania by the same traveler. These were placed for distribution in the hands of Nicholson and his council, who formally resolved to open them, "for the prevention of tumult and the divulging of such strange news." The substance of each letter was a confirmation of what had been already learned. They immediately sent two expresses, one by water and the other by land, to Governor Andros, who was in Maine bravely defending the frontier against the savages. He returned promptly to Boston, accompanied by ^{March 16.} three members of his council, Graham West, and Palmer.

Nothing further was learned either definitely or otherwise, until the 4th of April, when there entered Boston harbor a ship from Nevis April 4. in the West Indies, and John Winslow, one of her passengers, had copies of the Prince's declaration of the previous October. He also had in his possession some printed accounts of William's entrance into England. He exhibited the papers to several persons, but did not take them to the governor. Finally Andros sent for him and questioned him closely; but he refused to give any information or to produce the documents, and, in consequence of his contumacy, was committed to prison.

Dr. Mather had written private letters, which reached Boston by the same vessel; but they were dated a long time prior to the coronation of William and Mary. They were addressed to members of his own family. It was whispered, however, that in them he had expressed his belief that a charter with large powers for Massachusetts would immediately follow William's accession to the English throne. The Puritan prayer was henceforth, "success to the Dutch prince over the popish king."

It was not many days before Andros became convinced that something unusual was going on in and around Boston. He was a thoroughly loyal officer, and did not suspect the extent of the slanderous misrepresentations of his own conduct, which were inflaming the public mind. He wrote to Brockholls, whom he had left in command at Pemaquid, that he had good reason to believe that some of the Indians had been traitorously supplied with ammunition by Boston merchants, and ordered him to keep a strict guard to prevent surprise. He would have been surprised, himself, had he known what all the "buzzing and commotion" signified The people said he was about to oppose the lawful commands of the new sovereigns; that he was in league with the French; that he had hired the New York Mohawks to destroy Boston; that he had poisoned the soldiers in Maine; with a great many other equally absurd and inconsistent things, which found credence in a community which could see no escape from the evils of·Popery save in the restoration of the Puritan oligarchy.

On the evening of April 17, Andros entertained the gentlemen April 17. of his council at dinner. He retired at his usual hour and his sleep was undisturbed until late the next morning, when, while at breakfast, he was informed that people were coming into town in great April 18. numbers from the rural districts. The street soon had the appearance of an annual fair-day, only there were fewer women to be seen. Finally, the militia companies marched rapidly through one of the principal thoroughfares.

While Andros was investigating the nature of the disturbance, the prominent citizens were assembling in the Town House. Rev. Cotton

Mather read to them a " Declaration " which he had prepared, giving reasons for revolting against the present government. A summons was quickly signed for the arrest of the governor and his council. Andros was taken wholly unawares, and, of course, resistance was out of the question. He was escorted to prison, together with Graham, West, Palmer, and the other officers of the crown. A " Council of Safety " was chosen, to manage public affairs, whose purpose was said to be, " to preserve the government until directions should arrive from England." The old magistrates were reinstated in office, and quiet and good order soon prevailed throughout Boston.[1]

This proceeding had a singular tinge of secession; it was, as viewed from our present stand-point, uncalled for, and unjustifiable. But the stern New-Englander was unwilling to await the result of the political agitation in the mother country, and feared that the officers under James would attempt to re-establish their fallen monarch. The danger was imaginary to a great extent. And the dread of absolute power in a spiritual order blinded the eyes of the wise men of Massachusetts to the fact that the vigorous but narrow creed of Puritanism was only another form of religious despotism.

The idea of insurrection traveled with rapidity. Plymouth, sheltered under the wings of her more sanctified neighbor, Boston, _{April 22.} proceeded to place her former governor, Hinckley, in the chair of state, and adopted her old style of administration. Rhode Island did likewise. That is, she reinstated her old magistrates. It was accomplished _{May 1} quietly on the first day of May. Connecticut was reconstructed, _{May 9.} nine days later, on the skeleton of the copy of the famous charter, which was exhumed from the hollow oak at Hartford. Thus, without the knowledge and against the purpose of William, his dominion of New England was disunited forever.

Imperial New York rejoiced over the disseverment of the bond, freeing her from political connection with New England. Dutch New York eschewed all manner of religious fanaticism. The English families of New York were attached to the Church of England and had no symyathy with the meddling spirit of Puritanism. New York was intolerant of both Popery and Puritanism, and ready to plunge headlong into intense devotion to a Dutch prince who was so suddenly transformed into an English king.

New York was intrenched in prejudice, but prejudice as unlike that

---

[1] *Mass. Hist. Soc. Coll. Conn. Hist. Soc. Coll. Palmer's Impartial Account. Hutch. Mass. Chalmers' Annals. Barry. Arnold. Brodhead. Palfrey. Bancroft. Rhode Island Records. Force Tracts. Grahame. Hildreth. New York Col. Doc.*

which moved the people of Boston into rebellion as the Temperance Reform from Mahometanism, — the total abstinence from wine being the only like article in the two creeds. Popery was the horrible ogre. Protestants were everywhere united in their abhorrence and fear of it. There had been no complaint or even suggestion of misrule as far as Lieutenant-Governor Nicholson was concerned. He was a straightforward English official, obeying orders to the letter. He was a devout and consistent Episcopalian, never omitting his public Sunday devotions. All at once, however, he was suspected of intrigue and double dealing. Why might not he be a tool of Catholic James and secretly at work in the latter's interests? Some one told how he knelt to say mass in the king's tent on Hounslow Heath, three years before! It was retold again and again, and men's faces paled while they listened. Nobody stopped to consider that any courtly gentleman would have done the same thing if accidentally present on such an occasion.

The resident members of the Governor's council were Frederick Philipse, Stephanus Van Cortlandt, and Nicholas Bayard. They were all members of the Dutch Reformed Church, and the last two were deacons in good and regular standing. They were men of wealth and of aristocratic tastes. Philipse was sixty-three years of age, dignified, elegant, and conservative. He could balance himself between two fires with more tact and less danger than any other man in our history. Van Cortlandt was forty-six years of age, and, besides holding a commission from the crown as counselor to the governor, was the mayor of the city. He had been a popular public man for more than twenty years, but at this critical moment a whisper was started that he was a secret Catholic, and it seemed to be verified from the fact that he took part a few months before in the celebration of the birth of the Prince of Wales, and became so hilarious that he threw his periwig with its long flowing ringlets into the air. Bayard was the younger of the three and occupied a distinguished position as counselor to the governor and commander-in-chief of the New York militia. He was fond of display and conspicuously imperious. He was bright, genial, witty, quick-tempered and vindictive. He had many warm personal friends among his equals socially and politically, but he was feared and disliked by his inferiors.

Nicholson and his council met on the 2d of March, and re-
March 2. solved that Plowman, the king's collector (who was a Catholic), should bring the public money, which he had hitherto kept at his lodgings in a private house some distance away, to the port for safe-keeping. A strong chest was provided, and locked and sealed by the collector himself, until orders should arrive from England. This precautionary movement

was the immediate occasion of a wide-spread terror, which was confined, however, to the lower and more illiterate classes.

When news came of the imprisonment of Andros, Nicholson requested the common council of the city to meet in session with ^{April 26.} his special council in order to advise more intelligently as to the proper course to pursue in order to keep the country quiet. They met the next day in the City Hall. The common council consisted of John ^{April 27.} Lawrence, Francis Rombouts, William Merritt, Thomas Crundall, Paulus Richards,[1] Johannes Kip, Balthazar Bayard, Anthony De Milt, Teunis De Kay, and Peter De Lanoy. It was then resolved to call in the chief military officers in the afternoon. There was perfect harmony in the meeting ; and in view of the jealousies and fears of the inhabitants occasioned by a rumor that war had broken out between the English and French, it was unanimously agreed that the city must be fortified. Aldermen Crundall, Kip, De Lanoy, and Balthazar Bayard, together with Captains Abraham De Peyster and Jacob Leisler, were appointed a committee to survey the city, and determine upon the points most exposed. Money was scarce and it was decided to apply the revenues from the first of May, towards paying for the new defenses.

Nicholson and the three gentlemen of his council sent for the justices of the peace and the military officers of the various counties in the province and enjoined upon them strict care and watchfulness. They also wrote letters to Winthrop, Treat, Allyn, Younge, Pinchon, Clarke, Newbury, and Smith, of New England, of which the following is a copy, it being duplicated and sent to each.[2]

---

[1] Paulus Richards was the son of a French nobleman. The crest of his coat-of-arms was a lion's head in silver ; the motto, " I bend but break not." He was driven into Holland through religious persecution in 1650. Ten years afterward he came and settled in New Amsterdam, and in 1664, married Gelatié, daughter of the celebrated Anetje Jans. He became one of the leading men in the colony and city. He was an alderman from 1686 to 1697. His house stood upon the corner of Whitehall Street and Broadway. His son, Stephen Richards, born in 1670, married Maria, daughter of Johannes Van Brugh, and grand-daughter of Anetje Jans. They had nine children. One daughter, Elizabeth, married Nicholas Van Taerling. Paul Richards, the eldest son, organized a large mercantile firm, which included his five brothers, and transacted business on an extensive scale with Europe and the East and West Indies. They had business houses in New Haven, Philadelphia, Norfolk, and in the Island of Bermuda. He was a prominent man, an intimate personal friend of Lieutenant-Governor De Lancey, several years a member of the Assembly, and at one time, in 1734, appointed counselor to the governor in place of Rip Van Dam. In 1753, he was sent with Sir William Johnson to represent the city and county of New York in a conference between Governor Clinton and the Mohawk Indians. He was one of the gentlemen to whom the charter of Columbia College was granted, and made a bequest of four hundred pounds sterling to that institution. His brother, John Richards, married Elizabeth Van Rensselaer, and their son Stephen married Margaret Livingston.

[2] *New York Hist. Soc. Coll.*, 1868, p. 248.

Sʀ.

Having received the surprising news that the Inhabitants of Boston have sett up a Gouvernment for themselves and disabled his Excellency the Capt. Generall and Gouvernor in Chieff from acting in the gouvernment These are therefore to desire you That you would come with all expedition to advise and consult with us what proper is to be done for the safety and welfare off the Gouvernment this Citty and part of the gouvernment being resolved to continue in their station till further order. See not doubting off yʳ Complyance Remaine

Yʳ friends & humble Servants

Fʀ. Nɪᴄʜᴏʟꜱᴏɴ
Fʀᴇᴅ. Pʜɪʟɪᴘꜱᴇ
Sᴛᴇᴘ. Vᴀɴ Cᴏʀᴛʟᴀɴᴅᴛ,
Nɪᴄʜ. Bᴀʏᴀʀᴅ.

Nᴇᴡ Yᴏʀᴄᴋᴇ, 1689 Aprill the 27th.

The city militia consisted of six free companies called train-bands, embraced in a colonel's command. As many of the regular soldiers were in Maine it was the only defense of New York, with the exception of a sergeant's guard of royal troops which garrisoned the fort. Nicholson proposed that one of these train-bands should mount guard every night, supposing it would give the people a greater sense of security. Bayard was their colonel; and the six captains were Abraham De Peyster, Johannes De Bruyn,[1] Gabriel Minvielle, Charles Lodwyck, Nicholas Stuyvesant, and Jacob Leisler. De Peyster was a rich and aristocratic merchant of fine intelligence and excellent parts, the son of Johannes De Peyster. He was of French descent, as was also De Bruyn and Minvielle. The latter had been a resident of New York for about twenty years. His wife was the daughter of John Lawrence; and he was at one time mayor of the city. Lodwyck was an English merchant and an old-time Whig of the deepest dye. He was a man of irreproachable character, and of no mean ability. Five years afterward he was elected mayor of the city. Stuyvesant was the son of the old governor, and about forty years of age.

---

[1] Johannes De Bruyn was the first of the name in this country. He was of French descent, and the ancestor of the New York family of Brown. Indeed his name is sometimes spelled both ways, De Bruyn, and Brown, in the same manuscript document. He was an educated young man with considerable property. He commanded all the colonial forces in the war with the Indians just after the Colonial Revolution. His son, W. Brown, married Elizabeth Taerling, the granddaughter of Stephen Richards, and held many important positions. Their son Stephen Richards Brown, born 1765, had a daughter Maria who married Oliver Du Bois. The children of the latter were as follows : Stephen ; Richard ; Adeline ; Catharine. Adeline married Samuel Russel, and her daughter Almira married Major-General Hancock. Catharine married William Bennett, and her children were Helen, Emma, and Louisa. Helen married General S. S. Carroll, of Carrollton, and Emma married Leopold Bouvia. The children of the latter are Laura, Maurice, and Bertha.

He was in possession of the family estate and lived on the farm near Thirteenth Street. He had lost his first wife, Maria Beekman, and had recently married Elizabeth Slechtenhorst.

Jacob Leisler was the hero of the hour. He was a German, and not a Dutchman as has generally been supposed. He was born at Frankfort-on-the-Maine. Of his origin and early life very little is known. He had been a resident of New York about thirty years. He married, in 1663, Elsie (Tymens), step-daughter of Govert Loockermans, and widow of the wealthy Peter Cornelisen Vanderveen.[1] He was thus connected by marriage with Van Cortlandt and Philipse, and he was the brother-in-law of Balthazar Bayard. He was a deacon in the Reformed Dutch Church and a thriving man of business. He had never held any public office of importance, but his standing was respectable, such that in 1674 he was chosen one of the commissioners (Martin Cregier and Francis Rombouts being his associates) to provide means for the defense of the city, and he was assessed as "one of the most affluent inhabitants."[2]

He was a man of energetic will and great force of character, but he had little education and comparatively speaking no manners. He hated the crown, and the Church of England; he was a zealous champion of Belgian republicanism, and a rancorous though consistent party man. He was loud and coarse in conversation, and when angry would swear like a porter. He said bitter things which he readily forgot when pacified, but which others remembered to his sorrow and dishonor. His native quickness and sagacity would have rendered him eminent as a leader, but prosperity made him self-sufficient and boastful; and his want of knowledge of the world muddled his understanding. His integrity was unquestionable, his loyalty unimpeachable, and he had a strong but distorted sense of duty and honor. In short, he possessed the elements of executive power without the balancing characteristics. He

Leisler's Autograph.

---

[1] *Marriage Register of the Collegiate R. D. Church* in New York. Mr. and Mrs. Leisler had seven children : Susanna, b. February 10, 1664 ; Catharine, b. November 8, 1665 ; Jacob, b. November 13, 1667 ; Mary, b. December 12, 1669; Johannes, b. December 20, 1671 ; Hester, b. October 8, 1673 ; and Francina, b. December 16, 1676. *Register of Baptisms in Collegiate R. D. Church.*

[2] *Minutes of the Council of the Administration of Commanders Evertsen and Bincks*, Feb. 1, 1674. *Assessment Lists*, Feb. 19, 1674.

was of medium height, robust frame, full round figure, austere visage, dressed carelessly, made long prayers, and was rigid in the performance of every Christian duty. He had some legal knowledge picked up in practice of no very high kind, and he had used it in one or two lawsuits to the great pecuniary disadvantage of Van Cortlandt and Bayard, an offense which had terminated all social intercourse between the families.

He was an importer of liquors, and on the 29th one of his vessels entered the harbor with a cargo of wine on board. He refused **April 29.** to pay the duties, which amounted to one hundred dollars, on the ground that Collector Plowman being a Catholic was not qualified to receive the customs under the new power. The case was discussed at the meeting of the counselors, aldermen, and military officers, and the majority were of the opinion that the present official structure was sound until contrary orders came from the new sovereigns. Leisler became very much exasperated, and swore he would not pay a penny to Plowman ; he used language more forcible than elegant, and finally turned on his heel and left the council-chamber before the matter was adjusted.

As was feared, others declined to pay duties, shielding themselves **April 30.** under the excuse which Leisler had advanced. In apprehension of an attack from some foreign foe, watchmen were stationed at Coney Island to give an alarm if more than three vessels should come together within Sandy Hook. Nicholson and his council wrote to the Plantation Committee over the water, expressing their regret at the want of definite instructions, and picturing the painful embarrassment under which they groaned.

The greatest activity prevailed about the new fortifications. The council met daily. The Indians were carefully watched, and an order given that no rum should be sold them. But the most serious **May 11.** mischief was feared from the French. All at once an ominous cloud that had been hanging along the eastern end of Long Island took shape. The counties of Suffolk and Queens displaced their civil and military officers and chose others. Presently the Long Island militia began to clamor for their pay. Some ill-affected and restless men among them came to the city on foot in squads, and hanging round the fort discoursed largely upon individual freedom, and said Nicholson was preparing to betray New York into the hands of some foreign power. They picked up whatever gossip was afloat and told it, with additions, at every farm-house on their way home.

Every day developed some new source of alarm. The officers felt themselves surrounded by stealthy foes. And the common people were growing into the belief that their superiors were full of fiendish plans and purposes. Rumors when once started swelled into marvelous proportions as they passed from mouth to mouth. Some said that Staten Island was full of roaming papists. Others declared that Nicholson had been seen to cross the bay in a small boat to hold "cabals" with them; and that King James was soon to land on the Jersey beach with an army of French. A few of the Long Island militia actually took up arms and came within fourteen miles of the city, ostensibly to be near at hand in case of an attack, but as was supposed by the men in power, to watch their opportunity for seizing the fort and plundering the town.

It was clear that there were vague ideas being nurtured about a dawning millennium when the popular element should shoot miraculously to the top round of the governing ladder, and aristocracy come to earth and henceforth wield the plow and the hammer. The stupidity on that subject which prevailed among the humbler classes was by no means remarkable. The era of general intelligence, of printing-presses, newspapers, books, and schools, had not yet arrived to bless America. The condition of laborers was in no wise above the serfs in foreign countries. They were easily swayed and at the mercy of ignorant middle-men who were scarcely wiser than themselves. And no influence was quite as potent as what stirred their superstitious fears.

Many believed that the leading Dutch citizens were going over to popery. It was suddenly reported that Ex-Governor Dongan ^{May 15.} was the instigator of an infernal plot to destroy New York. It was true that he was fitting out an armed brigantine, but for quite a different object. On the evening of the 21st of May, some persons appeared before Colonel Bayard with a petition (unsigned) asking that the Roman Catholics in the city be disarmed. Their conduct indicated serious alarm. The next morning the subject and the petition were earnestly discussed in council. There were ridiculously few Catholics in either city or province. Among the soldiers there were not over twenty of ^{May 22.} that faith, "and they," said Colonel Bayard, "are old cripples." But it seemed best to gratify the people as far as possible, hence Mayor Van Cortlandt sent for the authors of the petition to come and sign their names. They refused, and at the same time demanded an answer in writing, or to have their petition returned. The mayor went to them and assured them that their wishes should be respected, but they received him ungraciously. Captains Leisler and Lodwyck were sent finally to return the petition and answer its writers verbally.

Major Baxter, one of the counselors from Albany, and commander of the fort in that place, arrived in New York on the 27th, ^{May 27} and requested of Nicholson and his council permission to withdraw from

22

the province, on account of the jealousies which had arisen concerning his religion. His judgment was approved, and he was permitted to retire. An ensign in New York was relieved from duty at the same time on account of his avowed Catholicity. The two men proceeded to Virginia.

But the tide was rising. Grievances seemed to multiply. The merest trifles became momentous. Every act of Nicholson was magnified into something of diabolical intent. On the evening of May 30, it was the turn of Captain De Peyster's company to mount guard. Lieutenant Henry Cuyler ordered one of his men to stand as sentinel at the sally-port. The sergeant of the regular soldiers in garrison objected that the lieutenant-governor had given no such directions. Upon Nicholson's return late at night, the incident was reported, and Cuyler was summoned to attend him in his bedchamber. Irritated at the breach of military discipline, Nicholson asked, "Who is commander in this fort, you or I?" Cuyler replied that he had acted under Captain De Peyster's orders. In a passion Nicholson exclaimed, "I would rather see the town on fire than be commanded by you"; then, seeing a stalwart corporal who had accompanied Cuyler as interpreter standing by the door with a drawn sword, he seized a pistol and ordered them both out of the room.

May 30.

Before sunrise the next morning the story was buzzed all over town with absurd exaggerations. It was reported and believed that Lieutenant-Governor Nicholson had threatened to burn New York. And it was said also that he was planning to massacre all the Dutch inhabitants who should attend church in the fort on the following Sabbath. The falsity of the rumor seemed to give it greater currency. No contradiction could satisfy the people.

May 31.

The lieutenant-governor went to the City Hall at the usual hour to meet his own and the Common Council, and Mayor Van Cortlandt sent for the militia captains. The latter appeared, all but Captain Leisler. Nicholson explained what had occurred the night before. But Cuyler maintained his version of the affair, and finally Nicholson in high temper dismissed him from the service for impertinence. Captain De Peyster sympathized with the disgraced officer and retired in anger.

Presently drums began to beat. Workmen dropped their tools and implements of labor, and rushed along the streets, and women and servants ran from the houses with white scared faces. A panic spread through the town. Terror, and a dread of no one knew what, rendered the scene almost hideous. Captain Leisler's company mustered tumultuously before the door of his house, led by Sergeant Joost Stoll. The latter brandished his sword, and shouted, "We are sold, we are betrayed, we are going to be murdered!" and then marched to the fort followed by the rabble. They were received and admitted by Lieutenant Cuyler; and a few minutes later Captain Leisler appeared and assumed command.

Colonel Bayard went at the request of the council at the City Hall to endeavor to bring the muti-
neers to reason, and induce
them to disperse; but he
was informed by Stoll in the
most insulting manner, that
they "disowned all authority
of the government." He returned to announce that his
commands were disregarded,
and that most of the city
militia were in rebellion. It
was then determined to hold
another session of the governor's and common council
during the evening.

Leisler's House in the Strand.

Captain Lodwyck's company was to mount guard that night, according to the previous arrangement of rotation in duty. A little before dark Leisler sent an armed posse to demand from Nicholson the keys of the fort. The lieutenant-governor was at the house of Frederick Philipse, where he had gone to supper. He declined to comply, and repaired to the City Hall to advise with his council how to act in such "a confused business." An hour later, Captain Lodwyck appeared at the head of his company, and entering the council-chamber claimed the keys. There seemed but one course to pursue. The military had turned against the government, and the government was powerless. Bloodshed must be avoided if possi-ble, and perhaps by yielding gracefully the people might be brought to their senses and their former obedience. The keys were accordingly sur-rendered.

Nicholson was a good soldier, but hampered in all his movements by English customs and forms. He was not blessed with a directing mind, and could act only under instructions. His counselors were in the same predicament. Instructions had, indeed, been sent to their imprisoned gov-ernor-in-chief at Boston, which had they reached New York would have saved the province from a series of disasters.

Meanwhile the militia captains were sadly perplexed. Some of them were afraid of the results of the outbreak, and regarded it as unnecessary and ill-timed. Captain Minvielle, Captain De Peyster, and Captain De Bruyn spent the greater part of the evening at the council-chamber in warm discussion with the officers of the government, who were their neighbors and friends. Leisler was at the fort, descanting largely upon liberty. He denounced popery and kings. He enlarged upon the uniform misrule by which James had brought matters to this crisis. He proclaimed his loyalty to the new Protestant sovereigns. He pictured the danger which threatened the city as imminent. Nicholson was a traitor. He had accomplices about him, and there was no question but that Sunday would be a veritable St. Bartholomew's day.

The captains came together late in the evening, and after much hesitation on the part of the majority, finally agreed to govern alternately until orders came from England. Leisler drafted a " Declaration," stating how New York was threatened by Nicholson, and promising to hold and guard the fort until the proper person should arrive to take command. This paper the captains signed upon a drum.[1]

June 1. The next morning there was a reaction in public feeling. The captains were not satisfied with the course events were taking. They were shrewd, sensible men, and doubted the policy of the movement. After an excited consultation, in which opinions differed materially, Captain De Peyster, Captain Stuyvesant, Captain Minvielle, and Captain De Bruyn visited Colonel Bayard, and requested him to take sole command in opposition to the lieutenant-governor. Bayard declined. "Gentlemen, there is no occasion for a revolution," he said. Nicholson was honest and trustworthy. A little patience, and orders would come to establish everything upon a proper basis. During the forenoon Philipse, Van Cortlandt, and Bayard mixed freely with the people, and tried to quiet their apprehensions respecting Nicholson. At one time it seemed as if they would succeed in restoring order and authority. But counter influences were at work. There were men who blazed forth in coarse invectives, and accused the counselors themselves of complicity in the traitorous designs of Nicholson. Leisler said they were all " a pack of rogues and papists," and were contriving together to hold the government for King James. It was a black Saturday for New York.

June 2. On Sunday it was Leisler's turn to mount guard, and he had matters pretty much in his own hands. He had wrought himself into a frenzy of political foresight, and probably believed his own prophecies. New York was to have a Dutch sovereign, who would favor his own people by permitting them to govern themselves. He was diffuse upon the subject of self-government. Down with aristocracy, down with tyranny and oppression. Let the people henceforth dictate. And the

---

[1] This " Declaration " was printed several weeks afterward by Samuel Green of Boston. In some of the reports it has been confounded with a second paper signed on the 3d of June.

"Gentlemen, there is no occasion for a revolution." Page 350.

"Let the people henceforth dictate." Page 350.

"During the forenoon, Philipse, Van Cortlandt and Bayard mixed freely with the people, and tried to quiet their apprehensions concerning Nicholson." Page 350.

people naturally enough shouted their applause. He went on and explained the nature of the conflict between church and state, — that is, according to his understanding of it, — and again the people applauded. He warned them against the " dogs and traitors " who were only waiting for the opportunity to commence a horrid massacre.

Many a wistful eye through that long and weary day watched with cruel expectation for indications of a death-storm. And the common soldiers boastfully declared that the town would have been running rivers of blood but for Mr. Leisler. He notified all the men belonging to the militia companies to come on Monday morning to the ^{June 3.} fort at a certain signal which would be given, and to obey no officer who should attempt to hinder them. The signal was to be the firing of guns. The maneuver was facilitated by the arrival of a ship from Barbadoes. A rumor spread that four or five French ships were inside of Sandy Hook. The soldiers ran in great disorder to the parade-ground in front of the fort. Captain Lodwyck hurried to the house of Philipse, where Nicholson, Van Cortlandt, and Bayard were assembled, and in behalf of Captains De Peyster, Stuyvesant, Minvielle, and De Bruyn, desired Bayard to take command as formerly, for without his orders each of the above-named captains had refused to appear in arms. Colonel Bayard replied that his orders had been so repeatedly disobeyed by both officers and men, and the government being powerless to sustain his commission while the fort was detained, he hardly thought it worth while for him to appear only as a private soldier. But an enemy was supposed to be approaching, and the lives and property of the citizens were at stake ; the captains had positively refused to act without his commands ; hence the lieutenant-governor and council gave order that he should proceed according to his commission as colonel of the regiment to give suitable orders in the emergency. In a few minutes he was on the ground. The captains met him with respectful deference ; but the men were rude and unmanageable.

The falsity of the alarm was quickly discovered, and the troops ordered to disperse. Instead of obeying the colonel or their captains, they crowded in a noisy and disorderly manner towards the fort, shouting, " To CAPTAIN LEISLER, TO CAPTAIN LEISLER," and threatened all those who tried to restrain them. They pressed inside the gate, and, seeing the discomfited captains halting in their rear, they wildly swore vengeance upon them unless they came in also. " We will pull down your houses over your heads," and " You are vile traitorous papists like Nicholson and his dogs," rang upon the air. Prudence seemed the better part of valor, and the unwilling officers yielded to the popular clamor.

Leisler had remained within the fort, and was ready with a document similar to the one prepared on Friday, which he read aloud as soon as he could obtain a hearing. It was received with riotous demonstrations of approval. Signers were called for, and over four hundred men put their names, or their marks to it, for a large proportion of them could neither read nor write. It was signed also by the captains and subordinate officers.

Colonel Bayard retired from the scene as soon as he saw that he could be of no use in stemming the rebellion. In the "west room" of Philipse's city mansion Nicholson and his three counselors remained all day; without soldiers and without fort, they were indeed but the figure-head of a disabled government. In the afternoon the master of the ship from Barbadoes landed, but Leisler took care to have him conducted directly to the fort, where his papers were examined. The mayor and aldermen of the city learned through a passenger that William and Mary had been proclaimed at Barbadoes. They even saw a copy of the London Gazette which contained the order for continuing all Protestants in office in England. The hope was thus created that relief would shortly arrive in the shape of direct instructions.

But Sir William Phipps had clogged the way. He was so zealous for the establishment of a commonwealth in Massachusetts that he prevented the transmission of William's order continuing all persons in office in the colonies. When he himself arrived in Boston, his first act was to advise the Puritans to bend to circumstances, and proclaim William and Mary without delay. The General Court convened and voted an address to the new sovereigns, which contained happily expressed felicitations, and a prayer for the restoration of the old Massachusetts charter with new privileges. Dr. Mather stood guard over the interests of Massachusetts in England, and so explained the proceeding against Andros, that William was half convinced of its justice. At least, he was too nearly overwhelmed with the complicated affairs of his new government to enter into any special investigation of its remote branches while there was an outward show of peace. He therefore directed that the government which the Bostonians had established for themselves should be continued until further notice.

The next occurrence of any note in New York was the arrival of Philip French, who had been in England on private mercantile business and had returned in the same vessel with Sir William Phipps. As soon as it was rumored that he was on the way from Boston, overland, Leisler placed sentinels and armed men some distance out of town to watch for him and conduct him to the fort. He was the bearer of letters

June 6.

to different persons, which were all opened, and such as were addressed to the lieutenant-governor and counselors were read aloud to the soldiers. French was able to give an intelligent account of what had transpired in England, but he had no idea where the orders for New York had gone to, if there had been any, which every one believed. The next day a vessel entered the bay from Boston, and Leisler, on the alert, received the captain with military parade and took his papers. Two letters addressed to Mayor Van Cortlandt were first opened and read aloud in the fort, and then forwarded to him. The act was regarded as an outrage, and the indignation of the helpless officers of the government was beyond expression. Nicholson thought it wise to go to England and render a personal account of the condition of affairs, and this course was warmly approved by his associates.

Leisler wrote letters to the leading men in Boston and in Hartford. In one addressed to Major Nathan Gold, under date of June 7, he said he wanted to have "one trusted man sent to England to June 7. procure some privileges"; and, assuming to speak for New York, he added, "I wish we may have part in your charter, being, as I understand, in the latitude." This last passage is a revelation of ignorance which shows that he was acting independent of advice at that time; for among the captains were men of education and intelligence, who might have told him better if he had not been too self-sufficient to ignore the necessity of counsel. He penned an address to William and Mary, for the "Militia and Inhabitants of New York," giving a tedious and long-drawn-out narrative of recent events, and promising entire submission to their pleasure. It was signed by all those who had signed the previous document, with the exception of Captain Minvielle, who was sick of the "hot-headed proceedings," and declined to act any further with the revolutionists. He went to Nicholson and solicited and obtained his discharge from the military service.

The address was sent to some Dutch merchants in London, who June 10. were requested to deliver it to the king, and add if possible "a seasonable word." The captain of the vessel who was to convey it across the water refused passage to Nicholson, and also to Rev. Mr. Innis, the Episcopal clergyman who was in haste to reach London with complaints. Nicholson went directly to Staten Island, and bought a share in Dongan's brigantine, and after much vexatious delay set sail on his voyage. He deputed Philipse, Van Cortlandt, and Bayard with the charge of New York affairs during his absence. The three gentlemen were each personally known to many of the prominent English statesmen, and their importance in the colony had been the steady growth of years. But now,

23

since aspersions had been cast upon their loyalty, it was esteemed best to counteract its effects as far as possible. Hence they wrote a letter to Secretary Shrewsbury, giving a detailed description of the overthrow of the government. To this letter was attached several confirmatory documents. One was a Latin certificate from Dominie Selyns, signed by the consistory of the Reformed Dutch Church, in which the three gentlemen were declared to be "pious, candid, and modest Protestant Christians, filling the offices of deacons and elders with consummate praise and approbation." Rev. Mr. Innis provided himself with written evidence from the Dutch and French clergymen, that he was a sincere and conscientious Protestant churchman.

Nicholson's departure gave Leisler unexpected advantage. He became stern and patronizing, magnified his questionable appropriation of authority into a noble patriotism, compared himself to Cromwell, and declared that the "sword must now rule in New York." He used lofty expressions in ordinary conversation, and put labored paragraphs into his letters, but he spelt like a washerwoman. He changed the name of the fort from James to William, and called a convention for the 26th of June to organize a "Committee of Safety," in imitation of Boston. He never fully understood the principles which underlay the movement in Boston, and had little or no conception of the singular tact and address which guided her through her perils. He was blindly infatuated with the new and novel idea of his own greatness, which had burst upon him like a meteor. Everything for the moment wore a silvery tinge. He commended his fellow captains for their dutiful deference to him. But erelong the ablest of them proved less tractable than he had anticipated ; while attempting to remove from office the Roman Catholic Collector, Plowman, he was met so squarely in opposition by Captain De Peyster and Captain Stuyvesant, who would have nothing to do with violence under any circumstances, that he was obliged to desist.

June 13. William and Mary were proclaimed at Hartford on the 13th. Shortly after, Major Gold and Captain Fitch set out for New York on horseback, with a copy of the printed proclamation and letters of advice and encouragement to Leisler. The news that they were on the way preceded them. The mayor and aldermen of the city had remained passive during the confusion, but it was agreed that they should meet the Hartford gentlemen, if possible, before their interview with Leisler. Therefore Mayor Van Cortlandt, accompanied by Colonel Bayard and several of the aldermen, rode out into Westchester, hoping to encounter June 20. them on the road, and finally stopped to dine at the house of Colonel Lewis Morris. They discovered there that they had been followed the whole distance by Leisler's son and Sergeant Stoll. They did not meet the travelers either, who entered the city by another route and held an interview with Leisler that same evening at the fort.

The next morning Mayor Van Cortlandt called upon Messrs. Gold and Fitch, and asked for the proclamation, in order that the city might do suitable honor to the new sovereigns. But it was already in the hands of Leisler. The following morning it was read to the soldiers in the fort. A little later, Mayor Van Cortlandt was visited at his residence by Leisler, Gold, and Fitch, accompanied by a file of halberdiers. Leisler accused him of shirking his duty, and ordered that William and Mary be proclaimed from the City Hall. Van Cortlandt replied with some asperity, that it was well known that he had made great efforts to obtain the proclamation for that very purpose, but now, as Leisler had taken it upon himself to read it in the fort, he might read it where else he pleased. Leisler flew into a rage and accused Van Cortlandt of siding with the Catholics and King James. Hot words followed. In the end Van Cortlandt expressed his willingness to summon the aldermen, and give notice to the citizens, if he could have an hour's grace.

When they had assembled at the City Hall, Leisler arrogantly ordered Van Cortlandt to read the proclamation. The latter was exasperated by the tone of command from a man who, although his senior by many years, was not his superior, and replied that the person who had read it in the fort in the morning should be called upon again, as he had no clerk. Leisler retorted, denouncing the mayor's conduct in strong language and calling him a "papist." The crowd, not understanding the drift of the dispute, became excited, and called out, "Seize the traitor!" and "Down with popery!" Van Cortlandt stepped forward and explained that he was not hindering the reading. Quiet was at last restored, and the proclamation was read by one of the captains.

The Hartford envoys listened to the stories of "hellish designs" until they said their "flesh trembled." They imbibed the popular belief that New York was full of "papists," who might at any moment rise and butcher peaceful Protestants. They congratulated Leisler upon his courage and invincible loyalty. As the people dispersed from about the City Hall, Colonel Bayard invited the mayor and aldermen to go with him to his house and drink the new king's health. The invitation was accepted. While going through the ceremony with great enthusiasm, a messenger came from Messrs. Gold and Fitch, asking them to join Captain Leisler and his officers in the fort and drink the new king's health. In order to let the people see that they were not lukewarm subjects of a new dynasty, they consented. The mob, however, gathered about them in a riotous manner, and were disposed to do them mischief. Alderman Crundall was violently ejected from the fort and seriously injured. The sheriff was pounded and kicked, and had his sword taken from him. Colonel William Smith was called a "devil and a rogue," and escaped rough usage by running. Philip French was struck on the side of his head with a musket and stunned. Van Cortlandt attempted to pass out, and was met with abuse on all sides, while a deafening shout rent the air of "We don't want you here."

A fire was discovered in the evening in the turret of the church in the fort, under which the powder was stored; it was supposed by many to be the work of the "papists," a demoniacal design to destroy the fort and the town.

Two days later Mayor Van Cortlandt obtained a copy of the royal proclamation which confirmed Protestant officers in their places in the colonies, and which had been, so disastrously for New York, detained in Boston. He convened the aldermen and the citizens at once, and published it in the same manner as William and Mary had been proclaimed on the 22d. Thus was established beyond question the authority of Philipse, Van Cortlandt, and Bayard, who held their commissions from the crown.

June 24.

Leisler was furious over the occurrence. He charged "Jacobitism" upon every one who would not join his standard. He called the three counselors "popishly affected, lying dogs." He saw undoubtedly that he was in danger of losing his position unless he labored vigorously to sustain it.

The next morning Van Cortlandt convened the counselors and the Common Council of the city at his house, and conferred long and earnestly. They thought it best to remove Collector Plowman, "for the peace of the restless community," and appointed commissioners to take his place until a successor should arrive from England. Colonel Bayard, Thomas Wenham, John Haines, and Paulus Richards were chosen, took the customary oaths and the keys, and entered upon their duties.

June 25.

In less than half an hour there was an uproar. They had only had time to change the "J" in the king's arms to a "W." Leisler came upon them with a company of soldiers, and ordered them out of the building. The resolutions of the mayor and council were pasted over the door. Leisler read these with contempt. Colonel Bayard attempted to argue the position, but was met with the old charge, "You are all rogues, traitors, and devils." The soldiers jerked Wenham into the street by the neckcloth, and battered and bruised him until some bystanders remonstrated to save his life, and were in turn assaulted and nearly murdered. Bayard was cut at fiercely, but the crowd was so thick that only his hat was injured. He succeeded in escaping into the house of Peter De Lanoy, which was immediately surrounded and in danger of being pulled down. Bayard made his further escape after a time. But the startling cry was raised, and spread from one end of the town to the other, that "the rogues had sixty men ready to kill Captain Leisler."

The next day Mrs. De Peyster, the mother of Captain De Peyster, and Mrs. Van Brugh went to Mrs. Bayard, and told her that ^{June 26.} her husband was in hourly peril of assassination, and advised that he should leave the city for a time. He was similarly counseled by some of the aldermen, who were amazed at the fury with which he was pursued. Assisted by his friends, who provided horses for him some miles above Philipse manor, he, attended by two negro slaves, managed to escape to Albany, where he was hospitably received and entertained by Mayor Peter Schuyler and Robert Livingston.

Leisler appointed Peter De Lanoy collector of the customs, having successfully routed the commissioners. Then the Convention which he had summoned came together. The excitements

Portrait of Hon. Peter Schuyler.
(From the original painting in the possession of the family.)

of the last few days had convinced half the town that the other half were concealing daggers and about to rise and sustain the Roman Catholics. To deny the charge was almost equivalent to a confession of guilt. Many of the delegates were men who were struggling with imperfect ideas of a democratic goverment, and openly promulgated the sentiment that "there had been no legal king in England since Oliver Cromwell." Two of the delegates seeing the tendency of the Convention to make Leisler com-

mander-in-chief, withdrew after the first session. The remaining ten
formed themselves into a " Committee of Safety." Their names were,
Richard Denton, Teunis Roelofse, Jean De Marest, Daniel De Klercke,
Thomas Vermilye, Samuel Edsall, Matthias Harvey, Peter De Lanoy,
Thomas Williams, and William Lawrence.

They appointed Abraham Gouverneur clerk of the committee.
June 27. He was a young man of nineteen, the son of the French Huguenot,
Nicholas Gouverneur. He had a remarkable education for one of his
years. He could read, write, and speak readily the three languages chiefly
spoken in New York, and kept the records with great clearness and precision.

The first business of the Committee of Safety was to appoint Leisler
"Captain of the fort." He was to open all letters and examine all
June 28. strangers that came into the city. Every person suspected of
popery was to be arrested and thrown into prison.

Six weeks afterward these ten men, assuming to represent a few of the
towns near the metropolis, issued a second commission appointing Leisler
commander-in-chief of the province. It was illegal, and served to illustrate the errors into which men will fall who are unaccustomed to rule.
Had the authority of such a commission been resolutely questioned it
would have tumbled into dust. Leisler argued the necessity of the
measure as a prevention against anarchy. He must have more power.
Should the French attack the province, or the " Jacobites " rise to carry
the colony by storm, the want of harmony in Albany and elsewhere
would prove fatal to all concerned. So the Committee of Safety gave
him what they did not possess, and he tightened his reins and became
more arbitrary than ever.

Meanwhile the time for the regular holding of the mayor's court was
approaching, and Leisler determined to put a stop to it. He sent
July 2. a message the evening before to Paulus Richards to the effect that
if the mayor undertook to hold court, "the people would haul the magistrates by the legs from the City Hall and he would not hinder them."
The morning came, and Mayor Van Cortlandt sent John Lawrence,
Francis Rombouts, William Merritt, and Thomas Crundall to the fort to
consult Leisler in regard to his intentions. But he, only repeated the
threat. The aldermen did not care to run the risk of encountering a
mob while they had no means of defense, so the mayor's court was adjourned for four weeks, presuming that by that time relief in some tangible shape would have arrived from England.

CHAPTER XX.

1689 – 1691.

NEW YORK UNDER LEISLER.

New York under Leisler. — The Elections of 1689. — Mrs. Van Cortlandt's Courage. — Leisler's Executive Ability. — Albany in Peril. — Independence of Albany. — Mayor Peter Schuyler. — Milborne's Defeat. — Connecticut to the Rescue. — Colonel Nicholas Bayard. — Captain Lodwyck in Disgrace. — Captain De Peyster in Disgrace. — The Rough Search for Colonel Bayard. — William III. of England. — The Tangle in New York. — The King's Letter to Nicholson. — New York threatened by the French. — Leisler's Agent at Whitehall. — Matthew Clarkson. — The King's Letter seized by Leisler. — Leisler's Assumption. — An Outburst of Rage. — Philip French in a Dungeon. — The Jails and Prisons filled. — Arrest of Colonel Bayard. — Arrest of William Nicolls. — Pursuit of Robert Livingston. — The French on the War-Path. — Burning of Schenectady. — Shocking Massacre. — Albany appalled. — Albany submits to Leisler. — The First Colonial Congress in America. — Leisler's Vigor. — Wholesale Complaints. — Connecticut's Rebuke. — Despotic Laws. New Rochelle. — Wedding of Leisler's Daughter. — Advice from Boston. — The Government of New York as ordained by William III. — Arrival of Lieutenant-Governor Ingoldsby. — The City in Tumult. — Leisler aggressive. — Bloodshed in New York. — Governor Sloughter's Arrival. — Leisler imprisoned. — The Sunday Sermon. — The Trial of Leisler and his Council. — Leisler and Milborne under Sentence of Death. — The Assembly of 1691. — Dr. Gerardus Beekman. — Sloughter's Character. — Signing of the Death-Warrant. — The Execution of Leisler and Milborne. — Impressive Scenes. — Effects of Leisler's Death. — The French and Indian War. — Death of Sloughter. — Ingoldsby Commander-in-Chief. — Etienne De Lancey.

THE summer passed away in tolerable quiet. The city of **1689.** New York was under a military despotism. Leisler counted all as " Papists " who would not recognize his authority. As none of the city magistrates would administer the oaths of allegiance in the fort, he sent for Dr. Gerardus Beekman, a Long Island justice, to perform that service. On one occasion four Cambridge students came into the city with Perry, the postman, and on suspicion of papacy were arrested and their letters seized and examined. Even the drums beat an alarm and four hundred soldiers appeared. But the modest travelers were found to be honest men, and were set at liberty. Several prominent citizens were arrested without warrant, and there was no time when many persons were not lying in prison for disaffection to the new government.

Aug. 25.   In August Jacob Milborne returned from Holland, where he had been staying for some months. His elder brother, William

Portrait of Dr. Gerardus Beekman.
(From an original painting in possession of the family.)

Milborne, was an Anabaptist minister who had taken an active part in the overthrow of the government of Andros. He himself declared that the English Revolution justified all that had been done in New York. He became an arm of strength to his old friend with whom he had formerly been associated in commercial ventures. He took up his abode in Leisler's family. He was by no means a genial companion; his disposition had been soured by early misfortunes, and his mind was one great uncultivated field of reformatory ideas. But his English education and his indomitable pluck were invaluable. Leisler's letters henceforth appeared in better dress, and were less subject to criticism. Ensign Stoll was sent to convey a document to Whitehall which was full of loyal asseverations. Leisler explained how in June he had been made captain of the fort, but omitted to mention his last absurd commission.

As the customary time for elections approached, Leisler ordered the towns and counties to proceed to choose new officers for the coming year. The charter of New York required that the mayor and sheriff of the city should be appointed annually by the governor and council, and the clerk by the governor, and that they should remain in office until others should be duly appointed in their places. The charter also ordained the Catholic feast of Michaelmas as the time to elect its aldermen. On that day the voting went on in the different wards, but the Leisler faction were alone in the field; their opponents denied the legality of the whole proceeding. Robert Walters, the son-in-law of Leisler, was returned as one of the aldermen.

Sept. 20.

Leisler was perplexed as to how to manage about the mayor and guber-natorial appointments. He finally summoned the Protestant freeholders of the city together to elect them. A few only were present, and the majority of votes were for Peter De Lanoy. This was the first election of a mayor by the city, or what was supposed to represent the city, of New York.[1] Johannes Johnson was returned as sheriff, and Abraham Gouverneur as clerk. Leisler issued a proclamation on the birthday of James II., as the charter dictated, confirming the election. Thus with characteristic inconsistency he violated one most essential _{Oct. 14.} point in the charter, and rigidly observed two others touching upon noted Catholic days.

A constable was sent to the house of Mayor Van Cortlandt to obtain the city charter, seals, records, etc., — for what were city officials without municipal paraphernalia! Van Cortlandt was not at home. A commit-tee was then appointed to wait upon Mrs. Van Cortlandt and demand them of her. She was a sister of Mayor Peter Schuyler of Albany, a tall, grandly proportioned woman, with a touch of imperialism _{Oct. 16.} about her, as if born to command. She received the committee politely, but declined to give up anything which had been left in her care by her husband. A sergeant-at-arms next visited her, but when she learned his errand she coolly shut the door in his face and defied his blustering threats. An effort was then made to find and imprison Van Cortlandt, but without success.

The French were already overshadowing the northern horizon and pre-paring to take advantage of the disturbances in the colonial government. Leisler acted promptly, used the public funds to put the fort in repair, and placed a double number of men at work upon the city fortifications. A new semicircular battery, for some time known as "Leisler's Half Moon," was built upon a flat rock west of the fort, and supplies of powder were obtained from Philadelphia.

Albany was seriously threatened, and a convention was called. It was presided over by Mayor Schuyler; and by his side, acting as sec-retary, sat his brother-in-law, Robert Livingston, who was also the _{Aug. 1.} brother-in-law of Mayor Van Cortlandt. The city recorder, Dirck Wes-sells, and Aldermen Wendall, Bleecker, Van Schaick, and other of the chief men were Hollanders, all Protestants, and members of the Reformed Dutch Church, of which Dominies Schaats and Dellius were the pastors. These magistrates had, as soon as they received a copy of the proc-lamation from New York, formed the citizens into a procession _{July 1.}

---

[1] Cornelius W. Lawrence was the first citizen elected mayor by the people of New York, in 1834.

and marched to the fort, and there, in the most dignified and solemn manner, proclaimed William and Mary, fired guns, and indulged in all other suitable demonstrations. They repeated the ceremony at the City Hall, rang the bells, and had bonfires and fire-works in the evening. They esteemed themselves in no wise subordinate to Leisler, but were determined to maintain their civil government until orders came from England.

But Albany, with her two little streets crossing each other at right angles, was the center of the great internal traffic of the province with the natives, and consequently second only in importance to the metropolis. It was desirable that every effort should be made to keep the Iroquois friendly, and no one understood the tactics required for that purpose better than Schuyler and Livingston. These warriors were in a deadly quarrel with the French, and the near Mohawks had asked assistance of men and horses to draw logs to fortify their castles, which was granted.

Several outside tribes had gone over to the French, and had recently fallen upon and destroyed Dover in New Hampshire, and Pemaquid in Maine. Albany might be attacked at any moment, and the " Convention" ordered that every gentleman present should bring a gun with half a pound of powder and ball equivalent, to be hung up in the church, and that the traders and other inhabitants should be persuaded to do the same, until the number of fifty was reached, these arms to be used in case of emergency. As some of the citizens were preparing to leave Albany, the Convention ordered, that, " as it was setting a bad example for the timorous and cowardly to run away, no able-bodied inhabitant should leave the county for the next three months, without a pass from the justice of the peace." After much hesitation a messenger was sent to ask Leisler for help. He forwarded four cannon and a small supply of powder and ball, at the same time commanding that commissioners be sent to him at once to consult for the public good. He addressed his letter to Captains Wendall and Bleecker, instead of the Convention, saying to the messenger that he had nothing to do with the civil power; he was a soldier, and would write to a soldier.

Aug. 7.

Sept. 4.

The Convention paid no further heed to him, but raised what money they could among themselves, and appealed to New England for aid. The latter sent delegates to enlist the Iroquois against the Eastern savages. The chiefs of the Iroquois were summoned to Albany, but declined to attack tribes who had done them no harm. The next day, at a private conference, the same sachems assured the Albany gentlemen that if the

French came to harm them, they would fight for them, and live or die with them.[1]

On the day appointed in her charter Albany proceeded to install her municipal officers, and in order to silence the misrepresentations of those who persisted in calling the Albanians "Jacobites," the civic and military officers, the citizens, and the soldiers in the fort, took oaths of fidelity to the new king and queen.

Oct. 14.

Thus there were two rival governments within the province of New York, and one was as rightful as the other. But the independent attitude of Albany galled Leisler. He shortly prepared a force of fifty-one men to proceed under the command of Milborne and take possession of the Albany fort. The Convention, learning what was in progress, sent Alderman Van Schaick to New York to tell Leisler that they would willingly accept reinforcements provided they came in an obedient spirit, but that no New York officer would be admitted to the command of the fort. Considering himself commander-in-chief of the province, Leisler determined to make his power felt, and dispatched three sloops full of armed men and ammunition up the river.

Oct. 26.

Van Schaick reached Albany before them, and reported how Leisler was bent upon "turning the government of their city upside down." The Convention summoned the citizens together, and a declaration was signed to the effect that they would not permit "them of New York or any person else, to rule over Albany, of which the Convention was the only present lawful authority." In order "to prevent jealousies and animosities," Mayor Peter Schuyler, who was a favorite with all parties and specially loved by the Indians, was appointed to the chief command of the fort. The principal men of Albany led him up the steep hill to the little fortress with great pomp and ceremony, and he was received by the garrison with cheers and huzzas.

Nov. 4.

Nov. 5.

Nov. 8.

The next morning the sloops from New York anchored a little below the city. Milborne sent a messenger to demand admission to the fort, and was promptly refused. Presently he made his appearance at the City Hall, where a crowd gathered, whom he harangued for some time, saying that all that had been done in the reign of James II. was illegal,

---

[1] *Doc. Hist.*, II. 19, 20, 50–55, 88. *Munsell*, II. 108. *Smith*, I. 99, 100. *Dunlap*, I. 158. *Mass. Hist. Soc. Coll.*, XXXV. 212, 217, 218. *Brodhead*, II. 583, 584, 585. *Colden*, I. 106–111. *Plymouth Records*, VI. 213. *Col. Doc.*, III. 610–783; IV. 349; IX. 387, 420–425, 440, 665. *Charlevoix*, II. 345, 415–419. *Belknap*, I. 198–206. *La Potherie*, III. 248. *Shea's Missions*, 277–325. *Garneau*, I. 305. *Bell*, I. 322. *Williamson*, I. 590–595. *Millet's Letter of July* 6, 1691, pp. 40–45.

and that the charter of Albany was null and void. Milborne had formerly lived in Albany, and not only knew the place well, but was well known by the people. He was answered briefly by Recorder Wessells, who said, "We have no arbitrary power here."

The following day Milborne appeared before the Convention. He produced his commission signed by Leisler and the Committee **Nov. 10.** of Safety. He was told that a commission granted by a company of private men in New York was of no force in Albany; that when he would show a commission from King William, he might command obedience. As he retired from the building he made a long speech from the steps to the people who had collected. He was interrupted constantly by shouts of "You want to raise mutiny and sedition," and "If things are carried on as you say, all authority will be overturned, and we shall run into confusion with the Indians."

In the course of twenty-four hours Milborne succeeded in winning some one hundred persons over to his interests, and they met and **Nov. 11.** chose Jochim Staats to command the soldiers from New York. **Nov. 12.** The Convention refused to accept the soldiers from New York as soon as they heard of it, unless they pledged themselves to come under the command of the Convention. On the 14th **Nov. 14.** Mayor Schuyler met the citizens at the City Hall, and explained why he had accepted command of the fort, simply to defeat Leisler's design to create a general disturbance among the people by making an absolute change of government. His course was warmly approved.

But Milborne was fully resolved to obtain the mastery. He assembled his complete force and marched valiantly up to the fort. He **Nov. 15.** halted with military precision and demanded possession. Schuyler ordered him away. Milborne attempted to force an entrance and was driven back. He ordered his men to load, and read to them a paper. Schuyler, upon one of the mounds of the fort, shouted a protest in behalf of the Convention, and directed Milborne and his troops to withdraw at once. A party of Mohawks upon the hill near by watched these proceedings, and all at once charged their guns and sent a hurried messenger to Schuyler, to say that if the New York soldiers were hostile they should fire on them. Schuyler sent Recorder Wessells and Dominie Dellius to pacify the savages, but the latter were thoroughly enraged and insisted upon the Dominie's going to Milborne with the same message which they had sent to Schuyler. Milborne was baffled, for he had met an unexpected foe. He dismissed his men and retired in humiliation.

He had some allies in Albany, and before he returned to New **Nov. 16.** York a private contract was signed by a few men of means to support the soldiers whom he was to leave behind under command of Captain Staats. He stopped at Esopus on his trip down the Hudson, but the people had been informed of his defeat at Albany and he could do nothing with them.

Ten days later eighty-seven soldiers reached Albany, sent at the request of the Convention by Governor Treat of Connecticut. They were led by Captain Bull, the same who courageously prevented ^{Nov. 28.} Andros from taking possession of Saybrook in 1775. The perils were so great that Lieutenant Enos Talmage of Captain Bull's company with twenty-four men were sent to garrison Schenectady. Captain Staats, instead of assisting in the common defense with his New York soldiers, worked industriously to promote faction. The condition of affairs became so lamentable that the Convention appointed the 4th of ^{Dec. 4.} December to be observed as a day of fasting and prayer.

Colonel Bayard in Albany, having been there since June, had been kept informed of all that transpired in New York, and was in constant expectation of royal instructions which would restore order. He learned in October that his only son, who had been lying dangerously ill for months, was in a dying condition, and he was very anxious to see him. He wrote to the justices of the peace in New York, asking personal protection from Leisler while visiting his family. He offered to give security in money, or to answer any complaints or accusations which could be brought against him and thereby satisfy the law. But the answer which he received was, " The sword rules, and we have no power in opposition to Leisler."

He then wrote to Captain De Peyster and Captain De Bruyn, with directions that the contents of his letter should be communicated to all the commissioned officers ; he ordered them "to bear good ^{Oct. 20.} faith and allegiance " to William and Mary, to be obedient to the civil

Autograph of Nicholas Bayard.

authority of the city, and to desist from aiding or abetting the illegal proceedings of Leisler and his associates. As a commissioned colonel of the regiment, as well as one of the counselors of the government, he considered that he was thus honestly and fearlessly doing his duty. The results, however, were most disastrous. The captains put his communication into the hands of Leisler, who flew into a terrible rage. He knew that Bayard, despite a little pomposity, stood high in the estimation of a large class of the inhabitants of the province. He knew that he was a man of orthodox religion and regular life, of ample fortune and high connections. He knew that he was a scholar, and notwithstanding his French and Dutch parentage, was an able expositor of the English law. He knew that his logic had already startled some of the captains as to the consequences of the revolt. He knew that Bayard was likely to be a continual thorn in his side. In short, he was afraid of him. The spirit of insurrection is always severe. Leisler determined to put his foot upon so dangerous a foe. Milborne added fuel to the fire by describing the effects of Bayard's influence in Albany. They feared he might overturn their whole structure.

Leisler called a public meeting, at which he announced that Nicholson had never shown his face in England, but had turned "privateer"; and that Bayard was "a traitor and a villain," and was coming upon New York with three hundred men to retake the fort for the late King James. As for Dongan, although he was living quietly on his farm near Hempstead, Leisler charged him with holding "cabals" at his house and at other places, preparatory to making an attempt on the fort. Captain Lodwyck denied this imputation upon Dongan, and was immediately dismissed from the service, with the scathing charge of being a friend to "popery and James."

Leisler called upon every man to take a new oath, which was, in substance, to be true to William and Mary, obedient to the Committee of Safety, and to the commander-in-chief of the province. Captain De Peyster was a man of strong practical sense, and, seeing the mischief which was likely to result from needlessly terrifying and exasperating the lower classes, warned Leisler to desist from such a course. The latter was in no mood to hear reproof, and angrily suspended him from office, appointing a more pliant captain in his stead. He thus lost one of the best men who had been among his adherents, and a counselor who might have saved him from destruction.

Meanwhile Bayard had privately arrived at his own house. It was evening, but a soldier saw him and ran with the news to the fort. A dozen armed men were sent at once to arrest him. They went through his house in a rough and riotous manner, greatly adding to the distress of his already afflicted family, by swearing that they would "fetch him from the gates of hell." Not finding him, they proceeded to search Van Cortlandt's house in the same brutal manner, and threatened Van Cortlandt himself so seriously that he was obliged to escape through the rear of his dwelling and hide himself in Connecticut and Albany for weeks. Mrs. Van Cortlandt and her children were grossly insulted, but she bravely maintained her ground, and after a while was left in peace. The house of Dominie Selyns was searched, and he was treated to the same coarse and vulgar language. Sixteen of the chief families of the city were obliged to submit to a similar indignity. Never was the pursuit of a culprit conducted in a more indecent manner. Last of all, Captain Stuyvesant was visited. He was an own blood cousin of Bayard, and the two had been intimate and confidential friends from boyhood. It had been reported recently that he had said that the stories about Bayard's being a Catholic were "a pack of lies." So perhaps he was concealing him. They invaded every room in his house from cellar to garret, and then went through all his barns and outbuildings. They acted like men infuriated, and many of them were intoxicated. The next day Captain Stuyvesant resigned his commission and retired from any farther association with Leisler. He possessed too much of his father's spirit to lend himself for the furtherance of dishonorable outrages.

The question will very naturally arise, Why was all this confnsion allowed to exist? Why came no orders from England? Why were not men established in power to whom power properly belonged? Why was William so oblivious to his own interests?

There was a complication of reasons. The year which had elapsed since William took up the English scepter had been to him one of torturing anxiety and incessant toil. The enthusiasm which had welcomed him to the throne was as brief as it was apparently sincere. He had himself, at the very moment when his fame and fortune reached its highest point, predicted the coming reaction. It is the nature of mankind to overrate present evil and to underrate present good, to long for what he has not and to be dissatisfied with what he has. Reaction is a law of nature as certain as the laws which regulate the succession of the seasons and the course of the trade-winds. Many of those who had at first taken up arms for William began to mutter among themselves before the end of two months, and not only found excuses for the maladministration of James, gross as it had been, but revealed unmistakable signs of heartfelt commiseration for his unhappy and exiled condition. They said he was their rightful and liege lord as the heir of a long line of princes, and had many of the qualities of an excellent sovereign. He was diligent, if he was dull. He was thrifty, with all his parsimony. He was brave, notwithstanding his weaknesses. He was even truthful when not under the fatal influence of his religion.

William was alive to the possible consequences of this change in public opinion. The power of a less watchful, less cautious, less determined ruler would have been quickly undermined. He knew that he must act, there was no standing idle, and his acts were criticised by his Privy Council, who were intriguing with each other. He wished to do justice to all parties, but justice would satisfy none of them. The Tories soon hated him for protecting the Dissenters. The Whigs hated him for protecting the Tories. Members of his own household were in correspondence with James. Insincerity lurked everywhere. He stood as it were upon a volcanic crater, and was perfectly aware of his danger. Great events were following each other, also, in rapid succession, — war with France, revolt in Ireland, anarchy in Scotland. What time had the worried monarch to think of his distant and less important American colonies ?

July 4.   But there came a moment when he was brought to a painful sense of their condition. It was when the reports which had been sent in May from New York and Boston reached Whitehall. He discovered that he had been duped into committing a deplorable mistake through the tact of Dr. Mather and Sir William Phipps. He saw that Andros had been imprisoned because he had executed the orders of his lawful English sovereign. Such orders it was not William's policy to undervalue. But even then, with European affairs pressing heavily upon him, he hardly managed with characteristic prudence and foresight. He inclined towards pouring oil over rather than probing wounds.

As for the tangle in New York, it had not yet burst in its full proportions upon the minds of either William or his ministers. Both parties having written to them in such a loyal strain, it was regarded as a mere internal dispute which a few royal words would quickly settle. They were accordingly penned to Nicholson.

The letter was addressed to "Our Lieutenant-Governor and Commander-in-Chief of our Province of New York in America, and in his absence, to such as for the time being take care for preserving the peace and administering the laws in our said Province of New York in America." And Nicholson was ordered to take up the government of the province, call to his assistance the chief freeholders, and "do and perform all the requirements of the office." John Riggs, who bore the letters from Nicholson and his council to the king, was intrusted with this important document on his return to New York. Before he sailed, Nicholson reached London. Supposing all communications addressed to him would be opened by the counselors Philipse, Van Cortlandt, and Bayard, no effort was made to have them altered, and as the vessel was under orders Riggs proceeded on his voyage.

Nicholson proceeded to Whitehall and had a personal interview with the king. He related what had occurred in New York; and a few hours later he repeated the same to the Plantation Committee. Aug. 31. It was quickly decided to send a governor to New York, and two days later William in council appointed Colonel Henry Sloughter to that office. Nicholson strove to obtain the post, but did not possess sufficient interest in court. He was, however, appointed lieutenant-governor of Virginia, which was an emphatic approval of his conduct in New York.

There was no reason why Sloughter should not have gone at once to his government, only that the troubles in Ireland absorbed universal attention just then. The English navy too was in a wretched condition, and all the vessels in the kingdom were in demand as convoys for William's army. Sloughter's commission and instructions did not pass the Great Seal until January 4, 1690. Meanwhile he had proposed that New York should include Connecticut, the Jerseys, and Pennsylvania. The suggestion was not favored by the king or council. Then he proposed to add Plymouth to New York, and Secretary Blathwayt actually included it in the draft of the commission. But Dr. Mather heard of it, and appeared in time to argue the question, and persuade the Lords that the addition of Plymouth would be more inconvenient than serviceable. Therefore it was stricken out.

Meanwhile it was rumored that the French had a design upon New York, and if successful " would put to the torture " some two hundred Huguenot families who had settled in the province. Louis XIV. had actually instructed Count Frontenac to prepare an expedition without loss of time, and proceed both by land and by water against the little city on Manhattan Island; Albany was to be surprised, and the army were to " cut in below, to secure the vessels on the river "; the English settlements in the neighborhood of Manhattan Island were to be destroyed, and " all officers and principal inhabitants from whom ransoms could be exacted, detained in prison." Louis ordered that the French refugees who should be found in New York, particularly those of the pretended Reformed religion, should be shipped to France.[1]

Prominent men in New York appealed to the king to send a large force to protect the " center of all the English plantations." Anxiety settled like a heavy cloud over the city. The Committee of Safety asked the Bishop of London to intercede with the king and obtain authority for Leisler, in order to defend New York until Sloughter's arrival,

---

[1] *Memoir of Instructions to Count Frontenac.* *Paris Doc.,* IV. *Doc. Hist. New York,* I. 295.

which it had been hinted might not occur until spring. But no such authority was given Leisler.

Ensign Stoll reached London with the August dispatches of Leisler, in November. William referred them quietly to Secretary Shrewsbury. Stoll was loud and opinionated, and elicited very little notice. His vapid talk wearied the courtiers. When he asked for a written approval of Leisler's acts, the question was evaded. He had the assurance to suggest a suspension of Sloughter's commission, which was treated with cool indifference. He made himself conspicuous in England only as a miserable failure, and he would have done Leisler far better service to have remained in New York.

Nov. 9.

Nov. 16.

Matthew Clarkson, who went to London in the same vessel with Stoll, fared differently. He was a gentleman. His father was an eminent divine, the Rev. David Clarkson, of Yorkshire. His family were well known at Whitehall; and, besides, he was a young man of culture and refinement. His sister was the wife of Captain Lodwyck, and coming here to visit her, three years before, he had determined to make New York his home. He obtained the appointment of Secretary of the province, with power to choose his own deputies, and returned with Sloughter. He soon after married Catharine, daughter of Gerritsen Van Schaick of Albany.[1]

Dec.

Riggs arrived in Boston in December. He learned that Colonel Bayard was in Hartford at the house of Governor Treat, and wrote to him to say when he should arrive in New York. Bayard hastened home privately, never doubting but that the king's orders were specific enough now to set the wheels of government rolling properly.

Riggs reached Bayard's house late on Sunday evening, and met with a warm welcome. But he had received advice in Boston which caused him great embarrassment. The wise men of that wise city had told him that he must give the king's letter to Leisler, who was in actual command of the province. It was his own private belief that Leisler would refuse to receive and act upon a royal communication which was clearly intended for other parties. In order to avoid personal difficulty, he requested that all three of the counselors should be present and witness

---

[1] One of the curiosities of historical research in New York is the confusion of orthography in the matter of proper names. There was no standard orthography in the old Dutch language at that early period. Each individual seemed to spell according to his own fancy. Dutch names became Anglicized in part, and Dutch, English, and French were often blended together. It is sometimes almost impossible to trace family names. We have an instance in Gerritsen Van Schaick. In some of the old documents his name is written Gosen Van Schaick; in others, Goose Van Schaick; and in very many, Gerrits Goose. A hundred instances of a similar character might be cited within as many pages.

his surrender of the packet. Philipse was sent for, but Van Cortlandt was out of town, too far away to be reached that night.

Early the next morning, before it was possible for the counselors to meet, Leisler sent a company of armed soldiers to convey Riggs from his lodgings to the fort. He had no alternative but obedience, yet he detained the escort under pretence of finishing his breakfast until he could dispatch an earnest request to Philipse to come with Van Cortlandt (who had been sent for during the night) to the fort and meet him in Leisler's presence. There was no time lost, and the two counselors arrived almost as soon as himself. They were warmed into violent excitement by the importance of the case, and sharply asserted that they were the persons to whom the packet was addressed. Leisler denied their claim. He held the reins of government, of which fact the king was aware, and to him, and to him alone, the address referred. Hot words accomplished nothing. Leisler's corollary was a weak one, and yet under the circumstances beyond refutation. Besides, he had the advantage of present power. The counselors were conscious of being in the right, but their exasperation only aggravated previous acrimony. New York long groaned under the complication of miseries which resulted from that singular interview.

Riggs gave Leisler the king's packet, and Leisler gave Riggs a written receipt for it. Leisler then turned upon Philipse and Van Cortlandt, and called them " popishly affected dogs and rogues," and ordered them to " be gone." As for the people who rallied wildly around their supposed democratic chief, they were kept entirely in the dark as to the contents of the king's letter to Nicholson. It never was read openly during Leisler's rule.

Leisler proceeded to announce publicly that he had received a commission from the king to be the lieutenant-governor of the province. He assumed the station and the title. He appointed a council, consisting of Peter De Lanoy, Hendrick Jansen, Dr. Gerardus Beekman, Samuel Edsall, Thomas Williams, and William Lawrence, administering the usual oaths. He made Milborne Clerk of the Council and Secretary of the province, and with great ceremony and military parade he caused William and Mary to be proclaimed anew.

There was no seal for the province of New York, as Andros had broken that of 1687, when New England was consolidated ; hence Leisler ingeniously manufactured one by altering the Duke's coronet in **Dec. 11.** his old seal of 1669, placing the crown of England upon his head. When Sunday morning came, Leisler with devout ostentation walked into the old Dutch Church, where he had so long been one of the deacons, and took his seat in the governor's pew. His new council seated themselves in the pew set apart for that august body of men. Angry breezes seemed to blow through the length and the breadth of the sacred edifice that day, and never in the memory of the oldest church-goer did Dominie Selyns find it so difficult to hold the attention of his congregation.

Leisler, transformed into a royal chief, sternly inculcated the doctrine of passive obedience. The larger portion of the intelligent class of inhabitants knew that his extraordinary assumption had no foundation in fact, and that his acts under the circumstances could not be sustained by law. He issued a proclamation that the customs and excise *Dec. 16.* duties settled by the Colonial Act of 1683 remained in force. The Act had been disallowed by James, but the duties it levied had been continued by the order of Dongan. Leisler had been the very first man to refuse to pay duties under that order. He had called it a "popish Act," and had made more noise and trouble in relation to it than any other merchant in New York. Now he was about to enforce it by his own arbitrary decree. It was the death-blow to democratic theories in the popular mind.

There was a bristle of opposition, and an outburst of rage that was something fearful. At first it was vented upon the .proclamation itself; it was torn down and a paper declaring its illegality affixed in its place. The next day a duplicate of the proclamation was posted, together with an order forbidding any person to deface or take it away. But as the shades of night fell over the city it met with the same fate as its predecessor. Several persons were arrested under suspicion of having done the mischief and were thrown into the prison in the fort. They were seized and dragged into confinement without the slightest opportunity for self-defense. Among them were two lads, one of whom was Cornelis, the younger brother of Captain Abraham De Peyster. Upon investigation it was found that the proclamation was undisturbed at the time of their commitment, but they were kept in custody, and refused bail, until their friends petitioned for their release, addressing Leisler as lieutenant-governor.

An Indian slave belonging to Philip French was arrested and imprisoned on suspicion of having a part in tearing down the proclamation. French was highly indignant, and expressed his opinion in contemptuous terms of the "self-styled lieutenant-governor." He was quickly arrested and thrown into the fort dungeon. He offered bail, but it was not accepted. The small high windows of his cell were nailed carefully, and a strict watch kept outside. His friends were not permitted to see him; even his lawyer was denied access, and he was treated more barbarously than a convicted felon. About the middle of February a message was surreptitiously conveyed to him that one of his vessels (he was a large shipping-merchant), containing a valuable cargo, was wrecked on the rocks near New London, and the urgent necessity for giving personal attention to the matter induced him to bend, and address a humble petition to Leisler, according him the title of lieutenant-governor, and asking for release upon the consideration of five hundred pounds bail. In a few days he was set at liberty.

Leisler was quick of superficial apprehension and acted with remarkable promptitude. He possessed the elements of administrative capacity, but ignorance and inexperience in matters of state effectually clogged his pathway. His proceedings were all attended with vexation, and with more or less danger. Many who hailed him in the first instance as their protector from the evils of despotism and popery were disappointed and became his bitterest opponents. His dogmatism bore him with the swiftness of an arrow into blunders which no after repentance could retrieve.

He issued new commissions, making justices, sheriffs, and military officers in the various counties of New York. Then he ordered all persons holding commissions from former governors to surrender them to the nearest magistrates. This last was in a multitude of instances openly and sneeringly disregarded. Officers prowled about the country arresting those who rebelled, and the prisons were soon found too small to hold such an army of captives. The jails and prisons were enlarged, and all rendered more secure. To try the prisoners Leisler commissioned courts of oyer and terminer, and to compel the payment of customs and excise duties he erected a court of exchequer. Thomas Clarke, a thorough English lawyer, appeared before this tribunal, and boldly declared that no member had a commission from the reigning king to be a baron of his exchequer.

Leisler wrote a long letter to King William, explanatory of his conduct; but it was a clumsy document. He said he had acted upon the royal letter to Nicholson, "although two of Sir Edmund Andros's council pretended thereunto." He stated that his course had given great satisfaction to most of the people in the province. At the very moment he was penning those lines, his son was acting the part of a spy, to prevent the transmission of a different style of communications from Philipse, Van Cortlandt, and others. When Leisler learned that Andros and his fellow-prisoners were about to be sent to London, he determined to prevent any letters from disaffected persons reaching Boston, to be conveyed by them to England, and caused the arrest of the post-rider, John Perry, about one fourth of a mile beyond the house of Colonel Lewis Morris in West-chester, where it was known he frequently stopped for postal matter. The mail-bag was opened, and found to contain private letters from Bayard, Van Cortlandt, Brockholls, Morris, Nicolls, Reed, and many others. All criticised Leisler and his associates virulently and unsparingly. The post-rider was thrown into prison, from which he was not released for many months. Leisler announced that he had detected a "hellish conspiracy" against the government. He issued warrants for the apprehension of each of the gentlemen who had written to White-hall.

Colonel Bayard was the first on the list, and the most rancorously pursued. The soldiers swore that they had orders to take him "dead or alive." They broke in the doors of his house, destroyed furniture as they went from room to room, and were profane and insolent to Mrs. Bayard and other members of his household. Bayard had secreted himself in the cellar of a cooper in the rear of his dwelling, where they found him at last, and dragged him in a most abusive manner to the fort. He was immediately manacled with irons, and the ponderous door of the prison closed upon him.

Van Cortlandt's house was broken open in the same riotous manner, but he had made his escape, and his wife, dreading a repetition of former scenes, had fled with him. Some weeks elapsed before Mrs. Van Cortlandt ventured to return, and even then her liberty was threatened and her children insulted. A serious illness broke out in her family and one beloved child died, but the husband and father could only learn of his affliction in his refuge at Hartford, and at the same time grieve that his loyalty was misinterpreted, his honor stained, his credit blasted, and his large estate running to decay.

William Nicolls, after escaping the soldiers through various stratagems, was finally seized at the Long Island ferry-house, and cast into the ill-ventilated dungeon beside Colonel Bayard. He was a spirited young man of thirty-three, the son of Matthias Nicolls, the former secretary of the province. Like his father, young Nicolls was an aristocrat; and he had been conspicuous in his denunciations of Leisler, whom he called a "German upstart." He was the attorney-general of the province (since 1687), and his character for courage and professional ability stood high. He was also a justice of the peace, and the chief ground of his imprisonment was his refusal to surrender his commission under Leisler's edict. He was a bachelor, but three years later married Anna, daughter of Jeremias Van Rensselaer.[1]

[1] *Van Cortlandt to Sir Edmund Andros,* May 19, 1690. *Robert Livingston to Sir Edmund*

It was rumored that both Bayard and Nicolls were to be tried for treason. Meanwhile Bayard was very sick in prison. His life was in imminent danger unless he could obtain medical attention and **1690.** physical comforts. He therefore penned a humble petition to Leisler, addressing him as " lieutenant-governor," and after promising respect and deference for the future, asked for pardon and release. Leisler was immensely gratified with the concession. But Bayard was too dangerous an enemy to be allowed to run at large with impunity, and the petition was denied. Abundant bail was offered and refused. Both Bayard and Nicolls were kept in miserable cells for thirteen months, until the arrival of Sloughter.

In spite of all these rigorous measures Leisler found that much of the fruit of leadership was exceedingly unpalatable. He could command little respectful consideration save at the point of the sword. He was called " Lieutenant Blockhead," " Deacon Jailor," " Governor Dog-driver," and other uncomplimentary epithets. Those who were fearless in the use of their tongues were unsparingly punished. Sometimes pardon was obtained through a deferential oath ; though such was the exception, not the rule. Christopher Gere was imprisoned for being heard to say that he was " just as much lieutenant-governor as Mr. Leisler."

Robert Livingston incurred Leisler's wrath, and was pursued until he was obliged to escape from the province to avoid prison fare. He found refuge in Hartford with his brother-in-law Van Cortlandt. Both gentlemen were made welcome at the hospitable home of Governor Treat. Livingston's offense was disloyalty to Leisler. His influence in the Albany Convention, and his great wealth and resolute character, made him a formidable adversary. Leisler charged him with being a " Jacobite," and the ground of the accusation was his having been heard to say, in the early part of the disturbance, that " a parcel of rebels had gone out of Holland into England with the Prince of Orange at their head." Livingston's lands were seized for taxes which he defiantly refused to pay. And all this time Albany stood out against Leisler, notwithstanding that he issued a commission to Captain Staats with an order to take possession of Fort Orange.[2] Mayor Schuyler and the Convention demanded

---

Andros, April 14, 1690. *Mr. Newton to Captain Nicholson,* May 26, 1690. *John Clapp to Secretary of State,* November 7, 1690. *The Address of New York Merchants to William and Mary,* May 19, 1690. *William Nicolls to George Farewell,* June 24, 1690. *" A Modest and Impartial Narrative." Doc. Hist. New York,* Vol. II. *Col. Doc.,* Vol. III. *New York Hist. Soc. Coll.* (1868). *Chalmers' Political Annals. Brodhead,* II. *Dunlap. Smith. Leisler's Memorials to William and Mary.*

[2] Captain Jochim Staats married for his second wife *Francina,* the younger daughter of Jacob Leisler.

sight of the king's letter to Nicholson.   As it was withheld they declined
to acknowledge Leisler as lieutenant-governor.

Events, however, were close at hand which were likely to subordinate
for a time all minor considerations.   The orders received by Count
Frontenac to commence hostilities against New England and New York
" afforded him," so he wrote, " considerable pleasure, and were very necessary for the country."   He immediately organized three different detachments, " to attack those rebels at all points at the same moment, and thus
punish them for having protected the Mohawks."   One of these ravaged
Maine and destroyed the village of Salmon Falls, now Berwick in New
Hampshire, and then, in conjunction with the second, burned Portland,
alarming the whole eastern frontier of New England.

The third and most important of the detachments marched towards
Albany.   It was composed of two hundred and ten men, ninety-six of
whom were savages, from the northern tribes of the Iroquois, and the
rest were " the best qualified Frenchmen for the purpose." [1]   When some
five or six days out, a council was called to determine the route they
should follow.   The Indians demanded of the French what was their
intention.   Upon being informed they objected.   They said it was rash
and desperate, for Albany was stronger than the French supposed, and
the attacking party was too weak.   It was finally decided to first destroy
Schenectady.   After a severe tramp over an intensely cold and moun-
tainous country covered with snow, the expedition halted within six miles
of the doomed town on four o'clock of Saturday afternoon.   A reconnoitering party soon reported its defenseless condition, and a little before midnight the benumbed and exhausted Canadians proceeded to their fiendish
task with barbaric ferocity.

The town was in the form of a parallelogram, and contained upwards
of eighty well-built and well-furnished houses.   It was surrounded by a
palisaded wall, and could be entered only by two gates.   These gates were
open, for no one apprehended the approach of an enemy from Canada in
such bitter weather.   Besides, Indian scouts were stationed in the vicinity of Lake Champlain, and they had seen nothing to occasion any alarm.
And, saddest of all, the town within was divided against itself, and in no
condition to make a defense.   Leisler had been trying to clinch his authority there as well as in Albany, and some were for him and some were
against him.   The magistrates had lost their authority, and Leisler's new
officers had not been able to establish their own.   Talmage and his garrison were half starving for the want of supplies which it was the business of the town to furnish, and by withholding which the Leisler faction
were determined to bring them to submission.

[1] *Paris Documents.   Doc. Hist. New York*, I. 297–302.

All unguarded the people slept, when with one war-whoop — a long, piercing, indescribable yell — the miserable work was begun. Schuyler, in writing of the massacre, said, " Neither pen nor tongue can express the horrors of that cruel night." There was little or no resistance. The fort was the only place under arms; it was set on fire, and Talmage and his men mercilessly slaughtered. The sack of the town lasted two hours. Sixty persons were killed, and about an equal number taken prisoners. It was ordered that the minister, Dominie Terschenmacker, should be taken alive, for the purpose of obtaining information from him, but he was slain and his papers burned before he was recognized, and afterwards his head was put upon a pole and carried to Canada. Twenty-five almost naked survivors made their escape from their burning homes, and pushed their way half frozen through the snow to Albany. Some thirty Iroquois who were lodging in the village were spared, as it was a part of the policy of the French to win over the remainder of the savages through kindness, and the striking of audacious blows against the English.

Some half-mile above the village lived the chief magistrate of Schenectady, Captain Alexander Glen. He was one of the members of the Albany Convention, and Leisler's partisans had threatened to burn his house. At daybreak a party of French visited him, and, finding that he had no intention of surrendering, but was putting himself on the defensive with his servants and some Indians, they assured him that in consequence of certain favors formerly received at his hands, he and his people and property should be safe from violence. He accordingly laid down his arms on parole, entertained the officers in his private fort, and finally accompanied them to the burning town. Several women and children who claimed affinity with him were released from captivity. The Canadian savages muttered because their prisoners were reduced so greatly in numbers, and said, " Every one seems to be a relation of Captain Glen!" The next day the conquerors set out on their homeward journey, taking with them considerable plunder, including fifty good horses. They suffered from cold, hunger, and disease on the way, ate thirty-four of the horses, were several times attacked by Indian war-parties, losing many of their tired warriors, and finally, with a mere remnant of the expedition, reached Montreal, to report a victory which was a lasting disgrace to the French nation.

The appalling news was carried to Albany by Simon Schermerhorn, who, wounded himself, and on a lame horse, entered the _{Feb. 9.} town Sunday morning. Schuyler at once ordered the guns of the fort to be fired to summon the people together. There was no church-going that day. All was hurry of preparation for carnage. An express was sent through the deep snow to Esopus, and to Claverack for assistance, it being

supposed Albany would be next attacked.   It was soon discovered, however, that the enemy had departed for Canada.   A party of men

Feb. 10.   were sent to Schenectady to bury the dead on Monday.   The Convention then wrote to the governments of Massachusetts, Connecticut,
Maryland, and Virginia, and to "the civil and military officers of New
York," proposing that all should join in an attempt to take Quebec by
water in the spring.   Thus from Albany in her distress came the first
suggestion of a union of the English colonies to attack the French.

Feb. 25.   Schuyler sent for the Mohawk sachems, who came and mourned
over the calamity that had befallen Schenectady.   They promised
to join the English in an effort to ruin the French country and bring the
war to an end.[1] The consolidation of American strength to intimidate the
foe at the north by this means received inspiration, as the savages were
worth a dozen armies such as the colonies could furnish.   Leisler was up
and doing as soon as he heard of the massacre.   He made it his first business to disarm and imprison about forty officers who held commissions
from Governor Andros.   He also issued warrants for the arrest of Ex-Governor Dongan, Ex-Mayor Willett, Thomas Hicks, and several others, under
the pretended supposition that they were in league with the French.
Dongan was obliged to leave his home, and fly into New Jersey, and
from there to Boston.   Several New Jersey gentlemen, among whom were
William Pinhorne and Andrew Hamilton, dared not venture within the
precincts of New York.   Leisler imagined that "cabals" were being held
and plans matured to annihilate his authority, and rested upon military
force to preserve his power.

The ugly aspect of French affairs led him to send ambassadors to the
various colonies to confer on measures for public safety.   For immediate
protection he raised a force of one hundred and sixty men and sent them
to Albany.   As it was a moment of extreme danger, the Convention
allowed them to enter the fort peaceably.   De Bruyn, Milborne, and Provoost were in command.   Leisler's authority was thus established.   He
immediately proceeded to confirm the mayor and other city officers in
their places, and to command all persons to respect and obey them.   He
also ordered that "no one asperse or reproach another under penalty of
the breach of the peace."   A common danger is the most potent of har-
monizing influences.

In April Leisler called an assembly for the purpose of raising money

[1] *Robert Livingston's Verbatim Account. N. Y. Hist. Soc. Coll.* (1869), 165–186. *Millet's
Letter of July 6, 1691. Doc. Hist. N. Y.,* II. 91–95.   *Colden,* I. 123–127.   *Smith,* I. 105,
106.   *N. Y. Hist. Soc. Coll.,* II. 105–109.   *N. Y. Col. MSS.,* III. 692–710.   *Brodhead,*
II. 609–613.   *Munsell's Alb. Col.,* III.

for the proposed expedition against the French. It met at the house of Alderman Robert Walters, Leisler's son-in-law. An act was passed to tax property real and personal. But before other business **April 24.** could be accomplished petitions came pouring in like hail-stones for the release of the suffering prisoners in the fort. Such was the excitement, and the number of people who gathered about Walters' house, that a riot seemed inevitable. Leisler was not in the humor for a popular inquisition, and hastily prorogued the Assembly until September.

He next convened a congress of the several colonies in New York. At Livingston's suggestion, Massachusetts had already **May 1.** called a New England meeting at Rhode Island. This, however, was abandoned; and the first North American Colonial Congress met at New York on the call of Leisler. The delegates from Massachusetts were William Stoughton and Samuel Sewall; from Plymouth, John Walley; from Connecticut, Nathan Gold and William Pitkin; and New York was represented by Leisler and Mayor De Lanoy. It was agreed that New York should furnish four hundred men, Connecticut one hundred and thirty-five, Massachusetts one hundred and sixty, Plymouth sixty, while Maryland promised one hundred. Rhode Island could not send men, but would raise money in reasonable proportion. Leisler at once, and with commendable vigor, fitted out three vessels for the capture of Quebec, — one a privateer of twenty guns, another a brigantine belonging to Captain Abraham De Peyster, and the third a Bermudan sloop. Two other sloops were also sent to cruise about Block Island, and to see that Long Island Sound was kept clear of the French. Schuyler at Albany had meanwhile apprehended the French agents who had been sent to treat with the Mohawks, and despoiled them of their letters and presents. **May 27.** Four Frenchmen were given to the savages, who burned two of them. D'Eau was sent to New York. Among his papers was the Latin letter of Lamberville to Millet, which contained certain expressions of good-will toward Dominie Dellius of Albany, which resulted in Leisler's charging that clergyman with "treasonable correspondence with the enemy."

In the midst of all this commotion Stoll arrived from London with information which greatly troubled Leisler. The king had taken no notice of him, and had appointed Nicholson lieutenant-gov- **May 20.** ernor of Virginia. There was significance in the fact. Leisler saw too that the tide of popular feeling was setting against him. There was a great outcry about the taxes. The right of an assembly called by Leisler to impose them was stoutly denied. Presently the demands for the release of Bayard and Nicolls assumed a black and threatening aspect. Leisler was one day assaulted in the street, and but that he never ven-

24

tured out without a guard, he would probably have been killed.   The assailants were quickly mastered, and some twenty or more of them were secured in irons.   Leisler then issued a proclamation, that all who would not sign a declaration of fidelity to him, as representing King William, should be esteemed enemies to the king and be treated accordingly. Through marvellous strength of will Leisler was enabled to go on performing the most unjustifiable acts of cruelty, and at the same time succeeded in convincing his adherents that he was in the conscientious discharge of a pious duty.

Complaints were not wholly checked with all his caution.   An address to William and Mary, signed by the French and Dutch Dominies, several elders and deacons, and many leading citizens, was dated May 19, and sent across the water.   It stated that New York was ruled by the sword, "at the sole will of an insolent alien, assisted by those who formerly were not thought fit to bear the meanest office, several of whom can be proved guilty of enormous crimes; . . . . and they imprison at will, open letters, seize estates, plunder houses, and abuse the clergymen."

May 19.

The expedition against Canada was well conceived.   Leisler intended to command it himself, but was defeated by the Albany Convention. He then appointed Milborne commander-in-chief, which offended New England, where Milborne had a very undesirable reputation.   Winthrop was the choice of the army, and the influence was so strong in his favor that Leisler revoked his unfit appointment and issued a commission to the more popular general.   All things being ready, Winthrop marched with the Connecticut forces to Albany, accompanied by Livingston, who was acquainted with the route, and from his long experience in diplomacy with the Indians, one of the most valuable counselors in the whole matter.   Winthrop was a guest in Livingston's family during his stay at Albany.   Winthrop wrote to Treat that the whole design was "poorly contrived and in confusion."   Milborne was acting as commissary, and was self-sufficient and incompetent.   The quotas of men were not equal to those promised at the Congress.   After many days spent in frivolous disputes the troops went north as far as the head of Lake Champlain.   But word followed them that Milborne could furnish no more provisions from Albany, and while they were trying to construct canoes to cross the lake, small-pox broke out in the camp, and they were obliged to return to Albany.

July 14.

Aug. 7.

Aug. 15.

Leisler was furious at this failure, and hastened to Albany.   Milborne charged it all to the interference of Livingston and the imbecility of Winthrop.   Leisler went through the mere form of an exami-

Aug. 27.

nation, and placed Winthrop and his principal officers in irons. This so outraged the Connecticut soldiers and the Mohawks, that Leisler in alarm set his prisoners at liberty, but he ordered Winthrop to appear in New York and make his defense. Connecticut at once administered a cutting rebuke. Her governor wrote to Leisler : "If you are concerned, so are we, since the army is confederate ; and if you alone judge upon the general's and council of war's actions, it will infringe our liberty. A prison is not a *catholicon* for all state maladies, though so much used by you."

One masterly achievement blunted the edge of disappointment as Canada escaped her threatened danger. Captain John Schuyler, a young man of twenty-two, led a band of forty Englishmen and one hundred and twenty Indians to La Prairie, opposite Montreal, where every house and haystack was burned, one hundred and fifty head of cattle destroyed, six men killed, and nineteen prisoners taken. Thus was Schenectady avenged.

A great naval expedition from Boston, under the command of Sir William Phipps, sailed the 9th of August. It consisted of thirty vessels, the largest of which carried forty-four guns. But the men ^{Aug 9.} who had been sent over from England were newly raised and badly appointed, and, owing to the want of pilots and the autumn storms, it did not reach Quebec until the 8th of October. It was then winter, or nearly, the expedition encountered a long list of disasters, and returned with heavy losses and without spoil. During the summer and early autumn, however, Leisler's vessels had been on privateering voyages, and brought into New York several French prizes.

The Assembly did not meet in September, owing to Leisler's absence in Albany. He accordingly issued writs, summoning it at a later day. When it came together it enacted a law requiring all per- ^{Sept. 18.} sons who had left the province to return within three weeks from the time of its publication, under pain of being "esteemed disobedient ^{Oct. 2.} to the government." Another law levied a new tax for the support of the garrison in the fort. A third law declared that any ^{Oct. 4.} person refusing to accept a civil or military commission from Leisler should be fined seventy-five pounds ; and that any one leaving Albany or Ulster without permission from Leisler should be fined one hundred pounds ; and that all persons who had left those counties must return within fourteen days, "at their utmost perils." It would be difficult to find in the annals of legislation more despotic enactments.

New Rochelle was founded that summer by a colony of French Huguenots. They purchased the land of Leisler, who had bought it of Mr. Pell. They were called upon almost immediately to pay taxes. They resented such a measure, as it was the first year of their sojourn upon the property, and sent petitions to Whitehall to be relieved from such insufferable duties.

The people of Queens County declared against the government of Leisler; and Milborne, who had been withdrawn from Albany, was sent to subdue "with violence all such as were refractory." Edsall and Williams were commissioned to assist him in searching houses and vessels and in securing suspected persons. Dominie Varick of Flatbush was arrested and imprisoned for too much freedom of speech. An attempt was made to imprison Dominie Dellius of Albany, for praying for the crown and not for the King of England, but he escaped to Boston. Dominie Selyns offered bail for Dominie Varick, and was grossly abused. Dominies Perret and Daillé, the French clergymen, were threatened for withholding their approval of these high-handed proceedings.

Oct. 20.   The last letter which Leisler wrote to the king was dated October 20, 1690. He charged the failure of the Canadian campaign to the perfidy of New England, the treachery of Livingston, and the cowardice of Winthrop. Not far from the same date the aggrieved

Nov. 7.   inhabitants of Hempstead, Jamaica, Flushing, and Newtown, met and wrote to the king's Secretary of State. They dwelt with bitter emphasis upon their oppressed condition, and upon the tyrannical acts of the "bold usurper," and his accomplices. They said Milborne, who was famous for nothing but infamy, had in "a barbarous and inhuman manner plundered houses, stripped women of their apparel, and sequestered estates." They begged of the king "to break this heavy yoke of worse than Egyptian bondage," and said the crimes which Leisler had committed would force him to take shelter under Catiline's maxim, "the ills that I have done cannot be safe but by attempting greater."

1691.   The new year dawned gloomily. The rising wrath of the people of the metropolis was held in check by the fort. They dared say, however, that much of the plunder which had been obtained from houses, shops, cellars, and vessels was shipped to the West Indies and elsewhere and sold at a high price. The most extreme measures were resorted to for the collection of taxes; even Leisler's friends were aghast at his hot-headed and rancorous persecutions. But they could not hinder them. He was deaf and blind to the common dictates of humanity, and heeded no advice, save that which was in harmony with his own severe notions. It is probable that fear had much to do with his conduct, as he saw no other way to hold the chair of state but by mere brutal force. Milborne insinuated himself into the good graces of Leisler's family, and kept their feelings lashed into fever-heat by declaiming against the aristocrats. He came every day with some new and dismal skeleton, which was to alienate them more effectually from their relatives and friends. He was always glowering, and how he came to win the affections of the gentle, fair-haired, blue-eyed Mary Leisler must always remain a mystery. They were married in the early part of the year, and all the circumstances in connection with the wedding were of a depressing instead of a joyous character. Dominie Selyns, who had been their pastor for a long series of years, and who married Catharine Leisler to Robert Walters in 1685, was not invited on this occasion. A few friends only, and not those who had formerly been most welcome in the household, were present; and there was heaviness in the air, and little light in the sunshine. That very evening came letters from Boston to Leisler, counseling him "to temper justice with moderation and mercy, since the king's own settlement of the matter was so near." Governor Sloughter was indeed upon the water and might arrive at any moment. But the very dread of his coming seems to have made Leisler more hard and implacable.

William had been brought to a sense of the condition of New York through the addresses and petitions which claimed his attention. The frigate *Archangel* and three smaller vessels were fitted, after much delay, to convey Sloughter to his government. Richard Ingoldsby, who had just returned from victorious service under William in Ireland, was commissioned lieutenant-governor. Two companies of soldiers accompanied these officers to America.

William was no less fond of sovereignty than James, but he took broader views, and was much the more politic of the two. He ordained a government for New York which continued substantially in operation for nearly a century. It consisted of a governor and council appointed by the crown, and an assembly elected by a majority of the freeholders in the several counties of the province. In their mimic sphere these authorities shadowed the king, lords, and commons of England. Sloughter's commission was in form like the one James gave Dongan and Andros, with the exception of the permitted Assembly. In case of the governor's death or absence, his duties were to be executed by the commander-in-chief, if the king should appoint one, or by "the first counselor," who was to act as "President." William's instructions were similar to those of James to his governors. The former order respecting the Church of England was renewed, by which the Bishop of London was to have ecclesiastical jurisdiction in New York. Liberty of conscience, which James had granted to all peaceable inhabitants, was restricted by William to all such persons "except papists." The liberty of printing was limited in the same language used by James.

William honorably discharged Andros and his fellow-prisoners, (who had been sent from Boston), finding no just cause of complaint against them. He also showed his appreciation of the former officers of the colonial government by appointing Frederick Philipse, Stephanus Van Cortlandt, Nicholas Bayard, William Smith, Gabriel Minvielle, Chidley Brooke, William Nicolls, Nicholas De Meyer, Francis Rombouts, Thomas Willett, William Pinhorne, and John Haines, as counselors to the new governor. Joseph Dudley of Massachusetts was subsequently added to this council, and also made chief justice of the province. James Grahame was appointed recorder and attorney-general.

The name of Leisler was not mentioned, and the sting was destined to be incurable. All the papers which had been received from Leisler, and the petitions from the inhabitants, were referred by the king and his Privy Council to Sloughter, with orders to examine strictly and impartially into the case, and return a true and perfect account.

Jan. 29. The fleet was a long time on the ocean. The vessels separated in a storm, and three, under the command of Ingoldsby, were the first to reach New York. They were at once visited by Philipse, Van Cortlandt, and several other gentlemen, who, impatient of delay, urged Ingoldsby to land and take possession of the fort. He accordingly prepared to do so, and sent a message to Leisler demanding the citadel for the king's soldiers and their stores. But Ingoldsby was only commissioned to obey Sloughter, and of this technical dilemma Leisler took advantage. He refused to yield the fort unless Ingoldsby should produce written orders from the king or governor. He sent Milborne, accompanied by Mayor De Lanoy, to the vessel to inspect Ingoldsby's documents, and to offer the City Hall for the use of the king's forces. Ingoldsby was indig-
Jan. 30. nant ; he knew that William had never recognized Leisler's authority, and in high temper he issued a mandate to Captain Samuel Moore of Long Island for aid against the " rebels " who opposed the king.
Jan. 31. Leisler issued a " protest," and a call to the neighboring militia to assist him in enforcing orders.
Feb. 2. A day or two passed, when Ingoldsby, learning that " malicious rumors " were afloat concerning his movements, issued a proclamation that he had not come to disturb but to protect the people. The
Feb. 3. next day Leisler proclaimed that he was ready to obey Sloughter when he should arrive, but forbade all persons from obeying Ingoldsby, who had no orders. It was not long before Ingoldsby was well assured that the current of popular favor was in his behalf; he therefore landed his troops with as much caution as if he had been making " a descent into the country of an enemy," and quartered them in the City Hall.

He then sent a message to Leisler with an order to release Bayard and Nicolls, who were named as counselors by the king. This was the roughest blow which had as yet descended upon the misguided man. "What!" he exclaimed, white and trembling with passion, "*those* **Feb. 14.** *popish dogs and rogues!*" The answer which was taken back to Ingoldsby was to the effect that they must remain confined "until his Majesty's further orders arrive."

Time moved on slowly. Where was the missing frigate, and Governor Sloughter? The soldiers on both sides were unruly. A story was circulated that Ingoldsby and his party were "papists" and disaffected persons fled from England, holding only forged commissions. Armed men and supplies of provisions were constantly arriving at the fort. Leisler forbade the king's soldiers from going the rounds, and issued voluminous threats. The city was in a great tumult. Six of the counselors named in Sloughter's commission met and tried to straighten matters. They finally issued a call for the neighboring militia, to prevent any **March 4.** "outrageous and hostile proceedings" on the part of Leisler. Leisler replied with a proclamation, declaring that he was constrained to take up arms in defense of "*their Majesties' supremacy*," and denounced the illegal proceedings of the king's own officers. He also wrote a flatteringly worded letter to Governor Sloughter, who, it was supposed, had stopped at Bermuda, expressing the hope that "his Excellency" might speedily arrive.

Matthew Clarkson, the new secretary, who had come on the vessel with Ingoldsby, wrote, by request of the counselors, to the gov- **March 11.** ernment of Connecticut for advice. A response came quickly from Treat and Allyn, who advised that anything "tolerable and redressible" had better be borne from Leisler until the arrival of Sloughter. At the same time they wrote to Leisler, urging him to "so act and demean himself as not to violate the peace and safety of the country." Dr. Gerardus Beekman, who had been a stanch friend of Leisler through his entire rule, was alarmed at the course the latter was pursuing, and foresaw bloodshed; he assembled the people of King's and Queen's Counties, who framed a peace address, and he took it upon himself to confer personally with Leisler and attempt to dissuade him from such "base and imprudent proceedings."

It was of no use. Leisler was obtusely stubborn. He prepared **March 16.** a long declaration against Ingoldsby and the counselors, and ordered them to disband their forces, — which they had collected to the number of several hundred, — otherwise they would be pursued and destroyed. He demanded an answer within two hours. It came; they said **March 17.** they wished to preserve the peace, and whoever should attack them would be "public enemies to the Crown of England." It would seem as if the judgment of Leisler was wholly unbalanced just at this crisis. He probably acted under the most intense excitement. He had not the slightest intention of disobeying his royal master, and yet he

placed himself in the direct attitude of rebellion. Within half an hour after he received Ingoldsby's temperate message he fired one of the guns of the fort at the king's troops as they stood on parade. This was followed by several shots at a house where some of them lodged. Several were wounded, and two killed, one of whom was an old soldier, Josiah Bowne. Consternation spread through the city. The guns of the fort were answered, but, safely entrenched behind the breastworks, Leisler's party did not suffer. Leisler ordered the

Beekman Arms.

block-house at Smit's Vlye to support the fire from the fort. The commander, Brasher, seeing Ingoldsby's soldiers preparing to attack him, went to the fort for further orders, and was imprisoned for not firing at once. In his absence the burgher-guard at the block-house laid down their arms and went to their houses.

This defection disheartened Leisler. The next day he fired a few more shots, which did no harm. Ingoldsby held his men on the defen-

March 18. sive, expecting a sally from the fort at any moment. To distinguish his men from those attached to Leisler he directed them to wear white bands on their left arms.

At this distressing moment word came that the *Archangel*, with the

March 19. governor on board, had anchored just below the Narrows. She had been nearly wrecked on the Bermuda rocks, and detained for repairs. The counselors hastened in a small boat to welcome the long-expected and much-desired commander-in-chief. As soon as he learned the state of affairs, he came at once to the city in the ship's pinnace. It was evening, but he proceeded to the City Hall, the bell was rung, and his commission read before a large assemblage. The shouts of joy and the noisy uproar made Leisler tremble. Sloughter took the oath of office, as did also the counselors who were present. Notwithstanding the lateness of the hour (it was eleven o'clock), Ingoldsby was sent with his troops to demand entrance to the fort. Leisler refused, but sent Stoll to Sloughter for "orders under the king's own hand directed to himself." Stoll with coarse effrontery expressed his gratification that "Governor

Sloughter was the same man whom he had seen in England," and received the quick and tart reply : " Yes, I have been seen in England, and intend now to be seen in New York." No further notice was taken of Stoll. Ingoldsby was sent back to the fort to order Leisler, and such as were called his council, to report themselves at the City Hall, and to release Bayard and Nicolls immediately from their confinement. Presently Ingoldsby returned, accompanied by Milborne and Mayor De Lanoy. Leisler said the fort could not be surrendered in the night-time according to military rules, and had sent the two last-named gentlemen to explain. They were not allowed to speak at all, but were committed to the guards. Ingoldsby was sent to the fort the third time with the same order, and was the third time " contemptuously " refused. It was now past midnight, and the governor directed the council to meet him early the next morning. And thus ended that eventful day.

The gentlemen assembled promptly on Friday morning at the City Hall. Leisler had prepared an apologetic letter, tendering the fort and government in the best English he could use, promising ^{March 20.} to give " an exact account of all his actions and conduct." His egotism on points which he did not clearly understand, not disloyalty, was what gave him the appearance of trying to capitulate. But Sloughter's plans were all matured before the document was received, and it was laid on the table unnoticed. He sent Ingoldsby to require the men in the fort to ground their arms and march out, promising pardon to all save Leisler and his council. The latter, having " been found in actual rebellion," were conducted to the City Hall, and committed to the guards. The great prison door was opened, and Bayard and Nicolls freed from their long confinement. They were brought to the City Hall, looking aged and emaciated ; they were hardly able to stand upon their feet. They took the oaths of office amid warm congratulations ; and a little later Leisler was conveyed to the same dungeon which they had occupied, and the chain which Bayard had worn was put upon his leg.

Sloughter at once took possession of the fort, which he named William Henry. He issued writs the same day for the election of representatives to an Assembly to meet on the 9th of April. He commissioned John Lawrence mayor of the city,[1] William Pinhorne recorder, and Thomas

---

[1] John Lawrence was seventy-two years of age, and few men of his time were held in higher esteem ; his letters evince remarkable energy and decision of character, and are evidently the production of a man of superior intellect and liberal education. His nephew, William Lawrence, was one of Leisler's council, a man already past middle life. Although so widely separated in their political views there was great confidence and affection existing between the uncle and nephew, and it was a painful position indeed when the one was appointed to the commission for trying the political offenders, and the other was one of those offenders.

Clarke coroner. Thomas Newton was made attorney-general of the province.

The following Sunday was the first time in months that the church-going community had breathed freely. The clergymen thanked God fervently for present blessings. Dominie Selyns preached from the twenty-seventh Psalm, his text being, " I had fainted unless I had believed to see the goodness of God in the land of the living." His sermon, penned through the fulness of joy at the turn events had taken, may have been a libel upon the Christian theory of mercy to a fallen foe, but it was the outpouring of a heart which had been sorely tried, and the reasonings of a spirit which had calmly reviewed the situation. It had its effect upon public opinion, and stimulated the demand which was everywhere rending the air for the punishment of the author of the wrongs which had been visited upon the community. Not a ray of pity for the mistakes of the humiliated Leisler seemed to penetrate the cell where he sat in a state of the most abject despondency.

March 22.

On Monday a committee was appointed to examine the prisoners. It consisted of Chief Justice Dudley, Van Cortlandt, and Brooke. They were committed for trial. Owing to certain recent transactions, Sloughter declined hearing the case, and ordered a special court of oyer and terminer. Dudley and Thomas Johnson were appointed judges in admiralty, together with Sir Robert Robinson, the former governor of Bermuda, Colonel William Smith, Mayor John Lawrence, Recorder Pinhorne, Captain Jasper Hicks of the frigate *Archangel*, Lieutenant-Governor Ingoldsby, John Younge, and Isaac Arnold. It was said that they gentlemen most capable of discerning the truth, and the least prejudiced against the prisoners. Bayard, Van Cortlandt, and Pinhorne were directed to prepare the evidence. William Nicolls, George Farewell, and James Emott were assigned as king's counsel, to assist Attorney-General Newton, who was then reputed the best lawyer in America.

March 23.

March 24.

The trial began March 30. The indictment found by the grand jury charged the prisoners with treason and murder, " for holding by force the king's fort against the king's governor after the publication of his commission, and after demand had been made in the king's name, and in the reducing of which lives had been lost." Eight of the prisoners pleaded " Not Guilty." Leisler and Milborne refused to plead until the court should decide whether the king's letter to Nicholson had or had not given Leisler authority to take upon himself the government. The court referred the question to Sloughter and his council, who declared

March 30.

that nothing whatever in the king's letter, or in any of the papers of the Privy Council which Sloughter had seen, could be understood or interpreted to contain any power and direction for Captain Jacob Leisler to assume control of the government of the province, and that such control could not be holden good in law.

The court announced this decision, but Leisler and Milborne still refused to plead, and appealed to the king. They were accordingly tried as mutes. After eight days the jury pronounced them guilty, together with Abraham Gouverneur, Dr. Gerardus Beekman, Johannes Vermilye, Thomas Williams, Myndert Coerten, and Abraham Brasher. De Lanoy and Edsall were acquitted. Chief Justice Dudley then proceeded to pronounce the sentence of death upon the eight condemned criminals, according to the barbarous English law then in full force.

The prisoners at once petitioned the governor for a reprieve until the king's pleasure should be known; and their petition was granted. Sloughter wrote to William: "Never greater villains lived, but I _{April 20.} am resolved to wait your pleasure if by any other means than hanging I can keep the country quiet." He also wrote: "I find these men against whom the depositions were sent, to be the principal and most loyal men of this place, whom Leisler and Milborne did fear and therefore grievously oppress. Many that followed Leisler were through ignorance put up to do what they did, and I believe if the chief ringleaders are made an example the whole country will be quieted, which otherwise will be hard to do." In a letter to the Plantation Committee, Sloughter wrote: "The loyal and best part of the country is very earnest for the execution of the prisoners. But if his Majesty will please grant his pardon for all except Jacob Leisler and Jacob Milborne, it will be a favor."

Sloughter investigated the various accusations as he was directed by the king. Those against Leisler, contained in the address of the people, he found "severally true." Those against Bayard and Nicolls, forwarded by Leisler, he pronounced of small consequence. Those gentlemen could prove that they had always been good Protestants, and only desired to continue the government in peace until orders should arrive from England.

The Assembly convened on the day appointed in a small coffee-house on Pearl Street. It was a proud era for New York, for it was the first popular representation under the direct authority of the _{April 9.} crown. James Graham was appointed speaker. He was a lawyer who had already attained distinction at the bar, and a man of great dignity, of fine presence, and a master of rhetoric. He was the second son of the Earl of Montrose, of Scotch notoriety, and in all his tastes and habits and methods of thought was a fair type of the ancient nobility of Great

Britain. The governor and Chief Justice Dudley each appeared, and made a speech. The latter was noted for legal acumen and sound principles. He had the appearance of a man whose body was at the mercy of a restless mind; he was tall, thin, pale, and wore the worn look which comes with constant study. He was afterwards a member of the British Parliament, lieutenant-governor of the Isle of Wight, and governor of Massachusetts (from 1702 to 1720). The members of the Assembly were not experts in legislation, but with Newton and Graham to draft their bills they accomplished no little business. They passed fourteen laws; one of the first was for settling the late disorders, and to provide against similar disturbances in the future. The old Court of Assizes was abolished, and a new Supreme Court, consisting of five judges, instituted in its stead. Dudley was to be chief justice, and Johnson, Smith, Van Cortlandt, and Pinhorne associate judges. A revenue for defraying the public expenses of the province was granted. But the law was limited to two years, which annoyed the succeeding governors, who wished revenue to be granted for longer periods. The Assembly was a thoroughly royalist body, and yet in language clear and forcible they asserted the right to a representative government, not as a consequence of royal favor, but as an English liberty inherent in the people.

A resolution was passed, unanimously, by the House, condemning Leisler's acts as illegal, arbitrary, mischievous, destructive, and rebellious, and charging the tragedy at Schenectady entirely to his account. This resolution was copied in full, signed by James Graham, Speaker, and sent to the governor, "that his Excellency might know that his acts had been approved."

Meanwhile petitions were coming in upon Sloughter and his council from every quarter. Dr. Gerardus Beekman prayed for pardon on the ground that he was only at the fort to persuade Leisler against inhumanly firing on the king's soldiers, and that he had very sick patients who needed his immediate attention. His wife, Magdalena Beekman, entreated in a most touching strain that better accommodations be given him in the prison until the king's pleasure should be known. She said that her husband had acted on the Committee of Safety only at the urgent request of the people of Long Island, and that he had had "true meaning and good intent"; but that he now "saw plainly that he had been misled for the want of a right understanding." William Beekman interceded for his son; and issued a government bond of £100 to Sloughter, as security for the use of certain property belonging to Dr. Gerardus before he was convicted of treason, and which in case of his non-pardon was forfeited to the crown.

Petitions from the families and friends of the other condemned prisoners were received in great numbers. One for the pardon of Leisler
was largely signed in Westchester and on Staten Island. But counter-
petitions were equally numerous, from those who had been wronged and
distressed, all praying that the ringleaders in the late administration
should be immediately executed. Many of the prominent and loyal
men declared that there was no security for life or fortune while such
" tyrants " were allowed to exist, for they might head an ignorant mob on
any occasion; they announced their intention of removing from the
province unless Leisler and Milborne, at least, were made to suffer the
extreme penalty of the law. Word came from Albany about the same
time that the Mohawks, disgusted with Leisler's mismanagement, were in
actual treaty with the French. It was imperative that the new governor
should quickly conciliate the savages, else the province would be lost.

Any estimate which can now be framed of the extent of the pressure
which was brought to bear upon Sloughter must necessarily be very inexact. He was a weak, avaricious, immoral man at the best; he was
also notoriously intemperate. But whether drunk or sober the facts of
the case remain the same. He was under the direct influence of men
who had suffered until human hate had well nigh exhausted every other
fountain of feeling. He was a guest in the house of Colonel Bayard.
Smith says, that " Sloughter was invited to a wedding-feast and when
overcome with wine was prevailed upon to sign the death-warrant,
and before he recovered his senses the prisoners were executed." This
statement, even if true in part, cannot be true as a whole, for the death-
warrant was signed on Thursday and the execution took place on Saturday.[1] It has been said that the three Dutch ministers constantly argued
for the administration of justice in the pulpit. It has been said that
ladies who had tears for highwaymen and housebreakers breathed nothing but vengeance, and earnestly pleaded with Sloughter to have com-
passion upon them, and upon the country, by removing forever the guilty
creatures. It has been said that large sums of money were offered the
needy governor to induce him to put his name to the fatal paper; and
that his own wife, from sheer covetousness, added her voice of entreaty
to the same effect.

Caution must be exercised in accepting such accounts as history,
penned as they were by violent partisans, and tinctured with the narrow-

---

[1] *Letter from Members of the Dutch Church in New York to the Classis of Amsterdam,*
October 21, 1698. *N. Y. Hist. Soc. Coll.* (1868), pp. 398 – 412. *Address of the New York
Legislative Assembly to Lord Bellamont,* May 15, 1699. *Governor Sloughter to Colonel Cod-
rington. Governor Sloughter to Mr. Blathwayt. Governor Sloughter to Lord Inchiquin.*

minded prejudice of that peculiar age. It appears that Sloughter hesitated through an imperfect apprehension that he should exceed his legal power by pronouncing death upon prisoners who had appealed to the king. He was finally led into the belief that this act would enable him to manage the Indians, for he had decided to go to Albany and meet the Mohawk sachems. At the meeting with his council May 14, the following was entered upon their records : —

" Present, His Excellency the Governor, Frederick Philipse, Nicholas Bayard, Stephanus Van Cortlandt, William Nicolls, and Gabriel Minvielle.

" Upon the clamor of the people daily coming to his Excellency relating to the execution of the prisoners condemned of treason, and having received the opinion of the greater part of the Representatives of the Assembly now convened, he was pleased to offer to the council his willingness to do what might be most proper for the quiet and peace of the country before he should go to Albany. And he demanded of the council their opinion whether the delay of the execution of justice might not prove dangerous at this conjuncture. Whereupon it was unanimously resolved, that for the satisfaction of the Indians, and the assertion of the government and authority, and the prevention of insurrections and disorders for the future, it is absolutely necessary that the sentence pronounced against the principal offenders be forthwith put in execution."

The next paragraph explains itself : —

COUNCIL-ROOM, May 16, 1691.

His Excellency having sent the minute of council of the 14th of May, referring to the execution of the principal criminals condemned of treason, to the House of Representatives to acquaint them of the resolve of this board, the same was returned underwritten in manner following : —

HOUSE OF REPRESENTATIVES FOR THE PROVINCE OF NEW YORK,
Die Veneris, May 15, P. M., 1691.

This House, according to their opinion given, do approve of what his Excellency and council have done.

By order of the House of Representatives,

JAMES GRAHAM, *Speaker.*

Thus the death-warrant was signed. Dominie Selyns was the messenger who was sent to break the terrible intelligence to the unhappy men. They petitioned Sloughter for a reprieve, but it was not granted. He respited all the sentence, however, save the hanging and the separation of the heads from the bodies.

The scenes within the cells were for the next few hours heart-rending. For all they had done, for all they had attempted to do, for their loyalty to the king, for their Christian zeal, only an ignominious death. Self-opinionated no longer, broken in spirit, overcome by the grief of his family and by unavailing regrets, Leisler humbled himself before his God and prepared for the end. As for Milborne, he never ceased his efforts to excite pity and clemency. Despair preyed upon his mind until he was almost a maniac.

Saturday dawned with a dark, northeast, melancholy rain-storm brooding over the city. The gallows was erected near the site of the old Tammany Hall. A ferocious rabble assembled to witness the execution; they said a grave under the gallows was too respectable a resting-place for the "black dogs"; they said they should have been tortured like Indians; and they hoped they might go to the place of wailing and gnashing of teeth. A strong guard of soldiers was esteemed necessary to prevent the prisoners from being torn in pieces when they should be led forth.

Dominie Selyns walked beside the doomed men and offered the last consolations of religion. Leisler made a short speech upon the scaffold. He said he knew that he had grievously erred in many ways, and asked pardon of God and of all those whom he had offended. He declared his loyalty to the king and queen, and prayed that all malice might be buried in his grave. He said he forgave the most implacable of his enemies, and begged his friends and relations to forget and forgive any injury done to him. He prayed for all in authority, and for his distressed and afflicted family, and requested charity and prayers for himself. Milborne spoke for a few moments in a pathetic strain, but, seeing Livingston in the crowd, he exclaimed, "You have caused my death. Before God's tribunal I will impeach you for the same." The sheriff asked Leisler if he was ready to die. He replied that he was, and that he did not fear death, for what he had done had been for the king and queen, the Protestant religion, and the good of the country. He then exclaimed, "I am ready!"

The drop fell. A wail of anguish rent the air, which for the moment drowned the gross ribaldry of those who regarded the scene with barbarous exultation. Women fainted, and sorrow-stricken mourners mingled their tears with the falling rain. It was a solemn and an ominous occasion, and it left its abiding mark upon New York history. Its effects are still with us. Better men have paid as dearly for their mistakes in all ages of the world, but Jacob Leisler and Jacob Milborne were the only two who were ever executed in New York for a political crime.

The event was variously judged. Candid jurists pronounced the whole proceeding perfectly lawful. "But," said others, "there were extenuating circumstances which were not allowed to appear at the trial." Concerning no public actor in colonial history has opinion more widely differed than in regard to Jacob Leisler. He has been held up as a champion of

Dutch democracy against English aristocracy, of Protestantism against Romanism, of republicanism against monarchism. It is evident, however, from a careful analysis of his official career, that there was no struggle in New York to call for championship in any of these directions. And his acts clearly negative all claim to democratic theories. He seized authority with honest intentions and with unquestionable belief in the plots his fancy created. He afterwards became infatuated with the novelty of the position, and his strong passions and feeble judgment led him into more unpardonable excesses than were ever committed by any of the governors placed over the colony by the Crown of England. And yet he was not a bad man, and his execution was a shocking blunder. He became a martyr in memory, not a convict, and his death was the stock of a party which for years, by its triumphs and its defeats, retarded seriously the prosperity of New York.

The outcry was at once raised that he had been murdered. " Barbarously murdered," wrote Dr. Mather to Chief Justice Dudley. " Revengefully sacrificed," wrote Jeremias Van Rensselaer to the Lords of Trade. The various accounts of the transaction produced a profound sensation in England. The touching appeals to the king from Mrs. Leisler and her children, and from the young widow of Milborne, that the estates of the deceased might be restored to their families, were carefully weighed. William declared in favor of the fairness of the trial, and the justness of the sentence, since they were not indicted for the part they had taken in the revolution, or in the subsequent violences, but simply for holding a fortress by arms against the legal governor, which in the judgment of law was levying war against the king. But he ordered their estates to be returned to their heirs, because the services of the fathers required some compensation.

This imperfect redress did not satisfy. The children and friends of Leisler persisted year after year until an act of Parliament reversed the attainder, which occurred in 1695.[1] It was almost entirely accomplished through the able Massachusetts agents; but it is said when the handsome, energetic young Jacob Leisler, Jr., appeared in England, and was favored in his suit by Lord Bellomont, that Robert Livingston, who was there at the time, and who was an intimate personal friend of the Earl, had several interviews with him and interested himself in recommending the subject, as well as young Leisler himself, to the notice of the Lords.

---

[1] Jacob Milborne, a son of the deceased by his first wife, was one of the petitioners named. It is recorded that Joanna Edsall, wife of Jacob Milborne, joined the Garden Street Dutch Church, November 29, 1688. She was the daughter of Samuel Edsall, and died, as is believed, during her husband's absence in Europe.

New York was now in a most critical condition, not only from internal faction but from foreign warfare. The French king was fully bent upon the conquest of a province which through the Five Nations had caused so

Portrait of Robert Livingston.
(From copy (of Gen. J. Watts de Peyster) of original painting in possession of Clermont Livingston.)

much bloodshed and desolation among his Canadian subjects. All the art of the French character was brought into requisition to win the savages to their standard. Sloughter arrived in Albany May 26. The Mohawks were there before him, and the meeting took place _{May 26.} the next day. The negotiations were managed by Mayor Schuyler and Robert Livingston, and were exceedingly interesting. Sloughter had brought presents from England, which were given to the Indians with much ceremony.[1] One of the Mohawk chiefs said that the late

---

[1] These presents were 1 doz. stockings, 6 shirts, 3 bags powder, 16 bars of lead, 30 gul strung wampum, 3 runlets rum, 3 rolls tobacco, and privately to the chiefs some coats of duffels. *Governor Sloughter's Answer to the Proposition of the Mohawk Sachems, Albany, May 26, 1691. New York Col. Doc., Vol. III. 771 – 781. Chalmers's Political Annals.*

disorders in the province had wellnigh confounded all their affairs, and that several of their white brethren had deserted Albany in the hour of danger, which must not happen again. Finally, in order to re-establish the confidence of the savages on a firm basis, it was decided that Mayor Schuyler should lead them on an aggressive campaign into Canada, and preparations were immediately made. Schuyler left Albany on the

June 21. 21st of June with four hundred men, five sixths of whom were Indians, and plunged into the dense forests to the north. He crossed Lake Champlain, and pushed directly into the enemy's country. With rapid strides he soon reached La Prairie, and surprised the governor of Montreal, who was encamped with a large force. Owing to the prowess of the Mohawks, Schuyler obliged his gallant opponents to retire into their fort, which he assaulted, though with a success hardly equal to his vigorous efforts. Apprehending danger of being cut off in his retreat, he prudently retired and conducted his warriors in triumph to Albany. His exploit stimulated the Iroquois, who continued their attacks upon the French unaided, and nobly protected New York while her exhausted resources enabled her to maintain only feeble frontier garrisons.

June 27. Sloughter remained in Albany until Schuyler's departure and then returned to New York. He found a multitude of duties awaiting him, and entered upon their performance at once. But his

July 21. career was soon checked. He was taken suddenly ill on the 21st of July, and died on the morning of the 23d. His symptoms were

July 21. of such a nature that the physician suspected he had been poisoned. A negro servant who had been seen to put something in his coffee at the table just before his attack was accused and examined, and in great terror called upon Heaven to witness that it was only sugar. A post-mortem investigation resulted in the opinion that he had died from natural causes, and the grateful negro was exonerated from suspicion. His body was placed in the Stuyvesant vault by permission of the family, next to that of the honored Dutch governor.

Chief Justice Dudley, to whom as president of the council the government would have fallen in this emergency, was in Curaçoa. In consequence, the council met two days after the governor's death, and unanimously declared Ingoldsby commander-in-chief, until the king's pleasure should be known.

It was not long before information reached New York that the French had been reinforced and were planning to attack Albany. Schuyler had not returned. It was next to impossible to raise more men and money. Therefore Ingoldsby and the council applied to New England for aid, which was "flatly denied." In this extremity they wrote to the Lords of Trade, begging earnestly for warlike stores. In explaining the condition of New York, they said "it had never ceased to groan under its insupportable pressures since its miserable union with Boston." They even charged all the recent calamities upon Boston. "New York had always been signal for her good affection to monarchy until poisoned with the seditions and anti-monarchial principles of Boston."

Ingoldsby hurried to Albany and conferred with some of the Mohawk sachems. He gave them presents, and they, more friendly than the New England people, continued their defensive warfare.

The Assembly met in September and made what appropriations seemed practicable. Schuyler had by that time returned, and the prospect was brighter. The city elections were comparatively quiet. The aldermen chosen were, William Beekman and Alexander Wilson for the East Ward, William Merritt and Thomas Clarke for the Dock Ward, John Merritt and Garret Dow for the Out Ward, Johannes Kip and Teunis De Kay for the North Ward, Robert Darkins and Peter King for the West Ward, and Brandt Schuyler and Stephen De Lancey for the South Ward.

Brandt Schuyler, although he took a less active part in public life than his brother Peter, was universally respected. In personal appearance he bore a striking resemblance to his sister Gertrude, Mrs. Van Cortlandt. His wife was Cornelia, the sister of Stephanus Van Cortlandt, hence the two families were doubly related, and lived on terms of great social intimacy.

Stephen, or, as he was more commonly known, Etienne De Lancey, was the son of a French nobleman of Caen in Normandy. He was the ancestor of all of that honorable name in this country. He brought with him many evidences of wealth and culture. He prosecuted a foreign trade, chiefly to Africa, and acquired a large fortune. His place of business was on Pearl Street; nine years later he married Ann, the daughter of Stephanus Van Cortlandt.

CHAPTER XXI.

1691 – 1701.

ABRAHAM DE PEYSTER.

ABRAHAM DE PEYSTER. — EFFECTS OF THE REVOLUTION. — THE TWO HOSTILE FACTIONS. — THE GARDEN STREET CHURCH. — ORIGIN OF WATER STREET. — PUBLIC PAUPERS. — CITY LEGISLATION. — CONDITION OF THE PROVINCE. — THE CORPORATION DINNER. — GOVERNOR FLETCHER. — FLETCHER STUDYING THE INDIANS. — THE GIFT OF A GOLD CUP. — FLETCHER'S DIFFICULTIES. — BOSTON MEDDLING. — CALEB HEATHCOTE. — A CURIOUS ROMANCE. — THE ASSEMBLY STIFF-NECKED. — FLETCHER IN TEMPER. — THE FIRST PRINTING IN NEW YORK. — SIR WILLIAM PHIPPS. — OFFICIAL STEALING. — LIVINGSTON IN ENGLAND. — YOUNG LEISLER AT WILLIAM'S COURT. — WRANGLING IN THE ASSEMBLY. — ACCUSATIONS AND COUNTER-ACCUSATIONS. — FLETCHER'S SPEECH. — SHOCKING BRUTALITIES. — FLETCHER'S CHARACTER ON TRIAL. — LIVINGSTON CRITICISED BY FLETCHER. — DE PEYSTER'S NEW HOUSE. — DE PEYSTER'S DESCENDANTS. — MILLER'S DESCRIPTION OF NEW YORK. — DOMINIE SELYNS'S PIRACY. — MRS. FLETCHER AND HER DAUGHTERS. — CAPTAIN KIDD. — THE EXPEDITION AGAINST PIRACY. — KIDD THE PRINCE OF PIRATES. — THE REPEAL OF BOLTING AND BAKING ACTS. — FIRST OPENING OF NASSAU STREET. — THE FIRST LIGHTING OF THE CITY. — THE FIRST NIGHT-WATCH. — THE EARL OF BELLOMONT. — BELLOMONT'S REFORMS. — BELLOMONT'S COLLISION WITH THE MERCHANTS. — THE ACTS OF TRADE. — THE PEACE OF RYSWICK. — THE LANDED ESTATES ATTACKED. — JAMES GRAHAM. — DOMINIE DELLIUS. — BELLOMONT'S MORTIFICATIONS. — THE DUTCH CHURCH. — BELLOMONT IN BOSTON. — THE BOARD OF TRADE. — DEATHS OF GRAHAM, VAN CORTLANDT, AND BELLOMONT.

A BRAHAM DE PEYSTER was appointed mayor of the city. Although he had attached himself to Leisler in the early part of the Revolution, he had been involved in none of the later indiscretions, and it was predicted that he would be a most effective agent in the way of restoring public tranquillity. He was a native of the city, interested in its growth and prosperity, and knew the temper of its people. He was also personally popular. He was about thirty-four years of age, with a frank, winning face, fine presence, and great polish and elegance of manners. His character was irreproachable, and his political judgment sound. He had married about seven years before, while on a visit to Holland, his cousin Catharine De Peyster. His father, Johannes De Peyster, had some time since died, but his

1691. **October.**

mother was living in the old homestead. His three brothers, Isaac, Johannes, and Cornelis, each acquired a large estate for the period, and each filled from time to time responsible positions in the city government. Isaac was a member of the Assembly for several years. Johannes, who

Portrait of Col. Abraham De Peyster.

(From original painting in possession of Hon. Frederic de Peyster, President of New York Historical Society.)

was reputed the handsomest man of his day, was mayor of the city in 1698 – 99, and was succeeded by David Provoost, who was the husband of their only sister Maria. This lady's daughter by a former husband became the wife of the celebrated James Alexander, and mother of Lord Stirling.

When De Peyster first robed himself in the mayor's gown and entered upon his judicial duties, he was harassed as few mayors have ever been either before or since his time. The Revolution had disturbed every man's private affairs. Property had been seized for taxes, neighbors were suing each other for debts and damages, and insubordination against the city laws was of daily occurrence. The virulence with which men complained of each other indicated the wells of bitterness beneath the surface of society, and foreshadowed the coming storms in the political horizon. A story was circulated that Leisler had never paid the soldiers whom he had taken upon himself to raise. This De Peyster promptly denied, as he had

personal knowledge of its falsity.   To say Leisler was dishonest in pecuniary matters was simply monstrous, for he had expended large sums of
his own money to keep the government from bankruptcy.   De Peyster did
not hold Leisler blameless; he had eschewed all connection with the
man as soon as he found him unpersuadable and infatuated beyond reason and justice (according to his private opinion), but he was lenient
towards him in his heart, and thought he had been harshly treated
at the last.

Two hostile factions were each trying to maintain untenable grounds,
and each trying to hoodwink and overreach the other.   The anti-revolu-
tionists were dominant, and manifested a constant disposition to retaliate
upon all such as had supported Leisler.   The Act of the Assembly promising pardon to every one not under actual sentence of death was coldly
received.   The families and friends of the six condemned prisoners were
making herculean efforts for their release, and the sufferers were full of
concessions and promises.   But both parties were smarting from wounds
for which there was no healing balm, and which were to culminate finally
in great incurable ulcers.

De Peyster projected city improvements with a lavish hand.   He donated a tract of land at " Smits Vlye " to the corporation, and presently
an act was published for the sale of a few of the lots, on condition that
the buyers help build wharves that were very much needed; one fronting King Street, thirty feet wide, and one on either side of Mrs. Van
Clyffe's slip, of about the same dimensions.   The site of the old Fly Market was a part of this donation.   A few years later De Peyster presented
to the corporation the site of the old City Hall where Washington was
inaugurated.

In December the subject of building a new Dutch church was
Dec. 19. again agitated.   There were a number of families who objected to
worshiping in the one in the fort, in any event, and, besides, that edifice was
getting old, and it was much too small.   A lot in the midst of a beautiful
and highly cultivated garden belonging to Mrs. Dominie Drisius was deemed
sufficiently up-town.   It fronted on a picturesque little lane called " Garden Alley," which in course of time and progress became Garden Street,
and is now Exchange Place.   The work was pushed forward at once, and
the building completed in 1693.   The style of it was an oblong square,
with three sides of an octagon on the east side.   It had a brick steeple in
front, resting on a large square foundation, which admitted room above
the entry for an apartment in which the consistory could hold their meetings.   The windows were small panes of glass set in lead, and burnt curiously into the glass were the coats-of-arms of the chief families who

constituted the church and congregation. There were also from time to time, subsequently, many painted coats-of-arms hung upon the walls. The pulpit, bell, and several escutcheons were from the church in the fort. This bell was placed in a church erected in 1807 on the spot where the

Portrait of Mrs. Col Abraham De Peyster.
(From original painting in possession of Hon. Frederic de Peyster, President of New York Historical Society.)

Garden Street Church stood. Some thought the bell too small, but Judge Benson, who was one of the elders at the time, said the bell was the first ever brought to the city, and that its silver tones had been the delight of the native Indians. For its antiquity, if for no other reason, it ought not to be substituted for modern castings. It consequently remained in its place, and shared the fate of the church in the great fire of 1835. A silver baptismal basin was procured in 1694, on which was engraved a sentence written by Dominie Selyns, indicating the significance of the baptismal rites. The basin cost "twenty silver ducats"; it is a curious relic, preserved and in use in Dr. Rogers's church on Fifth Avenue, corner of Twenty-First Street, in which the corporate title of the first Dutch church in New York is handed along.

The corporation assumed to own the land under water, and in order to fill in the shore along the East River lots were sold all the way from the City Hall to Fulton Street; hence the origin of Water **1692.** Street. These lots were chiefly purchased by merchants, who paid an average price of twenty dollars each; one of the terms of purchase re-

26

quired the buyer to cover the entire front of his lot with a building of brick or stone not less than two stories high. It was during this year (1692) that Pine, Cedar, and the neighboring streets were laid out through the old " Damen Farm " which was bounded north by Maiden Lane. The " Damen Farm " is described among the deeds as " Clover Wayters," — Clover Pastures. Maiden Lane was called " Maagde paetje " — Virgin's Path — from the fact that it was a resort for washerwomen, because of a little stream of spring water which ran through the valley at that point.

The investigation of patents caused an endless amount of wrangling. An interesting question came up as to the ownership of the vacant space in Hanover Square. It was found to be covered by a title of Govert Loockermans, and was claimed by his heirs. The claimants determined to build there, and as such a proceeding would shut off the fine water-view from a number of handsome dwellings in the neighborhood, great efforts were put forth to keep the property out of their hands. Johannes Van Brugh, who lived on the north side of the square, was one of the witnesses for the city in the suit. He remembered the spot to have been in common for forty-six years, and his wife, who was a daughter of Dominie Bogardus, remembered as far back as 1637.

It was through the suggestion of Mayor De Peyster that the city first assumed the support of public paupers. Each alderman was ordered to make a return of the poor in his ward. A poor-house was not then provided, but the paupers were recommended as objects of charity, and granted a small pittance of the public money. About the same time the corporation erected in front of the City Hall, on the river shore, a pillory, cage, whipping-post, and ducking-stool, as a perpetual terror to evil-doers. Vagrants, thieves, slanderers and truant-children were to be there exposed for public show, or to receive such chastisement as their offenses warranted. The ducking-stool was for the special punishment of excess or freedom of speech. It was a purely English invention. It had been used for a long period throughout the British Empire. This was the first introduction of it into New York. Its need must have been startlingly apparent twenty-two years before, when the Lutheran minister, having been prosecuted for striking a woman, pleaded in defense that *she provoked him to it by scolding.*

Street-cleaning was one of the subjects of city legislation this year. A law was passed requiring every householder to keep the street clean in front of his own door ; and another requiring the street surveyor to cause all " stramonium and other poisonous weeds rooted up within the city."

If the affairs of the province had been as ably managed as those of the city, it would have been fortunate. But Ingoldsby was illogical, inexact, and blundering. He was brave in war, and had some talent for administration, but he did not know his own mind. His interest was to stand well with the council, and his irritable and imperious nature was constantly impelling him to quarrel with them. His spleen was excited one day by a dry answer from Van Cortlandt; the next, by a suggestion from some other of the gentlemen. He kept actively at work, but accomplished little or nothing. The French worried the government into a continual state of unrest. The funds were wanting to satisfy the grumbling demands of the colonists for protection. It was finally determined to make another appeal to the king.

Matthew Clarkson drew up an address, which was signed by Ingoldsby, Philipse, Van Cortlandt, Bayard, Minvielle, Nicolls, and Pinhorne, setting forth the necessities of New York with great precision, and imploring supplies to carry on the war. It contained a carefully worded picture of the condition of the province, and of its sources of income, and argued the advantage of adding to it Connecticut, New Jersey, and Pennsylvania, in order to give it strength to defend itself. It was such a document as could not be passed by with inattention. It said, " The middle of Long Island is altogether barren. The west end is chiefly employed in tillage and supplies the traffic of New York. The east end is settled by New England people, and their improvements are mostly in pasturage and whaling. Despite our strict laws their industry is often carried to Boston. Esopus has about three thousand acres of manurable land, all the rest being hills and mountains not possible to be cultivated. The chief dependence of Albany is the traffic of the Indians. New York City is situated upon a barren island, with nothing to support it but trade which comes chiefly from bread and flour sent to the West Indies. All the rest of the province except Westchester, Staten Island, and Martha's Vineyard, consists of barren mountains not improvable by human industry." It was read by King William ; it was read by Queen Mary ; it was read by the Privy Council.

The result was the appointment of a governor for New York with broad instructions. The choice fell upon Colonel Benjamin Fletcher, a soldier of fortune, and an energetic officer. He was made thoroughly acquainted with the distresses of his government, and before sailing solicited presents for the Indians, warlike stores, and two additional companies of soldiers. It was all granted with an alacrity equal to the importance of his requests. In order to restore that internal peace which the inconsiderate folly of Leisler had destroyed, a general pardon was granted, and all prosecutions growing out of the late disorders prudently discharged.

The frigate which bore him to New York was to remain for the protection of its coasts. He arrived August 29, and was cordially

Aug. 29.

welcomed. His commission was formally published the next

Aug. 30.

morning. The same counselors were continued, with the addition of Peter Schuyler and Richard Townley, and they all took the customary oaths. Dudley, however, was still absent, and Colonel William Smith was appointed chief justice in his place. Fletcher was ordered to require all the English colonies to furnish their quota of men and money for the general defense; but he was never able to enforce such an order, and all his authority outside of New York was openly disputed, giving him repeated and unnecessary mortifications.

The city corporation tendered the new chief magistrate a dinner, which cost £ 20. Mayor De Peyster presided, and made a happily worded speech on the occasion. He requested Fletcher to use his influence with the king to obtain a confirmation of the city charter, and a continuation of the bolting and baking monopoly, which had become of great value to New York. Vigorous efforts were being made in the inland towns to break it up, and although various laws had been passed to prevent its infringement, the mayor and aldermen were apprehensive of its ultimate destruction. A few days later the corporation addressed a letter to Fletcher on the same subject, and with great earnestness entreated him "to take the afflicted city into favorable consideration, and be come its benefactor by saving it the monopoly without which it must perish."

Governor Fletcher was a stout, florid man, of easy address, showy and pretentious. He rolled through the streets in a carriage drawn by six horses. His wife and daughters were stylish ladies, who followed the latest European fashions. His servants wore handsome livery and were well drilled. He was fond of society, and never happier than when performing acts of hospitality. He was a great lover of high living and drank wine daily, but not to excess. It was a common practice during his administration for politicians and gentlemen concerned with him in the government, to drop in at their own convenience, without formal invitation, and dine at his well-filled table. He was not a man of extensive learning, but his mind was largely stocked with ideas, the result of acute observation. He talked rapidly and to the point, and his arguments always carried weight. He had a hot, hasty temper, but it was combined with so much decision of character that it only fitted him the more perfectly for a military commander, in which capacity he was successful; there was, however, about him an arrogance not so well adapted to the chair of state. He stumbled into errors and extravagances, and raised up against himself powerful foes. He was devoutly religious, and had the bell rung twice every day for prayers in his household. He exerted himself to found churches, and to pave the way for the extension of the gospel. With his rule commenced a distinct era in the civil and religious history of New York.

From the day of his arrival he was never idle, and to all outward appearances seldom weary. His first work was to study into the affairs of the Indians. They must not be allowed to go over to the French. He repaired to Albany and placed himself under the tuition of Mayor Schuyler. He was for weeks a guest in the Schuyler mansion. He made a trip with Schuyler into the Mohawk country, and was entertained by the warriors in their famous castles. He pried into the character, habits, and strength of these natives of the wilderness. He even learned somewhat of their language. In his subsequent transactions with them. his success was so marked that it was spoken of as his distinguishing excellence by those who would not give him credit for any other good thing.

Much was due to his instructor. Schuyler enjoyed the well-earned reputation in Europe as well as America of being the most consummate diplomat of his time. He had secured the undying friendship of the Iroquois, and his advice and suggestions carried with them the power of law. Colden says that he was " only a country farmer, who had on some occasions given proof of courage, but that he was in no way distinguished by abilities either natural or acquired."[1] The records show, nevertheless, that he possessed a depth of understanding that was always in advance of Indian instinct and treachery, with no inconsiderable fund of strength in reserve. And his exhibition of military skill on every occasion where there was a clash of arms seems fully to have justified the Indian sobriquet of the " Great Brave White Chief."

Fletcher placed Ingoldsby in command of the soldiers at Albany. Upon his return to New York he was waited upon by Mayor De **1693.** Peyster and the aldermen of the city, and presented with a gold cup which cost the corporation £ 100. Such presentations were then very much in vogue among all corporate bodies in Europe.

Presently news reached Fletcher that the vigorous old Count Frontenac had started from Montreal with an army of six or seven **Jan. 15.** hundred French and Indians, supplied with everything necessary for a winter's campaign, intending to descend upon the Five Nations. New York

---

[1] *Cadwallader Colden's Letters to his Son. N. Y. Hist. Soc. Coll.* (1868).

was alarmingly insecure, and the governor and the mayor went unitedly into the work of fortifications.   One cold snowy winter evening
Feb. 12. about ten o'clock an express reached Fletcher to the effect that the French were fighting the Iroquois in the neighborhood of Schenectady, and that Schuyler had started with a small force from Albany to the relief of the allied Indians.   Drums at once beat for volunteers, and within forty-eight hours Fletcher with three hundred men was *en route* for the scene of warfare.   He reached Schenectady on the 17th,
Feb. 17. and found that the French had been defeated and driven towards Canada with serious loss.   They were pursued until their pursuers were so distressed for provisions that they fed upon the dead bodies of the enemy.   The French were reduced to that degree of starvation before they got home that they ate their shoes.

The governor's promptness and the extraordinary circumstance of free navigation of the Hudson River in the month of February caused the Indians to regard him as a wonderful warrior, and they gave him the name of " Cayenguirago," — the Great Swift Arrow.   The Indians had lost their castles and suffered severely.   Fletcher did what he could to comfort them, assisted them to build wigwams, and furnished them with provisions.   The sachems told him that the English did not provide them with warlike stores as the French did their Indian friends, and that they could not continue the war unless they were better sustained.   They said, too, that if all the colonies would join in good earnest Canada might be reduced.

Fletcher returned to New York, leaving the frontiers distracted and comparatively defenseless.   The Assembly soon after convened, and voted him the thanks of the House for his energetic proceedings.   The defense of the province, which might be so easily invaded, was the first and most important subject for discussion.   Six hundred pounds for one year's pay of three hundred volunteers was granted.   Then Fletcher called attention to the establishment of the Church of England, according to the king's orders.   The indifference of the House in regard to what he had said on a former occasion angered him, and he remarked with much asperity :
" Gentlemen, the first thing I recommended to you at our last meeting was to provide for a ministry, and nothing is yet done.   You are all big with the privileges of Englishmen and Magna Charta, which is your right, and the same law provides for the religion of the Church of England.   As you have postponed it this session, I trust you will take hold of it at the next meeting and do something toward it effectually."

The two factions which had derived their existence from the Revolution would not agree upon anything.   Whenever Fletcher attempted to reconcile feuds, he found neither adversary inclined to be content with less than the other's neck. He was, indeed, as he expressed himself, ruler over "a divided, contentious, and impoverished people." And things grew worse instead of better. Some of his counselors, having suffered unjustly themselves, relentlessly persecuted those who had wronged them under the authority of Leisler's commissions. The Leislerians, on the other hand, accused the governor of being the tool of the aristocrats, and took exception to all his measures. Jacob Leisler, Jr., was now at the court of William and Mary, directing all his energies to the task of removing the stain of treason from his father's memory. He was aided by the depositions of many persons in New York, and his mother and six sisters were sending

Garden Street Dutch Church, built in 1693.

petition after petition to the queen. It occasioned continual commotion. The six prisoners in the fort, under sentence of death, appealed to Fletcher, immediately upon his arrival, for release from their "miserable confinement." He sent for Dr. Gerardus Beekman and Abraham Gouverneur to come before him in the City Hall, and, in the presence of Mayor De Peyster, told them that they had petitioned him separate from his council; that, even if the latter were their enemies, since he must rule the country in connection with them, they must address a petition in a suitable manner, before he could take any steps for their benefit. It was accordingly done. Then each of the prisoners was set at liberty, after giving bonds that he would not leave the province. Abraham Gouverneur quickly took advantage of his freedom, and escaped in a fishing-boat to Boston. Sir William Phipps, who had recently been made governor of Massachusetts, promised to take care of him and assist him in going to England. Phipps told Gouverneur that Fletcher was a "poor beggar," who only sought money and not the good of the country, and that the "old King James's Council" at New York spoiled every good thing, and must be got out of the way. Phipps's counselors talked in a similar strain to Gouverneur, who wrote an account of it to his parents, with a request that his letter might be shown to Dr. Beekman and Mrs. Leisler.

All at once Fletcher heard that there had been meetings, violent speeches, serious reflections upon some members of his council, and fresh demands of reparation for Leisler's blood. While he was wondering what had started such a storm, and just as he was flattering himself that he had somewhat abated the foaming of the waters, the letter of Gouverneur by a singular accident fell into his hands. Ah! it was Boston, the neighbor who, in the enjoyment of the tranquility of peace, disregarded the cries for help when New York was overawed by a murderous enemy, — it was Boston at the bellows, trying to fan the embers of former discontents. Fletcher wrote to Phipps, and demanded the surrender of Gouverneur, which was haughtily denied, and the latter soon joined young Leisler in London.

Fletcher's endeavor to establish a ministry was seconded with great zeal by Caleb Heathcote, who was appointed to the governor's council in the spring of 1693. He had been in New York but a few months, but his uncle Captain George Heathcote had been a property owner in the city for seventeen or more years. The uncle died a bachelor, and Caleb was his heir by will. The latter was a young man of promise, and his unusual talents brought him into immediate notice. He was the son of the mayor of Chester in England, and brother to Sir Gilbert Heathcote, the founder and first president of the bank of England, and Lord Mayor of London.

There was a curious romance in which these brothers were concerned. Caleb was engaged to be married to a lady of great beauty, and in the full pride of conquest took his elder brother to see his betrothed. Gilbert was not only struck with admiration, but actually fell in love with the lady himself. What is more, he finally supplanted Caleb in her affections and married her. The disappointed lover sailed for America, and was soon immersed in business both public and private. Succeeding to the estate of his uncle, who had large shipping interests, he found little time for heart-breaking regrets. Society was also a cordial balm for his slowly healing wound, for no one in those days who saw a gentleman could mistake his social position, and he was consequently received into the little circle which gathered around the governor with all the state and ceremony of a court. It was not long before he became a favorite guest in the house of Chief Justice William Smith, "Tangier Smith" as he was called from having been governor of Tangier before he came to New York. The chief center of attraction was Miss Martha Smith, that gentleman's daughter, and ere many months a gay wedding at St. George's manor furnished society gossip for a season. Heathcote built a manor-house on his extensive lands near Mamaroneck (which were erected into a manor in 1701), and was lord of the manor of Scarsdale to the end of a long and eventful life. At his death the title as well as the estate descended to his son Gilbert. He had other children, among whom a large legacy from his brother William was divided. His eldest daughter, Ann, married Lieutenant-Governor James De Lancey. His third daughter, Martha, married Dr. James Johnson of Perth Amboy, who was the friend and correspondent of Gronovius, and who succeeded Heathcote as mayor of New York.

In July word came to Fletcher that the French were offering presents to the Iroquois, who had suffered terribly from the war while they had received no material aid from the colonies which they had July. defended. The defection of these brave allies would be the ruin of New York. The governor hurried to Albany, and summoned the sachems to an interview. He made them large gifts of clothing, hatchets, knives, and ammunition. They were apparently pleased, and gave him furs as a tribute of esteem. But they delivered no belt of wampum as a token of sincerity, and although they promised to remain steadfast and loyal, they left behind them a feeling of insecurity. Fletcher wrote to the king that the warriors accused the neighboring English colonies of cowardice and laziness, and were extremely dissatisfied that they were involved alone in such bloody warfare. "And should we lose the affections of our Indian friends," he continued, "we should be instantly steeped in blood ourselves."

A new Assembly convened in September, and James Graham was elected speaker. Fletcher recommended two chief objects to the consideration of the House. One was the settling of a ministry, Sept. 14. the other was the establishment of the revenue during the life of the king. Business progressed slowly, for there was much coldness and backwardness among the members. Fletcher sent a messenger on the Sept. 20. 20th to remind the House of the value of time and the great expense of the session to the country. Shortly after, Jacobus Van Cortlandt presented the bill of the revenue, which was read for the first time. In the afternoon a committee from the House met a committee from the council at Stephanus Van Cortlandt's residence, where the bill was discussed at great length. The counselors were all for settling the revenue upon the king for life. The Assemblymen present, among whom were Jacobus Van Cortlandt, Johannes Kip, and Colonel Pierson, were firmly in favor of continuing it only for five years. An amendment warmly sustained by the counselors was voted down by the Assemblymen, and it passed the House in its original form.

The next day a bill for the establishment of a ministry, which gave the election of rectors to the vestry-men and church-wardens, was transmitted to the council. It was returned with an amendment investing the power of collation in the governor. The Assembly refused to assent to an alteration which deducted so much weight from the scale of popular power. The bill became a law, and it was couched in such language as led the Church of England to think it was enacted for her establishment alone, and gave room for the dissenters to contend that it was passed equally for their benefit. Fletcher was so exasperated that he summoned the House before him and broke up the session in high temper. He said : —

" You have shown a great deal of stiffness. You take upon you airs as if you were dictators. I sent down to you an amendment of three or four words in that bill, which, though very immaterial, yet was positively denied. I must tell you that it seems very unmannerly. There never was an amendment yet decided by the council but what you rejected ; it is a sign of stubborn ill-temper. But, gentlemen, I must take leave to tell you, if you seem to understand by these words that none can serve without your collation or establishment, you are mistaken ; for I have the power of collating or suspending any minister in my government by their Majesties' letters patent. Whilst I stay in the government I will take care that neither heresy, sedition, schism, nor rebellion be preached among you, nor vice nor profanity encouraged. It is my endeavor to lead a virtuous and pious life and to set a good example. I wish you all to do the same. You ought to consider that you have but a third share in the legislative power of the government, and ought not to take all upon you, nor be so peremptory. You ought to let the council do their part. They are in the nature of the House of Lords or Upper House. But you seem to take the whole power into your own hands and set up for everything. You have had a very long session to little purpose and have been a great charge to the country. Ten shillings a day is a large allowance and you punctually exact it. You have been always forward enough to put down the fees of other ministers in the government ; why did you not think it expedient to correct your own to a more moderate allowance ? Gentlemen, I shall say no more at present, but that you do withdraw to your private affairs in the country. You are hereby prorogued to the tenth day of January next, ensuing." [1]

At this time the Assembly had no treasurer, and the public money went directly into the hands of the receiver-general, who was appointed by the

[1] *Journal of the Legislative Council of New York*, Vol. I. 47, 48.   *Chalmers.   Smith. Bancroft.   Dunlap.*

Crown. It was issuable only by the governor's warrant, hence every officer from the auditor to the clerk of the Assembly must apply to Fletcher for their pay.

New York was afflicted with all the pressures which never fail to over-whelm any country whose resources are not equal to its enterprises. Be-sides, she was struggling alone against the common danger. Fletcher's letters to the king finally led the latter to send mandatory letters to the other colonies, ordering them to assist New York in the prosecution of the war. For greater union he sent a commission to Fletcher to govern Penn-sylvania, which Penn had neglected since the Revolution. By the same vessel came a letter to Fletcher from Penn himself, admonishing him " to tread softly and with caution," as that territory and its government was his own private property. Fletcher made a journey to Pennsylvania, and spent some six weeks in the province; but the Quakers had been instruct-ed how to evade his authority, and, finding he could accomplish nothing, he left the government to Lieutenant-Governor Markham, and wrote to William that the trust conferred upon him was " only a trouble," and, so far from adding strength to New York, his absence increased her embar-rassments.

It was during his brief stay in Pennsylvania that he presided at the trial of William Bradford, the printer, who, having been arrested and ar-raigned before two Quaker judges for having printed a pamphlet for the political party out of power without permission of the administration, had appealed to the highest tribunal in the province. He was triumphantly acquitted, and Fletcher, becoming greatly interested in him personally, and desirous of introducing the art of printing into New York, invited him to come to the metropolis and print for the government at a stated salary. Bradford accepted the call, and took up his permanent abode in New York.

Sir William Phipps had been commissioned to govern all New England, but his jurisdiction over the military of Connecticut was revoked and transferred to Fletcher. The latter went to Hartford to assume author-ity. He remained there twenty days, and tried in vain to prove the inhe-rent right of the Crown to control all matters appertaining to the militia. The General Court was intrenched behind the charter, and finally sent Winthrop to England for redress; the latter so pleaded his cause at court that the Crown lawyers decided in favor of the Connecticut charter, and that the king had only the right to appoint the quota to be furnished in times of great emergency. Fletcher's commission was consequently re-voked.

Fletcher next sent Mayor De Peyster and Counselor Brooke to Boston
26

to negotiate with Governor Phipps for assistance. He received them ungraciously. When they stated their errand, and told him of the weak
condition of New York, the great depopulation it had suffered in the defense of the frontiers, the wavering temper of the Indians, and the ruinous taxes repeated and repeated upon the people until they were weary
and disheartened, and asked for a proper quota from Massachusetts pursuant to the king's instructions, Phipps seemed disposed to answer them
in the same way that he reproved his servants, by throwing a chair at
their heads. He swore he would not furnish a man nor a farthing.
They told him that the governors of the different colonies were going to
send commissioners to New York in October to confer on the subject,
but he sharply interrupted them by declaring that none should come from
him. Some of Phipps's counselors were present, and seemed heartily
ashamed of his behavior. They apologized, aside, and hoped that De
Peyster and Brooke would blame his education for what they had seen
and heard. " His Excellency is needlessly hot," said Brooke. " Ah ! you
must pardon him ; it is dog-days," was the reply.

1694. In the spring a new Assembly was elected. When they con-
March. vened Colonel Pierson was chosen speaker. There was so much
disagreement among the members about the amount of taxes to be levied
upon the already overburdened people, that Fletcher became uneasy lest
the gallant Iroquois should make a separate treaty with the French before
he could furnish them the aid he had promised. Finally a dispute arose
about the number of men necessary to guard the frontiers. Fletcher,
worried out of all patience, testily informed the House that he was a
competent judge of such matters, and if they would provide a subsidy, he
would head the militia any moment when necessary. " Time runs away,"
he exclaimed. " You have now sat twenty days, and little or nothing is
done. It were much more pleasant if business went on cheerfully at
once." A bill was finally passed to raise a small sum, but it was insufficient. The House demanded an examination of the public accounts, particularly the muster-rolls of the volunteers in the pay of the province,
the members who were of the Leislerian faction having accused Fletcher
and his council of official stealing. It was granted ; but the malicious
warfare of words did not cease. The session was adjourned on the 26th
of March to meet again on the 25th of September.

During the summer the little printing-press of William Bradford
created quite a sensation in New York. He was among other things employed in printing the Corporation laws. The young printer was one of
the most industrious of men, and was constantly issuing something novel,
and from its rarity and freshness of course interesting to people who had

hitherto been obliged to obtain all printed matter from a distance. His first issue was a small folio volume. The second was a 24mo of fifty-one pages, entitled "A LETTER OF ADVICE TO A YOUNG GENTLEMAN LEAVING THE UNIVERSITY, CONCERNING HIS CONVERSATION AND BEHAVIOR IN THE WORLD ; by R. L. A." A copy of this antique work was sold at an auction sale of E. B. Corwin, a few years since, for the small sum of $ 12.50 !

Robert Livingston was in England the greater part of this year. He sailed in the early spring, and his vessel was shipwrecked upon the coast of Portugal. He had no alternative but to undertake the hazardous journey through Spain and France by land. He was about sixty years of age at the time, but in the full possession of all his remarkable gifts of intellect, and scarcely less reckless than in his adventurous youth. He accomplished the feat of getting through an enemy's country in safety, and in commemoration of the event altered the Livingston coat-of-arms from a demi-savage to a ship in distress, and changed the motto " Si je Puis " — If I am able, — to " Spero Meliora " — I hope for better things. He was cordially received by the lords at Whitehall.

He was surprised to learn that an order had passed the Privy Council for the pardon of the "condemned six " in New York, and that their estates had been restored to them ! He was still more surprised to meet Abraham Gouverneur in the antechamber of the king ! But when he met young Leisler at the dinner-table of the Earl of Bellomont his feelings underwent a change, and he entered with characteristic warmth into the iron purpose of the young man to secure complete restitution of blood as well as property ; and he, moreover, aided the latter to the extent of his influence, which was not inconsiderable. William having been successfully petitioned for leave to apply to Parliament, Constantine Phipps (one of the Massachusetts agents) framed a bill to reverse the attainder of Leisler and his adherents, and Sir **Henry** Ashurst sat as chairman of the committee to whom it was referred. Dudley was present, and opposed it with all his strength, and the whole court regarded it with disfavor. It nevertheless passed into a law in April, 1695. Massachusetts was triumphant, as it was supposed to contain a Parliamentary recognition of the rectitude of her violent proceedings. As for New York, this implied censure upon her administration engendered and continued civil distractions until it seemed as if she would be rent in sunder. Gouverneur returned and became one of the ablest and most persistent leaders of the Leislerian party. In 1699 he married Mary Leisler, the widow of Jacob Milborne. One of his daughters was the mother of the distinguished Gouverneur Morris.

Meanwhile September came and the Assembly once more convened.

Fletcher presented a detailed account of his transactions with the Indians, and explained to the House the ill effects of their late policy in abating fourpence per day from the soldiers' pay. These poorly compensated men had been running away in troops of seven at a time. Eightpence could hardly provide food and shoes. Men could not be found to serve for such a paltry sum. Fletcher said he knew how to exercise strict discipline, but it went against his nature to put men to death for desertion when they were starving and freezing, and it was impossible for them to do duty barefoot on the frontiers in the winter. The New York soldiers were the more discouraged because those from New Jersey received their full twelvepence per day.

Sept. 25.

He also pressed attention to the disagreeable duty of raising more money for forts, ammunition, and stores. But the Leislerians in the House were growing bolder every day. They were determined to crucify the men who surrounded and supported Fletcher. They expressed dissatisfaction with the disposition of the revenue. The books were again laid open for their inspection. They had no intention of being mollified, and picked flaws with many of the charges and disbursements, notwithstanding they were aware as well as others, that in time of actual war there will unavoidably be great and unexpected charges, indispensable to the welfare and safety of a country. Fletcher had, as soon as he found there was no prospect of help from the colonies (except New Jersey) applied himself to the work of obtaining recruits from England, and had so far succeeded that four hundred soldiers, as a standing force, about this time arrived. But they must be supported. While eightpence per day would enable an English soldier to live better in England, as far as meat and clothing were concerned, than twice that sum in New York, the Assembly were unwilling to grant any additional pay. Fletcher argued that they could not be kept together on that amount of money; they would soon have no means to buy shoes, stockings, and shirts. The dispute became very bitter. Fletcher accused the House of ingratitude, after all his efforts to secure the troops. The House muttered about the misapplication of the revenue. He finally prorogued them until the following March.

1695.
March 21.

When they then came together the wrangle was renewed with vigor. The House asked for an adjournment until the muster-rolls could be inspected. Fletcher refused, on the ground that the request was improper, and he demanded the immediate raising of funds for the subsistence and pay of the officers and men in the service of the province. A bill was framed to raise £1000, to secure the frontier for six months. It was pronounced insufficient by Fletcher, and rejected.

A committee from the governor's council met a committee from the Assembly, and placed the accounts of the province before them in order to show that a fraction over £1023 was at that moment actually due to the forces at Albany. The committee from the Assembly refused to look at these papers. They asserted that there was a surplus of funds somewhere, and demanded the balance of accounts, not the accounts themselves. They said they believed there was a voucher for every dollar which had passed the council-board, but would not credit the council. If Fletcher appointed more officers than the House made provision for, or detained the men longer in service, he must pay it himself. The committee from the council explained that the men were detained longer in the service on account of the delay in the arrival of the soldiers from England, and the intelligence that the enemy were marching towards Albany; there was also daily occasion to send out men to range the woods and defend isolated farms. Who so competent to judge in such matters as the commander-in-chief? The men had done their work, and now they must be paid. The next day there was another meeting of the two committees. The council were represented by Stephanus Van Cortlandt, Chief Justice Smith, and Caleb Heathcote. Peter De Lanoy was at the head of the committee from the Assembly. The council tendered the House the muster-rolls; they had before given the abstracts, they now put the original papers into the hands of De Lanoy, and desired him to compare it with the abstract in the presence of and for the satisfaction of every member of the Assembly. De Lanoy declined, saying, "There is no need of it."

But when the Assembly again voted, it was to raise only the £1,000. Fletcher was in a very trying position. He sent for the speaker and the whole Assembly, and in the council-chamber earnestly entreated them to "leave fruitless and causeless contention and jangling, which was a stagnation upon all business, and regard only the good and safety of the province." The counselors took the opportunity to acknowledge themselves witnesses of the governor's integrity, and expressed their unanimous belief that it was his sincere desire to promote the best interests of the people. It was to no purpose; suspicion had taken deep root, and the House would not recede from its position. The following morning the governor prorogued the Assembly for ten days. He said: —

April 11.

April 12.

April 13.

"You have spent a long time at the expense of the country for no purpose. The supply you give is no supply at all. If a man gives me £1000, and obliges me to pay £10,000, he gives me nothing. . . . . I am as sensible of the burden of detachments as you can be and have done much more to lighten it.

It is an oppression that falls wholly upon the poor. The most of you are sheltered by commissions, as justices of the peace or militia officers ; but you know that you must contribute some proportion to the taxes. The gentlemen who are of my council are riveted among you here. They have fixed down their stakes and have as much interest in the country as yourselves. Yea, more than all of you. They are as unwilling to bring a yoke upon their posterity as you are. I can name two of them who pay more taxes in one year than all of you pay. It seems strange that you will put no trust in them, and make doubts and scruples where there is no ground for it, in things which you yourselves confess you do not understand. There's never a man amongst you, except Peter De Lanoy, who pretends to understand an account. There is not one farthing of public money disbursed but by advice of the council, and there are good vouchers for it. . . . . Had you acted like men, if you found me out of my duty, it was your business to have provided for the safety of the province, then to have drawn up your accusation against me to their Majesties, which I should have taken care should have come to their hands."

The Assembly had on the 12th, in answer to a petition from five church-wardens and vestrymen of the city, declared that these church-wardens and vestrymen had power to call a dissenting minister, who should be paid and maintained according to the Act of September 22, 1693. Fletcher, who had very just notions on such subjects, sharply rebuked the members for meddling with what they did not understand. " The laws," he said, " are to be interpreted only by judges ; . . . . there are no such officers as church-wardens and vestrymen in any Protestant church but the Church of England."

On the 20th Fletcher dissolved the Assembly by proclama-
April 20. tion. Another was elected, and convened in June. Fletcher had been personally into the field, and influenced the election as far as it was in his power. Among the members were Colonel Henry Beekman,[1] Brandt Schuyler, Major Wessells, and Jacobus Van Cortlandt. James

---

[1] Colonel Henry Beekman was the eldest son of William Beekman, and brother of Dr. Gerardus Beekman. He settled in Esopus (Kingston). He was called the "Great Patentee" because of his extensive landed estate. A boy once asked a Dutch farmer on the Hudson, if there was any land in the moon. "I don't know," was the reply ; "but if you will go to Colonel Henry Beekman he can tell you, for if there is any there you may be sure he has got a patent for the bigger part of it." Colonel Henry Beekman was a deacon and elder in the Reformed Dutch church, and judge of the county of Ulster. He married Janet, the daughter of Robert Livingston (the nephew of Robert Livingston the first of the name in in this country) and his wife, Margaretta Schuyler. He was large-sized, of symmetrical figure, manly in bearing, with a handsome, intelligent face. His children were, 1, Henry, who married Margaret Livingston (children, Robert, Henry, John, Edward, Janet, Margaret, Alida, Catharine, Hannah) ; 2, Catharine, who married Mr. Paulding of Rhinebeck ; 3, Cornelia, who married Gilbert Livingston (children nine sons and five daughters) ; 4, Robert ; 5, Gilbert.

Graham was speaker. More harmony was obtained, and reasonable sums were raised to defray the debts of the government. Some important bills were passed, and then the House was adjourned until October. In the interim Fletcher visited Albany and conferred with the Indians, giving them many presents. He scolded them for allowing Count Frontenac to rebuild the fort at Cadaraqui, but commended them in turn for having made peace with one of the remote western tribes which had hitherto aided the French. One of the warriors of the latter tribe had been captured while negotiating the treaty, and put to death by the French in the most shocking manner. He was tied to a stake, and a Frenchman broiled the flesh of his legs with the red-hot barrel of a gun. A furrow was then split from the prisoner's shoulder to his garter, and filled with gunpowder, which was set on fire. The captors danced around and filled the air with shouts of laughter. When the poor fellow's strength began to fail his scalp was taken off and hot coals of fire placed upon his skull. He was then untied and ordered to run for his life. He reeled like a drunken man, and started in an easterly direction; they shut up the way and drove him to the west, which the Indians call the country of departed miserable souls. He had vitality enough left to throw stones at his pursuers. They finally put an end to his misery by striking him on the head. After this every one cut a slice from his body and concluded the entertainment with a feast. The Iroquois immediately served up their French and Indian prisoners in a similar manner. It was retaliation and it was re-retaliation. The cruelties of that long and bloody warfare are beyond the power of language to describe. Count Frontenac finally determined to carry the sword into the very midst of the confederate tribes. He raised an army which was so large and extensive that it created a famine throughout Canada, and he was himself carried in an easy-chair directly in the rear of the artillery. News reached New York, and recruits were hurried off to the help of the Indians.

When the Assembly came together in October the prospect was dark and dubious. The people had been paying heavy taxes and doing hard duty for a long time with no sign of peace. The neighboring October. colonies denied assistance, and covered and protected those of the soldiers who had deserted; they had also turned to their own account both trade and people. These things were not well understood in England, and the governor, council, and Assembly finally agreed to send two agents, William Nicolls and Chidley Brooke, to correctly represent the case to the king. They sailed, but were captured by the French on their voyage, and threw their papers and letters overboard. They lay for several months in a Paris prison, and it was a long time before they reached Whitehall.

27

While New York was in speechless fear of the approaching French army at the North, Livingston at the English Court was heaping red-hot coals of fire upon the head of Fletcher himself. He, Livingston, was trying to recover money which he claimed to have advanced to the government of New York from time to time for some twenty years past. He said that sums which had been raised by Act of the Assembly to reimburse him had been misappropriated by Fletcher. He, moreover, declared that the present Assembly had been illegally elected. He preferred so many startling accusations against the governor that the Lords of Trade took the matter up and went through the form of an investigation.

Philip French was in England, and testified to having learned (from hearsay) that Fletcher had threatened to pistol any man who dared vote for Peter De Lanoy; that he, French, went to dine with Fletcher, and asked if such reports were true, and that the latter did not deny them, but when told that the news came from Colonel De Peyster, angrily exclaimed, " De Lanoy and De Peyster are both rascals." French further testified that there was great confusion on the day of election, and that he saw many soldiers and sailors, with clubs in their hands, about the polls; and that there was much talk about " heats in the Assembly" concerning public money. Captain Kidd testified that the sheriff of New York asked him to let his crew come ashore to vote, but could not say that it was by the governor's order. Other sea-captains swore to having been asked to let their crews come ashore to vote, but no one could swear that it was by the governor's order, or that the votes were actually cast. Abraham Gouverneur and Jacob Leisler, Jr., testified that Fletcher hindered free elections, and passed soldiers and seamen off as citizens; that the latter prowled about all day armed with clubs and staves : and that false returns were brought in from many of the counties. They had heard it said that all the goldsmiths in New York were employed in making snuff-boxes and other plate for presents to the governor; also that the illegal Assembly had raised a large sum of money and sent agents to England to defend their actions. Letters were read from Peter De Lanoy, Robert Walters, and others, praying for the recall of Fletcher; they said they were not solicitous whether it was gently done or whether he fell into disgrace, only so they were rid of him.

The Lords of Trade were wary in coming to conclusions; after considerable delay Nicolls and Brooke appeared and put in strong counter-testimony. Gouverneur and Leisler tried to impeach them by showing how they had been instrumental in sending two heroes to the gallows. Fletcher heard in course of events of the charges against him, and denied them so utterly, and was so well sustained in all his explanations by the members of his council, and seemed to have labored so indefatigably to further the interests of the province in its great struggle with the French, that he was exonerated from blame; and but for a new complication of complaints would have been undisturbed in his position.

Livingston succeeded in collecting his claims of the government, and returned to New York as a commissioned agent for the Indians, at a salary, to be paid by the province, of £130 per annum. Fletcher was indignant. He said there was no need of this new office which Livingston had created; that it was an additional expense, could not be paid as long as the war lasted, and that all treaties would be negotiated by the governor in person under any circumstances. The council were of the same opinion. Fletcher declared that Livingston had warped the judgment of the Lords of Trade by false insinuations; that, instead of suffering by his loyalty to New York, he had been abundantly paid by fees and perquisites for his services, and had actually made a fortune out of his employment, never disbursing sixpence but with the expectation of twelvepence in return; that he had neither religion nor morality, and only thirsted to get rich, and had often been known to say that he "had rather be called knave Livingston than poor Livingston." He was an alien, too, born of Scotch parents, in Rotterdam, and thus disabled from executing any business of trust relating to the Treasury in the English dominions according to a late Act of Parliament. The governor and council met the strong-willed scion of nobility with the most determined opposition; and finally suspended him from the exercise of his office and laid the matter before the king.

The year 1695 was eventful in city improvements as well as political encounters. Notwithstanding all the inconveniences of war, there was a healthy, bustling activity among the people, and a rapid increase of population. There was more money in circulation than ever before, and merchants were extending their commerce and growing rich. The privateers and pirates whom the war sustained came here to buy provisions in exchange for gold and valuable commodities from the East. Many new houses and stores sprung up, and real estate suddenly advanced.

Colonel Abraham De Peyster built a palatial mansion on Queen Street, nearly opposite Pine. It was fifty-nine by eighty feet, and three stories high. It had a great double door in the center of the front, over which was a broad balcony with double-arched windows. This balcony was for nearly a century the favorite resort of the governors of New York when they wished to hold military reviews. The rooms of the house were immensely large (some of them forty feet deep), and the walls and ceilings were handsomely decorated. The furniture was all imported, and was elaborately carved and very costly. The grounds occupied the whole block, and there was a coach-house and stable in the rear. The style of life of the family was the same as that of the European gentry of the same period. They indulged in elegant hospitalities and costly entertainments; the chief people of the city and province, and stately visitors from the Old World, were often grouped together under this roof. The silverware in daily use upon the table was estimated as worth about $ 8,500, and the most of it was of exquisite workmanship. The finest

De Peyster Arms.

cut-glass and the rarest patterns of China adorned the quaint and massive sideboard; and the walls were hung with paintings from the old masters. They had sixteen household servants, nine of whom were negro slaves. De Peyster owned a tract of land on the north of Wall Street east of Broadway to William Street, and thence toward the river, which was called the "Great Garden of Colonel De Peyster," and which after his death was divided into lots and partitioned among his children.

Of the sons of De Peyster, Abraham figured the most conspicuously in public affairs. He was born in the new Queen Street mansion in 1696. He died in 1767 at the age of seventy-one. He was forty-six years treasurer of the province of New York. His descendants in the direct line represent this ancient and honorable family to-day.[1] One of the younger sons, Pierre Guillaume, married (in 1733) Catharine the daughter of Arent Schuyler; their son, Colonel Arent Schuyler De Peyster, entered the military service

---

[1] Abraham de Peyster, Jr., married Margaret, eldest daughter of Jacobus Van Cortlandt and Eve Philipse in 1722. He was treasurer of the province from June 2, 1721, till his death in 1767. He had eleven children, several of whom died young. James was the eldest son and inherited the estate. He was born in 1726. Frederic (known as the Marquis) was born in 1731 ; he succeeded his father as treasurer of the province. Catharine married John Livingston, and had thirteen children. Margaret married Hon. William Axtell, one of the king's counselors. Maria married Dr. John Charlton. Elizabeth married Matthew Clarkson.

James de Peyster married (in 1748) Sarah, daughter of Hon. Joseph Reade, one of the king's counselors. He had thirteen children. Frederic, the eldest surviving son, married Helen, only daughter of Samuel Hake (claimant of the title of Lord Hake) and granddaughter of Robert Gilbert Livingston. She died in 1801, and he afterwards married Ann, only daughter of Gerard G. Beekman and grand-daughter of Lieutenant-Governor Pierre Van Cortlandt. Frederic, the son of Frederic de Peyster, married Mary Justina, the daughter of Hon. John Watts. He rose to eminence at the bar of New York, and has ever been one of her most public-spirited citizens. He is now the honored President of the New York Historical Society. His only son, John Watts de Peyster, married Estelle, daughter of John Swift Livingston. He was Brevetted Major-General for meritorious services, by concurrent Resolution of the New York Legislature, in 1866 ; and has achieved a world-wide reputation as an author and military historian.

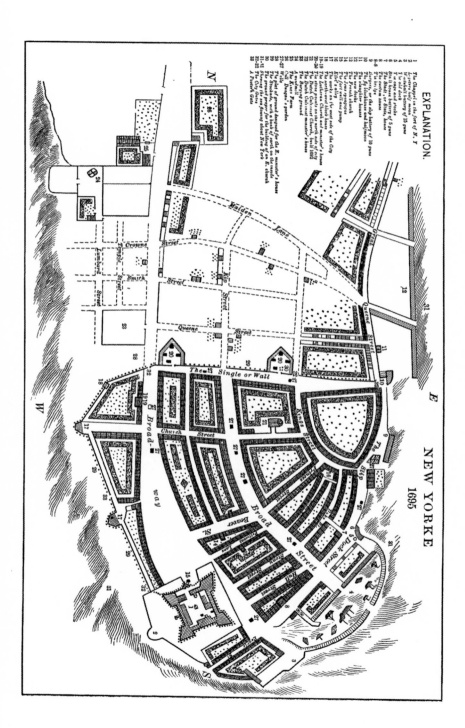

NEW YORKE
1695

in 1755, and held a royal commission for more than half a century. He commanded at Detroit and vicinity during the most stormy period of the French and Indian War, and contributed largely to the consolidation of the English possessions. His wife accompanied him everywhere, in camp and in quarters, amid savage tribes and in polished communities. His nephew and namesake, in one of his voyages round the world, discovered the De Peyster Islands in the Pacific Ocean.

Of the daughters of De Peyster, Catharine married (in 1710) Philip Van Cortlandt, son of Stephanus Van Cortlandt, and second lord of Cortlandt manor. She was the mother of Lieutenant-Governor Pierre Van Cortlandt. Elizabeth (whose godmother was Mrs. Governor Fletcher, in 1694) married Governor John Hamilton of New Jersey. Joanna, born in 1701, married her cousin Isaac De Peyster.

Fletcher, in his zeal for the good of the church, built a small chapel in the fort in 1693, and the queen sent plate, books, and other furniture for it. It was burned with the other buildings in 1741, and but little is known of its history. Rev. John Miller was the Episcopal clergyman. As soon as the Assembly passed the act for establishing a ministry in the province, he demanded induction into the living; but it was decided that he was not entitled to it. He accordingly sailed for England; while on the voyage he was taken prisoner by the French, and threw all his papers into the sea. During his imprisonment he wrote from memory a description of New York. He said the commerce of the city had become so extensive that forty square-rigged vessels, sixty-two sloops, and as many boats were entered at the Custom-House at one time.[1] The chief part of his little work was devoted to a labored and extraordinary plan for civil and ecclesiastical government on a new basis. This clergyman had greatly stimulated Fletcher in the work of building a church edifice, and had recommended a site. But Fletcher had his eye upon the " King's Farm," which was set apart for the use of the governor; it consisted of a garden, an orchard, a triangular graveyard in one corner, and pasturage for cows and horses. Andros had leased that portion of it under cultivation for twenty years, at sixty bushels of wheat per annum. As the lease was about expiring, Fletcher granted it to the use of the church-wardens for seven years without fine. A building was at once projected and in course of a few months was completed. A charter, bearing date May 6, 1697,

---

[1] The manuscript of Rev. John Miller, with a quaint map attached, found its way from the archives of the Bishop of London to the library of George Chalmers, the historian, and finally fell into the hands of Thomas Rodd, a London bookseller, who published it in 1843. Since then the original manuscript has been deposited in the British Museum. The city was then all below Wall Street, the wall remaining; also, the stone bastions at Broadway and William Street.

was granted by an act of the Assembly, approved and ratified by the governor and council, by which "a certain church and steeple lately built in the city of New York, together with a parcel of ground adjoining" (with full description) was to be known as Trinity Church. The wardens and vestrymen were duly named and constituted,[1] and with the Bishop of London for their rector,[2] were established a body corporate and politic, with all the privileges and powers usually pertaining to the same.

Up to that time the Episcopal service had been performed in the Dutch Church, and the clergymen of the two denominations had lived in all friendship. But Dominie Selyns was uneasy about the legal condition of the Dutch organization, and feared its privileges might at any moment be withdrawn. He and his consistory, therefore, applied to Fletcher for a charter. It was granted, prior to that of Trinity Church (May 11, 1696), and indeed was the first church charter issued in the colony. It secured the independence of the organization by giving it power to call its ministers, and to hold property acquired by gift or device. It also provided for compulsory payment of church rates for the support of the gospel. This last clause was never enforced, and was stricken out altogether as inconsistent with the principles of republican government, when the State Legislature confirmed the charter after the colonies became a nation. Dominie Selyns, in writing to the Classis of Amsterdam, said that there were several English ministers in the rural districts about New York who had been educated in New England; that the University of Cambridge had graduated very many in philosophy and the higher studies. He said that the French minister Dominie Perret, a man of great learning, officiated in New York; that Dominie Brodet had been called to preach to the Huguenots in New Rochelle, five hours' ride from New York; and that Dominie Daillé had gone to Boston. "Morals," continued the pious and accomplished dominie, "have much degenerated, and evil practices have been introduced by strangers and privateersmen. Our calamities spring from the bottomless pool of heaven-high sins, foreign but nevertheless without suspicion of foreigners. Money increases, high houses are built, and land is made in the water. Since I came the last time the city and its inhabitants have increased more than two thirds."

---

[1] The first church-wardens of Trinity Church were Thomas Wenham and Robert Lurting; the first vestrymen, Caleb Heathcote, William Merritt, John Tudor, James Emott, William Morris, Thomas Clarke, Ebenezer Wilson, Samuel Burt, James Everts, Nathaniel Marston, Michael Howden, John Crooke, William Sharpas, Lawrence Read, David Jamison, William Huddleston, Gabriel Ludlow, Thomas Merritt, William Janeway.

[2] The appointment of the Bishop of London for a rector, who could not actually perform the duties, was a temporary arrangement to provide the corporation with a head. *Book of Patents*, VII. 25, Secretary of State's office.

"He said Tew was agreeable and companionable—had good sense and a great memory, that he had often invited him to his table, and taken him to drive, because it was a source of diversion and information to talk with him." Page 423

Piracy had long been in existence. It had been encouraged rather than otherwise by the European governments. In time of war it was agreeable to annoy the commerce of an enemy without trouble or expense. Private armed vessels, sometimes licensed and sometimes unlicensed, roved the seas and robbed and plundered at pleasure. Many of these free-sailors held commissions from the king of England to annoy France. Presently the ships of all nations were seized, plundered and sunk or burned, not excepting those of Great Britain herself. The English government was roused only when ocean-commerce seemed nearly destroyed.

Just at this moment the Leislerians seized hold of the lever which fate seemed to have ordained for the complete overturn of political affairs in New York. They accused Fletcher of conspiracy with the pirates; that is, they declared that he encouraged and protected them. He had in common with the practice in England issued commissions for sea-captains to raise men and act as privateers against the French. He had also accepted bonds and promised protection. But he afterwards denied to the satisfaction of the Lords of Trade having ever aided in such manner known pirates. Meanwhile the evidence of commissions found in the possession of the high-handed sea-robbers, Coats, Hoare, Tew, and others, was used to prove his complicity in their crimes. He said they abused the favor shown them and turned pirates afterwards. He admitted his knowledge of the fact that Tew had been a pirate prior to his acquaintance with him, but said that the latter had promised not to engage in such business any more. He said Tew was agreeable and companionable, had good sense and a great memory; that he had often invited him to his table, and taken him to drive, because it was a source of diversion and information to converse with him. He said he had it in his heart to convert Tew from the error of his ways, to make him sober and reclaim him from the "vile habit of swearing." He had presented him with a book on the subject; on another occasion he had given his singular guest a gun of some value. Tew had seemed grateful, and bestowed in return a curious watch upon the governor. Rumor said that he also gave valuable jewels to Mrs. Fletcher and her daughters. But this, if true, was never proven. It was, however, a remarkable intimacy; and Tew subsequently proceeded to the Indian Ocean, where, harboring himself with others of his craft among the creeks of Madagascar, he plundered and murdered until humanity refuses to blot the pages of history with his deeds.

No sooner was Fletcher implicated than some of the wealthiest and hitherto most respectable citizens of New York were accused of sharing in the spoils of ocean robbery. Every new development seemed to justify the suspicion. The remarkable influx of strangers, the increasing quantity of rich goods exposed for sale, the rapid erection of expensive buildings, and the free circulation of Eastern gold pieces, pointed in the one direction.

The Lords of Trade brought the startling subject before the king as soon as he was capable of attending to business after the death of Queen Mary. It was some months before any action was taken, and then not until an event occurred which could not be passed by unnoticed. The pirates had destroyed some of the Mogul's ships in the Indian Ocean, one in particular that he was sending laden with presents to Mecca.

The East India Company learned that the Mogul had information that the corsairs were Englishmen, and also that he was about to take reprisals for damages. A man-of-war must unquestionably be sent to put a stop to such traffic. But Parliament had so appropriated the nation's funds that no money could be obtained for the purpose. " We can make it a private undertaking," said King William to his counselors. " I will give £3,000, and you can furnish the balance." Lord Somers and the Earls of Oxford, Rumney, and Bellomont, with Robert Livingston, who was still at court, discussed the question, and finally contributed the whole amount, some £6,000, the king failing to advance the sum which he had promised. Livingston introduced Captain Kidd to Lord Bellomont, and recommended him as a fit man to command the expedition. Livingston said Kidd had sailed a packet from New York to London for some years, was known to be honorable and brave, was well acquainted with the habits and haunts of the pirates in the Eastern seas, and was ready to perform deeds of valor for the good of the country. He was accordingly employed, receiving a commission from the Admiralty, which gave him power simply to act against the French. It was not deemed sufficient, and another commission was finally furnished under the Great Seal, dated January 26, 1696, giving him full authority to apprehend all pirates wherever he should encounter them, and bring them to trial. Livingston entered into bonds with Kidd to Bellomont, to account strictly for all the prizes secured ; and a grant under the Great Seal provided that all property taken from the pirates should vest in the parties at whose cost the vessel was fitted out, the king to receive one tenth of the proceeds. There was abundant ground for complaint, and great handle was made of the arrangement, for it was against law to take a grant of goods from offenders before conviction. But the case of pirates was manifestly different from that of other criminals. They could never be attacked except in the way of war, and whoever undertook such an enterprise ran a great risk, and it was reasonable that they should have a right to what they should find in the enemy's hands, whereas, those who seize common offenders have the strength of the law within immediate reach, and incur so little danger that the cases are by no means parallel.

Kidd set sail in April, 1696, under brilliant auspices. He stopped in New York and shipped ninety additional men, and in July was fairly at sea on his fatal mission. The sequel — how, instead of suppressing piracy, he became the prince of pirates, and nearly involved not only the Lords of Trade, but even the king of England himself, in the blackest of charges — is well known. The undertaking was in itself innocent and meritorious. Yet it was traduced until, in the House of Commons, it was voted as highly criminal, and but for energetic action on the part of a few, would have condemned its projectors forever.

Kidd was an attractive and cultivated man, and there was no occasion to distrust his intentions. As far as known his previous life had been irreproachable. He had a comfortable and pleasant home in Liberty Street, New York, and a wife beautiful, accomplished, and of the highest respectability. She was Sarah Oort, the widow of one of his fellow-officers; they were married in 1691, and at the time of his departure for the Eastern Ocean, they had one charming little daughter. Many supposed that he had secret orders from the government to pursue piracy. But the stain upon England's records did not prove indelible.

Dudley, the former chief justice of New York, was in London, taking advantage of his interest at court to obtain the governorship of Massachusetts, Sir William Phipps having recently died. He opposed the bill to reverse the attainder of Leisler and Milborne in the House of Commons with all his strength, which was not inconsiderable. The agents from Massachusetts took the opportunity in consequence to urge against him the conspicuous part he had borne in the trial and condemnation of the unfortunate men, and he lost his appointment for the time. Bellomont was the favorite candidate henceforth. When it became evident that Fletcher must be recalled, it seemed the part of wisdom to appoint one general governor over New York and New England for convenience during the continuance of the war. At the same time each colony was to have an Assembly and courts independent of each other. Bellomont had been created an earl by William as a reward for his many distinguished services to the royal pair; he had been the treasurer and receiver-general of Mary, and the personal and confidential friend of the king. He was esteemed one of the most honest as well as able men about the throne. William told his Lords that Bellomont would be more likely to put a stop to piracy than any other man he could think of. Bellomont received the appointment, but, owing to disputes about the salaries of both sovereign and statesmen, consequent upon the financial distress of the kingdom at that juncture, he did not reach his government for more than two years.

27

The year 1696 was distinguished by the repeal of the Bolting and Baking Acts in New York, which had added so many coffers to the **1696.** city's purse. The mayor and common council resisted to the last, but all to no purpose. Commerce in bread and flour was thrown open to all competitors. An alarming scarcity of bread soon began to prevail. The bakers declared they could not buy bread cheap enough to supply their customers at former prices. An account of stock was taken of the wheat, flour, and bread within the city, and only about a week's provision discovered for the seven thousand inhabitants. The repeal of the Bolting Act had enabled the farmers throughout the country to grind their own flour, and it had been sold largely to the pirates as a private speculation. A famine was actually threatened. A petition was signed by a majority of the citizens, and despatched to the king, asking for a restoration of the monopoly.

June. The first opening of Nassau Street occurred in June. Teunis De Kay successfully petitioned the mayor and common council for the privilege of making a cartway through *"the street that runs by the pie woman's leading to the city commons,"* and the land alongside was given to him as a compensation for his labor. About the same time the corporation of the city of New York appropriated the first dollar ever expended upon the cleaning of the streets. The amount set apart was £ 20.

1697. The following spring the streets were first lighted. The novelty of the decree issued by the corporation gives it a peculiar flavor : —

" The Board taking into consideration the great inconvenience that attends this city, for want of lights in the dark time of the moon, in the winter season, it is therefore ordered that the housekeepers of the city shall put out lights in the following manner, viz, every seventh house shall cause a lantern with a candle in it *to be hung out on a pole,* the charges to be defrayed equally by the inhabitants of the said seven houses."

The institution of the first night-watch was equally characteristic of the times : —

" Four good and honest inhabitants of the city shall be appointed whose duty it shall be to watch in the night-time from the hour of nine in the evening till break of day, until the 25th of March next ; and to go round the city each hour of the night with a bell, to proclaim the season of the weather, and the hour of the night."

1698. The arrival of Lord Bellomont was the great event of the spring of 1698.[1] He arrived on the 2d of April. He was met at the

---

[1] Richard Coote, Earl of Bellomont and Baron of Coloony, was the son of Sir Richard

wharf by prominent gentlemen from both political parties, and crowds of people. The corporation burned four barrels of gunpowder in their salute of welcome. He went through the usual forms of ^{April 2.} publishing his commission, and that of his lieutenant-governor, John Nanfan, a cousin of Lady Bellomont, who had crossed the ocean with them ; and then the new governor administered the oaths to the members of the executive council, who were continued without change.

A pretentious dinner was given to Bellomont by the corporation, according to the ancient custom.[2] Johannes De Peyster was the mayor, and he could preside over a banquet with as much grace as his distinguished brother Abraham. A loyal address had been prepared which greatly pleased the new executive, and he was delightfully affable to everybody.

Bellomont was a genuine nobleman. He was also a master of the art of politeness, and knew how to make even the commonest man or woman feel that they were the objects of his special regard. He was of attractive, commanding presence, large-sized, somewhat above the ordinary height, with finely shaped and well-poised head, a face stamped with iron firmness, dark, magnetic, kindly, expressive eyes, and small, soft white hands. His voice was low and musical, but capable of great modulation. No one could tell a story with more humor, or enjoy a hearty laugh better than he. And yet he was not cheerful as a rule, and his countenance was apt to wear an expression of painful thought. It was only at rare intervals that vivacity sparkled forth like foaming nectar, and then it was so charming that the memory of it remained whatever clouds followed. He bore himself with a certain dignity that was much admired. He sat in his saddle with an ease which equestrians tried in vain to imitate. His dress was a model of elegance and good taste, and it was a matter which no mental disturbance ever induced him to neglect. His table was filled with the choicest viands, and it was served with as much ceremony as William's own. His equipage was magnificent.

Coote, who on the restoration of Charles II. was made a peer of the realm with the title of Baron of Coloony. The family is of French extraction, and settled originally in Devonshire. From a branch of the family, which afterwards possessed large estates in Norfolk and Suffolk, those of Ireland are descended. *Lodge's Irish Peerage,* I. 299. *History of Ireland,* II. 83 ; III. 145. *Nichols's Irish Comp.,* 1735. Upon the death of the elder Baron of Coloony, July 16, 1683, Richard succeeded to his titles and estates. In March, 1689, he was one of the first to espouse the cause of the Prince of Orange, and was soon after appointed treasurer and receiver-general to Queen Mary. William advanced him to the dignity of the Earl of Bellomont. He married in 1660 Catharine, daughter and heiress of John Nanfan of Birch Morton, and had two sons, Nanfan and Richard, who successively inherited their father's titles. *Sketch of the Earl of Bellomont* by Moore, in Stryker's *American Quarterly Register.* Vol. I. 434.

[2] One hundred and fifty persons dined with the new governor on this occasion, the bill of fare embracing venison, turkey, chicken, goose, pigeon, duck, and other game, mutton, beef, lamb, veal, pork, sausages, with pastry, puddings, cakes, and the choicest of wines.

He was sixty-two years of age, but might easily have passed for fifty. Lady Bellomont was much younger, as he had married her when she was only twelve. He was very fond as well as very proud of her. A series of stately dinner-parties were given by the leading New York families, and the first few weeks of their American life were more pleasant than any which ever came afterwards.

Bellomont had from his youth up been accustomed to see power constantly associated with pomp, and found it difficult to believe that the substance existed unless people were dazzled by the trappings. Prejudice, not vanity, was his besetting sin. He took his measure of men with the eye instead of the rule, and was as sincere in his friendship as he was inflexible in his aversions. He had a sound heart, honorable sympathies, and an honest desire to do justice to the oppressed. But he formed opinions too hastily, and they were the result of impulse rather than reason. They were apt to be colored by the first hearing of a case. Thus the good he might have done was warped and defeated. And he, instead of preserving a steady mean between the two great party extremes, was carried swiftly into the political whirlpool. He indulged in the most implacable antipathy towards Fletcher, even long before he crossed the ocean. He had listened to the aspersions cast upon the character of the latter by the Leislerians at the court of William, and had never doubted the truth of the same. He came prepared to pronounce wholesale condemnation upon all the acts of his predecessor. Evidence was an after consideration in his mind. It would have been the part of wisdom to have sifted the grains of fact from the vast amount of fiction, but Bellomont was as precipitate as he was sincere.

The hopes of the Leislerians were greatly stimulated by his appointment, for he had openly declared in England that in his opinion the execution of Leisler was a judicial murder. His ears were consequently filled at once with exaggerated complaints. And things certainly had a singular look. Trade seemed to be traveling on a tangent. Arabian gold and East India goods were everywhere common. New York was getting rich at a most extraordinary rate.

Bellomont with characteristic conscientiousness charged all irregularities to the account of his predecessor, and then set about overturning the stones which hid the pool of corruption. It was not so easy to prove as to guess who had been immersed within it. He discovered something akin to green mould hanging from the garments of several of the landed lords, who represented the aristocratic party. The members of his council were reticent, and he soon learned that they were meeting daily at the lodgings of Fletcher, who had not yet sailed for England. They were owners of merchant-vessels, — at least many of them were, — and their friendship for Fletcher had an aroma of complicity. Besides, they did not come up manfully, in the eyes of the new executive, to his assistance when he attempted to enforce the laws of trade, and some of them expressed surprise that they must needs have such an unexpected disturbance.

Fletcher was quite determined to have his accounts with the government audited before he departed, that he might take his proofs and vouchers to the Lords of Trade, as he was confident that he could clear himself from all the charges which had been made against him. He said that after having held commission under the Crown of England for thirty-five years without the least reproach or impeachment of his reputation, he did not think he " should become a castaway in the rear of his days."

Bellomont had been in New York scarcely three weeks before he issued a writ of restitution to put Leisler's and Milborne's families in possession of their estates, which had hitherto been a tardy process through various obstacles. It created a popular tumult, for the property had passed through several hands, and innocent parties were obliged to vacate houses and stores to which they held title-deeds obtained in good faith. But a still greater excitement was caused by the seizure of ships and goods under the new administration. Chidley Brooke was the collector of customs and receiver-general. He was a blood relative and had been brought up in the home of the father of Bellomont. His first employ in the government had been through the influence of the late Baron of Coloony. Bellomont treated him haughtily, however, and in the execution of his duties, now more sharply defined than ever, granted him no quarter. He ordered him to seize a cargo of East India goods, and became very angry when Brooke showed a disposition to hold back by declaring that it was not his business, and that he had no boat with which to visit the vessel. He was compelled to obey orders finally, but he delayed the accomplishment of the task for some days, and then captured only a small portion of what the ship contained, the remainder being secreted. Bellomont was in high temper, but the merchants outrivalled him in that particular, and almost raised a mutiny over his proceedings; he was enraged at Brooke for what he styled " negligence " in allowing unlawful trade to get such headway, and said it would cost so much more trouble now to put it down.

Meanwhile the stories about Fletcher were thriving in New York as well as England. It was said in connection with his having issued commissions to piratical commanders, that he had received large sums of money for protecting pirates whenever they chose to land in New

York to dispose of their spoils. It was said that one pirate had given him a ship which he had sold for £ 8,000 to Caleb Heathcote. It was also currently reported that the great merchant-vessels of New York, which went to Madagascar for negroes, bought goods of the pirates, and that the owners of those vessels had money interest in the pirate vessels. There was no end to the gossip. William Nicolls was charged with having been Fletcher's chief broker in the matter of protections, and the place of rendezvous where he had often held interviews with piratical captains on the Long Island shore was confidently pointed out to Bellomont. The earl never gave the question the benefit of a doubt. With swift impetuosity he suspended his counselor without even a hearing in his own defense. Then he wrote to the Lords of Trade under date of May 8, 1698 : —

"Colonel Nicolls ought to be sent with Colonel Fletcher a criminal prisoner to England for trial, but the gentlemen of the council are tender of him, as he is connected by marriage to several of them, and I am prevailed upon to accept £ 2,000, for his appearance here when demanded. He is a man of good sense and knowledge in the law, but has been a great instrument and contriver of unjust and corrupt practices."

Bellomont dissolved Fletcher's late Assembly and issued writs for a new one. The election stirred up the old feud, but the Leislerians through the country were as yet not fairly awake to this possible deliverance and did not win a majority in the House. The new Assembly met as early as possible, and Philip French was chosen speaker. Bellomont's opening address was a review of the condition of public affairs. His legacy, he said, was a divided people, an empty purse, a few miserable, half-starved, naked soldiers, ragged fortifications, a tumble-down governor's house, and, in short, a whole government out of frame. The prospect was certainly anything but cheerful. Bellomont said he should pocket none of the people's money, and all his accounts should be furnished for inspection when and as often as desired. He declared against free elections, against piracy, against illegal trade, against disorders of whatever nature, and in favor of reducing the salaries of the officers of the government. He said the revenue which had been raised for five years was nearly expiring and must be renewed. He said that immediate provision must be made to pay the debts of the government.

Until now the Assembly had consisted of nineteen members. Bellomont warmly advocated the passage of a bill to increase the number to thirty, and to provide against the abuses attending elections. It created so much ill-natured discussion that no other business was attempted for a month, and finally six of the members seceded from the Assembly altogether. The only thing which had really been accomplished was an address to the king, and Bellomont dissolved the body in disgust.

The trouble with the merchants grew into such proportions, and it became so necessary to have officers who would execute justice promptly, that Bellomont peremptorily dismissed Brooke from all his positions, and appointed Hon. Stephanus Van Cortlandt with Mr. Monsay, searcher of customs, to act as commissioners until a new receiver-general should receive the sanction of the king. Two or three days afterwards some goods were to be seized, and each of three constables who were sent for in turn to perform the duty was missing. A report was communicated to Bellomont the same afternoon, to the effect that the sheriff himself was concerned in the receipt of some East India goods, and that a large quantity was concealed in his house. The earl sprang to his feet and sent an order to Mr. Monsay and Mr. Everts to seize them at once. They entered the sheriff's house without opposition, but while they were packing the goods for removal to the Custom-House, the doors were locked upon them, leaving them prisoners in a close, unventilated garret, where they were obliged to remain until they were nearly stifled. It was nine o'clock in the evening before Bellomont heard of their incarceration. He at once sent his own servants with three files of soldiers, who broke in the doors and liberated the gentlemen.

The next day Mr. Monsay was called upon to seize more goods, but he declined to serve longer in that vocation. Bellomont was surprised, for Monsay had been searcher of the customs for six years, and this late office advanced him an extra £ 200 in the way of salary. Brooke was accused of having influenced Monsay. But as the latter could not be persuaded to come in collision again with the angry merchants, who had threatened his life, the son of Sir George Hungerford, another relative of the Earl, was appointed in his place.

William Pinhorne disapproved of Bellomont's arbitrary proceedings, particularly in regard to the merchants, and took occasion to express his opinions in strong language. He was immediately removed from the council by the governor, on the ground of having used disrespectful words against the king. He retired to his plantation near Snake Hill on the Hackinsack River, and was appointed judge of the Supreme Court in New Jersey, and a member of the governor's council in that State.

A record of the various encounters of Bellomont in his efforts to enforce the Acts of Trade would fill a volume. He wrote to the king : —

" I am obliged to stand entirely upon my own legs, my assistants hinder me, the people oppose me, and the merchants threaten me. It is indeed uphill work."

That such was the case is no matter of wonder. Those Acts of Trade were despotic in their nature and contradictory to the rights of humanity. They were everywhere evaded. New York was not alone. The city had become a nest of pirates, it is true, but it was the English nation which fed and fostered them. Piracy did not originate in New York. The place was simply chosen on account of its central geographical position, and its nearness to the open sea. A brief review of the Acts of Trade will enable the reader to better judge why no voice of conscience declared their violation a moral offense, and how respect for them resolved itself into a mere calculation of chances; it is to be taken into account also that New York was a city chiefly of aliens, owing allegiance to England and to other European powers, and without the bonds of common history or tongue.

No commodities might be imported into any British settlement in Asia, Africa, or America, or exported thence, but in vessels built in England or in her colonial plantations, and navigated by crews of which the master and three fourths of the sailors were English subjects. The penalty was forfeiture of ship and cargo. No one but a natural-born subject of the English crown or person legally naturalized could exercise the occupation of merchant or factor in any English colonial settlement. No sugar, tobacco, cotton, wool, indigo, ginger, or dye-stuffs produced in the colonies should be shipped from them to any other country than England, and ship-owners were required at the port of lading to give bonds with security proportioned to tonnage. The prohibited articles were called *enumerated,* and as soon as any new articles were brought into notice through the ingenuity and industry of the colonists, they were added to the list. It forbade also the importation of any European articles into the colonies save in vessels *laden in England* and navigated as above. It was the policy of nations to keep the trade of colonies confined to the parent country. Charles II. imposed a tax of five per cent on all goods imported into or exported from any of the dominions of the crown. Parliament went a step farther and taxed the trade which one colony carried on with another.

The peace of Ryswick had interrupted hostilities between the French and English, but Count Frontenac was still pursuing the Iroquois with unabated vigor. Bellomont sent two agents, Captain John Schuyler and Dominie Dellius, to Montreal to confer with the French commander. The latter claimed that the Iroquois were French not English subjects and he must bring them to terms. An interesting controversy at once ensued. Bellomont took a very high and arrogant tone in his correspondence, and Count Frontenac was equally resolute and opinionated. Bellomont, although seriously ill with the gout, hurried to Albany to meet the Indians themselves. Before any settlement was reached in the matter the Count died at the advanced age of seventy.

When Bellomont returned to New York he found the gentlemen of his council sullen and estranged. He invited them to dine with him, and fancied he detected signs of displeasure when he drank the king's health, as was his custom. He made a lame effort to conciliate the merchants, who were grumbling more loudly than ever, by giving them a general invitation to come to his dinner-table at any time; but they never came. Brooke had gone to England to obtain redress for his grievances. He had sailed during the governor's absence in Albany, and had been visited by great numbers of prominent persons before his departure, and crowds of people attended him to the vessel. Bellomont discovered that petitions had been extensively signed, asking for his recall, and sent by Brooke to Whitehall.

The great bone of contention in the council was piracy. All were agreed in the necessity for its suppression. But as to its actual extent there was a vast difference of opinion. Bellomont was informed that Colonel Bayard had assisted Fletcher in giving protection to pirates. He proclaimed it with emphasis. He also startled his associates by making known his suspicions in regard to several others among their number, who had unquestionably been concerned in the encouragement of depredations upon the sea. The retort was in the very nature of things inevitable. It was now well known that Captain Kidd had raised the black flag; and the possible complicity of Bellomont himself was on men's lips all over the world. The iron entered the noble soul. But the Earl would not allow any such misrepresentations to come between him and the execution of what he considered his duty. He was trying to purify a corrupt government, and suspected men must not be allowed to stand in high places. He therefore proceeded to remove Colonel Bayard, Gabriel Minvielle, Thomas Willett, Richard Townley, and John Lawrence from the council. The following morning Frederick Philipse resigned.

The excitement was intense. Rumor distorted facts, and the displaced gentlemen were accredited with the darkest deeds. A beautiful diamond worn by Mrs. Bayard was said to have been taken from the finger of an Arabian princess, and romance quickly wove the story into a bloody murder. It was reported to have been the price paid to Bayard for obtaining the murderer's protection. It was for a time currently believed that Minvielle possessed a large box of Arabian gold pieces obtained in a similar manner. John Lawrence was said to have often entertained the freebooters at his house on Long Island. Frederick Philipse was the

28

subject of much speculation. He owned several great merchant-vessels, and it was said that three or four were coming in from Madagascar laden with jewels and costly wares; and that his son Adolphe Philipse had gone out in a small ship to meet them and conceal the treasures. This last story was the only one which had any tangible foundation. Adolphe Philipse did go out as reported, though his object was never made known. When the vessels were at last entered, the depositions of the crew substantiated the original statement of Philipse that the goods had been bought at low prices from African traders instead of pirates.

Bellomont wrote to the Lords of Trade in reference to the changes made in the council, without repeating the charges which he had so impulsively preferred. He said that Townley lived in East Jersey and never came to the meetings; that Philipse resigned on account of his great age, being seventy-two years old; that Lawrence was also superannuated, being eighty-two years of age; and that the other gentlemen were disposed to promote illegal trade. David Jamison, the clerk of the council, was removed because of grave impertinence, and the governor in excusing such a stringent course, said that Jamison had once been condemned to the gallows in Scotland for blasphemy and burning the Bible, but in mitigation of the sentence had been transported to America; and, also, that he had two wives, — one left behind him, and one in New York.

The new counselors appointed to fill the vacancies were Robert Livingston, Colonel Abraham De Peyster, Thomas Weaver, Dr. Samuel Staats, and Robert Walters.[1] Bellomont had reviewed Fletcher's action against Livingston and reinstated the latter in all his offices. The Leislerian faction were thus in the ascendant in the council, and the whole party took courage. Some went so far as to broach the subject of demanding a retrospect of all the events and quarrels during the period of the Revolution.

On the other hand, Colonel Bayard was so indignant with the treatment which he had received, that he made a voyage to England at once, and personally laid the subject before the Lords of Trade and the king. William Nicolls stood guard over party interests in New York. Clubs and "cabals" were held at stated intervals, and an uneasy time it was for the governor. The latter came into collision with William Brad-

---

[1] Dr. Samuel Staats married, while holding some appointment in India obtained for him by William of Orange, an East Indian "*Begum*" or princess, with whom and his children he returned to Holland and thence to New York. His daughter Catharine married Lewis Morris, and was the mother of the celebrated Staats Long Morris. *Gouverneur Kemble; New York Genealogical and Biographical Record,* January, 1876, p. 17.

ford, who was printing for the government, and high words many times ensued. Bradford's salary was cut down in the general reduction of governmental expenses, and he several times told the Earl he might do his own printing.

Bellomont, from all he could learn, was convinced that much of the wealth of the New York aristocracy had been dishonorably obtained. The enormous landed estates haunted his mind. Small men could not obtain a foothold in the province. Every acre of government land had been granted away to feudal lords ; in many instances, in tracts from twenty to forty miles square. It had a ruinous outlook. He finally leveled a fierce blow at the great landholders by an attempt to break all existing grants, and the shaping of a bill, which should be approved in England, to prohibit any one person from holding over one thousand acres under any circumstances.

Meanwhile a new Assembly was in contemplation. For months prior to the election, the country was canvassed by conspicuous leaders of both parties. They rode night and day, defied cold and fatigue, **1699.** and encountered snow-storms and freshets. William Nicolls slept more than once under a haystack, and Robert Walters twice swam a swollen stream when the ice was breaking. Bellomont removed the sheriffs in the different counties, and appointed new ones, such as leaned towards the party which he represented, in their stead. The struggle was the sharpest ever known at that time in America. In many places on the day of election there was fighting and broken heads at the polls. The Leislerians were victorious. When some one said to Bellomont, " The new members all seem to be Englishmen," he replied with a sarcastic smile, " There is Johannes Kip, Rip Van Dam, and Jacobus Van Cortlandt ! Their names speak Dutch, and the men scarcely speak English." Johannes De Peyster and Jeremias Van Rensselaer were also among these elected.

James Graham was one of those who attached themselves to Bellomont, and the warm-hearted Earl placed implicit confidence in him for a time. With all his democratic notions the nobleman governor had great respect for birth and blood. Graham was the son of the Earl of Montrose, who, although a Scotchman, was well known and highly esteemed in England. That was his first recommendation. Then, too, he was endowed with brilliant intellectual qualities, was witty, chivalrous, communicative, overflowed with anecdote, in short, was a man after the Earl's own heart, and he enjoyed such society. But Graham was not a friend who could be trusted, and a more cautious and less sincere man than the impulsive Bellomont would have sooner found him out. He was the attorney-general of the province, and had consequently drawn up all the necessary papers for Fletcher's land-grants. Inconsistent as it appears, he was one of the very first to suggest their illegality. If such was the fact, then he alone was responsible, for he understood the forms and methods of the province and Fletcher left the whole matter entirely to him. He was apparently in entire sympathy with the projects of the Earl, vouchsafed much information, said the grants were destructive to the best interests of the people, and ought to be broken. He recommended, however, that a few should be shattered at first, " as a sort of essay to see how it would be borne," and the rest destroyed afterwards. It was serious business, but Bellomont was undismayed and plunged straight into the fire. Graham knew how, like many another adviser since his time, to throw fuel into the flames and protect himself.

He had been chosen speaker of the House, and was ordered to prepare the bill for vacating the grants. The first estates under condemnation were, two of Dominie Dellius, one of Colonel Bayard, one of Captain Evans, one of Caleb Heathcote, and one belonging to Trinity Church. Before the subject was brought into the council for formal approval, Bellomont sent an invitation for Graham to dine with him one day, and remarked, among other things, that Colonel William Smith seemed very much averse to the passage of such a bill. Graham, to the Earl's astonishment, said the thing could not be done at all; that civil war would ensue should it be attempted. The following day Graham called upon the Earl, and told how he had found a quarter of meat significantly laid across the sill of his door on the previous evening, which none of his servants could account for, and which was undoubtedly a menace, meaning that he was to be quartered. Bellomont laughed at such nonsensical fears. The same day the bill was brought before the council. Three members were for it, and three against it, and, as there were only six present, Bellomont gave the casting vote. He wrote to the Lords of Trade that the three who were against it were the largest landholders in New York, except Dominie Dellius. He, with singular honesty of purpose, caused the bill to be so worded that his own and all future governors' hands were tied from granting any more, or even so much as leasing the demesne of the governor for more than his own time in the government. The House added a clause to deprive Dominie Dellius also of his benefice at Albany, to which the council agreed. While it was being discussed in the Assembly Graham opposed it, which greatly annoyed Bellomont, since it had been framed through his direct instrumentality. It passed the House, however, with a large majority.

The remainder of the grants were shortly to be attacked. Prominent among the landgraves was the chief justice of the province, and counselor, Colonel William Smith, of St. George's manor, near Brookehaven. It was said that he owned over fifty miles of sea-beach, and that his land crossed the whole breadth of Long Island. He was influential, and Bellomont apprehended that he would prove a formidable antagonist, but was fully determined to meet the issue. Personally he had no affinity for the cold, taciturn, self-righteous ex-governor of Tangier. He did not even respect his abilities. He admitted that Smith " had more sense, and was more gentlemanlike than any man whom he had seen in the province, but that did not make him a lawyer, and he really knew very little about law with all his legal pretensions."

While Bellomont was maturing his policy of grading the hills and building up the vales, a terrible commotion was being fomented. Dominie Dellius had sailed for England, carrying certificates of his piety and good life, and a purse for his expenses filled by the members of his church in Albany. He went in all confidence to the king, expecting to get the Act annulled which deprived him of his broad pastures. At the same time the church-wardens and vestry of Trinity Church appealed to the Bishop of London in the most earnest manner, asking his interference with the Lords of Trade to prevent Bellomont from wresting from them their property and rights. They particularly commended the great zeal, generous liberality, and indefatigable industry of Fletcher, who they said was the " sole founder, the principal promoter, and the most liberal benefactor " of the church ; and they prayed that the destruction planned by one who was a communicant and constant attendant might be averted. Rev. Mr. Vesey esteemed himself personally aggrieved in the matter. He had been on agreeable terms with Bellomont, had dined with him often, and had driven with him in his coach-and-six. The good divine at once left

Portrait and Autograph of Rev. William Vesey.

the governor and family out of his prayers altogether. And what was more, he prayed for Dominie Dellius by name each Sunday in the sanctuary, desiring God to give the latter a safe and prosperous voyage and great success with the king.[1]

Bellomont was confounded. He had not intended to injure the welfare of the church, only to recover the gubernatorial conveniences which the church enjoyed. He had, with the consent of the council, settled £ 26 per year upon the minister for house-rent; and it was his intention to propose to the Assembly a further settlement of £ 50 per year upon Mr. Vesey, and all his successors in that cure. As things stood he could no longer attend divine service in his accustomed place, and he wrote to the Bishop petitioning that Mr. Vesey be immediately deprived of his benefice in New York.

As for Dominie Dellius it is hardly probable that he obtained his Indian lands fraudently. He had been an agent among the savages, and during the long years of wars and alarms had been of great service to the government. At one time he had, in connection with Peter Schuyler and one or two others, petitioned Fletcher for liberty to trade with the Mohawks. Fletcher saw no objection, since the practice of buying large estates for a few knives and tobacco-pouches had been in vogue ever since New York was first settled; and, besides, he had been instructed by the king to use his own discretion in such matters. A short time subsequently, permission was granted to Dominie Dellius to make a second purchase, in which no one was concerned but himself. The sachems accepted the price offered, and signed and sealed the instrument of conveyance in the same solemn manner that other Indians had done before them. But as soon as Fletcher had gone and Bellomont began his reformatory movements, these treacherous men of the forest complained, and said they had been cheated and deceived. Dellius had been an active opponent of Leisler, hence appearances were made to tell seriously against him by the party in power. Not only his religion, but his morals were assailed. The customary epithets of the times, such as "incendiary" and "liar" and "proud person," were heaped upon him, and it was asserted that he did not pray for the king, only for the Crown of England.

The aristocracy of that decade sustained the clergy, and the clergy sustained the aristocracy; and the merchants sustained both the clergy and the aristocracy. Their grievances were of a kindred nature. Their cry of rage vibrated on one chord. Each sent angry petitions across the water asking for Bellomont's recall.

The Lords of Trade were worse confounded than Bellomont himself. With petitions as above filling up their tables, and with the indignant

---

[1] Vesey Street was named from this clergyman. Church, Chapel, and Rector Streets have the same clerical origin.

Bayard, Brooke, and Dellius standing boldly before them in defense of rights civil and political, the trial of Fletcher came on and occupied some days. The charges against him proved less formidable than had been expected before they were subjected to the light of careful analysis. Evidence was entirely wanting to convict him of any intentional wrong-doing. The result of the trial was only an expression of mild disapproval concerning some of his proceedings.

Bellomont was deeply chagrined; the more so when he received a friendly caution from the king to beware lest he encourage the Leislerians so far that they demand reparation for damages sustained during the Revolution. Such a course would involve property interests and drive many important families from the province. Bellomont responded quickly that he had no idea of such a foolish step. "You must think me out of my wits," he said. At the same time he defined his policy, that since many men of the Leislerian party in New York were competent to hold office, it was only fair to promote them.

The Act for breaking the grants was laid on the table for future consideration by the Lords of Trade, and that was another mortifying circumstance. Bellomont wrote as if stung by an asp. He said he had only carried out the instructions of the crown, and if he was not sustained in his course he should resign. He did not desire to have the Act to break the two grants of Dellius approved, unless he should be abundantly authorized to go on and break the others, meaning Schuyler's, Van Rensselaer's, Livingston's, Van Cortlandt's, Philipse's, — both father's and son's, — Smith's, Nicolls's, Beekman's, Morris's, etc. He asked the recall of Matthew Clarkson, the secretary of the province, saying that he was a "weak man, incapable of business," and that he was heartily tired of him. He declared that there was not a man in New York whose skill and integrity he could trust, and recommended that George Tollet be sent from England to fill the vacancy. He complimented the Dutch citizens of New York for their honesty, but said the English were quicker in accounts and more ready with their pens. As for himself, he said he was perpetually in business from nine o'clock in the morning until ten at night, except during meals, and that it was wearing upon his health and strength.

The Assembly settled the revenue upon the governor for six years, but it was not until after a long and tedious dispute. Graham several times waited upon Bellomont in the hope of persuading him to accept it for three years, and was haughtily rebuked for his pains. A bill passed the House during the same session for the building of a poorhouse. Bellomont smiled ironically when the news came to him, and remarked that there was no such thing as a beggar in city or country. And it is a significant fact that in no other part of the king's dominions at that time was there so rich a population as in New York.

About this time Abraham Gouverneur married Mary Leisler, the widow of Jacob Milborne. He was a member of the House, and drew up a remonstrance, addressed to the king, which arraigned all the proceedings against Leisler and Milborne. His intention was to compel Graham, the speaker, who had been one of the judges at their trial, and who was esteemed a two-sided politician, to proceed to the council-chamber, attended by the whole Assembly, and deliver the document to the governor; in case of his refusal, he was to be thrown out of the body. Dr. Staats told Bellomont what was in contemplation. A few moments later Graham himself appeared, and with considerable agitation said that he had just heard the paper read, and " would sooner be torn in pieces than bring it up and read it at the head of the House, for it would be in effect cutting his own throat." Bellomont resorted to an artifice to save Graham ; he sent for the Assembly, saying he had orders from the king to make Graham one of his council, and that they must choose a new speaker. Gouverneur was at once elected to the chair by general acclamation, and presented the remonstrance in due form. This movement did not accomplish its object; but it resulted in the disinterment of the remains of Leisler and Milborne, and with funeral honors they were given Christian burial in the Dutch Church. The service was performed at midnight, in presence of twelve hundred or more persons, and in the midst of a storm which was only equaled in fury by the one which deepened the gloom at the time of the execution. Order was maintained by a large detachment of soldiery.

At the same moment the Dutch Church was tottering upon its foundation. Bellomont had made an effort to annul the charter on the ground of its having been obtained through bribery. The only proof shown was that the consistory had on one occasion made Fletcher a present of a piece of plate. The charter itself was not agreeable to the Leislerians, because it gave the power of calling ministers to the minister and consistory. They battled for their old right of congregational vote. They carried their quarrels before the Classis of Amsterdam with such vigor that the first candidate who was called to act as colleague to Dominie Selyns declined the honor. The accomplished pastor, under whose ministration, since his return from Holland, the church had increased from four hundred and fifty to six hundred and fifty members, was growing old and must have assistance. The charter prevailed in the end, and the Rev. Mr. Du Bois accepted a call, and reached New York in the summer of 1699. The death of Dominie Selyns occurred shortly afterward, and his loss was deeply mourned. He was one of the acknowledged founders of the Dutch Church in America, and probably did more during his long, interesting, and honorable career to determine its position for all the future than any other man.

The time came at length when Bellomont must attend to that part of his commission which constituted him governor of Massachusetts and New Hampshire. He made the tiresome overland journey to Boston, while overwhelmed with care and perplexity, and suffering acutely with the gout in his right hand. He was accompanied by Lady Bellomont and a large retinue of servants. He found in each of the Eastern colonies two powerful parties, and the Acts of Trade violated and the collection of customs at loose ends. He found, too, that Boston was the seat of learning and fanaticism, and wondered how the two came to go hand in hand. Opposition to his measures was not so manifest as in New York, owing to the fact of there being less business done. New England was peopled with intellectual men of small means who wrung their subsistence from the earth. In the rural districts there was a general appearance of social equality. Bellomont had never seen anything like it, and contrasted it with the manors of New York, — the lords amid their tenantry and negro slaves, and their gilded trappings, coats-of-arms, and coaches-and-six. He was running over with democratic theories at the same time that all his tastes and habits of life were of the opposite character. But democracy was as yet imperfectly understood.

Boston was charmed with Bellomont. His noble bearing and easy elegant manners were everywhere admired. Crowds followed him through the streets. As in New York, his dinner-table was the resort of politicians. He instituted and encouraged their visits, but was oftentimes dreadfully bored. On one occasion, when his dining-hall was filled with Assemblymen from the country who were shabbily dressed and rough-mannered, he remarked aside to Lady Bellomont, " We must treat these gentlemen well; they give us our bread."

A larger revenue was voted to him in New England than had ever before been given to a governor. He favored the party in Massachusetts which opposed Dudley. There was comparative harmony in the General Court when he presided. We are told by historians that he was unparliamentary; he never, it seems, hesitated to propose business, recommend committees, or even leave his chair and mingle in the debates. In New Hampshire he quarreled with the lieutenant-governor (whom he had never liked) about having sent ship-timber to Portugal. At the time of the appointment of the latter he had said to Sir Henry

28

Ashurst, at whose instance it was done, " You seem to have a strong bias for carpenter-governors."

Bellomont kept his New York affairs constantly in mind during his stay in Boston. In one of his letters [1] to Colonel De Abraham Peyster he said : —

> " I wish you would tell Mr. Leisler that I can't move the king to get his father's debt ordered to be paid for want of government's and other people's testimony, on oath, that they saw Captain Leisler's books and that there was such a sum due as Dr. Staats and Gouverneur told me ; but the sum they mentioned I have forgot. Let this be done immediately, if they are able to swear to it ; it must be drawn up handsomely, that I may transmit it to England."

A little later he wrote, telling De Peyster, who had been in Boston with him for a short time, how high he (De Peyster) stood in the favor and good opinion of the New England people, and how much he was missed by everybody. He urged the latter " to get Mr. Leisler, Dr. Staats, Mr. Walters, and Mr. Gouverneur together and see if they cannot refresh their memories in the matter of the government debt. It will be ridiculous to ask the king to refund a debt when I do not know the amount." Lady Bellomont corresponded with several of the New York ladies while in Boston. At one time we find her desiring Mrs. De Peyster to buy her a pearl necklace if she could get one good and cheap.

Bellomont succeeded in arresting Captain Kidd before he left Boston. He had long felt that his honor and that of his government was deeply involved, and that the apprehension and punishment of the audacious pirate was essential to exculpation in the eyes of the world. Kidd had several times visited the American shores. He had buried a portion of his treasures on Gardiner's Island, which had afterwards been discovered. He fell directly into the trap which Bellomont had laid for him. He was sent to England for trial ; he was found guilty ; and he was executed on the 12th of May, 1701. His wife and daughter remained in New York, and lived in the strictest seclusion. The rumors of buried gold created a panic among the dwellers all along the Atlantic coast, and for years there was much digging and occasional " clicks of box-lids." But the fever at last died away, as have the wild romances and weird legends concerning Kidd.

When Bellomont returned to New York he wrote to the king that he should greatly prefer an honest judge and a trustworthy attorney-general to two ships-of-war. He said Graham " had changed his note and turned tail " ; that " Mr. Graham in the afternoon was always opposed to

---

[1] *Lord Bellomont to Colonel Abraham De Peyster*, August 3, 1699. *Miscellaneous Works of General J. Watts De Peyster*, p. 130.

Mr. Graham in the morning," and that he never knew when to depend upon his opinions, and was often led into ridiculous follies by him; that Graham never had rendered him any assistance only in the matter of hunting up testimony against Fletcher. He also said that piracy was on the wane, but he expected New York would be flooded with gold upon the arrival of one of Philipse's ships, which was expected.

About this time the new City Hall was built upon the site (donated by Colonel Abraham De Peyster), of the present Treasury building, Wall Street, opposite Broad. David Provoost, who was the mayor in 1699, laid the cornerstone. The building cost about £3,000. The arms of the king, also the arms of Belloment and of Nanfan, decorated the front. The old City Hall, which was in

City Hall, Wall Street.

an advanced state of decay, was sold to John Rodman for £920.

Public scavengers were first instituted this year, and two new markethouses were erected. Of the latter, one was on the corner of Coentis Slip and the other at the foot of Broad Street. A powder-house was built by the corporation, and in view of the recent Act of the Assembly in providing for a poor-house, a small building was hired where sick paupers might go for care and medical attention. The Brooklyn ferry was inspected and re-leased for seven years, and a ferry-house decided upon, which was subsequently erected. The rate of fare was established by law: it was eight stuyvers in wampum, or a silver twopence for a single person; half that sum each, when a number of persons traveled in company; one shilling for a horse; twopence for a hog (same as for a man); one penny for a sheep; and after sunset double ferriage for all. The dock was leased to Philip French for £40 per annum.

The Assembly met in the summer of 1700, but the business was unimportant and the session a short one. One law was enacted, however, which will never be read but with abhorrence. It was to hang every Popish priest who came voluntarily into the province of New York.

1700. Cruel and unaccountable as it appears, we have but to review the situation and dwell for a moment upon the bloody wars to the north, and the supposed tampering of the Jesuit emissaries with the Indians, to find cause for a measure rather of state policy than persecution. In directing severe penalties against the priests, the legislators fancied they were warding off the blows of the tomahawk.

The Board of Trade, consisting of a president and seven members, (the first in New York, and which had been established about three years,) should have exercised an immediate supervision over the commerce of the colony. It made the attempt, but the persistent violation of the revenue and other laws drove it to stringent measures, and it conse- . quently became as odious to the merchants as Bellomont himself. The latter interposed so many obstacles in the way of business that the London merchants were aroused and petitioned the king in behalf of the aggrieved people of New York. While it was under consideration another petition, praying to be reinstated in peace, safety, and prosperity, appeared, signed by thirty-three New York merchants, among whom were Nicholas Bayard, Philip French, Gabriel Minvielle, Rip Van Dam, Charles Lodwyck, Stephen De Lancey, Brandt Schuyler, Jacobus Van Cortlandt, David Jamison, and Elias Boudinot. There were thirty-two distinct accusations against Bellomont. The thirty-second was to the effect that the governor, in order to justify his arbitrary proceedings, had vilely slandered eminent and respectable persons; he had accused them of piracy and of trading with pirates, which was wholly false. The only ground he had ever had for such suspicions was that some of the rich gentlemen of New York owned ships which went to Madagascar for negroes, and sometimes met with India goods which they could buy at easy rates, but always gave true account of the same.

Before these papers were sent to England, the governors of Pennsylvania and Maryland tried to bring about a reconciliation between Bellomont and the merchants. Bellomont was irritated, and said he had no advances to make, unless it could be proven that he had acted contrary to law; if the merchants expected him to be reconciled and indulge them in unlawful trade and piracy, they would find themselves mistaken, for he should be " as steady as a rock on that point." He thought it was hard on him that the landholders should not have received their doom; he should expect insolence until the Act was ratified in England, " and until all who had obtained land by wholesale were brought under proper limits."

It was confidently asserted in New York that Bellomont was to be recalled, and some went so far as to say that Fletcher had been commissioned as his successor. This caused a disaffection among the Leislerians, and a number went over to the aristocracy. Bellomont was quite indifferent about being called home, and declared that no malice could spot his reputation. A letter from the Bishop of London to Rev. Mr. Vesey, however, cut him to the heart. The good divine seemed to have espoused the cause of Fletcher; he told the people of Trinity Church that " by Easter they would be rid of their grievances." " Ah !" said Bellomont, " if I am to find my services slighted in England, I may well be troubled."

The Lords of Trade had really taken no action in the matter. The contradictory stories perplexed them. They wrote a cheerful letter of encouragement to Bellomont, and appointed Judge Atwood and Attorney-General Broughton to go to his relief and assistance. They were a long time, however, in reaching New York. Bellomont was impatient with the delay, and said " the way some people shirked their duty and stayed away from their posts was intolerable." As for Weaver, who had loitered in England nearly three years, the governor asked the Lords to send him immediately home ; and at the same time he informed them that Major Ingoldsby had been in London four years, leaving his wife and children to starve, — the latter had now gone to stay at Judge Pinhorne's in New Jersey. Hungerford, who, on account of relationship, had been appointed assistant collector of the customs, was in jail, having " played the fool and worse." Augustine Graham (son of James Graham) had been suspended from the office of adjutant-general, " because," said Bellomont, " I esteem him a superfluous charge to the government." He was accused of intemperance, and Bellomont remarked " that the son would become sober when the father became honest." Lieutenant-Governor Nanfan was at Barbadoes, looking after his wife's fortune. Peter Schuyler never attended the meetings of the council, owing to the pressure of his duties in Albany. Robert Livingston could only come to New York at certain seasons of the year. Chief Justice Smith's home was a hundred miles away, and he was rarely present. Graham was at his country-seat near Morrisania, eight miles from the city, and was " either sick or sullen, for he had not shown himself for five months." It was thus that Bellomont pictured his hardships in being obliged to attend to the business of others as well as his own, and asked for an increase of salary. He expressed himself greatly hurt at having been " so pushed at," for supposed complicity with Captain Kidd, and said it was a cruelty that every honest man who served the king should have his name torn and villified.

In the early part of January, 1701, Bellomont publicly removed Gra-
1701. ham from the offices of attorney-general and city recorder. He
January. might have spared his former friend this infliction, and said he
should have done so had he known his illness was of a serious character.
Graham was dying, having been suffering from a serious malady ever
since his last visit to the council-chamber. He lived but a few days after
he was informed of the action of the governor. His large estate near
Morrisania was divided equally among his six children. Of his manner
of life a passing glimpse is handed along to us in his will, which makes
mention of an overseer, two white servants, and thirty negro slaves.

In November, prior to the death of Graham, Hon. Stephanus Van
Cortlandt had finished his eventful career. Bellomont felt his loss keenly
Although they differed in opinions upon almost every important subject
which came up for discussion in the council, they were warm personal
friends. Van Cortlandt had borne his years well, and was an excellent
public officer. His liberal views and large charities had greatly facilitated
the growth and prosperity of New York. His last sleep was full of
honors. His place in the council was filled by William Lawrence, who
was pronounced " a man of good estate and honest understanding."

Feb. In the latter part of February, Bellomont was attacked with the
gout, to which he had been subject for years ; but with characteristic energy he for several days dictated communications to the various
parts of his government, and, regardless of physical pain, wrote one or two
letters with his own hand. He grew worse, and on the 5th of
March 5. March ended his arduous and unsatisfactory labors, at the age of
sixty-five. His death caused a profound sensation. A general fast was
observed throughout the province. He was interred with appropriate
ceremonies in the chapel in the fort. When that structure was leveled in
1790, his leaden coffin was tenderly removed and deposited in St. Paul's
churchyard.

Lady Bellomont remained in New York about a year and a half after
the death of her husband, and then returned to England, where she subsequently married again. In her deep affliction she received the constant
attention and sympathy of Mrs. Abraham De Peyster, and Mrs. Stephanus
Van Cortlandt, — Lady Van Cortlandt, as she was then styled. The coach
of the latter, with its outriders wearing badges of mourning, made frequent
trips between the manor-house and city, although the ladies and their servants were much oftener seen wending their way through the woods on
horseback. Anne, the daughter of Van Cortlandt, had been married, a few
months before the death of the latter, to Stephen De Lancey,[1] and was now

---

[1] Stephen De Lancey soon afterward built a large elegant homestead upon land conveyed to

presiding over a pretentious mansion of her own on Broadway near Trinity Church. De Lancey was one of the merchants who had writhed under the imputation of piracy, and hated Bellomont with fiery intensity; but it did not prevent his beautiful bride from showing the utmost kindness to the bereaved widow.

What the results of Bellomont's policy might have been must ever remain a mystery. Few have been incited by more conscientious motives in their efforts to administer justice. His errors were chiefly in judgment; he allowed noble and praiseworthy impulses to carry him beyond the bounds of common prudence. But through his instrumentality piracy received a check from which it never had vitality enough to recover, and although he did not succeed in destroying the political influence and in lowering the social position of the gentry of the province, he did advance men who might not otherwise have had their talents recognized, and he produced something more nearly approximate to a common level than any one individual ever accomplished either before or since his time. Few would have had the courage to have raised an arm against so many adversaries, rarely another could have done so without falling in the fray. His death was the source of fresh troubles, and the only wonder is that New York did not resolve into a state of hopeless anarchy.[1]

him by his father-in-law, Stephanus Van Cortlandt, on the corner of Broad and Dock, now Broad and Pearl Streets. This same edifice attained celebrity at a much later period, as " Fraunces' Tavern." *Chamber of Commerce Records*, by John Austin Stevens, 307, 308.

[1] In my account of the brief administration of Lord Bellomont, as in many other instances, I abstain from citing authorities, because my authorities are too numerous to cite. My information has been derived, not only from the sources open to every student of history, but from thousands of old letters, sermons, tracts, records of trials, wills, and other musty and forgotten documents.

CHAPTER XXII.

1701–1710.

COLONEL WILLIAM SMITH.

Colonel William Smith. — Conflict in the Council. — Lieutenant-Governor Nan-
fan. — Illegal Voting. — Robert Livingston in Disgrace. — Mrs. Gertrude Van
Cortlandt. — The City Elections. — Extraordinary Confusion. — Mayor Noell.
— Chief Justice Atwood. — Manor-House of Caleb Heathcote. — Trial of Nich-
olas Bayard for Treason. — Death of William III. — Lord Cornbury. — Bay-
ard's Sentence reversed. — The Yellow Fever. — The Church Quarrel. — Lady
Bellomont. — The Leisler Bill. — Death of Frederick Philipse. — Philipse
Manor. — Philipse Will. — The French Church. — Trinity Church. — Queen
Anne. — Excitements. — The Treasurer of the Province. — Death of Lady
Cornbury. — Lord Cornbury and the two Presbyterian Ministers. — The Assembly of 1708. — Spirited Resolutions. — Lord Lovelace. — First Paper Money
in New York. — Five Indian Chiefs at Queen Anne's Court. — The Silver Vase
presented to Schuyler by Queen Anne.

THE sadness which fell like a pall over New York upon the death
of Lord Bellomont was quickly pierced by a clash in the political

1701. arena. Lieutenant-Governor Nanfan was in Barbadoes, and the
March 5. government was without a head. Colonel William Smith hastened to New York, but, owing to recent storms and swollen
streams, he did not arrive until the 11th. The ice was just breaking
in the Hudson River, which prevented Peter Schuyler and

March 11. Robert Livingston from reaching the city until the 21st of the
month.

Without waiting for the two latter, the council met to consider what
March 12. steps to take in the emergency. Colonel Smith claimed the chair
by virtue of being the oldest member. The four other gentlemen
present — Abraham De Peyster, Dr. Staats, Robert Walters, and Thomas
Weaver — thought a vote should be taken and the majority decide the
question. Smith said it was "an odd and doubtful way of proceeding,"
and since New York had never been so circumstanced before they must
look to other of the king's plantations for a precedent in the matter. The
discussion grew interesting and considerable heat was manifested. Smith

wrote out his opinion, and it was twice read before the meeting. They finally separated and came together again the next morning. A written reply to Smith's arguments was produced and read. It ^{March 13.} declared that one member had no more power than another, and that when the majority saw fit to meet as a council for the transaction of public business they should notify Smith, and if he refused to meet with them, they should act in the administration of the government without him. De Peyster acted as President of the Council.

The spirit and tone of the document offended Smith, but he maintained his position. After a long session the gentlemen separated without having arrived at any settlement. The next day and the next was but a repetition of the same. The question also came up as to whether the Assembly ought to sit on the 2d of April, the day specified at the time of their prorogation. Smith was inclined to believe that the Assembly was actually dissolved by the governor's death. Some of the gentlemen were so earnest in pressing for the meeting of the Assembly that Smith suspected they designed attempting to pass bills of private consequence, which Bellomont had only been prevented from doing by the superior discernment of the Lords of Trade. Such was the fact, as subsequent events proved. The Leisler family had never rested in the matter of securing an Act of the Legislature of the province to sustain them in instituting suits for damages, claimed to have been sustained during the revolution, and their estimates were alarmingly exorbitant. The wife of Robert Walters was Leisler's daughter, and she inherited her father's persistence in a purpose, as well as her share of the estate. It is easy to see why Walters was anxious to seize the opportunity to further her wishes and increase his own possessions. Dr. Staats had been one of Leisler's council, and had always advocated the exaction of some terrible retribution for the murder of two innocent men. Weaver was a new man in New York, and one of those blundering and shallow persons who always talk loudly, particularly upon those subjects which they least understand, and who are usually restrained with difficulty from talking all the time. The speaker of the Assembly was Abraham Gouverneur, who had not only suffered himself, but his wife was Leisler's daughter, and was doubly interested through her father and her first husband. This was certainly an opportune moment for carrying a long-determined plan into execution.

Schuyler and Livingston at last put in their appearance. They at once took the ground which had been held so valiantly by Smith. Livingston had, in the earlier part of Bellomont's administration, sided ^{March 21.} with the Leislerians. But it was more from personal regard for the gov-

29

ernor than for any sympathy in their cause. The Kidd affair, in which he had been accused of sequestering piratical treasures to a large amount, had produced coolness between himself and Bellomont. The remarkable interests now at stake brought him into his old groove. There was a sharpening of sabers and a rush to mortal combat. It was three against four, De Peyster being in sympathy with the Leislerians. The scheme of revenge was charged squarely upon the latter. In turn Livingston and Schuyler were accused of defrauding the government, and Smith was informed that he was considered a dangerous man by the late governor, and was just about to have been ousted from the council. Colonel Smith had actually been deprived of the office of chief justice in December, and De Peyster had been invested with the dignity — during the interim, until the arrival of Atwood — simply for necessary process without being expected to judge in any cause. The eloquent vituperation and stinging sarcasm which echoed from wall to wall in the council-chamber was unequalled in history. The clamor of the angry disputants was so loud and threatening that people in the neighborhood spread an alarm. Weaver outdid all the rest in the elevation of his voice and in the originality of his ideas. He said if the rest of the four were of his mind, they " would put those who would not submit to the majority fast in irons and chains," for it was nothing more or less than rebellion.

April 2. The Assembly met on the 2d of April, but owing to the quarrel in the council adjourned from day to day. Both parties sent a written explanation of the controversy to the House, and it was decided that the council had the right to govern by majority of voices. But in view of the irreconcilable nature of the singular affair the House adjourned until June. Meanwhile Nanfan arrived. There was no **May 10.** longer any question of pre-eminence, for, according to the provision in Bellomont's commission, the lieutenant-governor was now the commander-in-chief. Other questions arose, however, of even graver moment, and the spirit of antagonism increased to an unprecedented degree.

The Lords of Trade had advised Nanfan to avoid engaging himself " in the heats and animosities of parties," and in all things to use moderation. He attempted obedience, and his first act was to dissolve the Assembly and order a new election. The energy and tact of each party were brought into full play, and the contest was one of the most bitter and demoralizing that ever occurred in New York. There was illegal voting everywhere. The elections were sharply disputed. The Leislerians were in the majority ; when they came to choose a speaker for the House there was another painful disturbance. Out of twenty-one members, of which the House was composed, ten voted for Abraham Gouverneur and nine for William Nicolls. The minority undertook to prove that Gouverneur was an alien, for which several of the gentlemen were prosecuted. On the other hand, it was charged that Nicolls and Wessells were not properly qualified to act as members, because they were not actual residents of the counties where they were elected. They both retired from the House in anger, and sent written complaints of their treatment to England.

The oaths were administered to the Assemblymen by Atwood (who had arrived and been made one of the counselors), De Peyster, and Livingston. Two days later Nanfan named a committee, by urgent request from certain sources, to audit the public accounts. It con- Aug. 19. Aug. 21. sisted of Atwood, De Peyster, Dr. Staats, and Robert Walters, who were to meet a committee from the House at the residence of Roger Baker. It was a proceeding aimed directly at Robert Livingston. It was pretended that he had never accounted for the public money which he had formerly received out of the excise. He indignantly refused to appear before this tribunal. His conduct was pronounced " a determination not to render an account," although it was well known that his books and vouchers were in the hands of the government and detained from him. The two committees unanimously recommended that a bill be passed the House for the confiscation of his real and personal estate to the value of as much debt to the crown as could be charged to him.

A few days later Mrs. Stephanus Van Cortlandt was summoned before the auditing committee to pay an alleged deficit in her late hus- Sept. 9. band's accounts to the amount of £ 530. She took no notice of the mandate. She even withheld the books and papers when they were demanded. Quite an excitement was fomented on her account, but she stood out as fearlessly against threats as she had done in the time of the Revolution. She believed her husband to have been perfectly upright, and was determined to prevent his memory from being sullied through the implacable malice of the party in power. She hoped, too, that before matters came to a crisis a new governor and a new order of things might bless New York. Suits were instituted against her, but Lord Cornbury came just in time to save her from being publicly annoyed. Her resolute course of action was attributed largely to the influence of Nicholas Bayard, whose son Samuel had recently married her daughter Margaret, and the families were more intimate if possible than ever. She was supposed, too, to be very much under the guidance of Livingston, whose wife was her sister Alida, and who stayed chiefly at her house when in New York. Both suppositions were alike incorrect and did the lady injustice. She was a responsible, capable, and efficient member of society, abundantly able to judge and act for herself.

Nanfan informed the auditing committee, that while in Albany, in conference with the sachems of the Five Nations, just after his arrival from Barbadoes, the Indians had expressed great affection for Livingston, and desired that he should be sent to Europe to procure them some favors. The committee summoned Livingston before them, and this time he appeared. They told him that it had been made to appear that he had used some undue influence in prevailing upon the Indians to signify their pleasure that he should visit the king in their behalf; but that he could, if he thought proper, take a voluntary oath to clear himself from censure. Livingston was too well acquainted with English law and liberty to abet such insolence. He knew that there was not a shadow of proof against him. He contemptuously replied that he "did not think it worth his while."

The House immediately addressed Nanfan with a petition to be forwarded to the king for the removal of Livingston from the office of Secretary of Indian Affairs. A bill was prepared, obliging Livingston to account, which was passed, with an amendment by Nanfan, to the effect that time should be given him until the 25th of March, 1702.

October. Other bills passed, but the one entitled "An Act for the payment of the debts of the government made in the late happy Revolution," was delayed day after day by the persistent opposition of the minority. Finally young Leisler went to Nanfan with a petition that it might receive immediate consideration. Nanfan received him graciously, but coolly remarked that the Assembly had been sitting a long time, and the remaining bills must all be dismissed until the next session. The same afternoon he prorogued the House until the third Tuesday in March.

The city elections were as disorderly as those of the province. Both parties seemed lost to all sense of honor and decency. There was as much illegal as legal voting, and several bloody skirmishes among individuals. At last there was a violent dispute about which party had really won. As there were to be six aldermen and six assistants, should party division be equal, Thomas Noell, the new mayor, who belonged to the aristocracy, would have the casting vote. But the Leislerians claimed the victory, and, departing from the customary method, were severally sworn in by the retiring mayor, who was of their own party.

Mayor Noell was sworn, as usual, before the governor and council, and then repaired, in company with the elected aldermen, to Trinity Church to listen to an appropriate discourse by Rev. Mr. Vesey. From there they proceeded in solemn state to the City Hall, where the bell was rung, Mayor Noell published his commission and took the chair. The retiring mayor, De Riemer, arose and gracefully presented him with the city charter and seal. Abraham Gouverneur was city recorder, and took his seat by the mayor. Noell told the clerk to proceed with the ceremony of swearing in the members elect. Several responded, as their names were called, by saying they had been sworn in already. Shouts of " It cannot be done," and " It is not according to law," caused great confusion. There were crowds of citizens present, and all talked together, until the hubbub was deafening. Some declared that no one could be legally sworn by the old mayor, and others with equal emphasis maintained the right by law. Not only voices but fists were raised, and the uproar became of such magnitude that Mayor Noell apprehended a fight and arose and dissolved the meeting.

Noell declined to sit with aldermen, as a common council, who refused to be sworn by him. And as the common council was the only legal authority for scrutinizing disputed elections, the city was in danger of being without a government. The urgency of the case induced Noell to take upon himself the responsibility of appointing four men in each ward to inspect returns. The Leislerians whom he placed on these committees refused to serve. They pronounced the proceeding irregular, and claimed that the common council could only judge of the qualifications of its own members. The remainder of the committees went on with their labors, and returned the names of all the voters in the disputed wards, with the men for whom they had severally voted. It was found that the aristocratic party were in the majority.

Mayor Noell then called a meeting at the City Hall to swear in the new aldermen. Those who would be displaced by such action joined them, and they all marched along the streets and entered the hall ^Nov. 11. together. They took their seats side by side, with angry determination resting upon their countenances. Mayor Noell arose, and said he should use no violence to eject those who had no business there, and went on swearing in such as had been legally chosen. Voices were meanwhile protesting from every part of the hall. The clerk administered the oaths amid a deafening roar of tongues, and when the mayor proceeded to the transaction of business, all took part with audacious effrontery until the confusion became so great that he adjourned the Board for two weeks. The case went before the Supreme Court, which decided upon an ^Dec. 29. equal division of the aldermen and assistants between the two parties. As Mayor Noell and Recorder Gouverneur were opposed, the Board stood equally divided.

With Chief Justice Atwood came Attorney-General Broughton from England. A round of dinners and entertainments was given these gen-

tlemen, which, together with the great heat of the summer, caused Broughton a severe fit of illness. He had a family of eight, and houses were so
scarce that he could find no accommodations except in crowded lodgings.
He finally wrote to the Lords of Trade for special permission to occupy
one of Captain Kidd's vacant dwellings. He also petitioned that the
office of surveyor-general might be given to his son, in case Augustine
Graham, who had sailed for England to settle his father's estate, should
resign.

Weaver, as collector of the customs, made himself offensive to men of
all classes and opinions. He collided with the merchants concerning the
Acts of Trade so perpetually, that he was more cordially hated than any
other man who had ever filled the position. When he meddled with politics his dogmatic assertions and shallow understanding were brought so
conspicuously into the foreground, that even his best friends said he was
enough to ruin any cause.

During this autumn Madame Sarah Knight journeyed from Boston to
New York on horseback, and wrote some very pleasant notes about her trip.
She was obliged to ford some rivers, and cross others in a frail scow, and as
for taverns, there were no such conveniences as yet along the route. She
was a woman of culture as well as courage, and deeply interested in the
progress and development of the country. As she approached Mamaroneck
she was surprised to find so much of the land under successful cultivation, and good buildings erected. Presently she came to the manor-house
of Colonel Caleb Heathcote, with its broad lawns, handsome gardens, elegant shade-trees, and great deer-park after the most approved English
fashion. As for New Rochelle, she pronounced it a " clean, pretty place,
where many French gentlemen of learning resided, and where were pass-
able roads, and a bridge broad enough for a cart."

The city of New York was so very unlike Boston, that she regarded it
with special interest. The half-blending of Dutch and English customs,
the confusion of tongues, the variety of fashions, and the different styles
of equipage attracted and amused her. She said, " the prevailing style of
architecture was plain," the brick buildings were chiefly " in divers colors
laid in checks and glazed." The inside, as far as she had an opportunity
of judging, was more elaborate than the outside, and neat to a fault. The
hearthstones usually extended far into the room and were laid with tiles ;
the staircases were highly ornamented. The streets of the city were generally paved to the width of ten feet from the fronts of the houses on each
side of the way, while the center was constructed to serve the double purpose of gutter and sewer. A few " brick pathways " were the only sidewalks. Broadway was shaded with beautiful trees on either side.

The judicial jurisdiction of Chief Justice Atwood extended over New England, but he was not well received in the courts. He was many times affronted in the most premeditated manner. While attempting to suppress illegal trade in Boston he had a sharp conflict with the son of Robert Livingston, who had a vessel wrecked off the coast, filled with wines, brandies, and other European commodities. And he was instrumental in seizing the cargo of a vessel belonging to Samuel Vetch, afterwards governor of Nova Scotia, whose wife was Margaret, the daughter of Robert Livingston.

View of New York, 1704.

As for Robert Livingston himself, he was vilified, accused, and threatened on every side. Party ingenuity was constantly at work devising new ways for blackening his character. There were grounds for complaint against him, but insufficient to warrant the wholesale defamation to which he was subjected. And equally virulent were the attacks upon Colonel Nicholas Bayard, whose power as a political leader was well understood. The passage of the Leisler Bill, as it was called, was a foregone conclusion with the Leislerians, hence a proclamation was issued, ordering every person concerned to bring in claims and losses for settlement. The inventory that followed was a most extraordinary mathematical production, as might have been predicted. One old gun, and a small rusty sword, seized by Governor Sloughter, were together valued at £ 40 ; and hundreds of similar items might be cited.

The proceeding created intense excitement. The aggrieved appealed to the king, asking for a governor — one who understood the principles of government, and whose sentiments were in unison with those of Parliament. An address of congratulation was also prepared to forward to Lord Cornbury, who, it was reported, had been chosen to succeed Bellomont. These papers were burdened with over six hundred signatures, among which were those of the leading men of the aristocratic party. The movement was conducted with great secrecy; but it was discovered by Nanfan and the members of his council, who styled it "A CONSPIRACY." They said it was done to intimidate them from the performance of duty. Notwithstanding petitions had been the acknowledged right of Englishmen for ages, Chief Justice Atwood claimed that the present was a case of "sedition and rebellion." The most persistent effort was made by the government to secure the papers or their copies. Several persons were arrested and brought before the council, and by means of threats and promises the information was at last obtained, that the documents had been signed at a coffee-house kept by Captain Hutchings, one of the city aldermen. It also appeared that Colonel Bayard and his son Samuel were concerned. Hutchings and the two Bayards were accordingly summoned before Nanfan and the council, and examined. The result was unsatisfactory, since no new facts were elicited; Hutchings was committed to jail for not producing the papers, and Colonel Bayard and his son were compelled to enter into bonds to the amount of £1,500 each, to answer to an indictment to be filed against them in the Supreme Court.

A consultation took place the next day among the signers of the papers. It was unanimously decided that there was nothing whatever in the transaction contrary to the plain English law. Consequently Colonel Bayard, Rip Van Dam, Philip French, and Thomas Wenham signed an appeal, addressed to the governor and council, asking for the release of Hutchings, who could not produce the papers, because they were not in his possession. The petitioners frankly admitted that they held the documents, but denied any disloyalty. Chief Justice Atwood denounced the haughtiness in the tone of the communication. Dr. Staats and Robert Walters read and re-read and weighed the language of the petitioners, sentence by sentence. What could this passage mean? — "and another address to my Lord Cornbury, whom we understand by certain advice we have received from England to be nominated by his Majesty to succeed the late Earl of Bellomont." Was not such an expression literally disowning and casting off the authority of Lieutenant-Governor Nanfan? Nanfan himself did not so interpret it. But then, he was only the figure-head of the administration. Weaver saw more clearly through the film, and detected what he styled "an infernal plot."

Before noon of the same day Colonel Nicholas Bayard was arrested for

"High Treason," and committed to prison. The city militia were placed on guard above his cell, to prevent his being rescued by enraged friends.

Philip French and Thomas Wenham were given six days in which to produce the "treasonable addresses." They declined, and, not relishing the prospect of imprisonment, quietly left the province. Attorney-General Broughton saw no sufficient ground for the commitment of any of the petitioners; he was ordered with considerable asperity to give his reasons in writing for such an opinion. He did so, and Chief Justice Atwood was highly indignant, and ordered the grand jury of the Supreme Court to bring a presentment against him for neglect of duty; Weaver, as solicitor-general, put it into a formal indictment. **1702.** **Jan.**

Bayard and Hutchings were arraigned, indicted, and tried for high treason. They petitioned for a postponement of the trial until the usual sitting of the Supreme Court, but, instead, a special court was ordered for February 19. Samuel Bayard prayed earnestly that his father might have a jury composed of Englishmen. This, too, was without avail. Chief Justice Atwood was on the bench, and the associate judges were Colonel Abraham De Peyster and Robert Walters. Weaver was the prosecuting attorney, and insisted upon sitting with the jury. When the gentlemen of the jury differed from him materially in opinion, he threatened "to have them trounced." William Nicolls and James Emott appeared for the defense. They were both remarkable lawyers for the times in which they lived, but their sound reasoning and eloquence were wasted on this occasion, the prisoners having been condemned in advance by both judge and jurors. **Feb.**

Bayard pleaded "NOT GUILTY" to the charge of having conspired to produce mutiny among the king's soldiers by persuading them to sign "libels" against the government, and to the other treasonable acts specified. The defense attempted to show that the addresses were the opposite of treasonable, their design being simply to prove to the Lords of Trade that the signers were neither "Jacobites" nor "pirates," as had been represented, but good and loyal subjects ready to give up lives and fortunes at any moment in the king's service.

Weaver, in a violent speech, charged the Englishmen of New York with trying to introduce popery and slavery into the province, and pronounced Bayard the leader. He said they were a band of pirates, and had offered the late Lord Bellomont £10,000 to connive at their infamy. At one stage of the trial Nicolls moved for an adjournment until the next morning. "No," responded the chief justice, "we do not propose to give Mr. Vesey a chance for another sermon against us." The foreman of the jury was the brother of one of the judges upon the bench. When

29

the case was turned over to them, they were absent from the room but a few minutes before returning with a verdict of GUILTY.

Chief Justice Atwood immediately proceeded to pronounce the horrible English sentence upon traitors then in full force.

Bayard applied to Nanfan for a reprieve until his Majesty's pleasure should be known. This was denied unless he should acknowledge himself guilty of the crime of treason. Six several petitions were in like manner rejected by the lieutenant-governor. The governor and prominent gentlemen of the neighboring provinces interceded, but to no purpose. The day of execution was fixed. Of this he was duly notified and placed in irons. He was forbidden to see his wife, children, or other relatives. Finally friends drew up a petition worded so as to express his sincere sorrow for the offense of signing the addresses and encouraging others to sign, and begging pardon for the same. This, at the last moment, obtained a reprieve, but it did not liberate him from prison. Hutchings, however, was released on bail.

On the very day that Colonel Bayard was being denounced as a traitor, William III. of England was finishing his brilliant career.
March 7.
He had reigned a few days over thirteen years. His death would have been a great stroke to the nation at any time, but at this particular epoch nothing could have been more unfortunate. The insult of Louis XIV., who, upon the death of James II., a few months before, had proclaimed that ex-monarch's doubtful son king of England, rendered another war inevitable. William had formed a great alliance, and was about to consummate a critical scheme of warfare. He desired to live a little longer; and yet he met death with calmness and without fear. He expressed his firm faith in the Christian religion, and received the sacrament. His last act was to take the hand of one of his earliest friends and press it to his heart. When his remains were prepared for the coffin it was found that he wore next to his skin a small piece of black silk ribbon. The lords in waiting ordered it to be taken off. It contained a gold ring and a lock of the hair of Mary.

The crown, pursuant to previous Act of Parliament, devolved on Anne, the youngest daughter of King James by his first marriage. She was then in the thirty-eighth year of her age. The Privy Council waited upon her in a body, and she received them in a well-considered speech, which she pronounced with great distinctness and effect. The coronation took place on the 23d of April (St. George's Day); and Dr. Sharp, the Archbishop of York, preached an appropriate sermon on the occasion. The Queen immediately gave orders for naming the electress of Brunswick, in the collect for the royal family, as the next heir to the crown, and she formed a ministry.

Meanwhile the New York Assembly met in March and hastened to pass the celebrated Leisler Act. A bill was also worried through the House, in spite of determined opposition, to outlaw Philip French and Thomas Wenham. The other business consisted of the passage of an Act to increase the number of assemblymen by five; of an Act to continue the revenue two years longer; and of several Acts of minor importance. The House continued its sessions both night and day in order to accomplish all that was desired before the possible arrival of a new governor. A jury of inquiry returned estimates concerning Livingston's property, and under the conditions of an Act passed in September, the whole of his estate, real and personal, was confiscated, and he was deprived of his seat in the council and of all his other offices.

An arrival of importance created another sensation while the city was astir with these remarkable proceedings. It was Lord Viscount Cornbury, and he landed with much fuss and ceremony. All ^{May 3.} the prominent men gave him an eager if not a cordial welcome. The city corporation entertained him with a grand banquet. His commission as governor of New York was duly published, and his counselors sworn into office. His first business was to issue two proclamations; one for continuing all civil and military officers in their present positions until further notice, and the second for dissolving the Assembly.

Edward Hyde, Lord Cornbury, was the grandson of the Earl of Clarendon — the Lord Chancellor and Prime Minister of Charles II. — and the son of the present Earl of Clarendon, who was the brother-in-law of James II. Thus the new governor of New York was the first cousin of Queen Anne, and heir to an earldom. He had been one of the foremost in setting an example of defection in King James's army by leading a large body of cavalry, of which he was in command, to the camp of William. He had ever since held important commissions under the latter monarch. He had been appointed, and even set sail for his new government before the death of William. Queen Anne confirmed his commission immediately upon her accession to the throne. She also forwarded him additional instructions relative to necessary and vigorous preparations for the defense of the New York frontier against the French.

Cornbury had been a military chieftain for nearly twenty years, but of political power he had very little conception, except as it emanated from the self-will of a superior. He had genius for exacting obedience, and order and method were to him literally "Heaven's first law." But he was unfortunately destitute of tact and discretion. He stood among the mixed people of New York and New Jersey like an ogre come to crush one party and raise another. He had no sympathy with the primary notion of popular rights, he was without true nobleness of heart, and he was addicted to many private vices. He, in short, illustrated the most exaggerated feature of aristocratic arrogance. Yet his coming was

fortunate just at this juncture, else the excesses of the Leislerian party would have sowed discord beyond all hope of future reconciliation. Many merchants and property-owners had already removed into New Jersey. They came back, however, to watch the effects of the new administration.

Colonel Bayard's case was upon every person's lips, and Cornbury gave it his first attention. He found that Chief Justice Atwood had forbidden any one from taking notes in the court, not excepting

Portrait of Lord Cornbury.

the lawyers themselves. The whole trial seemed to have been conducted in an irregular manner. Prisoners had been convicted and sentenced to die for signing treasonable papers, when the papers themselves at the time of conviction had never been seen by the lieutenant-governor, by any member of his council, by Weaver, who filed the prosecution, by the grand jury who found the bill, nor by the petty jury who brought in the verdict of guilty. They were to be executed for *supposed written treason*, which was never produced in evidence nor proved to be treason.

Atwood and Weaver found themselves standing in a very odious light, and both suddenly absconded, notwithstanding the latter was under heavy bonds to render a true account of his Custom-House collections. The two were concealed in Virginia until they could sail for England; Atwood assuming the name of Jones, and Weaver that of Jackson. Cornbury formally suspended them from all their offices, and appointed Colonel Caleb Heathcote and Dr. John Bridges to succeed them in the council.

About the same time Cornbury was petitioned so earnestly by certain parties that he proceeded to suspend De Peyster, Dr. Staats, and Robert Walters from the council, on the ground of their alleged activity in promoting disorders in the province. Dr. Gerardus Beekman, Rip Van Dam,

Killian Van Rensselaer, and Thomas Wenham were sworn in their stead, the latter having returned from exile.

Cornbury was fully aware of the feeling the various accounts of the crime and trial of Bayard had awakened among the Lords of Trade. The prisoner was known personally to them, and party spirit was thoroughly understood. They had resolved, even before he sailed for New York, that Bayard and Hutchings should have a hearing before the queen in council. A letter to this effect was written to the Earl of Manchester on the first day of May. A royal order subsequently reached Cornbury for the release of Bayard on bail, and a few months later the queen by advice of her council reversed the sentences which had been pronounced upon both Bayard and Hutchings, and reinstated them in their property and honor " as if no such trial had been."

It was about the 17th of June that Cornbury received orders to proclaim Queen Anne in New York and in East and West New Jersey, and the duty was performed in the metropolis on the following day. The people of all stations in life manifested the most undoubted loyalty.

On Friday, June 19, Cornbury started for Burlington, the chief town in West New Jersey; but, owing to rough roads, or, in many **June 19.** instances, to the want of roads altogether, he did not reach his destination until late on Sunday night. He was received and entertained by Governor Hamilton, and on Monday at eleven o'clock the magistrates and people were gathered together and the new queen proclaimed " in the same happy manner as in New York." Cornbury's plan was to proceed to Amboy, the chief town in East New Jersey, but recent rains had flooded the lowlands, and he was obliged to defer his visit until a later day.

He had scarcely reached New York on his return than he was appalled by the amount of sickness which prevailed. The small-pox had raged all the spring, and now the yellow fever was sweeping over the city. Few persons who were attacked recovered. He made great haste to remove his family to a place of safety. Lady Cornbury[1] was an invalid, and they had three young children. Jamaica, Long Island, was where they finally took up their quarters for the summer. There were but few good houses in that little village, and the Presbyterian minister, Rev. Mr. Hubbard, offered his new parsonage to the governor, and with a large family sought more humble and less convenient accommodations.

---

[1] Lady Cornbury was Katharine, daughter of Lord O'Brien, who was himself the son of the Earl of Richmond in Ireland. She was married to Lord Cornbury in 1688. Upon the death of her mother, Lady O'Brien, she became Baroness Clifton, of Leighton Bromswold, Warwickshire, England.

Cornbury was an Episcopalian, and loved the church as a religion of state subordinate to executive power. In common with many others of his time he believed that its establishment in the colonies would be a safe-guard against popery. There were a few Episcopalians in Jamaica, but they had no place of worship. The town had been settled chiefly by New England Puritans, although there was an occasional Dutch planter in the neighborhood. The little church edifice had been built by vote of the town, and the minister's salary was raised in the same manner. As soon as it was practicable a substantial dwelling for a parsonage had been added to the church property. When the famous Ministry Act was passed, in 1693, the few Episcopalians, who as townsmen contributed their yearly dues for the support of the gospel, made investigations to learn whether the Presbyterians had really any better claim to the church property than any other sect, and came to the conclusion that it was held simply by virtue of priority of possession. As soon as Lord Cornbury came among them, a consultation took place which resulted in a determination to wrest the sacred edifice, parsonage, etc., from the Presbyterians altogether. Consequently, one Sabbath afternoon, between the morning and the even-ing service, a few zealous churchmen obtained the key, and took the sanc-tuary captive. The next day the outraged Presbyterians gathered round the building, and forcibly entered it, tearing up the seats and otherwise mutilating the interior. The Episcopalians rallied in as large a force as possible, countenanced by Cornbury, and, rushing into the church, turned out the enemy in a violent manner. The battle was a serious one, several persons being wounded. But, as the governor was within a stone's-throw of the belligerents, and, his own servants taking an active part in the fray, it is no matter of wonder that the Episcopalians were left masters of the field. Long and tedious litigations followed; many of the Presbyterians were prosecuted for damages to the building, and several men among them were heavily fined, and imprisoned. It was not until 1728, that the colonial courts finally decided that the church edifice belonged to the Presbyterians; and it was restored to that denomination.

Cornbury presented the parsonage to the Episcopacy, when the summer was over and he about to return to the city. The glebe he turned over to the sheriff, who laid it out in building-lots, and farmed it for the benefit of the church.

The fatal sickness of this summer deprived New York of more than five hundred of her citizens. Meanwhile Cornbury was not neglectful of the Indians, but for whom New York would have been at the mercy of the French. He went to Albany on the 5th of July, and five days later the sachems of the Five Nations and delegations from the river tribes met him in solemn conference. The chain of friendship was polished anew with the customary gifts from the government, such as guns, kettles, blankets, knives, beer, bread, powder, and rum. One of the sachems rose and requested that the rum might be put in some secure place until after the business of the meeting was all transacted, lest his people fall to drinking. It was accordingly lodged in Robert Livingston's cellar. Peter Schuyler and Robert Livingston were Cornbury's efficient aids, as indeed they had been the interpreters and tutors of every royal governor, as far as Indian affairs were concerned, for a long series of years. The sachems promised to report any hostile movement on the part of the enemy which should come within their knowledge, and to be subject at all times to the advice of their white leaders. Cornbury saw indications, however, of defection on the part of some of the northern tribes, and it was believed that they would eventually go over to the French. He consequently wrote to the Lords of Trade that, in his opinion, the only way to protect New York was to drive the French out of Canada.

As for Livingston, Cornbury was cordially determined to see him justified before the world. An application was made to Lady Bellomont for such accounts and vouchers as her late husband had transferred from the hands of his clerk to his own possession, shortly before his death; they were obtained and proved effectual in removing the aspersions from Livingston's character. His estates were restored in February, 1703, and two years later a commission from Queen Anne reinstated him in all his former appointments and honors.

Lady Bellomont left the city upon the first appearance of the fatal epidemic. She obtained quarters at a little farm-house on Long Island until she could make arrangements to sail for Europe. All at once she was accused of having in her possession money belonging to the government, which had not been accounted for by the late governor. She was not allowed to start on her voyage until she had given bonds to the amount of £10,000 for her appearance in New York in the following April to answer to the charges against her. She immediately upon her arrival in England petitioned the queen for an investigation of her affairs. She emphatically denied all the charges which had been "manufactured," and asked for an order to collect large arrears in Lord Bellomont's salary.

Nanfan made arrangements to remove to Barbadoes, but the course of his career did not run smoothly. His wife and children were safely embarked on the vessel, when he was arrested on a charge of not having accounted for the public money which had been in his hands; and also on another charge for having countenanced and abetted arbitrary arrests while in power. He was thrown into prison, and his family proceeded to their destination without him. He remained in close confinement one year and a half. The Lords of Trade finally ordered his release on bail. Plans were matured to re-arrest him, and he only escaped by taking refuge on a man-of-war in the harbor, and proceeded in a shabbily clad and despondent condition to England. Fraud was never proven in his case; he suffered the disgrace with none of the perquisites. No one pretended to hold him responsible for the atrocious proceedings of the last few months. He was young and inexperienced, and very much under the influence of Atwood and Weaver. Even Cornbury exonerated him from blame, and fixed the stigma upon the flying ex-chief-justice and certain members of the council.

The Lords of Trade were astonished when they learned that the New York Assembly had passed the Leisler Act for reparation of damages claimed to have been sustained during the Revolution! They

July 14. immediately sent Cornbury their former instructions to Bellomont, which they had intended should be a guide to Nanfan as well, and ordered, peremptorily, that no such irregular proceeding should be allowed. They also forwarded the queen's order in council for the restoration of Attorney-General Broughton to the execution of his official duties, the queen deeming it unfit that any person should be punished for giving his opinion in matters which had been referred to him. Broughton was subsequently made one of the governor's council.

About the same time Cornbury received a formal commission to govern New Jersey, the proprietors having surrendered all their powers to the queen. East and West New Jersey were henceforth united into one province. Counselors were named from among the most prominent inhabitants. An Assembly was elected by the majority of freeholders, as in New York, which was to sit first at Perth Amboy, then at Burlington, and afterwards alternate between the two places. All voters must possess at least one hundred acres of real estate, or personal property to the amount of £50 Liberty of conscience was granted to all persons except papists, and the solemn affirmation of the Quakers was to be taken instead of an oath. Cornbury was directed to take special care " that God Almighty be devoutly and duly served," and that ministers of the Church of England should be furnished with a parsonage and glebe at the common charge. He was also instructed to encourage traffic in merchantable negroes, which the African Company in England would furnish at moderate rates.

Even during that summer of distress (1702) while Cornbury was in the cosey enjoyment of the Jamaica parsonage, the elections were stirring up the old strife through the length and breadth of the province. Philip French was chosen a member of the new Assembly,[1] and in October of the same year appointed mayor of the city. Stephen De Lancey, Jacobus Van Cortlandt, and Henry Beekman were also elected to the Assembly, and William Nicolls was chosen speaker. The House met at Jamaica, and accomplished no little business. It continued the revenue for seven years; voted £ 1,800 for the defense of the frontiers;[2] raised £ 2,000 as a present to Cornbury towards defraying the expenses of his voyage; passed an Act for disciplining slaves who had become insolent and unmanageable; an Act for destroying wolves in New York; an Act for settling the militia; an Act to appoint commissioners to examine the accounts and debts of the province; an Act for maintaining the poor of the city; an Act for establishing a free grammar school in the city; an Act to enable the city to supply the vacancy when officers should be removed by death; and an Act for repealing some of the previous Acts of the Assembly. In reference to the money raised as a present for Cornbury, it is worthy of note that within the next twelve months the queen issued an order forbidding any similar gifts to governors in any part of the British dominions.

Colonel William Smith resumed his seat in the council, and was again made chief justice of the province. One of the first acts of Mayor French was to cause the arms of the late Lord Bellomont and of ^{Dec. 23.} Nanfan to be torn from the wall of the new City Hall on Wall Street, and broken in fragments by the city marshal.

The very next morning the Garden Street Church bell solemnly tolled the intelligence that Frederick Philipse had suddenly died at Philipse Manor. He was in the seventy-seventh year of his age. For more than half a century he had been intimately associated with every event of any note in city or province. He was called the " Dutch millionaire." But although classed among the "grandees," he had incurred comparatively little political enmity, and was not denounced as a wholesale foe to all the rights of humanity, as were many of his contemporaries. Philipseborough (or Philipse Manor), where he resided the greater part of every year, was under high cultivation. At the time he obtained the royal charter (in 1693) which gave him all the privileges and powers of a lord, the ferry, island, and meadow had been confirmed to his property,

---

[1] The Act of the late Assembly outlawing Philip French had been annulled by the English Lords.

[2] The raising of this money was as follows : each of the royal council must pay a poll-tax of 40 s. ; each member of the House, 20 s. ; every lawyer in practice, 20 s. ; every man wearing a periwig, 5 s. 6 d. ; every bachelor over twenty-five years of age, 2 s. 3 d. ; every freeman between sixteen and sixty years, 9 d. ; owners of slaves for each, 1 s.

30

also the right to build a bridge over "Spiken-devil ferry," as it was then called, and collect toll from passengers. The bridge was named Kings Bridge. Philipse commanded the same respect in New York which was accorded to men of his standing in England. He presided with baronial ceremonies in the administration of justice among his tenantry. He had two great rent-days, on which he feasted his people, — one at the Yonkers

Philipse Manor-house.

portion of Philipseborough and the other at Sleepy Hollow. His manor-house was a grand edifice for the times, although it was enlarged subsequently. Its rooms were spacious, with richly ornamented ceilings, and its hall immensely broad, with an imported staircase, which is still in existence. A beautiful lawn sloped gradually to the very edge of the Hudson, which was dotted with fine specimens of foreign trees brought from the different climes by the great merchant's vessels. A fine park was stocked with deer; and gardens, filled with fruits, shrubs, and flowers, extended to a great distance to the north and south of the dwelling. At the time of Philipse's death the household embraced over forty negro slaves. Forty-five years later, the servants or slaves required to keep the princely establishment in running order numbered fifty.

When Bellomont set his face like steel against the tendency to feudalism in New York, he had no personal dislike to Philipse. They met in social intercourse, and were friendly. Bellomont suspected Philipse of trading with the pirates, but he had no grounds upon which to frame an accusation. He never attempted to do so except on one occasion, and then with characteristic reticence and cold resentment Philipse retired from any further part in public affairs. Bellomont was almost a monomaniac in the matter of curtailing landed estates, because he firmly believed that great wealth in a few men was not conducive to the prosperity of an infant colony. There is more than one light in which to regard that question. As for New York, it is very apparent that she is indebted largely for her present commercial importance to the tireless activity and remarkable energy of those men who accumulated private fortunes prior to the beginning of the eighteenth century. Modern improvements and business facilities were not yet introduced into our country; the services of these same stirring men were constantly required in the administration of government; and they were liable with every turn of the political wheel to be thrown into the slough. They were obliged also to perform military duty, and wars and rumors of wars were perpetual. Their money in a multitude of instances saved the credit of the colony. Advances were constantly needed, for taxes were collected with difficulty at all times, and the expenses of a long-drawn-out war can never be properly estimated.

Castle Philipse (Tarrytown.)

The contents of well-filled purses encouraged the tradespeople, having a similar effect to rain upon growing crops; a drouth is always fatal, but a shower is a blessing even if it cause a freshet occasionally when and where water is not needed. The same wise power which gathers the mists loosens the rain-clouds and distributes the drops. New York received her mercantile impetus through the spirit which Bellomont found so formidable, when he began to question the motives and investigate the means by which men enrich themselves.

Frederick Philipse left by his will a valuable house and lot in the city, and a mortgage of Dominie Selyns, to his daughter Eve, who was the wife of Jacobus Van Cortlandt; another daughter was the wife of Philip French, who received a house and lot in the city, and an estate in Bergen. An immense tract of land at the Upper Mills in Westchester County, and other real estate was given to his son Adolphe Philipse; and the manor of Philipseborough descended to his grandson, Frederick Philipse, whose father, Philip Philipse, had died some two years before.

The winter was spent by Cornbury in examining into the resources of the province, and answering the inquiries of the Lords of Trade. **1703.** But he lacked the persistent industry of his two predecessors, was given to frivolous amusements, would often dress himself in women's clothes to show his remarkable resemblance to Queen Anne, and he spent many hours of each day at cards. He was excessively prodigal in the use of money, and he was negligent about paying his debts. The gentlemen of the council had counted upon his ability and good sense, and were mortified and disgusted with his exhibition of weakness and eccentricity.

When the Assembly met in the spring, Cornbury proposed the raising of a sum of money for the purpose of erecting two stone batteries at the Narrows, where the sea is not quite a mile broad. It would render the port safe from a hostile attack by water, since no ship could pass that point, and the logic was unanswerable. The House voted £1,500, but the question of appointing a treasurer to hold the money separate from the other public funds was argued at considerable length, greatly to the discomfiture of the governor. The reflection upon his honor met with a sharp rebuke. The House responded courteously through its speaker, William Nicolls, giving a diagnosis of the money accounts during the year past ; these had been examined from time to time by the legislators, according to the queen's directions, and the result was the discovery that considerable sums which had been raised by the people for the defense of New York had been otherwise appropriated. Nicolls, in behalf of the Assembly, explained the situation and cautiously added, "Your lordship will no doubt take care to see those mistakes rectified." He then went on to disclaim any desire of introducing innovations, but, the House having been entrusted by the people of the province with the care of their natural and civil liberties as Englishmen, it was a high duty to obey their wishes and protect their property rights, particularly when these same people "had literally outdone all mankind, and it was feared themselves, by the constant paying of taxes for the prosecution of the tiresome war."

One of the Acts passed at this session of the Assembly prohibited the distilling of rum, and the burning of oyster-shells or stone into lime within half a mile of the City Hall in Wall Street, as it was believed that business had much increased the mortality of the preceding summer. Another Act, of same date, enabled the French Church to erect a suitable edifice for public worship ; which was accomplished the following year. It was located in Pine Street, and was called Du Saint Esprit.[1] The first pastor was Rev. James Laborie. The Huguenots who had settled upon Staten Island came over in frail canoes to attend Sabbath worship, as did many from Long Island until such time as they were strong enough to build churches of their own.

1704. William Peartree was the mayor of the city in 1703, and retained the position until 1707. He was an English West Indian merchant, who removed to New York in 1700 from Jamaica, W. I. His place of business was on Beaver Street, where he also built a fine resi-

---

[1] See page 329 for a sketch of this church.

dence. He was a man of education, and interested himself in the establishment and improvement of institutions of learning. A free grammar school had been for a long time in contemplation, and Peartree was chiefly instrumental in its final accomplishment; Andrew Clarke was employed as teacher. About the same time the first effort was made in New York for the instruction of negro slaves. A catechizing school was opened for them by Rev. Mr. Vesey. The jail was remodeled during the winter and rendered more secure for felons; and a debtors' prison was arranged in the upper story of the City Hall. It was a rough room with coarse board partitions, without chairs, warmth, or comforts of any sort whatever. It remained substantially in the same condition for three fourths of a century. The punishment for a petty thief was to burn into the left cheek near the nose the letter " T."

The people of New Jersey were disappointed in Cornbury, as well as those of New York. His rather handsome face and bland manners attracted them at first, but his demand for an annual salary of £ 2,000 per annum for twenty years produced a sudden shock, like that of an earthquake. The stiff Quaker, Samuel Jennings, turned abruptly upon him with the quaint remark, " Then thee must be very needy."

The New Jersey Assembly had been accustomed to raise only moderate sums for the support of the government, and, after much debate, voted £ 1,300 per annum for three years. Cornbury was very angry, and when he found that he could not manage affairs, he dissolved the body. A new Assembly was elected, which was more pliable, and granted the £ 2,000 salary, but cautiously, for two years. This partial triumph would hardly have been accomplished had not Cornbury refused to admit three of the most important and intelligent of the newly elected members to their seats, on the feigned ground that their estates were not as large as the royal instructions required.

Lewis Morris was one of the members of Cornbury's New Jersey council. He had spent some time in England, where he had been one of the warmest advocates for the surrender of the proprietary government to the crown. The Lords of Trade were so much pleased with him that he received the first nomination for the governorship of New Jersey. But the original intention of giving the province an executive of its own was abandoned, and New Jersey was placed with New York under the administration of Cornbury.

Lewis Morris was at this time a dashing and somewhat erratic young man of thirty-three. His life had been a singular one. His father, Richard Morris, had been active in the service of Cromwell, and found refuge in New York upon the restoration of Charles II.; he obtained through

Governor Stuyvesant, about the year 1661, a grant of over three thousand acres of land upon the northern side of the Harlem River, with baronial privileges, and built a comfortable homestead. The property was called Morrisania. When his only and infant son Lewis was six months of age, his wife sickened and died, and he shortly followed her. The orphan babe was thus left to the care of entire strangers, and the government of New York assumed charge by appointing guardians to protect his interests. In 1674 Colonel Lewis Morris, an elder brother of Richard Morris, removed from Barbadoes to New York, and became the guardian of his nephew. He resided in Morrisania, but he purchased some four thousand acres of land in Monmouth County, New Jersey, upon which he located iron-mills; he also built a manor-house, and various buildings for his dependents, who in 1680 numbered seventy or more. Upon his death in 1691, this property fell to young Lewis, which, together with the large estate of his father, made him a very rich man.[1]

He had been a willful and capricious boy, given to all manner of mischievous pranks, and had been renowned for playing practical jokes upon his best friends. He had defied the restraints of schools and tutors, and finally ran away, and supported himself for some time in the capacity of a scrivener on the island of Jamaica. At twenty he was in New York again, and in full assumption of the airs and graces of manhood was paying court to Isabella, the beautiful daughter of Hon. James Graham. They were married on the 3d of November, 1691.

Where Lewis Morris studied law is unknown. His first appearance in public life was as one of the judges of the Court of Common Right in East New Jersey. He was also one of the counselors of Governor Hamilton. He was gifted with a certain amount of discernment into men's characters and springs of action, which subsequently won him a brilliant reputation at the bar. He possessed a mind of more than ordinary vigor and originality, which, in connection with great peculiarity of temper, bluntness of speech, and curtness of manner, rendered him as attractive to his friends as he was obnoxious to his enemies. He was an adept in the wily intrigues of colonial politics. His opinions were always advanced with emphasis and maintained with spirit.

From the day that Lewis Morris first met Lord Cornbury he entertained for him the most scornful contempt. When measures were in-

[1] "Mr. Mompesson, our chief justice, is dead. I have commissioned Lewis Morris, Esqr. in his room for these reasons amongst others, that he is a sensible, honest man, and able to live without a salary, which they will most certainly never grant to any in that station, at least sufficient to maintain his clerk. — *Postscript of a letter from Governor Hunter to the Lords of Trade, March* 28, 1715.   *Col. Hist. N. Y.*, Vol. V. p. 400.

troduced into the council which Morris conceived prejudicial to the interests of the province, he assailed them in a determined manner, and oftentimes with the most stinging ridicule, until Cornbury, finally, in sheer self-defense suspended him from office.

Ingoldsby returned to New York in the early part of 1704, with a commission as lieutenant-governor under Cornbury. But the two did not agree. And, one complaint after another reaching the Lords of Trade, they at last revoked the appointment.

Meanwhile Queen Anne had given her attention to the condition of Trinity Church. The king's farm, which had created so much painful disturbance through the generous granting of its use by **1705.** Fletcher to the struggling corporation, was augmented by the addition of the Anetje Jans estate, and formally presented by deed patent, signed by Lord Cornbury, to this church. It was only a farm at the time, and comparatively of little value, but it has long since become a compact portion of the city.

Colonel William Smith died at St. George Manor, just after the opening of the new year. He had retired from the office of chief justice nearly two years before, but had continued to meet with the governor's council until within a few weeks. Dr. Bridges succeeded him as chief justice; but he filled the office only for a brief period, his death occurring not far from that of Colonel Smith.

Roger Mompesson (the seventh chief justice of New York) was appointed in his stead. He was a new arrival. He was an English lawyer of ability, who had been recorder of Southampton, and a member of two Parliaments. He was descended from Rev. William Mompesson, who was Rector of Eyam, Derbyshire, during the plague of 1666. He became involved through engagements to pay some of his father's debts, and found it convenient to accept a judicial appointment which would bring him to America. He was sworn into the New York council, and continued a member of that body until his death. He was appointed chief justice of New Jersey as well as New York, and held the office, with the exception of the few months of Lord Lovelace's administration, also until his death. In 1706 he was sworn chief justice of Pennsylvania, but it does not appear that he sat on the bench of that colony. His wide experience and sound legal acumen enabled him to do more than almost any other man towards molding the judicial system of both New York and New Jersey.[1] John Barbarie and Adolphe Philipse were appointed to fill vacancies in the council, and a little later Mayor William Peartree

---

[1] Roger Mompesson married Martha, the daughter of Judge William Pinhorne, of Snake Hill, New Jersey. He had one son, Pinhorne Mompesson.

was added to the number in place of Attorney-General Broughton deceased.

The great excitement of the summer of 1705, was the discovery of an enormous tooth in the side of a hill near Claverack on the Hudson. It weighed four and three-fourths pounds, and had the appearance of having been taken from a human skull. Other bones were found, which, however, crumbled on exposure to the air. One, supposed to be a thigh bone, measured seventeen feet in length. The event was recorded as the first discovery of a mammoth in America. Eighty years afterwards the bones of the great beast were found in Ulster County, and Charles William Peale formed his skeleton for the museum.

Hardly had the sensation died away created by the marvelous tooth when a riot occurred which was something startling. Captain Cleaver, a noted privateer, brought a Spanish man-of-war into port which he had captured after a desperate struggle. The crew were elated by their victory, and under the influence of poor wine paraded the streets singing songs and uttering coarse and vulgar jests. The sheriff attempted to check them, and they fell upon him with drunken fury. He escaped to his house, which they surrounded, and, not being able to force an entrance, they assaulted every person who came to his assistance. Two army officers, who were in advance of the soldiers dispatched from the fort, were attacked and one killed, while the other was dangerously wounded. The soldiers put the sailors to flight, leaving one of their number dying in the street. The sailor who killed the officer was arrested, tried, and executed for the murder.

In the midst of these scenes a French privateer suddenly entered the harbor. The city was thrown into a great state of consternation. The batteries at the Narrows, which were to prevent such a catastrophe, had not been erected, notwithstanding the appropriation of £1,500 two years before! " Misappropriation " rang in Cornbury's ears. He highly resented the imputation, and said the money had never been collected. There was almost a panic. The mayor and common council petitioned the Assembly for help in the work of fortifications, and Cornbury himself talked forcibly on the subject. The House, meanwhile, was having a tempest within itself. Some of the members declared that the body was invested with the same powers as the House of Commons. They even went so far as to deny the right of the governor and council to amend a money bill. They clamored for a treasurer of their own. Risks could not be afforded. The province was impoverished by the increasing expenses of the government, and by the diminution of ocean commerce in consequence of the war. It was convenient party capital to be always prepared to accuse former administrators of having devoured the public funds, but the time had come when it was better to provide against mischief than complain of it. Cornbury contended to the last against the implied spot upon his honor, but he wielded little influence over the iron Assembly of 1705, and was obliged to submit the matter to the queen and her lords.

The result was an order transmitted to the New York governor " to permit the General Assembly of the province to name their own treasurer when they raised extraordinary supplies for particular uses." It was a strong point gained, for even the title " General Assembly " was conceded, about which there had been no small amount of undignified jangling. £ 3,000 was at once raised for the city fortifications, and Hon. Abraham De Peyster was appointed treasurer of New York.

The citizens had all this while been vigorously at work, — some four hundred men were employed daily on the defenses. The militia had been drilled and volunteers enlisted. It was estimated that between four and five thousand men could be mustered to arms within twenty-four hours notice. It was a season of alarms. At one time a French fleet was reported off the coast. But the city escaped her threatened danger.

Lady Cornbury was at this time wasting slowly away with a disease of many years' standing, and her husband, roused to devotion by the near prospect of losing her, bent his energies to the performance of loving attentions. He watched by her bedside night and day, and reprimanded nurses and servants for the most trifling negligence. She died at half past eleven o'clock on the night of Sunday, August 11, aged thirty-four years, and was buried in Trinity Church. She had given birth to seven children, but only three, one son and two daughters, survived her. For a time Cornbury was apparently overwhelmed with grief, but it soon lifted, and he returned to his former life and practices. He cared very little what people said or thought about his private character, for was he not of royal blood, and did not kings suit themselves ? His conduct told greatly to his disadvantage, nevertheless, and he lost favor with all classes. He performed religious duties with severe ostentation, but even Episcopalians had very little faith in his Christian zeal.

As for the Presbyterians, Cornbury had been simply odious to them ever since the church quarrel at Jamaica. There were few as yet in New York, and they had no church edifice. Their custom was to assem · ble in private houses on the Sabbath, and conduct worship among themselves. It happened that two Presbyterian ministers came to the city, Rev. Francis McKemie from Virginia and Rev. John Hampton from

Maryland, and sent a message to Cornbury asking for an interview. The reply was a courteous invitation to the two divines to dine with the governor that same afternoon. They proceeded to Cornbury's mansion, and were well received and hospitably entertained. They conversed upon general topics, but made no mention of any intention to preach in the city. The next day they visited some of the city clergymen, and were offered both the French and Dutch pulpits for the ensuing Sabbath, provided the governor would give his consent. The clerical strangers said it was not worth while to trouble the governor, since they had the queen's authority to preach anywhere in her dominions. They declined the tender of the churches, and made other arrangements. McKemie preached at a private house, and Hampton occupied the sacred desk of the little church in Newtown, Long Island.

Cornbury was no sooner informed of these events than he sent an order to the sheriff of Queen's County, to arrest the two ministers, who were staying in Newtown, and bring them into his presence. The order was executed in a coarse, rough, and exceedingly offensive manner. Attorney-General Bickly (the successor of Broughton) was with Cornbury when the gentlemen appeared. The governor proceeded to question them, and they to justify their course. The governor said the law would not permit him to countenance strolling preachers, for they might be papists for aught he knew. They must qualify themselves by satisfying the government that they were fit persons to occupy the pulpit before they could be permitted to preach. McKemie said he had qualified himself in Virginia, which was sufficient. The ministers were as ignorant of law as children, and Cornbury construed their seeming contumacy into intentional fraud. If the attorney-general had possessed tact and discretion, he might have guided both clergymen and governor out of the difficulty; but he was a voluble talker rather than a valuable counselor, and the interview resulted in the imprisonment of the innocent but opinionated men. Chief Justice Mompesson was absent, hence it was six weeks and four days before the prisoners were brought to trial. Meanwhile a deep sense of the injustice of the whole proceeding impressed itself upon the community, and Cornbury was stigmatized as a narrow-minded persecutor of Presbyterianism. The trial was attended with considerable excitement, but the jury acquitted the ministers; they were obliged, however, to pay all the expenses of the prosecution.

In April a new Assembly met in New Jersey, Cornbury having ordered an election with the specific purpose of having his salary renewed. What was his chagrin to find the majority of the members, with Lewis Morris at their head, opposed to all his measures. The fearless Quaker,

Samuel Jennings, was chosen speaker. The first business before the House was the disposal of a chapter of grievances. A petition was prepared to forward to the queen; and a remonstrance, drafted by Morris, was read to the governor. It was a bitter morsel, and it lost none of its force in the clear, distinct rendering of it by Speaker Jennings. Cornbury was charged with accepting bribes; he was accused of encroaching upon popular liberty by denying the freeholders' election of their representative; and his new method of government was criticised in a cutting manner. At the more pointed passages Cornbury, assuming a stern air of authority, would cry out, "Stop! What's that?" When thus interrupted, Jennings would look steadily into the governor's eyes for an instant, and then meekly, but emphatically, reread the offensive paragraph, bringing out every shade of meaning with stinging fullness of articulation.

Cornbury's reply was distinguished for its length and its weakness. He left no part of the remonstrance unanswered. He denied some of the charges and attempted to justify others; he charged the Quakers with disloyalty and with having tried to promote faction; and he abused Jennings and Morris to the extent of his ability, pronouncing them "men generally known to have neither good principles nor morals."

This elicited a second paper from the House, in which all former grievances were amplified. The Quakers responded to Cornbury's charge against them in the words of Nehemiah to Sanballat: "There is no such things done as thou sayest, but thou feignest them out of thine own heart."

Cornbury was greatly discomfited. He could positively obtain no money from New Jersey without disagreeable concessions. He returned to New York, and met an equally stubborn Assembly. **1708.** There was much business, and the session was a long and important one. But the revenue, which by a previous Act was about to expire, was not continued. The House passed a bill to discharge Cornbury from a contract of £250 with Mr. Hansen, and consented to an appropriation for Indian presents, claiming, however, an exact list of all that was needed in advance.[1] A difficulty with Thomas Byerly, the collector and receiver-general, occupied much valuable time at this session. He had announced that the treasury was exhausted. As the debts of the government were unpaid, the House was petitioned to provide means for their discharge. Peter Schuyler was one of the chief creditors, having loaned large sums of money, and he instituted an investigation by which Byerly would be compelled to account. Byerly could not comply be-

---

[1] *Journals of the Legislative Council of New York*, Vol. I. p. 248.

cause his predecessor in office, Mr. Fauconnier, withheld accounts as securities for back pay. The case provoked sharp arguments. It was the occasion of the appointment of a committee on grievances, of which William Nicolls, the speaker of the House, was chairman. This committee drafted a list of resolutions and sent them to the queen. They illustrate the temper and intelligence of the Assembly of 1708, and are as follows : —

" *Resolved,* That it is the opinion of this Committee, that the appointing coroners in this colony, without their being chosen by the people, is a grievance, and contrary to law.

" *Resolved,* That it is, and always has been, the unquestionable right of every free man in this colony, that he hath a perfect and entire property in his goods and estate.

" *Resolved,* That the imposing and levying of any moneys upon her Majesty's subjects of this colony, under any pretense or color whatsoever, without consent in General Assembly, is a grievance, and a violation of the people's property.

" *Resolved,* That for any officer whatsoever to extort from the people extrava· gant and unlimited fees, or any money whatsoever, not positively established and regulated by consent in General Assembly, is unreasonable and unlawful, a great grievance, and tending to the utter destruction of all property in this plantation.

" *Resolved,* That the erecting a court of equity without consent in General Assembly is contrary to law, without precedent, and of dangerous consequence to the liberty and property of the subjects.

" *Resolved,* That the raising of money for the government, or other necessary charge, by any tax, impost, or burden on goods imported or exported, or any clog or hindrance on traffic or commerce, is found by experience to be the expulsion of many, and the impoverishing of the rest of the planters, freeholders, and inhabitants of this colony ; of most pernicious consequence, which, if continued, will unavoidably prove the ruin of the colony.

" *Resolved,* That the excessive sums of money screwed from masters of vessels trading here, under the notion of Port-charges, visiting the said vessels by supernumerary officers, and taking extraordinary fees. is the great discouragement of trade, and strangers coming among us, and is beyond the precedent of any other port, and without color of law.

" *Resolved,* That the compelling any man upon trial by a jury, or otherwise, to pay fees for his prosecution, or anything whatsoever, unless the fees of the officers whom he employs for his necessary defense, is a great grievance, and contrary to justice."[1]

---

[1] Journals of the legislative council of New York.

The last resolution had direct reference to the case of Rev. Francis McKemie, in which William Nicolls was one of the lawyers for the defense.

The unfitness of Cornbury for his position had long been the subject of anxious discussion at Whitehall. When petitions for his removal multiplied, and were in every instance signed by men of character and influence in both New York and New Jersey, the warning was not allowed to pass by unheeded. A new governor was appointed in his stead. It was John, Lord Lovelace, Baron of Hurley, a nephew of the former New York governor of that name. He arrived in the city on the 18th of December, and was greeted with a noisy reception. In the midst of the sensation created by the event, the hungry creditors of Lord Cornbury hovered about his residence, and, finding he had no money with which to pay for his last joint of meat, they began to clamor and threaten. All manner of tradesmen's bills were presented for payment, and it was found that he had private debts of every sort and description. The unhappy ex-governor was arrested and lodged in the debtor's prison, where he was confined until he succeeded to the Earldom of Clarendon, made vacant by his father's death, and to the privilege of peerage. A sum of money forwarded at last from his father's estate set him at liberty. He left New York with few friends, if any, to mourn his departure. And yet he had been of service to the province, which is none the less worthy of notice because it was without design. He had toned and mellowed political animosity by uniting the two parties in one bond of opposition against himself. And he had taught men to be watchful, to withdraw confidence from foreign rulers, to canvass the rights of British subjects, and to study the necessities as well as the methods of resistance. He carried with him to England the unenviable distinction of having been one of the most disreputable of all the New York governors.

Lord Lovelace was ill all winter. He had taken a violent cold on the vessel while it lay off the coast near Sandy Hook in December, and a settled cough was the result. He was not confined to his room **1709.** at all times, and attended to such business as he was able. He dissolved the Assembly and ordered a new election. When the House met, and had again chosen William Nicolls speaker, he appeared, and, in a short speech, asked for a careful examination of public accounts, that it might be apparent to the world that the public debt was not incurred in his time ; and he also recommended the raising of the revenue for seven years, as formerly. The House responded cheerfully, saying that the beginning of the new administration promised peace and tranquillity, and that suitable measures would be taken for the good of the country, and the new governor's satisfaction. In the matter of the revenue, however, it was decided to raise it annually and appropriate it specifically.

The illness of Lord Lovelace assumed a more alarming character May 6. as the spring opened. His family suffered as well as himself, and one child died in April. His own death occurred very suddenly on the 6th of May. A little later, his only surviving son, the young Lord, was consigned to the tomb. Lady Lovelace excited universal sympathy in her afflictions; a widow and childless, she returned to England in July.

Ingoldsby, as lieutenant-governor of the province, assumed the government. All his actions were closely scrutinized, for he was not considered a man worthy of such a trust. Indeed, it was through a blunder that he retained the office, the Lords of Trade having never forwarded the order of 1704, revoking his appointment. As soon as the news of Lovelace's death reached Whitehall, Ingoldsby's commission was revoked the second time, and he was ordered to take no part in public affairs whatever, except in a military capacity.[1] After Ingoldsby's removal, Dr. Gerardus Beekman, as president of the Council, filled the executive chair until the arrival of a new governor.[2]

Ingoldsby's short administration was distinguished by an attempt to drive the French out of Canada. Such an enterprise had been long and earnestly desired by New York, but the want of harmony among the colonies and the backwardness of England had thus far stood effectually in the way. Colonel Vetch, the son-in-law of Robert Livingston, finally brought the project to a crisis. He had some years before visited Quebec, and he had sounded the St. Lawrence River, so that now he was prepared to lay intelligent plans. The English Ministry consented, and promised to send a large fleet to the assistance of the colonists. Colonel Vetch returned from England to Boston, and soon prevailed upon the New England colonies to join in the scheme. He then visited New York and perfected arrangements. Francis Nicholson, the former lieutenant-governor, was elected commander-in-chief. Peter Schuyler went among the Iroquois, and persuaded them to take up the hatchet once more against the French. These savages had been for some time maintaining a neutral ground between the two fighting nations, England and France, having entered into a treaty with the latter. The other colonies agreed to assist, and the bright, near prospect of getting rid of a troublesome and merciless foe to the north filled every heart with joy. The Assembly issued bills of credit, since the treasury was empty and it was the only expedient by which New York could contribute to the expense. Twenty

---

[1] Sunderland's order was signed on the 17th of April, 1710, but it did not reach New York until the next spring.

[2] See portrait, page 360.

"But the great event of the pilgrimage was their reception by Queen Anne"   Page 470

ship and house carpenters were impressed into the service; commissaries were appointed and empowered to break open houses and take provisions by force, if needful; and men, vessels, horses, and wagons, for transporting the stores, were to be forcibly employed whenever the exigency of the case required. The greatest activity prevailed. Presently all things were in readiness. New York had spent £20,000. The army set out in fine spirits, and marched through the wilderness to Lake Champlain. The Indians were under the command of Colonel Peter Schuyler. They halted for news of the British fleet which was to come to their assistance. They waited for weeks. The fleet never came. The disappointment was overwhelming. It seems that there had been a great defeat of the Portuguese, and the troops destined for Canada had been sent to their relief. But the news did not reach Nicholson, Schuyler, and Vetch, where they were camping in the woods and swamps, until September, and then the disgusted soldiers were conducted home.

Schuyler deplored the failure of the expedition more than any other man. He had a comprehensive appreciation of the ultimate results of this border warfare, and wished to see it brought to an end. He was thoroughly acquainted with the Indian character. He had in the early part of his life insinuated himself into the good graces of the savages by the performance of pleasant acts. From then until now the men of the forest had never been in Albany without coming to his house and eating at his table. He was continually making them presents, and by his liberality in that direction greatly impaired his own fortune. But it enabled him to maintain an ascendency over them, and obviate the jealousies arising through the efforts of the French Jesuits. His interventions and stratagems saved New York rivers of blood. He believed in the necessity for vigorous measures against the French. He said not only the safety, but the very existence, of the colonies was at stake. He finally resolved to go to England and lay the subject personally before the Lords of Trade. To make his mission more effective he took with him five Indian chiefs at his own private expense. As he predicted, the whole kingdom was stirred into curiosity and enthusiasm. Crowds followed them wherever they went. Their pictures were taken and offered for sale at every corner. The theaters were put in requisition to entertain them, and the Guards were reviewed .in Hyde Park for their special benefit.

But the great event of the pilgrimage was their reception by Queen Anne. The court was in mourning at the time for the Prince of Denmark; and by way of courtesy the Indians were dressed in black vests and breeches, and instead of their own royal blankets, wore about their shoulders scarlet cloth mantles edged with gold. Sir Charles Cotterel conducted them in two coaches to St. James's, and the Lord Chamberlain introduced them with the usual ceremonies of state to the queen. The chief orator among them made a speech, to the effect that the reduction of Canada was absolutely necessary for their free hunting, and that if the great queen was not mindful of her children of the forest they would be obliged to forsake her country for other habitations, " or stand neuter," each of which was very much against their inclinations. At the close of the interview they presented her with a belt of wampum.

Schuyler was the bearer of an appeal from the New York Assembly to the Lords of Trade, which, together with the presence of the Indians, moved the nation to promise to send an expedition against Canada. Schuyler was personally the recipient of all manner of distinguished attentions during his brief visit. Queen Anne presented him with an elegant silver vase as a token of respect. It has been handed along from one generation of the Schuyler family to another, in the direct descent, and is now in the possession of Mr. George L. Schuyler of New York, to whose generous courtesy we are indebted for the sketch.

Schuyler Vase.

(For inscription, see Appendix A)

CHAPTER XXIII.

1710–1720.

GOVERNOR ROBERT HUNTER.

Governor Robert Hunter. — Hunter's Life and Character. — Hunter's Corre-
spondence with Swift. — Hunter's Counselors. — John Barbarie. — Rip Van
Dam. — The Germans. — Livingston Manor. — Hunter's Country-seat "Andro-
borus." — The City Finances. — Negro Slaves. — Lobsters. — Origin of the
Debt of England. — Prophecies. — The Canadian Campaign. — The Disappoint-
ment. — The Negro Insurrection. — City Improvements. — The Assembly. —
Death of Queen Anne. — George I. — Chief Justice Lewis Morris. — Robert
Watts. — The New York Families. — James Alexander. — First Presbyterian
Church Wall Street. — Potatoes. — Hunter's Farewell Address. — Peter
Schuyler in Command of New York.

IN June, 1710, New York once more rejoiced in a governor. Robert
Hunter was unlike any of his predecessors. He was a strong, active,
cultivated man of middle age, with refined tastes and feelings, combined
with genial and persuasive manners; and he was a model of morality.
His attainments were such that he had for many years enjoyed the warm
personal friendship of Swift, Addison, Steele, and other distinguished literary men in England. He was something of a poet himself, although he
had always written under a *nom de plume.* He was fond of men of
learning, and encouraged the arts and sciences wherever and whenever
he had an opportunity. He was also a most agreeable and entertaining
social companion.

His early life was full of incident. He was one of the gentlemen who
served as guard under the Bishop of London to the Princess Anne when
she retired from her father's court. He soon after received a commission
in William's army; and he had in all the wars since that time given
proof of great courage and rare ability. One winter he was in command
of a regiment of troops who were quartered in a Holland town. The
following is one of many similar anecdotes related of him : —

The magistrates of the place had incurred the displeasure of the people,
and a move was made for a new election. The magistrates in great heat

31

appealed to Hunter to hinder the assembling of the people. He was too intelligent an officer not to know that it was dangerous for the soldiery to interfere in the civil government, while it was really best for all parties that the election should be prevented. The day came, and crowds gathered in the great church and were about to displace the old magistrates. Hunter, who had called his regiments together privately, without beat of drum, marched his whole force towards the church, and when quite near it ordered the drums to beat the Grenadier's March. The people were so startled and terrified that they rushed out through the doors, and jumped from the windows of the building, in the greatest dismay and confusion. Quite a number were seriously hurt and one or two killed. Of course all further business for the time was suspended. Meanwhile Hunter marched his soldiers directly past the church to the parade-ground, without apparently taking the least notice of the panic and its consequences, and when they had gone through with their usual drill, he dismissed them.

In 1707, while Addison was Under-Secretary of State, Hunter received the appointment of governor of Virginia.[1] He was captured by the French while on his voyage to that colony, and detained a long time as a prisoner in Paris. He corresponded with Swift while there, and from his letters we learn that the witty Dean had been expecting Hunter to use his influence to obtain for him a bishopric in Virginia. Under date of January 12, 1708, Swift says : —

"I am considering whether there be no way of disturbing your quiet by writing some dark matter that may give the French court a jealousy of you. I suppose Monsieur Chamillard or some of his commissaries must have this letter interpreted to them before it comes to your hands ; and therefore I think good to warn them, that if they exchange you under six of their lieutenant-generals they will be losers by the bargain. But that they may not mistake me, I do not mean as *Viceroy de Virginie, mais comme le Colonel Hunter.* . . . . Have you yet met any French colonel whom you remember to have formerly knocked from his horse, or shivered, at least, a lance from his breastplate ? Do you know the wounds you have given when you see the scars ? Do you salute your old enemies with

> " ' Stetimus tela aspera contra,
> Contulimusque manus ? ' "   .

Three months later, under date of March 22d, Swift wrote : —

"I find you a little lament your bondage, and, indeed, in your case it requires

---

[1] Smith erroneously states that Hunter was appointed lieutenant-governor of Virginia. His commission was that of governor-in-chief, but it was by a compromise with the Earl of Orkney.

a good share of philosophy. But if you will not be angry, I believe I may have been the cause you are still a prisoner ; for I imagine my former letter was intercepted by the French, and the most Christian king read one passage in it (and duly considering the weight of the person who wrote it) where I said, if the French understood your value as well as we do, he would not exchange you for Count Tallard and all the *débris* of Blenheim together." [1]

Hunter was finally exchanged for the Bishop of Quebec, and was at once named by the queen for the government of Jamaica, which happened to be vacant. He signified a decided preference for the government of New York, which was also- vacant, and his wishes were very graciously respected. He had married, while in the army, the lovely and accomplished Lady Hay, who accompanied him to New York. It was not an auspicious moment for comfort and the enjoyment of life, for the country was in perpetual agitation about the war, and the unpopular administration of Cornbury had rendered the whole community suspicious. But Hunter set an example of gentlemanly forbearance, kindly humor, sterling integrity, and purity of sentiment, which cooled the heated atmosphere, and by slow degrees public affairs assumed a more healthful aspect. The council was composed of Dr. Gerardus Beekman, Abraham De Peyster (who was also treasurer of the province), Peter Schuyler, Rip Van Dam, Dr. Staats, Robert Walters, Adolphe Philipse, Chief Justice Mompesson, Caleb Heathcote, John Barbarie, and Killian Van Rensselaer.

Barbarie was a wealthy Huguenot, whose father settled in New Rochelle in the time of Jacob Leisler. His wife was Gertrude Johnson, the granddaughter of Hon. Stephanus Van Cortlandt. He was French in all his tastes and habits, polite to a fault, and pleasing in address, though given to extravagant fits of temper. He was also notoriously arrogant on the subject of birth and family connections.

Van Dam ranked among the most prominent merchants of the city. He owned several ships, and was extensively engaged in the West India trade. For many years he had stood out openly and manfully against all abuses, and had regarded with interest whatever affected the commerce of the young colony. Indeed, his first entrance into the exciting arena of politics seems to have been on the occasion of the seizure of some of his vessels by Bellomont, for alleged infringements of the custom laws. He at once threw himself into the opposition, and henceforth was an active party leader. He attained great power and influence, and after having been one of the governor's council for nearly thirty years, he as

---

[1] *Contributions to East Jersey History.* Whitehead, p. 148. *Smith's New York : Smith's New Jersey.*

President of that body acted for more than a year (from July 1, 1731, to August 1, 1732) as governor of the province.[1]

Chief Justice Mompesson was probably of more real service to Hunter than any other counselor, as he had taken special care to inform himself in regard to the character, manners, morals, and peculiarities of the people of New York and New Jersey, and he was, moreover, less tinctured with party prejudice than the men who had been battling with grievances for a lifetime. He was a master of the English law, and his advice was always to the point.

At that epoch Germany was crying out in anguish through the draughts made upon her resources by the "Thirty Years' War." Thousands of the peasantry had no alternative but gradual starvation or immediate emigration to some foreign country. Many of them, flying before the French, took refuge in the camp of the Duke of Marlborough. Queen Anne sent a fleet to Rotterdam to convey a portion of them to London, and such was the eagerness of the unhappy people to accept of exile that England was threatened, as it were, with an invasion. At least thirty-two thousand were landed upon her shores. The Ministry thought it might be a possible public advantage to quarter a few shiploads of them in the American colonies, to be employed in making pitch and tar for the naval stores, and therefore a proclamation was issued offering free passage to such as might wish to cross the Atlantic. At that moment Hunter was about to embark for New York, and was intrusted with the charge of three thousand, who had pushed forward for transportation. The government entered into a contract to settle them upon lands which they might agree to pay for in labor after a certain time, and to provide them with present necessaries, such as houses, and household and working utensils.

Hunter had scarcely reached New York ere he was compelled to hasten to Albany to confer with the sachems of the Five Nations. He took the opportunity to prospect along the Hudson River for a suitable location for the German colony, and finally purchased about six thousand acres of land of Robert Livingston from the manor property, and adjacent to some

---

[1] Rip Van Dam was born in Albany. *Coll. R. D. Ch. Records.* He married Sarah Vanderspiegle, in the city of New York, on the 14th day of September, 1684. The baptisms of fifteen children are recorded in the Dutch Church between the years 1685 and 1707. Many of this large family lived to years of maturity. Rip, an elder son, married Judith Bayard. Richard married Cornelia Beekman. Isaac, who was baptized in the Dutch Church of New York, on January 9, 1704, was one of the executors of his father's will ; he had six children, the eldest of whom, Anthony, figured among the prominent merchants of New York for many years. *Chamber of Commerce Records,* by John Austin Stevens. Of the daughters of Rip Van Dam, Maria married Nicholas Parcel ; Elizabeth married, first, John Sybrant, second, Jacobus Kiersted ; and Catalyntic married Walter Thong, and their daughter Mary became the wife of Robert, third Lord of Livingston Manor

pine forests. The Germans were soon upon the spot, and, sheltered by cheap and hastily constructed dwellings, huddled together in five distinct villages. Others came after them, many proceeding to Pennsylvania, where they laid the foundation of the German population which is so large an element in that State. These earlier German emigrants were mostly hewers of wood and drawers of water, differing materially from the class of Germans who have since come among us, and bearing about the same relation to the English and Dutch and French settlers of their time, as the Chinese of to-day to the American population of the Pacific coast of the United States.

Presently a change in the English Ministry turned the affairs of these war-worn and poverty-stricken emigrants into hopeless confusion. The new Lords endeavored to render every measure of their predecessors unpopular. They raised a terrific howl about the importation of foreigners to their American colonies, and declared that the giving of them employment was going to endanger the Church. They attacked the legality of the agreement which the government had entered into with the Germans. Hunter soon found his drafts dishonored, and himself personally liable for the expenses of the German colony. It checked him in the carrying out of many plans for their comfort and prosperity, yet he stood bravely by them to the extent of his power. They were sore and discomfited. They grumbled about their land, and said it was unfit for cultivation. Some of them defiantly appropriated other tracts than what had been assigned to them. They quarreled with the overseer whom Hunter had appointed. They clamored for more seed for their gardens, for more bread, beer, beef, hoes, and grubbing-hooks, and were lazy, and disinclined to prepare trees for the manufacture of pitch and tar. Hunter explained to them his embarrassments and his inability to control the English purse. They did not believe him, or, if they did, they refused to be comforted. He enlisted as many of them as practicable for the expedition about to be sent to Canada, and when that proved a failure, allowed them to keep their arms. This last act of consideration he soon, however, had occasion to regret.

He was returning from Albany, after one of his many interviews with the Indian sachems, and stopped for a few days, as was his custom when going up and down the river, at Livingston Manor. This beautiful place was even then the seat of a broad and elegant hospitality. The most refined and cultivated people of the country resorted there for visits, which were often prolonged for weeks ; and every distinguished foreigner who landed upon our shores was sure to be welcomed in his own home by the lord of the manor, who had lost none of the courtliness of his younger years, and at seventy-six carried himself as proudly erect as at forty-five. He had always been courted, notwithstanding his political perversity, and never appeared to better advantage than when entertaining a house full of agreeable guests. His wife had grown more delicately fair and beautiful under the snows of her many winters, and presided over the establishment with queenly dignity, still charming every one by her conversation and winning all hearts by her sweetness of temper. Their children were well bred and highly educated. Philip, who afterwards succeeded his father as lord of the manor, was then about twenty-five. Robert Livingston had not yet retired from public life. He was still secretary of Indian affairs, although Philip often acted as his deputy, and was actively interested in all that concerned the welfare of the province. His jurisdiction as magistrate extended over the entire country between the manor and Albany. Application had been made to him on the very day Hunter reached the manor, by one of the German clergymen, for the dissolution of two unhappy marriages at the German Flats, — as the German settlement was called. Livingston declined to interfere on the ground that Dirck Van Wessells Ten Broeck had just been appointed magistrate over the district to the south.

The manor-house was brilliantly lighted on the evening of the governor's arrival. As the family, with their distinguished guest, were quietly dining, a party of Germans appeared at the great east door and asked to see " His Excellency." Hunter at once granted the request, but the interview was neither agreeable nor profitable. The visitors came with cloudy visages and covert threats to announce their intention of removing to "the Schoharie country," which they declared had been promised them in the queen's contract, and at the same time demanded money from the government to effect their purpose. They had already hindered the government surveyors from laying out any more lots where they were at present located, and had organized an association, with the avowed determination of compelling acquiescence to their wishes. Even during the conversation on the manor-house balcony a party of armed Germans were hanging about on the borders of a thicket near by. Hunter adroitly postponed a final settlement with them for two days. In the mean time he sent an express privately to Albany, forty miles distant, with orders for two independent companies of troops to come directly to his relief by water. They arrived in the night, and were landed with great secrecy, and kept close under the bank of the river out of sight. By appointment, Hunter met the German delegation at a little house on the shore, early the following morning. The latter were ill-mannered and would not listen to anything he had to say. He raised his voice and with much decision told them what he should and what he should not do. One of the Germans began to bluster, and use profane and threatening language; a signal at that moment brought the concealed soldiers briskly in front of the building with drums beating. Such an unexpected apparition so terrified the rude fellows, who had been plotting to seize the governor, that they retreated in great confusion to their villages. The soldiers followed them and took their arms away from them altogether. The salutary lesson restored order for a time, and the work of making pitch and tar once more commenced; but the German colony never ceased to be a thorn in Hunter's flesh.

The meeting of the Assembly occurred soon after Hunter's return to New York. He went before the House, and cordially admonished its members "to do away with unchristian division." Said he, "Let every man begin at home, and weed the rancor out of his own mind; leave disputes of property to the laws, and injury to the avenger of them, and like good subjects and good Christians, join hearts and hands for the common good." But this Assembly, like many another before and after it, was cold and suspicious, and backward about raising the necessary allowances for the government. The excuse was the former misapplication of the revenue, which had involved the country in debt; and a little later, the poverty of the people was pleaded, which had been caused by the tax to defray the expenses of the late expedition to Canada. Some of the members openly denied the right of the queen to appoint salaries for her colonial officers. No one made more forcible arguments to that point than Stephen De Lancey, whose ideas had been molded by European experiences. William Nicolls, the speaker of the House, lawyer-like and self-contained, favored the growing feeling that there should be a restraint upon the governor's prerogative. The support which was cautiously and after labored discussions granted to Hunter was on terms which he could not accept without breach of his instructions.

Autograph of Lewis Morris.

In New Jersey Hunter found a warm admirer and friend in Lewis Morris. The acquaintance had begun in England some months before. But the gentlemen in the council whom Morris had so violently opposed during Cornbury's administration set themselves like steel against both Morris and Hunter, until the latter was obliged to ask the Lords of Trade for the dismissal of Pinhorne, Coxe, Sonmans, and Hall. The New Jersey Assembly sustained him in this particular by declaring, in a memorial, that so long as these gentlemen remained in places of trust in the province justice could not be duly administered, nor liberty and property safe. Hunter about this time purchased a house in Amboy, on the knoll south of St. Peter's Church.[1] It commanded a fine view of the harbor, and of the bay and ocean beyond, and was his official residence while on his tours of duty in New Jersey; and it was where he often retired during the heat of summer, and on other occasions when desirous of recreation or relief from the weighty cares of state. He wrote to Dean Swift: —

" I thought in coming to this government I should have hot meals, and cool drinks, and recreate my body in Holland sheets, upon beds of down ; whereas I am doing penance as if I was a hermit ; and as I cannot do that with a will, believe in the long run the devil will fly away with me. Sancho Panza was indeed but a type of me, as I could fully convince you, by an exact parallel between our administrations and circumstances. . . . . The truth is, I am used like a dog, after having done all that is in the power of man to deserve better treatment, so that I am now quite jaded."

Hunter's pecuniary embarrassments were of the most vexatious kind. He had stripped himself for the government, and could not even command a salary. In a letter to Swift under date of March 14, 1713, he wrote : —

" This is the finest air to live upon in the universe ; and if our trees and birds could speak, and our Assemblymen be silent, the finest conversation also. The soil bears all things, but not for me. According to the custom of the country the sachems are the poorest of the people. In a word, and to be serious, I have spent my time thus far here in such torment and vexation, that nothing hereafter in life can ever make amends for it."

Another serious difficulty arose out of his not being a High-Churchman. The Church had become the political engine of the ministerial faction, and when Coxe and Sonmans found themselves relieved from legislative power, they set themselves vigorously at work to enlist the clergy and

---

[1] In addition to his property at Amboy, Hunter purchased Mattenecunk Island in the Delaware, near Burlington, and retained possession of it for some years after he left the province. In June, 1731, James Alexander wrote to Hunter that Governor Montgomery was so much delighted with this island, that he got vistas cut from it in various directions up and down the river for the agreeable prospects thus afforded. — *Whitehead's East New Jersey,* 154.

the missionaries in a plan to undermine the authority and compel the recall of Hunter, and obtain the appointment of the good Churchman, Nicholson, in his place. They informed the Ministry that Hunter was the protector of dissenters and Quakers, and the upholder of men of low and depraved tastes. They said many other things which it was supposed would be damaging to him at the Court of England. But Hunter's frank and manly answer to the accusations, appealing to the evidence of all sober men, clergy or laity, for a testimony to his straightforward conduct in relation to the furtherance of Christianity, restored the confidence of the Lords of Trade, which it must be confessed was for a time shaken. Hunter was excessively annoyed, as appears from his letters, but he bore himself with consistent dignity, and never seemed to suffer any dejection of spirits. He was an indefatigable worker; his days were divided for each duty with arithmetical precision. When hardest pressed for money, he was usually in his wittiest moods, and often jocosely remarked that he expected to die in a jail. In his leisure moments one winter, assisted by the facetious Morris, he composed a farce, called "Androborus," — The Man-Eater, — in which the clergy, Nicholson, and the Assembly were so humorously exposed, that the laugh turned upon them in all circles. From the merriment thus provoked grew a better liking for and a more generous appreciation of the governor himself.

Jacobus Van Cortlandt was the mayor of New York in 1710, as was he also in 1719. The city had grown very little since the commencement of the century. The city government, like the provincial, was embarrassed in its finances. It went beyond its resources when the City Hall was built on Wall Street. The corporation revenue failed to meet' loans and expenses, and an annual levy was the last resort. In 1703, £ 300 was raised, which was less than one third of one per cent on the value of estates. The citizens grumbled, and in 1704 the amount was reduced to £ 200, which did not abate the dissatisfaction. Various expedients were proposed to add to the revenue of the corporation for absolute necessities. Finally, an appeal was made to the general government for further ferry privileges, which resulted in the charter of 1708. To the city's former franchises was added the grant of land between high and low water along the East River (on the Long Island side from Wallabout to Red Hook) to prevent competition on the part of unlicensed ferrymen. The advantage of additional city ferries soon became apparent. The following table of income and expenditure in 1710 will interest such of our readers as may wish to compare it with the present financial structure and the sums involved : —

31

Annual Income of New York City in 1710	£	s	d
Rent of Ferry	180	0	0
" " Dock . . .	30	0	0
" " Swamp . . .	1	0	0
" " Land to Codrington	1	0	0
Rec'd from 68 Licenses . .	51	19	6
" " 15 Freedoms .	10	2	0
" " The Pound . .	2	0	0
" " Fines & Forfeitures	5	0	0
" " 4 Guagers & Packers & Cullers .	3	12	0
" " Lease to Mr. Van Evern . .	1	12	0
" " Lease to John Van Horne . .		12	0
" " Lease to Van Orden		12	0
" " Lease to J. Anderson	1	0	0
" " Lease to John Boss		12	0
" " Lease to Tuys Boss		12	0
" " Lease to Ryer Hanse		12	0
Total	294	7	6

Annual Expenditure 1710	£	s	d
Salary per annum Town Clerk .	20	0	0
" " " Marshall .	10	0	0
5 per c. Treasurer's Commissions	20	0	0
Bellmen's Salaries . .	36	0	0
Lanthorns & Hour glasses .	3	0	0
Fire and Candle for Constable's Watch	3	0	0
Bonfires on Nov. 5th & Feb. 6th & March 8th & April 13th .	20	0	0
Pens, ink & paper for Town Clerk	1	4	0
Books for Records . . .	2	0	0
Repairs on City Hall and jails	50	0	0
Repairs on Ferry House .	40	0	0
Repairs on the Dock . .	10	0	0
Incidental Expenses . .	42	0	0
Cage, Pillory & Stocks . .	10	0	0
Repairing the Sewer . .	10	0	0
Total	277	4	0

The importation of negroes was perhaps more lucrative at this date, than any other species of commerce. Buyers and sellers desired some special place of rendezvous, hence a slave-mart was erected at the foot of Wall Street. Considerable trade was carried on in clams, the Indians in the distant inland territories reckoning them among their best dishes. When they inhabited the coasts they caught them themselves; now they were only too glad to buy them of the Dutch and English.

An English writer, speaking of New York in 1710, said: —

"There is a kind of frog which lives there during the summer, and which is very clamorous in the evening, and in the night, especially when the days have been hot and rain expected. They quite drown the singing of birds, and frequently make such a noise that it is difficult for a person to be heard in conversation."

And the same writer goes on to introduce to our notice the mosquito: —

"The New York people are greatly troubled with a little insect which follows the hay that is made in the salt meadows, or comes home with the cows in the evening. This little animalculae can disfigure most terribly a person's face in a single night. The skin is sometimes so covered over with small blisters from their stings, that people are ashamed to appear in public."

But the most amusing part of the article, which by the way appeared in a London paper of that date, was in relation to New York lobsters. We will quote the passage entire : —

"Lobsters are caught thereabouts, and after being pickled in very much the same manner as oysters, are sent to several places. I was told of a very remarkable circumstance! The coast of New York had European inhabitants for a long time, and yet no lobsters were to be found there. The people fished for them, but never a sign of one could they find in that part of the sea. They were brought in great well-boats from New England, where they were plentiful. But it so happened that one of these lobster-laden well-boats struck a rock and broke into pieces near Hell-gate, about ten miles from New York, and all the lobsters in it got off. Ever since then there has been a great abundance of them in the waters about the metropolis."

The statesmen of the mother country were very much astonished at the importance which their colonies had begun to assume. Hunter's letters revealed the spirit of self-sufficiency which was pervading New York. It was time to look into affairs, if Colonial Assemblies dared set bounds to the royal prerogative. Hitherto the supreme power of the home government had seemed in accordance with justice and with policy. Indeed, nothing less would have kept the life-blood of the feeble infant in circulation. But as the child grew in strength and stature the fetters should have been loosened. No sensible parent deals with a son of fifteen in the same manner as with a son of five. It was folly to treat such a province as New York, in the early part of the eighteenth century, as it might have been proper to treat a little band of emigrants who had just built their huts on a barbarous shore, and to whom the protection of the flag of a great nation was an indispensable necessity.

England was already in debt, and the English mind was speculating upon the emoluments to be reaped from the colonies. The right of Parliament to tax at discretion was not yet maintained, but the way to it was being paved through illiberal legislation. The nation was comparatively free from pecuniary obligations when William III. ascended the throne. The war with France which followed was expensive. It was found impossible, without exciting the most formidable discontents, to raise by taxation the money needful for its continuance ; and at that very moment numerous capitalists were looking around them in vain for some good mode of investing their savings. They had hitherto kept their wealth locked up, or lavished it upon absurd projects. Riches sufficient to equip a navy which would sweep the entire Atlantic of French privateers, was lying idle, or passing from the owners into the hands of sharpers. No wonder that the statesmen of the realm thought it might with advantage to the proprietor, to the tax-payer, and to the whole British Empire, be attracted into the treasury. Italy, France, and Holland had set the example of incurring a national debt. Sir William Temple told his countrymen, how, when he was ambassador at the Hague, the single province of Holland, then ruled by the frugal and prudent De Witt, owed about five million pounds sterling, for which interest at four per cent was always ready at the day specified for its payment ; and when any part of the principal was paid off the public creditor received his money with tears, well knowing that he could find no other investment equally secure. Montague, one of the most inventive and daring of financiers, was among those who discussed this question. When England finally resorted to the expedient, it was popular; the moneyed men were delighted with the opportunity of lending, and the land-owners, hard pressed by the load of taxation, rejoiced at the prospect of present ease. It was the Tories who at a later period assailed the national debt with rancorous criticism. The rate of interest as first established was ten per cent. After the year 1700 it was only seven per cent.

Such was the origin of the famous debt which has since perplexed the brains and confounded the pride of statesmen and philosophers. At every stage of its increase a cry of anguish arose, and wise men prophesied bankruptcy and ruin. When the great contest with Louis XIV. was terminated by the peace of Utrecht, the nation owed about fifty millions. Acute thinkers declared that it would permanently cripple the body politic. But the nation grew richer and richer. After the war of the Austrian succession the debt had increased to eighty millions. Another war, and, under the energetic and prodigal administration of the first William Pitt, the debt rapidly swelled to one hundred and forty millions. Writers of every grade were in despair. They said it would have been better to have been conquered than oppressed with such a burden. David Hume, one of the most profound political economists of his time, declared that such madness exceeded the madness of the Crusaders. He gloomily predicted that the fatal day for the country had arrived. He could not see the prosperity around him, the growing cities, the marts too small for the crowd of buyers and sellers, the increase of commerce, and the general spread of culture. Adam Smith's vision was but a trifle clearer. He admitted that the nation had actually sustained the vast load, and thrived under it in a way which could not have been foreseen. But the limit had been reached. Even a small increase might be fatal. And he issued a solemn warning against the repetition of such a hazardous experiment. George Grenville, who was eminently practical, declared that the nation must eventually sink under the debt unless a portion of the burden was borne by the American colonies. We shall erelong see how the attempt to lay a portion of the burden upon the American colonies produced another war. And after that war England's debt had increased to two hundred and forty millions, and the colonies were gone, whose aid had been regarded as indispensable. Again the case was pronounced hopeless. England was given over by her state physicians, while, at the same time, the strange patient persisted in living, and was visibly more prosperous than ever before. Soon followed the wars which sprang from the French Revolution, and which exceeded in cost any that the world had ever seen. When they were ended, the debt of England was eight hundred millions. And it was as easy to pay the interest on that gigantic amount as on the original debt of fifty millions. For while the debt had grown all other things had grown as well. There was incessant progress of every experimental science, and there was the persistent effort of every man to get on in life. The resources of the country had been very much enlarged, and business had been doubling and redoubling itself.

There was no little incapacity and corruption prevalent in the State Department of England during Hunter's administration. The plowshare had not yet been put through old systems and fossilized methods of action; and the benefits arising from later experiences were entirely wanting. All rising power in the colonies was esteemed demoralizing. Those dependencies must be compelled to contribute to the defense of the frontiers. Parliamentary interference was suggested by the annoyed and perplexed Ministry. But when the New York Assembly found that the queen and her Lords were really about to fulfill the promise made to Schuyler, by an invasion of Canada, it was warmed into a generous outlay. £10,000 were issued in treasury bills, to be redeemed by taxation in five years, and six hundred troops were furnished, in addition to six hundred Iroquois warriors enlisted by Colonel Schuyler. An important Congress of colonial governors met at New London on the 1711. 21st of June, to decide upon the men and means to be contributed June 21. by the other colonies. There were present Governor Hunter, Governor Dudley, Governor Saltonstall, Governor Cranston, Colonel Schuyler, Livingston, Colonel Vetch, and other gentlemen of note. Every one was willing to assist, and the army, when organized, assembled in Albany, and was placed under the command of Colonel Francis Nicholson, who was to march by land and attack Montreal, while an immense fleet from England should at the same time appear and destroy Quebec. General Hill, a relative of Mrs. Masham, who had superseded the Duchess of Marlborough as the queen's favorite, commanded the fleet. When it arrived at the mouth of the St. Lawrence River a dense fog prevailed, and eight

vessels, containing eight hundred and eighty-four men, were wrecked and lost on the rocky coasts. This calamity so disheartened the officers that they held a council of war, and finally determined that it was im-
_{Sept. 14.} practicable to proceed farther. They anchored in Spanish River Bay; but, as they were provisioned for only ten weeks, they in a few days sailed for home, arriving in Portsmouth on the 9th of October,
_{Oct. 9.} where, in addition to all their previous misfortunes, the *Edgar*, a seventy-gun ship, was blown up, and four hundred troops, besides many friends who had come on board to visit them, were instantly destroyed.

The disappointment fell heavily upon the colonies. The new Ministry was blamed, and with just and sufficient reason, for the mismanagement of the whole matter. Why was not the fleet more fully victualed? Where was there any valid excuse for having tarried in Boston until the season for attack was over? It was supposed that the Ministry intended to save £20,000 to the government by obtaining supplies for the fleet from New England. This was denied by some, and affirmed by others; but whether true or false, it rankled all the same.

New York was in a much worse condition than before the attempted raid, for the enemy were apprised of all that had occurred, and were not only bolder, but threatened general destruction. Many inoffensive families who were comfortably settled on farms above Albany were murdered without the slightest provocation. The cruelties of the French and their allied Indians were without parallel in history. The people of Albany were in constant alarm, and it was not long ere the city of New York was thrown into great consternation by a rumor that the French contemplated an attack by sea.

Nicholson and his troops were recalled as soon as the news of the failure of the fleet reached the governor. But they were not disbanded until spring. Their support, together with the repairs on the fortifications, greatly increased the public debt. The council and the Assembly joined in an urgent appeal to the English government to renew the effort to drive the French out of Canada. Hunter went personally among the Indians, and made every effort in his power to pacify them, and keep them true to the colonies. The operations of England henceforward, in regard to the French, grew less and less momentous,
1712. notwithstanding New York's despairing cry, and the war was finally terminated by the treaty of Utrecht in 1713.

Meanwhile the city was disturbed by an alarming and mysteri-
April 6. ous movement on the part of the negroes. Ever since the West India Company introduced slavery into New York, the traffic in human flesh had been continued, and of late it had very greatly increased.

England was in favor of the system. She imported over three hundred thousand negroes from Africa between the years 1680 and 1700. Nearly half of the population of New York City in 1712 (then about six thousand) was colored. All the wealthy families owned slaves, some as many as fifty. People of moderate means were content with from three to half a dozen in their households, but those were esteemed as necessary as chairs or tables. There was no unity among the slaves, and it was not supposed that there could be any possible political danger from their joint action. They were as rude and ignorant as any other barbarians, and excessively stupid. In anger, however, it was found that they could prove themselves positively fiendish. A few who had received some hard usage from their masters planned a scheme of revenge, which was to kill as many of the citizens as possible without regard to whether they were the persons who had injured them or not. They met at midnight in the orchard of Mr. Crooke, which was not far from the present Maiden Lane, armed with guns, swords, hatchets, and butchers' knives. They set fire to an outhouse, and when the flames brought persons running to the spot, they fell upon and murdered them in the most shocking and brutal manner. Nine men were thus massacred, and six severely wounded. One or two narrowly escaped from the inhuman assassins, and quickly notified the authorities of what was taking place. The governor sent a detachment of soldiers from the fort on a brisk run to the scene of horror, which so frightened the cowardly fellows that they retreated into the woods. Sentinels were stationed at the ferries to prevent their leaving the island, and the next day, with the help of the militia, they were all captured and brought to trial, except six, who in terror and desperation committed suicide. Twenty-one were condemned and executed : several of these were burned at the stake ; some were hanged, one was broken on wheels, and one hung in chains to die of starvation. Many who were not directly implicated were arrested for supposed complicity in the plot, but were afterwards released for want of sufficient evidence or pardoned by the governor.

Shortly after the excitements consequent upon the negro insurrection had subsided, a duel was fought by Dr. John Livingston and Thomas Dongan, which resulted in the death of the former. Dongan was **1713.** tried for murder and found guilty of manslaughter. The mayor (from 1711 to 1714) was Colonel Caleb Heathcote, and chiefly through his instrumentality, Broadway was graded this spring from Maiden Lane to the Commons. Shade-trees, similar to those which graced the southern portion of the street, were planted on either side to the terminus of the improvements. The family homestead of the Beekmans stood on a bluff overlooking the East River, near the present corner of Pearl and Beekman Streets. It was built by Hon. William Beekman in 1670. An orchard of

fine old apple-trees stretched over several acres to the right, and pears and peaches were cultivated in large quantities on the rolling land in the vicinity. The garden hugged the mansion on two sides, and was one of the finest on Manhattan Island. The family coach, of which the sketch is an authentic

The Beekman Coach.

representation, is preserved, and in the possession of Hon. James W. Beekman, Vice-President of the New York Historical Society.

Although Hunter was in harmony with his council in almost all matters of public interest, he was in constant collision with the Assembly, which was opposed to the granting of a permanent revenue for the support of the government. The House took the subject finally into grave consideration, and sent to the council several bills which the latter attempted to amend; this provoked a warm controversy between the two branches of the legislature. The council argued from precedent, and its relative position as Upper House, or House of Lords. The Assembly resolutely maintained that both Houses were alike Commons, and that the council was only an advisory board, in other words, a cipher in the government. They claimed, by virtue of having been the free choice of the people, an inherent right to dispose of the money of the freemen of the colony, and declined to be influenced by the action of any former Assemblies, or by the opinions of the Lords of Trade.

Both Houses adhered so obstinately to their respective positions that the public debts remained unpaid. Meanwhile Hunter, by the advice of his council, established a Court of Chancery and exercised the office of chancellor himself. Rip Van Dam and Adolphe Philipse were appointed masters in chancery, Mr. Whileman, register, Mr. Harrison, examiner, and Mr. Sharpas and Mr. Broughton, clerks. A proclamation was issued to signify the sitting of the court on Thursday in every week. The Assembly immediately passed the two following resolutions : —

"*Resolved*, That the erecting of a Court of Chancery without consent in General Assembly is contrary to law, without precedent, and of dangerous consequences to the liberty and property of the subjects.

" *Resolved,* That the establishing fees without consent in General Assembly is contrary to law."

The council denounced the action of the Assembly in strong and bitter language. Hunter tried to modify the resentment of both Houses. The council wrote an account of the matter to the Lords of Trade, who replied, by unqualified approval of the court which Hunter had established, and dropped a few severe censures upon the course pursued by the Assembly. They said " her Majesty had an undoubted right to erect as many courts in her plantations as she might think necessary for the ends of justice." They also expressed themselves in favor of the right of the council to amend money bills.

There were a few astute lawyers in the Assembly who were skilled in the interpretation of the English law. William Nicolls predicted that the time was not far distant when the logic of the House would be honored by the ablest and best minds in England. And it is an interesting fact that the right of the King to erect a Court of Chancery without consent of Parliament, was warmly contested in England in 1734, and in 1775. Hunter and his council were in the wrong. No such court could legally have been instituted without consent of the Assembly.

The House immediately voted an address to the queen, declaring their willingness to support her government, but complaining of misapplications in the treasury; and intimating suspicions that it had been misrepresented. It prayed that Hunter might be ordered to consent to a law for supporting an agent to represent the House at the Court of England. Provoked beyond endurance at such proceedings, and to put an end to the unprofitable disputes between the Houses, Hunter, whose honesty of purpose was as clear as the sunlight, dissolved the Assembly.

Of course an election followed, and the politicians who had long been accustomed to the tactics of faction entered into the **1714.** contest, which was spirited and exciting. Several new members were returned, but the majority were of the same mind as those who had preceded them. The invincible William Nicolls was again elected speaker. Hunter met the new House with the announcement that he should pass no law whatever until it had made provision for the government. He said he had begged his bread for several years and should now take another course. Having no alternative but to comply or break up immediately, the House cautiously provided for a revenue for one year, and then proceeded to other business. The debts of the government remained unnoticed until the autumn session When the claims were called in, the amount was prodigious. It exceeded £48,000. The members were overwhelmed with consternation. Weeks were spent in discussing methods for its liquidation.

An Act was finally passed for the issue of bills of credit to the full amount, to be lodged in the hands of the treasurer, Colonel Abraham De Peyster, and circulated by him according to the directions of the Act. There was no such thing then as a science of finance, and but little to be learned from the financial experience of the civilized world. Neither was it a fixed fact that a government could make a currency to suit its own fancy, and carry on trade independent of the rest of mankind. It is not strange that our early legislators fell into blunders and were sometimes panic-stricken. It is more a matter of surprise that they did not make irretrievable mistakes, since they were obliged to act from the dictates of common-sense rather than precedent. And legislation was then, as well as at the present moment, a cheap prescription, purchased by a little public clamor.

Scarcely had this knotty question been settled, ere the news of Queen Anne's death, and of the accession of George I. to the throne of England, reached New York. In honor of the new sovereign there was a general illumination of the city, and bonfires and torchlight processions added brilliancy to the display.

Oct. 6.

The Assembly was dissolved by the death of the queen, and when the Assemblymen received their pay, Stephen De Lancey immediately donated his fee, £ 50, to the corporation, to be expended in a city clock, which with four dials soon graced the very respectable and substantial City Hall, and was found to be a great convenience to the citizens.

1715.
May.

The spring election of 1715 was more satisfactory to Hunter than any which had preceded it. The House came together in May, and the first subject discussed was naturally that of the revenue. Lewis Morris, the member from the borough of Westchester, put all the vigor of his intellect into a plan for the governor's relief. He said that narrow-mindedness and penury were sure to defeat their own ends. He painted in glowing colors Hunter's four years of patient and uncomplaining service, his struggle to live, his hardships and privations cheerfully borne, and his undeniable right to a liberal support. In spite of his unattractive temper and many glaring faults, Morris wielded a strong influence. A few conservative members resisted his logic to the last. Arguments were used which were concise, clear, convincing, and sometimes delivered with grave irony. Mr. Mulford from Suffolk County was the only one who descended to personal abuse. He denounced the whole question of the revenue as a " put-up job " of the government. He was a man of opinions, but of feeble judgment, and, his remarks becoming offensive, he was expelled from the House. The next day it was found that the revenue party were in the majority, and to facilitate matters Hunter consented to the Naturalization Bill, which resulted in the immediate settlement of a revenue for five years.

Mompesson died in June of this year, and Hunter immediately appointed Lewis Morris chief justice of the province in his stead. In asking the Lords of Trade for their confirmation of his choice, Hunter said that Morris was the fittest man in New York for the trust, for besides being honest he was able to live without a salary. The strongest argument in his favor, however, was his recent valuable services in the Assembly, "for the good of the government." He had many enemies, and it was whispered that he had paid Hunter a large sum of money, and that he had bribed some of the prominent counselors of the governor in order to prevent their interference and thus enable him to se-

Portrait of Chief Justice Lewis Morris.

(Copied through courtesy of Hon. William A. Whithead, from original pen miniature by Watson.)

cure his promotion. When that accusation was effectually contradicted he was sneeringly called the *governor's favorite.* "Very well," said Hunter, "no truer word was ever spoken. He is my favorite, and why should he not be when he is so well worthy?" Then it was argued that he was constantly liable to indiscretion, and that his knowledge of law had been gathered by experience and observation, rather than by profound study. His subsequent career showed him to have been one of the most searching and sagacious of judges, and even those who were the bitterest in their opposition at first, were constrained finally to admit that he was austerely just in his decisions.

George Clarke, the secretary of the province, was appointed to fill Mompesson's place in the council at New York, and David Jamison, the chief justice of New Jersey, was assigned to the vacancy in the council of that province. Clarke was descended from the Clarkes of Somersetshire, whose residence was at Swainswick, near Bath. His wife was of royal blood. She was Ann Hyde, a cousin of Queen Anne. Clarke had filled the office of secretary since 1703, and his abilities had won him deserved prominence in the colony. Twenty years later we shall find him lieutenant-governor of New York.

Dr. Samuel Staats died shortly afterward, and Chief Justice Jamison was appointed in his stead in the New York council. The Lords of Trade remembered Jamison as one not well spoken of by Lord Bellomont, and wrote to Hunter to inquire what manner of life he had led since that period. Hunter replied that he had constantly held important official positions, had acquired a large estate, had been noted for his art and management in legal processes, had been of unblemished life and conversation, and had enjoyed a large measure of distinction because of his exemplary piety and religious zeal. As for what had been formerly reported, Hunter said, " Lord Bellomont must have been grossly imposed upon, for although Jamison had been a little wild in his young days, he had never been sentenced to be hung for burning the Bible in Scotland, and the story of his having had two wives was notoriously false."

The residence of many of the counselors was some distance from the city, hence Hunter recommended five more names to the Lords of Trade. They were, Augustine Graham, who had ripened into a politician quite as polished and scarcely less subtile than his honored sire; Dr. John Johnson, the recently elected mayor of the city; Stephen De Lancey; Robert Lurting ; and Robert Watts. Hunter said they were all men of large wealth, which was an answer to the leading question invariably asked by the English statesmen when a candidate was proposed. Their first confidence was in real sterling business talent, and although the idea was then scarcely understood, and has since been mercilessly misconstrued, the root of the whole matter was in the fact that men are developed and made better by taking their lots and places in the tasks, enterprises, temptations, and vicissitudes of life, working their way, not only that civilization may be extended and Christianity strengthened, but that they themselves may represent a more perfect type of manhood. Inherited wealth has not unfrequently proven a bane to its possessor, and clogged instead of accelerated the wheels of progress ; but the creation of property is, and always has been, one of the best schools for bringing into full play the varied powers of which men's natures are compounded. The history of New York illustrates the assertion. It is said, and sometimes with a sneer, that the metropolis was founded by traders (that every man kept a store), and that in its present proportions it is only an outgrowth of commerce. We stand perpetually accused of being a money-making and a dollar-loving people. But we do not feel reproached. We have learned that whatever is strong, noble, just, and possible, whether it is the pursuit of wealth, art, or fame, is good for the world through the unfolding of individual character and the consequent uplifting of society. We have the satisfaction of knowing that our money-making citizens, through every decade since we were a little fur-station, have been second to none in generous impulse, in Catholic charity, in Christian progress, and in public spirit. We have seen money flow from their coffers like water from Croton Lake. We have seen churches built, we have seen schools and colleges established, we have seen asylums endowed, we have seen hospitals and homes provided, and we have seen the current of liberal giving making its way beyond our own limits, until, like Holland's canals, it extends through every habitable portion of our vast country. What it has done towards supplying human wants, encouraging thrift, and diffusing virtue and intelligence and education, we can only comprehend by a careful investigation of how American society has been built up from the foundation. Let us cease to under-value the one talent without which we should have been narrow-minded indeed. Let us bear in remembrance, also, that riches honestly acquired are entirely consistent with the spirit of Christianity, and without which Church and State would alike languish.

Robert Watts had been a resident of New York about five years. He came from Scotland. The home of the Watts family was Rosehill,[1] an ancient estate or district about a mile west of Edinburgh, on the old Glasgow road. Hunter named Robert Watts to the Lords of Trade, as "a gentleman of sound sense, high respectability, and known affection to the government." He seems to have been a young man of many personal attractions, of considerable culture, and of rare promise. He married, the year before, Mary, the daughter of William Nicolls and Anne Van Rensselaer. His son, the afterwards celebrated Hon. John Watts, was born April 5, 1715. The latter was precocious from his very

---

[1] The Rosehill estate is nearly all built over, and the Caledonian Railway passes through it. The Watts homestead is still standing, and in a fair state of preservation ; it is a quaint, old-fashioned building, some sixty feet square, and three stories high, with four windows in a row on every floor. Its situation is high, affording a splendid view to the west and south. There is a two-story building about twenty feet square a little to the rear of it, like a tower, separate for offices. The extensive grounds in connection with the place have been used for some years as a coal-depot by the Caledonian Railway Company.

babyhood, and as soon as old enough he was sent abroad to complete a finished education.[1]

The social attractions of the winter of 1715 – 16 were greater than they had ever been. Families who had been estranged for long and weary years, through political and other disturbances, became friends, and hospitably entertained each other. Dinner-parties were an almost every-day occurrence, and there were several notable weddings and other *fêtes*. In receiving guests the same etiquette and ceremony were observed as in the higher European circles. The governor was in a happier frame of mind than before the Assembly provided for his salary, and now he was hoping to have the £ 20,000 refunded to him from the English government, which he had expended from his own purse in his care of the Germans. He entered into the gayeties of the winter with a relish, and was the magnetic center of every assemblage. Lady Hunter, the bright particular star of his destiny, was always by his side and elicited the most sincere homage and admiration. She was a lady of superior education and rare accomplishments, gentle, self-contained, and unselfish, shining in society rather through the reflected light of her husband, but in domestic life radiating a steady luster all her own, which was the more charming because of her sweetness of disposition and strength of character. Among those who formed the "court circle," as it was aptly styled, were the Van Cortlandts (there were several families of Van Cortlandts; Philip, the second Lord of the Manor, had recently married Catharine, daughter of Hon. Abraham De Peyster, and, a little later, the daughter of Jacobus Van Cortlandt was married to Abraham De Peyster, Jr.), Bayards, Van Dams, (Rip Van Dam, Jr., was married the following year to Judith Bayard), Clarkes, Morrises, De Lanceys, De Peysters, Beekmans, Nicollses, Wattses,

---

[1] John Watts married, in 1742, Ann De Lancey. Their children were : 1, Robert, who married Mary, daughter of Lord Stirling ; 2, Ann, who married Archibald Kennedy, afterwards Earl of Cassilis ; 3 and 4, Stephen and Susanna, twins, both of whom died young ; 5, John, born in 1749 (died in 1836), who married his cousin Jane De Lancey ; 6, Susanna, who married Philip Kearny ; 7, Mary, who married Sir John Johnson ; 8, Stephen, who married in England, Miss Sarah Nugent ; 9, Margaret, born in 1775 (died in 1836), who married Major Robert Leake.

John Watts, the third son of John Watts, Senior, who married, in 1774, Jane, daughter of Peter De Lancey and Elizabeth Colden, had children as follows : 1, John, who never married ; 2, Henry, who never married ; 3, Robert, who never married, but took the name of Leake, and a fortune (died in 1830) ; 4, George, an army officer, who never married ; 5, Stephen, who never married ; 6, Ann, who never married ; 7, Jane, who never married ; 8, Elizabeth who married Henry Laight (had no children) ; 9, Susan who married her cousin Philip Kearny, and was the mother of the late lamented Major-General Philip Kearny ; 10, Mary Justina, who married Hon. Frederic de Peyster, and was the mother of Major-General John Watts de Peyster,

Gouverneurs, Provoosts, Staatses, Philipses, Van Hornes, and others. It is necessary for a clear understanding of the peculiar workings of the complicated political machinery of New York prior to 1776, to keep in mind the relationship of the chief actors on the public stage. Nearly all the prominent families were connected by marriage, and, in many instances, doubly and trebly connected.

The following summer Lady Hunter died, after a short and severe illness, and Hunter was so smitten by the affliction that he **1716.** never recovered his former cheerfulness during his stay in New York. Indeed, his subsequent failure of health, and consequent petition to the Lords of Trade to be allowed to return to England, was attributed to his great, hopeless sorrow for her loss.

There were two arrivals worthy of notice this season. James Alexander, from Scotland, the father of Lord Stirling, and William Smith from Buckinghamshire, England, the father of the well-known historian of New York.

James Alexander was a young lawyer of good birth and education. His special excellence was in the knowledge of mathematics. He had been an officer of engineers in Scotland. Hunter no sooner made his ·acquaintance than he perceived that such unusual talents might be turned to account in this country ; and he accordingly appointed him surveyor-general of New Jersey, where he shortly projected an advantageous boundary between New York and New Jersey, which, however, was not agreed upon at the time. Alexander was also in the secretary's office, and was attorney-general (for two years) of the New York province. Within five years he occupied a prominent seat in the councils of both New York and New Jersey.

He married, in 1721, the granddaughter of Johannes De Peyster (the first of that honorable name in this country).[1] Their only son was William, afterwards Earl of Stirling. They had four daughters, Mary, who married Peter Van Brugh Livingston ; Elizabeth, who married John Stevens ; Catharine, who married Walter Rutherford ; and Susanna, who

---

[1] An error in regard to the marriage of James Alexander having been many times repeated, the same is here corrected by the authentic genealogy of the lady whom he married. Maria De Peyster, daughter of Johannes De Peyster, married, 1, Paulus Schrick (who was born in Hartford, Connecticut, and whose house in 1686 was on the east side of Broad Street) ; 2, John Spratt, styled " Gentleman " in the old records ; 3, David Provoost, mayor of the city in 1699. Maria, daughter of John Spratt and Maria De Peyster, married, October 15, 1711, Samuel Provoost, and after his death, she married, in 1721, James Alexander. Thus it was not the widow of David Provoost whom Alexander married, as generally supposed, but the widow of Samuel Provoost, who was herself the daughter of Mrs. David Provoost by a former husband.

married John Reed, all ladies of marked ability and singular strength of character. Mrs. Alexander is described as possessing great mental vigor and business talent. She conducted the mercantile affairs of her husband in her own name for some years after his death.

James Alexander was a great acquisition to the community. He was not only a lawyer and mathematician, but he developed into a distinguished politician, statesman, and man of science. He found time amid his various labors for extensive study. He, with Dr. Franklin and others, founded the American Philosophical Society, and maintained a constant correspondence with Halley, the Astronomer Royal, and other learned dignitaries in different parts of Europe.[1]

Hunter was a Low-Churchman. He tried to sustain a certain amount of social intercourse with Rev. Mr. Vesey, of Trinity Church, but was treated with coolness and apparent suspicion. He finally contented himself with giving straightforward attention to matters which might properly be considered within his province as the head of the government, was active in promoting the general interests of religion, and the spread of the gospel throughout the province, and, having satisfied his conscience, allowed the clergy to nurse their prejudices. Rev. Mr. Vesey was one of the most excellent and useful of men, but, like his contemporaries across the water, exceedingly narrow and bigoted. All his studies, his mental faculties, his daily tasks — everything within him and without him was consecrated to his pastoral work. He was tender of the Church, spiritually and temporally, and watched over it with jealous care. One of his warmest friends and most cordial supporters was Colonel Caleb Heathcote, who was also an agent for the Society for Propagating the Gospel in Foreign Parts, and took personal interest in the missionaries who were from time to time sent among the Indians. The good divine was a grave, thoughtful man, his face often wearing the expression of deep melancholy; in the company of friends, however, he was affable and cheerful, and in his domestic relations he was most gentle and affectionate.[2]

One of the charges made by Rev. Mr. Vesey against Hunter to the Bishop of London was, that he favored the Presbyterians. The latter

---

[1] James Alexander died in 1756. He accumulated a large estate, and lived in the style of the English gentry. His country-seat was in New Jersey. Mrs. Alexander, in continuing the business of her husband after his death, was efficiently aided by her son William, until a contract for supplying the king's troops with clothing and provisions during the French war brought him under the notice of the military Shirley, who made him his aid and private secretary, and finally took him to England, where the young man found himself the nearest male heir to the Earldom of Stirling. Mrs. Alexander died in 1761.

[2] See portrait of Rev. Mr. Vesey on page 436.

were spoken of as dissenting Protestants.

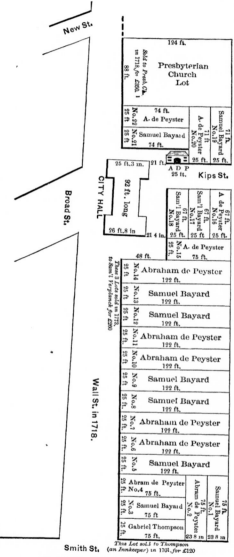

Map of the "De Peyster Garden,"

north side of Wall Street, in 1718. From the original parchment in possession of Hon. Frederic de Peyster, President of New York Historical Society.

There was as yet but a mere handful of them in New York, and since 1706 they had worshiped in private houses. Hunter firmly protected them in all their rights. Having finally gained sufficient **1718.** strength, they decided to purchase a lot in Wall Street, near the City Hall, and build a church.[1] The edifice was erected the following year. Rev. James Anderson was the first pastor; the congregation were allowed to meet for public worship, prior to the completion of the church, in the City Hall, by special act of the corporation. The same organization now worship in the elegant stone structure on Fifth Avenue, between Eleventh and Twelfth Streets.

The ancient "De Peyster Garden," which was purchased from Governor Dongan by Colonel Abraham De Peyster and Colonel Nicholas Bayard, and which embraced quite an extent of valuable territory to the north of Wall Street, was surveyed and laid out in lots in the early part of this year. There were twenty-two of these lots, besides the site of the City Hall, previously donated by De Peyster, and the one recently occupied by the trustees of the new Presbyterian Church. The map, which is an authentic copy of the antique

[1] The lot was purchased from the heirs of Gabriel Thompson, who had originally purchased it from the "De Peyster Garden."

32

original,[1] illustrates the condition of Wall Street at this date, and is too interesting to be omitted.

Not far from this time a party of Scotch-Irish Presbyterians, of the school of Knox, emigrated from Londonderry, Ireland, and found their Canaan in a little nook in New Hampshire, which four years afterward was incorporated into a town and called Londonderry. John Woodburn, the great-grandfather of Hon. Horace Greeley, was one of those pioneers of the New England forests. It was they who introduced the culture of potatoes into the northern settlements. Within twelve months the seed had been brought to New York and planted. The product was looked upon with marked disfavor at first. The tops, when in full bloom, were decidedly ornamental, and were cultivated in the gardens along the " Broadway road " simply for the flower. At least such was the case for a season or two. The native country of the potato is still a matter of doubt. Common report and general belief refers it to Peru. It is supposed they were introduced into Europe by the Spaniards, but their use as an esculent was very tardily adopted. Walter Raleigh carried some to England from Virginia in 1586. He had found them among the Indians, whose traditions seemed to warrant the conclusion that they had been brought a long distance from the south. There have been more than fifty different varieties cultivated since that period. Of these such have been perpetuated as were found best adapted to each climate or particular district.

1719. In June, 1719, vigorous measures were taken to establish the partition-line between New York and New Jersey, as also between New York and Connecticut. The marks which were left by the commissioners under Dongan in 1683 had been worn out by time, or destroyed by evil-disposed persons, and thus many people residing near the lines were shirking both the taxes and the laws, by claiming first to live in one province and then in the other, as policy prompted. Allan Girard, who had been appointed surveyor-general of New York in place of Colonel Augustine Graham (recently deceased) and James Alexander, took repeated observations to find the chief stream which formed the river Delaware, and finally fixed the line between New York and New Jersey. Their decisions, which were more nearly correct than any which followed, resulted in a chronic controversy between the two provinces, which had hardly been settled at the time of the Revolution.[2] In 1748 Lewis

---

[1] Copied through the courtesy of Hon. Frederic de Peyster.

[2] In regard to the extensive grants of lands along the frontiers of the provinces, Alexander said, that although they were doubtless productive of great evils to New York, the buyers had paid sums, first to the natives for their rights, afterwards government fees attending the

Morris made a speech before the New York Assembly, in which he said that the affair of the partition-line dated back as far as he could remember, and while he did not consider himself able to judge correctly as to whether it should be a mile farther north or south, as he was no master of mathematics, and had never examined the surveyor's reports, yet it had cost the provinces so much already that he did not esteem it worth while to meddle with it further. The people along the line were in constant jangle with each other, and quarrels with the government and serious litigations were continually multiplying relative to the rights of soil and jurisdiction. At one time two men, whose farms lay in the disputed territory, joined the New Jersey militia, and were promptly threatened with imprisonment by the commander of the New York militia if they ventured to serve. Others were arrested for nonpayment of taxes, which gave abundant business to the courts, and created no little asperity among the lawyers. It was the subject of warm discussions at the court of St. James, and the correspondence between the Lords of Trade and the leading men of New York and New Jersey forms almost a library of itself.[1]

More than a year had elapsed since William Nicolls, on account of failing health, had declined by letter his position as speaker of the Assembly, which he had held for sixteen years;[2] Robert Livingston was chosen in his stead. For some months Hunter had been quietly making preparations to return to England. But he greatly feared that

patents, amounting to quite as much as he thought as the land was worth, and to deprive such people of their possessions was a harsh, unjust, and dangerous proceeding.

[1] Ferdinando John Paris was the agent from New Jersey in London during many of the years while this controversy was going on, and has left the papers and letters relating to the partition-lines in a condition of most admirable arrangement.

[2] William Nicolls died in 1722, aged sixty-six years. His large estate on Long Island, which he called Islip, in honor of the ancient village of that name, six miles from the University of Oxford, where his father was born, was divided among his six children. They were : 1, Benjamin, who married his cousin Charity Floyd, and died in 1724, his widow subsequently becoming the wife of Rev. Dr. Samuel Johnson, first president of King's (Columbia) College, and mother of Samuel William Johnson, the first president of the same institution after it became Columbia College ; 2, William, who for many years was speaker of the New York Assembly, as his father had been before him, — a shy, timid, uncommunicative, but candid and sincere man, who never married, but spent the greater part of his life in perplexing lawsuits, occasioned by the unsettled condition of his father's and brother's affairs ; 3, Rensselaer, who married and resided near Albany ; 4, Mary, who married Robert Watts ; 5, Catharine, who married John Havens, of Shelter Island, and was the mother of Nicoll Havens, and grandmother of Hon. John Nicoll Havens ; 6, Frances, who married Edward Holland.

In a memorandum left by Hon. John Watts, Senior, is the following paragraph : "As my own father had added an *s* to his name (making Watt Watts), for what reason I have never heard, Mr. Nicolls left the *s* out of his name, calling himself, as all his descendants have done, Nicoll."

it might occasion intrigues if it should be known that he was to resign his government, and he therefore kept his affairs an absolute secret. Not one person knew of his intentions, until, on the 24th of June, he sum-
June 24. moned the House before him, and after transacting the special business for which they had been called, he arose and addressed them in the following words:—

"Gentlemen, I have sent for you that you may be witness to my assent to the Acts passed by the General Assembly in this session. I hope that what remains unfinished may be perfected by to-morrow, when I intend to close the session.

"I take this opportunity also to acquaint you that my uncertain state of health, the care of my little family,[1] and my private affairs on the other side, have at last determined me to make use of that license of absence which was some time ago graciously granted me, but with a firm resolution to return again to you, if it is his Majesty's pleasure that I should do so; but if that proves otherwise, I assure you that whilst I live, I shall be watchful and industrious to promote the interest and welfare of this country, of which I think I am under the strongest obligations for the future to account myself a countryman. I look with pleasure upon the present quiet and prosperous state of the people here, whilst I remember the condition in which I found them upon my arrival. As the very name of party or faction seems to be forgotten, may it ever lie buried in oblivion, and no more strife ever happen amongst you, but that laudable emulation who shall prove himself the most zealous servant and dutiful subject of the best of princes, and most useful member of a well-established and flourishing community, of which you, gentlemen, have given a happy example."

The reply of the Assembly through Robert Livingston, Speaker, was equally courteous and to the point:—

"Sir, when we reflect upon your past conduct, your just, mild, and tender administration, it heightens the concern we have for your departure, and makes our grief such as words cannot truly express. You have governed well and wisely, like a prudent magistrate, like an affectionate parent; and wherever you go, and whatever station the Divine Providence shall please to assign you, our sincere desire and prayers for the happiness of you and yours shall always attend you. We have seen many governors, and may see more; and as none of those who had the honor to serve in your station were ever so justly fixed in the affections of the governed, so those to come will acquire no mean reputation when it can be said of them their conduct has been like yours.

[1] The late Lady Hunter was heir to the estate of Sir Thomas Orly, and Hunter wished to confirm the property to his five children, Thomas, Charles, Catharine, Henrietta, and Charlotte. He also hoped to recover from the English treasury what was due him on account of the Germans.

"We thankfully accept the honor you do us in calling yourself our country-man. Give us leave then to desire that you will not forget this as your country, and, if you can, make haste to return to it. But if the service of our sovereign will not admit of what we so earnestly desire, and his commands deny us that happiness, permit us to address you as our friend, and give us your assistance when we are oppressed with an administration the reverse of yours."

No governor ever left New York with greater *éclat* or carried with him more substantial tokens of good-will and affection. He sailed in July, and the chief command of the province devolved upon Peter Schuyler, as the oldest member of the council. His short administration was marked by very few events of note. The Assembly was not convened, by special instructions from the Lords of Trade, as it was a mooted question whether it could legally act under Schuyler, and it was thought that an election at the present time would be prejudicial to the interests of the crown. The boundary between New York and Canada never having been established with any accuracy, the French were extending their settlements across the borders, and pushing themselves into the immediate country of the Five Nations. Robert Livingston called the attention of Schuyler to these alarming encroachments, and Myndert Schuyler and Robert Livingston, Jr., who had married Peter Schuyler's only daughter, were sent as agents to treat with the sachems individually, at their castles, hoping to prevent them from going over to the French. The result was a new treaty with these powerful and ever vacillating tribes, in order to confirm and preserve the ancient league. The records of that particular period are also crowded with the transactions respecting the partition-line between New York and New Jersey.

Schuyler was advanced in years, but was modest, brave, shrewd, and reticent, though less active than formerly. He trusted very much to the energetic counsel of Adolphe Philipse, and for lodging the king's seal in the hands of the latter was unsparingly criticised. Philipse had been a member of the council for fourteen or more years, and the agent for New York at the court of George I., for some months prior to Hunter's departure from the province. He was a sedate bachelor of fifty-four, and, though no scholar, he was a gentleman, and possessed a character of more than common accomplishments and strength. He was of a penurious turn of mind, and had been so pronounced in his opinions regarding finance and governmental outlays as to bring himself into direct antagonism with the warm personal friends of Hunter. By the king's instructions the president of the council was to receive one half of the salary and all the perquisites of a governor. A dispute arose whether the word "half" did not extend to "all the perquisites" as well as to the salary. Schuyler retained the whole, and in his right to do so was ably sustained by Philipse.

Upon Hunter's arrival in England he effected a change of business with William Burnet, by resigning the government of New York and New Jersey, and accepting an offer of comptroller of the customs in London. In 1727 he was appointed governor of Jamaica. He died in 1734. He maintained an active correspondence with his friends in New York and New Jersey from the time he left the provinces to the end of his life, and was kept informed of all events of consequence political and personal. He continued to be a property-owner also, and in 1730 wrote to James Alexander, expressing his desire to purchase six or seven hundred acres of land at New Brunswick, if it could be bought reasonably. Alexander in reply told him that the country about there was being settled very fast, and that "all the way for thirty miles south was a continuous line of fences and many good farmers' houses"; that a lot of ground in New Brunswick had grown to nearly as high a price as so much ground in the heart of New York.[1]

Thirteen months from the time of Hunter's farewell to New York, on the 20th of September, 1720, Schuyler was relieved from executive duties by the arrival of Governor William Burnet.

---

[1] *Whitehead's Contributions to East Jersey History. Rutherford MSS.*

Morris Arms.

(For description see page 545.)

CHAPTER XXIV.

1720 – 1732.

GOVERNOR WILLIAM BURNET.

GOVERNOR WILLIAM BURNET. — SOCIAL EVENTS. — BURNET'S MARRIAGE. — DR. CADWAL-LADER COLDEN. — ROBERT LIVINGSTON SPEAKER OF THE ASSEMBLY. — JOHN WATSON THE FIRST PORTRAIT-PAINTER. — ROBERT WALTERS. — BURNET'S INDIAN POLICY. — REV. JONATHAN EDWARDS. — BURNET'S COUNCIL. — YOUNG MEN GOING WEST. — BUR-NET'S THEOLOGY. — THE FRENCH PROTESTANTS. — STEPHEN DE LANCEY. — WILLIAM BRADFORD. — THE FIRST NEWSPAPER IN NEW YORK. — THE SILVER-TONED BELL. — BURNET AND THE INDIAN CHIEFS. — DEATH OF GEORGE I. — BURNET'S DEPARTURE FOR BOSTON. — THE NEW POWDER-MAGAZINE. — GOVERNOR JOHN MONTGOMERY. — CON-FERENCE WITH THE INDIANS AT ALBANY. — JAMES DE LANCEY. — THE FIRST LIBRARY IN NEW YORK. — THE JEWS' BURIAL-PLACE. — THE CITY CHARTER. — FIRST FIRE-EN-GINES IN NEW YORK. — FIRST ENGINE-HOUSE. — RIP VAN DAM PRESIDENT OF COUNCIL AND ACTING GOVERNOR OF NEW YORK.

THE advent of Governor Burnet was an event of special interest. New York was in holiday attire. Flags were flying, cannon speaking significant welcome, and the military on parade in full uni-form. It was a beautiful September day, and the balconies of all the houses along the route were filled with ladies, as the new governor was escorted with stately ceremony to the City Hall in Wall Street, according to ancient usage, to publish his commission. **1720.** **Sept 20.**

William Burnet was the son of the celebrated prelate, Bishop Burnet. He was named for the Prince of Orange, who stood sponsor for him at his baptism. He was a free-and-easy widower, large, graceful, of stately presence, dignified on occasions, but usually gay, talkative, and condescending. He was esteemed handsome, and greatly admired by the ladies, to whom he was specially devoted when in their presence. His gallantry was not a recommendation, however, to public favor. Some of the grave heads in high places were shaken dubiously. One gentleman wrote to Hunter, " We do not know yet how the fathers and husbands are going to like Governor Burnet, but we are quite sure the wives and daughters do so sufficiently."

He had been carefully educated by his learned father, who, it is said, saw nothing in the youth but faint promise of moderate scholarship, until he was at least twenty years of age, and had been so uneasy on the subject that he had counseled anxiously with Sir Isaac Newton in relation to the best methods for training so refractory a mind.   William took a sudden turn finally; books became his delight as well as his companions, and he began to hoard them as a miser hoards gold.   One of his relatives was charged with the buying of new books, and the frequent and expensive orders brought many a sharp and serious rebuke upon the young student's thoughtless head, for he was greatly exceeding his income. When this restraint became intolerable, he drew upon his brothers for

Portrait of Governor Burnet.

money.   But they only laughed at his bookish proclivities, and admonished him to browse in his own pastures.

His early life was passed in the atmosphere of William and Mary's Court.   As he matured into manhood he was in constant and daily intercourse with the most cultivated and polished men of the age.   He traveled extensively and became thoroughly conversant with the language and customs of the different nations of Europe.   He was free from affectation, and treated all classes with the most cordial politeness.   He possessed an exhaustless fund of humor and anecdote, but he was not always noted for the discrimination with which he made choice of friends.   His brother Gilbert wrote to him, shortly after he reached New York, in a strain of great caution, advising him against being "led by his genial and winning temper into too much familiarity, which might be turned to his great disadvantage."

He was pleased with the society of New York, which compared favorably with that to which he had been accustomed. He met, within a week after his arrival, the lady whom he married the following spring. She was Anne Marie, the daughter of Abraham Van Horne and Maria Provoost, a beautiful and accomplished young woman of eighteen summers. The Van Hornes were an ancient and eminently respectable family of Dutch ancestry. No one of the name had hitherto figured conspicuously in political life, but they were wealthy and refined people. Abraham Van Horne was a merchant, owning and occupying a large storehouse,

Portrait of Mrs. Burnet.

and a bolting and baking house, besides other property. He was appointed to the council of New York through the recommendation of Burnet in 1722, and held the office until his death in 1741.[1]

Burnet and Hunter were personal friends, and the affairs and leading characters of New York were thoroughly discussed by them before the former accepted the chair of state. He was better prepared, therefore, for active and efficient work from the beginning of his administration than his predecessors had been. His opinions and tastes differed materially from those of Hunter, and the friends of the latter were not altogether predisposed in his favor. He was treated with courtesy, however. Lewis

---

[1] Governor Burnet buried his wife, Anne Marie, or "Mary," as he calls her in his will, in 1727, while in New York ; also one child. He had one son, Gilbert, by his first marriage, who was sent to England upon his death in 1729. He had children by his second marriage. William, Mary, and Thomas. Mary married William Browne, of Beverly, Massachusetts. *New England Historical Genealogical Register*, Vol. V. p. 49.

Morris, bustling, penetrating, and in many things inconsistent, stood highest in his confidence, and still filled the office of chief justice. Burnet was exceedingly fond of him. Lewis Morris, Jr., was taken into the council in place of Caleb Heathcote, recently deceased. Hunter, as has been seen, was liberal in his religious views, and not disposed to make tenets and doctrines the test of friendship. Burnet, on the contrary, was inclined to theological arguments, and rarely let his heart go out towards those who differed from him in matters of religion.

The Lords of Trade deemed it wise that the Assembly, which had been so favorably disposed towards the government before Hunter resigned, should be continued without an election. This measure was opposed by Schuyler and Philipse, on the ground of its illegality. Hence Burnet removed them both from the council, and appointed Dr. Cadwallader Colden and James Alexander in their places. It was a hostile step, and provoked no little comment and criticism. Burnet's reasons for pursuing such a course were obvious. The members of the present Assembly were pledged to grant the revenue again for five years. Symptoms of the old tumult in the political atmosphere at once became apparent. Meanwhile the new members of the council were able and sagacious, and worthy the high place they afterwards held in the governor's esteem.

Dr. Cadwallader Colden was the son of Rev. Alexander Colden of Dunse, in the Merse, Berwickshire, Scotland. He was born February 7, 1687, O. S. He was educated at the University of Edinburgh with a view of settling in the Church of Scotland, but, after completing his studies in 1705, he applied himself to the study of medicine. He was attracted finally to Philadelphia, where his mother had a widowed and childless sister. After practicing his profession in that city for some three years, he visited New York. It was in the summer of 1718. He only stayed three days. He received, however, the most polite and complimentary attentions from Governor Hunter. He was invited to the executive mansion, and a ceremonious dinner was given in his honor. About two weeks after he returned to Philadelphia, he received a letter from Hunter, inviting him to New York, and offering him the office of surveyor-general of the province. Henceforth his name will be identified with our history, until we find him occupying the position of lieutenant-governor in the interesting Stamp Act period. We are indebted to him for much of our science, and some of our most important early institutions. Hence a brief outline of his career will not be amiss at this juncture.

He bought some three thousand acres of land in Orange County in 1719, which he named " Coldenham." He removed his family, a wife and six young children, there in 1728, having brought the land under cultivation, and built a fine large dwelling. This retired home gave him leisure for philosophical study, to which he was greatly inclined. He maintained a voluminous correspondence with the learned scientists of Europe for more than thirty years, — with Linnæus, Gronovius, Peter Collinson, of the Royal Society of London, Peter Kalm, of the Royal Academy of Stockholm, the Earl of Macclesfield, Dr. Franklin, and a host of others. The subjects embraced botany, history, natural history, astronomy, mathematics, philosophy, electricity, and medicine. His writings all bear evidence of indefatigable industry, of solid as well as varied acquirements, and of original conceptions. Mrs. Colden was a lady of genius, able to instruct her children, — indeed, took almost the sole charge of their education, — and assisted her husband materially in his literary labors and correspondence. Colden was the first New-Yorker who achieved an extensive transatlantic reputation, either as a historian, a man of scientific acquirements, or as a philosophic writer, or who was recognized abroad solely on account of his literary labors. His connection with the government of New York from time to time will appear in future pages. In 1672 he purchased an estate of one hundred or more acres near Flushing, Long Island, where he erected a substantial country-house, and called the place Spring Hill. It was here that he died, in 1776, and was buried in a private cemetery on the property.[1]

The speaker of the Assembly at this time was the venerable Robert Livingston. He was of great service to Burnet in the affairs of the Indians, which had become more complicated than ever. An active trade was going on between the French and Indians which would soon prove disastrous to New York. The French purchased English goods in New York and Albany, and sold them to the Indians. Aside from the profits of this commerce to the French themselves, it was clear that the Indians would soon get under their controlling influence; and there was no predicting the terrible power which might be used against the province. Burnet at once laid plans to prevent the circuitous trade, by the encouragement of direct intercourse with the red men.

Owing to his duties in the Assembly, Livingston desired to resign the office of Secretary of Indian Affairs in favor of his son Philip, and Burnet warmly seconded the arrangement by writing to the Lords of Trade and speaking of the younger Livingston in high terms. The

---

[1] The children of Lieutenant-Governor Cadwallader Colden were as follows : 1, Alexander, 2, David, died in infancy ; 3, Elizabeth, married Peter, third son of Hon. Stephen De Lancey ; 4, Cadwallader ; 5, Jane ; 6, Alice ; 7, Sarah, died young ; 8, John ; 9, Catherine ; 10, David. *Genealogical Notes of the Colden Family in America*, by Edwin R. Purple.

result was a commission promptly forwarded, and the son quietly assumed the father's duties.

Meanwhile Burnet actively favored a bill which had been drafted by Livingston and Morris, forbidding the sale of such goods to the French, under severe penalties, as would be merchantable to the Indians. By this means the French would be compelled to procure their wares from Boston or directly from England at advanced prices. The merchants strenuously opposed the measure in the House. They had been receiving cash in hand, and good profits on their goods, and the loss of such a valuable trade would materially affect their purses. The bill passed, however, and was cordially approved by the governor and council. Then the merchants in great heat appealed to the Lords of Trade. But the Act was sustained in England, and its manifold advantages were unquestionable.

Burnet purchased Hunter's country-seat in Amboy, and resided there a part of every year. His public duties in New Jersey were scarcely less onerous than in New York. But he easily overcame the slight opposition of his first Assembly, by consenting to increase the circulating medium of the province, and they granted him an annual salary of £ 500 for five years. Burnet made the acquaintance in Amboy of John Watson, the first portrait-painter who ever took up his permanent abode in America. He was from Scotland, having arrived in New Jersey in 1715. He was an eccentric man, of irascible disposition and penurious habits. His neighbors disliked him. They stood aloof and called him a miser. He was a crusty bachelor. His family consisted of himself and a nephew and niece. He was unquestionably a man of taste and talent, and devoted to art, but he never courted the favor of any one. Burnet became interested in him and allowed him to pen miniature sketches of himself and Mrs. Burnet in India ink, and from the originals, recently discovered by Hon. William A. Whitehead, the New Jersey historian, our engravings are copied. Between that time and the Revolution, Watson accumulated a collection of paintings, which entirely filled one of his houses in Amboy, but they disappeared during the war and have never since been traced. The painter himself lived to an old age. He became blind, and deaf, and bedridden, and still lived. His nephew waited with some impatience for the "dead man's shoes." " Hope deferred *actually* made his heart sick." He could not handle the bonds and mortgages and coin until the proper time, which was long in coming. Meanwhile he had an heir's affection for the old house, which was surely going to decay unless it had a new roof. So he set carpenters privately at work, and had it unroofed and reroofed while the owner was living in it, perfectly unconscious of the operation which was

"Governor Burnet met the Indian sachems in Albany during the summer of 1721; * * * they said they had heard that he was married in New York, they were glad, and wished him much joy. They also begged leave to present the bride with a few beavers for pin-money." Page 517

in progress over his head. One morning the nephew was startled by the inquiry, "What is the meaning of the pecking and knocking which I hear every day?" The heir hesitated a moment, then replied : "Pecking? pecking? Oh! ay! 't is the woodpeckers; they are in amazing quantities this year, leave the trees and attack the roofs of the houses, there is no driving them off." And the old man was satisfied.

Robert Walters was the mayor of the city from 1620 to 1625. He was one of the wealthy men of the period, liberal and public-spirited. He lived in style, kept several horses, owned a large number of negro slaves, and his family always dressed in the latest fashion ; but they never entertained guests except their own immediate relatives. Mrs. Walters had turned her face against society ever since her father's unhappy death. Although more than a quarter of a century had elapsed, and every reparation had been made by the government which was possible, the sting remained, and it was with her incurable.

About this time Hon. Abraham De Peyster retired from the office of treasurer of the province, which he had filled ably and to the satisfaction of all parties since 1706. He also resigned his office of counselor to the governor, much to the regret of his associates. He had, through all the bitter controversies attendant and consequent upon the Revolution, maintained a straightforward, conscientious course, rigidly adhering to the primitive principles of honesty and justice, and we find him in his advanced years commanding the respect and confidence of his political opponents, as well as the admiration and cordial regard of his more immediate friends. His public services were crowned with honor. His son, Abraham De Peyster, Jr., was appointed treasurer of the province in his stead, and remained in that position of trust forty-six consecutive years.

Governor Burnet met the Indian sachems in Albany during the summer of 1721, and was so affable and kind to them, ignoring 1721. their rude ways, and the stench of bear's-grease with which they were plentifully bedaubed, walking and talking (through an interpreter) and dining with them every day, that they became exceedingly fond of him, and were quite ready to bind themselves to his terms of peace. In order to preserve their good-humor the more effectually, he promised to found and encourage an English settlement in their wild country. They were greatly pleased, and said they had heard that he was married in New York ; they were glad, and wished him much joy. They also begged leave to present the bride with a few beavers, for pin-money, and added, significantly, that it was "customary for a brother upon his marriage to invite his brethren to be merry and dance."

Burnet laughed heartily, while thanking them for their good wishes.

When he had distributed the presents prepared by the crown, he ordered several barrels of beer to be given them, "to rejoice with and dance over."[1]

One of the sons of Colonel Peter Schuyler offered his services to lead the expedition into the Iroquois country, and Burnet appointed him at once, in order to prove that he had no personal dislike to the family, even if he had removed the father from office. Young Schuyler received a captain's commission, a handsome salary, and several substantial presents for his outfit. Ten young men joined him in the enterprise, and went prepared to purchase land, erect a trading-house, and start a settlement. Each took with him a stock of guns, and a few blankets, beads, and other trinkets, and a bark canoe. The object was to establish a permanent and direct trade with the Indians. The company were absent a year, when they returned, all in good health, having developed both physically and mentally, and laid the basis of not a few colossal fortunes. They had accomplished a noble work, the fruit of which was to bless New York in all the future. Within a brief period over forty young men had followed their example by plunging boldly into the Indian country as traders, which served to strengthen the precarious friendship existing among remote tribes.

It was in the autumn of 1721 that Jonathan Edwards, fresh from the study of divinity in Yale College, came to New York to preach the gospel to a small society of Presbyterians who had seceded from the new church in Wall Street. New York had an ill name in New England at that time, from being, as the Puritans expressed it, "too much given to Episcopacy." The "show and ostentation and purse-pride" which prevailed in the metropolis was supposed by the New Englanders to be an effectual barricade to the kingdom of heaven. Therefore a company of clergymen sent the young dominie to our shores, in much the same spirit that missionaries are now sent among the Bramins of Hindostan.

First Presbyterian Church, Wall Street.

He was a youth of only nineteen, silent and uncommunicative, but he had the air and dignity of mature

---

[1] *Governor Burnet to Lords of Trade*, October 16, 1721. *New York Coll. MSS.*, Vol. V. 630 – 640.

manhood. He was tall and slender, stooped slightly, his face was pale and somewhat wasted but singularly refined, and he always dressed in homespun gray. He had not then grasped the tenets of his sect, as he did at a later date with the eager, enthusiastic love which accompanies original conceptions, rather than with the languid assent with which an inherited creed is usually received. His education was not even completed, and in a few months he returned to Yale, where as pupil and then tutor he developed into one of the shining lights of Christianity. Writing afterwards of his brief labors in New York, he said : " If I heard the least hint of anything that happened in any part of the world that appeared in some respects or other to have a favorable aspect on the interests of Christ's kingdom, my soul eagerly catched at it ; and it would much animate and refresh me. I used to be eager to read public news-letters, mainly for that end ; to see if I could not find some news favorable to the interests of religion in the world. I very frequently used to retire into a solitary place on the banks of Hudson's River, at some distance from the city, for contemplation on divine things and secret converse with God ; and had many sweet hours there."

The subsequent career of Edwards is familiar to every American, and his influence is felt to this day by millions who never heard his name. While yet a young man sermons and volumes from his pen were republished in Europe and widely read. The picture of his removal into the wilderness with his wife and ten children, on a mission to the Indians, after he had passed middle life, has in it a touch of religious romance. Mrs. Edwards and her daughters, in order to solve the problem of daily food, made lace and painted fans, which they sent to Boston to be sold. One daughter married the accomplished Rev. Aaron Burr, the first president of Princeton College, and her son was the notable Aaron Burr of New York. Among the descendants of Rev. Jonathan Edwards are an army of distinguished individuals, — men of worth, talent, and high position ; women gifted, good, and beautiful.

Meanwhile the Five Nations had made frequent inroads into the province of Virginia, contrary to the treaty long since consummated with Lord Effingham at Albany, and which had been several times renewed by subsequent governors. A serious affair had occurred in Pennsylvania during the summer which resulted in the killing of an Indian from the Five Nations by one of the white settlers. Sir William Keith deemed it advisable to meet the sachems and come to some understanding in regard to the matter. Burnet was somewhat afraid of underhanded negotiations with subjects of the New York government, having had certain experiences of that character which had proved disastrous, and

1722.

went to see the sachems himself, expostulating with them for their conduct. They said, if some person of distinction would come from Virginia to renew the covenant chain, they would keep clear of that territory in all their future hunting and warlike expeditions; "which means," wrote Burnet to the Lords of Trade, "that a fine present would refresh their memories." Burnet proposed a congress of governors and commissioners from all the colonies to meet the Indian chiefs at Albany. The object was ostensibly to confirm treaties, but really to produce an impression upon the Indian mind that the English were going to act in unison as well as the French, and become stronger and more powerful than the latter. This august body met in September. Governor Spottswood of Virginia, at that time one of the most elegant and accomplished men on this side of the Atlantic, came in person, and with becoming deference submitted all his propositions to the Indians, first to Burnet and his counselors, for approval. Sir William Keith of Pennsylvania presided over the congressional deliberations. Burnet acted as an agent for Boston. The session occupied several days, and terminated satisfactorily to all parties.

This Congress framed a memorial to the English government, asking for orders and funds to erect trading posts and ports through the Indian countries, by which to anticipate and prevent the encroachments of the French. Such measures, then easily executed, would have saved the government millions of dollars and much innocent blood. But England gave no heed to the appeal, and the project was reluctantly abandoned.

The country beyond the Great Lakes had not yet been explored. It was only known as the *far West.* In May of the following year a tribe of **1723.** Indians appeared in Albany, bringing their calumet-pipe of peace, **May.** and singing and dancing, as was customary in visiting a place for the first time. The commissioners of Indian affairs could not understand their language, or make out from whence they came. They went away, but soon returned, bringing an interpreter from among the Iroquois, who said they were a great nation with six castles and tribes, from Michilimackinack, and wished to make arrangements to buy wares of the English. In July another tribe made their appearance, for the purpose of traffic, who said the French had built a fort in their country called Detroit; and before September eight other different parties of strange Indians had visited Albany, desiring free commerce, — thus the effect of Burnet's policy was becoming apparent.

The Lords of Trade wrote to Burnet, in June, 1724, that the **1724.** New York Act for laying a duty of two per cent on the importation of European goods had been repealed in England. They also directed him to allow the passage of no more such laws "upon any pretense whatsoever," hoping he would find some other method for raising money to build a fort, the purpose for which the Act was intended. They were in receipt of grievous complaints from the New York merchants, relative to his interference with the French trade; but they said, "While there is so great an appearance of advantage in the encouragement of the Indian traffic, you may depend upon it we shall duly consider their objections before we discourage so fair a beginning." [1]

Burnet was, like his father, of a theological turn of mind. He cultivated an intimate social acquaintance with the clergymen of New York, inviting them to his house and table in the most informal manner, and visiting them in their places of study with great frequency.

The French Protestants just at this juncture became dissatisfied with their pastor, Rev. Louis Rou, a man of learning, but proud and passionate, and dismissed him, in favor of his colleague, who was distinguished for dullness and goodness. Whereupon the injured divine appealed to the governor and council, protesting against the Act of the Consistory as "irregular, unjust, illegal, and without sufficient cause." The consistory were summoned before a committee of the council, of which Dr. Colden was chairman, and ordered to show by what authority they were a court with power to suspend their minister. Mr. Jamison argued at some length, that, although the authority of the officers of the church was not by commission, it was actually established by toleration of the government. Dr. Colden remarked, pointedly, that it was easy to show their power if they had any, and he expected it to be shown immediately. Mr. Jamison replied, that by the same power they called a minister they could suspend him. Dr. Colden insisted that the power should be shown. Mr. Jamison took refuge again under the indulgence of the government and usage. Dr. Colden told him he must show that usage. The interview was long drawn out, and resulted in a decision by the committee, that, no authority having been shown by the Consistory of the French Protestant Church for suspending their minister, they had therefore no such authority. The report of the transaction, signed by Dr. Colden, Rip Van Dam, Robert Walters, and others, contains the following paragraph : —

"But in regard to the French Protestant church which has suffered so much and is at this time suffering in France on Account of their Religion, and in regard to the great numbers of the French Congregation that live in good repute and credit in this place, We are of the Opinion that the said Congregation be admonished, that every person in it doe all in his Power to preserve peace and

---

[1] *Lords of Trade to Governor Burnet*, June 17, 1724. *New York Col. MSS.*, V. 707.

unanimity in their Congregation, for this End that they Endeavour to bring this present unhappy difference to an amicable conclusion.   That if this desirable End cannot be Effected the Partys who shall think themselves aggrieved ought to apply to the Courts of Justice in this Redress, with that meekness and charity to each other which may Encourage the Government to continue towards them the generous protection under which they have been long easy, and that there may be no reason now to think that they grow wanton under the abundance of Liberty and Plenty which they Enjoy here, and that the Ministers of the French Congregation who shall officiate next Sunday be ordered to Read Publickly the said Opinion and Admonition immediately after Divine Service in the forenoon."

Stephen De Lancey was one of the principal benefactors of this church, and was very indignant at the interference of the government.   He had been instrumental in removing the minister, and it was not agreeable to have that same minister reïnstated in the pulpit.   De Lancey was one of the merchants who had taken exceptions to Burnet's Indian policy, and had lost heavily through the obstruction of commerce with the French.   The two provocations rendered him a bitter foe, and his imperious conduct angered the governor.   The following summer De Lancey **1725.** was elected by the city of New York to the Assembly.   When **Sept.** the House came together Burnet refused to administer to him the oath of office on the ground that he was not a British subject.   De Lancey proved that he was made a denizen in England some years before, and, besides, he had served in several former assemblies.   The House decided in his favor, and with considerable show of arrogance (through Adolphe Philipse, Speaker, who was no admirer of Burnet) claimed the right of judging of their own members, and pronounced the governor's course unconstitutional.   An interesting feud arose, which, as months rolled on, several times assumed threatening proportions.   The De Lancey party criticised and condemned the Court of Chancery, and disputed Burnet's decrees as chancellor.

Meanwhile, a newspaper was born.   William Bradford, who introduced **Oct. 16.** the art of arts, printing, into New York in 1693, had up to this time been chiefly in the employ of the government.   On the 16th of October, he issued the first newspaper in New York City, which was purely an individual enterprise.   It was a *half*-sheet of *foolscap paper* filled with European news and Custom-House entries.   It was called *The New York Gazette*.   It was published weekly, and advertised to be sold by Richard Nicolls, postmaster.   Before the end of the following year Bradford, who was both editor and printer, received sufficient encouragement to induce him to increase its size to *a whole sheet of foolscap* *paper,* or four pages. Bradford was the founder of the first paper-mill in this country, and was also the father of book-binding and of copperplate engraving.[1] Lyne's map of New York in 1728 was his work.

The establishment of an English post at Oswego annoyed the French beyond measure. They feared the trade from the upper lakes would be drawn thither, and thus diverted from Montreal. Hence they determined to repossess themselves of Niagara, rebuild the trading-house at that point, and repair their dilapidated fort. The consent of the Onondagas to this measure was obtained by the Baron de Longueil, who visited their country for the purpose, through the influence of Joncaire and his Jesuit associates. But the other members of the confederacy, disapproving of the movement, declared such permission void. The chiefs met Burnet in council at Albany in 1726. They said, "We come to you howling, and this is the reason why we howl, that the governor of Canada comes upon our land and builds thereon." The governor responded in a frank, pleasing, dignified manner, using the figurative expressions of the Indian dialect, which his brawny audience seemed to highly relish. He could talk, however, better than he could perform. He was involved in political difficulties with a factious Assembly, and his administration was opposed by merchants in both New York and Albany, who, by the shrewdness of his Indian policy, and the vigorous measures with which he had enforced it, had been interrupted in their illicit trade in Indian goods with Montreal. He could do very little for the protection of the Indians. He at his own private expense, built a small stone fort at Oswego, and sent a detachment of soldiers to garrison it. The two hundred traders already there were armed as militia. At the same time the French secured and completed their fortifications at Niagara without molestation. In December, 1829, through representations made to the Lords of Trade, which were never clearly understood by those who sustained Burnet, an Act of the Crown repealed the measures which had been so advantageous to New York, and which in effect revived the execrable roundabout trade, and reopened the door of intrigue between the French and the Iroquois, which had been so wisely closed.

Up to the year 1726, the Reformed Dutch worshiped in the little Garden Street Church. But increasing numbers warned them to provide larger accommodations. They purchased a building-lot **1726.** (price £575) on the corner of Nassau and Liberty Streets, and built the Middle Dutch Church, late New York City Post-Office. The corner-stone was laid in 1727. It was opened for worship in 1729. It was

---

[1] William Bradford was of noble birth, as appears from his escutcheon ; for, although forbidden by his art from writing himself *armigero,* he always sealed carefully with arms.

not finished, however, until 1731; and even then it had no gallery for some years. It was dedicated to the "Hon. Rip Van Dam, *President of his Majesty's Council for the Province of New York.*" The ceiling was one entire arch without pillars. It was a substantial stone building, one hundred feet long and seventy wide, with a good steeple and bell. This bell was cast in Amsterdam in 1731. It was by order of Hon. Abraham De Peyster, who died in 1728, while the church was in process of completion. He directed in his will that a bell should be procured in Holland at his expense and presented to the new church. Tradition says that a number of Amsterdam citizens threw silver coin

The Silver-Toned Bell.

into the preparation of the bell-metal. It certainly has a silvery ring. It is still in existence, a trophy of antiquity, nearly a century and a half old, and hangs in the tower of the Reformed Dutch Church, corner of Fifth Avenue and 48th Street.[1]

About this time George I. died, and George II. ascended the throne of England. In the official changes which followed, Burnet was removed

[1] This ancient bell was secreted from the British soldiers, who occupied the Church during the Revolution, and when the edifice was repaired and reopened, it was restored to its original place in the belfry, where it remained until 1844. It was then transferred to the church in Ninth Street, until 1855, when it was placed on the church in Lafayette Place. The steeple of this latter church was taken down a few years since, and the bell was removed to the tower of Dr. Ludlow's church, corner of Fifth Avenue and 48th Street. See Appendix B.

from the government of New York to that of Massachusetts and New Hampshire. He had but little to take with him from New York, **1728.** save the love of his associates and his books, for he had had neither inclination nor opportunity to accumulate money. He regretted the change, as New York held many attractions for him. And he was deeply regretted by those who knew him best. His culture, learning, and conversation were the delight of men of letters, and his influence was healthful upon the community. Boston had heard of his scholastic attainments and elegant manners, and an agreeable reception was in store for him. He was escorted with more ceremony on his overland journey from New York to Boston than was ever accorded to a royal governor in the colonies. A committee from Boston met him on the borders of Rhode Island. Among the gentlemen of this committee was the facetious Colonel Taylor. Burnet complained of the long *graces* which were said at the meals where they had stopped along the road, and inquired when they would shorten. " The *graces* will increase in length until you get to Boston ; after that they will shorten till you come to your government in New Hampshire, where your Excellency will find no *grace* at all," replied Taylor. A more than ordinary parade marked the governor's entrance into Boston. Multitudes of people on horses and in carriages were congregated some distance from the city, and the display was long spoken of as something unprecedented in the history of the country. He did not rule long, however, over the New England colonies He died on the 7th of September, 1729, from a sudden illness caused by exposure while on a fishing excursion.

Governor Burnet's successor in New York was Colonel John Montgomery. He was fresh from Court, having been gentleman of honor to George II. while Prince of Wales. He was a soldier by profession, though a courtier by practice. He knew something of diplomacy, but very little of the world in general. He had spent an indolent, frivolous life, and was without sufficient character to inspire opposition.

He arrived, April 16, 1728. The corporation and citizens gave him a flattering reception, and presented him a congratulatory address in a gold box. He produced a favorable impression upon the Assembly through his unwillingness to sustain the Court of Chancery only as a matter of form, and he was therefore voted a five years' revenue.

The French were threatening the little fort at Oswego, and it became evident, before the summer was over, that the Indians must be once more mollified. A conference took place with the sachems in Albany, where Montgomery, as the figure-head of the government, was assisted by James De Lancey, (who had been appointed to the council in the place of

Mr. Barbarie, deceased), Francis Harrison, Robert Long, George Clarke, the provincial secretary, and Philip Livingston, and also by the mayor, recorder, and aldermen of Albany, and other gentlemen. It occupied several days. The sachems and attendant Indians entered Albany on the first day of October, about one o'clock in the afternoon. They requested an interview with the governor before he made any proposition to them. They were accordingly conducted to his lodgings, and after an interesting preamble, the chief orator of the party made the following speech : —

" BROTHER CORLEAR, — Last fall a message with a token was sent to each nation, acquainting us that his late Majesty, King George I., was deceased, for which we were very much concerned, and heartily sorry, because he was a king of peace, and Almighty protector of his Subjects and Allies, but at the same time we received the good news that the prince, his son, now King George II., was crowned in his place, and hope he will follow his father's steps."

They then gave some skins to the governor.

" We were acquainted at the same time that King George is a young man. We hope he will follow his father's steps, that he may be as a large, flourishing tree, that the branches thereof may reach up to Heaven, that they may be seen of all nations and people in the world. We engraft scions on the same branches, which we hope will thrive, and that the leaves thereof will never fade nor fall off, but that the same may grow and flourish, that his Majesty's subjects and allies may live in peace and quiet under the shade of the name."

They gave some more skins to the governor.

" We have now done what we intended to say at present."

Montgomery replied : —

" BRETHREN, — The concern you express for the loss of his late Majesty, the King of Great Britain, will recommend you very much to the favor of his son, the present king, who, as he succeeds to the throne, inherits all his virtues, and I hope the kind message I am to deliver to you from him to-morrow will comfort you for your father's death."

He then presented them with some blankets, shrouds, and a few barrels of beer, with which to drink the king's health.

The next day they all assembled in the council-chamber, and Montgomery opened the conference with considerable display of eloquence. He said : —

" BRETHREN, — It is with great pleasure that I meet you here, and I am very sorry that I could not do it sooner. But you will be convinced that it was not my fault when I tell you that in crossing the great lake I met with such violent storms that I was driven quite off this coast, and it being in the winter season was forced to go a great way southward to refit the man-of-war in which I came. So it was five months after I sailed from England before I arrived at New York. The business which was absolutely necessary to be done has detained me there ever since, and retarded the delivery of the kind message I bring you from my master, the King of Great Britain. His Majesty has ordered me to tell you that he loves you as a father does his children, and that his affection towards you is occasioned by his being informed that you are a brave and honest people, the two qualities in the world that most recommend either a nation or particular persons to him. He has been informed that you love his subjects, the English of New York, and desire to live with them as brethren. Therefore he has commanded me to renew the old covenant-chain between you and all his subjects in North America, and I expect you will give me sufficient assurances to do the like on your part."

He paused and presented a large belt of wampum.

"Besides the two qualities of bravery and honesty, his Majesty is convinced that you are a wise people, and good judges of your own interests. How happy you must think yourselves when the greatest and most powerful monarch in Christendom sends me here to confirm the ancient friendship between you and his subjects, and assure you of his fatherly care, and to tell you that he thinks himself obliged to love and protect you as his own children. You need fear no enemies while you are true to your alliance with him. I promise to take care that no one shall do you wrong, and if any of your neighbors are so bold as to attempt to disturb you, have no fear of anything they can do so long as the king of Great Britain is on your side, who is a prince initiated in war, and formed by nature for great military achievements, and who will, whenever there is any occasion for it, put himself at the head of the finest body of troops in the world. He has at present a fleet of ships in so good order and so well commanded that they would be master of the great lake, though the fleets of all the kings of Europe were joined against them."

One can almost hear the grunt of satisfaction with which this announcement was received by the Indian audience. Montgomery gave them another belt of wampum, and then proceeded : —

"After what I have told you I am convinced that so wise a people as you are will glory in behaving as becomes the faithful children of so great and powerful a king, who loves you."

Another grunt all round, and another gift of a belt of wampum.

"I expect you are now convinced that the garrison and fort at Oswego is not only for the convenience of the far Indians to carry on their trade with the people of this province, but also for your security and convenience. You can trade there, and on as easy terms as if none other Indians traded there ; therefore I make no doubt but that you will at all times defend this garrison against all enemies, according to your former promises. I desire you to give and grant to your kind father, his most sacred Majesty, a convenient tract of land near Oswego, to be so cleared and manured as to raise provisions for his men and pasturage for their cattle."

Another gift of a belt of wampum.

" I hear that you have been afraid that the trade with the far Indians would make the goods you want dear, but I can assure you that the woolen manufactories of Great Britain are able to supply the whole world. The greater trade that is carried on, the greater will be the supply and the cheaper the goods. I do entreat you to be kind to the traders, and not molest them as they go back and forth."

Another gift of a belt of wampum.

" I am informed that the Indians from Canada, who are gone with the French army against a remote Indian tribe have been among you, endeavoring to entice your young men to go with them to war against a people who have never molested you. I am glad your young men refused, whereby you show that you try to cultivate a good understanding with those Indians, and encourage the good design of a trade betwixt us and them. I expect you will persist in your good behavior towards these and all other remote Indian nations, as it will strengthen your alliances and make you a great people."

Another gift of a belt of wampum.

" His most gracious Majesty, the King of Great Britain, your indulgent father, has ordered me to make you in his name a handsome present of such goods as are most suitable for you, which you shall receive as soon as you give me your answer."

Montgomery gave them still another string of wampum, and after certain tiresome formalities, the savages withdrew to consult with each other and prepare their reply. On the 4th of October, all things being ready, the assemblage was once more convened. The orator from the sachems of the Six Nations delivered his speech thus : —

"BROTHER CORLEAR, — We are very glad you are arrived here in good health. You tell us that your master, the King of Great Britain, sent you. It is a very dangerous voyage, the coming over the great lake. We are glad you arrived in safety because of the good message you bring to us from your master. We would have been sorry if any accident had happened to your Excellency on this dangerous voyage. . . . . You tell us you are ordered by the great king, your master, to renew in his name the old covenant-chain with us, and not only to renew the same, but to make it brighter and stronger than ever. You have renewed the old covenant-chain with the Six Nations in the name of your master, the King of Great Britain. We, in like manner, renew the covenant-chain."

He gave a belt of wampum, and continued : —

" This silver covenant-chain wherein we are linked together, we make stronger and cleaner that it may be bright. We shall give no occasion for the breach of our covenant. . . . . You acquainted us, also, that the great King, your master and our father, bears great kindness to us as a father does to his children, and if any harm come to us he will resent it as if it was done to his children on the other side of the great lake. For which kind message we return our most hearty thanks."

He gave another belt of wampum.

" You tell us that the reason why his Majesty, our father, so affectionately loves us is because we are honest and brave. It is true, what you say, that the Six Nations, when they are sober and not in drink, will not molest or injure anybody, but the strong liquors which your people bring up into our country beget quarrels. . . . . Our ancestors brought their own rum from Albany when they wanted it. We desire that you shall not allow liquor brought to Oswego to be sold, but let such as want rum go to your city for it. Do not refuse our request, but grant it effectually. We have lost many men through liquor which has been brought up to our country and occasions our people killing one another."

The tall, straight, lithe, robust chieftain talked for hours, and said much that was sensible and indicative of sober reflection and civilized intelligence. He said the traders should be allowed to pass and repass freely through their country, without interference, provided they were laden with such goods as powder, lead, and useful wares, but not with rum. He said the Six Nations would mark out a tract of land near Oswego, where the English might plant and sow, and pasture cattle according to their desire ; but after the land was once marked out, the Indians would not be pleased to have the English go beyond the limits. As for defending the fort at Oswego if it was attacked, the orator dryly begged leave to acquaint the governor that the Six Nations gave permission to have the fort and trading-house established there, because they were told it was to be built on purpose to defend and protect them (the Six Nations), and they relied upon the performance of those promises. In regard to there being wool enough in England to supply all the world, he was very glad. Oswego was a convenient place for trade, and where all the far Indians

34

must necessarily pass. But the Six Nations thought goods ought to be sold cheaper to them than to anybody else. He thanked Montgomery for the present which he had brought from the great king, his master, but as night was approaching, asked him to delay delivering it until the morrow.

Montgomery responded briefly, saying that it was absolutely necessary to send rum to Oswego for the refreshment of the men in the garrison, but that he should give orders that none should be sold to the Indians. He thanked the savages for the promised land, and said no one should go beyond the bounds fixed ; as for the fort, it was indeed built for the protection of the Six Nations, but if attacked by any party whatsoever, he should expect them to assist the English garrison to defend it, as nothing could be more natural than for them to assist in the defense of a place which was maintained for their security. He then desired the Indians to send two of their number the next morning to receive the presents.

That same evening two of the principal sachems called at the governor's lodgings and requested a private interview. They wished to make some explanations concerning the defense of the Oswego fort if it should be attacked. They were quite willing to do their part, they said, and desired to correct the impression made upon the governor's mind by the orator's significant allusion to the subject. They wanted a magazine provided, and questioned pointedly in regard to the possibilities of another war between England and France. They were sorely troubled about the rum business. It was exceedingly mischievous in its effects. If rum must be brought to the trading-house at Oswego, they begged for strict orders that it should not be carried to their castles.

The minor details of the conference occupied the three following days. When the Indians finally departed, Montgomery enjoined upon them the necessity of watching their young men on the homeward journey, lest they do mischief to the cattle of the country people along their route.

This renewal of the ancient covenant-chain with the Indians was extremely seasonable, for the next spring the French prepared to demolish the Oswego fort. News reached New York in time, and a reinforcement was sent in great haste to the help of the little garrison, which, together with the understanding that the Indians were pledged to assist in the defense of the post, effectually prevented the attack, and from that time to 1754, it remained undisturbed, and was the source of great profit to New York.

James De Lancey, whose name appears in connection with this conference, was the elder son of Stephen De Lancey and Anne Van Cortlandt. He was a young man, only about twenty-six years of age, and a happy bridegroom, having recently married Anne Heathcote, the elder of the two daughters of Hon. Caleb Heathcote.[1] He had been educated, after attending the best schools New York afforded, in England, where he entered the University of Cambridge, as a Fellow - Commoner of Corpus Christi College, on the 2d of October, 1721. The Master of Corpus was then Dr. Samuel Bradford, afterwards Bishop of Carlisle, and Rochester. The gentleman whom young De Lancey chose for a tutor was the learned Dr. Thomas Herring, who became successively Bishop of Bangor, Archbishop of York, and Archbishop of Canterbury. The master and pupil kept up an intimacy by letter, long after the one became primate of all England, and the other chief justice and lieutenant-governor of New York,

Portrait of Caleb Heathcote.

and the richest man in America. In the various political controversies in which De Lancey was afterwards involved, the Archbishop's influence was exerted in his behalf at the court of Great Britain's sovereign.

De Lancey commenced the practice of law immediately upon his return to New York, and soon rose to eminence at the bar. He was one of the most brilliant and successful advocates of his time. His sound and cultivated judgment won him the respect and confidence of the community, and his influence broadened and deepened with every passing year. He possessed a large library collected in Europe, and was greatly devoted to books. The classics were to him as household words. He was ardently devoted to progress, and lent his careful attention to every topic of interest from law to agriculture. He had also many personal attractions and was a charming social companion.[2]

---

[1] In Governor Montgomery's letter to the Lords of Trade, dated May 30, 1728, in which he recommends James De Lancey as a suitable appointee for the council in place of Mr. Barbarie, deceased, he says " He is in every way qualified for the post ; his father is an eminent merchant, a member of the Assembly and one of the richest men in the province." James De Lancey started in life with a fortune, and his bride inherited half of her father's large estate real and personal. Hon. Caleb Heathcote was mayor of the city of New York for three years, was one of the governor's counselors, was the first mayor of the borough of Westchester, was judge of Westchester, was colonel of the militia all his life, was commander-in-chief of the colony's forces for a considerable period, and from 1715 to 1721 was receiver-general of the customs for all North America. His daughter Martha married Dr. Johnson of Perth Amboy.

[2] Étienne (Stephen) De Lancey — the name originally "de Lanci," and in the 16th and 17th centuries "de Lancy," was in the 18th Anglicized " De Lancey" — was born in

The year 1729 was marked by the gift of a valuable library, consisting of 1,622 volumes, to the city of New York. This favor emanated directly from the Society for the Propagation of the Gospel in Foreign Parts, the books having been bequeathed to that organization by Rev. John Millington. To these were added a small collection which had been donated to the city in the beginning of the century, by the Rev. John Sharpe, and the whole was carefully arranged in a room in the City Hall in Wall Street, and opened to the public as the "Corporation Library." Mr. Sharpe was appointed librarian. It became at once a popular resort; even gentlemen from Pennsylvania and Connecticut were permitted to borrow rare volumes, and keep them for an indefinite period. After Mr. Sharpe's death the books were without care, and the room which contained them seldom accessible. In 1754 a few public-spirited citizens founded the New York Society Library, and obtained permission from the Common Council to combine with it this old Corporation Library.

the city of Caen, Normandy, in 1663. At the revocation of the Edict of Nantes in 1685, his father the Seigneur Jacques (James) de Lancy was dead, and his mother was too aged to fly; she was concealed, while young Stephen escaped to Rotterdam in Holland. The following year he came to New York by the way of London, where he was denizened a British subject. He married, in 1700, Anne, the daughter of Hon. Stephanus Van Cortlandt and Gertrude Schuyler. Their children were: 1, James, born 1703, who married Anne, daughter of Hon. Caleb Heathcote and Martha Smith; 2, Peter, who married Elizabeth, daughter of Lieutenant-Governor Cadwallader Colden; 3, Stephen, who died unmarried; 4, John, who died unmarried; 5, Oliver, member of the governor's council, and brigadier-general; 6, Susanna, who married Admiral Sir Peter Warren; 7, Ann, who married Hon. John Watts.

James De Lancey's children were as follows: 1, James, who married Margaret, daughter of Chief Justice William Allen of Pennsylvania; 2, Stephen, who married Hannah Sacket; 3, Heathcote, who died unmarried; 4, John Peter, who married Elizabeth Floyd; 5, Maria, who married William Walton; 6, Martha, who died unmarried; 7, Susanna, who died unmarried; 8, Ann, who married Hon. Thomas Jones.

John Peter De Lancey's children were as follows: 1, Thomas James, who married Mary J. Ellison; 2, Edward Floyd, who died unmarried; 3, William Heathcote, who married Frances, daughter of Peter Jay Munro, and became Bishop of Western New York; 4, Anne Charlotte. who married John Loudon McAdam, the originator of macadamized roads; 5, Susan Augusta, who married James Fenimore Cooper, the novelist; 6, Maria, who died young; 7, Elizabeth Caroline, who died unmarried; 8, Martha Arabella, who never married.

Thomas James De Lancey's only child was a son, also Thomas James, who married Frances A. Bibby, but died without issue.

William Heathcote De Lancey's children were as follows: 1, Edward Floyd, who married Josephine M. De Zeng; 2, Margaret M., who married Dr. Thomas F. Rochester; 3, Elizabeth, who died young; 4, John Peter, who married Wilhemina V. Clark; 5, Peter Munro, who died unmarried; 6, William Heathcote, who died in infancy; 7, Frances, who died young; 8, William Heathcote, who married his cousin, Elizabeth D. Hunter.

The children of Peter De Lancey, second son of Stephen De Lancey, were: 1, Stephen, who married Esther Rynderts, and was recorder of Albany; 2, John, whose only daughter married Governor Joseph L. Yates; 3, James; 4, Oliver, who married Rachel Hunt; 5, Warren; 6, Peter; 7, Alice, married the celebrated Ralph Izard of South Carolina; 8, Anne, married John Coxe of the West Indies; 9, Jane, married Hon. John Watts (the younger); 10, Susanna, married Colonel Thomas Barclay.

A Jewish cemetery was laid out during the summer. It was bounded by Chatham, Oliver, Henry, and Catharine Streets. It was given by Mr. Willey of London, to his three sons, who were merchants in New York, with the expectation that it would be used as a burial-place for the Jews forever. Could the eye of the good Hebrew have penetrated into the future, what must have been his emotion! Warehouses of every size and description have for long years covered the site of this sacred enclosure, — commerce has effectually monopolized the space allotted for the sleeping dead.

The chief event during Montgomery's administration, which tended towards rendering his name interesting in history, was the granting of a new charter to the city, with an increase of powers and **1730.** privileges. It was accomplished chiefly through the exertions of De Lancey, and in courteous acknowledgment of the same, the corporation voted him the freedom of the city. This charter, henceforth known as Montgomery's charter, recited the charter of 1786; and extended the limits of the city to four hundred feet below low-water mark on Hudson River, from Bestaver's Rivulet southward to the fort, and from thence the same number of feet around the fort beyond low-water mark, and along the East River as far as the north side of Corlear's Hook. It gave the city the sole power of establishing ferries about the island, with all the profits accruing therefrom; it also granted or confirmed the lands held on Long Island, and all the docks, slips, market-houses, etc., upon Manhattan Island. It secured to the city the appointment of all the subordinate officers, and the power to hold a Court of Common Pleas every Tuesday; also authority to make or repeal such by-laws and ordinances as were desirable, and to erect all necessary public buildings.[1] The extent of the city at this period is best illustrated by the map, which was made from an actual survey by James Lyne in 1728.

It was not long afterward before Greenwich and Washington Streets were rescued from the water. Three new slips were also built, one opposite Morris Street, another opposite Exchange Place, and the third opposite Rector Street. In December of the same year a line of stages **Dec. 6** was established between New York and Philadelphia, which performed the tedious journey once a fortnight. The city was divided into seven wards the following spring, and the first steps taken to organize a fire department. Hitherto the leathern fire-buckets which every family was obliged to possess, were the only resource in case of fire. When the confusion and danger consequent upon such an occurrence were over, the buckets were thrown into a promiscuous pile, and the town-crier shouted for each bucket proprietor to come and identify his own. It was the har-

[1] *Kent's Book of Charters. Hoffman. New York City Records.*

vest moment for the boys, and there was often great strife among them who should carry home the richest man's bucket. Finally a committee was appointed to procure from London, " by the first conveniency," two fire-engines. They soon reported a contract effected with Stephen De Lancey and John Moore, for the importation, by the ship *Beaver*, " of two of Mr. Newsham's new inventions, fourth and sixth sizes, with suctions, leathern pipes and caps, and other materials thereunto belonging."

Men were employed the next winter to fit up a room in the City Hall for the reception of the two great wonders of the century. It was in 1736, April 15, that the first effort was made to build an engine-house. It was located on Broad Street, adjoining the watch-house. In October, 1737, the legislature appointed twenty-four able-bodied men from the city to work and play the engines upon all necessary occasions, and enacted a law regulating their duties. Thus was formed the first fire-company in the city.

And presently a new market was established a little to the north of the ferry on the Hudson River, for the accommodation of New Jersey people. The most notable market (simply a market stand) in the city just then was in the middle of Broadway, opposite Liberty Street; the country wagons that stood there on a market morning stretched quite a distance in the direction of Trinity Church, and the plenty and variety they afforded in the way of edibles were much commented upon by foreigners. The old market-place near Whitehall Street was about this time divided into lots and sold at auction, bringing an average price of about £ 260. Pearl Street was extended into a common road a little to the north of Wall Street in 1732. It took the line of the old cow-path which led to the common pasture.

1731. The year 1731 was distinguished by the settlement of the dis-
May 14. puted boundary-line between New York and Connecticut. An agreement was signed by the surveyors and commissioners of both colonies. A tract of land lying on the Connecticut side, consisting of above sixty thousand acres, and from its figure called the Oblong, was ceded to New York, as an equivalent for lands near the Sound surrendered to Connecticut. The very day after the transaction a patent to Sir Joseph Eyles and others, intended to convey the whole Oblong, was executed in London. A posterior grant, however, was issued here to Hauley and Company, of the greater part of the same tract, which the British patentees brought a bill in Chancery to repeal. The defendants filed an answer containing so many objections against the English patent that the suit was abandoned indefinitely, and the American proprietors have ever since held possession of the property. Francis Harrison of the council

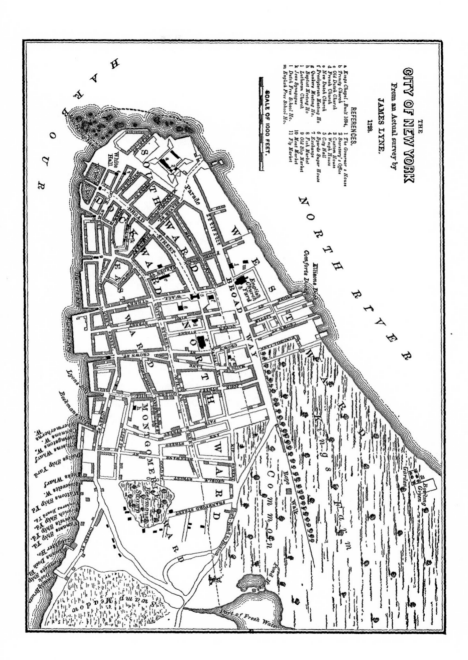

THE
CITY OF NEW YORK
From an Actual survey by
JAMES LYNE.
1728.

SCALE OF 1000 FEET.

REFERENCES.

a Kings Chapel, Built 1694.
b Trinity Church
c Old Dutch Church
d French Church
e New Dutch Church
f Presbyterian Meeting Ho.
g Quakers Meeting Ho.
h Baptist Meeting Ho.
i Lutheran Church
k Jews Synagogue
l Dutch Free School Ho.
m English Free School Ho.

1 The Governor's House
2 Secretary's Office
3 Custom House
4 Weigh House
5 City Hall
6 Exchange
7 Refined Sugar House
8 Fish Market
9 Old Slip Market
10 Meal Market
11 Fly Market

solicited this controversy for Sir Joseph Eyles and his partners, which
contributed in a large degree to the troubles so remarkable in the succeeding administration.[1]

The sudden death of Governor Montgomery on the 1st of July, 1731,
cast a brief shadow over the skies. He had avoided quarrels, consequently had made few enemies. He had had no particular scheme to pursue
for his own or others' aggrandizement, and, drifting along in a peaceful, uninterrupted stream of commonplaces, was regarded as amiable, and probably came as near inspiring affection as is possible for any good-natured
inactive man of moderate abilities.

The government devolved upon Rip Van Dam, the oldest member
and president of the council, and a well-known merchant of wealth and
high respectability. He was spoken of as "one of the people of figure."
He took the oaths of office in the presence of James Alexander, Abraham
Van Horne, Philip Van Cortlandt, Archibald Kennedy, and James De
Lancey.[2] The small-pox was raging throughout the city, and the Assembly, having been adjourned from one date to another, at last convened
at "the house of Mr. Rutgers near the Bowery Road." One of the first
subjects to which the attention of the legislators was called was the
startling encroachments of the French at Crown Point. They had actually
erected a fort, enclosed it with stockades, and garrisoned it with eighty
men, at the south end of Lake Champlain. The country belonged to the
Six Nations, and the very site of the fort was included within a patent to
Dellius, the Dutch minister of Albany, granted under the Great Seal of
the province in 1696. Nothing could be more evident than the danger
to which New York was thus exposed. It was through Lake Champlain
that the French and Indians made their former bloody incursions upon
Schenectady, the Mohawk castles, and Deerfield; and the erection of this
fort was apparently to facilitate inroads upon the English settlers along
the frontiers. It served as an asylum after the perpetration of inhumani-
ties, and was a depot for provisions and ammunition.

The Commissioners of Indian Affairs at Albany had discovered this
palpable infraction of the treaty of Utrecht, and sent a letter to Van
Dam by the hand of Colonel Myndert Schuyler.[3] Van Dam laid the

---

[1] Smith, Vol. I. 245.

[2] It seems that Lewis Morris, Jr., was suspended from the council for words dropped in a
dispute relating to the governor's drafts upon the revenue, on the same day that James De Lancey was elevated to that honorable position.

[3] Smith, the great authority of the history of this period, is evidently in an error respecting
the manner in which Van Dam received the first information of this encroachment. The
letter of Governor Belcher was not received until some time after Van Dam had been notified
by the commissioners at Albany, and it was in answer to one written to him by Van Dam.

subject before the House. It was duly considered, and ways and means discussed to put a stop to the audacious movements at the north. It was very clear that the French could march on Albany in three days from Crown Point, in case a rupture should happen between France and England, which was always possible at any moment. And in the mean time the beaver and fur trade might be obstructed at Oswego. The following resolutions were finally adopted : " 1, That the president represent the case to the king ; 2, That the Commissioners of Indian Affairs at Albany dispose the Six Nations, particularly the Senakas, to prevent the French from obstructing the trade ; and, finally, That his Honor be further addressed that he will be pleased to send copies of the above-mentioned letters and minutes to the governors of Connecticut, Massachusetts, and Pennsylvania, inasmuch as the said attempts may affect them likewise."

As acting governor of New York, Van Dam was singularly consistent in all his acts. He made no effort to overreach his authority, but quietly and resolutely maintained his views of right and justice, without apparent thought of himself. He was opposed to Courts of Chancery, and refused to take the oaths of Chancellor, notwithstanding direct instructions from the English government, and the damage it was likely to inflict upon the revenue. No other court possessed authority to compel the payment of quit-rents, or to adjudicate contested titles ; hence it will be seen that the anti-rentists were favored by this course, and it no doubt led to some of the serious subsequent events. Immediately after the news of the death of Governor Montgomery reached England, the government of the province was committed to Colonel William Cosby. This latter gentleman had formerly governed Minorca, and exposed himself to much criticism during his residence on that island ; among other offensive things he had ordered the effects of a Catalan merchant, residing at Lisbon, to be seized at Port Mahon in 1718, several months before the war of that year was actually declared against Spain, and he was charged with scandalous practices to secure the booty, by denying the right of appeal, and secreting the papers tending to detect the iniquity of the sentence. These rumors reached New York long before the new governor himself, who remained in London, leaving Van Dam to supply his place, for thirteen months. During part of this time New York was in dread of a law before Parliament, called the Sugar Bill, which was manifestly

Chamber of Commerce Records, by J. Austin Stevens, p. 108. "The error of Smith in his statement was first pointed out by Dr. O'Callaghan, in a MS. note, communicated to the New York Historical Society." *Letter of Van Dam to Secretary Popple*, October 29, 1731. *Letter of Van Dam to Lords of Trade*, November 2, 1731. *New York Col. Doc.*, V. 924 – 930.

34

in favor of the West Indies, and ruinous to the Middle Colonies of America. Cosby used his influence to oppose the bill, although without effect, the matter still remaining in abeyance at the time of his departure for New York. But he made it his first business, after reaching his desti-
1732. nation, to apologize for his long delay upon the other side of the
Aug. 1. water, on the ground of his friendship for New York, and his desire to defeat the odious bill in order to further her interests.

Cosby met the Assembly on the 10th of August, and delivered a well-
Aug. 10. prepared and flattering speech, with which the members were much pleased.[1] A revenue to support the government for six years was cheerfully granted, which included a salary for the governor of £1,560, with certain emoluments (to be gained out of supplies for the forts) amounting to £400; the new governor's expenses (£150) in a journey to Albany were also to be paid by the government, and a sum was raised to be laid out in presents for the Iroquois. It was some time before the House voted any special compensation to Cosby for his services in London, in assisting the agents from New York in opposing the Sugar Bill. When it was at last done, the sum named was £750.

Chief Justice Lewis Morris met Cosby the following morning on the street, and stopped to tell him the action of the Assembly. The smallness of the gift angered the haughty colonel, who had come to New York to make a fortune. "Damn them!" said he. "Why did they not add shillings and pence?"

Van Dam caused still fiercer emotions in the breast of the new-comer when a settlement of accounts was instituted. Van Dam, who had been in the governor's chair for thirteen months, received the salary. Cosby brought with him the king's order for an equal division (between himself and the president of the council) of the salary, emoluments, and perquisites of the office since the commencement of Van Dam's administration. Cosby proceeded to demand one half of the salary which Van Dam had received. The latter was willing to divide the salary, but it must be with division also of emoluments and perquisites, according to the sovereign's order. Van Dam was aware that Cosby had received, while yet in England, for pretended services and expenditures for Indian presents never given, for overcharges of clothing, subsistence, etc., for troops, sums of money which exceeded what had been paid to himself by over £2,400. The governor refused to divide, and Van Dam not only refused to refund any part of the salary, but demanded the balance due him.

The Assembly, prior to its adjournment, discussed at some length the subject of education. A bill for a free school, where Latin and Greek and the higher mathematics should be taught, was drafted by Adolphe Philipse, the speaker, and offered by Stephen De Lancey. It created an outburst of merriment, because of this curious preamble: " Whereas the youth of this colony are found by manifold experience to be not inferior in their natural geniuses to the youth of any other country in the world, therefore be it enacted," etc. It passed into a law, and Mr. Alexander Malcom, of Aberdeen, the author of a treatise upon book-keeping, was appointed teacher. The school was patronized by James Alexander, the Morris family, and many others, and became quite popular for a time.

Lewis Morris Mansion.
(Morrisania.)

CHAPTER XXV.

1732–1737.

GOVERNOR COSBY.

GOVERNOR COSBY. — RIP VAN DAM. — EXCITING LAW-SUIT. — OPINION OF CHIEF JUS-
TICE MORRIS. — THE COUNCIL. — THE JUDGES. — THE REMOVAL OF CHIEF JUSTICE
MORRIS. — JAMES DE LANCEY APPOINTED CHIEF JUSTICE. — COURTESY TO FOREIGN
VISITORS. — LORD FITZROY. — A LITTLE ROMANCE. — MARRIAGE OF GRACE COSBY. —
TAXES. — FASHIONS. — MORRIS AT THE COURT OF ENGLAND. — WILLIAM BRADFORD. —
THE NEW NEWSPAPER IN NEW YORK. — JOHN PETER ZENGER. — ARREST AND IMPRIS-
ONMENT OF ZENGER. — THE FAMOUS TRIAL. — CHIEF JUSTICE DE LANCEY. — ANDREW
HAMILTON. — DEFINITION OF LIBEL. — CHAMBERS'S ADDRESS. — HAMILTON'S ARGU-
MENTS. — ACQUITTAL OF ZENGER. — EXCITING SCENES. — PAUL RICHARDS. — THE CITY
WATCH. — CORTLANDT STREET. — THE POOR-HOUSE. — RIP VAN DAM. — COSBY'S
SICKNESS AND DEATH. — CONTEST BETWEEN RIP VAN DAM AND GEORGE CLARKE. —
GEORGE CLARKE LIEUTENANT-GOVERNOR OF NEW YORK. — MRS. CLARKE. — LEWIS
MORRIS GOVERNOR OF NEW JERSEY. — SOCIAL LIFE IN NEW YORK. — THE ELECTION
OF 1737.

G OVERNOR COSBY and President Van Dam were arrayed squarely
against each other, and neither seemed disposed to abate in the
slightest particular from his position. The governor proceeded to institute legal proceedings against Van Dam. As the matter was one of account, and cognizable only in a court of equity, an action could not be
brought in the Supreme Court, which was one of law. The governor was
shut out from the Chancery because he was Chancellor *ex officio*, and of
course could not hear his own cause. He therefore proceeded before the
justices of the Supreme Court as Barons of the Exchequer. This court,
as well as the Chancery, was extremely unpopular.

As soon as the bill was filed against Van Dam, he determined to
institute a suit at common law against the governor. This was overruled
in such a manner that Van Dam found himself compelled to a defense
before the judges in equity. The occurrences were of such an exciting
character that the whole community was interested. Van Dam was a
popular man, and his singular situation elicited warm sympathy.
1733. His counsel were William Smith (the father of the historian)
and James Alexander, both eminent lawyers. They excepted to the

jurisdiction of the court to which the governor resorted. Chief Justice Morris supported the exception. The two associate judges, James De Lancey (commissioned in 1731) and Adolphe Philipse, voted against the plea. The case was subsequently dropped without settlement, and Cosby never recovered any of the money. But the proceedings created two violent parties, and the most bitter feelings.

Chief Justice Morris delivered an opinion in favor of Van Dam, which irritated Cosby beyond measure, and the latter demanded a copy. Morris, to prevent any misrepresentation, caused it to be printed, and then sent it to the governor, accompanied by a letter, from which the following is an extract : —

"This, sir, is a copy of the paper I read in court. . . . . I have no reason to expect that this or anything else I can say will be at all grateful, or have any weight with your Excellency, after the answer I received to a message I did myself the honor to send to you concerning an ordinance you were about to make for establishing a court of equity in the Supreme Court, as being, in my opinion, contrary to law, and which I desired might be delayed till I could be heard on that head. I thought myself within the duty of my office in sending this message, and hope I do not flatter myself in thinking I shall be justified in it by your superiors, as well as mine. The answer your Excellency was pleased to send me, was, *that I need not give myself any trouble about that affair ; that you would neither receive a visit or any message from me ; that you could neither rely upon my integrity nor depend upon my judgment ; that you thought me a person not at all fit to be trusted with any concerns relating to the king ; that ever since your coming to the government I had treated you, both as to your own person and as the king's representative, with slight, rudeness, and impertinence ; that you did not desire to see or hear any further of or from me.*

" I am heartily sorry, sir, for your own sake, as well as that of the public, that the king's representative should be moved to so great a degree of warmth, as appears by your answer, which I think would proceed from no other reason but by giving my opinion, in a court of which I was a judge, upon a point of law that came before me, and in which I might be innocently enough mistaken (though I think I am not), for judges are no more infallible than their superiors are impeccable. But if judges are to be intimidated so as not to dare to give any opinion but what is pleasing to a governor, and agreeable to his private views, the people of this province, who are very much concerned both with respect to their lives and fortunes in the freedom and independency of those who are to judge of them, may possibly not think themselves so secure in either of them as the laws of his Majesty intend they should be.

" I never had the honor to be above six times in your company in my life : one of those times was when I delivered the public seals of the province of New Jersey to you on your coming to that government ; another, on one of the public days, to drink the king's health; a third, at your desire, to wait on my Lord Augustus Fitz Roy, with the lawyers, to tell him we were glad to see him in New York; and, except the first time, I never was a quarter of an hour together in your company at any one time; and all the words I ever spoke to you, except at the first time, may be contained on a quarto side of paper. I might possibly have been impertinent, for old men are too often so; but as to treating you with rudeness and disrespect, either in your public or private capacity, it is what I cannot accuse myself of doing or intending to do at any of the times I was with you. If a bow, awkwardly made, or anything of that kind, or some defect in the ceremonial of addressing you, has occasioned that remark, I beg it may be attributed to the want of a courtly and polite education, or to anything else, rather than the want of respect to his Majesty's representative. As to my integrity, I have given you no occasion to call it in question. I have been in this office almost twenty years. My hands were never soiled with a bribe; nor am I conscious to myself, that power or poverty hath been able to induce me to be partial in the favor of either of them; and as I have no reason to expect any favor from you, so I am neither afraid nor ashamed to stand the test of the strictest inquiry you can make concerning my conduct. I have served the public faithfully and honestly according to the best of my knowledge, and I dare, and do, appeal to it for my justification.

" I am, sir, your Excellency's most humble servant,

"LEWIS MORRIS." [1]

Cosby was highly exasperated, the more so when the opinion and the letter both appeared in the New York Gazette. Such an independent course could not be tolerated in the highest judicial officer in the colony, and Morris was almost immediately removed from the chief-justiceship.[2] In August of the same year James De Lancey was appointed in his stead. This appointment was made under the usual clause in governors' commissions which authorized them to " constitute and appoint judges "; a power which they exercised independently of the council, and not with its advice and consent, as in the erection of courts and the exercise of a few other powers. Morris henceforth became the active leader of the party in opposition to the administration, and De Lancey was the acknowledged chief of the governor's or court party. Morris, in spite of his peculiarities, was a popular man, and now,

1733.

Aug. 21.

---

[1] It will be seen by reference to the Resolutions of the General Assembly of New York in 1708 (page 476), that the doctrine had already been established that the erecting of courts of equity, without the consent of the legislature, was contrary to law.

[2] *Cadwallader Colden to the Earl of Hillsborough.* *James Alexander to Governor Hunter*, February 3, 1730. *New Jersey Hist. Coll.*, IV. 19 – 21. *Memoir of Hon. James De Lancey.* *Doc. Hist. N. Y.*, IV. 1041. *Bolton's History of Westchester*, II. 307; *Governor Cosby to the Duke of Newcastle, May* 3, 1733. *N. Y. Col. MSS.*, V. 942 - 952.

in the season of discontent, he became more than ever an object of regard by the class of people who esteemed themselves oppressed. In the autumn he was chosen to the Assembly to represent the county of Westchester, in the place of a de- ceased member. When he entered the city, can- non were fired from the merchant-ships in the harbor, and a large number of citizens met and escorted him with cheers and flying ban- ners to an elegant en- tertainment. It was the last day of the session, but at the next meeting of the Assembly, his son, Lewis Morris, Jr., took his seat among the members, notwith- standing the most vigor- ous efforts had been made to de- feat his elec- tion. The social world of New York had

Seal and Autograph of James De Lancey.

during all these public excitements been variously agitated. Governor Cosby had brought his wife and young lady daughters to this country with him, and they commanded no little attention. A series of brilliant entertainments were given during the winter and spring, which brought together the beauty, wit, and culture of the capital. Lord Augustus Fitzroy, son of the Duke of Grafton, who was lord chamberlain to the king, spent some weeks in Governor Cosby's family. It was customary for the city authorities to extend courtesies to distinguished strangers; hence, upon the arrival of the young nobleman, the mayor, recorder, aldermen, assistants, and other officials, waited upon him in a body, with a well-prepared speech, thanking him for the honor of his presence, and presented him with the freedom of the city in a gold box.[1] The following day the lawyers went in a body, with Chief Justice Morris at their head (it was just prior to his suspension from office), to show respect and welcome the traveler to our shores.

There was quite a romance connected with this visit of Lord Fitzroy. He was in love with one of the governor's daughters. According to the standard of society in England the match was beneath him, and neither the governor nor Mrs. Cosby dared give consent to the marriage. Through the intrigues of Mrs. Cosby, however, the young people were allowed to settle the matter for themselves. A clergyman was clandestinely assisted to scale the rear wall of the fort, and they were married in secret and without license. To secure Cosby from the wrath of the

The gold box presented to Lord Fitzroy cost £14 8 *s.* *New York City Records.*

Duke of Grafton, who was a great favorite of the king, a mock prosecution was instituted against Dominie Campbell, who had solemnized the nuptials without the usual form.

Another wedding shortly occurred in the governor's household. Miss Grace Cosby was married to Thomas Freeman. Three days later the mayor, recorder, aldermen, assistants, and other city dignitaries, marched in solemn procession to the governor's residence in the fort, and after congratulating the lovely Grace upon her good fortune, made the following speech : —

"This corporation being desirous upon all occasions to demonstrate the great deference they have and justly entertain for his Excellency, William Cosby, and for his noble family, have ordered that the honorable Major Alexander Cosby, brother to his Excellency, and lieutenant-governor of his Majesty's garrison of Annapolis Royal, recently arrived, and Thomas Freeman, the governor's son-in-law, be presented with the freedom of the city in gold boxes."

The style of dress at this time was very showy and conspicuous. Gay pendants were worn in the ears, costly crosses were suspended about the neck, and diamonds and rich brocades were esteemed essential to respectability among the wealthier families. Tight-lacing and wide skirts prevailed, though not as extensively as a few years later. The hair was frizzled and curled and arranged in a great variety of fantastic ways. The gentlemen outdid the ladies. They concealed their hair altogether by enormous wigs, which were supposed to greatly beautify the countenance. An advertisement in the New York Gazette (in 1733) throws a glimmer of light upon the prevailing fashion : —

"Morrison, peruke-maker from London, dresses ladies and gentlemen's hair in the politest taste ; he has a choice parcel of human, horse, and goat hairs to dispose of."

And another : —

"Tyes, bobs, majors, spencers, fox-tails, and twists, together with curls or tates [tetes] for the ladies."

Bright colors everywhere prevailed. The most gorgeous combinations appeared in the fabrics for a lady's wardrobe, and gentlemen wore coats and other garments containing all the hues of the rainbow. Large silver buttons adorned coats and vests, often with the initial of the wearer's name engraved upon each button. Occasionally an entire suit would be decorated with conch-shell buttons silver-mounted. Even coaches were painted and gilded in an extraordinary manner. A writer of the day, seeing the equipage of Lewis Morris rolling down "the Broad

Way " towards the fort, speaks of its silver mountings glittering in the sunshine, and of the family arms emblazoned upon it in many places. The crest was a spacious stone castle, with little turrets and battlements, the motto being *Tandem vincitur,* which was supposed to declare the virtue, perseverance, magnanimity, and success of the Morris family against oppression of whatever character.

The newspapers were crowded with advertisements and descriptions of runaway slaves, and since servants proverbially ape their masters, they furnish a grotesque view of the costumes of that decade.

" Ran away, a negro servant clothed with damask breeches, black broadcloth vest, a broadcloth coat of copper color, lined and trimmed with black, and black stockings." October 3, 1731.

" Ran away, a negro barber ; wore a light wig, a gray kersey jacket lined with blue, a light pair of drugget breeches with glass buttons, black roll-up stockings, square-toed shoes, a white vest with yellow buttons, and red linings." October 28, 1734.

After the death of General Montgomery his effects were sold at public auction : the advertisements specify four negro men, and four negro women, " the times of two men and one woman servant," a variety of fashionable wrought plate, a collection of valuable books, several fine saddle, coach, and other horses; and particularize somewhat in making mention of the household articles, as, for instance, — " A fine new yellow Camblet Bed, lined with silk and laced, which came from London with Captain Downing; also the Bedding. One fine Field Bedstead and curtains ; some blue Cloth lately come from London for Liveries ; some white drap Cloth, with proper trimming ; and some broad gold Lace. Twelve Knives and twelve forks with silver handles gilded. A large lined Fire skreen. Two Demi Peak saddles, one with blue cloth laced with gold,' etc., etc. It will thus be seen that furniture and decorations partook of the same tendency towards fanciful display as dress and equipage.

As months rolled on, the proceedings of Cosby so irritated his opponents that they resolved to lay their grievances before the **1734.** king. It was decided that Morris should himself be the messenger, as his private wrongs would incite him to special exertion, and his intimate acquaintance with all that related to the interests of the province would render him an intelligent adviser concerning future measures for its prosperity. The chief purpose in view was to obtain the removal of Cosby. The utmost secrecy was deemed advisable in regard to the contemplated movements of Morris. He asked for and obtained leave of absence to visit his New Jersey plantation, so wording his application that

it might be interpreted to cover his voyage to England.   He embarked at
Sandy Hook, accompanied by his son, Robert Hunter Morris.   Suspicion
was not excited among the "court party" until he had actually sailed.

Morris communicated his opinion of the British Ministry to James

Portrait of Rip Van Dam

Alexander, in a letter written shortly after his arrival in England, of
which the following is an extract : —

"We talk in America of applications to Parliaments!   Alas! my friend,
parliaments are parliaments everywhere; here, as well as with us, though more
numerous.   We admire the heavenly bodies which glitter at a distance; but
should we be removed into Jupiter or Saturn, perhaps we should find it composed of as dark materials as our own earth. . . . . We have a Parliament and
Ministry, some of whom, I am apt to believe, know that there are plantations
and governors, — but not quite so well as we do ; . . . . and seem less concerned
in our contests than we are at those between crows and kingbirds. . . . .
And who is there that is equal to the task of procuring redress ?   Changing the
man is far from an adequate remedy, if the thing remains the same ; and we
had as well keep an ill, artless governor we know, as to change him for one
equally ill with more art that we do not know.   One of my neighbors used to
say that he always rested better in a bed abounding with fleas after they had

filled their bellies, than to change it for a new one equally full of hungry ones; the fleas having no business there but to eat. The inference is easy."

Again he writes (March 31, 1735) : —

" You have very imperfect notions of the world on this side of the water, —

Portrait of Mrs. Van Dam.

I mean the world with which I have to do. They are unconcerned at the sufferings of the people in America. . . . . It is not the injustice of the thing [referring to Cosby's acts] that affects those concerned in recommending of him, provided it can be kept a secret and the people not clamor; and when they do, if they meet with relief, it is not so much in pity to them, as in fear of the reflection it will be upon themselves for advising the sending of such a man, the sole intent of which was the making of a purse. . . . . Everybody here agrees in a contemptible opinion of Cosby, and nobody knows him better or has a worse opinion of him, than the friends he relies on; and it may be you will be surprised to hear that the most nefarious crime a governor can commit is not by some counted so bad as the crime of complaining of it, — the last is an arraigning of the Ministry that advised the sending of him."

It is evident that Morris was treated with deference by the British Lords, but the affair was subjected to disheartening delays. The question of a separate governor for New Jersey was discussed; and a direct proposal was made to him, that, if he would withdraw the complaints against Cosby, he should receive the appointment, which he declined.

The Assembly of 1834 passed an important bill by which the Quakers were restored to the rights and privileges which that denomination enjoyed in England, — henceforth they could vote without taking the oaths prescribed by law. This and several other popular acts, countenanced by Cosby, propitiated the people, and the clamor and complaint in a measure subsided. But erelong an event happened which stirred New York from center to circumference. John Peter Zenger started a new paper, calling it the Weekly Journal. It was filled with witticisms on the government officials, low satire, lampoons, squibs, and ballads. The public relished it exceedingly. Now and then some well-written articles appeared, criticising the governor, council, assembly, the permanent revenue, and everything generally. Zenger had learned the printer's trade of Bradford.[1] He served at a later date as collector of sundry public taxes, and, through mismanagement, found himself in arrears, for which he was prosecuted; having no means to liquidate the debt, he left the city. He afterwards applied to the Assembly for leave to do public printing enough to discharge the debt, and was refused.[2]

He was a man of much persistence, and some native talent, but of very limited opportunities. He was encouraged, assisted, and very ably supported in this newspaper enterprise by James Alexander, William Smith, Lewis Morris and his son, Rip Van Dam, and others.

Bradford was the government printer, and the editor and publisher of the New York Gazette. He replied to many of the remarkable statements which appeared in the Weekly Journal, but he was not equal to the adversary in sarcasm. Cosby and his counselors were driven almost to madness.

Mingled with this singular controversy was a charge brought against Francis Harrison, one of the counselors, of having written a letter threatening Alexander and his family, unless money was deposited in a certain designated spot for the writer. This letter was found in the entrance-hall, shoved under the outer door of Alexander's residence. Harrison denied the imputation, and his associate counselors pronounced him incapable of such an act. Suspicion, however, still rested upon him, which was industriously fomented by the new newspaper. Out of this, in part, grew the imprisonment and trial of Zenger.

---

[1] John Peter Zenger was born in Germany in 1697. He came to New York with his widowed mother, and a brother and sister in 1710, being one of the party brought over by Governor Hunter at the expense of the Crown of England. The following year he was apprenticed to William Bradford for eight years.

[2] *Doc. Hist. N. Y.*, IV. 1042. *N. Y. Assembly Journal*, I. 627, 636.

Chief Justice De Lancey, in order to procure an indictment against Zenger, called the attention of the grand jury in October to certain low ballads in the Weekly Journal, which he designated as "libels." He said: "Sometimes heavy, half-witted men get a knack of rhyming, but it is time to break them of it when they grow abusive, insolent, and mischievous with it." The ballads being examined were ordered to be burned by the common whipper. The council shortly after made an effort to discover the author of certain other "libels." They addressed the governor, requesting that the printer should be prosecuted. The governor sent this document to the Assembly, where it was laid upon the table.

There came a moment, finally, when affairs assumed a serious aspect. The council pronounced four of Peter Zenger's Weekly Nov. 2. Journals, "as containing many things tending to sedition and faction, and to bring his Majesty's government into contempt, and to disturb the peace thereof," and ordered them to be burned by the common hangman, or whipper, near the pillory, on Wednesday the 6th instant, between the hours of eleven and twelve in the forenoon; it was also ordered that the mayor, Robert Lurting, and the rest of the city magistrates should attend the burning.

When this order was offered by the sheriff, the court would not suffer it to be entered, and the aldermen protested against it, as an arbitrary and illegal injunction. Harrison was the recorder, and made a lame effort to justify the council by citing the example of the Lords in the Sacheverel case, and their proceedings against Bishop Burnet's pastoral letter, but it was of no avail and he withdrew. The corporation declined, emphatically, to attend the ceremony, and forbade their hangman from obeying the order. The burning of the papers was performed by a negro slave of the sheriff; the recorder and a few dependants of the governor were the only spectators.

A few days subsequently, Zenger, in pursuance of a proclamation, was arrested and thrown into prison, where he was denied pen, ink, Nov. 17. and paper. In his paper of November 25, the editor apologizes Nov. 25. for not issuing the last Weekly Journal, "as the governor had put him in jail," but adds, "that he now has the liberty of speaking through a hole in the door to his assistants, and shall supply his customers as heretofore." His dictations, however, were carefully watched.

He was brought before the chief justice on a writ of *habeas corpus,* but his counsel, Smith and Alexander, objected to the legality of the warrant, and insisted upon his being admitted to bail. He swore that he was not worth £40, the tools of his trade and wearing apparel excepted, and could not give bail. Consequently he was recommitted.[1]

[1] *Chancellor Kent.*

The grand jury found no bill against him, therefore on the 28th of
1735. January, Bradley, the attorney-general, filed an *information* for
Jan. 28. "false, scandalous, malicious, and seditious libels."
The trial excited the attention of all America.

Smith and Alexander were the most eminent lawyers in the city, and
were well prepared on this occasion. They commenced by a spirited
attack upon the court itself, aiming at the legality of the commissions of
Chief Justice De Lancey and Judge Philipse, which, as has before been
stated, read, *during pleasure*, instead of *good behavior*, and had been
granted by the governor independent of the council.[1]

Such a proceeding was esteemed a gross contempt of court, and Chief
Justice De Lancey, addressing Smith, remarked, "You have brought it to
that point, sir, that either we must go from the bench, or you from the
bar." And he ordered their names struck from the roll, and thus
April 16. they were excluded from further practice. It would be difficult
to designate any other course which De Lancey could have taken under
the circumstances, consistent with his own dignity and self-respect, but
it caused almost a panic.

The court assigned John Chambers as counsel for the printer, who
pleaded NOT GUILTY for his client, and obtained a struck jury. The
silenced lawyers omitted no effort on their part which would tend to the
acquittal of the prisoner. They made it appear that their own suppression was a stratagem to deprive the defendant of help. They artfully
exhibited the "libels" to the public by the press, and at clubs, and in
other meetings for private conversation. It was easy to let every man
qualified for a juror into the full merits of the defense. The services of
the eloquent Philadelphia lawyer, Andrew Hamilton, were also secretly
engaged.[2]

The trial came on in July and occupied the entire summer. It was an
July. important feature in the early history of the press of New York,
and as it has been variously styled, "the germ of American freedom," and "the morning star of that liberty which subsequently revolu-
tionized America," etc., etc., it will be pardonable to go somewhat into
details on the subject. Hamilton presented himself promptly, and was
eagerly welcomed as the champion of liberty. He asserted that the
matter charged was the *truth*, and therefore no *libel*, and ridiculed some

[1] *Doc. Hist. N. Y.*, IV. 1043. Zenger's Report of the trial published in Boston three years
afterward.

[2] Hamilton was a lawyer of great note, although the famous trial of Zenger widely increased his reputation. He was educated and in practice in England before coming to this
country. He filled many stations of trust during his long residence in Pennsylvania with
honor and ability. He died in 1741.

of the notions advanced by the judges. The words charged as " false, scandalous, malicious, and seditious libels " were as follows : —

" Your appearance in print at last, gives a pleasure to many, though most wish you had come fairly into the open field, and not appeared behind retrenchments made of the supposed laws against libelling ; these retrenchments, gentlemen, may soon be shown to you and all men to be very weak, and to have

Portrait of Andrew Hamilton.
(From original painting in the Pennsylvania Historical Society.)

neither law nor reason for their foundation, so cannot long stand you in stead ; therefore, you had much better as yet leave them, and come to what the people of this city and province think are the points in question. They think, as matters now stand, that their liberties and properties are precarious, and that slavery is likely to be entailed on them and their posterity, if some past things be not amended ; and this they collect from many past proceedings.

" One of our neighbors of New Jersey being in company, observing the strangers of New York full of complaints, endeavored to persuade them to remove into Jersey ; to which it was replied, that would be leaping out of the frying-pan into the fire ; for, says he, we both are under the same governor, and your Assembly have shown with a witness what is to be expected from them : one that was then moving from New York to Pennsylvania, to which place it is reported several considerable men are removing, expressed much concern for the circumstances of New York, and seemed to think them very much owing to the influence that some men had in the administration ; said he was now going from them, and was not to be hurt by any measures they should take, but could not help having some concern for the welfare of his countrymen, and should be glad to hear that the Assembly would exert themselves as became them, by showing that they have the interest of their country more at heart than the gratification of any private view of any of their members, or being at all affected by the smiles or frowns of a governor ; both which ought equally to be despised when the interest of their country is at stake. ' You,' says he, ' complain of the lawyers, but I think the law itself is at an end. We see men's deeds destroyed, judges arbitrarily displaced, new courts erected without consent of the legislature, by which it seems to me trials by juries are taken away when a governor pleases ; men of known estates denied their votes, contrary to the received practice of the best expositor of any law. Who is there in that province that can call anything his own, or enjoy any liberty longer than those in the administration will condescend to let them, for which reason I left it, as I believe more will.' "

The court-room was crowded almost to suffocation ; every kind of business was neglected. The freedom of the press was at stake, as was also liberty of speech, and men looked at each other anxiously and conversed in undertones. Hamilton admitted the publication. Bradley, the attorney-general, remarked that the jury must then find a verdict for the king.

"By no means," exclaimed Hamilton, in his clear, thrilling, silvery voice. "It is not the bare printing and publishing of a paper that will make it a libel; the words themselves must be libelous, that is, false, scandalous, and seditious, or else my client is not guilty."

Bradley said "the truth of a libel could not be taken in evidence."

"What is a libel ? " asked Hamilton.

Bradley gave the usual definition. He said : —

"Whether the person defamed be a private man or a magistrate, whether living or dead, whether the libel be true or false, or the party against whom it is made be of good or evil fame, it is nevertheless a libel, and as such, must be dealt with according to law ; for in a settled state of government every person has a right to redress for all grievances done him. As to its publication the law has taken such great care of men's reputations that if one maliciously repeats it or sings it in the presence of another, or delivers a copy of it over to defame or scandalize the party, he is to be punished as the publisher of a libel. It is likewise evident that it is an offense against the law of God, for Paul himself has said, ' I wist not, brethren, that he was the high priest ; for it is written, Thou shalt not speak evil of the ruler of thy people.' "

"By no means," exclaimed Hamilton, in his clear, thrilling, silvery voice "It is not the bare printing and publishing of a paper that will make it a libel: the words themselves must be libelous, that is, false, scandalous, and seditious, else my client is not guilty." Page 582.